CLOUD COMPUTING

CLOUD COMPUTING

(An Innovative Technology for Linux and Android Platforms)

By

Dr. S. Anandamurugan
Kongu Engineering College, Perundurai, Tamil Nadu

Ms. T. Priyaa
Kongu Engineering College,
Perundurai, Tamil Nadu

Mr. M.C. Arvind Babu
Wipro Technologies,
Chennai, Tamil Nadu

(An Imprint of Laxmi Publications Pvt. Ltd.)
An ISO 9001:2008 Company
BENGALURU • CHENNAI • COCHIN • GUWAHATI • HYDERABAD
JALANDHAR • KOLKATA • LUCKNOW • MUMBAI • RANCHI • NEW DELHI
BOSTON (USA) • ACCRA (GHANA) • NAIROBI (KENYA)

CONTENTS

PREFACE

Cloud Computing is a buzzword in today's fast growing Information Technology (IT) industry. This technology has given a new dimension and vast agility across the entire IT development and services area to the whole business community and to the common end user. In less than decade of its popularity cloud computing has created a big revolution in the computer platform.

All the upcoming technologies are in tune with the cloud platform. In the upcoming years cloud itself can get through several layers of advancement to be more user friendly in all possible scenarios. Cloud computing is no more a future term or upcoming one, it's almost a truly reality one now. A basic internet technology of client server model scenario has transferred into the highly powerful dynamic and virtual cloud technology. Cloud computing can further make lots of dynamic changes in all the existing platforms in the next few years, ending all the traditional old practices.

As the industry requires new technology for its dynamic work culture and powerful output to the customer so as young technocrats and smart engineers need to be aware of all new technology platforms. Hence, this book has been prepared as a highly informative and an innovative book on cloud computing imparting all possible information to satisfy all types of reader. Almost every rare information has been presented in this book in all possible sections. Apart from cloud enough importance has been laid to the Linux technology, which is an important launch pad for any real time cloud technology projects. Linux is certainly a new world of operating system exclusively meant for all networking and server related operations in a highly secured manner.

As we are living in the days of highly insecure and hackers out in open. Linux is certainly a wise choice for every secured application. Along with cloud and Linux, an in-depth discussion has been done on android technology. We all know that we are living in the age of hand held mobile devices of smart technology and android has almost replaced the traditional desktop based machine work to the endless mobile apps. Android has defined a new meaning of usage to mobiles phone. Today android application development is simply aligned with the cloud technology. All the android apps are designed to support the end user in the cloud platform.

This book is designed to satisfy the needs and expectation of both the basic reader and an expert person from the industry. It is presented in a way to satisfy the ever dynamic IT industry requirement too. It can be used by students, teachers, scholars, researchers, technocrats and even by a basic reader who is not aware of many things in computing technology. The subject has been presented in a very simple, precise and also in a good depth manner covering all the corners of both common and innovation facts about the cloud technology and all its supporting platforms.

The book has totally fourteen chapters with each chapter presented from the very basic point to the top most advanced scenario of concepts. It contains ten chapters on cloud technology and Linux platform, three chapters on android technology using the cloud platform and the last chapter contains five case studies, which includes the real time executed projects. Throughout the book about many cloud based tools and software, notable about some Indian based technocrats and government funded cloud tools and projects have been discussed. The effort will be fruitful if the students and the teachers of this subject are benefited from it. Any suggestion regarding the subject of this book is cordially welcome.

—Authors

ACKNOWLEDGEMENT

In the first place, we would like to express our sincere gratitude to *Thiru. V.K. Muthusamy,* Correspondent, Kongu Engineering College, for having provided us with all the necessary facilities to undertake this work.

We feel extremely grateful for the strong support which we have received from *Prof. S. Kuppuswami,* Principal and *Prof. S. Balamurugan,* Dean, School of Communication and Computer Sciences.

Next, we would like to thank *Dr. S. Varadhaganapathy,* Head of the Department, Information Technology, Kongu Engineering College for his commendable help and support during this work.

Especially, we would like to submit our special thanks from the bottom of our heart to our friends from Wipro Technologies *R.T. Omprakash, M.S. Vignesh Sundaramurthy, G. Anusuya, S.M. Kalaiselvi,* for their moral support which we cannot express in a few words.

We extend our sincere thanks to all our colleagues for their comments and suggestions. Finally, we would like to thank everyone who has encouraged us at every step in the successful completion of the book.

—Authors

Chapter 1

Introduction to Cloud Computing

OBJECTIVE

- *To learn about the new cloud computing technology*
- *To know the list of all computing techniques and the evolution of cloud*
- *To know the characteristic and need for cloud computing*
- *To know the overall architecture of cloud computing*

1.1 WHAT IS CLOUD.....?

The word *cloud* literally makes us think of the meteorological cloud in the sky. But technically speaking cloud refers to a set of devices connected using internet. It is an advanced networking technology evolved from the various predecessor computing techniques. A group of devices connected together in a remote fashion to perform the end user task in a highly reliable and concurrent way refers to the term cloud. A cloud can consist of several devices of various types ranging from a traditional desktop based computer, hand held mobile devices of smart technology to powerful servers connected by a high speed internet. It refers to sharing of:

- Data
- Resources both software and hardware
- Workspaces
- Running process or application

Thus a cloud involves a sharing of more active and a dynamic resource rather than a static one. The cloud involves the migration of loosely coupled resource to the end user independent of the location and platform. The concept of sharing resource in cloud has a broader meaning which we will see in detail in the upcoming chapters.

Apart from sharing of resources cloud capabilities include:

- Clouds can host a variety of different workloads, including batch-style back-end jobs and interactive, User-facing applications.

- Clouds allow workloads to be deployed and scaled-out quickly through the rapid provisioning of virtual machines or physical machines.
- Clouds support redundant, self-recovering, highly scalable programming models that allow workloads to recover from many unavoidable hardware/software failures.
- Monitor resource usage in real time to enable rebalancing of allocations when needed.

Clouds also support non grid environments such as a three-tier Web architecture running Standard or Web 2.0 applications. A cloud is more than a collection of computer resources because a cloud provides a mechanism to manage those resources. Management includes provisioning, change requests, reimaging, workload rebalancing, deprovisioning, and monitoring. A cloud infrastructure can be a cost efficient model for delivering information services, reducing IT management complexity, promoting innovation, and increasing responsiveness through real time workload balancing.

A typical cloud consist of a collection of interconnected and virtualized computers or any other devices that are dynamically provisioned and presented as one or more unified computing resources based on service-level agreements established through negotiation between the cloud service provider and consumers. Clouds are clearly next-generation data centers with nodes virtualized through hypervisor technologies and dynamically provisioned on demand as a personalized resource collection to meet a specific service-level agreement, which is established through a negotiation and accessible as a service via Web 2.0 technologies in a modern web browser.

Along with cloud one must also understand the meaning of the word *Computing*. It is usually defined as the activity of using and developing computer technology, computer hardware, and software. It is the computer-specific part of information technology. Computer science or computing science is the study and the science of the theoretical foundations of information and computation and their implementation and application in computer systems.

Generally we can define computing to mean any goal-oriented activity requiring, benefiting from, or creating computers. Thus, computing includes designing and building hardware and software systems for a wide range of purposes processing, structuring, and managing various kinds of information doing scientific studies using computers making computer systems behave intelligently creating and using communications and entertainment media finding and gathering information relevant to any particular purpose, and so on. The list is virtually endless, and the possibilities are vast.

The NIST definition of cloud computing

Cloud computing is a model for enabling convenient, on-demand network access to a shared pool of configurable computing resources (e.g., networks, servers, storage, applications, and services) that can be rapidly provisioned and released with minimal management effort or service provider interaction.

Thus, cloud computing is a relatively new way of referring to the use of shared computing resources, and it is an alternative to having local servers handle applications. Cloud computing groups together large numbers of computer servers and other resources and typically offers their combined capacity on an on demand basis. The end users of a cloud computing network usually have no idea where the servers are physically located or where the applications are executed or data is stored they just start their application and start working.

Cloud computing is fully enabled by the virtualization technology and virtual appliances. A virtual appliance is an application that is bundled with all the components that it needs to run, along with a streamlined operating system. In a cloud computing environment, a virtual appliance can be instantly provisioned and decommissioned as needed without complex configuration of the operating environment.

Cloud computing environment provides a great flexibility and availability of computing resources at a lower cost. This emerging technology has opened a new era of e-services in different disciplines. Today cloud computing has become a buzzword in IT sector with all major companies moving towards this new technology. Some of the early corporate houses into this technology include Amazon, Google and Microsoft. Thanks to the revolution of Internet and Android system which has made the usage of cloud very easy, faster and user friendly. With the cloud revolution the typical web technology is getting advanced to the cloud platform. Often people get confused with the web based application and a dynamic cloud application. We will see their differences in the section 2.7 of chapter 2. Thus the advancement of Web 2.0 is regarded as cloud computing.

Cloud computing has a given a new meaning to the usage of internet from a traditional client-server model. Cloud computing is more of a service oriented technology by the vendor than a dedicated one. Today all Corporate IT companies are shifting to this technology giving its usage a new dimension to the business world from the traditional location and workspace dependence to the independent one now. There are lots of advantages to the corporate IT companies from cloud. Hence all companies have designed, developed and are managing their own cloud with multiple tie up with many other MNCs (Multi National Companies).

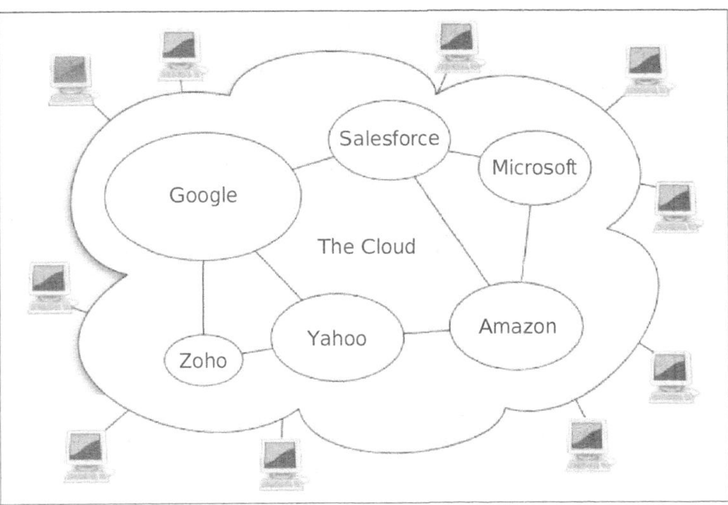

Figure 1.1 Typical cloud.

Cloud computing is a technology fully based on the usage of internet. The history of cloud computing dates back to 1950 but its major revolution started in late 2007. With the revolution of android system in 2008 and tablet PCs in 2009 cloud is certainly seen as a new networking technology to satisfy the needs of the business world and end user. A typical cloud is accessed using the web browser similar to accessing our e-mail from browser. Cloud technology is designed to provide the service to the end user task. Currently everyday a new cloud vendor is entering to the market. Each vendor provides a new feature to the end user and the business world. Every new hardware product being designed is in accordance with the cloud technology and advanced networking techniques.

Cloud technology is also closely associated with Linux platform. As we all know Linux is mainly for networking applications and server operations. Linux fully supports all the concepts of cloud computing and the virtualization techniques. Many cloud companies are having tie up with Linux platforms and are developing tools to work in their platforms. Today Linux is seen as the best platform that can support many other virtual tools and software. The server edition of various Linux operating systems is best suited for all networking and advanced computing techniques.

As of 2013 cloud computing is moving towards the mobile based android system called mobile cloud computing. With the revolution of android system, the next target of cloud is mobile based cloud technology. The smart technology in mobile phones and tablet PCs has given a new dimension to the usage of them from the Windows platform. Today millions of mobile applications are designed to satisfy the end user. The designed applications are in tune with cloud technology. The applications can easily connect to remote cloud servers and can furnish all the user task.

1.2 HISTORY OF CLOUD COMPUTING

Everything in the world has a past, nothing comes like what it's of today in the beginning. Lets us see the overall history of cloud computing in this section. The evolution of cloud technology dates back to 1950s when the concept of sharing resources was realized. The internet technology was in initial stages. The computer in those days was a large machine, far complex and not as advanced as it is today. Every small invention in the computer technology has changed the way computer functions and increasing its applications to the end user. The networking technology further made the computer technology to grow faster making it an intelligent super machine for communication purpose and to handle all real time problems.

Mainframes in 1950

The concept of resource sharing dates back to 1950 when there was a mainframe revolution in corporations. The large mainframes were installed in a specific room from where the users used to share the data storage and CPU power. Thus this was the first instance where the resource was shared. From here the sharing concept came into being.

IBM in 1970

In 1970 the IBM developed an operating system called VM, which can run multiple virtual machines with guest operating system. Virtual machine can be defined as the several operating systems running in a same hardware with the user working in them as if it the only OS running at a time. It was intended to leverage investments in expensive mainframe computer. The idea was to enable multitasking running multiple applications and processes for different users simultaneously. Thus the hardware virtualization technology came into existence with several virtual machines running in a same platform. Every VM can run the guest operating system with dedicated memory, processing and networking power. IBM was also the early leader in computer hardware and networking technology.

Communication revolution of 1990s

In early 1990s the telecommunication companies started the revolution of internet and infrastructure growth in the field of communication. The users were connected to a virtualized private network connection which provided the same service as of the dedicated point to point connection. Thus the revolution of internet had started and the data traffic increased by infinite times. The internet itself had undergone several layers of advancements and changes. The web domain World Wide Web (WWW) was seen as the beginning of the revolution of web technology and its service to the mankind in the milestone of computer technology. The concept of OSI layer was made as a standardization of the networking technology.

The concept of Electronic – mail was realized by several section of the society. Thus the growth of internet was in full revolution and the migration of computer technology from the traditional machines also took place in this period of time. By the beginning of 2000 the super communication internet was ready to reach the end user. Many hardware devices were introduced into the market. Each one had their specific functionality, making the task of end user very simple. Many large companies began to manufacture the computer with advances in their size, computation and efficiency in the end user task. Thus the shape of computer also saw a major changes in the late 90s technology revolution. In late 2000s the more portable computer laptops began to replace the desktop based machines.

Early 2000 and aftermath

With the high speed internet in place and the foundation of large data centers like Google, Amazon, Microsoft in place the concept of cloud computing began to arise. The concept of web 2.0 reached its full peak in the revolution of web technology. The concept of internet was now a more reality and a very common technology everywhere. In the initial years of internet revolution Google search engine was seen as major usage by the people. By 2003 more and more web pages were added to the pool of internet technology. Further more corporate IT companies were out in large number to solve the end user tasks. Internet became a common mode of communication, the web hosting of every organization became a fashion of the time. The standardization of the internet was also largely realized due to increase in the number of hackers and intruders in the market. Thus the governance and monitoring of internet came into existence with a set of well defined protocols adopted in the management of internet. Internet became a large ocean which connected the people from remote places to communicate and furnish the end user task.

Internet technology made the life so advanced with the revolution of web 2.0 and its application to the end user. The usage of social networking, online marketing and advertisement, live streaming, blogging and etc., formed the foundation of web 2.0. In late., 2008 accessing internet from hand held mobile devices made the technology a more user friendly and advanced. The traditional client server model was replaced with dynamic and heterogeneous distributed computing technology. The distributed technology along with the virtualization gave the birth to the age of new cloud computing technology.

The service oriented cloud technology took the full revolution in late 2007 with several open source cloud tools introduced in the market. It also saw the growth of many cloud vendors in the market to satisfy the demands of the end user. In early years of 2000 the windows platform of operating system was a common one in many machines. From there the windows operating system also went through many changes and new versions were released. The open source Linux platform was also growing simultaneously over fear of security reasons in windows operating system.

Cloud computing supported all forms of operating system. The Linux OS included Redhat, Fedora, Centos, Ubuntu and etc., which all closely worked with cloud computing technology and supported all the cloud tools. Since 2010 all the versions of advanced Linux were designed to support cloud computing. The tie up between the Linux platforms and the open source cloud tools gave rise to new Cloud operating based operating system being designed. Some of which includes Ubuntu and Eucalyptus cloud combined to give Ubuntu enterprise cloud in 2011. In 2012 Ubuntu combined with Openstack cloud to develop many cloud platform tools and software. In windows platform the windows OS 7 in 2009 and windows OS 8 in 2012 were designed to support the growing networking technologies.

In 2008 the smart technology of Android changed the entire world with hand held mobile devices replacing the desktop based PCs and the cloud further revolutionized in the mobile apps. More and more mobile applications were designed in accord with cloud technology in the android platform. The revolution of tablet in late 2009 further made the portability of devices easier. By 2010 tablets became a more common devices and an attractive hardware for the people. In 2012 the windows OS 8 was designed in tune with the tablet display of apps in the first screen using the metro language.

Today millions of applications are designed to satisfy the end user. For every function there is a mobile app being developed which is hosted in android web market from where the user can easily download, install and use them quickly. Today the cloud technology is as user friendly such that it is platform independent. All mobile apps are designed in accordance with the cloud technology. Today as of 2013 all major IT companies are shifting towards the cloud technology to satisfy the demands of business processing unit and the end user.

1.3 LIST OF COMPUTING TECHNIQUES

In the previous section, we saw the history of cloud computing and the revolution in the advancement of computer technology. Now, we see in detail the evolution of cloud computing from various predecessor computing techniques in the modern computer. Cloud computing is evolved from a various computing techniques of the past. Each computing technique changed the functioning of computer and its applications. Each technique had both advantages and disadvantages. Every predecessor technology matured and was popular in those times. Cloud shares the properties from each of them and is closely associated. Thus, cloud can be described as the combination of all previous techniques with some features addition or eliminated to enhance its usage effectively. The various predecessor technologies includes:

- ***Client server model*** – it is one of the basic computing model and the commonly used one. With the growth of internet technology the traditional client server technology came into existence. A typical user views the front end in a client machine which in turn depends on the back end server machine mostly includes database storage. It's the base of the networking concept and has led to the evolution of various other advanced computing techniques. A good example of this technology is the early internet. The drawback of this technique is the saturation of the server, leading to the crash of the back end server due to high data traffic and more prone to hackers attack.
- ***Mainframe technology*** – these are the large scale computers to perform the bulk work in offices and other business organizations. IBM mainframe made the revolution to this platform. Today most of the mainframes are from IBM based developed machines which have undergone several layers of advancement which includes the concept of virtualization, a principle of cloud computing. Modern mainframes can run multiple different instances of operating systems at the same time. This technique of virtual machines allows applications to run as if they were on physically distinct computers. Mainframe technology is used in large research labs and high processing business units for critical processing. The drawbacks include high cost, large size and produce more heat.
- ***Parallel computing*** – the advancement of processors lead to development of parallel processing of the task. In a parallel computing the large task is split into smaller ones and is solved concurrently. There are several forms of the parallel computing like task level, instruction level, data level and bit level. Today all processors are designed to satisfy the parallel computing technique. It has made a big revolution in the design of the computer hardware.
- ***Distributed computing*** – it can be defined as the components in the network which communicate to achieve a common goal. A best example of a distributed system is the Remote Procedural Call (RPC) between a stub and a skeleton where the message is packed and unpacked in the communication process between the two end systems. Another good example of a distributed system is the file system, which is distributed to easily migrate to various systems in the network. The

terms concurrent computing, parallel computing, and distributed computing have a quite similar meaning in them. Parallel computing may be seen as a particular tightly coupled form of distributed computing, and distributed computing may be seen as a loosely coupled form of parallel computing. The major goal of the distributed computing involves the migration, relocation and replication of resources. The migration of resources takes place using the virtualization concept. They are also highly scalable. The architecture of a distributed technology is either two tier or three tier or even multi tiered with each layer having their specific functionalities. Today most of the applications in internet and World Wide Web (WWW) are distributed in nature. It has made a major shifting of applications in the networking area. The distributed system is robust and is tolerant to any fault in the communication process. The distributed technology plays a major role in cloud computing principle.

- ***Cluster computing*** – the word cluster means a group or a collection of things. Cluster computing can be defined as the combinations of computers using the Local Area Network (LAN) to achieve the task of the end user. A computer cluster may be a simple two-node system which just connects two personal computers, or may be a very fast supercomputer. The ultimate objective of the technology is high performance delivery to the growing demands of the end user with scalability of the resource and cost reduction. The concept of message passing and data sharing became another important aspect to the networking area from the cluster computing technology.
- ***Utility computing*** – a perfect predecessor computing technology that shares most of the features of cloud computing is utility computing. Utility computing involves the renting of resources to end user in a metered fashion. The resources include the data, storage and computation services. Cloud computing is built on a Pay per usage scenario. The utility computing is of service oriented architecture. It involves the concepts of distributed and virtualization, through which the resources are made available to the end user. IBM, HP and Microsoft were early vendors in the new field of Utility Computing with their business units and researchers working on the architecture, payment and development of the technology. Google, Amazon and others started to take the lead later, as they established their own utility services for computing, storage and applications.
- ***Grid computing*** – it can be defined as a distributed system in which all systems interact to achieve the user goal. It can be known as a special form of parallel computing. Grids tend to be more loosely coupled, heterogeneous, and geographically dispersed. Grids are often constructed with middleware software libraries. The potential for massive parallel CPU capacity is one of the most attractive features of a grid. In addition to pure scientific needs, such computing power is driving a new evolution in industries such as the bio-medical field, financial modeling, oil exploration, motion picture animation, and many others. Grids are used in large research laboratories like NASA and other high computation projects to the mankind. They are popularly known as super virtual computer. Job scheduling is

a common example of the grid technology. Globus toolkit is the common software tool kit to establish a grid environment and analyze its features. Grid-enabled applications are specific software applications that can utilize grid infrastructure.

- ***Edge computing*** – it is closely related to grid computing. It can be defined as the pushing of the service like computation memory, data, storage and application from a central location of the network to the outer point in the network. Edge computing helps in the replication of information in the distributed environment. Topologically edge computing is also referred to as mesh computing, peer-to-peer computing, autonomic (self-healing) computing, and grid computing respectively.
- ***Green computing*** – it is an advancement of computer technology to make it an eco-friendly. The goals include reducing the use of hazardous materials, maximize energy efficiency during the product's lifetime, and promote the recyclability or biodegradability of defunct products and factory waste. The concept of virtualization is a form of green computing. The awareness of environmental friendly is spreading faster everywhere, hence green computing is seen as a need of the hour in computer field. All corporate IT companies are spending the part of their profit in eco friendly measures both inside and outside the company premises.

1.4 REVOLUTION AND MATURITY OF CLOUD COMPUTING

In the last section we saw the emergence of cloud computing from a list of various computing techniques. Cloud is derived from those techniques and its character appears closely related to each one of them. Thus in simple words we can say today's cloud are nothing but the combination of the various predecessor technologies. In this section, we see the maturity of the cloud and how this technology has become a success story to every end user. The maturity of a technology refers to the awareness among the people, ultimately leading to the usage of it. People analyze how a new technology is efficient and advanced compared to the existing ones. Many times the technology fails if the people are not taught how to work with them. If the technology is not user friendly or a major loop hole in its core functionality it loses its shine among the people in spite of some other additional new feature.

Above all every computing technology has to be business friendly so that it is well applied in the corporate IT sector. The concept of maturity is also incremental in nature. Like in a span of 2–3 years the same technology goes a higher version in a step wise approach to satisfy the needs of the end user and the business world. Generally a technology takes some time to attain its full maturity in the market. The incremental approach is the best way a technology can survive on a long run. If a technology is introduced completely in a single phase, if it fails to satisfy the end user and the business community it is completely rejected and loses its ultimate objective. With the maturity of a technology also marks the revolution of it among the people in full scale and making it popular. The business world switch to the new technology, all the previous works are transformed to the new technology workspace. The future work is carried in the new technology environment.

Early to mid-2000s

During the early to mid-2000s, the cloud was praised for its ability to reduce capital expenditure. Cloud applications were cheaper to implement, upkeep, and upgrade. Since these applications weren't tied into expensive hardware and were updated regularly, they freed the IT team from spending hundreds of thousands of dollars a year on maintenance and upgrade fees. So, for the cloud's earliest adopters, price was a core component of the value proposition.

While the cloud offered much more even back then, buyers often viewed cost savings as the predominant benefit due to shortcomings in other areas. Like any new technology, a lack of general knowledge created misconceptions, and in some cases, people just weren't amenable to change. But, technological roadblocks like downtime, inability to customize products, lack of feature parity with on-premise software, and slow load times all detracted from the cloud experience.

Mid 2000 – 2010

By the mid 2000s, the conversation around the cloud had changed drastically and so the knowledge and exposure of the corporate IT firms. The value proposition had evolved from purely cost savings although those were still largely in play to giving users the ability to access their data from anywhere. At this point, the cloud was not only saving significant capital, it was actually capable of changing the way people worked. It was liked by the business processing units.

A few significant advances during this time period helped to change the value proposition drastically. Availability and ubiquity of high-speed internet and the revolution of communication devices like Wifi. The evolution of mobile devices made working from anywhere a possibility while the cloud made it a reality. The android technology revolution started to influence more people into the advanced computing techniques. In the cloud, users could easily gain access to the same data from their laptop, Smartphone, tablet or desktop. Hardware took a backseat to software. More cloud vendors plunged into the market. The service oriented cloud was deeply analyzed to solve the end user problems.

By the end of the 2000s, the conversation around the cloud had changed from tactical to strategic. Cloud was becoming a more and more a real time based concept from just the theory oriented technology. Its importance and need was felt by the industry and the user.

2010 – Today

Today, the value proposition of the cloud comes from the ability to connect disparate applications to form one seamless web of IT. In a 100 percent web environment, APIs from dozens of applications can be integrated to allow data to flow across systems.

The rise of handheld devices and the Internet's ubiquity in the mid to late 2000s led to the proliferation of SaaS (Software as a Service) applications built to meet very specific needs of marketplaces like Salesforce.com App Exchange and the Google Apps Marketplace even emerged to support these growing ecosystem. While these applications fulfilled their original purposes and brought about efficiency for their end users, the number of individual applications installed and used across different departments and devices in one organization became unmanageable and risky for IT.

Using APIs from different applications, a company's internal IT department or an outside cloud services brokerage can now easily integrate these applications and let data flow between them. Whether the connections are included out of the box, you use a Chrome extension to pull data from one application into another, or you actually use a third-party product to integrate different applications, the cloud's value proposition for this era is clear as it creates efficiency across organizational departments by permitting disparate applications to communicate and share data with one another. In essence, the newest SaaS providers act as glue holding together larger, more established platforms.

Since 2010 many open source clouds have been introduced into market like Eucalyptus cloud, Openstack cloud, Cloudstack and so on. These open source clouds are extensively used in the Linux platform to accomplish the end user task. Every year the open source clouds are getting updated and new versions of more advanced, bug free one is dedicated to people. Recently Eucalyptus cloud 3.4 version was released in 2013 and Openstack new versions have been introduced. More and more cloud applications are designed and hosted in remote cloud, scaled to the needs of the end user. The windows platforms have also undergone a major change to satisfy the cloud technology. A good example is the design of windows OS 8 in 2011 using the metro language to support the advanced networking concept.

The cloud today is about changing the way organizations, employees, and partners interact and work together. Using cloud technology, we not only become more efficient and more effective, but the technology truly becomes an enabler for collaboration. Everyday cloud is undergoing some advancement. A new feature by a new vendor is added from time to time to satisfy the needs of the end user.

1.5 CHARACTERISTICS OF A CLOUD

A cloud exhibits several characters, which make it a quite unique and an advanced computing technology for the growing needs of the end user and the business units in the IT sector. Though some features of the cloud resemble previous computing technologies with some newly added and some ignored. A characteristic of a technology determines its efficiency and the core functionality in solving the user problem. The characteristics of cloud includes:

- ***Anytime, Anywhere Technology*** – a typical cloud can be used by the user anytime and independent of the location mainly due to its migration capabilities of a dynamic cloud using high speed internet device.
- ***Pay per usage*** – the resources in a cloud are metered based on the usage of the user, thus making the cloud technology an economic one and reducing the burden of the user by shared resource than a costly dedicated resource.
- ***On demand self-service*** – the resource in cloud are available to the user automatically from the various service provider as the demand required.
- ***Online access*** – the entire cloud technology functions using a high speed internet connected to various devices. It involves a thin client technology with a highly placed runtime server in the backend.

- ***Resource pooling*** – the deployed resources are made available to multiple end users at a time in a highly dynamic manner by creating the instances of it. The resources are allocated and reallocated based on the demand of user in a Multi – tenant model and independence of the location.
- ***Rapid elasticity*** – the resources in cloud are highly elastic in nature as the user can dynamically consume and release the resource based on the demand. The user can view the resources as if they are infinite and can be purchased in any quantity at any time.
- ***Scalability*** – the infrastructure of cloud computing is very scalable. Cloud providers can add new users and servers to cloud with minor modifications to cloud infrastructure and software.
- ***Reliability*** – it is achieved in cloud computing by using multiple redundant sites. High reliability makes the cloud a perfect solution for disaster recovery and business critical tasks.
- ***Loosely coupled*** – the resources in the cloud are loosely coupled so that they can easily migrate and can be scalable to the demand of the user.
- ***Multi tenancy*** – the cloud technology involves a wide range of end users being connected to a single cloud provider.
- ***Cost effective*** – an another feature of cloud computing is the cheap economy by the renting and sharing of all resources in the cloud than buying all the costly hardware, software and other resource. It is mainly useful for all small business organizations.
- ***Customization*** – a cloud is a reconfigurable environment that can be customized and adjusted in terms of infrastructure and applications based on the user demand.
- ***High performance*** – cloud computing technology provides users with a high performance computing environment compared to all other computing techniques. It is due to extremely large storage and powerful computing resources of the cloud infrastructure.

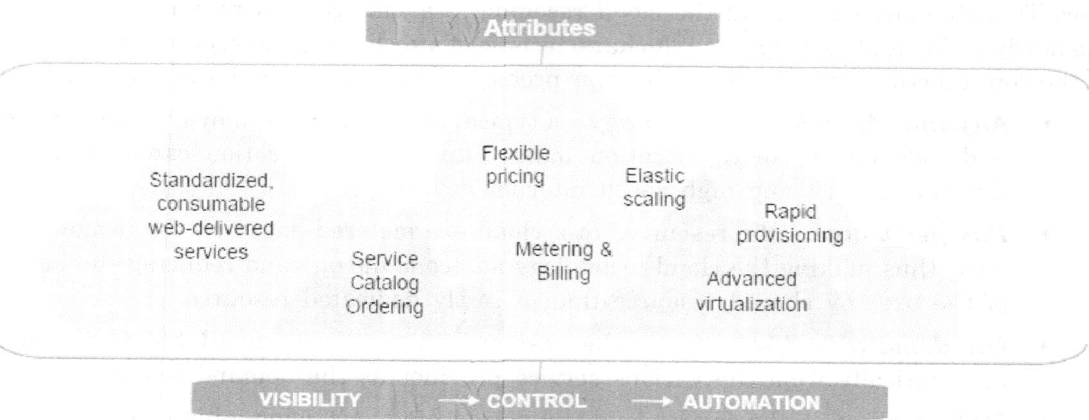

Figure 1.2 Characteristic of cloud.

1.6 NEED FOR CLOUD COMPUTING

In the earlier section, we saw the list of computing techniques from which the cloud is derived and the maturity of it in the recent years in various fields. We also saw the various characteristics of cloud. Now let us see the actual necessity of this technology. A necessity of a cloud technology can be described as the growing demands of the end user task. All the predecessor technologies have failed to satisfy the advancement required at that time. The other reason can also be due to the far user friendly and efficiency of the new technology when compared to the previous techniques. Thus the best technique which satisfies the advancement of that time and is business friendly to the corporate IT sector is adopted rather sticking to the outdated technology.

Well the need of a cloud can be due to

- ***Economic*** – cloud computing reduces the overall hardware and software cost due to the sharing of resource. After all cloud computing is based on the concept of pay per usage scenario.
- ***Automatic updating*** – well in traditional software the user is frequently required to update the latest version, but in cloud everything is auto updated with the changes being made available to the end user.
- ***Synchronization with other technology*** – cloud computing is a new technology, it works with all new and older platforms of other technologies. Cloud works with mobile applications of smart technology giving rise to mobile cloud computing. Cloud also works with Windows, Linux, Solaris, iOS platforms respectively.
- ***Scalability*** – the cloud is dynamic in nature such that the resources are scalable up and down based on the demands of the end user. Suppose in an IT organization suddenly the need of hardware resource goes up, we need to add the extra resource. But, this is not a worry factor using a cloud based workspaces in business organization.
- ***Service oriented technology*** – compared to all the previous computing technologies cloud computing quietly varies from its basic point of utilization. The cloud is a service oriented technology unlike a dedicated technology. It helps in the needs of the business processing unit and the aspiration of end user.
- ***Advanced networking*** – compared to all the previous computing technologies cloud computing is quite more advanced form of a networking technique. It can be said as the combination of all previous techniques satisfying the needs of the end user and business world.
- ***Remote access*** – the easy migration of all resources in cloud makes the user to access the cloud technology from anywhere, location independence and is user friendly.
- ***Robustness*** – the cloud technology is far robust than the traditional internet in handling any crisis situation like data traffic, hardware issues, security to resource

and etc. It is quite dynamic and more powerful computing technology. The concept of distributed technique makes the cloud far better to handle the data traffic. The data traffic is equally distributed in the network systems to handle any crashing of the network.

- ***Response Time*** – Cloud computing accomplishes a better response time in most cases than standard server and hardware. If the response time is too long it is unfriendly to the end user.
- ***Future technology*** – in the future if there is more advancement in computing technology further, the new computing technology will be based on the basis of cloud computing. As cloud itself has inherited from past computing technology. One cannot completely isolate the previous technology from the current one. After all cloud has utilized the much of the networking concepts and is platform independence in functioning. Thus cloud can be predicted as the base of further advancement in computing techniques.

1.7 CLOUD ARCHITECTURE

In this section, we explain the basic architectural layout of a cloud. Architecture represents a skeleton layout of the entity giving the details of its various components, interaction between them and the overall function of each component. Architecture gives a clear picture of how a specific function takes place in a step wise approach. We explain the cloud architecture using a set of diagrams which can be easy to imagine the overall layout and the way it functions.

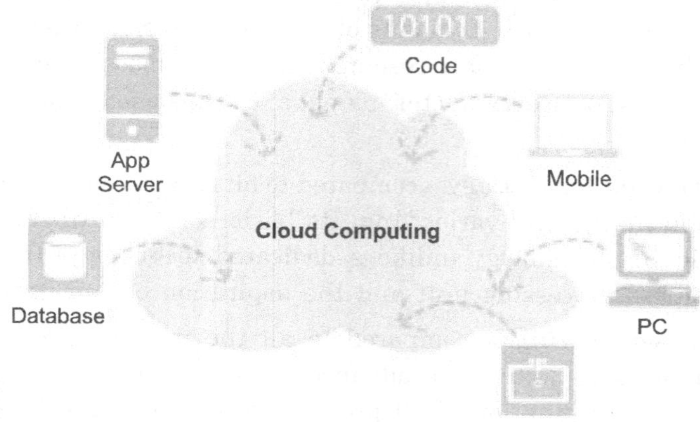

Figure 1.3 Devices connected to cloud.

Basic cloud architecture involves the resources being pooled in the cloud, which is represented as a literal cloud in the center and all the devices are connected to the cloud. Devices can range from traditional desktop based PCs, laptops, smart technology mobiles, tablets and other advanced hardware. The resources pooled in cloud include the database storage, app server, computation memory and other required resources of the end user. The pooled resources are provided as a service to the end user by creating instance of the resource and made available to the connected device using the high speed internet. The cloud is highly scalable to adjust the demand of the user based on the demand. The cloud is robust enough to overcome any fault or crash in the network when the capacity increases rapidly. Resources are allocated and reallocated in a uniform way.

A cloud involves many vendors who provide their service to the end user. In the current scenario everyday a new vendor is stepping into the market to provide their service to the end user. Thus day by day cloud is getting more popular and is advancing soon. Each vendor provides some extra or advanced feature in the cloud, making it a popular among the end user and the business world. Some vendors provide their service free while some charge. All the users of the cloud are regularly monitored and managed in a well defined manner by the vendor. The used resources are exactly calculated and are charged based on the consumption. Each user has a separate account by registering to the vendor initially and logging by the secured credentials. Any suspicious activity or any misuse of things can lead to the removal of the registered user from the cloud by the vendor. The major vendors include Amazon, Google, Microsoft, IBM, HP, EMC square, and so many. Today every major corporate IT companies have tie up with Amazon cloud and are working with them to enhance and solve all business related functions. Amazon is seen as a major cloud vendor in the market compared to all others. It is also more popular with other web services too.

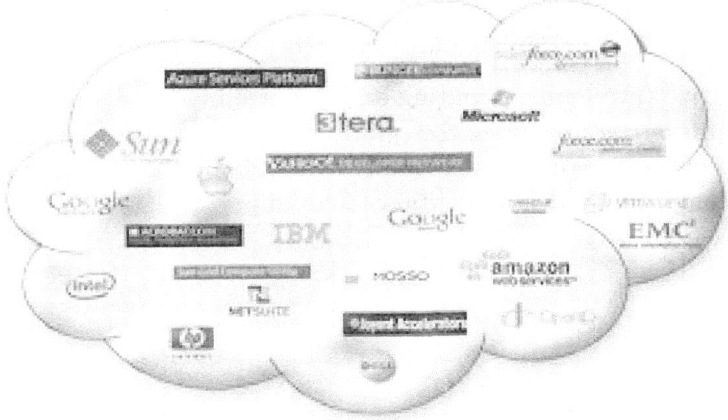

Figure 1.4 Cloud vendors.

Each service vendor in the cloud provides the required infrastructure for the end user to design their application and host their application into the cloud platform with all the necessary resources in the cloud. A good example of this can be Amazon elastic compute EC2 cloud and Microsoft windows Azure. They are proprietary and cannot be used as free. (We will see in details of this in the upcoming chapters)

Thus to combine all the above diagrams a typical cloud looks like this. A typical cloud involves multiple thin clients accessing the thick backend server. The cloud is highly advanced such that multiple instances of the same resource are shared by many clients at a time (virtualization).

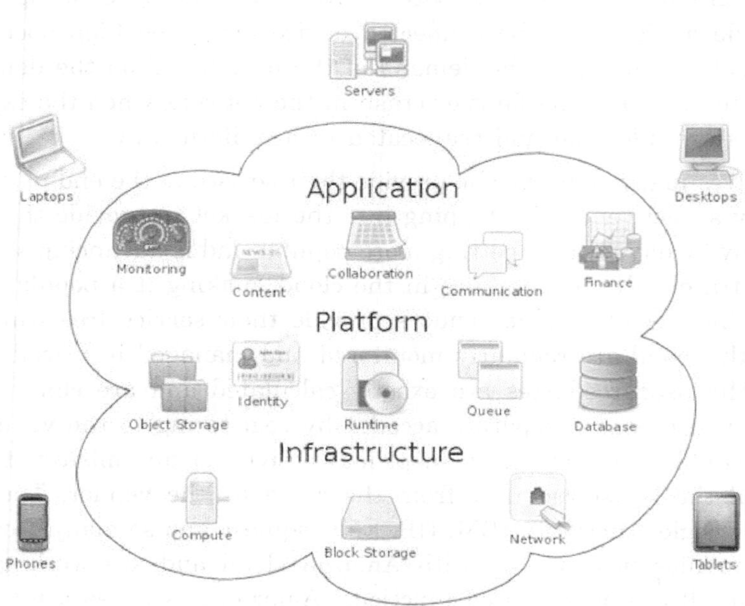

Figure 1.5 Cloud architecture.

We can summarize the cloud computing architecture by this diagram. The overall cloud provides the basic infrastructure using this platform the user develops the applications and it is hosted in a remote virtual cloud. It is made available by the enabling services. The core principal of cloud computing is virtualization technique.

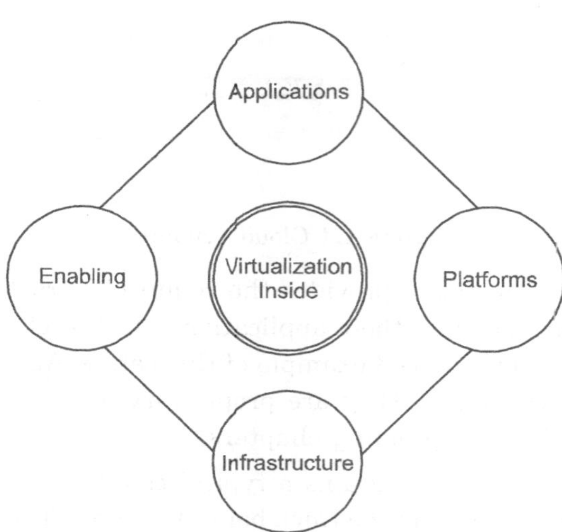

Figure 1.6 Overview of cloud architecture.

SUMMARY

- *Cloud computing is a recent trend in IT platform involving the sharing of resources by connecting to a remote cloud.*
- *Cloud involves the sharing of highly dynamic resources than a static web contents, regarded as the advanced networking technology.*
- *Cloud computing involves sharing of data, software, hardware, running process or application and even more than this.*
- *The NIST definition of cloud computing is - Cloud computing is a model for enabling convenient, on-demand network access to a shared pool of configurable computing resources (e.g., networks, servers, storage, applications, and services) that can be rapidly provisioned and released with minimal management effort or service provider interaction.*
- *The evolution of cloud technology dates back to 1950s when the concept of sharing resources was realized, it started with the mainframes revolution in 1950 and the virtual machines concept in 1970.*
- *In 1990 the revolution of internet had started and the data traffic increased by infinite times. The internet itself had undergone several layers of advancements and changes. The web domain World Wide Web (WWW) was seen as the beginning of the revolution of web technology and its service to the mankind in the milestone of computer technology.*
- *In late 2008 accessing internet from hand held mobile devices made the technology a more user friendly and advanced. The traditional client server model was replaced with dynamic and heterogeneous distributed computing technology.*
- *Cloud computing is evolved from a various computing techniques of the past. Each computing technique changed the functioning of computer and its applications. The computing techniques include client server, mainframe technology, parallel computing, distributed computing, cluster computing, utility computing, grid computing, edge computing and green computing.*
- *Maturity of a technology marks the revolution of it among the people in full scale and making it popular. The business world switch to the new technology, all the previous works are transformed to the new technology workspace. The future work is carried in the new technology environment.*
- *During the early to mid-2000s, the cloud was praised for its ability to reduce capital expenditure. Cloud applications were cheaper to implement, upkeep, and upgrade. By the end of the 2000s, the conversation around the cloud had changed from tactical to strategic. Cloud was becoming a more and more a real time based concept from just the theory oriented technology.*

- *Since 2010 many open source clouds have been introduced into market like Eucalyptus cloud, Openstack cloud, Cloudstack and etc. These open source clouds are extensively used in the Linux platform to accomplish the end user task. Every year the open source clouds are getting updated and new versions of more advanced, bug free one is dedicated to people.*
- *The characteristics of cloud computing includes Anytime Anywhere Technology, Pay per usage, On demand self-service, Online access, Resource pooling, Rapid elasticity, Scalability, Reliability, Loosely coupled, Multi tenancy, Cost effective, Customization and High performance.*
- *Cloud computing is favored by the users and the IT companies due to its Economic, Automatic updating, Synchronization with other technology, Scalability, Service oriented technology, Advanced networking, Remote access, Robustness,* ***Response Time and*** *Future technology.*
- *Basic cloud architecture involves the resources being pooled in the cloud, which is represented as a literal cloud in the center and all the devices are connected to the cloud. Devices can range from traditional desktop based PCs, laptops, smart technology mobiles, tablets and other advanced hardware.*

Chapter 2

PRINCIPLES AND WORKING OF CLOUD COMPUTING

OBJECTIVE

- *To know all the principles of cloud computing*
- *To know in depth about virtualization, distributed technology and thin client*
- *To know about the underlying working of cloud computing*
- *To know the differences and similarities about the web technology and cloud technology*

In the previous chapter, we saw the introduction to the cloud computing technology. We also saw the evolution of cloud, list of various predecessor computing techniques, maturity of cloud, characteristic and the overall architectural layout of the cloud. Now in this chapter let us see in detail about the list of various technological principles behind cloud computing. How these technologies are helping in the overall functioning of the cloud. We will learn about the overall picture of the revolution and the usage of internet in modern IT age of today. We will also see how the dynamic cloud is different from a static web page.

2.1 PRINCIPLES BEHIND CLOUD COMPUTING

For every new technology there is a foundation principle. Only based on that principle the technology is evolved, built, matured and revolutionized. The principle defines the overall functioning and the properties of the technology. By using the principle of the technology its applications are designed and are used. Without a basic principle no entity can exist or can be defined. In order to learn a technology we must first know the fundamental principles behind it only then we can understand it better and get a clear idea of it. Cloud computing is based on combination of previous computing techniques and some new ones. For cloud computing there are several principles which define its overall picture in terms of functioning using which all the applications are designed to fit in the cloud environment.

They include:

- Virtualization technology
- Distributed technology
- Thin client technology

Though these are the most important principle but there are many more techniques like networking, internet, web technology and web services, service oriented architecture, database management and still many more. Without the basic networking concept none of the above mentioned techniques can exist. Thus only by basic networking technique all of them have evolved.

Cloud computing can be defined as advanced networking technology. Using the basic networking concepts, web services and internet it functions. One cannot isolate cloud and the networking technology. Internet act as transmission mode for cloud computing. Cloud is accessed and used only using the traditional and basic internet technology. Cloud computing is also closely associated with all its previous computing techniques which we already saw in the previous chapter.

The principle of a technology also defines the amount or the overall requirement of the basic infrastructure required to support the technology. If the required infrastructure is unavailable the technology fails in the half way itself. Cloud computing is a highly dynamic technology it must be supported with a high speed internet, virtual data centers to process all the user requests, handle all the user task and above all the huge resources are pooled into the cloud. Cloud computing involves the migration of everything from a remote virtual cloud to the user location thus one must imagine the overall infrastructure to support such migration concept. Every technology is supposed to be robust, fault tolerance and even automation to some extent. Hence the underlying principle must provide and satisfy all these.

There are similarities between the technologies as the underlying principles are similar. They are based on same technologies but some differences in their actual usage and functioning. Two technologies can have same principle and we cannot completely isolate them. When a technology is evolved from the predecessor technologies then it must have evolved from the principles of the predecessor technologies.

2.2 INTERNET AND WEB 2.0

In the major principle related to cloud is the *internet* and basic networking technologies. Let us discuss in this section, how internet has changed from time to time and has led to a mass technological revolution which has ultimately led to revolution of various computing techniques.

Almost every one of us must have heard the term called *internet.* The words internets, web, net and so on are often popularly used which ultimately refers to internet. Today as of 2013 more than 75 percentage of the people have heard or exposed to the internet technology in just more than decade of its revolution. India is the third major usage of internet technology in the world. Every day millions of web pages and online contents are getting added day by day. Internet has become a large world today with people easily getting connected to it. Today's youth are grown only under the internet shadow. One cannot imagine the life without internet today.

The commonly used term for internet in many textbook versions is *network of networks.* The history of internet is a very large story we don't discuss much about this here for principles of cloud computing. The basic internet technology is of the WWW or World Wide Web consortium. The internet is of the TCP/IP protocol suit. All the web pages in internet are designed using the various scripting languages and are hosted in the server. The basic architectural model of internet is client server model. Today internet is such a large ocean that the data traffic and congestion is on the rise. Internet is growing day by day by huge contents in the internet. The security is of the prime concern in today's internet.

The previous internet or the outdated one was called as *web 1.0*. The modern and advanced internet of today is called as *web 2.0*. Web 2.0 is the term given to describe a second generation of the World Wide Web that is focused on the ability for people to collaborate and share information online. Web 2.0 basically refers to the transition from static HTML Web pages to a more dynamic Web that is more organized and is based on serving Web applications to users. Web 2.0 was previously used as a synonym for Semantic Web, but while the two are similar, they do not share precisely the same meaning. This advanced internet has paved the path for higher computing techniques and of course to cloud computing. The concept of web 2.0 generally includes three major parts:

- ***Rich Internet application*** – It defines the overall new experience brought from desktop based machines to browser whether it is from a graphical point of view or usability point of view. Some of the commonly used terms include related to rich internet application are Ajax and Flash. Quite such rich and interactive web pages have made the web 2.0 a more popular one.
- ***Web-oriented architecture*** – It is a key piece in Web 2.0, which defines how Web 2.0 applications expose their functionality so that other applications can leverage and integrate the functionality providing a set of much richer applications. It can also be defined as the advanced web technology. Examples are feeds, RSS, Web Services, mash-ups.
- ***Social networking*** – Defines how Web 2.0 tends to interact much more with the end user and make the end-user an integral part. Today's modern world there is a huge revolution of social networking technology. More and more social networks are out in today's internet. One can easily understand the concept of web 2.0 with its attractive features like.

Figure 2.1 Web 2.0 and its revolution.

- ***The Web is a platform*** – We have gone from installable software on our PC, to software-services that are accessible online. All data and software is now available online. One must not confuse internet with dynamic cloud.
- ***The Web is functionality*** – The Web aids in the transfer of information and services from websites.
- ***The Web is simple*** – It facilitates the access and usage of web services using user-friendly interfaces.
- ***The Web is light*** – The models of development, the processes, and the models of business become light. The lightness is associated with the ability to share information and services with ease, and made possible through the implementation of intuitive modular elements.
- ***The Web is social*** – People create the Web, populate the Web by socializing and gradually moving members from the physical world to the online world.
- ***The Web is flow*** – The users are seen as co-developers, while Web 2.0 remains in perpetual beta where it remains at the beta development stage for an indefinite period of time.
- ***The Web is flexible*** – The software is on a more advanced level because it enables access to previously unavailable digital content. This idea is similar to the Long Tail concept, which focuses on the less popular content that couldn't previously be accessed.
- ***The Web is mixable*** – The expansion of codes in order to modify web applications allows individuals who are not necessarily computer professionals to mix different applications in order to create new ones. Web 2.0 gets its power through this mashup capability.
- ***The Web is participatory*** – Web 2.0 has adopted a structure of participation that encourages users to enhance the application while they use it, instead of keeping it rigid and controlled.
- ***The Web is in our hands*** – Its increased organization and characterization of information emphasizes its user-friendly interaction through deep linking. Thanks to phenomena such as social tagging, information is always more and more easily available.

One of the most significant differences between Web 2.0 and the traditional Web 1.0 is greater collaboration among Internet users and other users, content providers, and enterprises. Originally, data was posted on Web sites, and users simply viewed or downloaded the content. Increasingly, users have more input into the nature and scope of Web content and in some cases exert real-time control over it. There are many other differences between web 1.0 and 2.0. Some of them include:

- Usage and designing of higher scripting technologies in web 2.0
- Web 2.0 involves full fled user participation

- Web contents in web 2.0 are too dynamic and more advanced
- Better resource sharing and communication from web 2.0
- Applications of web 2.0 are very rich and are platform independent
- Web 2.0 applications are easily accessed from not just computers it include hand held devices like mobile, tablet PCs and so on.

Web 1.0		**Web 2.0**
DoubleClick	-->	Google AdSense
Ofoto	-->	Flickr
Akamai	-->	BitTorrent
mp3.com	-->	Napster
Britannica Online	-->	Wikipedia
personal websites	-->	Blogging
evite	-->	upcoming.org and EVDB
domain name speculation	-->	search engine optimization
page views	-->	cost per click
screen scraping	-->	web services
publishing	-->	Participation
content management systems	-->	Wikis
directories (taxonomy)	-->	tagging ("folksonomy")
stickiness	-->	Syndication

Figure 2.2 Comparison between web 1.0 and web 2.0.

A simple comparison table between web 1.0 and web 2.0 applications and their core functionalities can be understood from the above table. Revolution of web 2.0 has led to mass popularity of the term internet. The advanced web 2.0 has led the foundation for higher networking areas and computing techniques.

The client side technologies used in web 2.0 includes Ajax and JavaScript Framework. YUI Library, Dojo Toolkit, MooTools, jQuery, Ext JS and Prototype JavaScript Framework Ajax programming uses JavaScript to upload and download new data from the web server without undergoing a full page reload. Today many scripting technologies are available to design the front end app.

To allow users to continue to interact with the page, communications such as data requests going to the server are separated from data coming back to the page (asynchronously). Otherwise, the user would have to routinely wait for the data to come back before they can do anything else on that page, just as a user has to wait for a page to complete the reload. This also increases overall performance of the site, as the sending of requests can complete quicker independent of blocking and queuing required to send data back to the client.

On the server-side, Web 2.0 uses many of the same technologies as Web 1.0. Languages such as PHP, Ruby, Perl, Python, as well as Enterprise Java (J2EE) and Microsoft.NET Framework, are used by developers to output data dynamically using information from files and databases. What has begun to change in Web 2.0 is the way this data is formatted. In the early days of the Internet, there was little need for different websites to communicate with each other and share data. In the new participatory web or web 2.0, however, sharing data between sites has become an essential capability. To share its data with other sites, a website must be able to generate output in machine-readable formats such as XML (Atom, RSS, etc.) and JSON. When a site's data is available in one of these formats, another website can use it to integrate a portion of that site's functionality into itself, linking the two together. When this design pattern is implemented, it ultimately leads to data that is both easier to find and more thoroughly categorized, a hallmark of the philosophy behind the Web 2.0 movement.

Some of the interactive features of web 2.0 include:

- Very interactive and communicative feature of internet which can be supported in many hardware devices not just restricted to desktop PCs, it supports mobiles phones, tablet PCs and other smart technology devices.
- Most of the web contents are highly dynamic in nature rather a static one before.
- All the printed contents are available as online documents in internet like newspapers, magazines and so on. Thus all of these have reduced the paper waste.
- Users can work in offline with some web applications, typical example being the web page being downloaded and viewed later in browser
- Mass online chatting and communication sites with several interactive chatting apps in both internet and mobile version along with live video.
- Social networking age where people are easily connected to each other using the social networking sites like Facebook, Twitter, Linkdin and so on.
- Many online applications to track the locations and other mappings facilities, quite a very interesting and useful one for mainly travelers.
- Many online downloading sites to download movies, videos, images and etc., which has put an end to viewing videos from CDs and other small storages.
- Online blogging sites they are very helpful to gather much information about various fields.
- Online streaming of videos in internet in many video sites like Youtube and etc. Today everything is available as videos and images in online apart from the traditional data.
- Online marketing and mass e-shopping websites like ebay, flipkart and so on. A very convenient and easy option to purchase everything in online with home delivery.

- Online banking and monetary transactions. A fast approach to all forms of user transactions on monetary issues.
- Online e-learning and tutorials web sites with several interactive forums.
- A another major revolution of web 2.0 is online booking of all tickets be it rail, air, bus, movie, and all other appointments.

And still lot more is web 2.0 features, this is just the tip of it. Along with android today internet has changed the whole world by millions of applications.

As we already know cloud computing is accessed using the internet technology. Without internet cloud computing cannot exist at all. Web 2.0 has laid the base for advanced computing technology.

2.3 VIRTUALIZATION TECHNOLOGY

In this section, let us see in detail about the virtualization technique, its types and how this technology is helping in the overall functioning of cloud computing. Virtualization is a very big area and has a very broad meaning. One can also say the maturity of virtualization has paved the path for new cloud computing area.

A very important and the basic fundamental principle of cloud computing is *virtualization*. The term *virtual* literally refers to an imaginary or something that does not exist but is assumed to be existing. Virtualization technology has been proposed and developed over a relatively long period. The earliest use of VMs was by IBM in 1960, intended to leverage investments in expensive mainframe computers. The idea was to enable multitasking running multiple applications and processes for different users simultaneously. We have already seen this in chapter 1. To speak technically the meaning of virtualization is quite vast and it varies from place to place based on its usage. There are several types of virtualization. Based on the type the real meaning and its underlying functionality of virtualization also varies. We will see the types of virtualization below in this section.

From cloud computing point of it virtualization can be defined as the duplication or a replication of a resource from a remote cloud and it is migrated to the end user. It is popularly referred as the *instance* of the resource. The term resource in virtualization can be hardware, memory, storage, operating system, application and network. The instances are generated in large number and are assigned to each user at a time based on their need. The instances are migrated from the remote cloud to the user. The generation and migration of instances is the prime concept involved in cloud computing. For this process a very high memory and the infrastructure is required in real time.

It is this virtualization technique that is making the cloud computing a more dynamic and powerful one. Compared to all other previous computing technique cloud computing can be more distinguished well with virtualization technique. Throughout all the discussion of cloud computing the word virtualization is used in every material or technical papers. It is the overall backbone of this technology. Virtualization technology is also quite eco friendly and is seen as the base for green computing techniques too.

There are various reasons that virtualization is effective in practical scenarios which includes:

- ***Server and application consolidation*** – Under virtualization concept we can run multiple applications at the same time on the same server resulting in more efficient utilization of resources.
- ***Configurability*** – Virtualization allows dynamic configuration and bundling of resources for a wider variety of applications than could be achieved at the hardware level.
- ***Increased application availability*** – Virtual migration allows quick failure recovery from unplanned outages with no interruption in service. Thus they are more fault tolerant.
- ***Improved responsiveness*** – Resource provisioning, monitoring, and maintenance can be automated, and common resources can be cached and reused.

Linux is the best platform to work with the virtualization technology. More than Windows or any other operating system platform Linux is acknowledged as the best operating system to work in real time and analyze the concepts of virtualization. The overall architecture of the Linux is designed to work with networking and virtualization concepts in a very user friendly manner. We can install any virtualization tool and work with it in Linux platform. All cloud tools are based on virtualization only. That is why almost all the cloud tools are installed under the Linux platform. We must enable the virtualization feature in operating system before installing any cloud tool else it will fail at the time of installation itself. One can easily enable the virtualization using the commands in terminal. We can also check using commands in terminal whether the virtualization is enabled or disabled currently.

There are several types of virtualization. Each one has different function and its application. The types include:

- Hardware virtualization
- Desktop virtualization
- Network virtualization
- Data virtualization
- Application virtualization including operating system and software
- Memory virtualization
- Server virtualization

And many more types of virtualization. Out of all these we will discuss in detail about the hardware virtualization.

Hardware virtualization is a type of virtualization in which several applications or operating system is run on a single hardware itself. It appears to us as if multiple applications are running in different memory but in reality they are running in a same memory. A good example of it is the virtual box software in which we install another operating system inside the software it is called guest machine. The virtual box itself is another software running in the base machine called host machine. The software that creates a virtual machine on the host hardware is called a *hypervisor* or *Virtual Machine Manager*. Some of the examples of hypervisor include:

Type	Description	Vendors
Application virtualization	Application Virtualization takes applications and their supporting OS capabilities and creates a logical package for each application that runs as an independent layer on an OS so applications don't affect each other or the underlying OS.	VMware, Microsoft, Citrix
Desktop virtualization	Desktop virtualization puts an entire PC environment on a virtual machine so it can be provisioned to users from a common, centrally stored "image."	Citrix, VMware, Ceedo, InstallFree, Xenocode
Server virtualization	Server virtualization puts an entire server environment (operating system, hardware, and connectivity) onto a virtual machine so it can be run on any compatible server, typically in parallel with other virtual machines on the same server to increase hardware utilization.	VMware, Microsoft, Citrix Red Hat, Oracle
Storage virtualization	Storage virtualizatio pools together multiple physical data stores into one logical pool.	EMC, Fujitsu, HP, Hitachi, IBM, NetApp
I/O and memory virtualization	Emerging types of virtualization include I/O and memory virtualization, both of which break down physically separate sets of computing resources into more flexible logical groupings.	Intel, AMD, RNA, Networks
Network virtualization	Network virtualization creats logically separate communication channels within and across local area networks (LANs) to allow multiple types of network channels on the same infrastructure.	Networking vendors

Figure 2.3 Types of virtualization.

LynxSecure, RTSHypervisor, Oracle VM, Sun XVM Server ,VMware VSX & ESXi, Xen, KVM, Microsoft HyperV and VMware Fusion.

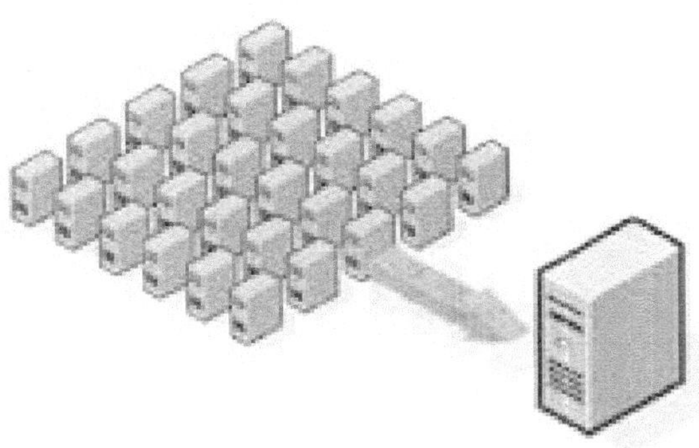

Figure 2.4 Virtualization.

We can better understand the hardware virtualization concept with virtualizing x86 architecture.

Virtualizing the X86 Architecture

Now we see how the hardware virtualization actually works with the x86 architecture. The x86 architecture has proven to be the dominate platform in enterprise computing, moving from its humble beginnings in desktop systems to now, powering the large enterprise applications that run businesses across the globe. The current generation of x86 CPUs include features such as large scale multi-threading with 8 or more processing cores, support for large memory systems with Non Uniform Memory Access (NUMA) and integrated memory controllers, high speed CPU interconnects and chipset for support for advanced Reliability, Availability and Serviceability (RAS) features.

In order to provide a secure operating system environment x86 architecture provides a mechanism for isolating user applications from the operating system using the notion of privilege levels. In this model the processor provides 4 privilege levels, also known as *rings* which are arranged in a hierarchical fashion from ring 0 to ring 3. Thus the overall hardware virtualization concept involves the privilege levels popularly known as rings.

Ring 0 is the most privileged with full access to the hardware and is able to call privileged instructions. The operating system runs in ring 0 with the operating system kernel controlling access to the underlying hardware. Rings 1, 2 and 3 operate at a lower privilege level and are prevented from executing instructions reserved for the operating system.

In commonly deployed operating systems such as Linux and Microsoft Windows the operating system runs in ring 0 and the user applications run in ring 3. Rings 1 and 2 historically have not been used by modern commercial operating systems. This architecture ensures that an application running in ring 3 that is compromised cannot make privileged system calls, however a compromise in the operating system running in ring 0 hardware exposes applications running in the lower privileged levels. While this model provides benefit for traditional bare metal deployments it presents challenges in a virtualized environment.

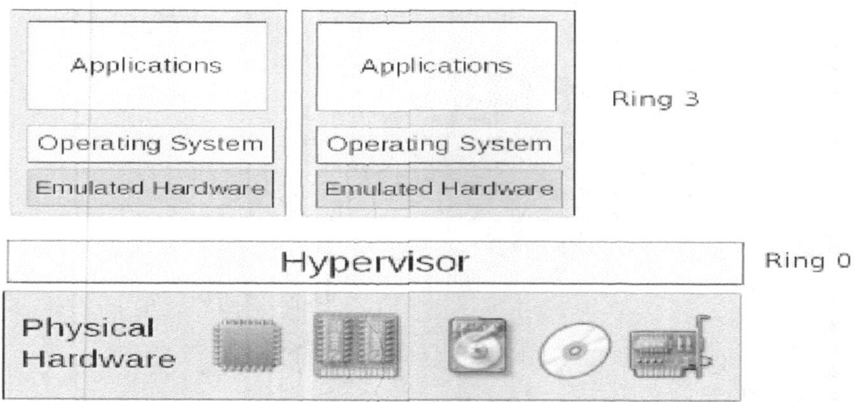

Figure 2.5 Virtualization in x86 architecture.

In a virtualized environment the hypervisor must run at the most privileged level, controlling all hardware and system functions. In this model the virtual machines run in a lower privileged ring, typically in ring 3. Within ring 3 we can see the virtual machine running with an operating system running on virtual hardware. Since the operating system was originally designed to run directly on hardware it expects to be running in ring 0 and will make privileged calls that are not permitted in ring 3. When the operating system makes these privileged calls the hardware will trap the instructions and issue a fault, which will typically destroy the virtual machine.

Generally we can classify the hardware virtualization into two types they include:

- ***Full virtualization*** – In this form of virtualization the entire hardware is virtualized. This enables multiple virtual systems to run concurrently totally isolated from each other in the same hardware. The hypervisor or virtual machine monitor provides access to memory, devices, network, including the CPU.
- ***Paravirtualization*** – It requires the guest operating system kernel to be modified to become aware of the hypervisor since the entire hardware environment is not virtualized. The guest operating systems are executed in their own isolated domains, as if they are running on a separate system. Paravirtualization can attain better performance than full virtualization.

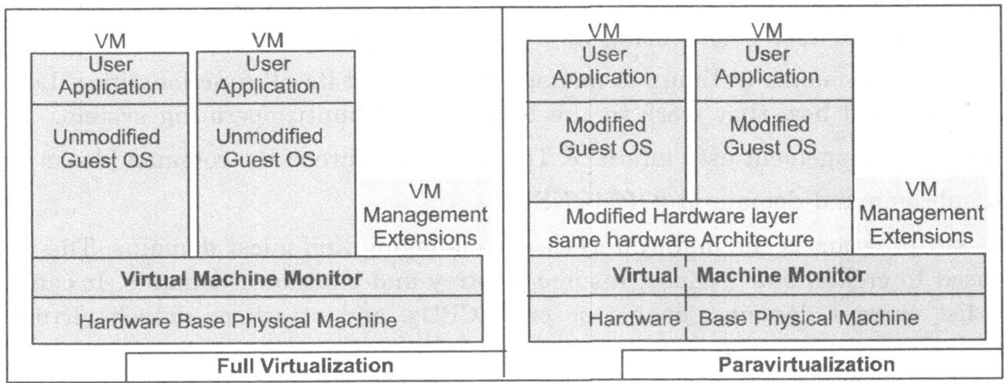

Figure 2.6 Types of virtualization.

Full virtualization is best suited for:

- sharing a computer system among multiple users
- isolating users from each other
- emulating new hardware to achieve improved reliability, security and productivity

Virtualization is accomplished by the use of a hypervisor tool to logically assign and separate physical resources running in a same hardware. The hypervisor allows a guest operating system running on the virtual machine to function as if it were solely in control of the hardware unaware that other guests are sharing it. Each guest operating system is protected from the others and is thus unaffected by any instability or configuration issues of the others.

Let see some of the hypervisors in detail and their functions.

Xen

The Xen hypervisor was created at the University of Cambridge at the end of the 1990's as part of the Xenoserver research project. The Xen community develops and maintains Xen as free and open source software. The first open source release of the Xen hypervisor was done 2002, and the current version of the hypervisor is 4.3 as of 2013. It can thus be considered a mature and stable product. Commercial support is provided by XenSource Inc. Xen is also provide as the virtualization solution by solution providers like Red Hat, Novell, and Sun. Xen is currently marketed by Citrix.

Responsibilities of the hypervisor include memory management and CPU scheduling of all virtual machine and for launching the most privileged domain popularly referred as dom0 the only virtual machine which by default has direct access to hardware. From the dom0 the hypervisor can be managed and unprivileged domains domU can be launched. Xen boots from a bootloader such as GNU GRUB, and then usually loads a paravirtualized host operating system into the host domain.

Xen is usually considered a paravirtualization solution, although version 4.0 adds capabilities for system virtualization. Xen handles device drivers by running a special operating system in a special high-privilege Xen domain (dom0). This operating system handles all device driver requests and has optimized device drivers for the available hardware. The guest operating system then has to be modified to work against these interfaces. One needs to enable the hypervisor before using any virtual tool or cloud tool.

There are commands in Linux to manage the Xen and its all functionalities. Let us see the commands and how they work in the terminal of Ubuntu operating system.

xm – xen management user interface. The basic structure of the command looks like this

xm subcommand domain-id [OPTIONS]

The **xm** program is the main interface for managing Xen guest domains. The program can be used to create, start, pause, resume, destroy and shutdown domains. It can also be used to list current domains, enable or pin VCPUs, and attach or detach virtual block devices.

The status of the host and guest systems may be viewed at any time using the list option of the xm command.

xm list

It displays the list of host and guest systems with the current state which includes:

- ***r - running*** – The domain is currently running and healthy.
- ***b - blocked*** – The domain is blocked, and not running or runnable. This can be caused because the domain is waiting on IO (a traditional wait state) or has gone to sleep because there was nothing else for it to do.
- ***p - paused*** – The domain has been paused, typically as a result of the administrator running the xm pause command. When in a paused state the domain will still consume allocated resources like memory, but will not be eligible for scheduling by the Xen hypervisor.

- ***s - shutdown*** – The guest has requested to be shutdown, rebooted or suspended, and the domain is in the process of being destroyed in response.
- ***c - crashed*** – The domain has crashed. Usually this state can only occur if the domain has been configured not to restart on crash.
- ***d - dying*** – The domain is in process of dying, but hasn't completely shutdown or crashed.

VMware

VMware is a major company which has worked in the field of virtualization and cloud computing for the past several years. It has developed many more products and solutions in these fields. It is seen as a big player in both virtualization and cloud computing. VMware offers a commercial hypervisor called ESX.

ESX runs on a bare metal and does not require a separate operating system. Instead it comes with an included Linux kernel that is booted first and used to load special device drivers and other features required by the hypervisor. The Linux kernel provides access to all devices of the system to the guest operating system using these drivers. In principle VMware is thus a paravirtualization solution. However Scan-Before-Execution the VMware marketing term for its run-time pre-virtualization technology, allows the guest operating system to run unmodified on VMware.

ESX uses a Linux kernel to load additional code it is referred as the vmkernel. In the event of a hardware error, the vmkernel can catch a Machine Check Exception. This results in an error message displayed on a purple diagnostic screen. This is colloquially known as a purple diagnostic screen, or purple screen of death.

Live migration (vMotion) in ESX allows a virtual machine to move between two different hosts. Live storage migration (Storage vMotion) enables live migration of virtual disks on the fly. During vMotion Live Migration of a running virtual machine (VM) the content of the (RAM) memory of the VM is sent from the running VM to the new VM. The content of memory is by its nature changing all the time. ESX uses a system where the content is sent to the other VM and then it will check what data is changed and send that each time smaller blocks. At the last moment it will very briefly freeze the existing VM, transfer the last changes in the RAM content and then start the new VM.

KVM

It is the recent hypervisor technology to be made available in the market. Its feature and working are quite very interesting and useful. KVM consists of two parts the KVM module that is used to virtualize memory and QEMU an emulator for virtualization of I/O. KVM provides solution to make a Linux kernel into a hypervisor by loading a module. Each guest operating system is now a process in user mode of the KVM hypervisor. KVM assumes that it is running on a processor with hardware support for virtualization.

KVM is implemented as a loadable kernel module that converts the Linux kernel into a bare metal hypervisor. There are two key design principals that the KVM project adopted that have helped it mature rapidly into a stable and high performance hypervisor.

Firstly the KVM was designed after the advent of hardware assisted virtualization it did not have to implement features that were provided by hardware. The KVM hypervisor requires Intel VT-X or AMD-V enabled CPUs and leverages those features to virtualize the CPU. KVM was able to design an optimized hypervisor solution without requiring the supporting of any legacy hardware or requiring modifications to the guest operating system.

Another key design principle used was not to reinvent all the core features which already exist. Since the Linux kernel already includes the core features required by a hypervisor and has been hardened into a mature and stable enterprise platform by over 15 years of support and development it is more efficient to build on that base rather than writing all the required components such as a memory manager, scheduler, etc., from the ground up.

Another key decision made by the KVM team was to incorporate the KVM into the upstream Linux kernel directly. The KVM code was submitted to the Linux kernel community in December of 2006 and was accepted into the 2.6.20 kernel in January of 2007. At this point KVM became a core part of Linux and is able to inherit key features from the Linux kernel.

In the KVM architecture the virtual machine is implemented as regular Linux process, schedule by the standard Linux scheduler. In fact each virtual CPU appears as a regular Linux process. This allows KVM to benefit from all the features of the Linux kernel. Device emulation is handled by a modified version of QEMU that provides emulated BIOS, PCI bus, USB bus and a standard set of devices such as IDE and SCSI disk controllers, network cards, etc.

Figure 2.7 KVM architecture.

KVM supports live Migration which provides the ability to move a running virtual machine between physical hosts with no interruption to service. Live Migration is transparent to the end user, the virtual machine remains powered on network connections remain active and user applications continues to run while the virtual machine is relocated to a new physical host.

KVM inherits the powerful memory management features of Linux. The memory of a virtual machine is stored as memory is for any other Linux process and can be swapped, backed by large pages for better performance, shared or backed by a disk file.

KVM is able to use any storage supported by Linux to store virtual machine images, including local disks with IDE, SCSI and SATA, Network Attached Storage (NAS) including NFS and SAMBA/CIFS or SAN with support for iSCSI and Fiber Channel. Multipath I/O may be used to improve storage throughput and to provide redundancy. Again, because KVM is part of the Linux kernel it can leverage a proven and reliable storage infrastructure with support from all the leading storage vendors with a storage stack that has been proven in production deployments worldwide.

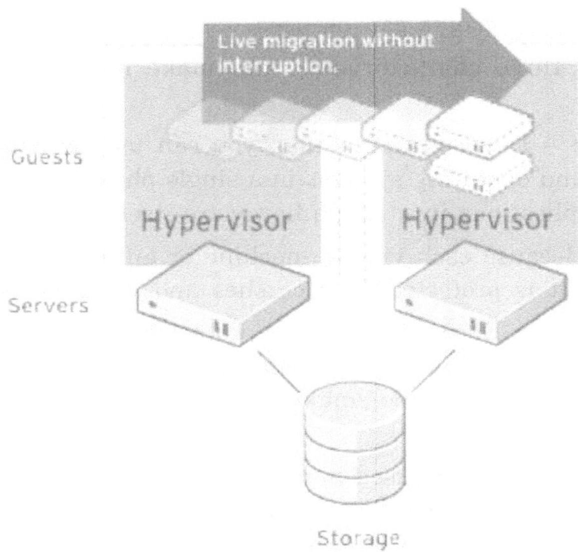

Figure 2.8 Live migration in KVM.

KVM also supports virtual machine images on shared file systems such as the Global File System (GFS2) to allow virtual machine images to be shared between multiple hosts or shared using logical volumes. Disk images support thin provisioning allowing improved storage utilization by only allocating storage when it is required by the virtual machine rather than allocating the entire storage up front. The native disk format for KVM is QCOW2 which includes support for snapshots allowing multiple levels of snapshots, compression and encryption.

There are commands in Linux to know whether the CPU supports the hardware virtualization or not. We can use them to check it. We will see how to check it in Ubuntu operating system. Type these commands in the terminal to check whether CPU supports hardware virtualization or not

egrep '(vmx|svm)' /proc/cpuinfo

egrep-c '(vmx|svm)' /proc/cpuinfo

If **0** it means that your CPU doesn't support hardware virtualization.

If **1** or more it does support but you still need to make sure that virtualization is enabled in the BIOS.

Alternatively one can also use

Kvm-ok

It gives output as

KVM acceleration can be used

or

KVM acceleration can NOT be used

Any one of the two commands can be used.

Virtualization has three characteristics that make it an ideal for cloud computing which are:

- ***Partitioning*** – Using virtualization, you can use partitioning to support many applications and operating systems in a single physical system itself. Thus we can run many applications in a single hardware itself by virtualization.
- ***Isolation*** – Because each virtual machine or an application is isolated from one another each it is protected from crashes and viruses in the other machines.
- ***Encapsulation*** – Encapsulation can protect each application so that it doesn't interfere with other applications. Using encapsulation, a virtual machine can be represented as a single file, making it easy to identify and present to other applications.

Thus this how virtualization is used in cloud computing and this principle is acting as a backbone for this technology. There several IT companies that are working in this field of virtualization. There are lot more projects and opportunities in this area. Some of the notable companies working in virtualization include:

- Vmware
- Citrix
- Oracle
- Red hat
- EMC square
- Virtual bridges
- parallels

And so on. Everyday many applications and tools are designed, are introduced into the market.

2.4 DISTRIBUTED TECHNOLOGY

Another principle which is very much essential for cloud computing is the *distributed technology*. It is a very commonly known technology and is used extensively in today's modern age of computing. We must have worked with it often and in several circumstances. Let us see in detail about this technology and functionalities helping the cloud computing working in a very efficient manner.

The word *distributed* literally refers to the passing or sharing an entity among a group or network. To speak technically the term distributed system can be defined as the system in a network which communicates with each other to accomplish the task. They have a common goal in the network. The distributed system can be imagined as a set of computers connected to each other using the networking devices like LAN cable, switch, router and so on. They communicate and coordinate with each other to accomplish the user task. This underlying technology is called as *distributed technology* and the computing technique is popularly known as *distributed computing*. In distributed computing a problem is divided into many tasks each of which is solved by one or more computers which communicate with each other by message passing. The systems in distributed network are commonly known as *nodes*. A distributed system may have a common goal, such as solving a large computational problem. Alternatively each computer may have its own user with individual needs and the purpose of the distributed system is to coordinate the use of shared resources or provide communication services to the users The network can be small or large with a fixed or a dynamically number of systems in the network. The systems can be in remote or local network too.

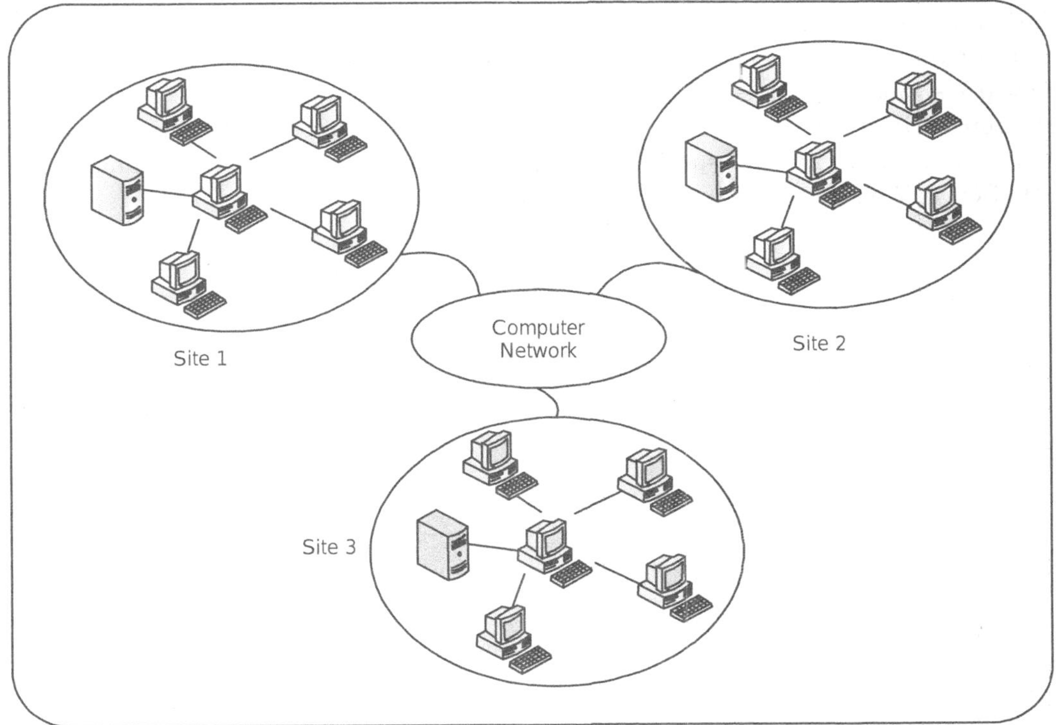

Figure 2.9 Distributed system.

Distributed technology is serving as the base for all other higher computing technologies and in the networking area. Be it cluster computing or utility computing or grid computing or cloud each of these technologies are from this basic concept of distributed. All the applications and the overall functioning of all these computing techniques are from underlying distributed nature. The resources are easily shared or migrated or instances of them are used by all the systems in the network primarily using the distributed techniques. One must imagine how two remote computers in internet communicate with each other so easily, concurrently and faster. It is all based on the distributed nature of communication in the network.

Almost every networking technology which is evolved after distributed computing shares its feature from it. Today most of the applications found in the internet are distributed in nature. It has become a very common term in today's age of advanced computing domain. To be more precise today's web is almost distributed architecture rather than the conventional and traditional client server model of computing. Today many remote applications of various applications are designed with the growing needs and the high expectations of end user and the IT companies. Hence so the data traffic and congestion in internet is increasing day by day.

The commonly developed and used distributed applications include distributed databases, distributed file system, distributed operating system and so on. The distributed applications are also popularly known as *middleware*. Middleware in the context of distributed applications is software that provides services beyond those provided by the operating system to enable the various components of a distributed system to communicate and manage data. Middleware supports and simplifies complex distributed applications. It includes web servers, application servers, messaging and similar tools that support application development and delivery. Middleware is especially integral to modern information technology based on XML, SOAP, Web services, and service-oriented architecture.

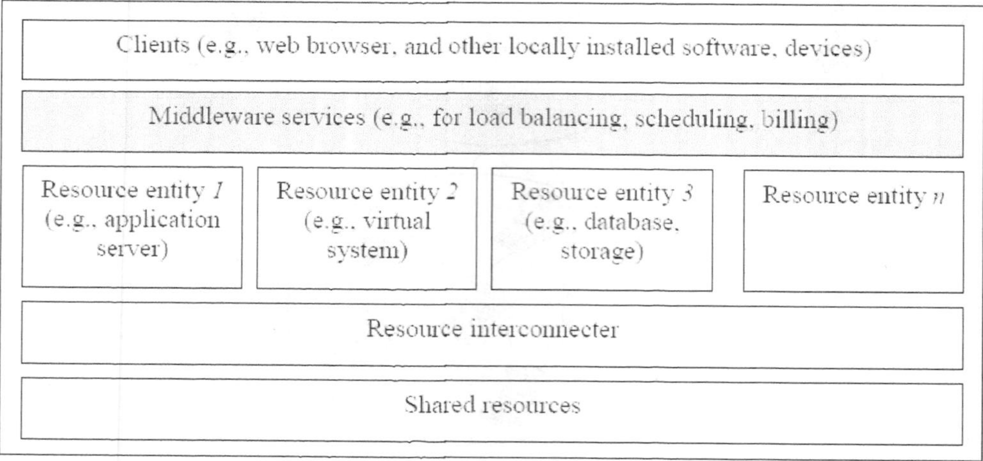

Figure 2.10 Layers of distributed network.

The overall functioning architecture of a distributed system is either 3 tiered architecture or multi tiered. The common one is the three tier architecture. In three tier architecture the front end is the user interface to handle and manage the application by the user. In this tier all user applications run. In the middle there is the processing stage to process all the user request and in this tier are the application server. In backend there is the database to store all the user transaction. This model is quite basic and a common one. But today's complex distributed applications are multi tiered to satisfy all the complex needs of the end user. There are several service models too for distributed system some of them include centralized model, client server model, peer to peer model and so on.

In business enterprises, distributed computing generally has meant putting various steps in business processes at the most efficient places in a network of computers. In the typical transaction using the 3-tier model, user interface processing is done in the PC at the user's location, business processing is done in a remote computer, and database access and processing is done in another computer that provides centralized access for many business processes. Typically, this kind of distributed computing uses the client/server communications model.

Some of the issues we need to consider while designing applications for distributed systems include:

- autonomy of the computing systems
- transparency and openness in communication
- heterogeneous in nature
- they must be fault tolerant in network
- they must be highly reliable
- flexibility in nature
- platform independence
- well secured during communication
- highly scalable
- highly replicated
- high performance too in terms of all computation

There is a lot of overlapping in the word distributed, parallel and concurrent. Almost all these three words mean the same meaning. Their functionalities are also closely same with a quite small exception. Parallel computing may be seen as a particular tightly coupled form of distributed computing and distributed computing may be seen as a loosely coupled form of parallel computing. Parallel Systems are typically finer-grained Distributed Systems. Distributed Systems are typically the most coarse-grained. In parallel computing, all processors may have access to a shared memory to exchange information between processors. In distributed computing, each processor has its own private memory known as *distributed memory*. Information is exchanged by passing messages between the processors. Thus one must not confuse with these closely related technologies and their functions.

A computer program that runs in a distributed system is called as a *distributed program* and *distributed programming* is the process of writing such programs. Today there are several algorithms available for distributed computing. The algorithms are written in a highly efficient manner to reduce the complexity in the communication of distributed systems.

Efficiency is also an another criteria to be considered for such algorithms. The choice of an appropriate distributed algorithm to solve a given problem depends on both the characteristics of the problem, and characteristics of the system the algorithm will run on such as the type and probability of processor or link failures, the kind of inter-process communication that can be performed, and the level of timing synchronization between separate processes. One must not forgot algorithms are the fundamental concepts to define the working part of any technology. It is also the algorithm code which defines the overall functionality to be executed by the system. The algorithms can be modified or advanced to satisfy the needs and requirements of the end user.

A very common term we often use in the discussion about distributed technology is *Remote Procedural Call* (RPC). It is an inter process communication. It can be defined as the communication between the two remote systems called as *stub* and *skeleton* as if they are executing in a local one. The messages are packed in the stub and it is unpacked in the skeleton. It is technically called as *marshalling* and *unmarshalling* process. Using the object oriented principles RPC is called as *Remote Method Invocation* process (RMI). Using this simple technique today millions of applications are designed and are working in internet. The history of RPC style distributed computing was fairly complicated in the past. More or less it started with Sun Microsystems Open Network Computing (ONC) RPC system in 1987 as the basic communication mechanism for its Network File System (NFS). NFS is now supported on UNIX, Linux, and many other distributed operating systems. NFS is used to access directories and files located on remote computer as if those directories and files were located on the local computer.

The first major effort toward language independent and platform-neutral distributed computing was taken by the Object Management Group (OMG) in 1989. OMG is a consortium that includes over 500 members. In 1991, OMG delivered the first version of Common Object Request Broker Architecture (CORBA), a distributed objects platform. CORBA allowed programs located in different parts of the network and written in different programming languages to communicate with each other. The term Object Request Broker (ORB) gained popularity to denote the infrastructure software that enabled distributed objects. In 1996 CORBA version 2 introduced the Internet Inter-ORB Protocol (IIOP) as major enhancements in the core distributed computing model and higher-level services that distributed objects could use. IIOP established CORBA's dominance in distributed computing for the next 5 years until the advent of Web services.

Microsoft started its own distributed computing initiative around 1990. In 1996 Microsoft delivered the Distributed Component Object Model (DCOM), which was closely tied to previous Microsoft component efforts such as Object Linking and Embedding (OLE), non-distributed COM (or OLE2), and ActiveX (lightweight components for web applications). To compete with CORBA, the next year in 1997 Microsoft introduced COM+ to bring DCOM much closer to the CORBA model for distributed computing.

Some of the major advantages of distributed technology include:

- The overall performance of the network is high due to distributed technology
- It reduces the overall cost and other expenditure involved in networking

- One of the major advantage of distributed technology is the replication of all resources in the network thereby making the availability of the resources to all the users
- It is highly scalable to meet the demands of the network
- In this technology all systems are highly independent in terms of all computation
- This technology is highly reliable and can overcome any fault in the network
- Distributed technology can further act as a base for higher and advanced networking technology in an incremental manner.

2.5 THIN CLIENT TECHNOLOGY

In the last major principle of cloud computing is the thin client technology. In the previous sections, we saw how the virtualization and distributed techniques are helping in the design and overall functioning of cloud computing. Now let us see in detail about thin client technology.

In terms of the computational power systems can be classified into two major types in the network called as *thin client* and *thick client* respectively. It is quite a very interesting technique. It tells us how the machines are dependent on each for their computation. It also gives the broad picture of remote computation of the end user task in a very user friendly manner. For cloud computing thin client is quite an essential feature need to be supported by the computer. This principle of cloud computing is naturally seen in the end user side.

To speak technically *thin client* also known as *slim machine* is a system without any hard disk and is stateless. The overall computation does not occur in this machine. It is fully dependent on the remote thick server. All the user task and requests are handled in the thick machine in the backend. A typical example of the thin client can be an operating system with just a user interface applications like web browser. It has no other major features to support or accomplish the end user task. Using the thin-client computing model, you won't need to purchase or upgrade hardware just run the latest software instead, you'll be able to let it comfortably evolve, leveraging your existing hardware, operating systems, software, networks, and standards. Thin-client/server computing extends the life of your computing infrastructure considerably. One can imagine a huge network with several thin client machines being accessed by the end user which are managed by the backend thick server.

One needs to imagine a stateless machine in the front end with just user interface and all other transactions being done in the backend. This is how the overall thin client technology works. The backend machines are the intelligent one with all the computation power in their processor. As the user transaction gets executed the final output is displayed to the end user in the front end machine. The user feels as if all the operations are taking place in his machine but in reality it is executed in the backend. The time period to process the user request is also too short and it is so fast that user never feels the impact of the thin client technology. The application logic is separated from the user interface at the server and transported to the client machine. The thin client software accesses and takes advantage of the server system software. MultiWin, the extension to Windows NT Server, allows multiple concurrent thin-client users to log on and run applications in separate, protected Windows sessions on the server.

A thin client machines running Remote Desktop Protocols (RDP), like Citrix ICA and Windows Terminal Services, and/or virtualization software, accesses hard drives in the data center stored on servers, blades, etc. Thin clients, software services, and backend hardware make up **thin client computing,** an **alternative desktop computing model.**

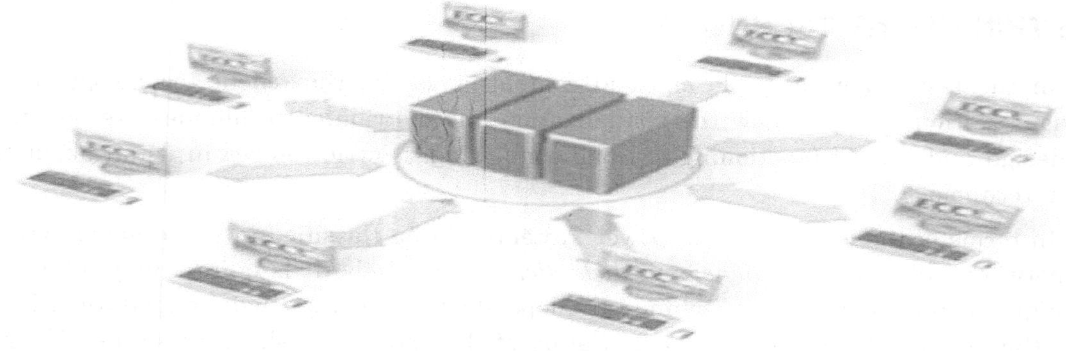

Figure 2.11 Thin client technology.

In cloud computing all the users are connected to the remote cloud. There is a migration of all resources and even the high power workspaces into the user machine. Migration word refers to the instances of the resources being sent to several users at a time. In cloud all the computation takes place in the high powered remote cloud which needs a huge infrastructure to support them. There comes the thin client computing usage in cloud. Thus all user tasks are executed in the remote virtual cloud not in the user machine. All the resources are pooled in the remote cloud to satisfy the needs of the end user. After the task is executed it is again saved back to the virtual remote data center. One must imagine the large number of users accessing the cloud, executing all their task and saving in the cloud data center. This is how the real time cloud works.

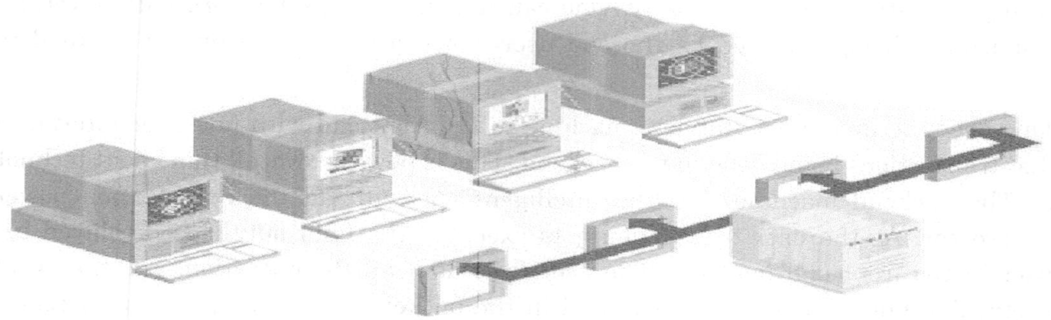

Figure 2.12 Processing in thin client technology.

Some of the major advantages of thin client technology include:

- Reduced cost of client machine
- No hardware issues
- More robust hardware provision in backend server machine
- No major problems in any computational aspects
- Better software environment
- No update or maintenance of software required
- Faster access to GUI applications
- Support heterogeneous systems
- Centralized management of transactions
- Ease of use.

Thus most of the IT professionals clearly prefer single-point control like in the thin client computing. They don't want to travel around a company providing support for each desktop computer that has an operating system. The thin-client architecture allows departments to consolidate databases, file servers, and application servers in the same location in which they manage user access. This consolidation means that users worldwide can access the same centralized information and that companies can avoid the security, cost, reliability, and management issues involved in having widely dispersed databases.

2.6 WORKING AND MIGRATION OF CLOUD COMPUTING

Till now we saw the various principles of cloud computing. We saw how virtualization, distributed and thin client technology are helping in the underlying cloud technology. Now let us see the overall working of the cloud technology. We will see two important things that happen in the backend of the cloud, dynamic resource allocation and live virtual machine migration.

To understand exactly how cloud computing works, let us consider that the cloud consists of two layers mainly the back end layers and the front end layers. One can imagine every application has both front end and back end. Front end is the graphical user interface of the application, while the back end is the database to store all the contents. The front end layers are the parts you see and interact with all resources in the cloud. Thus the front end is the view through which the user views and realizes the cloud in the real time. The back end consists of the hardware and the required software architecture that delivers the data and all other applications that you see on the front end. The back end in the cloud is the large virtual cloud server where all the activities take place.

The user data, application and workspaces are all stored and processed only in the back end highly dynamic, remote and virtual cloud servers. The back end is very important in cloud as it is the place where all the activities takes place, even by mistake if the cloud server is accidently attacked by hacker or the server is down, the user data is completely inaccessible and the work completely gets affected for the user. Thus storing and maintaining the virtual servers in cloud is a very important task. The virtual servers are in a very remote location such that the user might not know where the actual processing takes place, its all a mystery in cloud.

In the first step the user registers with the cloud vendor, the user enters all his personnel details and the banking transaction details for paying the money to the vendor based on the utilization. Only after the vendor confirms the user registration, the separate user account is created. In the registration step the user must confirm to all the service level agreements with the cloud vendor before accepting the cloud technology usage. After this the user can login to the cloud with his credentials and use all the resources and tools in the cloud provided by the cloud vendor. Thus all the interaction in the cloud takes place using the web browser, similar to internet. The user might feel all the operations are taking place in his local machine but actually they are happening in a remote location.

The vendor might provide the user with free trial for some time, later charge for all the usage. At the end of the month the user gets the billing amount from the vendor based on the overall resource usage and is requested to pay the amount in a given time, else the account is locked. There will be several layers of security for the cloud by vendor, the user must not tamper or involve in any other unwanted suspicious activities inside the cloud, else the account of the user is disabled by the vendor.

Clouds use a network layer to connect user end point devices, like computers, smart phones, tablet and all other hardware devices to resources that are pooled in a remote virtual data centre in the cloud technology. Users can access the data centre via a company network or the internet or both of them. Today the technology is fast advancing such that people can access cloud using many interactive apps in smart phone and tablets. Almost all the mobile apps are cloud based and are linked to the aspiration of the users. Clouds can also be accessed from any location, allowing mobile workers to access their business systems on demand.

Applications running on the cloud take advantage of the flexibility of the computing power available. The computers are set up to work together so that it appears as if the applications were running on one particular machine. This flexibility is a major advantage of cloud computing, allowing the user to use as much or as little of the cloud resources as they want at short notice, without any assigning any specific hardware for the job in advance.

Dynamic Resource Allocation and Scheduling Algoriths

Well we must understand how the resources are dynamically assigned in the cloud. This is one of the major criteria in the working of cloud.

Well one must not forget cloud is a vast technology with several users working and accessing all the resources at a time, hence we need a specific way of handling all the users and allocate the resources to them in a very dynamic way. There are several scheduling algorithms available to dynamically allocate resource and execute all tasks in cloud. When a job is submitted to the clouds, it is usually partitioned into several tasks. Following things are need to be consider when applying parallel processing in executing these tasks.

How to allocate resources to all the tasks?

In what order in cloud tasks are executed?

How to schedule overheads when VMs prepare, terminate or switch tasks?

Task scheduling and resource allocation can solve these three problems. In embedded systems technology and in high performance computing areas task scheduling and resource allocation have to be addressed very carefully. Typically, efficient provisioning requires two distinct steps or processes:

- ***Initial static planning step*** – the initially group the set of VMs, then classify them and deployed onto a set of physical hosts
- ***Dynamic resource provisioning*** – the allocation of additional resources, creation and migration of VMs, dynamically responds to varying workload. Second step runs continuously at production time where in contrast first step is usually performed at the initial system set up time and may only be repeated for overall cleanup and maintenance on a monthly or semi-annually schedule.

In this VM-based architecture of cloud all hardware resources are pooled into common shared space in cloud computing infrastructure so that hosted application can access the required resources as per there need to meet Service Level Objective (SLOs) of the application. The adaptive manager use in the architecture is Multi-Input Multi-Output (MIMO) resource manager, which includes mainly three controllers CPU controller, memory controller and I/O controller, its goal is regulate multiple virtualized resources utilization to achieve SLOs of application by using control inputs per-VM CPU, memory and I/O allocation. Thus this how the allocation of resource is controlled in VM based architecture of cloud.

Today several high performance algorithms are available for scheduling resources some of them include, adaptive resource allocation algorithm for the cloud system with preempt able tasks in which algorithms adjust the resource allocation adaptively based on the updated of the actual task executions. Adaptive List Scheduling (ALS) and Adaptive Min-Min Scheduling (AMMS) algorithms are use for task scheduling which includes static task scheduling, for static resource allocation, is generated offline. The online adaptive procedure is use for re-evaluating the remaining static resource allocation repeatedly with predefined frequency. In each re-evaluation process, the schedulers are re-calculating the finish time of their respective submitted tasks, not the tasks that are assign to that cloud.

Virtual Machine Monitors (VMMs) like Xen provide a mechanism for mapping virtual machines (VMs) to physical resources. This mapping is largely hidden from the cloud users. Users with the Amazon EC2 service, for example, do not know where their VM instances run and even others too. It is up to the cloud provider to make sure the underlying Physical Machines (PMs) have sufficient resources to meet their needs at that time. VM live migration technology makes it possible to change the mapping between VMs and PMs while applications are running. However, a policy issue remains as how to decide the mapping adaptively so that the resource demands of VMs are met while the number of PMs used is minimized. This is challenging when the resource needs of VMs are heterogeneous due to the diverse set of applications they run and vary with time as the workloads grow and shrink. The capacity of PMs can also be heterogeneous because multiple generations of hardware co-exist in a data center.

There are two major goals in several algorithms which include:

- ***Overload avoidance*** – the capacity of a PM should be sufficient to satisfy the resource needs of all VMs running on it. Otherwise, the PM is overloaded and can lead to degraded performance of its VMs.
- ***Green computing*** – the number of PMs used should be minimized as long as they can still satisfy the needs of all VMs. Idle PMs can be turned off to save energy.

The dynamic resource allocation is based on distributed multiple criteria decisions in cloud computing. It is of tow-fold, first distributed architecture is adopted, in which resource management is divided into independent tasks, each of which is performed by Autonomous Node Agents (NA) in ac cycle of three activities:

- ***VM Placement*** – in it suitable Physical Machine (PM) is found which is capable of running given VM and then assigned VM to that physical machine
- ***Monitoring*** – in it total resources use by hosted VM are monitored by NA
- ***VM Selection*** – if local accommodation is not possible, a VM need to migrate at another PM and process loops back to into placement.

And secondly, using the PROMETHEE method, NA carry out configuration in parallel through multiple criteria decision analysis. This approach is potentially more feasible in large data centers than centralized approaches.

Live Virtual Machine Migration

Well an another important activity that takes place in cloud while the user is working involves the live migration of the virtual machines. It is a very interesting concept but the front end user is not aware or cannot feel all these while working.

Live migration of Virtual Machines (VMs) is the process of transitioning a VM from one Virtual Machine Monitor (VMM) to another without halting the guest operating system, often between distinct physical machines, it has opened new opportunities in computing area. The user is unaware of all these in the front end. It is implemented by several existing virtualization products, we have already seen several hypervisors in the section 2.3. Live migration can aid in aspects such as:

- High-availability of all services
- Transparent mobility
- Consolidated management
- Workload balancing.

There are many ways in which a virtual machine can be moved from one VMM to another. Since virtual systems are typically stored as regular files on disk in the data center, the files associated with a halted system can be copied to another VMM using a network or using portable storage devices such as USB drives. In addition to the migration of halted virtual systems, many popular VMMs support live migration, the process of transitioning a VM from one virtual machine monitor to another without halting the guest operating system.

While various virtual machine monitors have different wire protocols for live migration, the underlying algorithms are similar. Live migration techniques usually begin by copying memory pages of the VM across the network from the source VMM to the destination while the VM continues to run within the source VMM. This process continues as pages are dirtied by the VM. When the source VMM reaches a threshold and deems that no additional significant progress is being made in the transferring of dirty pages, it will halt the VM, send the remaining memory pages, and signal the destination VMM to resume the execution of the VM. The point at which the VMM decides to halt the source VM and copy the remaining pages is usually an implementation-specific heuristic that attempts to balance and minimize both the duration of migration and the downtime of the migrating VM. Other variations include the destination VMM resuming the VM early and requesting pages from the source VMM on-demand.

While one might assume that networks across which VM images are migrated are secure, this is not an entirely safe assumption anymore. As live VM migration becomes more common in many organizations, it is likely that the migration transit path may span multiple commodity networks and significant geographic distances. Indeed, virtual machines have been successfully migrated across continents with application downtimes as low as 1 to 2 seconds. In addition, a compromised system inside a network employing live migrations can facilitate untrusted access to migrating VM images. The ability to view or modify data associated with live migrations or influences the migration services on source and destination VMMs raises several important security questions.

While virtualization and live migration enable important new functionality, the combination introduces several other security challenges in the underlying. A virtual machine monitor that incorporates a vulnerable implementation of live migration functionality may expose both the guest and host operating system to attack and result in a compromise of integrity. Given the large and increasing market for virtualization technology, a comprehensive understanding of virtual machine migration security is essential. However, the security of virtual machine migration has yet to be analyzed.

Well there are three classes of threats to the migration process:

- ***Control Plane*** – The communication mechanisms employed by the VMM to initiate and manage live VM migrations must be authenticated and resistant to tampering. An attacker may be able to manipulate the control plane of a VMM to influence live VM migrations and gain control of a guest OS.
- ***Data Plane*** – The data plane across which VM migrations occur must be secured and protected against snooping and tampering of guest OS state. Passive attacks against the data plane may result in leakage of sensitive information from the guest OS, while active attacks may result in a complete compromise of the guest OS.
- ***Migration Module*** – The VMM component that implements migration functionality must be resilient against attacks. If an attacker is able to subvert the VMM using vulnerabilities in the migration module, the attacker may gain complete control over both the VMM and any guest OS.

Thus one must be very careful with the security with the live migration.

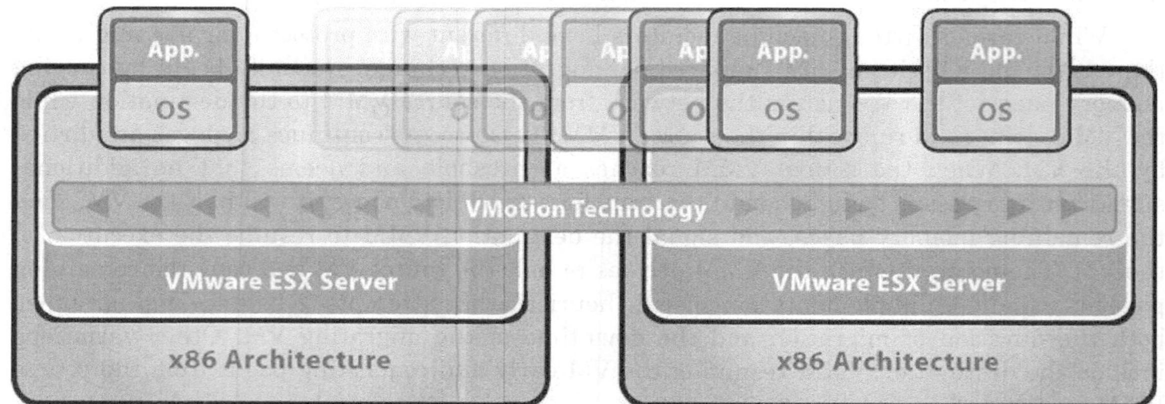

Figure 2.13 Live virtual machine migration.

2.7 WEB TECHNOLOGY AND CLOUD TECHNOLOGY

In the whole chapter till now we saw the various principles of cloud computing. How these principles are helping in the core functionality of cloud. Notably virtualization, distributed and thin client play a major role in the virtual remote cloud functioning. Now in this section let us see in detail about the differences between the traditional web technology from the advanced cloud computing.

There is a very common confusion between web technology and cloud technology. Most of them don't know which is a web application and cloud app exactly. They interchange both of these technologies. People sometimes find it difficult in distinguishing them. Many are not aware of the differences between them. Let us see how these two technologies vary and even how both of them are dependent.

Before understanding the differences between them we must consider some of the issues:

Are web technology and cloud technology interrelated to each other?

Are web apps and cloud apps vary in their function?

What is the difference between web hosting and cloud hosting?

Is web technology not a solution to handle the growing data traffic and congestion in internet?

Is web technology an outdated one with the evolution of various computing techniques?

What is the relation between web 2.0 and cloud computing?

In what way cloud is advanced and dynamic compared to traditional internet?

Are cloud servers more efficient and robust compared to web servers?

With the revolution of cloud are we shifting towards cloud technology ignoring the traditional web based technology?

Thus these are some of the things we need to consider in broadly classifying two technologies.

The web can be closely associated with the word called internet and WWW. Web technology refers to the underlying technology used to build some simple web applications using scripting languages like HTML, PHP, python, java script and still many more languages. Today currently DOT NET is the most used one. These designed web application are hosted in a server and it is accessed by the end user using the respective URL in the web browser. One can just imagine them as a simple client server model way of communication. The backend servers are powerful enough to handle all the requests but sometimes the web applications crash due to over traffic and congestion in network.

The process of designing web applications is popularly known as *web designing*. The term used to host the web apps in a server is called a *web hosting*. The web pages in internet are popularly known as *web sites*. There are millions of web sites and web apps in the internet.

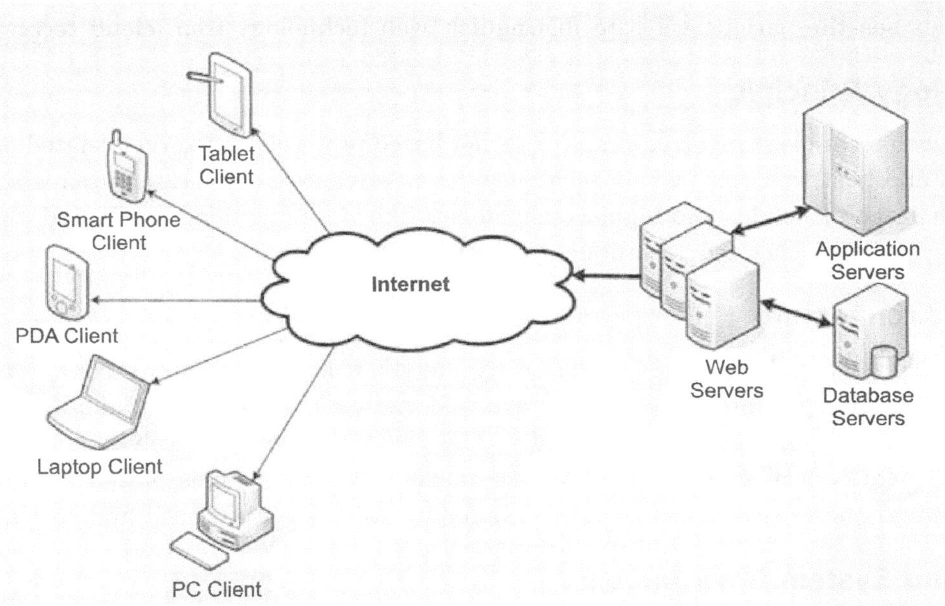

Figure 2.14 Typical web architecture.

As we all know cloud computing deals with the remote and highly dynamic systems in which all the resources are pooled into the cloud. The technology is generally based on the service oriented model. Multiple vendors are available in market to provide the cloud technology to the end user. Cloud computing is an advanced networking technology where the instances of the resources are created and it is migrated from a remote place to the user machine. Several users are connected to the single remote cloud, they use multiple resources at a time from the cloud. The term resource involves the memory, storage, computation, networking and all other user requirements to accomplish the task. The term migration refers to the huge set of resources and even the workspaces to the end user machine.

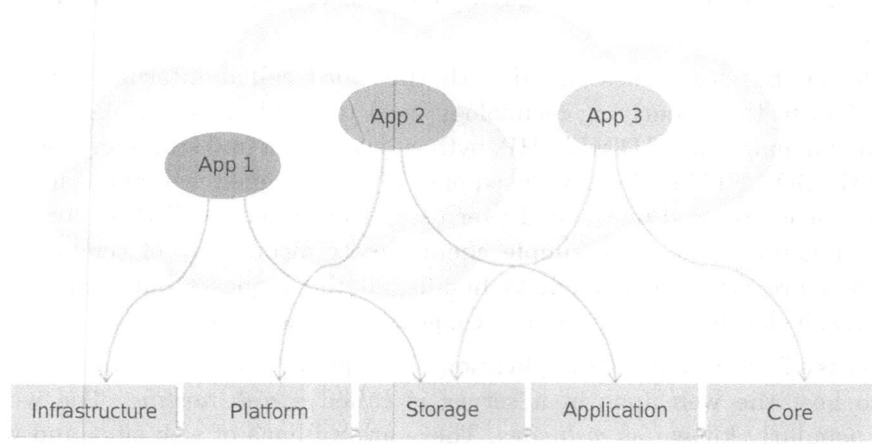

Figure 2.15 Cloud app.

Let us see the various ways to distinguish web technology from cloud technology

Technology Principle

The web technology involves simple internet based protocols and server related principles to design and host web apps. Cloud technology is an advanced networking area with several basic web based principles and higher technologies like virtualization, distributed, thin client technology, service oriented techniques and etc.

Overall Architecture

The web technology concept generally involves a simple client server model of architecture. Though there are many advanced networking models available today but commonly they are of client server model. The cloud technology involves far higher and advanced architectural models called service models. Which includes platform as a service (PaaS), Infrastructure as a service (IaaS), Software as a service (SaaS) and so on.

Operating System Environment

Well to design and host web applications it can be implemented in both Windows and Linux operating system environment successfully. But for cloud computing the concepts of virtualization can be worked in real time only under Linux environment. Almost all the cloud tools are installed only in Linux environment.

Operational Difference

The web based technology is quite comparatively static in its core functionalities though even they get updated from time to time. Cloud computing is a highly dynamic technology where the overall functionalities keep on changing from time to time based on the needs of the end user. It is highly flexible, elastic and scalable.

Sharing Resources

The word sharing has a quite different meaning in two technologies. In web technology only the static web contents are shared to the users. While in cloud computing the term sharing is quite broader with many pooled resources into the cloud. The instances of the pooled resources are used by the registered cloud users.

Data Storange and Computation

An another major difference between the web based applications and cloud applications is from the storage and computation aspect. The data is stored in the normal database servers in web technology. The data can be accessed easily from the backend. All the computation takes place in the client machine only. In the cloud technology all the computation takes place in the virtual remote cloud. All the data is also stored in the virtual data center which is far more advanced than a mere database server.

Infrastructure

Web technology comparatively requires a less amount of IT infrastructure compared to cloud. A commonly available server can be used to host and maintain web apps easily with few underlying configurations. The cloud computing technology needs a very high infrastructure to support the vast virtualization of all pooled resources to several users at a time. The instances of the resources are created and it is used by all the registered end users at a time.

Reliability

Web technology is a quite very basic networking area compared to advanced cloud. The web applications sometimes crash or the server is down due to huge traffic and congestion in network. But cloud computing is a very robust technology as it involves the instances of the resources and is highly distributed in nature to overcome any crash or failure. The cloud technology is highly flexible, elastic, fault tolerant and scalable. Thus the cloud is highly reliable than web based technology.

Availability

The web technology is not more replicated or distributed compared to cloud technology. The cloud apps are more replicated by the virtualization techniques. The several instances of the same resources are created to be used by several users at a time. Thus cloud apps don't crash or are unavailable due to traffic and congestion in network compared to web apps.

Ease of Use

Compared to all web applications and their usage the cloud apps are far higher easy, user friendly and accomplish the user task in a very reliable way. Cloud apps are also more advanced in their overall functioning. Cloud technology is now getting combined with Android technology to provide more advanced mobile based apps and techniques to the end user.

Economic Issue

The web technology involves a static content being designed and hosted onto the server. One needs to spend money in buying and maintaining the server and other web tool kits. Cloud technology involves a renting model with pay as you go model. The user pays the money for the resource being used. The renting model is quite less expensive than buying all the resources.

Security Issues

The web based apps are facing a huge security threat from many high powered hackers and intruders. Many websites are hacked from time to time in internet. It is very difficult to manage them and provide security cover over the large ocean of internet. The cloud technology also has serious security and privacy issues but can be well controlled and governed compared to the web apps. Providing security by the cloud vendor itself brings down some security issues and overhead in them.

Thus one most not confuse with web and cloud technology. There are several distinguish in them.

Now let us see how both the web technology and cloud technology are interlinked.

Cloud computing involves the applications being designed using the basic networking principles and the advanced technologies too. Internet is the basic transmission mode in cloud computing. Without internet one cannot access cloud at all. A very high speed internet is required to access the virtual remote cloud. The cloud is accessed using the common web browser only. Even the web technology requires internet and web apps are accessed using the web browser. There is a close relation between web apps and cloud apps. Which goes like this

All cloud apps are from basic web apps but all web apps are not cloud apps

The explanation goes like this all cloud apps are designed from the basic networking and web concepts. While the web apps are very basic apps and do not involve any major cloud concepts in a very broader meaning. Thus this how both the web technology and cloud technology are interlinked.

SUMMARY

- *For every new technology there is a foundation principle. Only based on that principle the technology is evolved, built, matured and revolutionized. The principle defines the overall functioning and the properties of the technology.*
- *Cloud computing is based on several principles but mainly based on Virtualization technology, Distributed technology and Thin client technology.*
- *In the major principle related to cloud is the internet and basic networking technologies. The previous internet or the outdated one was called as web 1.0. The*

modern and advanced internet of today is called as web 2.0. Web 2.0 is the term given to describe a second generation of the World Wide Web that is focused on the ability for people to collaborate and share information online.

- *A very important and the basic fundamental principle of cloud computing is virtualization. From cloud computing point of it virtualization can be defined as the duplication or a replication of a resource from a remote cloud and it is migrated to the end user. It is popularly referred as the instance of the resource.*
- *Linux is the best platform to work with the virtualization technology. More than Windows or any other operating system platform Linux is acknowledged as the best operating system to work in real time and analyze the concepts of virtualization.*
- *x86 architecture provides a mechanism for isolating user applications from the operating system using the notion of privilege levels. In this model the processor provides 4 privilege levels, also known as rings which are arranged in a hierarchical fashion from ring 0 to ring 3.*
- *There are two types of virtualization which include Full virtualization in this form of virtualization the entire hardware is virtualized. This enables multiple virtual systems to run concurrently totally isolated from each other in the same hardware. The hypervisor or virtual machine monitor provides access to memory, devices, network, including the CPU and the another is Paravirtualization It requires the guest operating system kernel to be modified to become aware of the hypervisor since the entire hardware environment is not virtualized.*
- *The Xen hypervisor was created at the University of Cambridge at the end of the 1990's as part of the Xenoserver research project. The Xen community develops and maintains Xen as free and open source software. Responsibilities of the hypervisor include memory management and CPU scheduling of all virtual machine and for launching the most privileged domain popularly referred as dom0.*
- *VMware offers a commercial hypervisor called ESX. ESX runs on a bare metal and does not require a separate operating system. Instead it comes with an included Linux kernel that is booted first and used to load special device drivers and other features required by the hypervisor.*
- *KVM is the recent hypervisor technology to be made available in the market. Its feature and working are quite very interesting and useful. In the KVM architecture the virtual machine is implemented as regular Linux process, schedule by the standard Linux scheduler.*
- *In distributed computing a problem is divided into many tasks each of which is solved by one or more computers which communicate with each other by message passing. The systems in distributed network are commonly known as nodes. A distributed system may have a common goal, such as solving a large computational problem.*

- *Remote Procedural Call (RPC) is an inter process communication. It can be defined as the communication between the two remote systems called as stub and skeleton as if they are executing in a local one. The messages are packed in the stub and it is unpacked in the skeleton. It is technically called as marshalling and unmarshalling process.*
- *Thin client also known as slim machine is a system without any hard disk and is stateless. The overall computation does not occur in this machine. It is fully dependent on the remote thick server. All the user task and requests are handled in the thick machine in the backend.*
- *Cloud consists of two layers mainly the back end layers and the front end layers. The front end layers are the parts you see and interact with all resources in the cloud. Thus the front end is the view through which the user views and realizes the cloud in the real time. The back end consists of the hardware and the required software architecture that delivers the data and all other applications that you see on the front end. The back end in the cloud is the large virtual cloud server where all the activities take place.*
- *Today several high performance algorithms are available for scheduling resources some of them include, adaptive resource allocation algorithm for the cloud system with preempt able tasks in which algorithms adjust the resource allocation adaptively based on the updated of the actual task executions. Adaptive List Scheduling (ALS) and Adaptive Min-Min Scheduling (AMMS) algorithms are use for task scheduling which includes static task scheduling.*
- *Live migration of Virtual Machines (VMs) is the process of transitioning a VM from one Virtual Machine Monitor (VMM) to another without halting the guest operating system, often between distinct physical machines, it has opened new opportunities in computing area. The user is unaware of all these in the front end. It is implemented by several existing virtualization products.*
- *The process of designing web applications is popularly known as web designing. The term used to host the web apps in a server is called a web hosting. The web pages in internet are popularly known as web sites.*
- *Cloud computing is a highly dynamic and advanced networking area where the resources are pooled into the remote cloud, mainly based on the service oriented model to the end users. There are several differences between the cloud apps and the traditional web apps. One must not get confused with them.*
- *There are similarities between the web based applications and cloud applications it goes like this all cloud apps are from basic web apps but all web apps are not cloud apps.*

Chapter 3

CLASSIFICATION OF CLOUD

OBJECTIVE

- *To know about the classification of cloud*
- *To learn and analyze the types of cloud*
- *To learn about the management of cloud and various management tools*

In the last two chapters, we saw the basic introduction to cloud computing and the various principles behind this new technology. We came to know how a traditional web technology differs from the dynamic cloud. In this chapter, let us see in detail how the clouds are classifieds. How classification of cloud helps in the security, business aspect of the technology and how the cloud is managed based on its scope. Classification of cloud is the best way to analyze its functions, limitations and its application. Classification of clouds can also help us in understanding the concept of sharing resources in cloud much more effectively. At last we will see the management of cloud and the various cloud management tools available.

3.1 TYPES OF CLOUD

We classify the clouds based on their scope within which the cloud can be accessed and is managed within that limit. As we have already learnt cloud computing can be defined as the technology in which group of devices are connected together in a remote fashion to perform the end user task. Hence we must define the boundaries of the cloud so that cloud can be easily managed and secured from people outside the boundaries. Speaking technically the word boundary can be defined as the accessibility of the cloud by the registered user. Some of the issues we need to consider while defining the boundary for a cloud include:

How do we define a boundary for a cloud?

Is defining the boundary a right way to secure and manage the cloud?

How can resource inside the boundary of a cloud be managed?

Are clouds powerful enough to prevent the unauthorized people from entering the defined boundary?

Are there any well defined standards for defining boundaries in cloud?

By defining the boundary in cloud will it affect the overall core functionality of the cloud?

By defining a boundary for the cloud are we making it a limitation in several aspects?

By defining a boundary in cloud cant we integrate or negotiate between the clouds for better services?

Thus, we must define boundaries to address all these issues. We must define boundaries to manage cloud which are robust and smart enough to prevent any intruder into the protected cloud. The defined boundary must satisfy the overall infrastructure and the capability of the corporate IT companies or the public cloud vendor. But a boundary must not be designed to affect the overall functionality of a cloud, which will defeat the whole objective of the new cloud technology. Securing and managing a cloud itself is a separate task in the corporate IT companies. All the resources and technical workspaces are well secured in the corporate IT companies as they are confidential and owned by them. We classify the cloud into four categories based on the scope which defines a well defined boundary to secure and manage the cloud in a very user friendly manner. The types of cloud includes:

- Private cloud
- Public cloud
- Hybrid cloud
- Community cloud

Thus, we classify clouds mainly to manage them within the well defined boundary. We will see each type of cloud in detail in the upcoming sections and how each type differs from one another. It gives us a broad picture about the new technology.

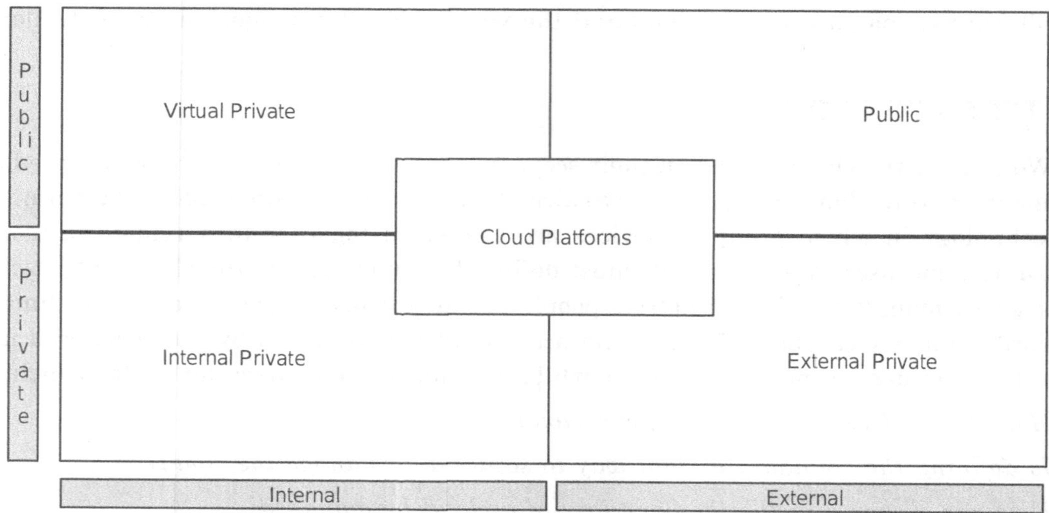

Figure 3.1 Types of cloud with a well-defined boundary for deployment.

Each type of cloud has some advantage and disadvantage. Each type of cloud has its own functionalities and limitations. Each type of cloud can be used in some business solutions based on their usage. The classification of cloud helps us in the right choice of cloud for the organization based on the needs and requirements of the user. The classification also helps us in analyzing the functions of the cloud in real time.

3.2 PRIVATE CLOUD

Lets us now see the first category of the cloud, it is *private cloud*. The word private means something isolated not known to everyone. To speak technically the private cloud is well managed cloud inside a protected organization. The private cloud inside the organization has a well-defined boundary to protect the cloud. The private clouds are generally set up behind the firewall of the organization in a well secured manner from the hackers and intruders. Only the native employees of the organization can access the cloud with the right credentials. The private clouds are also known as internal cloud. Thus a private cloud is private in nature to the organization. It has a well-defined boundary beyond which the private cloud cannot be accessed and used. Any attempt to use the cloud outside the organization ends up throwing a security alert to the cloud administrator of the IT company. A private cloud is accessed within the various locations of the same organization. Thus the organization is responsible for:

- Setting up their own private cloud
- Manage the private cloud users and functionality
- Manage the required infrastructure (storage and computation power) to support the private cloud
- Pool all the required resource into the private cloud
- Track the usage of resources by individual employees and by the individual project team
- Allocate and reallocate the resource inside the private cloud
- Design the suitable application to satisfy their cloud functionality
- Deploy the designed application into the cloud
- Update the application and other software resources from time to time
- Scale the application and resource based on the demand
- Secure the private cloud from outside the organization
- Define a set of standards and protocols to govern the cloud and its functionality
- Protect the privacy and security of the internal confidential information in the cloud.

  (Internal confidential information can be defined as information about a project which cannot be disclosed to other project officials within the same company)
- Manage the overall capital expenditure of the private cloud
- A separate set of team is formed to manage all the aspects of the private cloud inside the organization

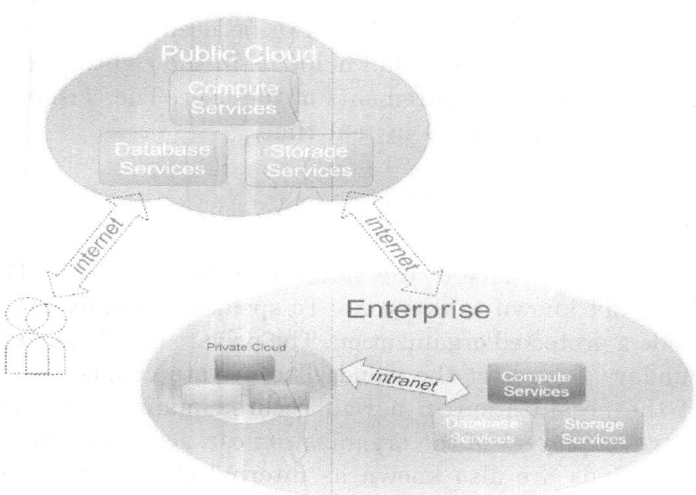

Figure 3.2 Private cloud.

Thus these are things to be done while an organization wants to have their own private cloud. Sometimes it is not possible to maintain all the functions of the cloud by the organization, they outsource the work to some other third party service provider. Among all the four types of cloud private cloud is the best secured cloud environment than the public, hybrid and community clouds. We might imagine public clouds like giant Google or Amazon, when we think of computer resources in the cloud. To overcome security and availability issues, private clouds are the best option for most of the IT companies. A good example of the private cloud can be the clouds setup by the corporate IT companies and using for their own internal purposes. Some of the private cloud by IT companies includes:

- Wipro technologies cloud
- Cognizant technologies cloud
- Accenture cloud
- Cisco cloud and so on

Over half of local and central governments across Europe are using or planning to use private clouds hosted by third parties. Meanwhile, 56% of local governments and 42% of central governments use or will use internally hosted private clouds. UK government cloud computing known as G-cloud promotes government-wide adoption of cloud computing.

There are numerous cloud tools available to configure a private cloud. They are installed under the Linux platform. The client machines are known as node and the server machine is called cloud controller. Setting up a private cloud in Linux is quite a tedious task as it involves a wide set of steps or instructions to be fallowed. But today to overcome them there are script file method of installation where all the steps are put in a huge file, running the file finishes the entire task. The tools are getting updated to newer versions from time to time. By using these tools we can setup a real private cloud, test and analyze the cloud environment. It is often used by all researchers and other educational institutions for study purposes. (We will see in detail about configuring a private cloud in detail in chapter 8)

3.3 PUBLIC CLOUD

The next classification of cloud is the *public cloud*. The word public literally refers to open or a common one. A public cloud is open to all the users and to the business world. Any user can register themselves to the public cloud vendor and can become a cloud user. A public cloud is quite broader in its structural aspect and the application when compared to the restricted private cloud. A public cloud is quite vast than a restricted private cloud. Public cloud has to support all the registered users from different location. It must pool all the resources into the cloud. It has to be more robust and dynamic in nature to allocate and reallocate the resources between the cloud users. Some IT companies may not be able to set up their own private cloud hence they depend on the public cloud vendor. It has to support the end user needs and expectations of the corporate IT sector. The public cloud is designed and managed by the cloud vendor.

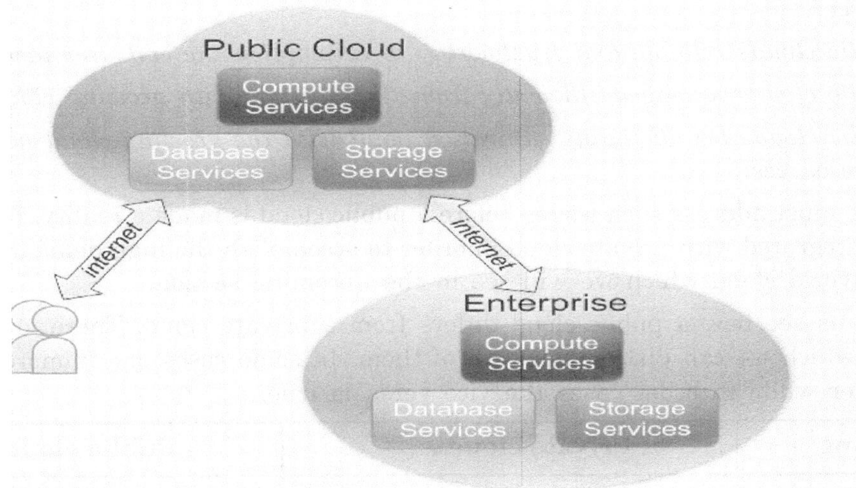

Figure 3.3 Public cloud.

The cloud vendor can be a giant corporate IT company. These giant IT companies work to make their cloud popular by user friendly measures and by huge advertisements everywhere. IT professionals are recruited and trained on the specific cloud technology domain. A best example of a giant corporate IT company as cloud provider is Amazon. It is one of the most popular cloud provider and a huge company in several platforms. (We will see in detail in chapter 7). The vendor charges the cloud user based on the usage. The vendor may give a free accessing of resource for some time like giving the user a trial period, later they charge based on the usage. The vendor charges the user based on the well defined slab rates for the resource usage. The slab rates are revised from time to time based on the vendors business requirements.

The public vendor must advance the computing resources pooled in the cloud from time to time to satisfy the needs of the end user and the business requirements. Vendor can also add some extra feature or functionality in the public cloud. Though the public cloud is open for all but it must provide some security feature too. The public cloud must detect any suspicious activity, maintain the privacy of registered user and their data, must not manipulate or tamper with user workspaces. Above all the public cloud vendor must be trustworthy. All the user data and business workspaces must not tracked by any third party or the vendor itself. Public vendor must limit itself to the service point in the cloud to the end user, rather involving in tracking, manipulating, and any other spying works makes the vendor company subject to cyber crime which can lead to legal action being taken by the concerned cloud user. Some of the issues we need to consider for a public cloud include:

What is the overall range of a publicly open public cloud?

Are public clouds safer with large section of users from different location registered as cloud user?

Are public cloud more transparent and openness in its core functionality?

How are the security and privacy of every registered cloud user maintained from another cloud user?

Are public clouds reliable and trustworthy to accomplish the end user task?

Are public clouds managed efficiently from time to time with growing cloud users?

Are public clouds bound to any saturation point with the growing cloud users and the pooled resources?

Thus, we must address such issues before a public cloud is made a reality. Public clouds can also be integrated with private cloud in order to accomplish the high demand of the user it is called hybrid cloud which we will see in the upcoming section.

Now let us see how a public cloud differs from a private cloud. There are numerous functions in which we can distinguish both of them. In some cases one is more advantage than the other while in other cases the vice versa is true.

Functions	**Private cloud**	**Public cloud**
Accessibility	Only inside the defined boundary	Can be accessed from anywhere
Scalability	Easily scalable	Easily scalable
Data security	Well secured	Not much secured
Resource sharing	Easy to share	Easy to share
Administration	Comparatively easy	Difficult with endless users and resource demand
Business agility	Highly agile	Medium
Capital expenditure	Depends on the organization and usage	Comparatively high
Data backup	Quite easy inside the organization	Huge loads of data storage is necessary

Some of the examples of a public cloud include:

- Amazon web services
- Google cloud
- Windows azure
- Salesforce
- Gogrid
- Cloudbees

Most of the clouds today are public as any user can easily sign in and use them. They may charge or may be free.

3.4 HYBRID CLOUD

In last two sections, we saw two types of cloud namely the private and public cloud respectively. Now let us see the third category in cloud called *hybrid cloud*. The hybrid clouds are extension to the private cloud by using both the local and remote resources. It is generally used when the capacity or cloud traffic suddenly increases. It is known by the term called *cloud bursting*. It can be defined as the sudden increase in the access to the remote cloud by multiple users at a time for their task. Thus a hybrid cloud is created when the remote resources are integrated into the private cloud.

Imagine a situation when the IT company has its own private cloud. Suddenly it extracts lots of resources from the cloud to accomplish all the task in the company. At a particular stage the saturation of the cloud reaches, where the pooled resources are unable to fulfill all the request of the cloud users. In such cases the private cloud can be extended or integrated with the other remote resources to satisfy the cloud user task. Thus the concept of hybrid cloud comes into existence.

Speaking from the business point of view some of the advantages of the hybrid cloud includes:

- ***Optimal utilization*** – generally in cloud only 5 to 20 percentage of the resources are used on average basis. Rest of the time the clouds are idle. But at the cloudburst time the traffic and demand of cloud users is too high. Hybrid cloud helps in the optimal utilization of the pooled resources in the cloud especially at the time of cloudburst.
- ***Data center consolidation*** – instead of having to provide capacity or the resources for worst-case scenarios only, a private cloud only requires resources for the average case. The option to burst out allows server consolidation and hence the reduction of operating costs. In particular, this includes the costs for hardware, power, cooling, maintenance, and administration. Thus using hybrid clouds the private clouds are becoming dependent on other cloud.

- ***Maintenance and risk*** – in the private cloud the organization is responsible for its maintenance and all the risks it faces. When it is integrated with the public provider to form the hybrid cloud some of the task gets reduced. It is up to the public cloud vendor to maintain all the services of the cloud and make the services run without any failures or down.
- ***Availability*** – ensuring high availability in the corporate data center is difficult and expensive, because it requires redundancy, backups, and geographic dissemination. As we all know corporate IT companies are vast in numbers and geographically scattered. Especially in companies where IT is not the core business, the expertise in this area is rather limited. In a hybrid cloud environment, the public cloud can scale up or take over operations completely if the company's data center is unavailable due to failures or any other issues.

Though the hybrid clouds are very business friendly but there are some issues and challenges in them. They include:

- ***Cost*** – from the business point of it the major drawback of hybrid cloud is the cost associated. It involves both the local and remote resources from a public cloud vendor. The operation cost and setup of hybrid cloud infrastructure is also high. Depending on utilization, data center cost and the costs of the cloud provider, businesses have to decide whether or not moving to the cloud is profitable. Some of the best way to reduce the excess cost is the metering of the resource from the public cloud separately to the user.
- ***Data security*** – most of the data in the company are highly confidential and cannot be disclosed to others. From the hybrid cloud as it involves the combination of cloud vendors to overcome cloud bursting there is high chance of secured data being misused or tampered from a safe private cloud to the hybrid cloud.
- ***Availability*** – though we saw the availability as an advantage in hybrid cloud but availability strongly depends on how public resources are integrated in the complete system. In case the public cloud is only used for cloud bursting, the local resources are extended in peak times the use of multiple providers can limit the risk significantly. However, if the cloud resources are interweaved with important business processes, the impact of a public cloud failure is considerably higher.
- ***Interoperability*** – the issue of interoperability is particularly important in hybrid cloud environments because they integrate different cloud solutions. While a completely compatible system would allow exchanging cloud providers and virtual machine images transparently, current hybrid cloud toolkits have to deal with numerous existing incompatibilities. If the clouds are incompatible to each others functionality then they cannot be integrated to give a hybrid cloud solution. Today each cloud provider is from different platforms and has their own way of functioning.

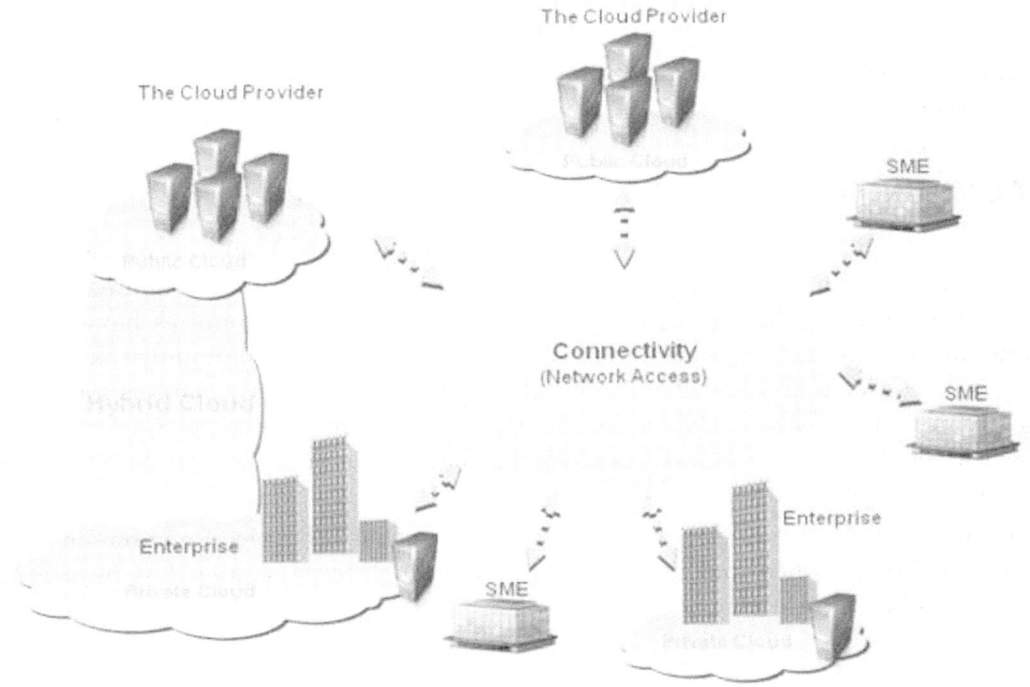

Figure 3.4 Hybrid cloud.

Some of the examples of hybrid cloud include:

- Rackspace hybrid cloud
- Red hat open hybrid cloud
- VMware hybrid service

And other combinations of clouds are suitable examples of hybrid cloud.

Figure 3.5 Comparison between private, public and hybrid cloud.

If you need varying levels of security, control and scalability a hybrid cloud option is worth considering. Ensure that all internal IT resources and multiple cloud provider solutions are engineered with standard operating procedures in mind, to make a complete, interoperable cloud solution.

3.5 COMMUNITY CLOUD

The last classification of the cloud is the *community cloud*. Well a community cloud is a type of cloud where the cloud service is provided as a service to the limited number of users or organizations which is managed by a vendor. These communities have a common goal and have an objective to achieve their own business target. A community cloud can also defined as a restricted and a well secured public cloud. A community cloud is more secured and has limitations over who should use the resource and other services. Community cloud involves the set of various organizations using the pooled resources based on their requirement and paying the price for the usage.

A community cloud is a lot like a private cloud, in that it's a cloud environment that is collectively defined, owned and governed, not by a single organization but by a group of organizations that form a community.

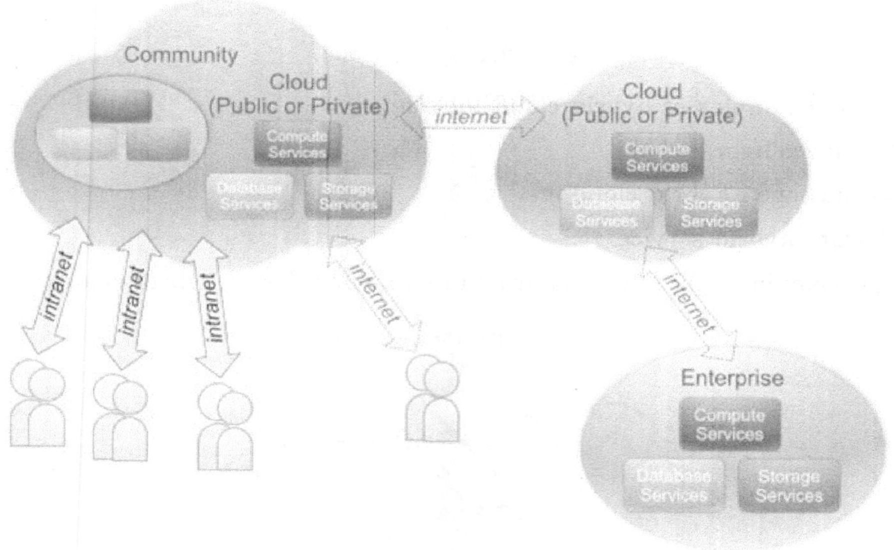

Figure 3.6 Community cloud.

Community clouds are often designed for businesses and organizations working on joint projects, applications, or research, which requires a central cloud computing facility for building, managing and executing such projects, regardless of the solution rented. The key to an effective community cloud is having a business interconnect service provider that can act as the central provisioning house for connectivity and ongoing operations. One can imagine a typical community cloud as combinations of cloud resources shared by a set of IT companies. The community cloud is managed by another vendor or a third party.

The organizing principle for the community will vary, but the members of the community generally share similar security, privacy, performance and compliance requirements. Community members may wish to invoke a mechanism that is often run by themselves to review those seeking entry into the community. The new member can join the community cloud based on their resource needs and the requirements. The new member is added into the community cloud by the service provider.

For example, take a certain industry, like the financial sector. A group of banks might want to form a community cloud for collaboration or for the sharing of information or documents or other types of services. That group of banks would work together to build this environment and own it and evolve it, and they would share the responsibility for it. They might bring out outside help to do so, but it's all under their control.

Some of the issues we need to consider for a community cloud include:

How is the cost of resources calculated between the organizations using the common community cloud?

What happens if a particular organization extracts huge amount of pooled resources creating a huge stagnation for others at a time?

How do we ensure safety and privacy in a common community based cloud?

How about the legal procedures between the various organizations in a community cloud?

The major advantage of community cloud includes:

- ***Cost*** – Compared to the private cloud the cost is reduced in community cloud as there are several organizations using the same cloud.
- ***Control*** – Compared to the public cloud the community clouds are under the control of the registered organizations or set of users under the cloud vendor. Thus they are well controlled and managed.
- ***Sharing*** – The another advantage of community cloud is the sharing of knowledge or resources between the registered organizations. But we need to be careful with the private and confidential contents.

A new study has revealed that the total value of community cloud can be up to 2.49 billion American dollars by 2018. The IT research firm MarketsandMarkets that released the study said community cloud technologies are built around cloud computing and include various software and hardware technologies, professional services, verticals and regions. It also signifies the growth of the cloud and its usage by all the users. The study also reveals the growth of community cloud as 34.5 percentage.

Some of the key areas where the community cloud is used include:

- Business intelligence software
- Enterprise application
- Health care

- BFSI industry
- Government organization

A typical example of community cloud is established in Singapore. The Singapore government has completed a whole-of-government community cloud project, which will support over 100 government agencies, 2,000 public e-services and 136,000 users. Thus a community cloud can be imagined a local network with all pooled resources into the cloud for various uses by the users or organizations.

Such kind of community cloud can also be established for educational, research, government offices and for other purposes.

3.6 CLOUD MANAGEMENT

In the previous sections, we saw in detail about the classifications of cloud. We also saw the various advantages and other applications of the respective type of cloud. In the last section of this chapter let us discuss in detail about the management aspects of cloud.

The word management has a quite big meaning and it is quite a very important term too. We may buy some new product or invent something or develop something but all of them require a proper *management.* To speak technically every major product developed or the task assigned in a major corporate IT company needs a proper and well defined management. Without a proper management the product or project may fail and it might prove to be a big mistake.

The term *cloud management* refers to all the aspects of the cloud environment and its task. A virtual remote cloud needs a proper management of its functioning and all its tasks. Cloud management means the software and technologies designed for operating and monitoring applications, data, users and all services residing in the remote virtual cloud. Cloud management tools helps ensure a company's cloud computing-based resources are working optimally and properly interacting with all the users and other services.

The cloud management is required for all types of cloud be it a private, public, hybrid and community cloud. Cloud management is required for all types of service models in the cloud. The cloud management is done by the cloud vendor or any other third party vendor not the registered user in the cloud. Some the major activities involved in the cloud management includes:

- Designing a suitable application for cloud
- Deployment of application into cloud
- Analyze the deployed application
- Monitoring the application, users and resources
- Proper delivery of cloud services
- Proper utilization of all resources in the cloud
- Better allocation of resources to every user

- Metering and billing phase of resources in cloud
- A proper governance of cloud
- Auditing task in the cloud
- A good tracking system of all resources and users in cloud
- In A well planned security and recovery from any accidental mistake in the cloud

And still many more.

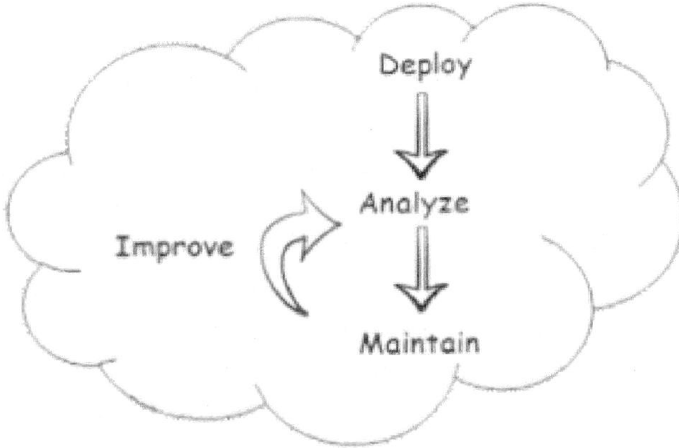

Figure 3.7 Cloud management.

Today several cloud management tools are available in the market. It is used by all the companies in the management of cloud. Some of the famous cloud management tools available include:

- ***Cloudability*** – it is a financial management tool for monitoring and analyzing cloud expenses. It aggregates expenditures into reports, helps identify opportunities for reducing costs, offers budget alerts and recommendations via SMS and email and provides APIs for connecting cloud billing and usage data to any business or financial system.
- ***Cloudyn*** – it is designed to help corporate IT companies from over-buying Amazon cloud resources. Cloudyn's suite of services gives users a dashboard showing detailed information on all of their virtual machine instances, databases, and storage. Cloudyn then provides insights into inefficiencies and suggestions on how to get rid of them.
- ***Dell boomi*** – it is a cloud-based software Platform as a Service used by customers who want to integrate their various cloud-based applications with each other and with on premise apps. New functionality allows usage of multiple data sources and reservation of cloud resources for real-time data transfer in integration processes.
- ***En stratius*** – it provides cross-platform cloud infrastructure management for public, private, and hybrid clouds that can be closely aligned with an enterprise's governance and security requirements. Features include self-service provisioning/

de-provisioning, multi-currency cost/chargeback tracking, customizable role-based access controls, single login to manage all cloud resources and support for enterprise authentication systems including SAML 2.0 and OpenID.

- ***Informatica*** – the new Informatica Cloud Data Masking service reduces the risk of data breaches during application development and testing. And the new Informatica Cloud Extend workflow service is geared toward business process creation and management in the cloud.
- ***Mule soft*** – it offers CloudHub a cloud-based integration platform as a service (iPaaS) for connecting SaaS, cloud and on-premise applications and APIs and Mule ESB, an open source enterprise service bus for connecting enterprise applications on-premise and to the cloud.
- ***Opscode*** – it lets cloud system administrators programmatically configure virtual systems thereby cutting down on repetitive, manual operations. It focuses on provisioning, configuring and integrating cloud resources.
- ***PuppetLabs*** – it is an IT automation software that gives system administrators the power to easily automate repetitive tasks, quickly deploy critical applications, and proactively manage infrastructure changes, on-premise or in the cloud. The product can automate tasks at any stage of the IT infrastructure life cycle. New features include enabling sys admins to view and respond to requests graphically support for third-party authentication services and support for Windows.
- ***RightScale*** – it was one of the first companies to address cross-platform cloud management. Its platform lets organizations easily deploy and manage business-critical applications across public, private and hybrid clouds. RightScale provides configuration, monitoring, automation and governance of cloud computing infrastructure and applications

Some of the business related reasons to consider the cloud management tools and technique includes:

- ***Spot issues*** – business companies may lose millions of money if their cloud is not properly functioning. The cloud management tools can spot any issues and them and report it early thereby preventing loss of money or productivity.
- ***SLA reporting*** – the cloud management tool can monitor the cloud providers ability to stick to the service level agreement or SLA. It mainly includes the uptime, latency, response time and so on. The cloud manager is alerted in case of any decline in the overall cloud output.
- ***Compliance management*** – it deals with the overall security and compliance of the cloud. Cloud management tools provide a good defense by both remaining in compliance with existing rules and regulations, as well as reporting to auditors who are constantly managing the cloud technology.
- ***Accidental recovery*** – cloud management technology allows tracking the operations of a cloud-based system including what happened in the lead up to a failure. Thus, they help in case of any failures of accidental disaster.

With cloud computing growing more complex day by day and a wide variety of private, hybrid and public cloud-based systems and infrastructure already in use a company's collection of cloud management tools needs to be more flexible and scalable as its cloud computing strategy.

SUMMARY

- *We classify the clouds based on their scope within which the cloud can be accessed and is managed within that limit. Speaking technically the word boundary can be defined as the accessibility of the cloud by the registered user.*
- *We classify the clouds based on their boundary as Private cloud, Public cloud, Hybrid cloud and Community cloud. Each type of cloud has some advantage and disadvantage, has its own functionalities and limitations.*
- *Private cloud is well managed cloud inside a protected organization. The private cloud inside the organization has a well defined boundary to protect the cloud. They are generally set up behind the firewall of the organization in a well secured manner from the hackers and intruders.*
- *Among all the four types of cloud private cloud is the best secured cloud environment than the public, hybrid and community clouds.*
- *There are numerous cloud tools available to configure a private cloud. They are installed under the Linux platform. The client machines are known as node and the server machine is called cloud controller. By using these tools we can setup a real private cloud, test and analyze the cloud environment. It is often used by all researchers and other educational institutions for study purposes.*
- *A public cloud is open to all the users and to the business world. Any user can register themselves to the public cloud vendor and can become a cloud user. A public cloud is quite broader in its structural aspect and the application when compared to the restricted private cloud.*
- *The cloud vendor can be a giant corporate IT company. These giant IT companies work to make their cloud popular by user friendly measures and by huge advertisements everywhere. IT professionals are recruited and trained on the specific cloud technology domain.*
- *The public cloud must detect any suspicious activity, maintain the privacy of registered user and their data, must not manipulate or tamper with user workspaces. Above all the public cloud vendor must be trustworthy.*
- *The hybrid clouds are extension to the private cloud by using both the local and remote resources. It is generally used when the capacity or cloud traffic suddenly increases. It is known by the term called cloud bursting. It can be defined as the sudden increase in the access to the remote cloud by multiple users at a time for their task.*

- *The issue of interoperability is particularly important in hybrid cloud environments because they integrate different cloud solutions. While a completely compatible system would allow exchanging cloud providers and virtual machine images transparently.*
- *A community cloud is a type of cloud where the cloud service is provided as a service to the limited number of users or organizations which is managed by a vendor. These communities have a common goal and have an objective to achieve their own business target. A community cloud can also defined as a restricted and a well secured public cloud.*
- *A community cloud is a lot like a private cloud, in that it's a cloud environment that is collectively defined, owned and governed, not by a single organization but by a group of organizations that form a community.*
- *Cloud management means the software and technologies designed for operating and monitoring applications, data, users and all services residing in the remote virtual cloud.* A virtual remote cloud needs a proper management of its functioning and all its tasks.
- *The cloud management is required for all types of cloud be it a private, public, hybrid and community cloud, all types of service models in the cloud too. The cloud management is done by the cloud vendor or any other third party vendor not the registered user in the cloud.*

Chapter 4

Services of Cloud

OBJECTIVE

- *To know about the service oriented aspect of cloud*
- *To know about the various service models of cloud*
- *To analyze about the cloud cube model*

The basic objective of a cloud is to provide service to the ends user and the business world. The overall architecture of the cloud itself is service oriented architecture, enabling it service based advanced networking technology. Most of the previous techniques were not that much of service model in its structure or functionality aspect. Cloud technology is quite unique in the aspect of service oriented. In this chapter let us see the various services the cloud provides and the service oriented architecture. How these services are helping in the revolution of this brand new computing technology.

4.1 SERVICE ORIENTED ARCHITECTURE

As we have been saying from the first cloud computing is based on service oriented model to the end user. In this section let us see in detail how the cloud architecture acts as service oriented model.

Service Oriented Architecture (SOA) can be defined as architecture style the supports the communication between the services. The word service refers to the functionality available to the end user that can be used to accomplish the task. In the service oriented model the services are exposed by service provider application and are invoked by service consumers. The service provider and service consumer are loosely coupled by the concept of *service contract* and *data contract*. They are well communicative using messages. The term service contract can be defined as interface for the exchange of communication message between the service provider and the consumer.

The term data contract refers to the understanding between the service and the client to exchange the data. A service consumer invokes the operations provided by a service contract as part of the service call and exchange data as per the data contract. The service provider registers all the services with a *service registry* which the consumer looks up to dynamically discover the services offered by the provider.

The service oriented architecture become famous with corporate IT companies due to its business friendly dimensions. The SOA techniques are highly reusable elements which can be integrated using an agile IT infrastructure. SOA can provide a compelling business proposition when combined with cloud computing and an enterprise that needs the various IT solution.

The relationship between cloud computing and SOA is that cloud computing provides IT resources you can leverage on demand, including resources that host data, services, and processes. Thus, you have the ability to extend your SOA outside of the enterprise firewall to cloud computing providers, seeking the benefits of it. One can also say cloud computing as the extension of SOA with the on demand services.

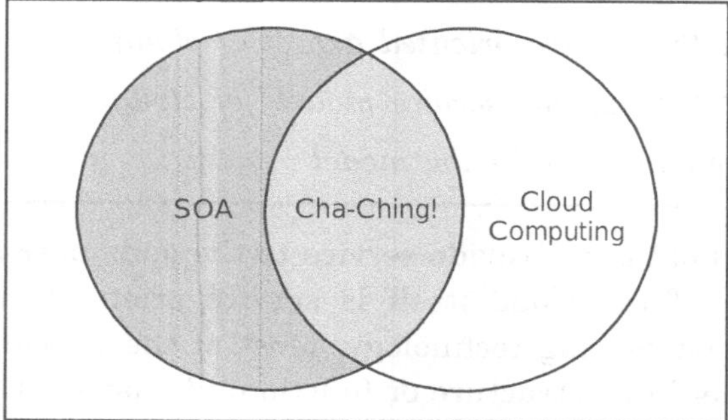

Figure 4.1 SOA and cloud computing.

Interest in cloud computing is also driving an interest in SOA. Both SOA and cloud are interlinked in several aspects. SOA not only is a mechanism to drive more reuse and agility but also offers the ability to figure out what should stay local and what should find a place in the clouds. Good SOA leads to a good cloud computing strategy, which leads to reduced costs, enhanced agility, and more excitement around enterprise computing than we have seen in awhile.

4.2 SERVICES OF CLOUD

The cloud computing technology is full of service oriented model to the end user. The cloud service providers can provide the business functionality as a service on the cloud that may be consumed by the cloud user. Corporate IT companies can build the services and applications that are core to the business functionality in the cloud that can accessed by all the employees in organization. Let us see all the services provided by the cloud in this section. This is the most vital feature of the entire cloud computing technology.

The services provided by the cloud is generally known as everything as a service (XaaS) including all the virtualized physical resources, virtualized infrastructure, as well as virtualized middleware platforms and business applications are being provided and consumed as services in the Cloud. While there are several services provided by the cloud but the most commonly used and the one that are often mentioned in cloud are only three of them (last three in the list). There are multiple vendors for each service even the same vendor may provide multiple services not just one. We must not confuse these services with the static web pages or the online based services. Cloud services are far advanced and dynamic than the web based apps. Cloud services also have quite wider meaning in terms of usage and their core functionality. The various services include:

- Storage-as-a-service
- Database-as-a-service
- Information-as-a-service
- Process-as-a-service
- Integration-as-a-service
- Security-as-a-service
- Management/governance-as-a-service
- Testing-as-a-service
- Network-as-a-service
- Hardware-as-a-service
- Platform-as-a-service
- Infrastructure-as-a-service
- Software-as- a-service

And still many more services are available.

- ***Storage-as-a-service*** – from this service model cloud provides the user with the required storage space as a service in the remote cloud. The user can store all the data into it and can easily access them using the high speed internet. There is no more need to carry pen drives or memory card or any other storage devices. Everything is stored in cloud and can be accessed with just internet in hand.
- ***Database-as-a-service*** – in this service model cloud provides the database for all the user operations from the remote cloud. It appears as if we are working in the local database, but all the work is being done and saved in the remote virtual cloud center. This is quite different from the usual online database. The cloud based database is more distributed in nature and can be accessed by multiple users at a time.
- ***Information-as-a-service*** – it includes any type of information being utilized by the end user from the remotely hosted cloud using an application interface. Examples can be stock price, news, and so on. One must not confuse this with any basic web page in internet.
- ***Process-as-a-service*** – it is a remote resource that can bind many resources together, such as services and data, either hosted within the same cloud computing resource or remotely, to create business processes. These processes are typically

easier to change than are applications and thus provide agility to those who leverage these process engines that are delivered on demand.

- ***Integration-as-a-service*** – it is the ability to deliver a complete integration stack from the cloud, including interfacing with applications, semantic mediation, flow control, integration design, and so on. In essence, integration- as-a-service includes most of the features and functions found within traditional Enterprise Application Integration (EAI) technology but delivered as a service.
- ***Security-as-a-service*** – it is the ability to deliver all the security features and the functionalities as bundled services in a remote cloud to the end user. Sometimes for a small organization it may be not possible for itself to provide all the security cover required, hence they can depend on such services in cloud.
- ***Management/governance-as-a-service*** – it is any on demand service that provides the ability to manage one or more cloud services. These are typically simple things such as topology, resource utilization, virtualization, and uptime management. Governance systems are becoming available as well offering for instance, the ability to enforce defined policies on data and services.
- ***Testing-as-a-service*** – it can be defined as the ability of the cloud to provide all the testing functionalities as a service in the cloud. Using these services the end user can test all the cloud apps, web apps and other internal apps.
- ***Network-as-a-service*** – it involves the various networking functionalities provided as a service in cloud. It involves the optimization of resource allocations by considering networking and computing resources as a unified whole. The services include flexible and extended VPN, and bandwidth on demand.
- ***Hardware-as-a-service*** – it refers to the various hardware functionalities provided as a service in the cloud. It involves the servers, memory and all other computational facilities in the cloud. It does not refer to any physical devices, only the functionalities.

4.3 PLATFORM AS A SERVICE

In the last section we saw the list of various service models and the function of them. Now lets us see in detail about the *Platform as a Service* (PaaS) model of the cloud in detail. The word platform can be defined as a stage or an opportunity to show cause something. Speaking technically platform can be defined as the workspace or the environments were the technical work is done based on the business requirements. In the cloud technology the term platform as a service can be defined as the development environment being provided as a service to the software developer or end user over the internet through the web browser. It helps the developer to easily accomplish their task with the independence of the location. The entire development environment which is provided as a service in PaaS model is easily migrated from the cloud to various devices connected to it by the *distributed technology*. The same development environment can be shared by multiple users at a time using the *virtual instances* of the resource in the cloud.

Speaking from the corporate IT companies point of view, PaaS model became a very friendly service model. It is best suited for small business organization working environment. Every IT company needs several set of software and tools to accomplish the client task. It may not be economic and quite practical to buy all the licensed software at least for a small organization. In the current scenario creating a company is easy enough, but buying all the hardware and software resources needed to effectively create a quality application become quite expensive. PaaS works like a middleware, helping an organization to create and test an app without having to worry about the underlying architecture. PaaS helps the developer to write the code of the application, test in the working environment, launch the app and continuously fix the bugs to make it a stable product for the end user and business world.

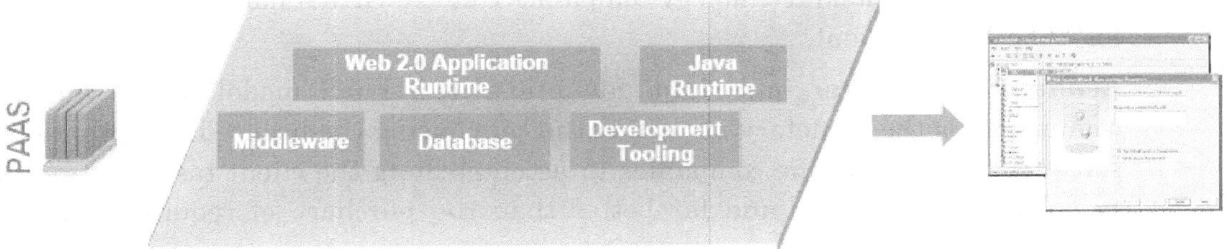

Figure 4.2 PaaS model.

The PaaS services are provided by the private vendors also which can include giant IT companies whose ultimate task is to provide the cloud technology to the end user and the business world. The features provided by the PaaS vendors include multi-tenancy, user self service account management, subscriber management, metering & analytics and resource management respectively. Everyday a new vendor is stepping into the market with far advanced features to satisfy the needs of the end user and business world.

The benefits of PaaS is utilized mainly by software developers, web developers, testing team, quality assurance team, maintenance team and so on. PaaS is very effective from developing a new application, maintaining the existing application and hosting the application in its working environment respectively. PaaS Companies are sometimes referred to as *cloud middleware* providers, since their services make up the middle layer of the basic three tiered architectural model for cloud computing service delivery, known as a *cloud stack*. PaaS Companies also provide services that support SaaS (Software as a Service) delivery on the top layer of the cloud stack. For any company that specializes in software, PaaS solutions invariably create a more secure development and testing environment. Some of the features provided by PaaS include:

- Development and design tool
- Application hosting environment
- Testing and maintenance environment
- Database management
- Server side workspace
- Storage facility
- Networking facility
- A running Operating System

Each of these is critically important in the software development industry. It creates a ring-fenced environment for development and testing, meaning greater levels of protection against external infiltration or simple data loss by the intruder and hackers. Some of the core benefits provided by PaaS to the corporate business world making it a perfect business solution include:

- ***Independent of physical infrastructure*** – PaaS model provides the cloud user the full fledged physical working environment on rent by the virtual infrastructure as a service. Corporate IT companies can concentrate on building, testing and maintaining applications rather on purchasing expensive hardware for servers and storage. Thus by cloud technology companies can use virtual hardware and software for their requirement.
- ***Economic*** – another important advantage of a PaaS model to the business community is the monetary investment in purchasing the licensed and proprietary software required by the companies in accomplishing the client task. The renting model is quite cheaper and far better than the purchase of required dedicated resources.
- ***Dynamic and advanced*** – the PaaS model is designed in such a way that all the resources in the working environment get easily updated with the advancement in the market to satisfy the business world. PaaS also provides list of various types of resources than sticking to a single type. The resources are quite dynamic to use by the end user.
- ***Flexibility*** – the business world has control over what tools they install on the platform in order to create the ideal software development environment required for them to satisfy the client request.
- ***Adaptability*** – the PaaS features are highly business friendly and are dynamic to the changes and advancement of the corporate IT sector. Thus they are easily adaptable to the business needs. They provide a win – win situation between the developer and the client.
- ***Team work from geographically separated places*** – the corporate IT companies are situated in different geographical locations with large number of employees working in same project with each module of the same project being distributed among them, in such situation the PaaS model is very useful in the development, testing and maintenance of the application. In the final stage the application of multiple modules is combined to give the final product which can be easily done by the cloud technology.
- ***Security*** – with hosting hardware under the company responsibility the difficulties of employing adequate levels of physical and digital security arises. By using PaaS, a business can pass off the responsibility of ensuring the protection of their data through the hosting service's own data center security redundancies.

Some of the notable PaaS service model vendors include:

- Microsoft Windows Azure
- Google app engine
- Amazon EC2
- SalesForce.com
- VMware cloud foundry
- CloudBees. com
- Orange scape
- Grid gain cloud computing
- Right scale

4.4 INFRASTRUCTURE AS A SERVICE

The next service model we will see in detail is *Infrastructure as a Service* (IaaS). The term infrastructure means the required platform or a basic architecture using which many services or functionalities can be delivered. To speak technically in terms of the cloud technology IaaS provides the required infrastructure as a service for the computation of the end user task. The infrastructure varies from the virtual data centers, virtual servers, virtual hardware, networking connections, load balancers and so on. It is quite interesting to know that such a large infrastructure itself is provided as a service in cloud by the underlying techniques of virtualization and distributed computing.

The core idea behind the IaaS is that the hardware required for various task are provided as a service from the remote centers. The remote centers are managed by the various service providers which also include the giant IT companies. An organization simply pays a monthly fee to use these resources as needed internally, and the cloud host is responsible for ensuring the ongoing care of the hardware and virtualized services. The service providers of IaaS need to maintain the large pool of all the required infrastructure by the end user or business community. The data centers and servers in the cloud must be powerful enough to handle multiple requests by several clients at a time. They must be robust enough to overcome any failure at the time of usage by multiple clients. The remote centers are so vast and scattered that the cloud user itself will not know the exact location were the requests are handled. The IaaS model is designed in such a way that the results of computation by virtual servers and data centers are accurate, faster and reliable.

Figure 4.3 IaaS model.

To speak from the corporate IT business point of view every IT company needs the IT infrastructure to run the basic functionality inside the company. The infrastructure include the servers for computation, data storage to store all the confidential business documents and client data, required hardware to accomplish the user task, networking technology for sharing and communication purposes. If all these basic infrastructures are provided as a service to the business world delivered by high speed internet in cloud technology, it reduces the overall investment money by the IT companies. IT companies can utilize such service models of cloud technology and spend their energy in other aspects of development, testing, deploying and maintenance process. IaaS typically follows a pay-as-you-go model, allowing a business company to determine how much it can afford each month or how many resources it actually needs. Thus IaaS provides services for creating an effective business infrastructure in the form of server and network resources, allowing for the availability of a private cloud and virtualized local network. Some of the benefits of IaaS model include:

- ***Enterprise level network*** – IaaS establishes a private cloud and a virtual local network inside the internal business networking for its functioning using the huge servers from the cloud. This basic structure allows for easy business expansion while still providing necessary data protection in a cloud setting.
- ***Cloud based server*** – instead of storing all the hardware inside the business unit, using the cloud technology all the computation takes place using the virtual servers in the remote cloud which consists of the pooled resources. It has many advantages like security redundancies and the on demand scalability.
- ***Virtual data centers*** – the major aspect of IaaS model is storage of all the computational data in the remote virtual data centers. This form of storing cut downs the storage expenses required for IT infrastructure for the business requirements.
- ***Scalability*** – as the IT companies are growing in size and dimensions in the business unit all the necessary IT infrastructure also need to be increased, further intake of required engineers and train them in the business unit. IaaS model cuts down the expenses of expanding IT infrastructure.
- ***Hardware investment*** – inside the business unit large amount of money in the project is spent in buying and maintaining the required infrastructure like PCs, servers and other necessary hardware from time to time. Using the IaaS model it reduces the investment on these issues due to its service provided by the remote virtual cloud technology.
- ***Pay as you go model*** – the cost of hardware can be quite higher but the same hardware can be used as a service by paying as rent model based on the usage limit. It reduces the overall cost of the IT infrastructure required in the business unit.
- ***Location independent*** – as we already saw in the PaaS model the cloud technology helps in the working environment independent of location. The same advantage also goes for the IaaS model of the cloud. The user can work from any suitable place by connecting to the cloud using the high speed internet and accessing all the resources and the workspaces respectively.

- ***Failure management*** – Due to the redundant nature of cloud, if one server or network switch were to fail, the data center would remain unaffected due to the numerous hardware resources it would naturally reroute activity levels through. Even if an entire data center were to fail, the host would have secondary and tertiary centers to ensure continued online function. Thus it typically varies from the web technology where if a server is down or fails the entire user activity is affected.

Some of the notable IaaS model providers in the cloud include:

- Amazon web services
- Openstack cloud
- Rackspace
- Terremark
- Savvis
- IBM
- CSC
- Gogrid

Now let us see the comparison between PaaS and IaaS service models of cloud computing.

Characteristic	**Infrastructure as a service (IaaS)**	**Platform as a service (PaaS)**
Sharing and multi tenancy	Multiple users	Multiple applications
Scalability	Scalable based on demand servers	Applications scale linearly
Agile and adaptability	VM placement	Load balancing and workload management
Reliable and fault tolerance	Reliable infrastructure	Reliable application
Service level agreement	Proactive system monitoring	Resources are allocated to meet SLAs
APIs	Infrastructure management via APIs	Application management via APIs
Virtualization	Server virtualization	Application virtualization

4.5 SOFTWARE AS A SERVICE

In this section let us see in detail about the *Software as a Service* (SaaS) model in cloud computing. Well all of us must have heard the term called software in computer technology. To accomplish every task in computer we need an interface with hardware and other platforms inside the computer which is achieved using the coded user interface called *software*. In the service model of SaaS in cloud, the required software is provided as a service to the end user and the business world to accomplish their task. The migration of the entire software for the user task in the cloud takes place by creating several virtual instances of the same software to be used by multiple users in the cloud. Hence in SaaS model the delivery of software as service takes place. It is one among the most used cloud service model by the end user and the business community. One can imagine SaaS model as software application, which is so dynamic and robust that it can be used by any number of online users at a time that it won't crash unlike a static web page. But one must not confuse with a static web application with the dynamic cloud application.

The SaaS model of cloud began to mature and became popular in late 1990s with the revolution of the internet technology and the advances in computer hardware. From there more and more online applications began to arise. With the cloud technology maturity in late 2007 the SaaS model was commonly used by all the end user and the business world. The vendors began to rent the software for the user task. Using which the process of downloading, installing and updating of software was not required for the end user. It can also be economic to use rented software than the purchase of the licensed software. In SaaS model the entire software and tools are migrated from the powerful virtual servers of the cloud centers. The techniques of virtualization and distributed made the SaaS model a reality. The execution of user task takes place in far remote cloud servers but appears to the end user as if the execution takes place in the user machine. The SaaS model is so user friendly and handy that a user connected to the internet using the web browser can easily access all the cloud software and tools. Among all the service models of cloud SaaS is the most commonly used one.

Speaking from the corporate IT companies point of view SaaS is another boon to their fortunes in business. The SaaS model is so effective that it reduces the required time and energy to be spent in the maintenance of various software inside the company. Prior to SaaS model companies had to purchase, maintain, update and troubleshoot all the licensed software. They also needed skilled IT professionals in managing the internal software and tools of the company. Though most of the IT companies use their internally developed tools and software which are quite confidential, but SaaS has provided a right solution to the business world. The SaaS model is also quite less economic compared to purchase of licensed software by the companies. SaaS removes the need for on-premise hardware or software. SaaS vendors house the hardware to run the software in their own facilities. They likewise store all customer data there as well. Clients then access the software and data remotely in a cloud-like environment. Many SaaS options are available for use through an internet browser, whereas others require a simple application install on the client's computer to access the software and receive updates. Thus similar to PaaS and IaaS SaaS is also location independence.

Figure 4.4 SaaS model.

SaaS model involves the subscription of the software by the companies and the end user. The project team in the company might use the software for a time period till the work gets completed and pay the rent based on the usage limit. Businesses also pay a monthly or yearly fee to utilize the services offered by the vendor, whether it is cloud storage, project management, or automated updates. And they also receive access to software updates as a regular part of the service's monthly maintenance from the vendor. The SaaS vendor can be giant IT company with large amount of pooled resources into the remote virtual cloud. They have a huge cloud infrastructure to support the large number of cloud users simultaneously by the virtual instances of the resources. Some of the commonly available software from SaaS model includes:

- Downloading software
- Word processing software typically text editors
- Databases and presentation tools
- Virtual CPU processing software
- Application development tools
- Bug testing tools
- Web development and hosting software
- Mobile application software
- Programming compilers
- A full fledged operating system
- Data storage software
- Simple tools like calendars, calculators and etc.

Thus these are the various tools available to the end user and business community in SaaS model of cloud technology. Some of the notable vendors of SaaS model include:

- Cloudswitch
- Cloudtran
- Apprenda
- Abiquo
- Accelops
- Cloud9

One of the major concerns of the SaaS is the data security and ownership. The real problem arises if the vendor accesses the confidential business data in the cloud. Thus the cloud user needs to be aware of any malicious process by either the vendor or intruders. During the negotiation of Service Level Agreement (SLA) the data ownership is not given to the vendor. SLAs typically spell out the parameters for such problems, outlining data ownership, security requirements and typical maintenance schedules. Vendors typically have many security measures in place from storage redundancies to multi-tiered firewalls to protect against hardware failure and theft of data.

Software as a service fulfills a real need that many companies and individuals have sought. Moving applications to a cloud environment allows not only businesses, but individuals

to access enterprise-level software at a more affordable monthly rate. As a model of software production and on-demand licensing, it provides many customers with benefits beyond a simple software solution, creating real long-term value and savings.

SaaS
Gmail. Google Doc. Finance. Collaboration.
Communication. Business. CRM. ERP. HR
Ex. Zoho. Salesforce. Google apps
PaaS
Web 2 application run time. Java 2 run time.
Developer tools. Middleware
Ex. Windows Azure. Aptana. Google apps engine
IaaS
Servers. Storage. Processing power. Networking.
Bandwidth
Ex. Amazon web service. Dropbox. Akamai

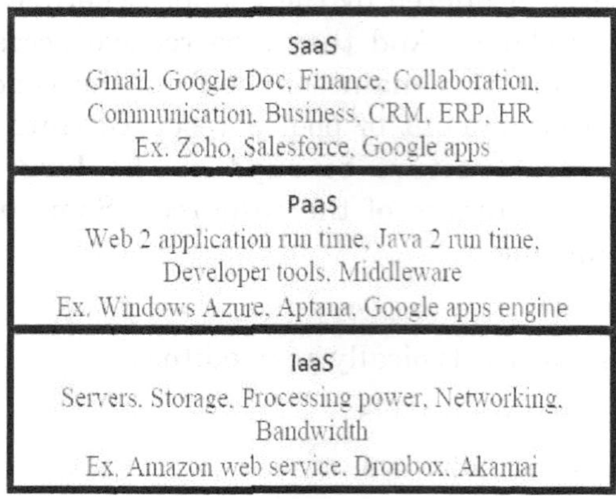

Figure 4.5 Service models of cloud and their examples.

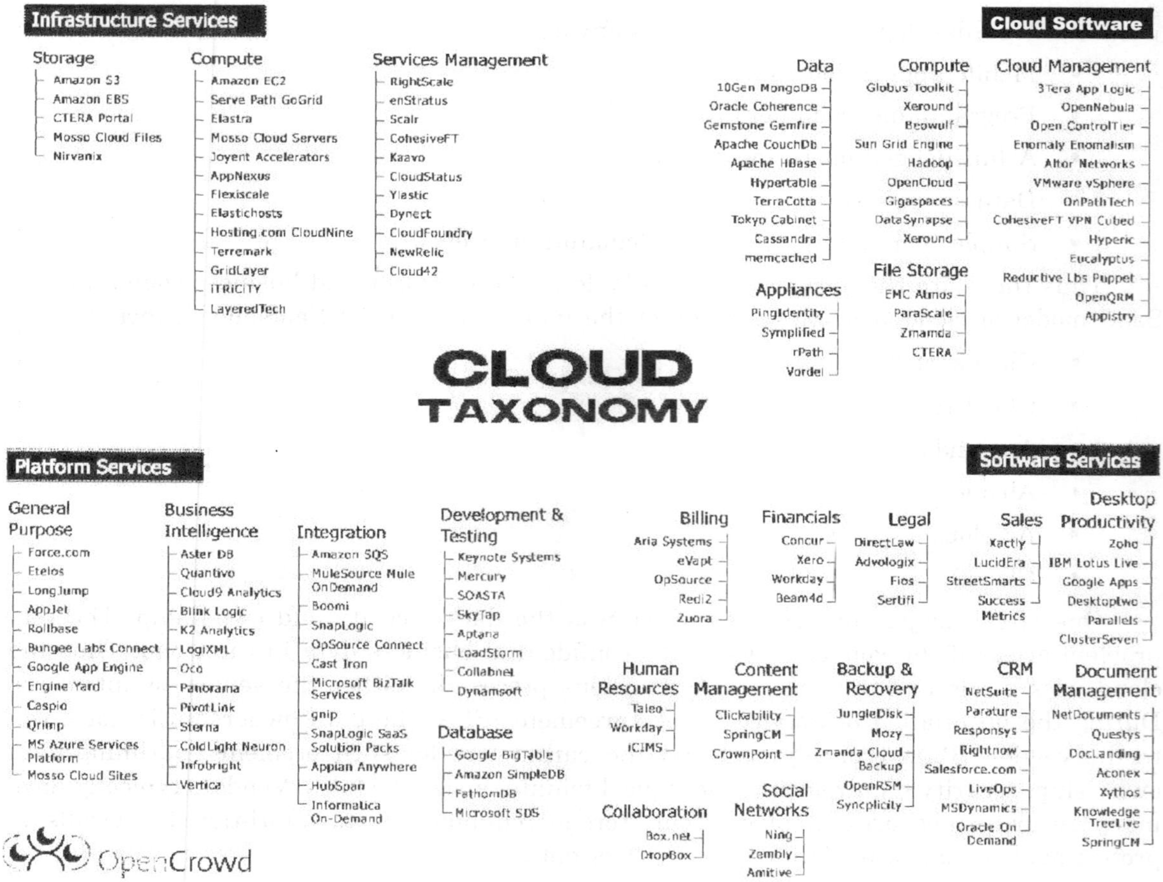

Infrastructure Services
Storage
Amazon S3
Amazon EBS
CTERA Portal
Mosso Cloud Files
Nirvanix
Compute
Amazon EC2
Serve Path GoGrid
Elastra
Mosso Cloud Servers
Joyent Accelerators
AppNexus
Flexiscale
Elastichosts
Hosting.com CloudNine
Terremark
GridLayer
iTRiCITY
LayeredTech
Services Management
RightScale
enStratus
Scalr
CohesiveFT
Kaavo
CloudStatus
Ylastic
Dynect
CloudFoundry
NewRelic
Cloud42
Cloud Software
Data
10Gen MongoDB
Oracle Coherence
Gemstone Gemfire
Apache CouchDb
Apache HBase
Hypertable
TerraCotta
Tokyo Cabinet
Cassandra
memcached
Compute
Globus Toolkit
Xeround
Beowulf
Sun Grid Engine
Hadoop
OpenCloud
Gigaspaces
DataSynapse
Xeround
Cloud Management
3Tera App Logic
OpenNebula
Open ControlTier
Enomaly Enomalism
Altor Networks
VMware vSphere
OnPathTech
CohesiveFT VPN Cubed
Hyperic
Eucalyptus
Reductive Lbs Puppet
OpenQRM
Appistry
Appliances
PingIdentity
Symplified
rPath
Vordel
File Storage
EMC Atmos
ParaScale
Zmanda
CTERA
CLOUD
TAXONOMY
Platform Services
General Purpose
Force.com
Etelos
LongJump
AppJet
Rollbase
Bungee Labs Connect
Google App Engine
Engine Yard
Caspio
Qrimp
MS Azure Services Platform
Mosso Cloud Sites
Business Intelligence
Aster DB
Quantivo
Cloud9 Analytics
Blink Logic
K2 Analytics
LogiXML
Oco
Panorama
PivotLink
Sterna
ColdLight Neuron
Infobright
Vertica
Integration
Amazon SQS
MuleSource Mule OnDemand
Boomi
SnapLogic
OpSource Connect
Cast Iron
Microsoft BizTalk Services
gnip
SnapLogic SaaS Solution Packs
Appian Anywhere
HubSpan
Informatica On-Demand
Development & Testing
Keynote Systems
Mercury
SOASTA
SkyTap
Aptana
LoadStorm
Collabnet
Dynamsoft
Database
Google BigTable
Amazon SimpleDB
FathomDB
Microsoft SDS
OpenCrowd
Software Services
Billing
Aria Systems
eVapt
OpSource
Redi2
Zuora
Financials
Concur
Xero
Workday
Beam4d
Legal
DirectLaw
Advologix
Fios
Sertifi
Sales
Xactly
LucidEra
StreetSmarts
Success Metrics
Desktop Productivity
Zoho
IBM Lotus Live
Google Apps
Desktoptwo
Parallels
ClusterSeven
Human Resources
Taleo
Workday
iCIMS
Content Management
Clickability
SpringCM
CrownPoint
Backup & Recovery
JungleDisk
Mozy
Zmanda Cloud Backup
OpenRSM
Syncplicity
CRM
NetSuite
Parature
Responsys
Rightnow
Salesforce.com
LiveOps
MSDynamics
Oracle On Demand
Document Management
NetDocuments
Questys
DocLanding
Aconex
Xythos
Knowledge TreeLive
SpringCM
Collaboration
Box.net
DropBox
Social Networks
Ning
Zembly
Amitive

Figure 4.6 The taxonomy of cloud computing.

4.6 CLOUD CUBE MODEL

Another way to understand the various service models, deployment and other attributes to manage the cloud is using an well defined model called *cloud cube* model from Jericho forum.

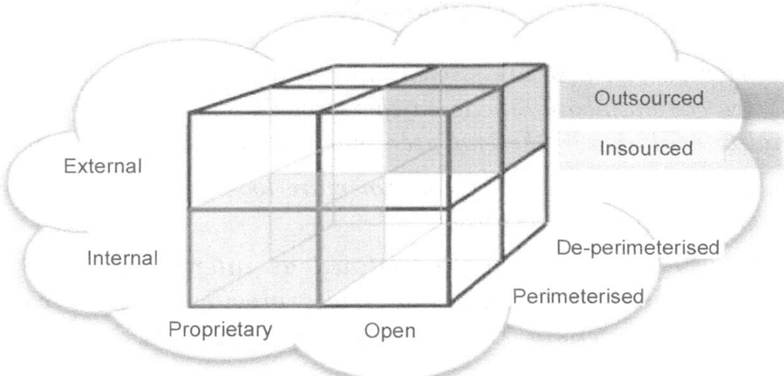

Figure 4.7 Cloud cube model.

The Cloud Cube Model illustrates the many permutations available in cloud offerings today and presents four criteria/dimensions in order to differentiate cloud formations from one another and the manner of their provision, in order to understand how cloud computing affects the way in which security might be approached.

The Cloud Cube Model also highlights the challenges of understanding and mapping cloud models to control frameworks and standards such as ISO/IEC 27002, which provides a series of guidelines and general principles for initiating, implementing, maintaining, and improving information security management within an organization.

Standards are very important in every technology. Standards define the way the technology is to be shaped and governed. Any deviation from the mentioned standards marks the violation of activities. The security in cloud is also monitored and handled by various deviations from the standard procedures.

The cloud cube model gives the overall parameters of the cloud, which is very useful in the management of it. One can imagine the vastness of the cloud both technically and in reality. Large number of users ranging from giant IT companies to small organization using the same pooled resources for various purposes at a same time. Each one of the registered cloud user using the same cloud resources for various purposes. Some of the cloud vendors provide the cloud for free while some for pay called proprietary. The cloud types help us in managing them by defining a well secured boundary. There are various types of cloud like private, public, hybrid and community. Based on the user needs and expectations one can use the required type of cloud. Security is a key issue in cloud due to its openness in nature. Only a well secured cloud can be trusted and be used by all the people.

Clouds are either managed by some vendors or by some third party vendors. Vendors can be giant company like Google, Amazon and Microsoft so on. The clouds are outsourced sometimes if the organization is unable to spend resources in its management.

SUMMARY

- *Service Oriented Architecture (SOA) can be defined as architecture style the supports the communication between the services. The word service refers to the functionality available to the end user that can be used to accomplish the task.*
- *The service provider and service consumer are loosely coupled by the concept of service contract and data contract.*
- *The term service contract can be defined as interface for the exchange of communication message between the service provider and the consumer. The term data contract refers to the understanding between the service and the client to exchange the data.*
- *The relationship between cloud computing and SOA is that cloud computing provides IT resources you can leverage on demand, including resources that host data, services, and processes. Interest in cloud computing is also driving an interest in SOA. Both SOA and cloud are interlinked in several aspects.*
- *The cloud computing technology is full of service oriented model to the end user. The cloud service providers can provide the business functionality as a service on the cloud that may be consumed by the cloud user.*
- *The services provided by the cloud is generally known as everything as a service (XaaS) including all the virtualized physical resources, virtualized infrastructure, as well as virtualized middleware platforms and business applications are being provided and consumed as services in the Cloud.*
- *Platform as a Service (PaaS) can be defined as the development environment being provided as a service to the software developer or end user over the internet through the web browser. It helps the developer to easily accomplish their task with the independence of the location.*
- *PaaS works like a middleware, helping an organization to create and test an app without having to worry about the underlying architecture. PaaS helps the developer to write the code of the application, test in the working environment, launch the app and continuously fix the bugs to make it a stable product for the end user and business world.*
- *Some of the features provided by PaaS include Development and design tool, Application hosting environment, Testing and maintenance environment, Database management, Server side workspace, Storage facility, Networking facility, A running Operating System.*

- *Infrastructure as a Service (IaaS) provides the required infrastructure as a service for the computation of the end user task. The infrastructure varies from the virtual data centers, virtual servers, virtual hardware, networking connections, load balancers and so on.*
- *The core idea behind the IaaS is that the hardware required for various task are provided as a service from the remote centers. The remote centers are managed by the various service providers which also include the giant IT companies.*
- *The service providers of IaaS need to maintain the large pool of the entire required infrastructure by the end user or business community. The data centers and servers in the cloud must be powerful enough to handle multiple requests by several clients at a time. They must be robust enough to overcome any failure at the time of usage by multiple clients.*
- *In the service model of SaaS in cloud, the required software is provided as a service to the end user and the business world to accomplish their task. The migration of the entire software for the user task in the cloud takes place by creating several virtual instances of the same software to be used by multiple users in the cloud.*
- *The SaaS model is also quite less economic compared to purchase of licensed software by the companies. SaaS removes the need for on-premise hardware or software. SaaS vendors house the hardware to run the software in their own facilities.*
- *SaaS model involves the subscription of the software by the companies and the end user. The project team in the company might use the software for a time period till the work gets completed and pay the rent based on the usage limit. Businesses also pay a monthly or yearly fee to utilize the services offered by the vendor.*
- *The Cloud Cube Model illustrates the many permutations available in cloud offerings today and presents four criteria/dimensions in order to differentiate cloud formations from one another and the manner of their provision, in order to understand how cloud computing affects the way in which security might be approached.*
- *The Cloud Cube Model also highlights the challenges of understanding and mapping cloud models to control frameworks and standards such as ISO/IEC 27002, which provides a series of guidelines and general principles for initiating, implementing, maintaining, and improving information security management within an organization.*

Chapter 5

Cloud in Action

OBJECTIVE

- *To understand the need and purpose of cloud migration process*
- *To know the hosting of cloud apps in data center servers using the virtualization technique*
- *To know the concept of inter cloud technology*
- *To know the various applications of cloud and the various proposed models of cloud in future*
- *To know the overall advantages and disadvantages of cloud technology*

5.1 MIGRATION TOWARDS CLOUD PLATFORM

Well we have seen the various types of cloud and service models. We must not forget that only in the last decade cloud computing has made so much revolution which means we were using the traditional IT approach and networking concepts to accomplish the user task rather than advanced cloud technology. Now in this section let us see in detail about the entire process, techniques and the methodology followed towards migrating to the cloud platform from the traditional approach.

The term *cloud migration* refers to the transition of the entire work done in the previous technology or platform into this new cloud computing platform. It involves the transition of the companies data, services, applications, internal tools, workspaces, official data and so on into the remote virtual cloud. It can also be defined as the overall transition of the working technology into a higher version of advanced cloud computing technology rather than sticking to the outdated mode of operation in the company.

One must imagine the whole tireless work needed in transforming such a large company working data and workspace from one technology to another. The new platform must be user friendly and it must support the previous technology and other previous approaches too. The new technology must not create any problem in the execution of the previous technology work and support its entire working environment. Well in the initial stages of the migration it takes time for a new technology to fully become operationalize and all employees get a smooth way of functioning. One must not immediately underestimate or overestimate the underlying technology and the overall process. It needs some time to fully mature and its full affect is acknowledged by all users.

Well the word migration is quite a very big term here. The full meaning of migration involves:

- Migrating all the data, application and services
- Migrating the entire workspace
- Migrating the overall infrastructure
- Migration of the entire underlying technology

It involves a whole set of change or transition rather than a mere shifting of platform.

While a cloud migration can present numerous challenges and raise security concerns, as we already know data security and privacy is a big issue in cloud computing. Cloud computing can also enable a company to potentially reduce capital expenditures and operating costs while also benefiting from the dynamic scaling, high availability, multi-tenancy and effective resource allocation advantages cloud based computing offers. As we already know cloud computing is a service oriented technology with the renting all pooled resources into the remote virtual cloud. Thus, there are several advantages to the company in migration to this new technology. Especially for small business enterprises migration to cloud can be a big boost to the company fortunes.

The process of cloud migration is quite a wide task considering the large dimension of IT companies. One must be careful in migration process as it involves some unexpected risks and accidents too during the whole transition period. One must not get confused with the overall migration process as there will be several data and working platform with both modified and unmodified platforms. A systematic transitional process must be initiated by the user to achieve the required target. Well there are four simple steps that can be fallowed in a very systematic way in the cloud migration process. Following these four steps of migration is much more enough to achieve the target required and one can have a smooth transition.

1. Plan

- Determine key business drivers which typically varies from the company perspective
- Define business objectives and the overall requirements
- Get executive sponsorship
- Set project guiding principles and goals
- Form project team made up of IT and business representatives with a clear depth about the underlying work
- Develop project plan for the transition which includes

- Define business requirements
- Set key success metrics and evaluation parameters
- Set timeline to finish the task
- Identify decision making authorities

2. Execute

- Execute the plan and set the stage of actual implementation
- Stay focused on original project scope, do not get diverted to other issues in the execution process
- Remember to follow the guiding principles at all times
- Communicate to all stakeholders regularly and update the underlying work
- Train users how to work in a new platform and all other constraints

3. Monitor

- Monitor adoption of the new technology
- Analyze the whole working process of the new technology
- Track all the success metrics and all the evaluation parameters taken into account in the initial stages of planning
- Stay focused with the major goals and objectives of the work
- Follow guiding principles and all other fault tolerance advices
- Only implement changes based on quantifiable business need and the changing requirements

4. Manage

- Proper management of the new working environment is a very important for a transition
- All the future work must be initiated and executed in the new platform rather going back to the previous one
- One must maintain a proper set of reference materials and documents for future use
- One must troubleshoot all the new problems and issues in the new platform
- One must refine and iterate the whole underlying work in the new environment so as the stabilize the new environment
- Finally one must get a good hands on experience with the new working environment

Thus following this systematic steps and methodology is more than sufficient for the cloud transition.

Once such a vast transition of the cloud technology is completed one must validate the overall transition. Practically speaking there are many problems associated with such a large transition. Thus after the full fledged cloud migration there is a need for the through checking of all the working, all tools and technology in the new platform. One can set up a list of all test cases and execute them to check the overall migration process effectiveness. It could prove to be a disaster if a new platform does executes the same application of old platform in a different way and gives a wrong output. The simple reason can be the mismatch of the new and old platforms. Thus full fledged interoperability is required else this entire migration process is totally waste.

One must ensure that the systems have been migrated to the new platform without loss of fidelity in functional and non-functional requirements. All the required set of issues are satisfied in the new platform at the post migration work. As systems are migrated to the cloud, it is necessary to allocate the right amount resources for them. Compute instances, storage devices and network bandwidth must all be appropriately aligned to the system needs based on the needs of the user. Thus this marks the full fledged working environment in the new platform.

Well one must imagine for a long term view too. What happens if there is an another new technology in the upcoming years and again there is a full fledged revolution for that new technology. Then the current migrated cloud computing technology must be further supportive into the migrated of that new technology also.

5.2 CLOUD HOSTING

Now in this section let us discuss in detail about a common term in cloud computing called *cloud hosting*. We will also discuss about the term *cloud server* too.

Well most of us must have heard the term called web hosting or application hosting. These were the traditional terms associated with the broader networking area of web technology. Now in cloud computing we use the term called *cloud hosting*. We can simply understand the term cloud hosting as the application which is designed in a suitable platform is hosted into the remote virtual cloud. As we already know the term cloud is quite vast in its technical meaning with dynamically pooled resources into it. Although one must not confuse cloud hosting with the traditional web hosting.

Traditional web hosting refers to the hosting of a simple static page written in any scripting language in a single server. But whereas the cloud is very dynamic in nature as it can migrate from one virtual server to another virtual server and is quite very much available at all situations to every remote users mainly due to virtualization and distributed technology. These highly advanced and dynamic servers for cloud are popularly known as virtual servers. We have already seen the overall distinguish between the web technology and cloud technology.

Traditionally there are two types of hosting:

- ***Shared hosting*** – Where the same server is shared between the users for hosting the contents. It is quite cheaper but inflexible too.
- ***Dedicated hosting*** – In this, user purchases a full fledged dedicated server for their own usage. It is not shared with others.

The cloud hosting process makes use of both the types of hosting based on the situation. Resource can be scaled up or scaled down accordingly in the cloud, making it more flexible and, therefore, more cost-effective. When there is more demand placed on the servers, capacity can be automatically increased to match that demand without this needing to be paid for on a permanent basis.

Cloud hosting describes the best method available to configure the virtual server in a very flexible way as required by the user or even the provider. It provides a more reliable, scalable and a well advanced networking based infrastructure required dynamically by the user. It provides a well-defined framework required for the business growth with the minimal expenditure. Cloud hosting provides the user with the interface to control the data stored in the virtual server. Like secure the data, manage the data, edit the data, create a new set of data, modify data and so on. Apart from all this it also allows to create a new server with few set of steps, resize servers and other networking operations. It also allows the users to customize the cloud hosting servers with the requirements like allocate processing power required, operating system, data residing location and configure it the way you like and assist in presenting content and graphics as the user feels.

We can easily achieve economies of scale with increased productivity with fewer personnel, stop spending heavily on technological infrastructure or other costly resources enjoy pay-as-you-grow pricing plan of Cloud Hosting. As we already know cloud computing involves the metering of resources with paying only for that. Increase reliability is ensured by better uptime and consistent online presence using this advanced cloud hosting process. Cloud Hosting uses multiple servers at different location to make certain that web presence won't be compromised or affected in any situation.

We have already seen the virtualization and distributed technology, how they are changing this advanced cloud technology with multiple instances. If one server goes offline, assistance is available from various other virtual servers, quite it's a very big process that takes place in the backend. One must never forget the term virtual server is quite technically very big in its function compared to a traditional server to host web pages. Multiple data centers with robust infrastructure reduce the risk of being affected by any accidental or any other natural damage. To an extent we can even say the data in cloud is quite comparatively better secured than the data in traditional internet.

With Cloud Hosting, the user is provisioned to avail on demand resources in real time. Resources are not limited to capacity of one server or any other physical constraints. As we know cloud is very dynamic in nature and supports multiple users by the creating the instances of the resources. Cloud Hosting would make the life very easier, accessibility is possible anytime from anywhere and also platform independence. It is all about the advancement of the technology in a step wise approach.

Some of the good examples of cloud hosting can fall under both the Infrastructure as a Service (IaaS) and Platform as a Service (PaaS) service models of the cloud computing. Under IaaS service model offerings the client or the end user is simply provided with the virtualized hardware resource on which they can install their own choice of software environment before building their web application. One can imagine them as the required infrastructure needed to work in the cloud environment. On a PaaS service model however, the client or end user is also provided with this software environment like operating system, database support, web server software, and programming support on which they can go straight to installing and developing their web application. It can also defined as the required platform to work by the user. Businesses with complex IT infrastructures and experienced IT users may wish to opt for the more customizable IaaS service model but others may prefer the ease of a PaaS service model. Thus the various service models of cloud can be best described for the example of the cloud hosting.

The another more obvious example of cloud hosting involves the use of public cloud models that is hosting websites or applications on virtual servers which pull resource from the same pool as other publicly available virtual servers and use the same public networks to transmit the data. Data which is physically stored on the underlying shared servers which form the cloud resource. One can imagine giant companies like Google, Amazon and Microsoft for the public cloud offerings. But today most of the cloud providers are charging money and it is not available for free. These public clouds will include some security measures to ensure that data is kept private and would suffice for most website installations. However, where security and privacy is more of a concern, businesses can turn towards cloud hosting in private clouds as an alternative that is clouds which use ring-fenced resources, whether located on site or with the cloud provider. As we already know private clouds are more secured than the public cloud.

Some of the features or the characteristics of the cloud hosting include:

- ***Simplicity*** – Compared to the web technology based web hosting, cloud hosting is quite very simple with just few steps to achieve the target.
- ***Pay as you go model*** – Like the other cloud computing tools, cloud hosting also charges for the used resources and it is metered.
- ***Scalable*** – Cloud servers are highly scalable based on the demand of the user unlike the traditional server.
- ***Reliability*** – Cloud servers are highly reliable in nature. Cloud hosting isolates each server, ensuring that possible stress on one does not affect another server's performance.
- ***Customizable*** – Cloud hosting is very much user friendly with which allows the user to customize all the requirements. User can specify the server's processing power, location, and operating system, as well as configure the server itself to present your content in the best possible way.
- ***Secure*** – The data or application hosted in the cloud server is quite very much secured compared to the traditional server. By distributing the server data across redundant servers, information hosted in the cloud is protected against any hardware failure or any other accidents. Automated backups and snapshots ensure that server content stays safe and up-to-date.

Cloud Server

When we are talking about cloud hosting we must not forget about an another important term called *cloud server*. The era of the traditional server based hosting of web pages is almost over now with the advanced cloud technology. The concept of virtualization mainly server virtualization type has given a new meaning to the usage of servers. For the cloud hosting we generally use the highly dynamic and virtual server called cloud server. Cloud servers are very powerful virtual environments created within a very strong cluster of servers. Cloud servers carry many benefits that are not offered within a dedicated server.

Quite a far more advanced and unique in its functionality are the cloud servers compared to the traditional server. Well there are lot of differences between the cloud server and the traditional server. It includes:

Cloud server	Traditional server
They involve the concept virtualization mainly the server virtualization technique in addition to all the networking concepts	It involves the minimal networking concepts.
It is highly dynamic in nature and scalable, better prepared to handle user traffic	Though they are scalable but in worst case the server crashes with the huge traffic
It is resilient and redundant in nature of its functioning	Comparatively not redundant in nature
Unlimited scaling of disk space	There is a limit for the disk space
In cloud computing technology cloud servers are available as a service to the user or organization	They are dedicated and owned by the users or organization
Based on the service model, there is no need for maintenance of hardware or configuration of any other feature required	A well defined set of maintenance and configuration of servers is required
It is based on the pay as you go model of cloud computing, quite economic	They are dedicated and hence costly in price

When we are opting for cloud hosting, users are renting virtual server space rather than renting or purchasing physical servers which we normally do. They are often paid for by the hour depending on the capacity required at any particular time. As we already know the pay as you go model in cloud computing or renting of resources. Today there are millions of cloud server providers in the market. Unlike dedicated servers in the traditional internet, cloud servers can be run on a *hypervisor* or *virtual machine manager*. The role of a hypervisor is to control the capacity of operating systems so it is allocated where needed. With cloud hosting there are multiple cloud servers which are available to each particular client. This allows computing resource to be dedicated to a particular client if and when it is necessary. Where there is a huge data traffic, additional capacity will be temporarily accessed by a website. Cloud servers also offer more redundancy. If one server fails, others will take its place and they are more dynamic in nature.

Cloud servers are a genuine win-w provider and the user. The vendor passes on reduced overhead through better resource allocation and more densely populated data centres while the cloud user enjoys flexible hour-by-hour rental charges on a platform and the benefits of rescaling from time to time based on the demand. For the many businesses still sitting on a depreciating asset as large as their seasonal peak, Cloud servers are a very wise choice for all business organization and mainly for the small business.

The advantages of cloud server are almost same as cloud hosting, it includes:

- On demand scalability of all resources in the cloud servers
- Well the overall setup and configuration of cloud servers are very easy compared to the traditional server
- Cloud Servers are completely customizable, and all resources such as firewall, load balancing, snapshots, and images can be added on demand. Fully support both Linux and Windows operating systems platform
- Cloud servers are highly cost effective with the pay as you go model of cloud computing
- Cloud servers are also highly secured from any accidents and disaster with the highly placed data backup and recovery system.

5.3 VIRTUAL DATA CENTER

Throughout the entire conversation from the first we have been using the words *remote center, virtual center, data center* and so on, all of them mean the same thing. Now in this section let us discuss in detail about the term *virtual data center*. Let us first understand the overall purpose and functioning of a data centre before we see the cloud based virtual data center.

Have we ever thought where are all the data, contents, images, video and so on we see in internet stored?

From where are all of them fetched within few seconds?

It all happens in a well secured storage medium called *data center*. Ultimately all the data and other workspaces are stored in this large remote data center. Data centers consist of large number of machines packed in a specific format storing all the contents. Data centers are owned and maintained by giant IT companies. There will be multiple data centers each one of them in a very remote location but are connected by large data cables which run through the land and oceans giving the connectivity. Data centers are situated in a very remote location mainly due to its high infrastructure needs and also due to security issues. Data centers are quite a very unique and highly secured place even more secured than a normal IT company with several security blankets around them.

A data center can occupy one room of a building, one or more floors, or an entire building they can be very vast, one must not wrongly assume them to be of just few computers and so. Most of the equipment is often in the form of servers mounted in 19-inchrack cabinets, which are usually placed in single rows with corridors between them. This allows people access to the front and rear of each cabinet. Servers differ greatly in size, from 1U servers which occupy one of 42 slots in a standard rack to large freestanding storage silos that occupy many tiles on the floor.

Mainframe computers and storage devices may be as big as the racks themselves and are placed alongside them. Large data centers may use shipping containers packed with 1,000 or more servers each when they need to repair or upgrade, they replace the whole container. Clean, unwavering power and lots of it is essential and important too. Data centers need to keep their computers running at all times, one must not shut them down even accidently. The data centers are shut down at the time of maintenance works only. They should be prepared to handle brownout sand even power outages. The power must be conditioned, and backup batteries and diesel generators must be available to keep power flowing no matter what.

As you can imagine, all that power generates a lot of heat with a huge set of computers. Data centers must cool the heat generated by the equipment. The most common mode of cooling is air-conditioning, water cooling is also an option when it's easily available, such as at some of the new data centers along the Columbia River in Washington State. Air-conditioning not only cools the environment but also controls humidity to avoid condensation or static electric buildup. Network connectivity and ample bandwidth to and from the network backbones are vital, to handle the input and output from the entire collection of servers and storage units. All these servers will be idle if no one can access them. Another important aspect is physical and logical security.

Bigger data centers are targets for hackers all over the world. Some freestanding data centers begin with security through obscurity and disguise the fact that a data center even exists at that location. Guards, mantraps, and state-of-the-art authentication technology keep unauthorized people from physically entering. Firewalls, VPN gateways, intrusion-detection software, and so on keep unauthorized people from entering over the network. Finally, data centers must always assume the worst and have disaster recovery contingencies in place that avoid loss of data and experience the minimum loss of service in case of disaster.

Even by mistake if a large data centre is technically attacked by an innovative hacker it is all over for the users and the company. They will be simple sent back to the Stone Age without any data and the workdone.

Well when we are talking about cloud computing even data centers needs to support the virtualization concept and all other principles of cloud. The data centers specifically meant for all cloud based operations and storage is known as *virtual data center*. A Virtual Datacenter in the context of cloud computing services falls within the Infrastructure as a Service (IaaS) service model. It enables the user to quickly access cloud infrastructure from a service provider. Which means virtual data center comes under the service model of cloud based on its functioning.

Virtual datacenters are populated by virtualized resource pools of storage, compute, network, and security of cloud infrastructure and securely managed via the online portals that are accessed by the user. The virtual data center service enables businesses and other organizations to roll out on-demand hosting, storage and computing resulting in the creation of their own private Clouds.

A Virtual Datacenter contains both the public and private catalogues of virtual machine templates using which the user can build new virtual machines quickly, or upload VMs that are already running in the internal environment or all other needs of the user. You can also build virtual applications within your own Virtual Datacenter and maintain them. A virtual application is used when you have an application that requires more than one VM, custom security and networking settings, custom startup parameters and want the application to be stored and provisioned from catalogues.

For example, you may occasionally need to create an instance of one of your websites with web servers, a database server and specific security settings for purposes of doing testing for each upgrade. This entire instance can be stored as a virtual application in the catalogue and then later used to create the upgrade test environment in your own Virtual Datacenter. When the testing is finished, you can power off the virtual application.

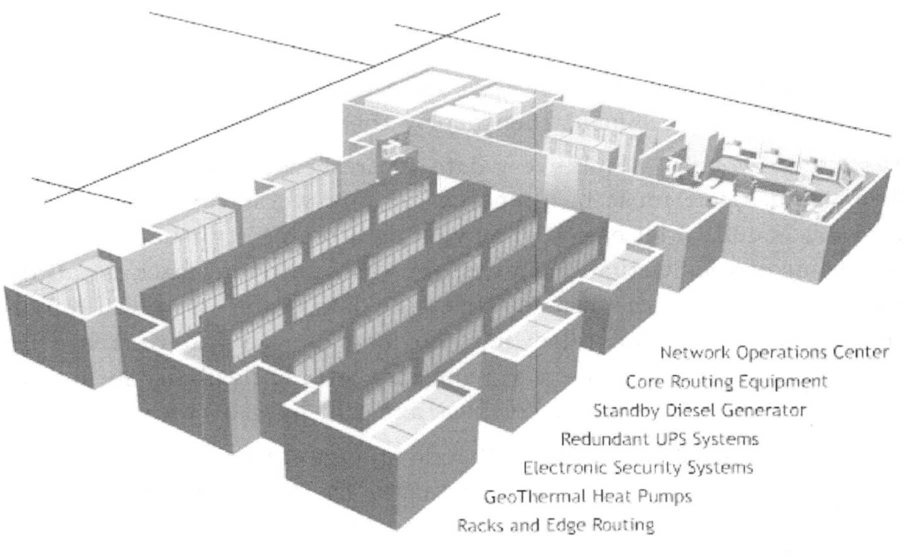

Figure 5.1 Virtual data center.

The virtual data centers with virtual servers provide more advantage than the common data centers with physical servers. Some of them include:

- ***Less heat production*** – Well we already know the virtualization is a form of green computing, saving energy. Running several machines in a same hardware saves the whole power consumption and also produces less heat too. Virtualization in data centre reduces the heat energy produced by the several machines running there by reducing the cooling mechanism required. One must not forget that companies spent huge amount of money in cooling solutions for a data center.

- ***Cost reduction*** – As usual as we already know the virtualization of the hardware saves the investment money in the purchase of all the required infrastructure equipments. The concept of virtualization in data centers reduces the overall cost.
- ***Faster deploy*** – Compared to the physical servers, in case of the virtual data centers with virtual servers all the user contents and the images are deployed faster in just few clicks and in a simple configuration steps.
- ***Easier backups*** – With the virtual servers data backup and recovery process is quite easy and simple as the data in virtual servers can easily move from machine to another incase of any accident or crash.
- ***Green computing*** – Well as we already said, virtualization is a form of green computing which is very much eco friendly and in the long term we can see only the use of virtual servers than the traditional physical servers. Such form of adoption is the need of the hour considering the mass impacts of the global warming.
- ***Testing environment*** – Another unique advantage is the best testing environment in a virtual platform. You can also isolate these testing environments from end users while still keeping them online. When you've completed the work, deploy it as live. Thus the virtual servers are a good platform for testing of application in a isolation environment then deploy them in the real environment.
- ***Disaster recovery*** – Well every data centre needs to be fully prepared with any form of disaster, must be prepared for any worst case scenario too. Disaster recovery is quite a bit easier when your data center is virtualized. With up-to-date snapshots of your virtual machines, you can quickly get back up all the data and running. And when the disaster strike the data center itself, you can always move those virtual machines elsewhere so long as you can re-create the network addressing scheme and so on. Having that level of flexibility means your disaster recovery plan will be easier to enact and will have a much higher success rate.
- ***Vendor independence*** – An another advantage of the entire virtualization concept is the independence of vendor to the user. The unique thing about virtualization is the abstraction between software and hardware layers. This means the user does not have to be tied down to one particular vendor the virtual machines don't really care what hardware they run on, so the user is not tied down to a single vendor, type of server, or even platform. Thus giving the user the platform independence.
- ***Towards cloud technology*** – Well the virtualization in data center is quite the user is towards the full fledged cloud technology platform. With a move to virtual machines and the virtualization concepts, you are that much closer to enjoying a full fledged cloud environment and all its applications. You may even reach the point where you can deploy VMs to and from your data center to create a powerful cloud-based infrastructure. But beyond the actual virtual machines, that virtualized technology gets you closer to a cloud-based mindset, making the migration all the more easy.

5.4 INTER CLOUD

Now in this section let us see an another interesting term called *inter cloud*. We will discuss in detail about the combination of cloud and the need of them. Though inter cloud is often regarded as the future perspective of cloud computing.

Well we all must have heard the term called *network of networks* as internet, the commonly used term in several books and so on. Similarly in cloud computing the term inter cloud or combination of clouds called as *cloud of clouds*. The idea behind them is that a single common functionality would combine many different individual clouds into one seamless mass in terms of on-demand operations in the cloud. Though one must not confuse intercloud with the hybrid type of cloud. Though this is quite new and a future view of the cloud computing. This inter cloud concept is still in very initial stages only we can expect the revolution and maturity of it in the upcoming years.

Inter cloud Systems is a global single-source provider of value-added services for both corporate IT enterprises and service providers. Inter cloud offers cloud and managed services, professional consulting services and voice, data and optical solutions to assist its customers in meeting their changing technology demands. Its engineering, design, installation and maintenance services support the build out and operation of some of the most advanced enterprise, fiber optic, Ethernet and wireless networks. Inter cloud provides consulting and professional solutions to the service provider and enterprise market in support of all facets of the telecommunications business. Inter cloud provides an array of applications and services, including unified communications, Interactive Voice Response (IVR) and SIP based call centers.

The Inter cloud scenario is based on the key concept that each single cloud or a service provider of a cloud does not have infinite physical resources or the capacity to support all of them. Well one must imagine what happens if a single cloud itself gets completely saturated with several users and all the resources are completely used, it reaches the saturation point of that cloud. In such situation the concept of inter cloud comes into the picture. If a cloud saturates the computational and storage resources of its infrastructure, or is requested to use resources in a geography location where it has no footprint, it would still be able satisfy such requests for service allocations sent from its clients. The Inter cloud scenario would help in such situations where each cloud would use the computational, storage, or any kind of resource of the infrastructures of other clouds.

Thus different clouds work together to overcome their saturation issue. Clouds combine to help each other attaining their full functionality. It also helps in the full operation of an idle cloud with the sharing of the cloud platform using the inter cloud technology when the other cloud is fully saturated. This is a precise analogy to how the Internet works, in that a service provider to which an endpoint is attached, will access or deliver traffic between source and destination addresses outside of its service area by using Internet routing protocols with other service providers with whom it has a prearranged exchange or peering relationship. It is also analogous to the way mobile operators implement roaming and inter carrier interoperability. Such forms of cloud exchange, peering, or roaming may introduce new business opportunities among cloud providers if they manage to go beyond the theoretical framework.

The inter cloud concept has lot of advantages. It can help the users in case of any accidents or any issues in a particular cloud, with all the users temporarily transferred to the another cloud. In case of any maintenance or the cloud operations are down due to unavoidable circumstances then in case cases the grouping or combination of cloud platforms is an exact solution. In the long run we can see the giant cloud providers like Google, Microsoft, Amazon and so on combining together to provide the inter cloud technology.

Well the evolution of inter cloud started only in 2009. In July, 2009 in Japan, an effort called the Global Inter-Cloud Technology Forum (GICTF) was launched with the stated goal of *We aim to promote standardization of network protocols and the interfaces through which cloud systems interwork with each other, and to enable the provision of more reliable cloud services than those available today*. As of 2012 they have over 85 member companies and have published proposed use cases as well as technical documents in the field of cloud computing and inter cloud.

In July, 2010 in France the First IEEE International Workshop on Cloud Computing Interoperability and Services popularly known as Inter cloud 2010 was held bringing researchers together and yielding many published papers about the various innovations in cloud computing. One must not forget in 2010 cloud computing was in its quite initial stages. The workshop became an annual meeting with Inter cloud 2011 later held in Turkey and Inter cloud 2012 held in Madrid too.

In February, 2011 the IEEE platform launched a technical standards effort called P2302 - Standard for Intercloud Interoperability and Federation (SIIF). The stated goal of the working group is to produce a standard as such *This standard defines topology, functions, and governance for cloud-to-cloud interoperability and federation. Topological elements include clouds, roots, exchanges which mediate governance between clouds, and gateways which mediate data exchange between clouds. Functional elements include name spaces, presence, messaging, resource ontologies including standardized units of measurement, and trust infrastructure. Governance elements include registration, geo-independence, trust anchor, and potentially compliance and audit. The standard does not address intra-cloud (within cloud) operation, as this is cloud implementation-specific, nor does it address proprietary hybrid-cloud implementations*. As of 2012 they have over 50 member companies and have published a Working Draft 1.0 in it.

In March, 2012 the famous cloud term *Inter cloud* made the Wired Magazine Jargon Watch list, quite making its presence and exposure to the entire technical and corporate IT sector. In June, 2012 at the 5th International Conference on Cloud Computing (CLOUD 2012) the IEEE announced an Intercloud Test Bed with stated goal of *The test bed will be a cloud infrastructure comprised of assets from participating universities and industry partners. It will be used to develop and test protocols that will be formalized in the IEEE P2302 interoperability standard*.

In October, 2013 the IEEE announced a Global Testbed initiative. The 21 cloud and network service providers, cloud-enabling companies, academic and industry research institutions from the United States, the Asia-Pacific region, and Europe. The members have volunteered to provide their own cloud implementations and expertise to a shared testbed environment. They will also collaborate to produce a working prototype and open-source global Intercloud.

To better understand the clouds we classify them into two major categories based on their organization which includes:

- ***Governmental*** – These are owned and managed by the government organizations. Well in the long run we can see the government too spending their money in several computer related solutions and platforms to move from the traditional management of all records and documents.
- ***Private*** – Well as usual they are the internal clouds inside an private organization for their own operations.

Well we can classify the inter clouds into various categories which include:

- ***Volunteer federation*** – It can be defined as the voluntary collaboration between the cloud providers to offer the exchange of resources and share all their platform in a very interactive way.
- ***Independent*** – When multiple clouds are used in aggregation by an application or its broker. This approach is essentially independent of the cloud provider and can be used to utilize resources from both governmentally and private clouds. They are also known as Multi-Cloud.

From the architectural point of view volunteer federation can be further classified as:

- ***Centralized*** – It includes a central entity in the sharing of resources and platform. Thus it can be defined as the store house of resources from where the entire management takes place.
- ***Peer to peer*** – In this group clouds communicate and negotiate directly with each other without any mediators. It is very direct in the communication.

The independent clouds can be further classified into:

- ***Services*** – Application provisioning is done by a service which can be hosted either externally or in house by the cloud clients. Most such services include broker components in themselves. Typically application developers specify an SLA or a set of provisioning rules and the service performs the deployment and execution in the background, in a way respecting these predefined attributes.
- ***Libraries*** – Often custom application brokers that directly take care of provisioning and scheduling application components across clouds are needed. Typically such approaches make use of inter-cloud libraries that facilitate the usage of multiple clouds in a uniform way.

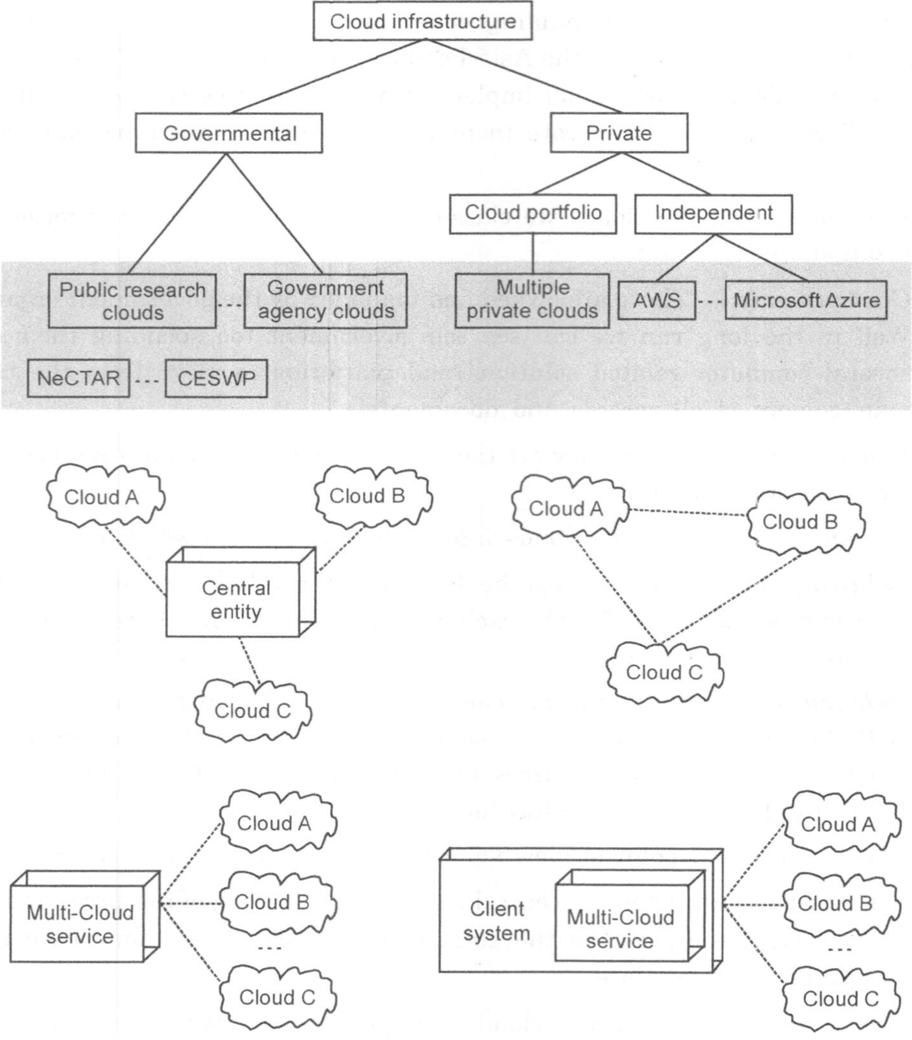

Figure 5.2 Classification of Intercloud.

There are some requirements for intercloud environments which include:

- ***Data location awareness*** – Ideally the persistent data and the processing units of an application should be in the same data centre may be even on the same rack in a data center and should be connected with a high speed network. If they reside on remote clouds the performance penalty could be grave. Well in cloud computing as we know the entire applications and workspaces to reside in the remote servers in a data centers.

- ***Client location awareness*** – Apart from the data even all the incoming requests also need to be known for better operations in the inter cloud platform. Ideally requests should be scheduled near the geographical location of their origin in order to achieve better performance. Though we have said throughout our entire discussion that cloud operations take place in a very remote place such that the user itself is unaware of any back end locations, but it is good if the operations take place in a nearby cloud centers.

- ***Pricing issue*** – Well we must never forget in cloud platform everything is charged, nothing is free. A common consideration for all types of applications deployed in multiple clouds is the pricing issue. Different providers have different pricing policies and mechanisms and minimizing the overall hosting price is a non-trivial task. An application broker would need detailed and up to date information about provider price and policies in order to perform fiscally efficient provisioning.
- ***Legislation and policy awareness*** – Well one must be very carefully in storing or any other cloud operations with confidential data and contents. For some applications the application broker should take into account both the legislative and political considerations upon provisioning and scheduling. For example, such a broker could avoid placing part of the data outside a given country or can avoid using cloud services of a specific vendor.
- ***Local resources awareness*** – Well working in a vast technology of combination of clouds by inter cloud platform one must have good awareness on the local resources in the particular cloud. Without knowing the real status of a single, merging several clouds or handling all the remote operations of different clouds can have many practical problems and issues.

5.5 APPLICATIONS OF CLOUD

Well in this section let us see in detail about the various applications of cloud computing. We will see how this technology is being used in various fields. Well at the end of reading the entire book you will feel that we have presented all the applications of cloud in some way or other in all sections. We will also discuss the usage scenario of cloud computing based on the user needs at the situation. Some of the commonly available applications of cloud in various fields and domain include:

- ***Data storage*** – One of the major area where the cloud technology is used include the data storage in the remote virtual cloud. It helps the user to easily access and use the data anywhere and anytime.
- ***Software and hardware*** – Many software tools and hardware functionalities are available in cloud for the end user. They help the user and business community to easily use them anywhere and anytime rather depend on the machine for the software installation and hardware configuration. Today there are many advanced cloud software and hardware designed to run in the virtual server. The word software includes operating systems, specialized tools, compliers and all other user needed items. Hardware refers to the server, memory, networking and all other infrastructures required.

- ***Cloud database*** – Cloud databases give developers and IT a powerful and scalable database that just works. From the infrastructure to the database software to the tuning and monitoring everything is done as a service. For many task database is required, hence today there are many cloud based databases available.
- ***Data backup and recovery*** – In tune with the data storage in cloud, it is also used to maintain the secured copy of data from disaster and other accidents. It is a another major usage of cloud computing.
- ***Email*** – Email is another mission critical application that is fairly mature and standardized, prime to move to the cloud. For years, CIOs have expressed a desire to outsource email. Independent professionals to large multinational companies should move their email to the cloud as soon as possible, for advancement. At a personal level, we all use cloud-based consumer email services like Hotmail and Gmail, and we enjoy the benefits of access anywhere and not having to think about capacity or server uptime. There is a right cloud email solution for every business, be it hosted low-cost email, Hosted Exchange for small businesses, or even managed dedicated Exchange environments for large customers.
- ***Sharing workspaces*** – The major application of cloud computing in the PaaS service model is the sharing of the required platform to achieve the required task. It is very much useful for all the business companies. Using this several remote users can interact and work together.
- ***E-commerce*** – Scalability and availability are critical concerns for online stores. Every minute of downtime can result in lost sales. A slow website can result losing a customer for life. E-commerce is also known for seasonal high peaks, such as the holiday season. Online stores no longer have to pay for and deploy infrastructure to support peak times, the cloud allows them to dynamically scale as their traffic scales. When a spike in interest at an e-commerce website occurs, the demand could bring down or significantly slow down traditional servers, preventing customers from being able to make a purchase. However, the cloud allows that same website to quickly spin up additional resources and handle the load. When the rush subsides, those resources are turned off. The cloud also makes it easy to deploy web servers in different locations with load balancing to accelerate local page load times and increase availability. Adding the services of a Content Delivery Network (CDN) makes it easy to distribute high-bandwidth content like images and video across the world in a very efficient and cost effective way.
- ***Testing and development*** – All the service models of cloud are designed to satisfy the testing and the overall development of the applications inside the corporate IT companies. These are the major and the full fledged uses of cloud technology. Development teams will benefit from the agility of creating instances in minutes, the efficiency of paying only for the infrastructure needed at any given point in time and from the efficiency of not having to manage and maintain the infrastructure. Additional instances can be set for testing and training purposes with the same efficiency. Load testing and simulation under different hardware configurations is also a no-brainer for the cloud.

- ***Private and hybrid cloud usage*** – Private clouds give IT departments many of the benefits of the public cloud with the added benefit of having an isolated network and computing resources that bring additional security. Rackspace offers private clouds that give IT departments a lot more control over the resources deployed and the architecture. Hybrid clouds, enabled by various underlying technologies, allow IT departments to connect public cloud, private cloud, dedicated hosted and on-premise infrastructure to gain the optimum combination of control and agility. For example, a web server can be set up in the public cloud, transaction processing can be in a dedicated server where PCI compliance is easier to attain, order processing can be on-premise and the ERP system can be on a private cloud with automatic backups going to storage on the public cloud.

  Well these may be the applications of cloud computing in IT industry, let us see some of the uses of cloud in various fields.

- ***Cloud in retail store*** – Cloud computing can be used in the management and the overall maintenance of the huge back end database used in the retail store. It is very unique and user friendly to use cloud computing in various sectors.
- ***E-governance*** – All government offices, records and their entire functionality can be made a one stop place for all, by using the e-governance model using the cloud technology. May be in the upcoming years we can see this advanced way of governance.
- ***E-learning*** – Cloud computing can be used for the learning purpose with a highly advanced learning methodology supported by then cloud servers. This king of learning process is becoming famous in several institutions, may be these will the future learning education system.
- ***E-polling*** – The voting process in election can also be implemented using the cloud computing technology with a highly secured and location independence manner. Online polling can be a good substitute to the existing election process.
- ***Medical research*** – Cloud computing is effectively used in the medical field too for all research and highly advanced telemedicine purpose. Apart from these cloud computing can be used to store all the database and effective management of all records in the hospital.
- ***Clouds computing in agriculture*** – In agriculture, cloud services are increasingly being used on a highly available, virtual server system from external providers. Access is via a secure Internet connection via VPN client. We are moving towards the modern agriculture technique with the usage of all advanced techniques.
- ***Mobile technology*** – Cloud computing technology is used to design and use all the mobile apps. Today the mobile technology is getting combined with the cloud to give the mobile cloud computing. Both of them are aligned to each other and are advanced.

Well lot more are the applications of cloud computing, but we stop this discussion here. In the upcoming chapters one can understand still lot more how the cloud technology is used.

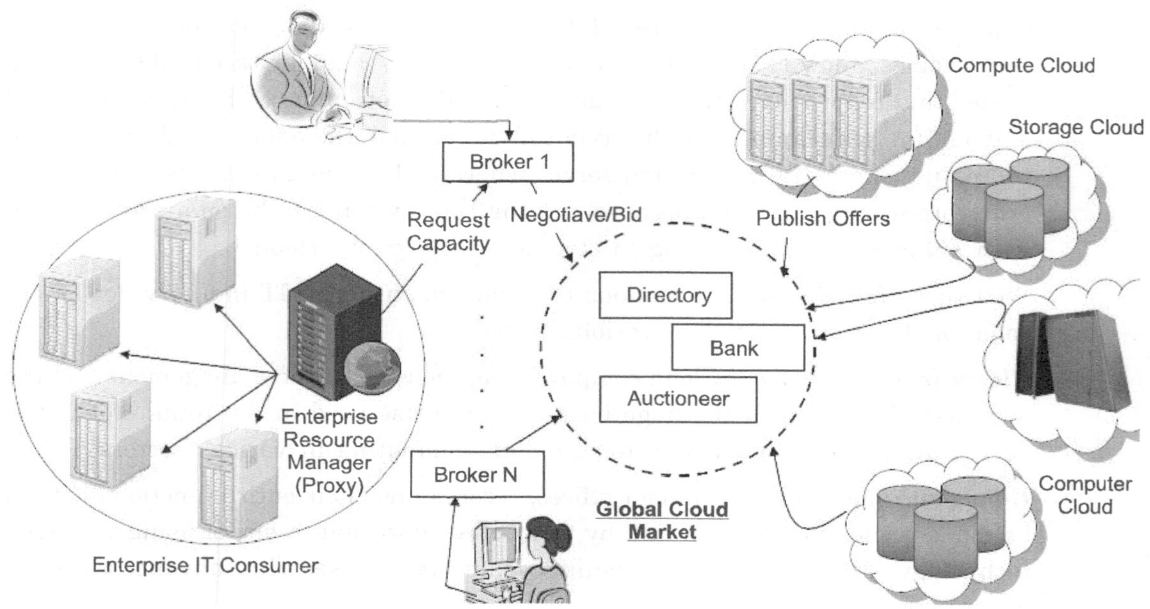

Figure 5.3 Applications of cloud computing.

Usage Scenerio

It is equally important to know when to use a technology and at places to be avoided in a very precise manner. It can prove to be disaster if a new user is unaware of this basic information, the wrong choice of a wrong platform can finish off the whole user task. From a business point of view it is must to know the exact usage scenario and the right platform to be used for that specific task. Some of the right usage scenario of cloud computing involves:

- ***When the processes, applications and data are largely independent*** – When they are not tightly coupled with other applications or information. The idea is that if they are tightly coupled, they are difficult, if not impossible, to decouple, and thus will not operate independently on a remote platform. If they are loosely coupled, fit is not an issue. Loosely coupled applications are a much better fit for cloud computing. Thus in a remote cloud apps need to be loosely coupled only then applications can easily migrate and work in the virtual environment.
- ***When the points of integration are well defined*** – When there are well defined points within an application where that application can share data, behavior, and processes. Thus, they are easy to integrate with applications back in the enterprise. Cloud applications must be well integrated so that it can be provided as a service to the end user.

- ***When a lower level of security will work just fine*** – When the information to be contained within the cloud computing environment requires a low level of security, and the world will not end if the information somehow got out. Cloud computing systems typically provide good enough security, even though security is an issue in the cloud computing but they are far secured than the traditional internet.
- ***When the core internal enterprise architecture is healthy*** – When you have your own house in order, and thus it is much easier for cloud computing systems to become part of that architecture. For any organization to adopt the cloud technology into its function, it must be first well designed and governed in its existing approach, else adopting cloud can complicate everything creating a big mess in its overall function.
- ***When the Web/Internet is the desired platform*** – When you are okay with deploying the user interface within a browser. Today, with the advent of Rich Internet Applications (RIAs), you have browser-based applications that look and function like native applications. Well today more and more technology and tools are designed to work in alignment with the traditional internet and browser.
- ***When cost is an issue*** – When there is a clear cost benefit to cloud computing, as discussed earlier. If you are looking to build and deploy an application on the cheap, cloud computing is typically the way to go. As we already know cloud computing is based on the pay as you go model of resource usage in a metered fashion.
- ***When the applications are new*** – It is much easier to deploy new applications on cloud platforms than it is to port existing applications there. As of today more and more applications are designed to align with the advancing technologies.

Cloud Computing is Unfit to Use When

- ***When the processes, applications and data are largely coupled*** – If the applications are interdependent, then it is not a good idea to move any of them to a remote cloud platform. They will quickly break or will not migrate which is typically expected in cloud. Remember, loosely coupled is good with cloud computing technology, tightly coupled is bad with cloud computing and must be avoided.
- ***When the points of integration are not well defined*** – When there are not good mechanisms in place to synchronize the information and processes hosted on cloud computing providers with those systems that exists the enterprise. Integrating those sorts of systems in which the interfaces are ill-defined places a lot of risk in the movement toward cloud computing and is not a good fit. Thus cloud technology needs a proper synchronization and a better integration.
- ***When a high level of security is required*** – When security is so much of a risk that you just cannot trust systems that you do not completely control. These types of systems should be rare. When control is critical to your business, it is better to avoid the cloud platform.

- ***When the core internal enterprise architecture needs work*** – If your enterprise architecture is dysfunctional, then extending it out to cloud delivered platforms is not a good idea. Get your house in order first, at least to the extent that externalizing systems to cloud resources will not cause harm.
- ***When the application requires a native interface*** – If you need to leverage native APIs such as Win32 and browsers are not an option, then cloud computing may not be a good fit to use.
- ***When cost is an issue*** – Again, consider the costs holistically. While in many cases cloud computing is a fit, in some cases it is not. Cloud is unsuitable for high economic based complex projects.
- ***When the application is legacy*** – Just as new applications are much easier to move to cloud computing, older or legacy applications are not, better to avoid cloud.

5.6 APPLICATION MODELS OF CLOUD

In the last section, we saw the various applications of cloud, now in this section let us see in detail about the various proposed future application models of cloud computing. We propose four major future application models though there are lot more. We will discuss each one them in detail.

E- Governance in Cloud

Today almost all government offices too are shifting to computer based working environment like the giant corporate IT companies. Gone are the days when the traditional paper and pen method was used to store all records, today to a very large extent computer based data system is used to bring down the paper waste which is a purely environmental friendly.

Some of the typical uses of computer based data system in governance field especially in India include:

- Storing large amount every citizen information in all government offices for various use
- Information about the various government departments, schemes, policies and announcements in web portals
- Issuing the birth certificate, death certificate, ration card, voter id, community certificate, electricity bills, water bill, house tax and still lot more government schemes and policies
- The entire banking transaction from the opening of account to the whole set of transaction process
- Issuing the online based complaint or viewing all user information or status in all government offices

- Even in healthcare, agriculture, transport and so on fields require the information using the database system and still lot more.

But there are some bottlenecks and problems associated with the traditional approach, some of them include:

- Resources need to be scaled up and down. There is no elasticity in the traditional approach one needs to know that the technology must always support the growing demands must not be saturated at one stage
- Software and hardware need to maintained and upgraded from time to time
- New licenses or tools need to be purchased
- Need to provide the system for 24 × 7 approach
- Need to provide secure environment with authentication and access control
- Need to provide the sufficient data storage facilities.

And so on are the issues associated with them. Now we propose a well advanced cloud based networking model which can be far more efficient and easy to store and maintain all records, *e-governance* using cloud technology.

A cloud based governance system can be built with all the data being stored in the highly dynamic and virtual cloud server in the backend. This is quite advanced and easy to access. It is also very friendly and can handle any amounts of traffic. Cloud computing technology can significantly improve the way a government functions, the services it provides to its citizens and institutions and its cooperation with other governments. It is like moving one step towards the e-information system, saying good bye to traditional paper and pen format of functioning. It can help address the challenges by providing elastic scalable, customized and highly available environment to all the users. It is easily connected to all the remote departments of the government, making an one stop approach to all the user needs and the information required.

It also relieves governments from the burden of upgrading, maintenance and licensing software and allows them to focus on the core work, improving the whole delivery and management system. Scalable and cost effective data storage can also be provided and file replication, multiple installations in geographically separated locations can be used for data recover in case of any disasters. Security approaches a technique can be deployed on the Cloud to prevent malicious behavior and protect data integrity and confidentiality.

Such king of huge governance model using cloud computing can be handled by the government appointed set of software engineers or can be outsourced to a third party vendor. Thus such models can also generate the large amount of employment to the people with the computer knowledge. This form of governance is required in all countries making the consumer friendly and fast, better administration without any loopholes in between. Files easily move from one department to another faster and the user task gets easily executed unlike the traditional approach. E-governance can also bring down the overall corruption or any other malpractices between the government departments with a well defined way of transparent functioning. We need to enhance the overall functioning of the government departments for the better growth and the prosperity of the nation.

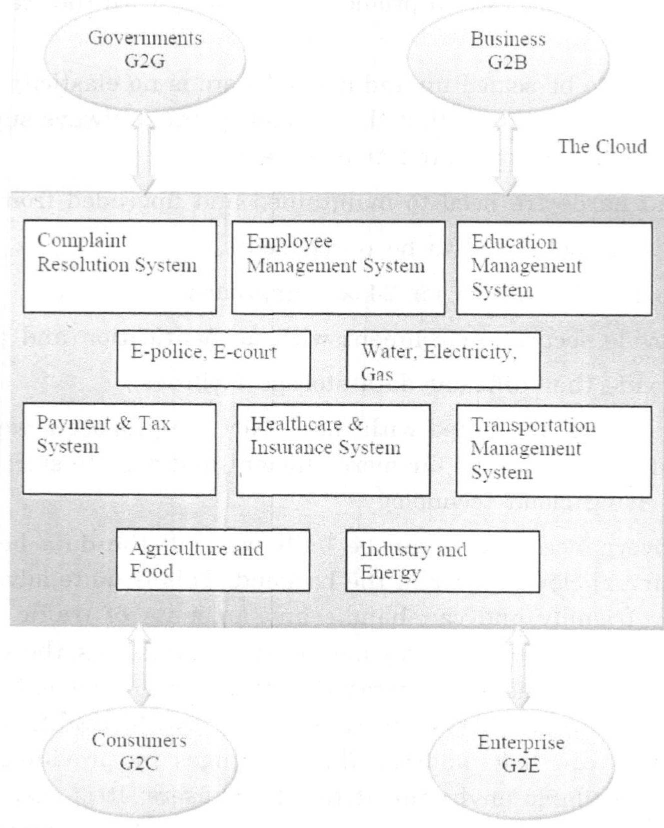

Figure 5.4 E-governance model using cloud computing.

E- Learning Using Cloud Computing

An another innovative and unique model of cloud computing application can be the e-learning methodology using the cloud computing platform.

Let us first understand the term *e-learning*. Well e-learning is an advanced way of learning using the electronic method rather using the traditional books and other stuffs. E-learning is a term used to describe any form of electronically-based learning and teaching, including computer-based teaching both in and outside of the classroom, such as the streaming of university lectures on an institution's website. E-learning is the computer and network-enabled transfer of skills and knowledge.

E-learning applications and processes include Web-based learning, computer-based learning, virtual education opportunities and digital collaboration. Content is delivered via the Internet, audio or video tape, satellite TV, and CD-ROM. It can be self-paced or instructor-led and includes media in the form of text, image, animation, streaming video and audio. It also includes the innovative way of learning using the multimedia technology, usage of power point based presentation, use of CDs and other computer based devices for learning. It major back bone includes internet as the mode of communication. E-learning is getting popular everywhere. It is the need of the hour with the growing challenges and the tough competition.

E-learning includes all forms of electronically supported learning and teaching methodology. The information and communication systems, whether networked learning or not, serve as specific media to implement the learning process electronically. This often involves both out-of-classroom and in-classroom educational experiences via technology, even as advances continue in regard to devices and curriculum. Abbreviations like CBT (Computer-Based Training), IBT (Internet-Based Training) or WBT (Web-Based Training) have been used as synonyms to e-learning.

Now we are proposing an innovative model of e-learning using cloud computing. This entire model of learning takes place using the cloud computing technology replacing the traditional approach of internet and other networking technology. E-learning model using cloud computing involves the usage of the highly dynamic and virtual servers for the storage of all the learning contents. As we already know there are lots of difference between the traditional servers and the cloud servers. The data stored in cloud servers are accessed by all the registered cloud users using the well designed web portal.

The e-learning content is made available to them. Not just computers, all other hardware devices can connect to the remote virtual cloud platform. Thus this form of advanced learning using the high performance computing is a very wise choice and need of the hour. We can have a better storage, better traffic maintenance and a well managed platform of e-learning using the cloud computing.

The e-learning model using cloud computing can be maintained by the same university/ college or can be outsourced to a third party vendor. There are several advantages of this e-learning model using cloud computing, both speaking technically of the technology and the e-learning model. It includes:

- ***Economic*** – One of the major advantage of the entire e-learning using cloud computing is the overall cost reduction. E-Learning users need not have high end configured computers to run the e-learning applications. They can run the applications from cloud through their PC, mobile phones, tablet PC having minimum configuration with internet connectivity. Since the data is created and accessed in the cloud, the user need not spend more money for large memory for data storage in local machines. Organizations also need to pay per use, so it's cheaper and need to pay only for the space they need. As we already know cloud computing is a purely service oriented technology, with a minimal cost being paid by the cloud user based on the pay per usage scenario.
- ***Improved performance*** – Since the cloud based e-learning applications have most of the applications and processes in cloud, client machines do not create problems on performance when they are working. After all cloud computing is highly dynamic with the virtualization and distributed techniques.

- ***Data storage*** – Cloud computing involves the usage of advanced virtual servers and the data storage techniques making the storage of data a far more efficient and advanced compared to the traditional approach. E-learning involves the storage of large amount of data in various formats, cloud based storage is the wise choice.
- ***Better infrastructure*** – The overall infrastructure to support the e-learning technique is quite supported by the principles and working of cloud computing in a very effective manner. The traditional approaches of e-learning are prone to data traffic and crashing of the servers. With the underlying virtualization and distributed technology are suitable to handle all these issues in the cloud technology.
- ***Software updates and management*** – Since the cloud based application for e-learning runs with the cloud power, the software's are automatically updated in cloud source. So, always e-learners get updates instantly. Thus the need of the updating and management task is considerably reduced.
- ***Improved document format compatibility*** – Since some file formats and fonts do not open properly in some PCs/mobile phones, the cloud powered e-learning applications do not have to worry about those kinds of problems. As the cloud based e-learning applications open the file from cloud. Cloud computing is also platform independent in many ways.
- ***Benefits for students*** – Students get more advantages through cloud based e-learning. They can take online courses, attend the online exams, get feedback about the courses from instructors, and send their projects and assignments through online to their teachers. Thus this form advancement in education can change the overall system and reduce the overall burden on the student.
- ***Benefits for teachers*** – Teachers also get numerous benefits over cloud based e-learning. Teachers are able to prepare online tests for students, deal and create better content resources for students through content management, assess the tests, homework, projects taken by students, send the feedback and communicate with students through online forums. Thus the overall e-learning process brings down the burden and the valuation task on the teachers. This king of user friendly methods is the need of the hour.
- ***Data security*** – A very big concern is related to the data security because both the software and the data are located on remote servers that can crash or disappear without any additional warnings. Even if it seems not very reasonable, the cloud computing provides some major security benefits for individuals and companies that are using/developing e-learning solutions.

And so on are the advantages of the cloud based learning system.

One of the most interesting applications of cloud computing is the educational based cloud application platform. The educational cloud computing can focus the power of thousands of computers on one problem, allowing researchers search and find models and make discoveries faster than ever. It makes the things quite faster, easier and more innovative. It is also very user friendly. The universities can also open their technology infrastructures to private, public sectors for research advancements, thus making an independent platform for research. The efficiencies of cloud computing can help universities keep pace with ever-growing resource requirements and energy costs. Students expect their personal mobile devices to connect to campus services for education.

As already most of the education premises are connected with a well designed and advanced wireless internet facility. Faculty members are asking for efficient access and flexibility when integrating technology into their classes. Researchers want instant access to high performance computing services, without them responsibility of managing a large server and storage farm. The role of cloud computing at university education should not be underestimated as it can provide important gains in offering direct access to a wide range of different academic resources, research applications and educational tools.

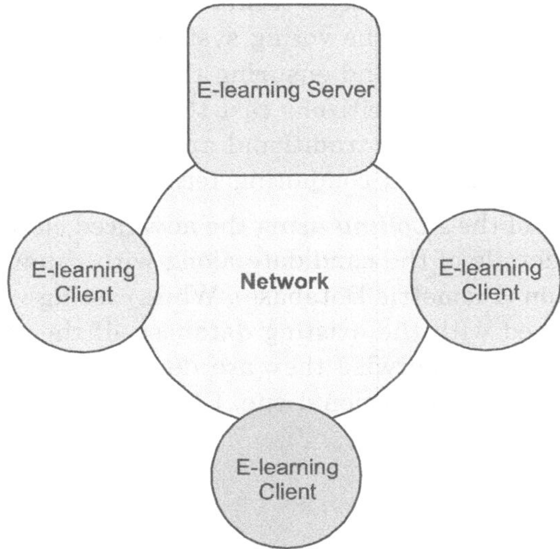

Figure 5.5 E-learning model using cloud computing.

Thus, there is a need to implement the high performance computing technique in the education field for better research, advancement and overall better efficiency in the whole education field for the future generation.

One of the best and advanced e-learning platform using cloud computing is http://www.docebo.com/. It is highly advanced and can be used in variety of ways.

As of 2103 the cloud based e-learning system is used in government schools in Tamil nadu, India. MoU has been signed between the School Education department and an NGO, Learning Links Foundation (LLF), school has become one of two government schools in the State where technology will drive learning in a major way. The school has been given 11 laptops, 13 tablets, one interactive board, a projector and a wi-fi connection. However, the major advantage is the introduction of cloud computing solution, which provides the school access to a digitized version of Samacheer Kalvi syllabus for classes VI to XII in Tamil and English.

E-polling in Cloud

Cloud computing technology can further be a back bone of the online voting based system. Though this model is quite new and has lot more to go in the upcoming years. The security level in existing voting system is not up to the mark and there are lots of controversies. As we do not have any back up, consider the case of EVM (Electronic Voting Machine) data reliability is not assured. EVM is based on microcontroller on which the program and the memory can be protected from external read, but that is very low level security and chip centric. In case of chip failure data loss occurs. In many voting system the candidate are restricted to vote at their respective places.

Internet voting system SERVE (Security Electronic Registration and Voting Experiment) is found to be vulnerable to denial of service attack and website spooling. This can compromise the results. Moreover there are a number of technical issues, including authentication and validation of the end-point, protecting the voting system against the inevitable attempts by hostile parties to disrupt the election, and ensuring that the network is capable of handling traffic storms if potentially millions of citizens cast their e-ballots in a short period of time. We can overcome the drawbacks of the traditional approach way of voting using the online polling system supported by the cloud computing technology.

In the proposed system of the *e-polling* using the advanced cloud computing the database creation is done with the details of the candidate along with thumb impression which serve as the key for authentication (Biometric Database). While casting vote the thumb impression of candidate is being matched with the existing database. If the match is found candidates are allowed to caste their vote, otherwise they are denied. This system provides safe and secure polling, far better than the traditional one. Cloud provides a service for voting to all authenticated user.

Scheduling Algorithm

The polling processing application may need to process millions of transactions per day, store the biometric information of the people. The main purpose of using the scheduling algorithm is to improve the communication overhead between the local cloud server to the main server. Due to a huge number of concurrent workflow instances, the algorithms should focus on minimizing the mean execution time of all process in order to maximize the overall throughput rather than minimizing the execution time of individual process.

Mean execution time is the time spent from the beginning of the first task to the end of the last task for a workflow instance. Throughput is the ability of a resource to process a certain number of instances in a given period of time. Hence they can be modeled as instance-intensive cloud workflows with considerable communication overheads. The main characteristic of such workflows is a huge number of relatively simple concurrent instances of which may involve considerable communication overheads among relevant tasks. Thus it is necessary to consider multiple instances of multiple workflows with communication overheads when designing scheduling algorithms for such workflows. Work flows on service-based cloud computing environment, we construct the simulation environment focusing for the algorithm, we use testing nodes located in different places connected via the Internet, thus the communication overheads vary.

In the cloud computing technology we can store the details of the people along with their thumb impression. The database creation is done with the details of the candidate along with thumb impression which serve as the key for authentication (Biometric Database).While casting vote the thumb impression of candidate is being matched with the existing database. If the match is found candidate are allowed to caste their vote , otherwise they are denied. This system provides safe and secure polling. Cloud provides a service for voting to all authenticated user. The cloud computing mainly works based only on the internet facility. All your data is stored online, so you don't have to worry about the capacity.

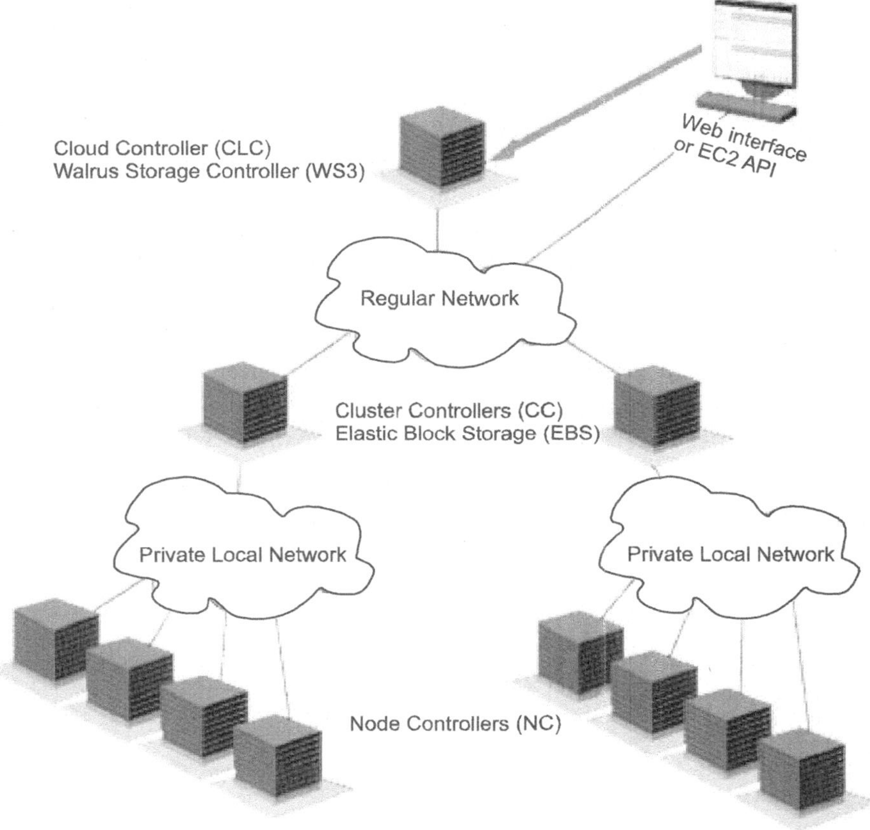

Figure 5.6 E-polling model using cloud computing.

Thus this how the overall polling process takes place in the cloud computing. Though the model of e-polling has many other issues need to be considered but it can be a big tool in the future for the polling purpose.

Enterprise Resource Planning in Cloud

Cloud computing is another boon in a large enterprise for the management of all tasks. One can imagine a big enterprise with several departments with their own function. In such places cloud computing makes the things very easy with its unique principle and working. Traditional *Enterprise Resource Planning* (ERP) systems have several limitations. As the business grows inside an organization, different software applications may be needed to manage information in many areas such as human resources, payroll, finance and administration. Obviously, purchasing, installing and maintaining such multiple types of software applications represent a challenge for business growing. Furthermore, traditional ERP systems are limited in terms of multiple user accessibility, performance and availability of resources. This approach is not user friendly and has many limitations with the going expansion of the company.

ERP cloud refers to installing the ERP applications on the cloud infrastructure with the highly dynamic and virtual servers so that they can be accessed by the organizations ubiquitously through a network connection. It is far advanced compared to the traditional one. One can imagine the large amount of software and tools used inside the business unit of the company, it needs a separate set of technical team to manage and troubleshoot all the issues. All these issues are removed using the service oriented cloud technology. Therefore, with this technology, project managers do not need to worry about installing, upgrading and maintaining applications inside their organizations. In addition, ERP cloud provides organizations with cost-effective scalable resources, high availability of data and applications and multitenant accessibility. Organizations can reduce their capital expenses and achieve higher Return on Investment (ROI) and shorter payback period by leasing resources and services on the cloud rather than purchasing new equipments and software applications. This is important especially for small and medium scale business where budgets are limited.

This form of working inside the organization makes the things far effective, advanced, well governed and far user friendly to all users. Cloud based ERP is the need of the hour at least in some big companies where there are large number of employees using several tools.

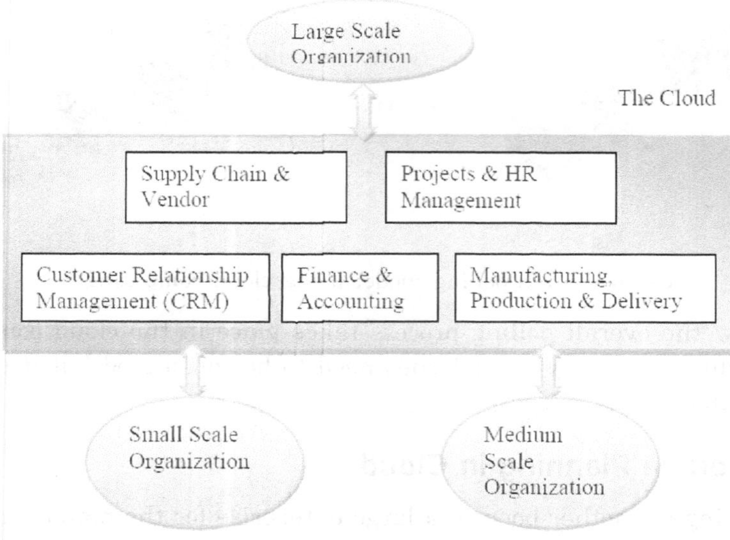

Figure 5.7 ERP model using cloud computing.

Apart from these four application models, there are many more fields where cloud technology can be used to help the users in a better way. In the upcoming years we can see cloud computing almost a reality rather just a proposed model.

5.7 ADVANTAGES OF CLOUD COMPUTING

Now in this section let us discuss in detail about the various advantages of the cloud computing technology. These advantages can better help us in understanding them. It includes:

- ***Cost efficient*** – The first major advantage of cloud computing is the economy of the technology. As we already know cloud computing is purely a service oriented technology with the resources being made available to the user in a pay per usage scenario, metered fashion. Cloud computing is probably the most cost efficient method to use, maintain and upgrade. Traditional desktop software costs companies a lot in terms of finance. Adding up the licensing fees for multiple users can prove to be very expensive for the establishment concerned. The cloud, on the other hand, is available at much cheaper rates and hence, can significantly lower the company's IT expenses. Besides, there are many one time payments, pay-as-you-go and other scalable options available, which makes it very reasonable for the company.
- ***Data storage*** – Cloud computing involves the storing of all data and workspaces in online with unlimited storage, making the independence of data location and usage by the user.
- ***Backup and recovery*** – Since all your data is stored in the cloud, backing it up and restoring the same is relatively much easier than storing the same on a physical device. Furthermore, most cloud service providers are usually competent enough to handle recovery of information. Hence, this makes the entire process of backup and recovery much simpler than other traditional methods of data storage.
- ***Robust and elastic*** – Cloud computing technology is far robust and powerful to overcome any crash or any technical failure compared to the internet. It is highly elastic and flexible in nature mainly due to the virtualization and distributed technology.
- ***High scalable and performance*** – Scalability is a built-in feature for cloud deployments. Cloud instances are deployed automatically only when needed and as a result, you pay only for the applications and data storage you need. Hand in hand, also comes elasticity, since clouds can be scaled to meet your changing IT system demands. Regarding performance, the systems utilize distributed architectures which offer excellent speed of computations. Again, it is the provider's responsibility to ensure that your services run on cutting edge machinery. Instances can be added instantly for improved performance and customers have access to the total resources of the cloud's core hardware via their dashboards.

- ***Optimal resource utilization*** – Servers, storage and network resources are better utilized as the cloud is shared by multiple users, thus cutting down on waste at a global level. Cloud computing is more environment-friendly and energy efficient. Down-time is cut and optimization of resources across enterprises on the cloud is achieved.
- ***Automatic software integration*** – Another major advantage of cloud computing is the automatic updation and maintenance of software in the cloud server by the cloud provider. This means that you do not need to take additional efforts to customize and integrate your applications as per your preferences. This aspect usually takes care of itself. Not only that, cloud computing allows you to customize your options with great ease. Hence, you can handpick just those services and software applications that you think will best suit your particular enterprise.
- ***Dynamic technology*** – Compared to all other previous technology cloud is far more dynamic in its functionality and resources in cloud are easily available to all the users who are accessing it from any remote location.
- ***Easy access*** – One of the most uniqueness and user friendly about cloud is the easy registration and usage of cloud anywhere, anytime by the user with just the internet facility. Putting an end to all the traditional dependence of machines.
- ***Quick deployment*** – Designing applications for cloud computing, can be easily and quickly deployed into the remote virtual cloud. Once you opt for this method of functioning, your entire system can be fully functional in a matter of a few minutes. Of course, the amount of time taken here will depend on the exact kind of technology that you need for your business.
- ***Compatibility*** – Another advantage of cloud computing is the compatibility with all other platforms and technology. Cloud supports all its predecessor computing techniques and is very platform friendly. Suppose if a company decided to shift to cloud platform, all its work in the previous technology and workspaces are well supported by cloud without any mismatch or technical issues in them.
- ***Eco friendly*** – The concept of cloud computing and virtualization are highly eco friendly with a form of green computing by saving all the excess of power using the virtual platform for its functioning, declining the usage of hardware by individual users therefore bringing down the e-waste problem too.
- ***Innovation and research*** – Enterprises can focus on innovation, as they do not have to own or manage resources. Cloud computing facilitates faster prototype development, testing and validation. Research and development projects or activities where users have to collaborate for a task/project are especially benefited.
- ***Business friendly*** – Compared to all other technology, cloud is fully business oriented technology. All its principle, service, usage and working all of them are aligned to the needs and requirements of business community. For small business organization cloud computing is a boon in its initial startup.

5.8 DISADVANTAGES OF CLOUD COMPUTING

Well every technology has some drawbacks in it. Not that they are fully advantageous. Some of the drawbacks of cloud computing include:

- ***Security concern*** – The biggest problem with the cloud computing is the overall security associated with the data. One needs to be careful to store and use the business related critical data in the cloud. This the major drawback of the technology, though the security provided in cloud is far more advanced than the traditional approach.
- ***Malicious attack*** – The number of intruders and hackers are on the rise these days hence the overall cloud computing technology needs to be far more robust enough to overcome any advanced tactics being used by hackers to hack all the confidential and business critical data.
- ***Technical issues*** – Though it is true that information and data on the cloud can be accessed anytime and from anywhere at all, there are times when this system can have some serious dysfunction. You should be aware of the fact that this technology is always prone to outages and other technical issues. Even the best cloud service providers run into this kind of trouble, in spite of keeping up high standards of maintenance. Besides, you will need a very good Internet connection to be logged onto the server at all times. You will invariably be stuck in case of network and connectivity problems. Even by mistake the cloud server is down, not even a single data can be accessed.
- ***Vendor dependence*** – One of the major disadvantages of cloud computing is the implicit dependency on the provider. This is what the industry calls vendor lock-in since it is difficult, and sometimes impossible, to migrate from a provider once you have rolled with him. If a user wishes to switch to some other provider, then it can be really painful and cumbersome to transfer huge data from the old provider to the new one. This is another reason why you should carefully and thoroughly contemplate all options when picking a vendor.
- ***Limited control*** – Since the applications and services run on remote, third party virtual environments, companies and users have limited control over the function and execution of the hardware and software. Moreover, since remote software is being used, it usually lacks the features of an application running locally.
- ***Vulnerability*** – Related to the security and privacy mentioned before, note that cloud based solutions are exposed on the public internet and are thus a more vulnerable target for malicious users and hackers. Nothing on the Internet is completely secured and even the biggest players suffer from serious attacks and security breaches. Due to the interdependency of the system, If there is a compromise one of the machines that data is stored, there might be a leakage of personal information to the world.
- ***Compliance*** – Compliance means that those who have to live with audit compliance issues may find that cloud computing providers do not provide the logging and

auditing features you need to stay compliant with the many laws that corporate America has to follow. The trend is that cloud computing providers will get better at this, so make sure to understand what your issues are and what the providers are offering as compliance solutions before moving forward.

- ***Service level agreement*** – Service-level agreements record a common understanding about services, priorities, responsibilities, guarantees, and warranties between the cloud provider and the cloud user. Many cloud providers do not offer them, but that will change as larger enterprises with stricter requirements begin to leverage cloud computing. The trend is for cloud computing providers to offer SLAs, but of course they do so by passing the cost of the risk down to the cloud computing platform consumer. It is another issue and cost to consider.

SUMMARY

- *The term cloud migration refers to the transition of the entire work done in the previous technology or platform into this new cloud computing platform. It involves the transition of the companies data, services, applications, internal tools, workspaces, official data and so on into the remote virtual cloud.*
- *While a cloud migration can present numerous challenges and raise security concerns, as we already know data security and privacy is a big issue in cloud computing. Cloud computing can also enable a company to potentially reduce capital expenditures and operating costs while also benefiting from the dynamic scaling, high availability, multi-tenancy and effective resource allocation advantages cloud based computing offers.*
- *The process of cloud migration is quite a wide task considering the large dimension of IT companies. One must be careful in migration process as it involves some unexpected risks and accidents too during the whole transition period. One must not get confused with the overall migration process as there will be several data and working platform with both modified and unmodified platforms.*
- *Cloud hosting is process in which the application which is designed in a suitable platform is hosted into the remote virtual cloud.*
- *Cloud hosting describes the best method available to configure the virtual server in a very flexible way as required by the user or even the provider. It provides a more reliable, scalable, and a well advanced networking based infrastructure required dynamically by the user. It provides a well defined framework required for the business growth with the minimal expenditure.*
- *With Cloud Hosting, the user is provisioned to avail on demand resources in real time. Resources are not limited to capacity of one server or any other physical constraints.*

- *For the cloud hosting we generally use the highly dynamic and virtual server called cloud server. Cloud servers are very powerful virtual environments created within a very strong cluster of servers. Cloud servers carry many benefits that are not offered within a dedicated server.*
- *Cloud servers can be run on a hypervisor or virtual machine manager. The role of a hypervisor is to control the capacity of operating systems so it is allocated where needed. With cloud hosting there are multiple cloud servers which are available to each particular client. This allows computing resource to be dedicated to a particular client if and when it is necessary.*
- *All the data and other workspaces are stored in this large remote data center. Data centers consist of large number of machines packed in a specific format storing all the contents. Data centers are owned and maintained by giant IT companies. There will be multiple data centers each one of them in a very remote location but are connected by large data cables which run through the land and oceans giving the connectivity. Data centers are situated in a very remote location mainly due to its high infrastructure needs and also due to security issues.*
- *Data centre needs to be fully prepared with any form of disaster, must be prepared for any worst case scenario too. Disaster recovery is quite a bit easier when your data center is virtualized. With up-to-date snapshots of your virtual machines, you can quickly get back up all the data and running.*
- *Inter cloud or combination of clouds called as cloud of clouds. The idea behind them is that a single common functionality would combine many different individual clouds into one seamless mass in terms of on-demand operations in the cloud.*
- *The Inter cloud scenario is based on the key concept that each single cloud or a service provider of a cloud does not have infinite physical resources or the capacity to support all of them. Clouds combine to help each other attaining their full functionality. It also helps in the full operation of an idle cloud with the sharing of the cloud platform using the inter cloud technology when the other cloud is fully saturated.*
- *Cloud databases give developers and IT a powerful and scalable database that just works. From the infrastructure to the database software to the tuning and monitoring, everything is done as a service.*
- *Private clouds give IT departments many of the benefits of the public cloud with the added benefit of having an isolated network and computing resources that bring additional security. Rackspace offers private clouds that give IT departments a lot more control over the resources deployed and the architecture. Hybrid clouds, enabled by various underlying technologies, allow IT departments to connect public cloud, private cloud, dedicated hosted and on-premise infrastructure to gain the optimum combination of control and agility.*

- *All government offices, records and their entire functionality can be made a one stop place for all, by using the e-governance model using the cloud technology.*
- *Cloud computing can be used for the learning purpose with a highly advanced learning methodology supported by then cloud servers. This king of learning process is becoming famous in several institutions, may be these will the future learning education system.*
- *The voting process in election can also be implemented using the cloud computing technology with a highly secured and location independence manner.*
- *It is equally important to know when to use a technology and at places to be avoided in a very precise manner. It can prove to be disaster if a new user is unaware of this basic information, the wrong choice of a wrong platform can finish off the whole user task.*
- *The first major advantage of cloud computing is the economy of the technology. As we already know cloud computing is purely a service oriented technology with the resources being made available to the user in a pay per usage scenario, metered fashion. Cloud computing is probably the most cost efficient method to use, maintain and upgrade.*
- *Cloud computing involves the storing of all data and workspaces in online with unlimited storage, making the independence of data location and usage by the user.*
- *Scalability is a built-in feature for cloud deployments. Cloud instances are deployed automatically only when needed and as a result, you pay only for the applications and data storage you need. Hand in hand, also comes elasticity, since clouds can be scaled to meet your changing IT system demands. Regarding performance, the systems utilize distributed architectures which offer excellent speed of computations.*
- *The biggest problem with the cloud computing is the overall security associated with the data. One needs to be careful to store and use the business related critical data in the cloud. This the major drawback of the technology, though the security provided in cloud is far more advanced than the traditional approach.*
- *One of the major disadvantages of cloud computing is the implicit dependency on the provider. This is what the industry calls vendor lock-in since it is difficult, and sometimes impossible, to migrate from a provider once you have rolled with him.*

Chapter 6

Real Time Cloud and its Application

OBJECTIVE

- *To know about the various cloud providers*
- *To learn in detail about all the cloud products and their functions*
- *To know about the list of all cloud based operating system*

Till now we saw the introduction to cloud computing, principles of cloud, cloud types, various service models and so on. In this chapter, let us discuss some of the real time cloud examples and their applications available today. We will also see some of the giant companies in the world which have developed many cloud computing products and business solutions. Reading them one can get a good idea about cloud computing technology and its application. Though most of the products are proprietary we need to pay money for usage, there are some available for free which we can use. Some of the free cloud applications are used by many people today.

6.1 AMAZON CLOUD AND ITS PRODUCT

When we talk about cloud we must never forget to use the word called *Amazon*. Amazon is a giant IT company in the world spread across several nations and has developed several products in cloud. Amazon has also has its work spread in several other areas too but it has given a new meaning to the cloud technology. Amazon has emerged as the undisputed leader in cloud technology today. Amazon Web Services (AWS) officially known as provides a cloud computing platform for all business sizes. AWS can provide a flexible, cost-effective IT infrastructure and services that can be scaled up and down based on the needs of the end user and companies. AWS helps companies select the platform that is suitable for the problem they face and pay only for what they use.

After all we know cloud computing is purely a service oriented technology with pay as you go model of charging. In addition, AWS applies advanced physical security and data privacy techniques to protect user data. AWS has security certifications and audits such as

ISO 27001, FISMA moderate, HIPAA and SAS 70 Type II. AWS is a comprehensive cloud service platform which provides many web services. It was one of the early IT giant to begin operations in cloud technology and other advanced web services. Almost all the Amazon products are proprietary. They need to be paid based on the usage and during free trial itself credit card details are prompted to the user.

Figure 6.1 Amazon web services official logo.

The various cloud products and solutions developed and owned by Amazon include

AMAZON ELASTIC COMPUTE CLOUD (EC2)

The Amazon web services provide the cloud hosting service using the platform EC2. It allows using the web service interfaces to launch instances with a variety of operating system platforms, load them with the custom application environment, manage network access permissions, and run the image using as many or few systems as the user desires. It is proprietary not for free. User has to pay the money based on the Amazon slab rate under the pay as you go model. Amazon EC2 provides a number of powerful features for building scalable, failure resilient, enterprise class applications needed for today's world. To use the Amazon EC2 fallow these steps:

- First select a pre-configured, templated Amazon Machine Image (AMI) to get up and running immediately or create an AMI containing your applications, libraries, data, and associated configuration settings.
- Configure security and network access on your Amazon EC2 instance.
- Choose which instance type you want, then start, terminate, and monitor as many instances of your AMI as needed, using the web service APIs or the variety of management tools provided.
- Determine whether you want to run in multiple locations, utilize static IP endpoints, or attach persistent block storage to your instances.
- Pay only for the resources that you actually consume. It is not for free.

Amazon Simple Storage Service (S3)

Amazon simple storage service provides the user to store all their data into the cloud. Using these cloud storage user can access the data anywhere, independent of machines and it reduces the need of hardware storage devices. Amazon S3 provides a simple web-services interface that can be used to store and retrieve any amount of data, at any time, from anywhere on the web. It gives any developer access to the same highly scalable, reliable, secure, fast, inexpensive infrastructure that Amazon uses to run its own global network of web sites. The service aims to maximize benefits of scale and to pass those benefits on to developers.

Data stored in Amazon S3 is secure by default only bucket and object owners have access to the Amazon S3 resources they create. Amazon S3 supports multiple access control mechanisms, as well as encryption for both secure transit and secure storage on disk. With Amazon S3 data protection features, you can protect your data from both logical and physical failures, guarding against data loss from unintended user actions, application errors, and infrastructure failures.

Amazon Glacier

Amazon Glacier is an extremely low-cost storage service that provides secure and durable storage for data archiving and backup. In order to keep costs low, Amazon Glacier is optimized for data that is infrequently accessed and for which retrieval times of several hours are suitable. With Amazon Glacier, customers can reliably store large or small amounts of data for as little as $0.01 per gigabyte per month, a significant savings compared to on-premises solutions. Amazon Glacier changes the game for data archiving and backup as you pay nothing upfront, pay a very low price for storage, and can scale your usage up or down as needed, while AWS handles all of the operational heavy lifting required to do data retention well. It only takes a few clicks in the AWS Management Console to set up Amazon Glacier and then you can upload any amount of data you choose.

Amazon Virtual Private Cloud (VPC)

It connects the company's existing IT infrastructure to AWS cloud via a Virtual Private Network (VPN). Amazon Virtual Private Cloud (VPC) lets the user provision a logically isolated section of the Amazon Web Services (AWS) Cloud where one can launch AWS resources in a virtual network that you define. You have complete control over your virtual networking environment, including selection of your own IP address range, creation of subnets, and configuration of route tables and network gateways. Additionally, you can create a Hardware Virtual Private Network (VPN) connection between your corporate datacenter and your VPC and leverage the AWS cloud as an extension of your corporate datacenter. With virtual private cloud one can:

- Create an Amazon Virtual Private Cloud on AWS's scalable infrastructure, and specify its private IP address range from any range you choose.
- Divide your VPC's private IP address range into one or more public or private subnets to facilitate running applications and services in your VPC.
- Control inbound and outbound access to and from individual subnets using network access control lists.
- Store data in Amazon S3 and set permissions such that the data can only be accessed from within your Amazon VPC.

- Assign multiple IP addresses and attach multiple elastic network interfaces to instances in your VPC.
- Attach one or more Amazon Elastic IP addresses to any instance in your VPC so it can be reached directly from the Internet.
- Bridge your VPC and your onsite IT infrastructure with an encrypted VPN connection, extending your existing security and management policies to your VPC instances as if they were running within your infrastructure.

Amazon Cloudfront

Amazon CloudFront is a content delivery web service that transfers customer's data with high speed and minimum delay using a global network of edge locations. It integrates with other Amazon Web Services to give developers and businesses an easy way to distribute content to end users with low latency, high data transfer speeds, and no commitments.

With Amazon CloudFront, there are no additional costs for serving dynamic content beyond Amazon CloudFront's existing low prices for data transfer and requests, and no required long term commitments for use. There are also no up-front fees, no monthly platform fees, and no need to hire expensive consultants to help with configuration.

Amazon Rout 53

Amazon Route 53 is a highly available and scalable Domain Name System (DNS) web service. It is designed to give developers and businesses an extremely reliable and cost effective way to route end users to Internet applications by translating names like www.example.com into the numeric IP addresses. It is designed such that computers use to connect to each other. Route 53 effectively connects user requests to infrastructure running in AWS such as Amazon EC2 instances, Elastic Load Balancers, or Amazon S3 buckets and can also be used to route users to infrastructure outside of AWS.

Amazon Relational Database Services (Amazon RDS)

Amazon Relational Database Service (Amazon RDS) is a web service that makes it easy to set up, operate, and scale a relational database in the cloud. It provides cost-efficient and resizable capacity while managing time-consuming database administration tasks, freeing you up to focus on your applications and business. Such cloud databases are highly dynamic and replicated in nature allowing multiple users to use them at a time.

Amazon RDS gives you access to the capabilities of a familiar databases like MySQL, Oracle, Microsoft SQL Server, or PostgreSQL database engine. Thus allowing the code, applications, and tools already used today with your existing databases can be used with Amazon RDS. Amazon RDS automatically patches the database software and backs up your database, storing the backups for a user-defined retention period and enabling point-in-time recovery. The user benefit from the flexibility of being able to scale the compute resources or storage capacity associated with your Database Instance (DB Instance) via a single API call.

Amazon Workspaces

Amazon WorkSpaces is a fully managed desktop computing service in the cloud. Amazon WorkSpaces allows customers to easily provision cloud-based desktops that allow end-users to access the documents, applications and resources they need with the device of their choice, including laptops, iPad, Kindle Fire, or Android tablets. With a few clicks in the AWS Management Console, customers can provision a high-quality desktop experience for any number of users at a cost that is highly competitive with traditional desktops and half the cost of most virtual desktop infrastructure (VDI) solutions.

Amazon WorkSpaces offers you an easy way to provide a fully managed, cloud-based desktop experience to your end-users. You don't have to worry about procuring or deploying hardware or installing complex software to deliver a desktop experience to your users. Amazon WorkSpaces takes care of all the heavy lifting of managing hardware and software, and tasks such as patching and maintenance, enabling you to deliver a high quality desktop experience to your users.

Amazon Cloudsearch

Amazon CloudSearch is a fully-managed service in the AWS Cloud that makes it easy to set up, manage, and scale a search solution for your website or application. Amazon CloudSearch enables you to search large collections of data such as web pages, document files, forum posts, or product information.

With Amazon CloudSearch, you can quickly add search capabilities to your website without having to become a search expert or worry about hardware provisioning, setup, and maintenance. With a few clicks in the AWS Management Console, you can create a search domain, upload the data you want to make searchable to Amazon CloudSearch, and the search service automatically provisions the required technology resources and deploys a highly tuned search index. As your volume of data and traffic fluctuates, Amazon CloudSearch seamlessly scales to meet your needs. You can easily change your search parameters, fine tune search relevance, and apply new settings at any time without having to reupload your data.

Amazon CloudSearch enables customers to offload the administrative burden and expense of operating and scaling a search service. With Amazon CloudSearch, there's no need to worry about hardware provisioning, data partitioning, or software patches. And like all AWS services, Amazon CloudSearch offers low, pay-as-you-go pricing with no up-front expenses or long-term commitments.

Amazon Elastic Map Reduce

Amazon Elastic MapReduce (Amazon EMR) is a web service that makes it easy to quickly and cost-effectively process vast amounts of data. Amazon EMR uses Hadoop, an open source framework, to distribute your data and processing across a resizable cluster of Amazon EC2 instances. Amazon EMR is used in a variety of applications, including log analysis, web indexing, data warehousing, machine learning, financial analysis, scientific simulation, and bioinformatics. Users launch millions of Amazon EMR clusters every year.

6.2 GOOGLE CLOUD AND ITS PRODUCT

Another major company which has developed ocean of computer products and services is Google. The word Google makes us think of the popular Google *search engine* but there are lot more products developed and owned by Google in several areas. Google integrates many applications and provides many services to customers in cloud. This integration makes Google one of the best service provider since it allows customers to have their tasks accomplished easily. It also saves money and time since developing and maintaining software to provide all of these services and applications is a time consuming and an expensive process. Google has developed many products in the field of cloud computing. Some of them include:

Google App Engine

It comes under the Platform as a Service (PaaS) concept of cloud service model where it provides the required software development tools to be used by the user to design the cloud application, host the cloud app into the Google cloud and scale it based on the demand of the user. Using this concept a user can host ten apps freely from their Google account. App Engine applications are easy to build, easy to maintain, and easy to scale as your traffic and data storage needs grow. With App Engine, there are no servers to maintain just upload your application, and it's ready to serve users. Mostly the apps are designed using the Eclipse software. We will see its demo in chapter 15 case study.

Google Compute Engine

Compute Engine is Google's Infrastructure-as-a-Service (IaaS) service model of cloud. Google Compute Engine is a service that provides virtual machines that run on Google infrastructure. Google Compute Engine offers scale, performance, and value that allows to easily launch large compute clusters on Google's infrastructure. There are no upfront investments and can run up to thousands of virtual CPUs on a system that has been designed from the ground up to be fast, and to offer strong consistency of performance. An instance is a virtual machine hosted on Google's infrastructure. All instances run Linux, using a standard image provided by Google Compute Engine, or a modified version of one of these images, customized by the user. User can optionally choose a machine type that specifies the number of CPUs, RAM, and other machine properties.

Google Cloud Drive

Similar to Amazon simple storage service (S3). Google has developed a storage medium popularly known as Google drive and it is for free till a specific limit not for rent completely unlike the Amazon storage. It can store about 15 Gb of data free for a user. We can get extra storage space but with the rental basis, it is not free afterwards. It was introduced only in April 2012. User can store any data they want and can use it anywhere with just a Google account and internet facility. Using such advanced storage facilities it makes the independence of machines. Google drive synchronizes with other Google applications easily. User can create folders in them, share with multiple people and so on. Thus it is more comfortable and easier to work with cloud apps than the traditional method.

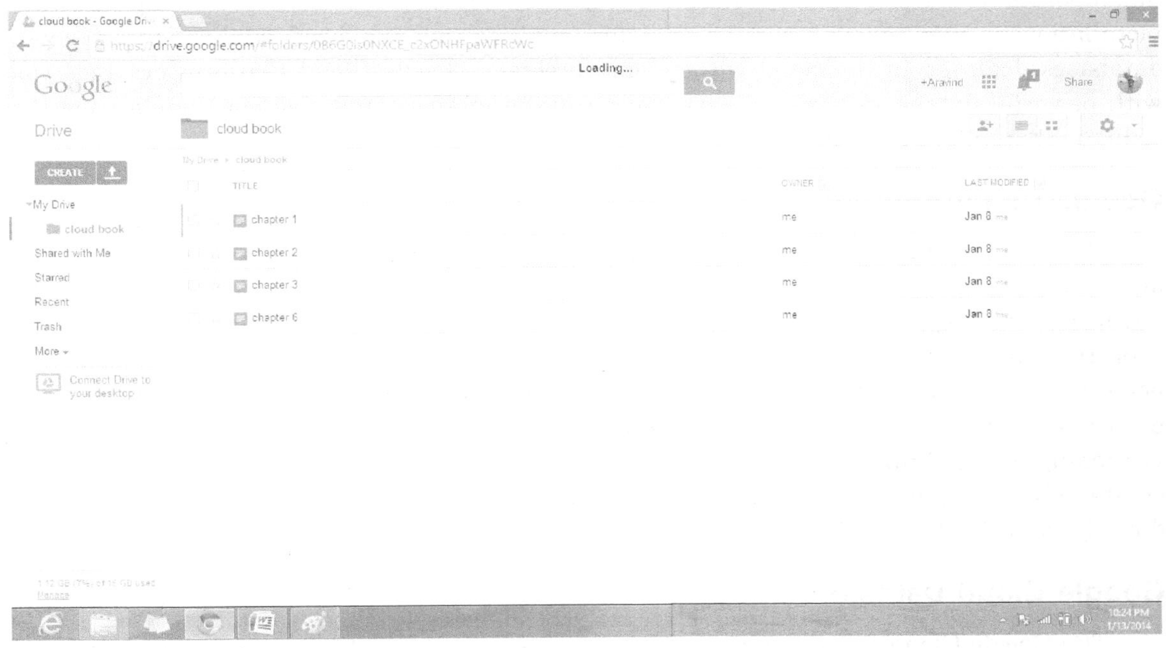

Figure 6.2 Google drive account.

Google Docs

Most of us use many word processors software to write any letter or any content. Cloud computing makes things far easier with the online cloud based software. One can easily write all contents using the Google docs. It is synchronized with Google drive. Google Docs is a tool for real time collaborative editing. Documents can be shared, opened, and edited by multiple users at the same time. Users cannot be notified of changes, but the application can notify users when a comment or discussion is made or replied to, facilitating collaboration. However, users can usually see where in the document or file a particular editor is currently writing, since in most of the suite's products, an editor's current position is represented with an editor-specific color or cursor.

Also the revision history included in the service allows users to see the changes made to a document, distinguished by editor, using their specific color. The application supports two ISO standard document formats which are OpenDocument which are for both opening and exporting and Office Open XML which is for opening only. It also includes support for proprietary formats such as .doc and .xls. Along with Google docs Google also provides the presentation, spreadsheet, forms and drawing software.

Google Cloud SQL

Google Cloud SQL is a MySQL database that lives in Google's cloud infrastructure. It has all the capabilities and functionality of MySQL, with a few additional features and a few unsupported features. Google Cloud SQL is easy to use, doesn't require any software installation or maintenance and is ideal for small to medium-sized applications. MySQL databases deployed in the cloud without any problem. Google Cloud Platform provides you with powerful databases that run fast, don't run out of space and give your application the redundant, reliable storage it needs.

Google Cloud Storage

Google Cloud Storage allows world-wide storing and retrieval of any amount of data and at any time. It provides a simple programming interface which enables developers to take advantage of Google's own reliable and fast networking infrastructure to perform data operations in a secure and cost effective manner. If expansion needs arise, developers can benefit from the scalability provided by Google's infrastructure. Though Cloud Storage can be accessed with a simple API, advanced feature sets add flexibility and power. Object versioning, parallel uploads and CRC-based integrity checking gives developers the ability to create robust, sophisticated applications. User can access the API using XML or JSON directly, or use libraries for several popular programming languages.

Google Cloud Datastore

The Google Cloud Datastore provides a set of tools and client libraries for accessing and managing Google Cloud Datastore from clients running on Google Cloud Compute Engine instances or elsewhere. It provides an RPC-based API that is hosted by the same Google service that hosts Google Maps, YouTube, and Google Apps APIs. User can use it with most applications and languages, for example, with a node.js web app running in a virtual machine or an on-premise Java application server. The Datastore is a schemaless object datastore providing robust, scalable storage for the application, with the following features like no planned downtime, atomic transactions, high availability of reads and writes, strong consistency for reads and ancestor queries, and eventual consistency for all other queries.

Google Bigquery

Querying massive datasets can be time consuming and expensive without the right hardware and infrastructure. Google BigQuery solves this problem by enabling super-fast, SQL-like queries against append-only tables, using the processing power of Google's infrastructure. Simply move the data into BigQuery and it handles the hard work. Queries are written in BigQuery's SQL dialect. BigQuery supports both synchronous and asynchronous query methods. Both methods are handled by a job, but the synchronous method exposes a timeout value that waits until the job has finished before returning.

Google Cloud Print

In the world of Google Cloud Print, one can print anything, from any device, to any cloud-connected printer. Google Cloud Print is a new technology that connects the printers to the web. Using Google Cloud Print, user can make home and work printers available to the user and anyone else user chooses, from the applications user uses every day. Google

Cloud Print works on phone, tablet, Chromebook, PC, and any other web-connected device user wants to print from. When you print through Google Cloud Print, your file is securely sent to your printer over the web. Because it's the web, Google Cloud Print works whether you're in the same room as your printer, or on another continent. It also doesn't matter whether you're on a phone, a traditional desktop, or anything in between like a tablet.

With ***Cloud Ready printers*** the Google Cloud Print experience is ready right out of the box. Cloud Ready printers register themselves directly with the Google Cloud Print service over your home or office's wireless network, so they're always available. And because they're always connected to the web, they can keep their drivers and firmware up to date without requiring your intervention. Google Cloud Print also works with conventional non-cloud printers, so you can get started today with any printer you already own.

6.3 MICROSOFT CLOUD AND ITS PRODUCT

The word Microsoft makes us think of the term *operating system software* but Microsoft is a world giant company with several technologies, products and services provided by them. In the last few years Microsoft has acquired several other companies and has started its work in other areas apart from the operating system platform. Microsoft has dominated the windows platform operating system. Started with desktop based computer then moved to server machines now to cloud computing. Microsoft is also a major player in today's mobile platform giving a tough competition to the Android platform. Microsoft also has developed many cloud products and solution which include:

Skydrive

Similar to Amazon simple storage service (S3) and Google drive Microsoft has developed a cloud based storage platform called Skydrive. It was previously known as Windows Live SkyDrive and Windows Live Folders. The service offers 7 GB of free storage for new users and for one year, an additional 3 GB of free storage to students. Additional storage is available for purchase based on pay as you go model. Users who signed up to SkyDrive prior to April 22, 2012 could have opted-in for a limited time offer of 25 GB of free storage upgrade. The service is built using HTML5 technologies and files up to 300 MB can be uploaded via drag and drop into the web browser, or up to 2 GB via the SkyDrive desktop application for Microsoft Windows and OS X. SkyDrive supports viewing of Portable Document Format (PDF) as well as Open Document Format (ODF), an XML-based file format supported in a number of word processing apps including Microsoft Office, OpenOffice.org, and Corel's WordPerfect. SkyDrive integrates with several other sites like social networks such as Facebook, Twitter and LinkedIn to enable users to quickly share their files with their contacts on these social networks. SkyDrive integrates with Bing's Save & Share feature, allowing users to save search histories into a SkyDrive folder.

When users delete any files on SkyDrive, the service will allow the user to undo the action and restore the deleted file from the recycle bin back to the original folder. Items in the recycle bin do not count against the user's SkyDrive storage limit. All items stored in the recycle bin are kept for a minimum of 3 days and a maximum of 30 days. If the content in a user's recycle bin exceeds 10% of the user's storage limit SkyDrive will delete the oldest content from the recycle bin provided that the files have been in the recycle bin for at least 3 days. From windows 8 onward Microsoft has made the Skydrive an inbuilt application itself. Thus Windows 8 is popularly known as cloud supported operating system.

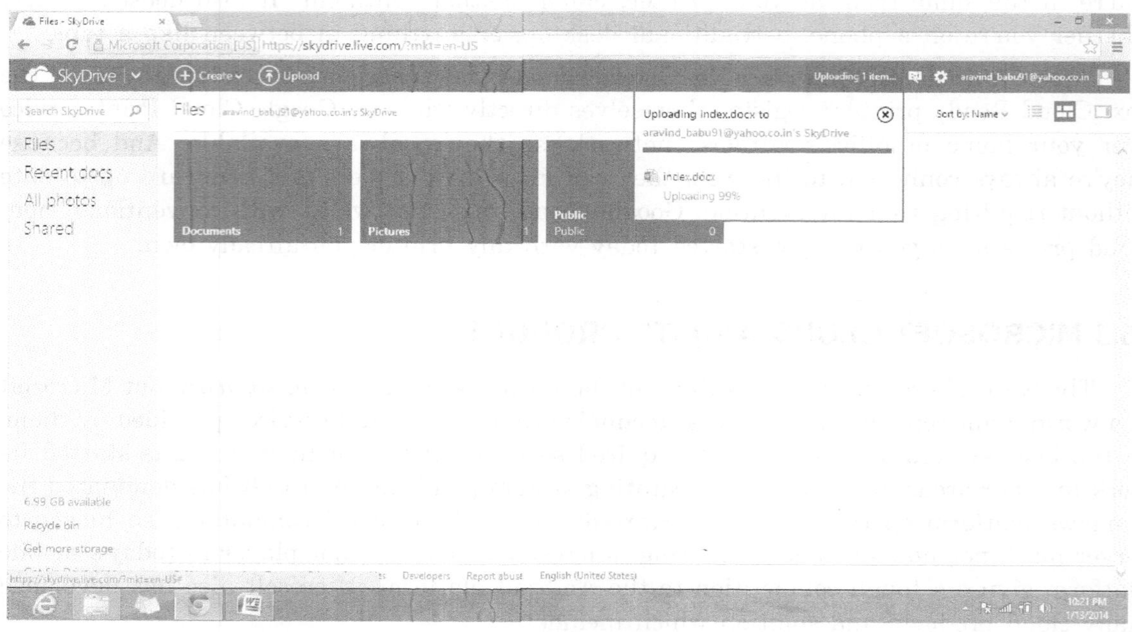

Figure 6.3 Skydrive account to store all data.

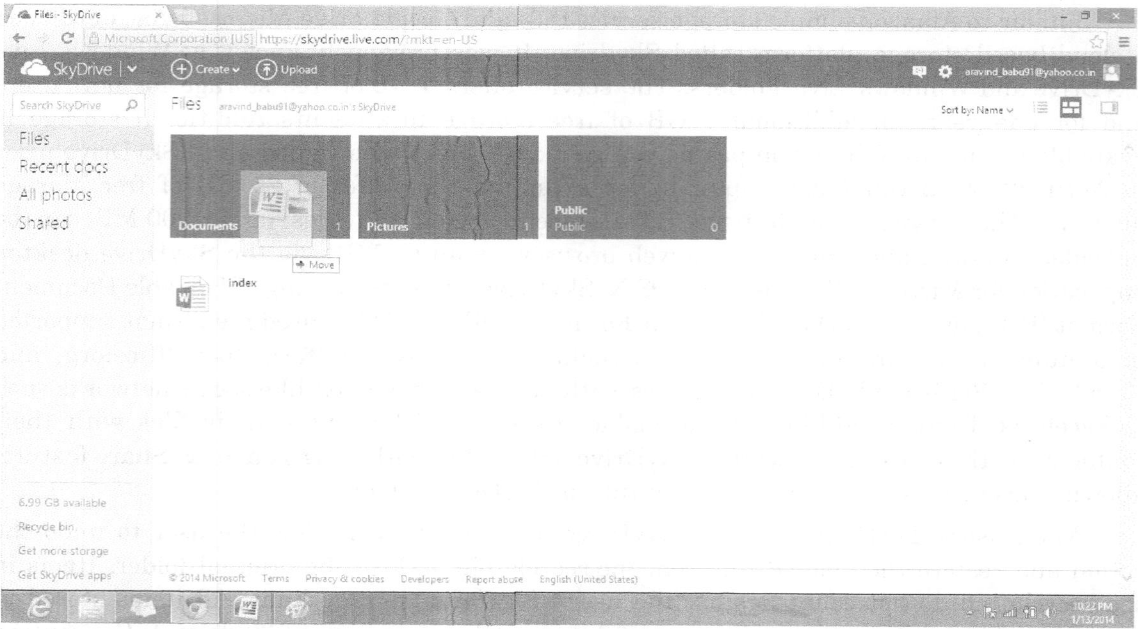

Figure 6.4 Moving data into Skydrive account.

Windows Azure

Windows azure is a proprietary cloud platform developed by Microsoft. Windows Azure is a cloud computing platform and infrastructure created by Microsoft for building, deploying and managing applications and services through Microsoft-managed datacenters. It provides both PaaS and IaaS service models of cloud and supports many different programming languages, tools and frameworks, including both Microsoft-specific and third-party software and systems. Windows Azure was released on February 1, 2010. Windows Azure can be used to build a web application that runs and stores its data in Microsoft datacenters. It can connect on-premises applications with each other or map between different sets of identity information. Some of its features include:

- ***Web sites*** – it is used to rapidly deploy highly scalable web sites on Windows Azure. It allows using languages and open source applications of a site administrator's choice and deploying content with FTP, Git, and TFS. Integrations with Windows Azure services include SQL Database, Caching, Content Delivery Network (CDN) and Storage. This is an optimal solution for a web presence to start small and scale as traffic grows with scalability, high availability, and built-in monitoring of performance and usage data. This is also a perfect turnkey for running ephemeral. short-live and transitory sites, for contests, promotions, campaign, prototype, proof of concept, and so on.
- ***Virtual machines*** – it is Windows Azure's IaaS solution. This much needed and long waited capability enables enterprise IT to provision infrastructure and deploys VMs on demand. An administrator can now easily deploy and configure Windows Server and Linux VMs in minutes in cloud. Migrate workloads without having to change existing code and modify network configuration, while able to securely connect those VMs to on-premises corporate networks.
- ***Mobile services*** – it offers a secure turnkey backend-as-a-service solution readily available for mobile applications. This offer accelerates mobile application development by incorporating structured storage, user authentication, and pushes notifications, and shortens the process dramatically. The Return On Investment (ROI) of this offering for mobile application development and deployment is almost immediate.
- ***Media services*** – it has everything for delivering content to a variety of devices, from Xbox, Windows phone, Windows 8, to MacOS, iOS and Android while ingesting, encoding, converting, and protecting content with both on-demand and live streaming capabilities. As media increasingly becomes part of a delivery in both business and social settings, Windows Azure Media Services arrive with tremendous business opportunities and growth.
- ***Cloud services*** – it is a PaaS offering, provides an on-demand runtime environment. Published API enables developers to build or extend enterprise applications onto Windows Azure with high availability and elastic scale. This is a PaaS environment

to deploy applications delivered as SaaS solutions to customers anywhere around the world.

Some of its newly added features include:

- Websites allows developers to build sites using ASP.NET, PHP, or Node.js and can be deployed using FTP, Git, Mercurial or Team Foundation Server.
- Virtual machines let developers migrate applications and infrastructure without changing existing code, and can run both Windows Server and Linux virtual machines.
- Cloud services such as Microsoft's Platform as a Service (PaaS) environment that is used to create scalable applications and services. Supports multi-tier scenarios and automated deployments.
- Data management such as SQL Database, formerly known as SQL Azure Database, works to create, scale and extend applications into the cloud using Microsoft SQL Server technology. Integrates with Active Directory and Microsoft System Center and Hadoop.
- Media services which includes a PaaS offering that can be used for encoding, content protection, streaming, and/or analytics.

And many more. We will the demo of it in chapter 15 under case study. The Windows Azure Platform provides an API built on REST, HTTP, and XML that allows a developer to interact with the services provided by Windows Azure. Microsoft also provides a client-side managed class library which encapsulates the functions of interacting with the services. It also integrates with Microsoft Visual Studio, Git, and Eclipse.

One must not think windows azure as an operating system with a word windows in it. It is completely charged not free. One has to give credit card details while registering it.

6.4 APPLE CLOUD

Most of us must have heard the famous Apple company and must have used many of its products. Apple has designed many smart technologies ranging from smart phones, laptops, tablets, music player, TV, operating system and so on. All its products start with the name called i like iphone, ipad, ipod, iOS and so on. Apple is a major giant company in the world with its product extremely famous for its unique brand and name. For cloud computing discussion we restrict with Apple cloud icloud only.

The cloud computing platform owned by Apple company is icloud. It was introduced in 2011 only but it has become very popular now. Millions of people are using it today. As we all know all Apple company applications are restricted only to their platform, outsiders or other platforms cannot use them. icloud is mainly used for cloud storage but has other functions too.

Figure 6.5 Apple icloud.

Some of the features of icloud include:

- Icloud helps in storing and viewing the music, movies, apps, book and etc which the user has purchased and downloaded from the iTunes store, app store and ibook store. It is automatically available on all Apple devices and whenever we start something on one device, all other devices automatically remember where we left off.
- Using the icloud one can easily share all photos and videos to other people using the Apple devices.
- A very important security feature provided by Apple is the searching of the lost device. One cannot easily steal someone's Apple product and sell it in market. There is an application to track and find the lost Apple products.
- icloud supports the iwork apps allowing the Apple users to work from anywhere. It supports all the Apple product platforms.
- icloud supports millions of application that help the users to easily use them and make their task simple. The applications are of various domains and have a very broad usage.
- They support an easy and user friendly browsing session using safari. icloud keeps the tabs you have open in Safari up to date on your iPad, iPhone, iPod touch, and Mac. So you can go from one device to the next and pick up browsing wherever you left off. Safari also saves web pages not just links in your Reading List, so you can get caught up on any device, even when you're not connected to the Internet.
- icloud supports a unique feature called keychain. Today users have multiple accounts in various websites it can be hard to remember every account information. Now icloud can keep track of account names, passwords, and credit card numbers for

the user. It doesn't just remember them, it can help create them. Password Generator suggests unique, hard-to-guess passwords for your online accounts. Then Safari can enter your passwords automatically whenever you need to sign in or complete an online purchase. icloud Keychain works on all iOS 7 devices and Mac computers running OS X Mavericks. And it's highly secure thanks to 256-bit AES encryption technique.

- icloud supports the best cloud storage of emails, calendars, contacts, notes, remainders and so on. It updates them from time to time and makes changes to all Apple platforms.
- icloud helps in the easy backup and restore of all the data. When the user sets up a new iOS device or need to restore information on one you already have, icloud Backup does the job in a very simple way. Connect your device to Wi-Fi and enter your Apple ID and password. Your personal data along with your purchased music, movies, TV shows, apps, and books will appear on the device, automatically.
- When you sign up for icloud, you automatically get 5GB of free storage. Your icloud storage is used for icloud Backup, app data and documents stored in icloud, and icloud Mail (icloud.com email accounts). If you need more storage, you can easily purchase an upgrade right from your device.
- icloud also provides a better security and privacy issue. icloud secures your data by encrypting it when it is sent over the Internet, storing it in an encrypted format when kept on server and using secure tokens for authentication. This means that your data is protected from unauthorized access both while it is being transmitted to your devices and when it is stored in the cloud. icloud uses a minimum of 128-bit AES encryption technique.

6.5 VMWARE CLOUD AND ITS PRODUCT

A very famous company that has delivered so many products and solution in virtualization and cloud computing is VMware. When we use the word VMware we think of the virtual operation system software. But it has developed so many products in both cloud computing and virtualization. It primarily started as a leader in virtualization technology but today has equally grown and developed up in cloud computing technology. Some of the cloud products include:

vCloud Director

VMware vCloud Director is a software solution that enables enterprises to build secure, multi tenant private clouds by pooling infrastructure resources into virtual datacenters and exposing them to users through Web-based portals and programmatic interfaces as fully automated, catalog-based services. By building secure and cost-effective private clouds with VMware vSphere and VMware vCloud Director, internal IT organizations can act as true service providers for the businesses they support, driving innovation and agility while increasing IT efficiency and enhancing security. This solution provides a pragmatic path to cloud computing by giving customers the power to leverage existing investments and the flexibility to extend capacity between clouds. Its features include:

- ***Create virtual datacenters*** – Virtual datacenters are logical constructs that include compute, storage, and networking capacity to enable complete abstraction between the consumption of infrastructure services and the underlying resources.
- ***Support multi-tenant environments*** – Administrators can group users into organizations that can represent any policy group, such as a business unit, division, or subsidiary company. Each has isolated virtual resources, independent LDAP authentication, specific policy controls, and unique catalogs. These features enable secure multi-tenancy and safe sharing of infrastructure.
- *vShield security technologies* – Integrated vShield Edge technologies such as perimeter protection, port-level firewalling, network address translation and DHCP services, offer virtualization-aware security, simplify application deployment, and enforce boundaries required by compliance standards. Upgrading to the full vShield Edge solution adds advanced services such as site-to-site VPN, network isolation, and Web load balancing.
- ***Infrastructure service catalog*** – Users are empowered to deploy and consume pre-configured infrastructure and application services, such as virtual appliances, virtual machines, operating system images, and other media with the click of a button from central catalogs. This enables IT teams to standardize offerings, simplifying troubleshooting, patching, and change management.
- ***Self-service portal*** – Users get direct access to their catalogs and virtual datacenters through a user-friendly Web portal.
- ***VMware vCloud API and Open Virtualization Format*** – The vCloud API is an open, REST-based API that allows scripted access to consume cloud resources, such as vApp upload/ download, catalog management, and other operations. The vCloud API makes basic transfer between clouds possible using the Open Virtualization Format (OVF), which preserves application properties, networking configuration, and other settings.
- ***Automation and orchestration*** – Leveraging the APIs in conjunction with the VMware vCenter Orchestrator plug-in and integrations with other orchestration and service management software, administrators can automate routine tasks, build ITIL workflows, and script complex operations with ease.

vCloud Hybrid Service

VMware vCloud Hybrid Service is a secure, dedicated infrastructure-as-aservice cloud, owned and operated by VMware and built on the trusted foundation of vSphere and the software defined data center architecture. The service supports existing workloads and third-party applications, as well as new application development, with unified networking that spans your existing and new data center capacity. It also offers common management and security and the same reliability and performance you expect from your internal VMware infrastructure. And with vCloud Hybrid Service, you have only one number to call for VMware support for both your onsite and offsite environments.

Broadest Operating System and Application Support

vCloud Hybrid Service supports the thousands of applications and dozens of operating systems that are certified to run on vSphere, so you can run your applications in the cloud with no changes required. This support addresses a shortcoming of many other cloud providers' offerings the complexity and effort required to rewrite applications for a specific cloud provider's platform.

Seamless Network Integration

vCloud Hybrid Service is built on a virtualized network that is quickly customizable to support your application and security needs. You can stretch your Layer 2 and Layer 3 networks from your data center to vCloud Hybrid Service without the need for manual configuration changes. Network virtualization enables you to configure your firewalls and network as if they were in your own data center, so that you can replicate the network your applications need to operate. The service provides common identity and access management across your onsite and offsite environments.

High Performance, Reliable Platform

vCloud Hybrid Service includes automated replication, monitoring, and high availability of your applications at no additional fee, so you don't have to rewrite or rearchitect existing applications to ensure their availability. Leveraging the same platform you already run internally, you can extend your management tools into the cloud, gaining an integrated IT capability across your data center and the cloud. By utilizing your existing investments, processes, and expertise, you can lower your total cost of ownership.

Choice of Service Options

vCloud Hybrid Service is available in two service options that can be deployed individually or in combination, giving you the flexibility and scalability you need to meet your organization's requirements:

- Dedicated Cloud provides you with a physically isolated infrastructure, giving you your own private cloud instance and the most control over your resources. This service is ideal for production workloads, including mission-critical applications, new application development, security- and compliance-driven applications, and high-performance applications that will benefit from physical isolation.
- Virtual Private Cloud provides you with logically isolated infrastructure, including fully private networking and resource pools. This service is ideal for short-term projects, development and test workloads, and projects with lower capacity requirements.

vSphere

VMware vSphere leverages the power of virtualization to transform datacenters into simplified cloud computing infrastructures and enables IT organizations to deliver flexible and reliable IT services. VMware vSphere virtualizes and aggregates the underlying physical hardware resources across multiple systems and provides pools of virtual resources to the datacenter. As a cloud operating system, VMware vSphere manages large collections of infrastructure such as CPUs, storage, and networking as a seamless and dynamic operating environment, and also manages the complexity of a datacenter. The following component layers make up VMware vSphere.

Infrastructure Services

Infrastructure Services are the set of services provided to abstract, aggregate, and allocate hardware or infrastructure resources. Infrastructure Services are categorized into several types.

- VMware vCompute, which includes the VMware capabilities that abstract away from underlying disparate server resources. vCompute services aggregate these resources across many discrete servers and assign them to applications.
- VMware vStorage, which is the set of technologies that enables the most efficient use and management of storage in virtual environments.
- VMware vNetwork, which is the set of technologies that simplify and enhance networking in virtual environments.

Application Services

Application Services are the set of services provided to ensure availability, security, and scalability for applications. Examples include High Availability and Fault Tolerance.

VMware vCenter Server

VMware vCenter Server provides a single point of control of the datacenter. It provides essential datacenter services such as access control, performance monitoring, and configuration.

Clients

Users can access the VMware vSphere datacenter through clients such as the vSphere Client or Web Access through a Web browser.

We stop our VMware discussion here. There are many more products by VMware company but it is above the scope of the book.

6.6 DROPBOX

In this section let us see in detail about the cloud storage software called Dropbox. Its features and attractive uses provided.

Dropbox is an another cloud storage software used to store all the user data. Dropbox company was founded in 2006 by Drew Houston and ArashFerdowsi as a Y Combinator startup company. Today it has become so much popular with supporting almost all hardware platforms ranging from computer, mobile, tablet and so on.

Dropbox offers cloud storage, file synchronization and client software. Dropbox allows users to create a special folder on each of their computers, which Dropbox then synchronizes so that it appears to be the same folder with the same contents regardless of which computer is used to view it. Files placed in this folder also are accessible through a website and mobile phone applications. Dropbox provides client software for Microsoft Windows, Mac OS X, Linux, Android, iOS, BlackBerry OS and web browsers, as well as unofficial ports to Symbian, Windows Phone, and MeeGo.

Some of the features by dropbox include:

- ***Encryption*** – the files stored on drop are encrypted with 256 bit AES encryption and SSL.
- ***Privacy*** – the privacy policy is designed to safeguard the collection, use, and disclosure of the team's information.
- ***Safety*** – If a computer is lost or someone leaves the business, remotely delete the Dropbox folder to keep business's most important data safe.
- ***Certification*** – Dropbox storage is SSAE16/SOC1, SOC2, ISAE 3402 and ISO 27001 certified on Amazon S3 and may provide data mirroring across other secure data centers.
- ***Two step verification*** – dropbox provides an additional layer of security by securing Dropbox accounts with a password and a phone.
- ***Reliable*** – it keeps the work safe with storage designed for 99.9% durability.

Dropbox uses a free business model, where users are offered a free account with a set storage size and paid subscriptions for accounts with more capacity. The desktop client machine has no restriction on individual file size, files uploaded via the web site are limited to no more than 10 GB per file. To prevent free users from creating multiple linked free accounts, Dropbox includes the content of shared folders when totaling the amount of space used on the account. Dropbox uses Amazon's S3 storage system to store the files.

Both the Dropbox server and desktop client software are primarily written in Python scripting language. The desktop client uses GUI toolkits such as wxWidgets and Cocoa. Other notable Python libraries include Twisted, ctypes, and pywin32. Dropbox ships and depends on the librsync binary-delta library which is written in C language. The version history is paired with the use of delta encoding technology. When a file in a user's Dropbox folder is changed, Dropbox only uploads the pieces of the file that are changed when synchronizing, when possible. Dropbox also provides a technology called LAN sync, which allows computers on a local area network to securely download files locally from each other instead of always hitting the central servers. LAN sync was developed by Dropbox Engineer Paul Bohm.

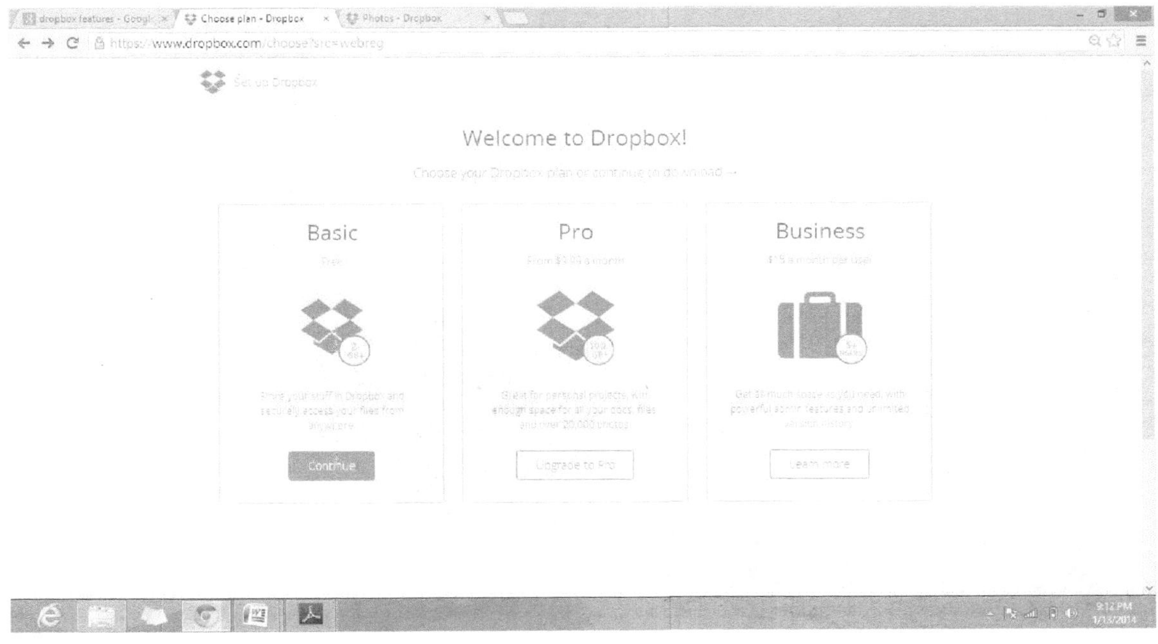

Figure 6.6 Dropbox plans.

Figure 6.7 Dropbox account with the data storage.

Figure 6.8 Dropbox easily helps to store all the data from the system itself.

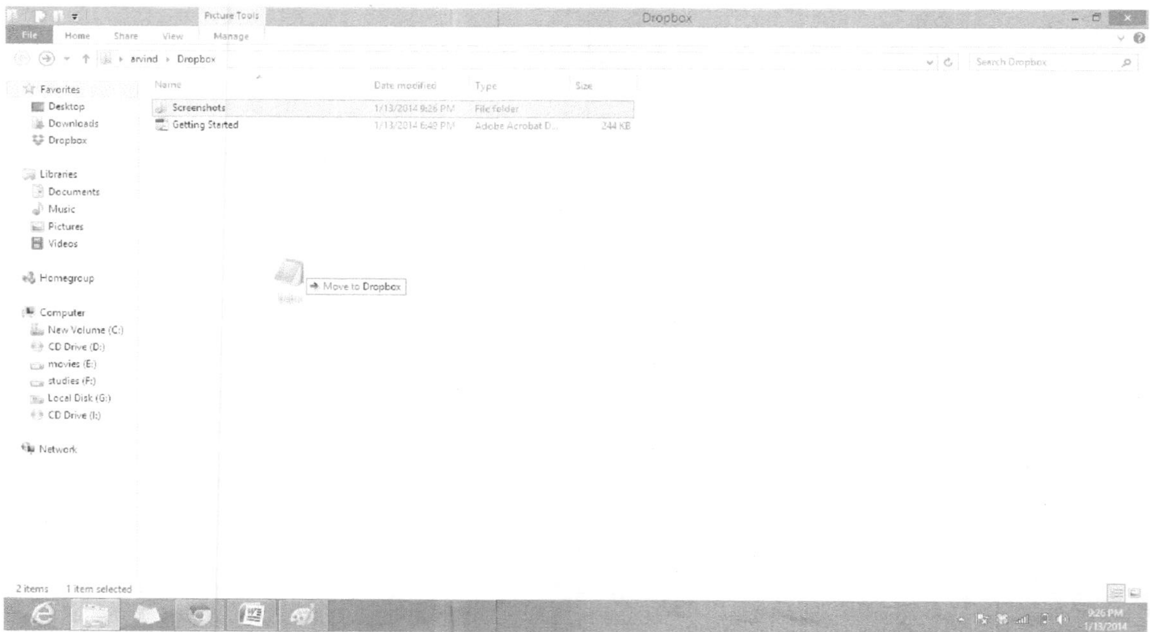

Figure 6.9 Moving files into Dropbox from the system.

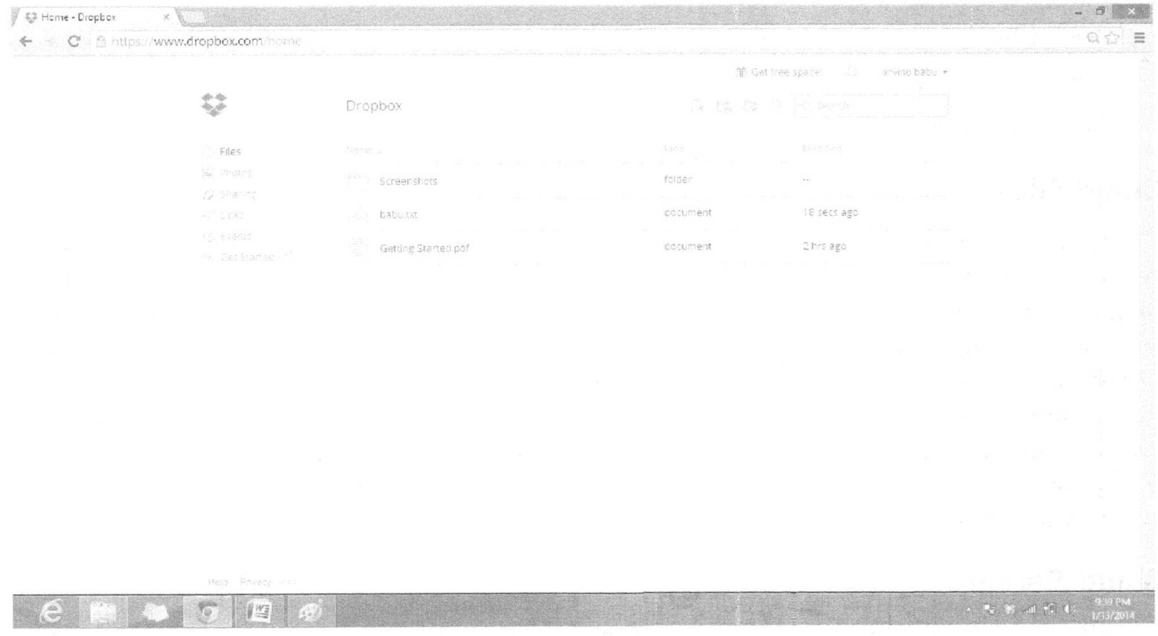

Figure 6.10 Data stored in the Dropbox account.

As of February 2013, Dropbox was responsible for 0.29% of all worldwide Internet traffic. In 2013 Dropbox acquired the email management application for iOS Mailbox and mobile coupon startup Endorse. On November 13, 2013, Dropbox announced it had reached 200 million users. On November 21, 2013, Dropbox released new versions of its apps for iOS. The new design now has a whiter and simpler user interface which brings the app in-line with other iOS 6 offerings.

6.7 RACKSPACE CLOUD

An another famous company in the field of cloud computing which has done lot of work is Rackspace. It has developed so many products and solution for cloud. They include:

- Public, private and hybrid cloud
- Cloud servers
- Cloud database
- Cloud files
- Cloud sites
- Cloud files and storage
- Cloud monitoring
- Cloud networks
- Cloud load balancers

- Cloud DNS
- Cloud big data platform
- Cloud queues

We will discuss some of the products in detail.

Cloud Files

Cloud files is a cloud hosting service that provides unlimited online storage and content delivery network for media on a utility computing basis. It was originally launched as Mosso CloudFS on 2008 and is similar to Amazon Simple Storage Service (S3). Unlimited files of up to 5 GB can be uploaded, managed via the online control panel or RESTful API and optionally served out via Akamai Technologies Content Delivery Network. In addition to the online control panel, the service can be accessed over a RESTful API with open source client code available in languages like C#/.NET, Python, PHP, Java, and Ruby. Rackspace owned Jungle Disk allows Cloud Files to be mounted as a local drive within supported operating systems like Linux, Mac OS X, and Windows.

Cloud Servers

CLOUD SERVERS IS a cloud infrastructure service that allows users to deploy one to hundreds of cloud servers instantly and create advanced, high availability architectures similar to the Amazon Elastic Compute Cloud (EC2). The cloud servers are virtual machines running on the Xen hypervisor for Linux-based instances, and Citrix XenServer for Windows and Linux instances. Each quad core hardware node has between 16 and 32 GB of RAM, allowing for allocations between 256 MB and 30 GB. Disk and CPU allocations scale up with memory, with disk sizes ranging from 10 GB to 620 GB. Various distributions of Linux are supported, including Arch, CentOS, Debian, Fedora, Gentoo, Red Hat Enterprise Linux and Ubuntu.

The technology behind the service was purchased in Rackspace's 2008 acquisition of Slicehost and the servers were formerly known as slices. These are much cheaper and generally easier to use than a traditional dedicated server, though it is still necessary to maintain the operating system and solution stack which is not required for the Cloud Sites product. This is one of the main differentiations between the two services where Cloud Servers includes full root access and thus allows for more customization, the Cloud Sites product is less flexible but requires less maintenance.

On December 14, 2010, Rackspace began offering a managed service level on the Cloud Servers product, which added additional support for the operating system and common applications as well as patching and other routine services. This additional support level does come at an increased cost, however.

Cloud Tools are applications and infrastructure software built to run on the RackSpace cloud. Applications listed include Zend, a PHP stack, Cloudkick, a cloud performance testing services,CopperEgg, a real-time cloud server and application monitoring service, Xeround, a MySQL cloud database, and MongoLab, the cloud version of the popular NoSQL database MongoDB.

Cloud Sites

Cloud Sites is a platform as a service offering, similar to traditional web hosting only built on horizontally scalable hardware infrastructure. A fixed monthly credit card payment gives users access to the service with an allocation of compute, storage and bandwidth resources. Should this allocation be exhausted then subsequent usage is billed on a utility computing basis. It allows an unlimited number of sites, databases and email accounts and includes reseller options such as client billing and support. Known as the fastest way to put sites on the cloud, it runs Windows or Linux applications across hundreds of servers.

Cloud Sites supports the PHP 5, Perl, Python, MySQL, .NET 2.0+, ASP and Microsoft SQL Server 2008 application frameworks.

Openstack Cloud

In 2010, RackSpace contributed the source code of its Cloud Files product to the OpenStack cloud tool project under the Apache License to become the OpenStack Object Storage component. From here the Rackspace became a far more major player in the cloud computing technology.

In April 2012, Rackspace announced it would implement OpenStack Compute as the underlying technology for their Cloud Servers product. The change will come a new control panel as well as add-on cloud services offering databases, server monitoring, block storage, and virtual networking. Today OpenStack is the major cloud tool used in the industry and everywhere. We will see in detail about OpenStack in chapter 8, 9 and 15.

6.8 SALESFORCE CLOUD PLATFORM

An another famous cloud computing platform which has designed several cloud products and services is salesforce. It popularly referred as salesforce.com. It is an American based company whose headquarters is situated in San Francisco, California. It is currently ranked the most innovative company in America by Forbes magazine, as well as number 19 in Fortune magazine's 100 Best Companies to Work For in 2013. It has acquired many other companies in the recent years.

Salesforce is popularly known for its Customer Relationship Management (CRM) products.

CRM cloud apps need to be easy to use for sales, marketing, and service professionals in any industry. That is why smart companies rely on a CRM platform that gives them complete freedom to customize CRM for their business. It is the best way to boost adoption and make sure CRM apps are working the way user wants. Successful CRM customers rely on a proven, trusted infrastructure the servers and software in a data center for running their CRM applications. For CRM to work effectively, it must have three characteristics:

- ***High reliability*** – uptime that exceeds 99.9%
- ***High performance*** – data access in less than 300 ms
- ***High security*** – industry certifications such as ISO27001 and SAS 70 Type II

An effective CRM infrastructure is based on multi tenancy multiple customers sharing common technology and all running on the latest release, much like Amazon.com or Google. With multi tenancy, you don't have to worry about application or infrastructure upgrades they happen automatically. In fact, multi tenancy lets companies focus on managing CRM, not managing technology.

Speaking from the sales and marketing view for sales managers CRM cloud apps provide real-time visibility to the team's activities so that they can forecast sales with confidence. For sales reps, CRM cloud apps make it easy to manage customer information so reps spend less time handling data and more time with customers.

For marketers, nothing is more important than tracking the sales that result from leads generated through marketing campaigns on the Web site, in email, or with Google AdWords. CRM cloud apps let marketers track leads and sources, route leads to the right salespeople in real time, and provide the analytics to see what is working and what can be improved further.

Service Cloud

Service Cloud allows to deliver revolutionary customer service from anywhere, anytime, on any device. So the user can embed one touch service directly into products. It is the full power and functionality of Service Cloud wherever you are.

Figure 6.11 Service cloud of Salesforce.

The Service Cloud delivers the world's first enterprise-grade knowledge base to run entirely on an advanced, multitenant cloud platform. That means you get all the cloud-computing benefits that salesforce.com is known for delivering. No expensive data centers. No software. No complex upgrades. Just powerful knowledge management, without the hassle of on-premises software. Unlike stand-alone applications, this knowledge base is fully integrated with everything else the Service Cloud has to offer, all the tools you need to run your entire service operation. When your knowledge base is a core part of your CRM solution, you can manage your knowledge as a process, not a snapshot in time. You can continually create, review, deliver, analyze, and improve your knowledge. Your agents get smarter, your customers get better service, and your costs go down.

The Service Cloud gives you the tools you need to manage your knowledge at enterprise scale. But it also delivers the same great ease of use that salesforce.com is known for. That means you'll benefit no matter what size or how complex your business is.

- ***Rich knowledge articles*** – Easily create rich articles, include images or videos and custom formatting with WYSIWYG editors. Even add navigation elements like tabs and or a table of contents.
- ***Review and approvals workflow*** – Everything you need to automate the authoring, review, and approval processes. Assign knowledge tasks, create deadlines, and update the status of your articles. Use the version control tools to help your organization work in sync.
- ***Usage analytics*** – Keep tabs on what's really valuable with analytics that show how often people read specific articles and how highly they rate them.
- ***Easy administration*** – Point-and-click administration tools let business users define processes, set up dimensions, and create article templates.

Sales Cloud

The Sales Cloud gives you everything you need to connect with customers from complete, up-to-date account information to social insights, all in one place and available anytime, anywhere.

Everything you need to know is automatically pushed to you in real time, from contact information to deal updates and discount approvals. What's more, the information is automatically shared with the members of your team who need it. The result is you close more deals faster and collaborate instantly on what matters.

Salesforce.com created the Sales Cloud to be as easy to use as a consumer website like Amazon and built it in the cloud to eliminate the risk and expense associated with traditional software. By pioneering the concept of cloud computing, salesforce.com showed that applications could be delivered over the Internet in the same way that electricity is carried into our homes. With its open architecture and automatic updates, the Sales Cloud does away with the hidden costs and drawn-out implementations of traditional CRM software. Today, it's the trusted sales app for more than 100,000 customers around the world.

By continuing to innovate and embrace technologies like mobile, collaboration, and social intelligence, the Sales Cloud has continued to pull ahead of the competition. Now you can stay on top of everything that's happening in your deals in real time, with updates on people, documents, accounts, and deals automatically delivered in your Chatter feed. And with native apps for the Android, BlackBerry, iPad, and iPhone platforms, you're always connected to your customers and teammates no matter where in the world you are.

Connected to both the right information and their colleagues, sales teams are more in sync and seeing dramatic improvements in performance.

6.9 CLOUD OPERATING SYSTEM

When we use the term called software one must never forget operating systems are also software. Cloud computing barrier has not let them also. Today there are many cloud based operating systems available today. One must not think them just as an online application. These operating system are available in the web browser with various software readily available in them. The operating system and software are based on the company that owns and manages this cloud operating system. One can just use them readily in online with a simple account and high speed internet. Thus cloud has made the life so much advanced and easy that one does not say

"I don't have that version of software in my system" or "I did not install that software in my PC"

Some of the cloud based operating system available today include:

ZeroPC

ZeroPC offers the user with 1GB of free storage and lets to connect cloud storage services like Box, DropBox, Google Drive, SkyDrive, SugarSync and 4Shared for access to all the required paperwork. ZeroPC is also available on the Android, iPhone and iPad, giving you access while on the go. For photo loving users, it is also a great photo management tool, linking photo & video services like Facebook, Flickr, Instagram, PhotoBucket, Picasa and Recood. It also has native apps for instant messaging, a text editor as well as productivity tools for managing documents and spreadsheets online.

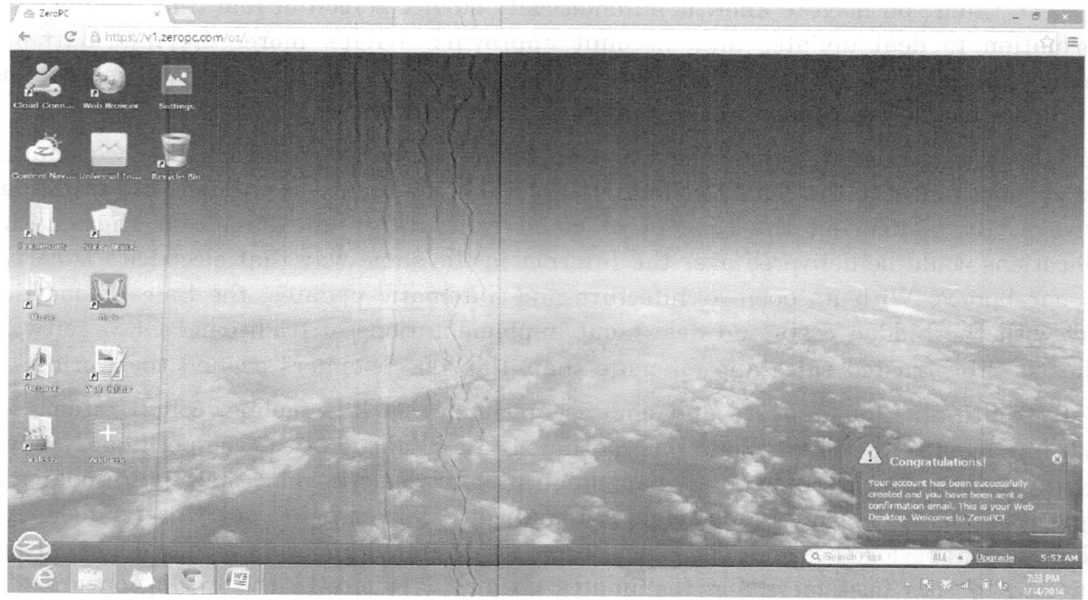

Figure 6.12 ZeroPC cloud OS running in the web browser.

Jolicloud

Jolicloud offers Joli OS, which you can download and install in your system even if the system is 10 years old or use it in the browser. Joli OS provides with the full cloud experience keep and use your favorite apps any time, any where. Jolicloud has over 15,000 web apps you can access using the system.User can integrate your DropBox and Google Drive accounts with Jolicloud and there is also a Jolicloud Me version where you can manage all of your online life at a single place Jolicloud Me currently supports Facebook, Flickr, Instagram, Picasa, Tumblr and Twitter.

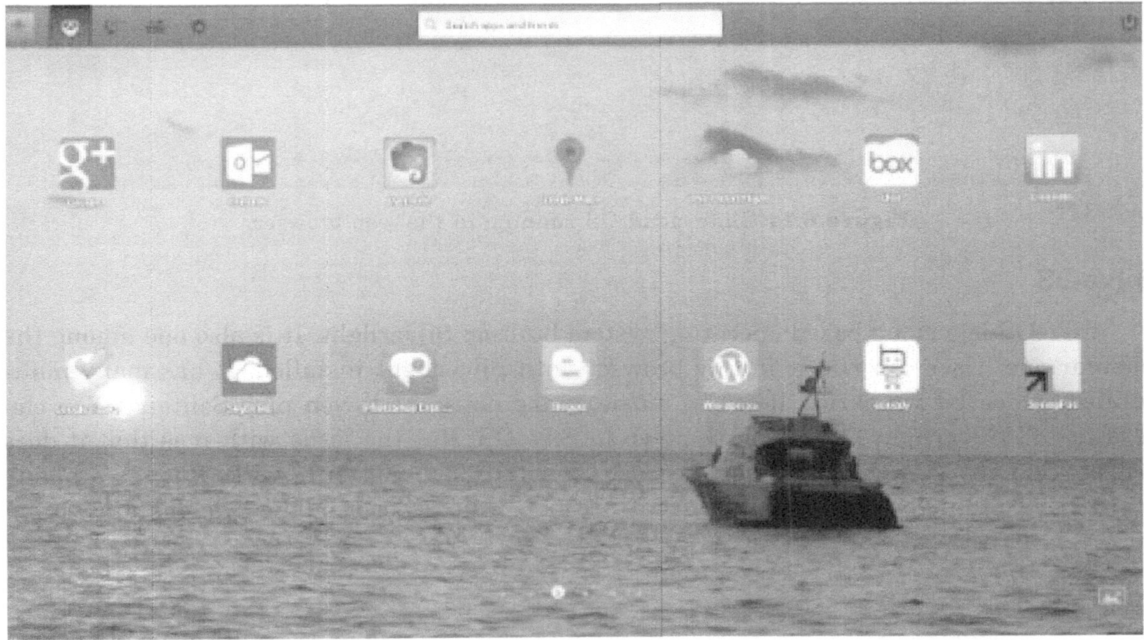

Figure 6.13 Jolicloud OS.

Glide OS

Glide OS is a right cloud based operating system when the user is working in a group project. Glide team offers 30GB of free storage and you can add a total of 6 users in a single account. The OS is not very pretty but is quite useful it has additional features like email and profiles as well as basic tools like Calendar, Notes, Text editor, Presentation maker and so on required for the paperwork. Glide operating system also provides synchronizing software for all other operating systems like Windows, Mac OS and Linux so that you can easily sync your files between Glide hard disk and the local storage. It also has browser extensions and a mobile version.

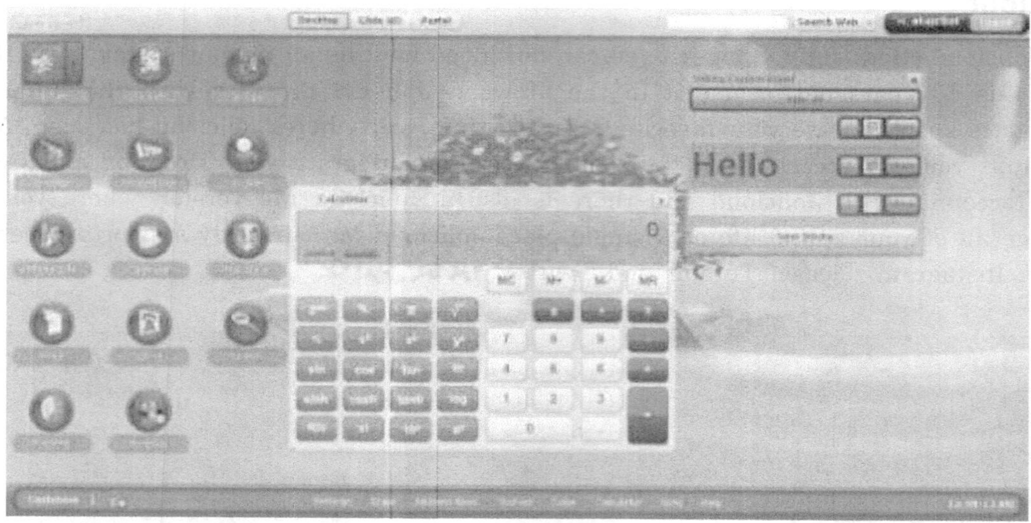

Figure 6.14 Glide cloud OS running in the web browser.

SilveOS

SilveOS is a cloud based operating system built on Silverlight. It is also one among the popular one. User can run it in any browser with Silverlight installed. It has many built-in apps which let you write, listen to music, make notes, and even play Solitaire. You can also install Silverlight apps from the web in SilveOS. But the issue with it is that it does not provide any storage so it's not the best Cloud OS for long term work. But it's a handy tool if you often work on computers that are not owned like a public systems and so on.

Figure 6.15 Silve cloud OS running in the web browser.

Ispaces Cloud Computer

iSpaces cloud operating system has only the basic features for you to manage your work like Browser, File manager, Notes, Office suite and so on. It also has 3 Workspaces accessible from the task bar. It lets you keep your working environments organized with quick access from one Workspace to the other. You can work on your files from Box and DropBox using the file manager. iSpaces has a simple environment for you to access your files on Box and DropBox in the same view, and you can move your files from one space to another just by drag and drop. The changes will be reflected in your respective cloud storage accounts.

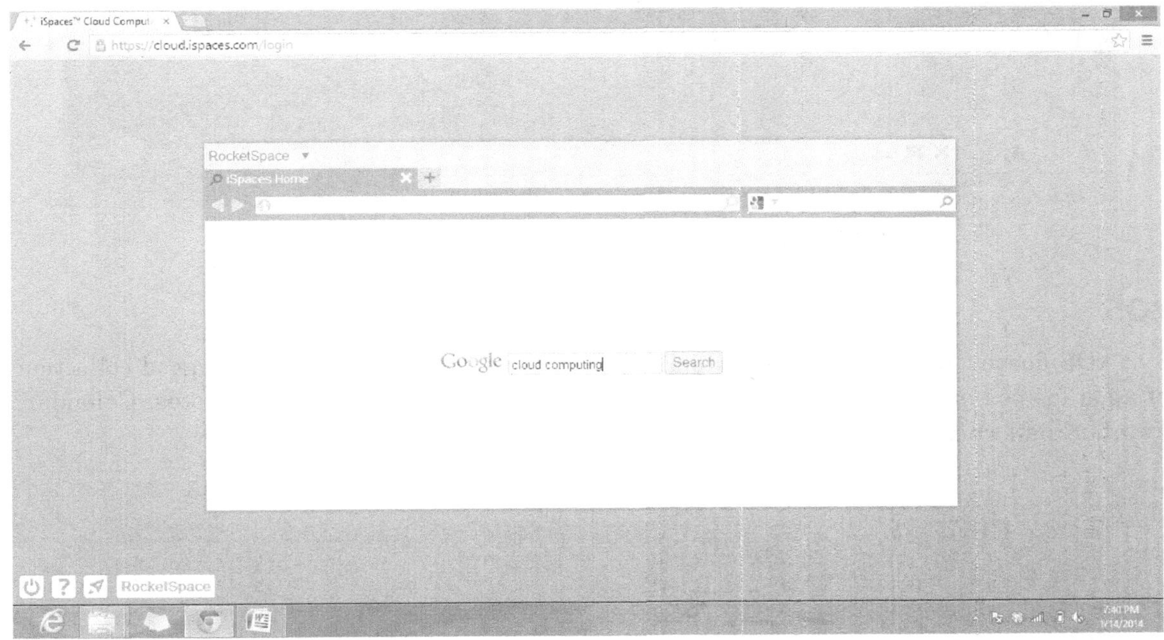

Figure 6.16 Ispace cloud OS running in the web browser.

Cloudo

Cloudo is an interesting operating system built to run in a web browser. It is packed with apps like Mail, Calendar, Audio Player, RSS reader, Contact manager, Word processor, Notepad, Command Line Interpreter, Finder. It provides a good interface like an operating system where you can run commands, install apps, play music etc. It handles multi-tasking quite efficiently and let you do your tasks efficiently. It also offers an Application Manager which you can use to install more apps in your Cloudo.

Figure 6.17 Clouddo OS running in the web browser.

xOS

xOS doesn't provide a lot of customization options but they do provide a good collection of apps for personal use. It offers Web browser, File manager, Text editor, Notes, Calendar, Paint, Email client, and Canvas Rider game among others.

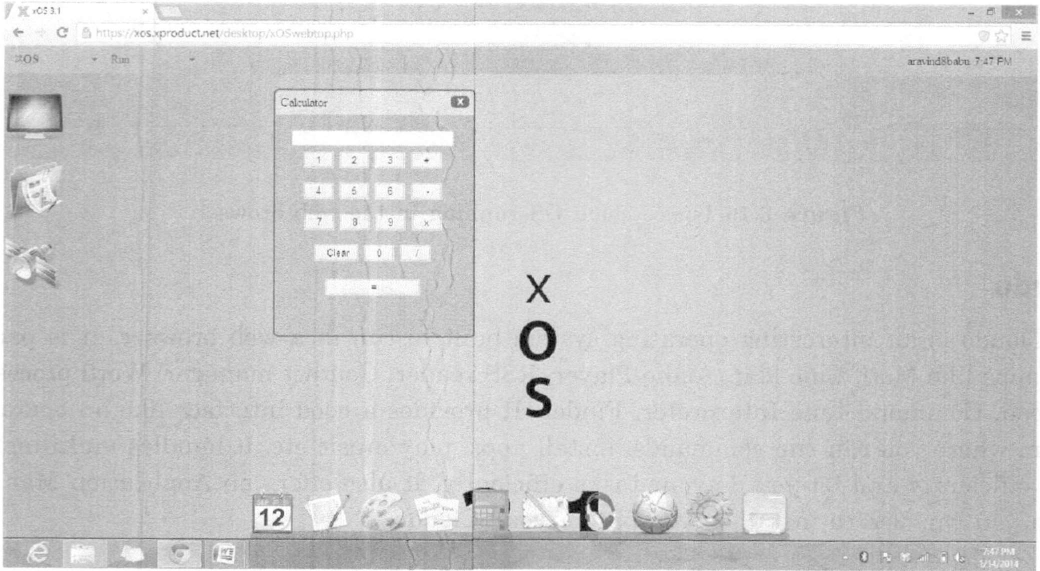

Figure 6.18 xOS cloud OS running in the web browser.

Zimdesk

ZimDesk is a cloud operating system full of apps and features. It has got Custom wallpapers, Office Suite, Contact Manager, RSS reader, Calendar, Mail client, FTP client, File uploader and manager and so on.

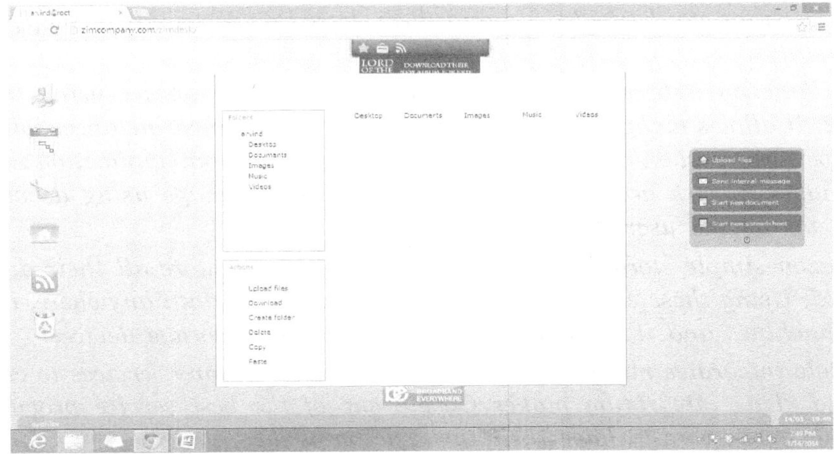

Figure 6.19 Zimdesk cloud OS running in the web browser.

The Places A

It is an another cloud operating system which offers basic apps like Radio, Calendar, File manager, Bookmark manager, Notes, Email client, etc. You can add web apps to it as links which will be opened in new tabs. It also supports instant messaging between its users. Cloud OS is unique such that one can have all the user documents, designs, music, personal files, photos and videos kept online and accessible via a virtual working environment. Working on a Cloud OS, all you need is an Internet connection and you're all set.

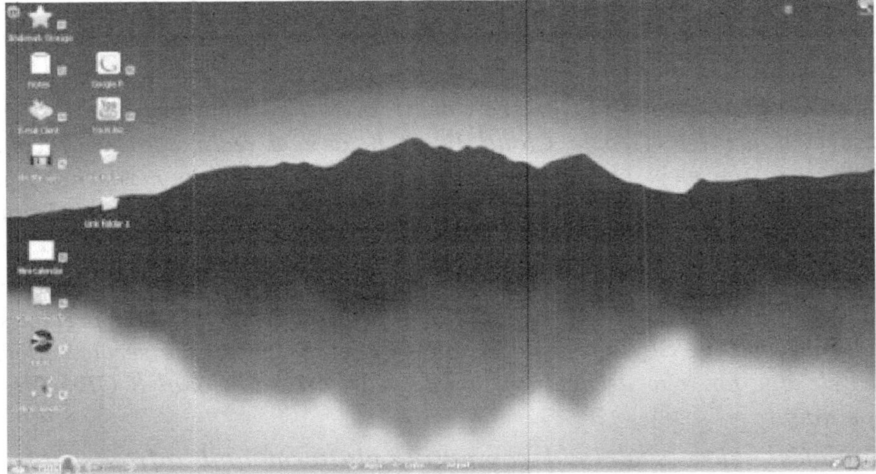

Figure 6.20 The place a cloud OS running in the web browser.

SUMMARY

- *Amazon has emerged as the undisputed leader in cloud technology today. Amazon Web Services (AWS) officially known as provides a cloud computing platform for all business sizes. AWS can provide a flexible, cost-effective IT infrastructure and services that can be scaled up and down based on the needs of the end user and companies.*
- *The Amazon web services provide the cloud hosting service using the platform EC2. It allows using the web service interfaces to launch instances with a variety of operating system platforms, load them with the custom application environment, manage network access permissions, and run the image using as many or few systems as the user desires.*
- *Amazon simple storage service provides the user to store all their data into the cloud. Using these cloud storage user can access the data anywhere, independent of machines and it reduces the need of hardware storage devices.*
- *Google integrates many applications and provides many services to customers in cloud. This integration makes Google one of the best service provider since it allows customers to have their tasks accomplished easily.*
- *Google app engine comes under the Platform as a service (PaaS) concept of cloud service model where it provides the required software development tools to be used by the user to design the cloud application, host the cloud app into the Google cloud and scale it based on the demand of the user.*
- *Similar to Amazon simple storage service (S3). Google has developed a storage medium popularly known as Google drive and it is for free till a specific limit not for rent completely unlike the Amazon storage. It can store about 15 Gb of data free for a user.*
- *Google Docs is a tool for real time collaborative editing. Documents can be shared, opened, and edited by multiple users at the same time. Users cannot be notified of changes, but the application can notify users when a comment or discussion is made or replied to, facilitating collaboration. It is synchronized with Google drive.*
- *Using Google Cloud Print, one can print anything, from any device, to any cloud-connected printer. Google Cloud Print is a new technology that connects the printers to the web. Using Google Cloud Print, user can make home and work printers available to the user and anyone else user chooses, from the applications user uses every day.*
- *Similar to Amazon simple storage service (S3) and Google drive Microsoft has developed a cloud based storage platform called Skydrive. It was previously known as Windows Live SkyDrive and Windows Live Folders. The service offers 7 GB of free storage for new users and for one year, an additional 3 GB of free storage to students.*
- *Windows Azure is a cloud computing platform and infrastructure created by Microsoft for building, deploying and managing applications and services*

through Microsoft-managed datacenters. It provides both PaaS and IaaS service models of cloud and supports many different programming languages, tools and frameworks.

- *The cloud computing platform owned by Apple company is icloud. It was introduced in 2011 only but it has become very popular now. Millions of people are using it today. icloud is mainly used for cloud storage but has other functions too.*
- *VMware vCloud Director is a software solution that enables enterprises to build secure, multi tenant private clouds by pooling infrastructure resources into virtual datacenters and exposing them to users through Web-based portals and programmatic interfaces.*
- *VMware vCloud Hybrid Service is a secure, dedicated infrastructure-as-aservice cloud, owned and operated by VMware and built on the trusted foundation of vSphere and the software defined data center architecture.*
- *Dropbox is an another cloud storage software used to store all the user data. Dropbox company was founded in 2007 by Drew Houston and ArashFerdowsi.*
- *Dropbox offers cloud storage, file synchronization and client software. Dropbox allows users to create a special folder on each of their computers, which Dropbox then synchronizes so that it appears to be the same folder with the same contents regardless of which computer is used to view it. Files placed in this folder also are accessible through a website and mobile phone applications.*
- *Cloud files is a cloud hosting service that provides unlimited online storage and content delivery network for media on a utility computing basis provided by Rackspace cloud. It was originally launched as Mosso CloudFS on 2008 and is similar to Amazon Simple Storage Service (S3).*
- *In 2010, RackSpace contributed the source code of its Cloud Files product to the OpenStack cloud tool project under the Apache License to become the OpenStack Object Storage component. From here the Rackspace became a far more major player in the cloud computing technology.*
- *Salesforce is popularly known for its Customer Relationship Management (CRM) products. CRM cloud apps need to be easy to use for sales, marketing, and service professionals in any industry.*
- *Service Cloud allows delivering revolutionary customer service from anywhere, anytime, on any device. So the user can embed one touch service directly into products.*
- *Salesforce.com created the Sales Cloud to be as easy to use as a consumer website like Amazon and built it in the cloud to eliminate the risk and expense associated with traditional software.*
- *Cloud based operating system are available in the web browser with various software readily available in them. The operating system and software are based on the company that owns and manages this cloud operating system. One can just use them readily in online with a simple account and high speed internet.*

Chapter 7

Linux and Open Source Cloud

OBJECTIVE

- *To learn about the Linux working environment*
- *To learn about the relation between Linux and cloud computing*
- *To know about the list of all open source cloud tools*
- *To know about the Indian developed cloud products and C-DAC*
- *To know about the Hadoop and its feature*

Linux is an open source environment commonly used in all back end server machines. Most of us would have worked with the Linux platform, it is quite different from Microsoft windows, Apple iOS and etc. Linux is regarded as a safe environment for all confidential work. Let us see in detail about the Linux environment and how it is useful for cloud computing. Let us also discuss in detail about all the open source tools available to implement the real time cloud primarily under Linux platform. We will see the Indian organization CDAC developed operating system, cloud and other computing tools. In the last section we will see the another recent topic Hadoop environment.

7.1 LINUX ARCHITECTURE

While we discuss about the open source Linux and cloud computing in detail we must be aware of the overall architecture of the Linux environment. The architecture of Linux gives the whole picture of how the Linux environment actually works and its unique features to the end user.

In Linux operating system there are generally two modes:

- ***Kernel Mode*** – It is used to execute all the operating system process. It is also known as the system mode. When the CPU is in kernel mode it is assumed to be executing trusted software and thus it can execute any instructions and reference any memory addresses. The kernel which is the core of the operating system and has complete control over everything that occurs in the system is trusted software but all other programs are considered untrusted software.

- ***User Mode*** – It is used to execute all the applications of the user. It is a non privileged mode. Thus all user mode software must request use of the kernel by means of a system call in order to perform privileged instructions such as process creation or input output operations.

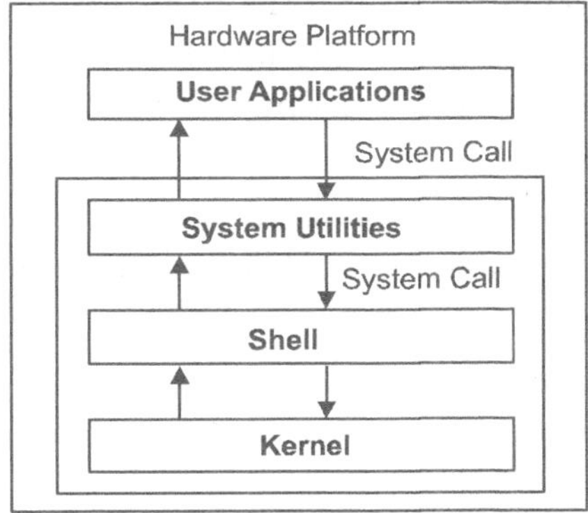

Figure 7.1 Linux architecture and its components.

The architecture of the Linux operating system consists of five major components:

- ***Kernel*** – It act as an **interface between operating system and other hardware resources.** It is the main part of the operating system that loads firsts and remains in the main memory. Kernel is the core part of operating system. When someone makes any changes to the kernel files it affects the whole operating system. It is the bridge between the application and the actual data processing to support the application. It is responsible for task management, memory management and disk management. Its primary function is to manage the computer resources and support other programs who want to use these resources.

The Linux kernel presents a virtual machine interface to user processes. Processes are written without needing any knowledge of what physical hardware is installed on a computer. The Linux kernel abstracts all hardware into a consistent virtual interface. In addition Linux supports multi-tasking execution in a manner that is transparent to user processes. Each process can act as though it is the only process on the computer, with exclusive use of main memory and other hardware resources. The kernel actually runs several processes concurrently and is responsible for mediating access to hardware resources so that each process has fair access while inter-process security is maintained.

The Linux kernel is composed of five main subsystems which include:

- ***The process scheduler*** – It is responsible for controlling process access to the CPU. The scheduler enforces a policy that ensures that processes will have fair access to the CPU while ensuring that necessary hardware actions are performed by the kernel on time.

- ***The memory manager*** – It permits multiple processes to securely share the machine's main memory system. In addition the memory manager supports virtual memory that allows Linux to support processes that use more memory than is available in the system. Unused memory is swapped out to persistent storage using the file system then swapped back in when it is needed. Thus there the swapping of memory by swap in and swap out takes place.
- ***The virtual file system*** – It abstracts the details of the variety of hardware devices by presenting a common file interface to all devices. In addition the VFS also supports several file system formats that are compatible with other operating systems.
- ***The network interface*** – It provides access to several networking standards and a variety of network hardware. Most of the networking operations are done only under Linux platform.
- ***The inter-process communication*** – It is a subsystem that supports several mechanisms for process-to-process communication on a single Linux system.

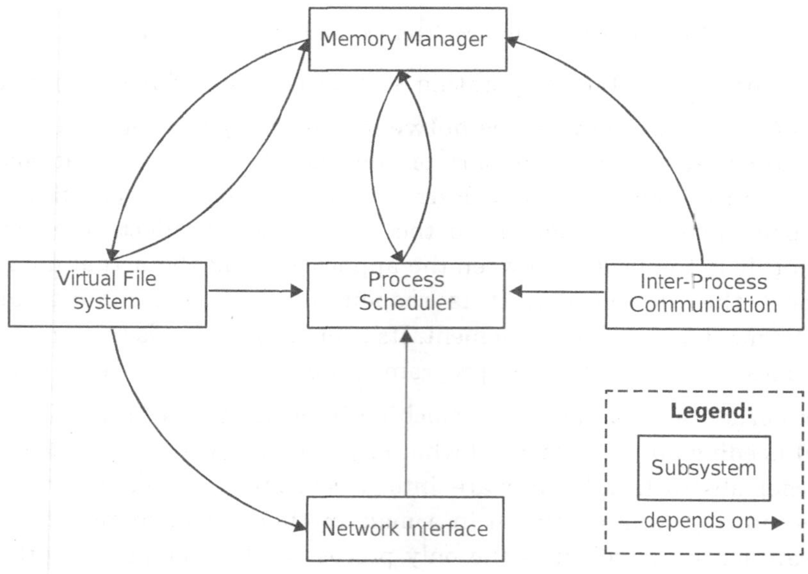

Figure 7.2 Linux kernel and its subsystem.

Once during the cloud tool installation we made a change to the kernel files, accidently it affected the whole operating system and we could not boot the OS next day. Our entire work was lost and it proved to be a mistake.

- ***Shell*** – It act as an interface between user and the operating system. It is a software that provide an interface for user of an operation system which need services of a kernel. When user gives the command for performing any operation from the command prompt the request goes to the **shell**. The Shell then translates these human programs to machine language and then transfers the request to the kernel. The kernel receives the request from shell, processes the request and then displays the result on the screen. All these functions are performed by the kernel in a transparent manner. An operating system shell is divided into two parts they include Command line and GUI.

Command Line

Well most of us know Linux operating support command line interface with various commands for the user task. It is the part of the operating system which receives and executes the operating system command by the user. The commands are then send to the kernel for execution. If the command is valid the kernal starts the execution else error will be produced. Thus one can imagine it is as intermediate for the command execution.

Graphical User Interface (GUI)

This provides a user friendly environment for user task. User cannot remember the syntax of all the command thus it help to simply point toward the object by the mean or mouse or some other pointing device which a user required for its execution. Thus is a desktop based execution environment unlike the command oriented.

- ***System utilities*** – The System Utilities consist of various system interrupts and system calls which are to transfer the control for the user mode to the kernel mode containing the kernel and shell for further execution of the commands. The control can be transfer using *System calls*.

  System call is an **interface between a process and the operating system**. In simple words the system call is the request for running any program and for performing any operation on the system that the user has requested.

System Calls are of Several Different Types

File management system call – It is used for performing open, close, read, write and for all other file operations.

Process control system call – It is used for performing all process control operations like Load, execute, create and other operations.

Device management system call – It is used for performing request device, write device, release device and other operations.

Communication system call – It is used for performing Send message, transfer status and other operations.

- ***User application*** – It includes all the application which a user requires to perform its task. Today there are millions of Linux application are available, some already inbuilt, some can be downloaded and so on. Kernel is used to generate processes to support these applications.

- ***Hardware platform*** – It includes all the hardware resources of the system such as keyboard, monitor, printer and etc., with which user can communicate with input output the request.

7.2 LINUX AND CLOUD COMPUTING

All of us are aware of both the Linux and Windows operating system. Most of us have easily worked in the graphical user interface (GUI) environment of Windows platforms. Among the commonly used Windows OS include XP, Windows7 and Windows8. The Linux platform is quite both GUI and command line interface based one. Commonly used Linux OS include Red hat, Centos, Ubuntu, Fedora and so on. The overall architecture of Linux is totally different from Windows. Linux is best suited for all the networking operations in the server side. Linux has both desktop based GUI version and the server version making it a very ideal choice for all networking functions. Linux working environment is very interesting, useful and even advanced compared to Windows. Linux is best suited for virtualization and cloud computing tools. Linux is modular, performant, power efficient, scalable, open source, and ubiquitous above all the major cloud infrastructures in the world are built in Linux platform only. Linux is purely open source technology and its versions are getting updated from time to time and quite interesting to work in them.

"Every time you use Google, you're using a machine running the Linux kernel,"

By Google's Chris DiBona

Some of the Linux features which makes it a right platform for cloud computing include:

- ***Linux architecture*** – Linux kernel supports the concept of componentization to a large extent that no other OS supports effectively. Linux kernel supports all the computing environments irrespective of its shape and size. Linux also supports the infinite types of hardware devices than any other previous OS. Another major advantage of Linux by cloud providers is that they can modify the open source code of Linux based on their needs and functionality. Linux is also best suited to work in networking area and in all storage medium.
- ***Compatible*** – Linux supports millions of applications from wide ranging of platforms. It is highly compatible and user friendly. Linux is the best architecture for all web based apps, databases, server scripts and all other open source projects into the cloud. Linux is also the best deployment platform for all the vendors mainly due to its open source, ubiquitous and overall quality.
- ***Licensing issue*** – There is a quite misconception that Linux is always free. In reality, the overwhelming majority of enterprise and governmental production deployments are commercially licensed and supported. For cloud platform providers, however, the option to run non-commercial distributions does exist, and may be compelling. Platform providers will choose this path because creating a cloud infrastructure composed of thousands or tens of thousands of licensed nodes would

be uneconomical with traditional per-server or socket models. By leveraging this lower cost approach, cloud providers are able to pass on the savings to customers.

- ***Power economic*** – Apart from several other advantages Linux is quite less power consumption platform in computer technology. Combined with the power saving efforts within cloud data centers, Linux is helping to lower the total solution cost for cloud customers.
- ***Management*** – For enterprises questions of resourcing and personnel are an important factor in technology deployment and purchase. In addition to evaluating the merits of a given product or project, organizations must consider how their existing skill sets map to the technologies. Managing and developing for Linux are common skills, the ubiquity of Linux within cloud platforms means that customers deploying to the cloud can avoid costly re-training for system administrators and developers. Hence the overall management in Linux is easier and not a hard business issue. In addition to re-purposing existing personnel, deployed IT management systems that already target Linux can be better leveraged with regard to Linux-based cloud nodes.
- ***Standardization*** – One of the most common concerns that analysts and other advisers have for potential cloud customers is the lack of standards, and the resulting potential for lock-in. Linux is seen as the right standard platform for designing, deploying and scaling the cloud app. The differences between Linux instances hosted in cloud environments and those hosted locally or at a data center are generally less technical than geographical. By standardizing on Linux workloads, customers will have the flexibility to deploy locally or remotely as the economics and circumstances dictate.
- ***Virtualization*** – It is one of the backbone principle of cloud computing. Linux is the right platform for working with virtualization and view the real time cloud. Linux supports the virtual tools like KVM and XEN. The images or application virtual instances can be run on the top of the Linux platform. Linux also supports the concept of migration, using which the virtualization can bridge from local environments to cloud based hardware. More than Windows or any other operating system Linux is the best one to support the concept of virtualization.

Linux was the startup for a new architectural approach and a new generation of web oriented businesses after the revolution of internet. Thus Linux was the beginner in the advancement of computing technologies and the networking approach helping the corporate IT business and the end user.

Almost all the cloud vendors are directly or indirectly have utilized the Linux kernel. Many Linux platforms have tied up with the open source tools and have developed many advanced cloud tools. A best example is Ubuntu tied up with Eucalyptus cloud to give Ubuntu Enterprise Cloud (UEC) in 2010. Then in 2012 Ubuntu joined hands with OpenStack Cloud to give a stable cloud environment in Ubuntu 12.04 version. The fact is that Linux is already the de facto operating system of choice for cloud computing. Linux is nothing less than the foundation upon which cloud platforms will be built going forward.

Some of the cloud products developed under the Linux platform includes:

Vendor	Products	URLs
10gen	Mongo	http://www.10gen.com/
3Tera	AppLogic Cloud Computing Platform	http://www.3tera.com/
Amazon EC2	Amazon EC2, Amazon S3, Amazon SimpleDB	http://aws.amazon.com/
Cassatt Corporation	Cassatt Active Response	http://www.cassatt.com/
CohesiveFT	Elastic Server	http://www.cohesiveFT.com/
Dell DCS	Cloud Computing Solutions	http://www.dell.com/cloudcomputing/
Elastra	Enterprise Cloud Server	http://www.elastra.com/
ElasticHosts Ltd.	ElasticHosts	http://www.elastichosts.com/
EMC	Mozy	http://www.mozy.com/
Enomoly	Elastic Computing Platform	http://www.enomoly.com/
Flexiscale	Cloud Computing On-Demand	http://www.flexiscale.com/
Google	Google Apps	http://www.google.com/apps/
IBM	Blue Cloud	http://www.ibm.com/ibm/cloud/
Media Temple	(mt)	http://www.mediatemple.net
Morph Labs	Morph eXchange	http://www.morphexchange.com/
Mosso	Cloud Sites, Cloud Files	http://www.mosso.com/
SalesForce.com	Force.com Cloud Computing	http://www.salesforce.com/
VMware	vCloud	http://www.vmware.com/technology/cloud-computing.html
Zimory	Public Cloud	http://www.zimory.com/

Figure 7.3 Cloud products developed under Linux platform.

7.3 LIST OF OPEN SOURCE CLOUD

In the earlier section, we saw the Linux environment and its platform for cloud computing. Now let us see the list of open source clouds commonly available today to set up a real time cloud environment. To design, deploy and manage the application in the cloud environment. The open source technologies as we all know it is free of cost. It can be used by educational institutions, researchers, academicians and even business organizations. These tools get updated from time to time. A user friendly blog is made available by the company to all users where everyone can post all their issues, problems and all related news. The users can also find any bugs in the tool and report it to the company. Today millions of blogs, tutorial videos and forums are available for all the open source clouds.

These cloud tools can be installed in a single machine or in any virtual operating system software. In order to work in Linux platform one must know some of the basic commands and must have some experience with them. The user also must have a good knowledge in all the networking concepts and settings. The user must get updated with the new version of Linux platform released from time to time. The Linux commands vary from one Linux OS to another Linux OS but are basically same and somewhat resemble each other.

Virtualization must be enabled in the operating to install these tools. The overall principle of cloud technology is virtualization hence without enabling or installing the suitable virtualization tools the cloud installation fails at a particular stage. Thus, it is completely waste of time in installing cloud tool without enabling the virtualization.

Some of the basic requirements needed for the cloud installation include:

- Minimum two computers and more
- Specific Linux version OS with virtualization enabled
- Installing all required packages in OS installation step
- Virtual OS software in case of virtual installation
- Minimum 32 GB RAM and more for the system
- High speed internet, without any firewall
- Specific cloud tool version in the respective format for Linux platform
- Specific Hypervisor for the cloud tool
- LAN cable
- Networking switch
- Router
- Network IP address and other networking configuration.

Lets us see the various cloud tools available:

- ***OpenStack*** – An ongoing trend in cloud computing as of 2013 is OpenStack. OpenStack is used to configure both private and public cloud respectively. It consists of various components which are used in the functioning of the cloud. We will see in detail about the OpenStack cloud in the next section.
- ***Eucalyptus cloud*** – It stands for Elastic Utility Computing Architecture Linking Your Programs To Useful Systems. It is an open source tool available to configure a cloud, create the virtual instance of the tiny image which is inbuilt in the application. It is compatible with the Amazon Web Services (AWS). It has five components managing it an overall cloud functions. They include node controller, cluster controller, walrus, storage controller and cloud controller. Eucalyptus combined with Ubuntu to give a cloud operating system called Ubuntu Enterprise Cloud (UEC) in 2010. Today there are several ways and techniques to configure the cloud using the Eucalyptus tool. In 2013 Eucalyptus came with a new and advanced version 3.4.
- ***OpenNebula*** – OpenNebula is an open-source virtual infrastructure engine that enables the dynamic deployment and re-placement of virtual machines on a pool of physical resources. The OpenNebula VM Manager is a core component of

Reservoir cloud. It's an open-source answer to the many virtual machine management offerings from proprietary players, and interfaces easily with cloud infrastructure tools and services

- ***Enomaly elastic computing*** – A programmable virtual cloud infrastructure for small, medium, and large businesses. Their Elastic Computing Platform (ECP) helps users to design, deploy, and manage virtual applications in the cloud, and also significantly reduces administrative and systems workload. A browser-based dashboard enables IT personnel to simply and efficiently plan deployments, automates VM scaling and load-balancing, and analyze, configure, and optimize cloud capacity.
- ***Nimbus*** – Nimbus has been developed in part within the Globus Toolkit 4 framework and provides interfaces to VM management functions based on the WSRF set of protocols. There is also an alternative implementation implementing Amazon EC2 WSDL. It uses XEN as the hypervisor.
- ***VNIX*** – It is used to configure a cluster cloud. With VNIX, administrators can deploy various VMs rapidly and easily on computing nodes, and manage them with related configuration from a single easy-to-use management console. In addition, VNIX implements several specialized features, involving easy monitoring, fast deploying, and auto configuring. It also uses XEN as hypervisor.
- ***Cloud era*** – The open-source Hadoop software framework is increasingly used in cloud computing deployments due to its flexibility with cluster-based, data-intensive queries and other tasks. It's overseen by the Apache Software Foundation. Cloudera is a promising startup focused on providing commercial support for Hadoop.
- ***Puppet*** – Virtual servers are on the rise in cloud computing deployments and Reductive Labs open-source software, built upon the legacy of the *Cfengine* system are hugely respected by many system administrators for managing them. You can use it to manage large numbers of systems or virtual machines through automated routines, without having to do a lot of complex scripting.
- ***Red hat cloud*** – Linux focused open-source player Red Hat has been rapidly expanding its focus on cloud computing. Red Hat held its Open Source Cloud Computing Forum, which included a large number of presentations from movers and shakers focused on open-source cloud initiatives.
- ***Traffic server*** – Traffic Server is used in-house at Yahoo to manage its own traffic, and it enables session management, authentication, configuration management, load balancing, and routing for entire cloud computing software stacks. Acting as an overlay to raw cloud computing services, Traffic Server allows IT administrators to allocate resources, including handling thousands of virtualized services concurrently.
- ***Joyent*** – Joyent cloud hosting infrastructure and cloud management software incorporate many open-source tools for public and private clouds. The company can also help you optimize a speedy implementation of the open-source MySQL database for cloud use.

- ***Reservoir*** – This is the main European research initiative on virtualized infrastructures and cloud computing. It is a far-reaching project targeted to develop open-source technology for cloud computing, and help businesses avoid vendor lock-in.
- ***Usher*** – The design philosophy of Usher is to provide an interface whereby users and administrators can request VM operations. While delegating administrative tasks for these operations out to smart plugins. Usher's implementation allows for arbitrary action to be taken for nearly any event in the system.

And many more cloud tools are coming to market everyday with far advanced, user friendly and new features in it.

We now compare the various features of Eucalyptus, OpenNebula and Nimbus cloud.

	Eucalyptus	**OpenNebula**	**Nimbus**
Disk Image Options	Options set by admin	In private cloud, most libvirt options left open.	Depends on configuration
Disk Image Storage	Walrus, which imitates Amazone S3	A shared file system, by default NFS, of SCP	Cumulus (recent update from GridFTP)
Hypervisors	Xen, KVM (VMware in non-open source)	Xen, KVM, VMware	Xen, KVM
Unique Features	User management web interface	VM migration supported	Nimbus context broker

Figure 7.4 Comparisons between cloud tools.

Setting up a private cloud in Linux is quite a tedious task as it involves a wide set of steps or instructions to be fallowed. But today to overcome them there are script file method of installation where all the steps are put in a huge file, running the file finishes the entire task and the cloud is configured. The tools are getting updated to newer versions from time to time. By using these tools we can setup a private cloud, test and analyze the real time cloud.

Though there are many cloud tools available to install private cloud. The output of all of them is quite similar to some extent but vary at some stage. The common output of all the cloud tools is viewed in the web browser in the specific network IP address only. Generally the output includes two phases one for admin and another for the registered cloud user.

The admin window generally includes:

- Log in window for the admin
- Overall usage of cloud resources by all users currently
- List of available services
- Adding new user and workspace for them
- List of all users of the cloud
- Available virtual images or software in the cloud
- Available set of virtual memory flavors for running application in cloud

The user window generally includes:

- Log in window for the registered user
- Available active image that can be used by the user
- Creating the instance of the image
- Active instance of the image and the IP assigned to it
- Overall usage summary of the cloud by the corresponding user

7.4 OPENSTACK CLOUD

In the previous section, we saw many cloud computing tools and how the overall output of them will be. In this section let us see in detail about the most famous and highly used cloud tool currently by almost all IT companies and the users its *OpenStack cloud*.

Till 2010 the cloud tool *Eucalyptus* was the most widely used on. But later it lost its hold due to its commercial availability, many unsolved bugs and inactive forum. Then came the OpenStack cloud into the picture.

OpenStack cloud is product developed by both NASA and Rackspace cloud. Rackspace contributed their Cloud Files platform to power the Object Storage part of the OpenStack, while NASA contributed their Nebula code to power the Compute part. OpenStack makes its services available through Amazon EC2/S3 compatible APIs and hence the client tools written for AWS can be used with OpenStack as well. OpenStack offers open source software to build public and private clouds. OpenStack is a community and a project as well as open source software to help organizations run clouds for virtual computing or storage.

Figure 7.5 OpenStack symbol.

OpenStack is more easily defined once the concepts of cloud computing become apparent but it is on a mission to provide scalable, elastic cloud computing for both public and private clouds, large and small. At the heart of its mission is a pair of basic requirements clouds must be simple to implement and massively scalable.

OpenStack is made of several components with each one of them with a particular function. They include nova, swift, glance, horizon and keystone. Let us discuss in detail all its function.

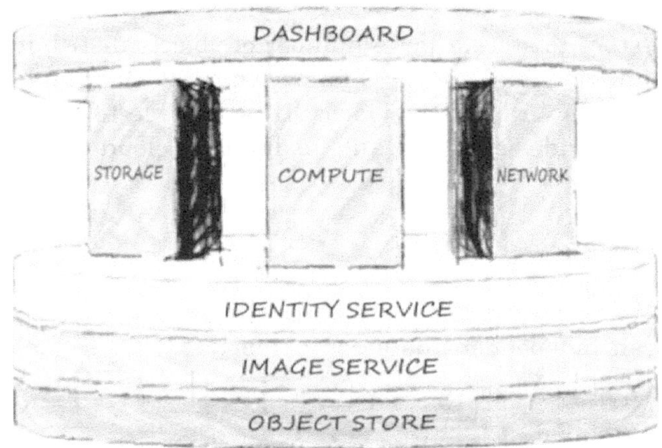

Figure 7.6 OpenStack architecture and its components.

Nova

Nova is the underlying cloud computing fabric controller for the OpenStack cloud. All activities needed to support the life cycle of instances within the OpenStack cloud are handled by Nova. It manages all the compute resources, networking, authorization, and scalability needs of the OpenStack cloud. Nova is a management platform and does not provide any virtualization capabilities by itself; instead, it uses libvirt APIs to interact with the supported hypervisors. Nova exposes its capabilities through a web services API that is compatible with that of EC2 of Amazon Web Services.

Functions and Features

- Instance life cycle management
- Management of compute resources
- Networking and Authorization
- REST-based API
- Asynchronous eventually consistent communication
- Hypervisor agnostic : support for Xen, XenServer, KVM, UML and Hyper-v

Nova Cloud Fabric is composed of the following major components:

- API Server (nova-api)
- Message Queue (rabbit-mq server)
- Compute Workers (nova-compute)
- Network Controller (nova-network)

- Volume Worker (nova-volume)
- Scheduler (nova-scheduler)

Swift

Swift is an object store to store a large number of objects distributed across commodity hardware. Swift has built-in redundancy and failover management and features like backing up or archiving data, serving graphics or videos. It is scalable to multiple petabytes and to billions of objects. Swift provides elasticity and flexibility of cloud based storage for your web applications.

Functions and Features

- Storing the machine images
- Working as an independent data container
- Redundancy and Failover
- Backup and Archival
- Extremely scalable

Glance

OpenStack Imaging Service is a lookup and retrieval system for virtual machine images. It can be configured to use any one of the following 3 storage backends:

- OpenStack Object Store to store images
- S3 storage directly
- S3 storage with Object Store as the intermediate for S3 access.

Functions and Features (Glance)

- Provides imaging service

Components of OpenStack Imaging Service (Glance)

- Glance-api,
- Glance-registry

Horizon

Horizon provides a modular web-based user interface for all the OpenStack services. With this web GUI, perform most operations on cloud like launching an instance, assigning IP addresses and setting access controls.

Keystone

Keystone provides authentication and authorization for all the OpenStack services. It also provides a service catalog of services within a particular OpenStack cloud.

There is a very active forum for OpenStack where people can post all their queries and all this can be helpful in working with OpenStack. One can easily install OpenStack cloud with script file installation in Ubuntu platform. We will see in detail on OpenStack installation in the chapter 15 case study.

Like every software undergoes updating from their current version to higher, OpenStack cloud has also under gone several versions update. Each version is more advanced and has several components than the normal five components. Each version has specific name like OpenStack Essex, Folsom and so on. The most recent one as of 2013 is grizzly and now Havana is the another new OpenStack release recently. The recent versions of Openstack cloud are more advanced and its very user friendly.

OpenStack Releases

Series	Status	Releases		Projects
Grizzly	Under development	Due	Apr. 4, 2013	Nova Swift Glance Keystone Horizon Quantum Cinder
Folsom	Current stable release	2012.2	Sep. 27, 2012	Nova Swift Glance Keystone Horizon Quantum Cinder
Essex	Supported	2012.1	Apr. 5 2012	Nova Swift Glance Keystone Horizon
		2012.1.1	Jun. 22, 2012	Nova Glance Keystone Horizon
		2012.1.2	Aug. 10, 2012	Nova Glance Keystone
Diable	Community-Supported	2011. 3	Sep. 22, 2011	Nova Swift Glance
	Security Supported,	2011.3.1	Jan. 19, 2012	Nova Glance
Cactus	Deprecated	2011.2	Apr. 15, 2011	Nova Swift Glance
Bexar	Deprecated	2011.1	Feb. 3, 2011	Nova Swift Glance
Austin	Deprecated	2010.1	Oct. 21, 2010	Nova Swift

Figure 7.7 List of various OpenStack versions.

One can see all the names of the various OpenStack versions, status of the product, release date and the components of it.

7.5 C-DAC AND ITS PRODUCT

Till now we saw all the cloud software designed by many giant IT companies and from research institutions from other countries. Now in this section let us see the Indian developed cloud technology and the ongoing research work by Indians. We will also discuss the Indians developed products and government funded IT department C-DAC. The various work done and the ongoing activities by C-DAC respectively.

C-DAC stands for Center for Development of Advanced Computing, is a research and development organization under the information technology department and the government of India. The National Centre for Software Technology (NCST), ER&DCI and CEDTI were merged into C-DAC in 2003.

Figure 7.8 CDAC official image.

C-DAC is the premier R&D organization of the Department of Electronics and Information Technology (DeitY), Ministry of Communications & Information Technology (MCIT) for carrying out R&D in IT, Electronics and associated areas. Different areas of C-DAC, had originated at different times, many of which came out as a result of identification of opportunities.

- The setting up of C-DAC in 1988 itself was to built Supercomputers in context of denial of import of Supercomputers by USA. Since then C-DAC has been undertaking building of multiple generations of Supercomputer starting from PARAM with 1 GF in 1988.
- Almost at the same time, C-DAC started building Indian Language Computing Solutions with setting up of GIST group (Graphics and Intelligence based Script Technology); National Centre for Software Technology (NCST) set up in 1985 had also initiated work in Indian Language Computing around the same period.
- Electronic Research and Development Centre of India (ER&DCI) with various constituents starting as adjunct entities of various State Electronic Corporations, had been brought under the hold of Department of Electronics and Telecommunications (now DeitY) in around 1988. They were focusing on various aspects of applied electronics, technology and applications.
- With the passage of time as a result of creative echo system that got set up in C-DAC, more areas such as Health Informatics, etc., got created; while right from the beginning the focus of NCST was on Software Technologies; similarly C-DAC started its education & training activities in 1994 as a spin-off with the passage of time, it grew to a large efforts to meet the growing needs of Indian Industry for finishing schools.

C-DAC has today emerged as a premier third party R&D organization in IT&E (Information Technologies and Electronics) in the country working on strengthening national technological capabilities in the context of global developments in the field and responding to change in the market need in selected foundation areas. In that process, C-DAC represents a unique facet working in close junction with DeitY to realize nation's policy and pragmatic interventions and initiatives in Information Technology.

As an institution for high-end Research and Development (R&D), C-DAC has been at the forefront of the Information Technology (IT) revolution, constantly building capacities in emerging/enabling technologies and innovating and leveraging its expertise, caliber, skill sets to develop and deploy IT products and solutions for different sectors of the economy, as per the mandate of its parent, the Department of Electronics and Information Technology, Ministry of Communications and Information Technology, Government of India and other stakeholders including funding agencies, collaborators, users and the market-place.

The vision of C-DAC is to emerge as the premier R&D institution for the design, development and deployment of world class electronic and IT solutions for economic and human advancement.

The mission of C-DAC includes:

- Expand the frontiers of Electronics and Information Technology.
- Evolve technology solutions - architectures, systems and standards for nationally important problems.
- Achieve rapid and effective spread of knowledge by overcoming language barriers through application of technologies.
- Share experience and know-how to help build advanced competence in the areas of Electronics and Information Technology.
- Bring benefits of Electronics and Information Technology to society.
- Utilize the Intellectual Property generated by converting it to business opportunity.

The core values of C-DAC includes:

- Innovation and pursuit of excellence in 'Applications', 'Research' and 'Technology' (ART).
- Integrity, transparency and openness in all our actions.
- Working with and through the 'Teams' is our way of life.
- Distributed Leadership across the organization at various levels.
- Strive to continuously improve our processes and quality.
- Address the needs of the society through user centric initiatives.

C-DAC has developed several products and research work in various areas including:

- ***High Performance Computing*** – Including the Param series of computers, Garuda national grid initiative, development of scientific computing applications on these platforms, and cloud computing.

- ***Multi-lingual Computing*** – Spanning the entire range from fonts and encoding to speech and language translation, which includes fonts for Indian languages, encoding standards, information extraction and retrieval, machine aided translation, speech recognition and synthesis, etc.
- ***Professional Electronics*** – Covering electronic devices and embedded systems. This area covers work such as underwater electronics, software radio, ubiquitous computing.
- ***Information and Cyber Security*** – Including intrusion detection and prevention, malware analysis, cyber forensics, network security, etc.
- ***Health Informatics*** – Including hospital information systems, electronic medical records, telemedicine, and cancer networks.
- ***Software Technologies*** – Including e-governance solutions, e-learning technologies, geomatics, open source software, accessibility, etc.

And they also provide education and training facilities in various technologies.

Some of the notable products and solutions developed by C-DAC include:

- PARAM series of supercomputers
- Namescape, the search engine for the Aadhar unique-ID project
- Bharat Operating System Solutions, a Linux-based general purpose operating system
- TaxoGrid, a grid-based molecular phylogenetics and drug discovery system
- GIST, Graphics and Intelligence based Script Technology
- Anvaya, a workflow environment for automated genome analysis
- Darpan, DARPAN is a real time network monitoring, visualization and Service Level Agreement monitoring tool developed by C-DAC Thiruvananthapuram

They have developed many more products in several areas.

Garuda

C-DAC launched the Indian National Grid Computing Initiative called GARUDA, with a vision to facilitate solutions to scientific, engineering and socio-economic development. GARUDA is a collaboration of scientific and technological researchers on a nationwide grid comprising of computational nodes, mass storage and scientific instruments. The aim is to provide the technological advances required to enable data and compute intensive science and engineering applications for the 21st Century. One of GARUDA's most important challenges is to strike the right balance between researchers and deployment of the innovation into complex scientific and engineering endeavors undertaken today.

The Department of Information Technology (DIT), Government of India has funded the Centre for Development of Advanced Computing (C-DAC) to deploy the nation-wide computational grid 'GARUDA' which will connect 17 cities across the country, with an aim to bring "Grid" networked computing to research labs and industry. A total of 45 institutions have been connected during the Proof of Concept phase of Garuda.

The various components of GARUDA include:

Grid Middleware Engineering

- Enabling SOA on GARUDA
- Compiler Service

Tools

- Monitoring tool - Paryavekshanam
- Integrated Development Environment - GIDE
- Grid Debugger - Gridhra
- Grid Service Generator - Automatic Grid Service Generator
- GARUDA Distribution Package - SIGMA
- Portal
- IGCA - Indian Grid Certification Authority
- Data Grid Solutions - SRB

Grid Applications

- Disaster Management
- Protein Structure Prediction
- EU- India Grid

Grid Users

- GARUDA Grid Operation & Administration
- GARUDA Partners Information

Grid Infrastructure

- GARUDA Backbone - NKN
- GARUDA Resource Information

The Indian Grid Certification Authority (IGCA) provides X.509 certificates to support the secure environment in grid computing. IGCA is an accredited member of the APgridPMA (Asia Pacific Grid Policy Management Authority) for Grid Authentication. IGCA is located at Centre For Development of Advanced Computing(C-DAC), Knowledge Park, Bangalore, India.

They issue User Certificates and Host Certificates to users of GARUDA Grid, Foreign collaborators or institutes related to Grid research and scientific collaborations from India. The IGCA is operated by Garuda Grid Operation Centre (www.garudaindia.in).

C-DAC has offices in Bengaluru, Chennai, Hyderabad, Delhi, Kolkata, Mohali, Mumbai, Pune, Thiruvananthapuram and Noida. The headquarters is situated in Pune. C-DAC provides several courses in the field of advanced computing and software development. Among these are the htc certification course C-DAC Certified HPC Professional Certification Programme (CCHPCP). C-DAC organises advanced computing diploma programmes through the Advanced Computing Training School (ACTS) located all over India, GIST Programme for Advancing Computer Education (PACE) and corporate training. The PG Diploma courses include specializations in Embedded System Design, VLSI, etc.

Some of the cloud tools developed by C-DAC include:

Cloud Vault

It has a simple web services interface that can be used to store and retrieve any amount of data, at any time, from anywhere on the web. Extremely Scalable in terms of Storage Size (Several Petabytes) and Storage Capacity (Number of objects). Pay as you use- no user or device licensing.

Cloud Vault provides academic and research communities with a convenient and affordable way to store data, including extremely large data sets. The object based storage system and multiple interface methods make the Cloud Vault easy to use for the average user, but also provide a flexible, configurable and expandable solution to meet the needs of more demanding applications.

Directories or Files of any size can be stored in the cloud, from small document to multi-terabyte data sets. Users can upload, download, delete and navigate files and directories via very simple User interface. And with on-demand storage, you never have to worry about running out of space your storage scales as needed. Once objects are in the cloud they are immediately available over the web to other users, the public or just to you.

Job Submission Portal For HPC

This Portal provides a web interface for submitting sequential and parallel jobs to HPC cloud computing environment which is offered as IAAS of Scientific Cloud. It also provides monitoring the job status and viewing/downloading the output/error data. This portal is specifically designed for the scientific application developers of the cloud to access the virtual cluster and run their jobs without getting into the difficulties of typing commands on command line.

Salient Features:

- Job Submission through Torque job scheduler.
- Job monitoring to know the status of submitted jobs.
- Output/Error files can be Viewed/Downloaded from the Portal.
- New user creation facility: New user can be created for login into the Job Submission Portal.

Scientific Cloud For HPC

High Performance Computing (HPC) allows scientists and engineers to solve complex science, engineering and business applications that require very high compute capability, massive storage, high bandwidth and low latency networking. Scientists and engineers either wait in long queues to access shared cluster resources or acquire expensive hardware (clusters) at their organization. Cloud computing is a useful model for on-demand access to the shared pool of configurable HPC resources (e.g., servers, storage, networks, applications, software, and services) that can be easily provisioned as and when needed.

For research groups, cloud computing will provide convenient access to reliable, high performance clusters and storage, without the need to purchase and maintain sophisticated hardware. C-DAC scientific cloud is an IaaS Cloud which provides virtual machine and virtual cluster on demands. Scientific Cloud Web portal provides you the GUI to the service for Creating, Destroying and saving the virtual machines. It also provides one click cluster having the MPI or HADOOP platform enable on it.

7.6 BOSS OPERATING SYSTEM

Most of us have worked with Windows, Linux, Apple and other operating systems which are developed by other countries. They are either open source or proprietary. Now in this section let us see the Indians developed operating system called *Bharat Operating Systems Solutions (BOSS)*. We will discuss in detail about this operating system and its feature developed by Indians.

National Resource Centre for Free & Open Source Software (NRCFOSS) at C-DAC Chennai as a part of its objective has been working on localized Indian distribution of GNU/ Linux called Bharat Operating Systems Solutions (BOSS) based on Debian. BOSS GNU/ Linux is available as Desktop edition, Server edition and as EduBOSS. BOSS Linux is targeted towards Government departments, SME's, schools and the first time user. A second target group is the Linux distro (distribution) developers so that they can develop a new distro based on BOSS Linux. Thus BOSS has been developed with the intention of spreading the Indian based technology and the golden work done by Indian engineers.

The various versions of BOSS desktop include:

- BOSS1.0 (Tarang) - released in January 2006
- BOSS 2.0 (Anant) - released in September 2007
- BOSS 3.0 (Tejas) - released in September 2008
- BOSS 4.0 (Savir) - released in April 2011
- Current version - BOSS 5.0 (anokha) Kernel - 3.2 GNOME 3.4 desktop Libreoffice 4.0

BOSS Gnu / Linux 5.0

BOSS Linux 5.0 features the latest Kernel 3.2.0-4, Supports Intel 32 bit & 64 bit architectures, a 3D desktop environment, Graphic installer, Office application software suite Libreoffice 4.0 , Internet access software (eg: web browser , email, chat etc.), and file sharing / converter and multimedia applications. The new version features a Media center to allow the user to easily browse and view videos, photos, podcasts, and music from a hard drive, optical disc, local network, and the internet. There is a personal and small-business financial-accounting software to extend the use of BOSS GNU / Linux to SMEs.

The desktop comes with an on-screen keyboard with Indian language support. The Smart Common Input Method tool provides input mechanism for Indian languages Unicode 6.1 support. The Orca Screen reader and Magnifier & E-Speak applications helps the people with visual impairments for using the BOSS desktop. The Bulk document converter helps people to easily migrate from other Operating system to BOSS GNU / Linux.

Currently BOSS GNU/Linux Desktop supports all the Official Indian Languages such as Assamese, Bengali, Gujarati, Hindi, Kannada, Malayalam, Marathi, Oriya, Punjabi, Sanskrit, Tamil, Telugu, Bodo, Urdu, Kashmiri, Maithili, Konkani, Manipuri etc., which will enable the non-English literate users in the country to be exposed to ICT and to use the computer more effectively.

BOSS Linux 5.0 is packaged in DVD and the user has the option to install, try and use the utility tools like PHP scripting language, fonts etc., all packed in a single DVD. BOSS 5.0 comes with support for more devices, application search tool with installation support for GUI / Network / installation from Windows / LTSP. Apart from the updates the new release is focused mainly on the security part of the Linux. It brings a new BOSS Security tool to harden desktop with more tightened password security, disabling unavailable services, hosts, ports etc., disabling USB, CD / DVD ports, enabling audit and SELinux to monitor user actions. BOSS GNU/Linux activities are coordinated by C-DAC Chennai centre, led by Shri.M.R.Rajagopalan and a team of 25 engineers who are involved in developing the BOSS GNU/ Linux operating system.

EduBOSS

It is an educational variant of BOSS Linux is a full-featured, user-friendly Linux operating system, has educational applications that are useful for schools (primary and higher levels). Adapted from BOSS GNU/Linux, it features graphical installer, office application suite, onscreen keyboard, Smart Common Input Method, web browser, educational games, paint & graphic tools, typing tutor, screen reader, text to speech application and a host of tools and packages for learning, and also for teaching. EduBOSS comes in a single DVD easily installable on a desktop. It also contains utility with add-on applications.

7.7 MEGHDOOT CLOUD

Now in this section let us see the Indian developed cloud computing tool called *MEGHDOOT CLOUD*. This tool is used to configure a cloud environment in real time. View the cloud, design and deploy the app into the cloud.

C-DAC has established a Private cloud environment to offer basic cloud services such as Infrastructure, Platform, and Software service to cater the needs of PAN C-DAC Applications. The primary focus of Research and Development activities are development of Open Source Cloud Middleware, providing an end to end security framework for Cloud, achieving Interoperability among various cloud service providers. C-DAC has come out with complete open source free software suite called *MEGHDOOT* for establishing cloud with value added features that converts the data centre to cloud centre. This product installs the

BOSS Operating system along with the cloud stack. Thus this cloud is integrated with the BOSS operating system as its base component. C-DAC has successfully completed various implementation and consultancy services to Government and SMEs for establishing Cloud, porting existing applications into Cloud and Development of cloud enabled applications. Various customized corporate training programs are offered for corporate, academicians, researchers, students and Government officials.

One of the remarkable activities ongoing is Integration of Private Cloud computing environment with existing Garuda Grid (India's National Grid Computing Initiative).

Meghdoot is one stop solution to implement state-of-art cloud environment completely based on Free and Open source software. This single suite incorporates tools across all layers to establish your own cloud with regard to open standards. Meghdoot is an indigenous cloud suite developed with enormous research efforts on top of various open source tools. Meghdoot integrated suite comprises of enhanced open source tools across all layers of cloud providing all required functionalities with the installation of tools is abstracted from the user, configuration of cloud is done made simple through the graphical user interface.

All the cloud administration activities including addition and removal of resources from cloud are made in a way that from single location the entire cloud resources and services can be managed through Web based Self servicing portal. The entire operation of cloud is completely automated with less overhead to the administrators. The core features and functionalities are as follows but not limited to Customizable advanced algorithm provides rapid elasticity that keeps track of the virtual machines and the application. The high availability feature ensures that all cloud services, application and the resources in cloud environment are available to the users all the time even when the primary server fails. The suite has a provision to deploy software packages owned by users into cloud. The solution is interoperable with various other clouds and supports live migration of virtual machines. The storage volumes for virtual machine users can be auto formatted. At the virtualization layer, servers with heterogeneous hypervisor can be brought in to single cluster.

Suite offers complete data encryption with high level of data portability. Provides backup of user data, applications and other critical management information and easy recovery of the entire cloud environment in case of any disaster, supports choreography and orchestration for the application developed and deployed in Meghdoot cloud, supports automated scale-in and scale-out features. Meghdoot cloud environment is completely secured with advanced security mechanism providing end-end security framework. The security mechanism available in Meghdoot cloud can be categorized into application level security, VM level security, data level security, VM resource and data isolation framework, PKI – CA signed certificate based VM access, Data Verification Service with 2 level authentication, Encryption Service with Client Side; Server Side and EBS Volume Encryption, Web application firewall, Host intrusion detection, Security for Data at rest, Identity and Access management in the cloud, Security for Data at Transit, Data remanence offering Data sanitization, Form based authentication and role base access control mechanisms and provision to integrate 3rd party CAs.

The complete solution is based on open API such that it can be extensible and based on open standards and the research components are contributed to the open source community.

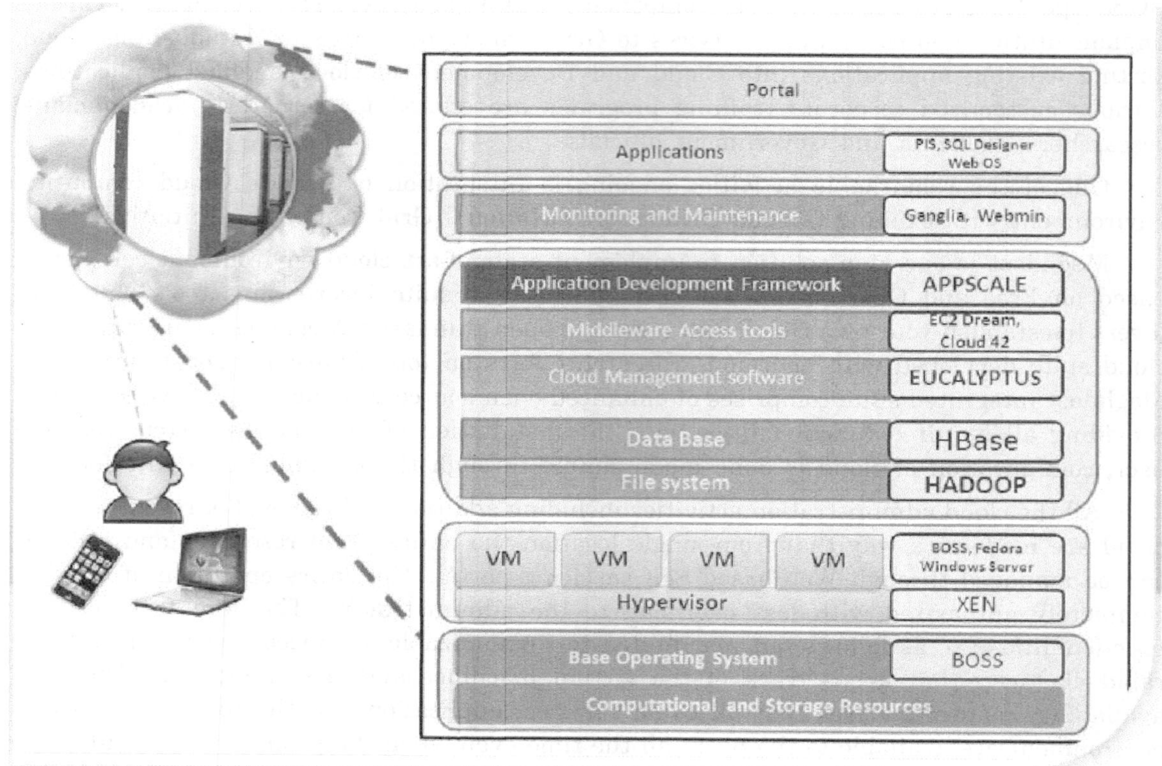

Figure 7.9 Meghdoot cloud stack.

The Meghdoot cloud components include:

- Linux Kernel – 2.6.32-5 & 3.0.0 -1
- Xen Hypervisor – 4.0
- Eucalyptus - 2.0.2
- Euca2ools
- Web management interface for Cloud (Meghdoot Portal)
- Standard tools of Linux Operating System
- GUI for Cloud Configurations
- Hyperic Hq Monitoring Tool

The hardware requirements for installing Meghdoot cloud include:

- Hard Disk – 50.0 GB (un-partitioned space)
- RAM – 4 GB
- DVD-ROM drive

We can install the Meghdoot cloud by its DVD. Insert the Meghdoot DVD into the drive, restart your computer and boot from DVD by editing the BIOS setup. The screen appears with three options:

- Start Meghdoot (BOSS CLOUD) Live
- Install Meghdoot (BOSS CLOUD)-Graphical
- Install Meghdoot (BOSS CLOUD)-Text Mode

Hence we can choose the required mode and install the Meghdoot cloud.

Successful deployment of Meghdoot cloud include:

Indian Banking Community Cloud

Indian Banking Community Cloud is established using Meghdoot in Institute for Development and Research in Banking Technology, Hyderabad (Established by Reserve Bank of India). The community cloud was inaugurated by Governor, Reserve Bank of India and currently 6 Banks application ported into Meghdoot cloud.

Poc- Government

As Proof of Concept, Meghdoot is deployed in the following Government organizations:

- Government of Kerala (KSITM - C-DAC, Chennai + IIITMK, Trivandrum)
- Government of Chhattisgarh (CHiPS, Raipur)
- Government of Assam (e-District)
- Tamil Nadu State Data Centre (ELCOT, Chennai)
- Naval Dockyard, Visakapatnam
- Institute for Development and Research in Banking Technology, Hyderabad.
- Maharashtra State Data Centre, Mumbai

In Small and Medium Enterprises (SME) sector:

- Y3 Technologies (Chennai and Singapore)

Academic Institutes

In academic institutions, CDAC conducted workshops & deployed cloud in the following institutions:

- Anna University, Chennai
- Curriculum Development Centre, Ernakulam
- P.S.G. Institute of Technology, Coimbatore
- Sri Venkateswara College of Engineering, Chennai
- Jerusalem College of Engineering, Chennai
- Madras Institute of Technology, Chennai

Corporate Trainings

C-DAC also conducts Corporate Training on Cloud technology (deployment, management, application development) wherein till Nov. 2013 following organizations were trained:

- Y3 Technologies, Chennai & Singapore
- Indian Navy

Certificate program (4 batch) with participants from:

- DIETy, Ministry of Communication & IT, Govt. of India.
- World Bank, Chennai
- IBM, TCS, CTS, Tech Mahindra, WIPRO, HCL : Chennai & Bangalore
- Sri Ramachandra Medical College and Research Institute, Chennai
- Other Universities across the country

Committee Memberships

C-DAC is contributing to standardization of cloud through memberships in the following committees:

- GI Cloud Task Force - Cloud App store (Chair : Addl. Secretary, DietY, MCIT, GOI)
- Cloud Working Group - Standardization for Cloud (Chair : Kris. Gopalkrishnan)
- Cloud Innovation council - Cloud middleware stack, Interoperability (Head : Sam Pitroda)
- Cloud working Group – IDRBT, Hyderabad

We browse so many sites for various purposes. It is estimated that the size of the whole data in internet was 0.18 zettabytes in 2006 and is forecasting a tenfold growth by 2011 to 1.8 zettabytes.

7.8 HADOOP

In the last section of this chapter, let us discuss in detail about another major area called *Hadoop*.

We see so much of data in the internet. Not the mere data alone we also see images, videos and so on. We browse so many sites for various purposes. It is estimated that the size of the whole data in internet was 0.18 zettabytes in 2006 and is forecasting a tenfold growth by 2011 to 1.8 zettabytes.

One must think

How are all this plenty of things stored?

How do we manage them?

How do we retrieve them?

Some of the large data processing needed areas include

- The New York Stock Exchange generates about one terabyte of new trade data per day.
- Facebook hosts approximately 10 billion photos, taking up one petabyte of storage.
- Ancestry.com, the genealogy site, stores around 2.5 petabytes of data.
- The Internet Archive stores around 2 petabytes of data, and is growing at a rate of 20 terabytes per month.
- The Large Hadron Collider near Geneva, Switzerland, will produce about 15 petabytes of data per year.

The exponential growth of data in the recent years is proving to be a big challenge to all the IT companies. Thus to overcome all these problems companies have started using the Hadoop platform.

Hadoop is an open source framework for writing and running distributed applications that process large amounts of data. Distributed computing is a wide and varied field, but the key distinctions of Hadoop are that it is:

- ***Accessible*** — Hadoop runs on the large clusters of commodity machines or on cloud computing services such as Amazon's Elastic Compute Cloud (EC2).
- ***Robust*** — It is intended to run on commodity hardware, Hadoop is architected with the assumption of frequent hardware malfunctions. It can gracefully handle most such failures. Thus it is highly robust and fault tolerant.
- ***Scalable*** — Hadoop scales linearly to handle larger data by adding more nodes to the cluster.
- ***Simple*** — Hadoop allows users to quickly write efficient parallel code.

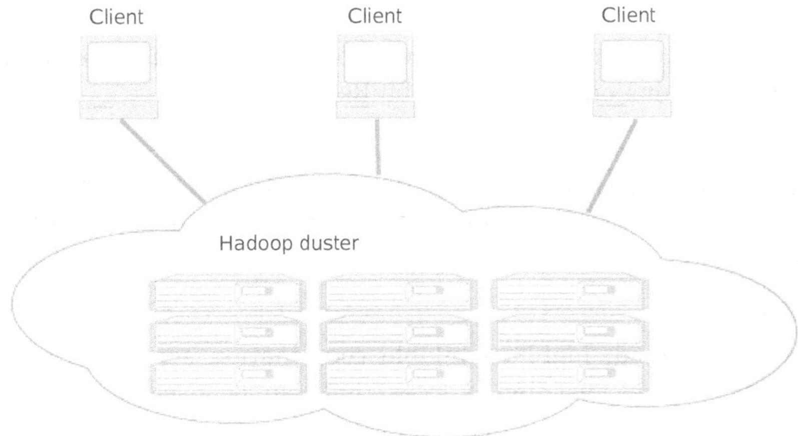

Figure 7.10 Hadoop cluster.

Hadoop clusters are a set of machines networked together in one location. Data storage and processing all occur within this machine. Different users can submit computing jobs to

Hadoop from individual clients, which can be their own desktop machines in remote locations from the Hadoop cluster.

Hadoop accessibility and simplicity give it a clear edge over writing and running large distributed programs. It is very easy to write such programs. Even college students can quickly and cheaply create their own Hadoop cluster. Today Hadoop is a core part of the computing infrastructure for many web companies, such as Yahoo, Facebook , LinkedIn , and Twitter. Many more traditional businesses such as media and telecom are beginning to adopt this system too.

Well there are several projects in Hadoop which include:

- ***Core***

  It is a set of components and interfaces for distributed file systems and general I/O process like serialization, Java RPC, persistent data structures and so on.

- ***Avro***

  It is a data serialization system for efficient, cross-language RPC, and persistent data storage.

- ***Mapreduce***

  It is a distributed data processing model and execution environment that runs on large clusters of commodity machines. It is one among the popular one in hadoop.

- ***HDFS***

  It is a distributed file system that runs on large clusters of commodity machines. It is a very common one in hadoop.

- ***Pig***

  It is a data flow language and execution environment for exploring very large datasets. Pig runs on HDFS and MapReduce clusters.

- ***HBASE***

  It is a distributed, column-oriented database. HBase uses HDFS for its underlying storage and supports both batch-style computations using MapReduce and point queries.

- ***Zookeeper***

  It is a distributed, highly available coordination service. ZooKeeper provides primitives such as distributed locks that can be used for building distributed applications.

- ***Hive***

  It is a distributed data warehouse. Hive manages data stored in HDFS and provides a query language based on SQL and which is translated by the runtime engine to MapReduce jobs for querying the data.

- ***Chukwa***

  It is a distributed data collection and analysis system. Chukwa runs collectors that store data in HDFS and it uses MapReduce to produce reports.

Well we will discuss in detail about HDFS and MapReduce.

Hadoop Distributed File System

The Hadoop Distributed File System is a distributed file system designed to hold very large amounts of data and provide high-throughput access to this information. Files are stored in a redundant fashion across multiple machines to ensure their durability to failure and high availability to very parallel applications.

The Hadoop Distributed File System (HDFS) will split large data files into chunks which are managed by different nodes in the cluster. In addition to this each chunk is replicated across several machines so that a single machine failure does not result in any data being unavailable. An active monitoring system then re-replicates the data in response to system failures which can result in partial storage. Even though the file chunks are replicated and distributed across several machines they form a single namespace, so their contents are universally accessible.

HDFS is a file system designed for storing very large files with streaming data access patterns running on clusters on commodity hardware. Let us see some of the features:

- **Very large files**

  Very large refers to the files that are hundreds of megabytes, gigabytes, or terabytes in size. There are Hadoop clusters running today that store petabytes of data.

- **Streaming data access**

  HDFS is built around the idea that the most efficient data processing pattern is a write once Read many times pattern. A dataset is typically generated or copied from source then various analyses are performed on that dataset over time. Each analysis will involve a large proportion if not all of the dataset so the time to read the whole dataset is more important than the latency in reading the first record.

- **Commodity hardware**

  Hadoop does not require expensive highly reliable hardware to run on. It's designed to run on clusters of commodity hardware like commonly available hardware available from multiple vendors for which the chance of node failure across the cluster is high at least for large clusters. HDFS is designed to carry on working without a noticeable interruption to the user in the face of such failure. It is also worth examining the applications for which using HDFS does not work so well. While this may change in the future these are areas where HDFS is not a good fit today.

- **Low-latency data access**

  Applications that require low-latency access to data in the tens of milliseconds range will not work well with HDFS. Remember HDFS is optimized for delivering a high throughput of data and this may be at the expense of latency. HBase is currently a better choice for low-latency access. Lots of small files since the name node holds file system metadata in memory, the limit to the number of files in a file system is governed by the amount of memory on the name node. As a rule of thumb, each file, directory, and block takes about 150 bytes. So, for example, if you had one million files, each taking one block, you would need at least 300 MB of memory. While storing millions of files is feasible, billions is beyond the capability of current hardware.

- **Multiple writers, arbitrary file modifications**

  Files in HDFS may be written to by a single writer. Writes are always made at the end of the file. There is no support for multiple writers, or for modifications at arbitrary offsets in the file.

Mapreduce

Hadoop MapReduce is a software framework for easily writing applications which process vast amounts of data like multi-terabyte data-sets in-parallel on large clusters (thousands of nodes) of commodity hardware in a reliable, fault-tolerant manner.

A MapReduce job usually splits the input data-set into independent chunks which are processed by the map tasks in a completely parallel manner. The framework sorts the outputs of the maps, which are then input to the reduce tasks. Typically both the input and the output of the job are stored in a file system. The framework takes care of scheduling tasks, monitoring them and re-executes the failed tasks.

Typically the compute nodes and the storage nodes are the same that is the MapReduce framework and the Distributed File System are running on the same set of nodes. This configuration allows the framework to effectively schedule tasks on the nodes where data is already present resulting in very high aggregate bandwidth across the cluster.

A MapReduce job is a unit of work that the client wants to be performed it consists of the input data, the MapReduce program, and configuration information. Hadoop runs the job by dividing it into tasks, of which there are two types map tasks and reduce tasks. There are two types of nodes that control the job execution process a jobtracker and a number of tasktrackers. The jobtracker coordinates all the jobs run on the system by scheduling tasks to run on tasktrackers. Tasktrackers run tasks and send progress reports to the jobtracker, which keeps a record of the overall progress of each job. If a task fails the jobtracker can reschedule it on a different tasktracker. Hadoop divides the input to a MapReduce job into fixed-size pieces called input splits, or just splits. Hadoop creates one map task for each split, which runs the user defined map function for each record in the split.

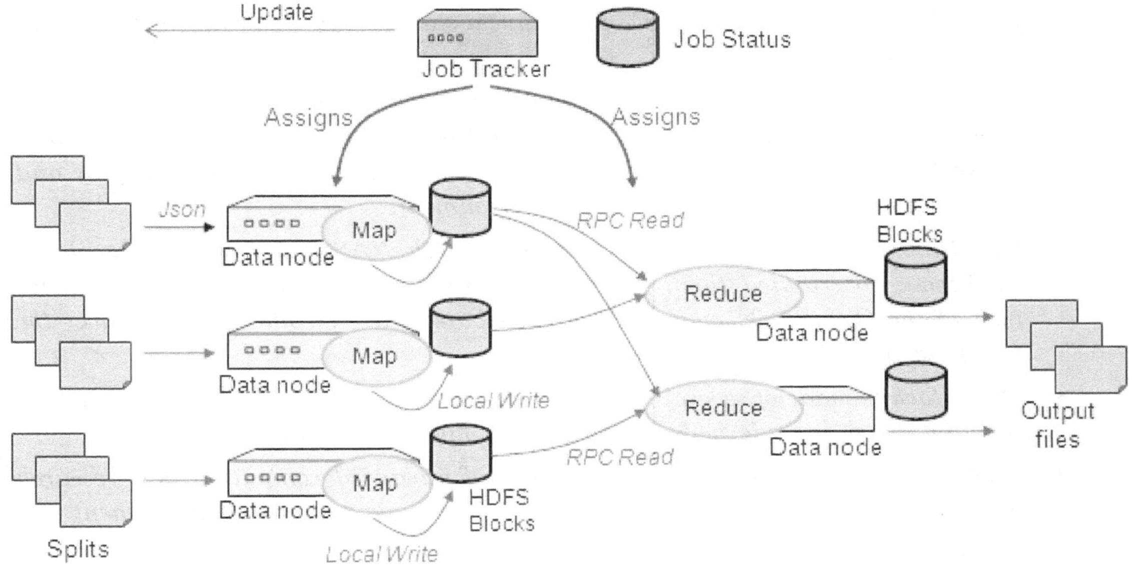

Figure 7.11 MapReduce and its function.

SUMMARY

- *In Linux operating system there are generally two modes, firstly Kernel mode is used to execute all the operating system process. It is also known as the system mode. Secondly User mode is used to execute all the applications of the user. It is a non privileged mode.*
- *The Linux kernel is composed of five main subsystems which include process scheduler, memory manager, virtual file system, network interface and inter process communication.*
- *System call is an interface between a process and the operating system. System calls are of several different types File Management System call, Process Control System Call, Device Management System Call and Communication System call.*
- *Linux is best suited for all the networking operations in the server side. Linux has both desktop based GUI version and the server version making it a very ideal choice for all networking functions.*
- *Linux is best suited for virtualization and cloud computing tools. Linux is modular, performant, power efficient, scalable, open source, and ubiquitous above all the major cloud infrastructures in the world are built in Linux platform only.*
- *Many Linux platforms have tied up with the open source tools and have developed many advanced cloud tools. A best example is Ubuntu tied up with Eucalyptus cloud to give Ubuntu Enterprise Cloud (UEC) in 2010. Then in 2012 Ubuntu*

joined hands with OpenStack Cloud to give a stable cloud environment in Ubuntu 12.04 version.

- *The open source technologies as we all know it is free of cost. It can be used by educational institutions, researchers, academicians and even business organizations. These tools get updated from time to time. They are used to design, deploy and manage the application in the cloud environment.*
- *OpenStack cloud is product developed by both NASA and Rackspace cloud. Rackspace contributed their Cloud Files platform to power the Object Storage part of the OpenStack, while NASA contributed their Nebula code to power the Compute part.*
- *OpenStack is made of several components with each one of them with a particular function. They include nova, swift, glance, horizon and keystone.*
- *C-DAC stands for center for development of advanced computing is a research and development organization under the information technology department and the government of India.*
- *C-DAC has developed several products and research work in various areas including High Performance Computing, Multi-lingual Computing, Professional Electronics, Information and Cyber Security, Health Informatics, Software Technologies and so on.*
- *C-DAC launched the Indian National Grid Computing Initiative called GARUDA, with a vision to facilitate solutions to scientific, engineering and socio-economic development. GARUDA is a collaboration of scientific and technological researchers on a nationwide grid comprising of computational nodes, mass storage and scientific instruments.*
- *C-DAC scientific cloud is an IaaS Cloud which provides virtual machine and virtual cluster on demands. Scientific Cloud Web portal provides you the GUI to the service for Creating, Destroying and saving the virtual machines.*
- *National Resource Centre for Free & Open Source Software (NRCFOSS) at C-DAC Chennai as a part of its objective has been working on localised Indian distribution of GNU/Linux called Bharat Operating Systems Solutions (BOSS) based on Debian. BOSS GNU/Linux is available as Desktop edition, Server edition and as EduBOSS.*
- *BOSS Linux 5.0 features the latest Kernel 3.2.0-4, Supports Intel 32 bit & 64 bit architectures, a 3D desktop environment, Graphic installer, Office application software suite Libreoffice 4.0 , Internet access software, and file sharing / converter and multimedia applications.*
- *C-DAC has come out with complete open source free software suite called MEGHDOOT for establishing cloud with value added features that converts the data centre to cloud centre. This product installs the BOSS Operating system*

along with the cloud stack. Thus this cloud is integrated with the BOSS operating system as its base component.

- *Meghdoot is one stop solution to implement state-of-art cloud environment completely based on Free and Open source software. This single suite incorporates tools across all layers to establish your own cloud with regard to open standards.*
- *Hadoop is an open source framework for writing and running distributed applications that process large amounts of data. It is easily accessible, robust, scalable and simple.*
- *Hadoop clusters are a set of machines networked together in one location. Data storage and processing all occur within this machine. Different users can submit computing jobs to Hadoop from individual clients, which can be their own desktop machines in remote locations from the Hadoop cluster.*
- *The Hadoop Distributed File System is a distributed file system designed to hold very large amounts of data and provide high-throughput access to this information. Files are stored in a redundant fashion across multiple machines to ensure their durability to failure and high availability to very parallel applications.*
- *Hadoop MapReduce is a software framework for easily writing applications which process vast amounts of data like multi-terabyte data-sets in-parallel on large clusters (thousands of nodes) of commodity hardware in a reliable, fault-tolerant manner.*

8

UBUNTU AND CLOUD COMPUTING

OBJECTIVE

- *To know about the evolution and working environment of Ubuntu*
- *To know about the list of all commands to work in terminal*
- *To know about the contribution of Ubuntu to cloud computing platform*
- *To learn how to configure a live cloud*

In this chapter, we will mainly discuss about the Ubuntu operating system and its products. We will see how Ubuntu is useful for cloud computing and its advancements. Let us see how to work in a command line interface with set of various commands. We will also see how Ubuntu has made a tie up with many cloud tools and has designed operating systems to easily configure cloud environment. Ubuntu has played a major role in revolutionizing cloud computing since 2010 all due to its tie up with several cloud companies. Working with Ubuntu is really a very interesting and a good option. Ubuntu has also developed many cloud tools which can be used to manage the cloud effectively.

8.1 INTRODUCTION TO UBUNTU ENVIRONMENT

In the first section of the chapter, let us see in detail about the Ubuntu operating system and its revolution. We will see how Ubuntu has become a major source of operating system in Linux world in less than a decade of its evolution.

Ubuntu is an African word meaning *humanity to others or I am what I am because of who we all are*. The Ubuntu symbol in the official logo is called *Circle of Friends*, and represents freedom, collaboration, precision and reliability. Mark Shuttleworth is the founder of the Ubuntu Project. As its founder Mark Shuttleworth puts it, Ubuntu is all about total commitment to everyday users, making things just work for them. It came into existence in 2004. A total of 131 Linux distributions are based on Ubuntu, of which 77 are currently active. The official website of Ubuntu is www.Ubuntu.com.

It has a very active forum where one can discuss all the recent trends and the happening. As we all know Linux platform are open source one can easily download the Ubuntu operating system from the website and install the operating system. From time to time Ubuntu keeps on releasing various versions of the operating system. It supports GUI based desktop version, command line version and server edition operating system. In each version of operating system more and more new features and advancements are added from time to time.

Figure 8.1 Ubuntu OS symbol.

Canonical Limited, the commercial company behind Ubuntu, is famously known as a virtual company with no national and geographic boundaries. According to its official source, Canonical has over 600 employees in nearly 200 cities across 30 countries, while the company has offices only at six locations which include London, Boston, Montreal, Shanghai, São Paulo and Taipei. Most of the employees are working remotely, communicating via IRC or email.

The code names of Ubuntu releases come from a combination of an adjective and an animal with the same first letter. Code names are chosen in an alphabetical order, so you can tell which release is newer from code names.

The various platforms Ubuntu supports include:

- Computer OS either desktop, command line and server editions
- Can be used in phone
- Tablets also support Ubuntu version
- Ubuntu supports TV device for user
- Cloud computing domain
- Several management tools.

Ubuntu is one among the most used Linux operating system. Ubuntu Linux has been powering millions of PCs around the world. It supports all forms of virtualization making it an ideal platform for cloud computing and other networking based technologies. Ubuntu has become very popular for the last few years mainly after the cloud revolution.

The largest desktop migration to Ubuntu is the upgrade of 85,000 desktop PCs from Microsoft operating system to Ubuntu by La Gendarmerie Nationale's IT team, under the French police force.

Ubuntu features a comprehensive package management system for installing, upgrading, configuring, and removing software. In addition to providing access to an organized base of over 35,000 software packages for your Ubuntu computer, the package management facilities also feature dependency resolution capabilities and software update checking. As of Ubuntu 13.04 the total number of Ubuntu packages is over 37,500, and total package size is over 45 GB. According to survey dpkg package is ranked first in terms of the number of people who use the package regularly, and ncurses-base package is number one in terms of the number of people who installed the package.

The version number of a particular Ubuntu release is actually the release year and month. So for example, the very first Ubuntu release is 4.10 because it was released in October, 2004. The recent Ubuntu 13.10 was released in October, 2013. A new release of Ubuntu becomes available every six months, and every fourth release becomes a Long-Term-Support (LTS) version.

Google's self driving car is powered by a stripped version of Ubuntu. Google is known to be a customer of Ubuntu Advantage, Ubuntu's enterprise services, in managing their Goobuntu desktops, a modified LTS version of Ubuntu.

Ubuntu One, which is personal cloud storage integrated with Ubuntu, runs on Amazon S3. According to the cloudmarket.com, Ubuntu Linux is ranked first on Amazon EC2 in terms of the number of EC2 images created by users; 54% of created EC2 images are Ubuntu images. Across all the major public cloud offerings be it Amazon, Rackspace, HP and others the number one guest OS is Ubuntu. Whether you measure by the total number of instances running, or the diversity of customized images available from vendors, Ubuntu is the preferred guest OS on the public cloud, for large institutions and startups alike.

Today most of the clouds are built on Linux platform than on any another Linux operating system. Some of the key benefits of using Ubuntu for cloud include:

- Compatibility with established cloud standards including the Amazon EC2 and OpenStack APIs. This gives organizations the freedom to move between cloud providers, or push private workloads out to public clouds on demand
- Freedom of choice with support for a widerange of hypervisors, network components, storage components, presentation technologies and more
- Massive scalability based on fast, lightweight messaging between cloud components
- High availability with features such as node evacuation, that keep the cloud running normally if a component fails or any other issues in between
- Backing from a worldwide community that incorporates more than 70 leading technology companies and tens of thousands of developers. This community delivers new, value-added features regularly and fixes issues as they arise
- Access to management tools like Landscape which provide reporting and monitoring on your workloads wherever they are running in the public cloud, private cloud, or plain old on-the-metal deployments

- Use of Cloud Deck for hybrid cloud coordination, giving your organization a single set of credentials for employees that can give controlled access to multiple public and private cloud regions through a single cloud API, with quotas and reporting.

Thus, Ubuntu has a clear edge than all other open source Linux operating system for cloud technology.

For cloud computing platform to install the OpenStack cloud we use Ubuntu 12.04 LTS server edition. Today both Ubuntu and OpenStack have tied up to develop many more cloud tools and solutions. As of 2013 it is commonly used by all the users and the IT companies. The term LTS stands for long term support it will support for 5 years. The recent Ubuntu version released includes 13.10 for desktop. Ubuntu server edition 12.04.03 LTS is the another commonly used one.

Ubuntu Cloud is built into Ubuntu Server 12.04 LTS. Like the rest of the Ubuntu operating system, it is free from licensing restrictions, enabling Ubuntu to deliver on the promise of open-source software using which one can deploy as much cloud as you want without needing to count licenses, anywhere. That flexibility has made Ubuntu the rising star of large-scale deployments, for web and big data.

Widely certified and supported for the long term, Ubuntu 12.04 LTS till 2017 is the most reliable platform on which to move from a pilot or proof of concept to a large-scale production deployment. It offers the robustness and agility you need for rapid scaling of the underlying cloud, while offering first-class support for the key virtualization technologies that underpin successful OpenStack deployments with the longest track record of support for KVM and LXC. Thus at least for few years from now Ubuntu is seen as the trend for the cloud computing mainly for OpenStack cloud at least.

Some of the new features added to Ubuntu 12.04 LTS include:

- Unity Dash's default home screen has changed. Now, it shows Recent Apps first, Recent Files next and lastly, your most recent Downloads
- Unity Dash now has quick lists support, which is really nice and user friendly
- A new home folder quick lists has been added to Ubuntu 12.04
- Apart from the usual three Unity lenses (Applications, Files and Music), there is now an additional Video lense too. (Keyboard Shortcut Super + V). It lets you select and play videos from a variety of sources ranging from your local collection to YouTube Movies, BBC iPlayer and TED Talks to name a few
- Head up display popularly known as HUD is a default now. Earlier it was said HUD will replace the menu options in utility applications but not done
- Size of launcher icons can now be changed directly changed from Wallpapers menu. No need to install CCSM just to do that anymore
- The default launcher behavior has been changed. This is perhaps the biggest visible change to new Unity. Launcher won't be in the dodge windows state anymore (by default) and instead will be always visible
- Dodge windows is not even an option anymore. It is completely removed

- Initiating Alt + Tab shows you just the open windows in the current desktop and not from all the desktops like it used to be
- Rhythmbox has just replaced Banshee in Ubuntu 12.04
- Finally, upgrading from the second alpha release of Precise Pangolin, this new beta version includes the 3.2.0-17.27 Ubuntu kernel, which is based on version 3.2.6 of the upstream stable Linux kernel.

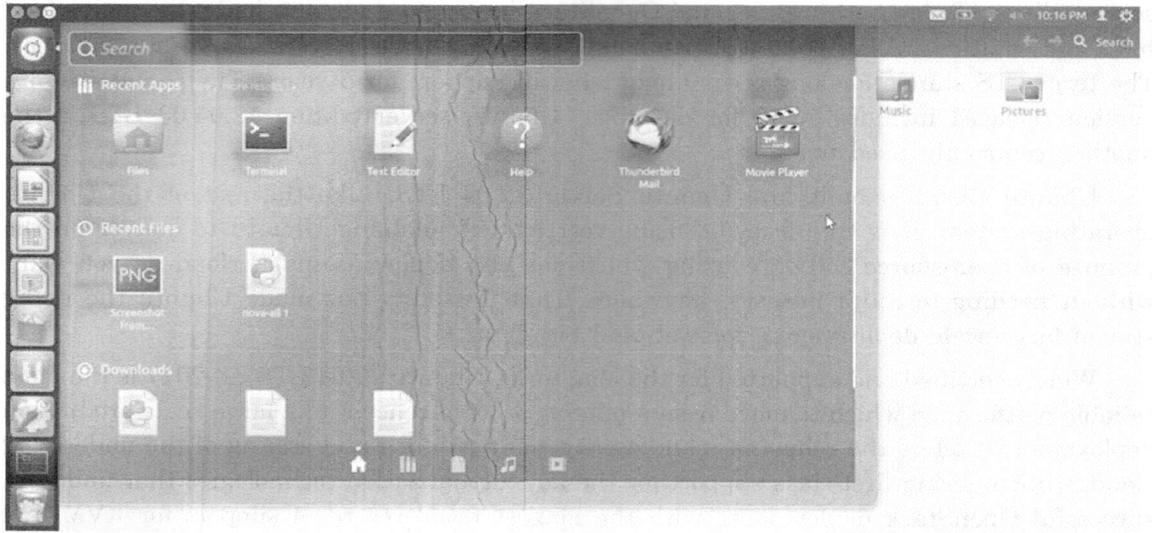

Figure 8.2 Ubuntu 12.04 operating system.

Thus, working with Ubuntu is very user friendly and a right choice for all networking technologies.

8.2 WORKING WITH COMMAND PROMPT

In the previous section, we saw the Ubuntu environment and its functionalities that are making it a popular one. We will see some of the useful commands to work in Linux environment. Though the lists of commands are huge in number and it is not possible to remember all of them. So let us discuss some of them now. The operating systems in Linux are GUI based but certain functionalities can be handled well only by using commands.

Terminal is a core part of Linux working environment. While in GUI mode of operating system everything is seen in the form of icons or visible one. But in Linux though most of them are in the form of icons too but working with commands in terminal is seen as the right way of handling several operations. When we talk about Linux we mainly use for all server related functions and networking purposes. After all Linux is seen as the safe environment for all confidential networking purposes.

Former Indian president and scientist APJ ABDUL KALAM was a firm supporter of open source technology. Once he asked the Indian army to use the Linux operating system environment for all confidential works.

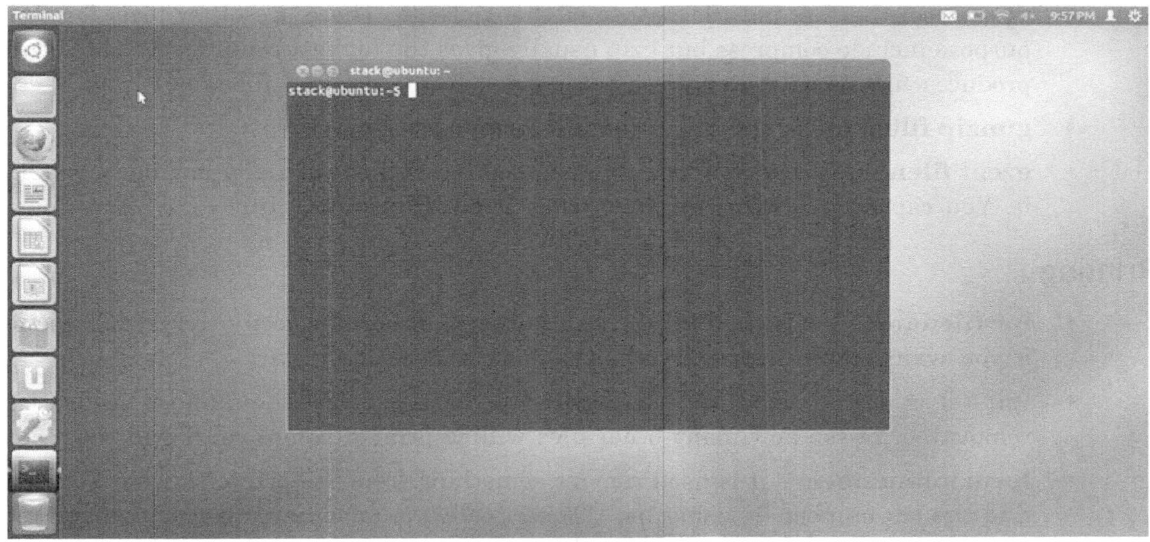

Figure 8.3 Ubuntu terminal.

File Related Commands

- **ls** – lists all files in the directory
- **mv filename1 filename2 –** it moves the file
- **cp filename1 filename2** – it copies the content from one file to another
- **rm filename –** removes the file
- **cat file name** – it displays the contents of the file in the standard output device
- **file filename** – it provides the type of data within the file
- **wc filename** – tells you how many lines, words, and characters there are in a file
- **emacs filename** – is an editor that lets you create and edit a file
- **diff filename1 filename2** – compares files, and shows where they differ
- **chmod options filename** – lets you change the read, write, and execute permissions on your files
- **chown filename** – it changes the owner of the file
- **ff** – find files anywhere on the system
- **tail file name** – displays the last n lines of the file
- **touch filename** – creates an empty file with the specified name
- **tar filename** – it allows to store and extract files from the tarfile

File Compression

- **gzip filename** – compresses files, so that they take up much less space. Usually text files compress to about half their original size, but it depends very much on the size of the file and the nature of the contents. There are other tools for this purpose include compress but gzip usually gives the highest compression rate. gzip produces files with the ending gz appended to the original filename

- **gunzip filename** – uncompresses files compressed by gzip
- **gzcat filename** – lets you look at a gzipped file without actually having to gunzip it. You can even print it directly, using **gzcat filename | lpr**

Printing

- **lpr filename** – it is used to print . Use the -P option to specify the printer name if you want to use a printer other than your default printer
- **lpq** – it is used to check out the printer queue, e.g. to get the number needed for removal, or to see how many other files will be printed before yours will come out
- **lprm jobnumber** – it is used remove something from the printer queue. You can find the job number by using lpq. Theoretically you also have to specify a printer name, but this isn't necessary as long as you use your default printer in the department
- **genscript** – it converts plain text files into postscript for printing, and gives you some options for formatting
- **dvips filename** – it is used to print **.**dvi files these are the files produced by LaTeX. You can use **dviselect** to print only selected pages

Directories

- **mkdir dirname** – it is used to make a new directory
- **rmdir dirname** – it is used to remove the empty directory
- **cd dirname** – it is used to change directory
- **cd** – it is used to go to the parent directory
- **pwd** – it tells you where your currently in

User Related Command

- **w** – it tells you who's logged in, and what they are doing
- **who** – it tells you who's logged on, and where they are coming from
- **whomi** – it returns the username
- **su** – switch to another user account
- **finger username** – it gives you lots of information about that user, e.g. when they last read their mail and whether they're logged in. Often people put other practical information, such as phone numbers and addresses, in a file called **.**plan. This information is also displayed by 'finger'
- **last -1 username** – it tells you when the user last logged on and off and from where. Without any options, last will give you a list of everyone's logins

- **talk username** – it lets you have a (typed) conversation with another user
- **write username** – it lets you exchange one-line messages with another user
- **elm** – it lets you send e-mail messages to people around the world and read them. It's not the only mailer you can use, but the one we recommend
- **date** – it shows the current date and time
- **cal** – it shows the calendar of the current month
- **man** – it gives the usage of various commands in the Linux

Web Related Commands

- **rlogin hostname** – it lets you connect to a remote host
- **telnet hostname** – it lets you connect to a remote host
- **ftp hostname** – it lets you download files from a remote host which is set up as an ftp-server. This is a common method for exchanging academic papers and drafts. The most important commands within ftp are **get** for getting files from the remote machine, and **put** for putting them there. **mget** and **mput** let you specify more than one file at once.
- **lynx** – it lets you browse the web from an ordinary terminal
- **ssh user@mahine** – it allows you to remotely login to the another Linux machine in the network. You can exit the ssh by typing exit in the terminal

Miscellaneous Commands

- **echo $VARIABLE** – it shows the value of an environment variable
- **setenv** – it lets you set environment variables
- **unset VAR** – it lets you un-set environment variables
- **| (piping)** – it lets you execute any number of commands in a sequence. The second command will be executed once the first is done, and so forth, using the previous command's output as input.
- **Passwd** – it is used to change the password
- **Clear** – this commands cleans the command prompt to begin the fresh start
- **Df** – it displays the available disk space
- **Du** – it shows how much space each file takes up
- **Ps** – provides the snapshot of the currently running process
- **Top** – displays the resources being used by the system press q to exit
- **Kill** – it is used to stop the process from running
- **Killall** – it is used to stop the process using its name
- **Shutdown** – shutdown or restart the Linux

Now let us see some of the Ubuntu commands in specific. These commands are also useful to install the cloud computing tools in the Ubuntu platform.

- To get the list of all built in ubuntu commands type this in terminal

  compgen -b
- To get the full list of all ubuntu commands type this in terminal

  Compgen –c

  Or

  Compgen –c | more
- To gain the root privilege in root we can use sudo in front of all commands called super user

  sudo X where X is the command
- To run the GUI application in root privilege use gksudo

  gksudo --app name--
- To update any package or any version of operating system use

  sudo apt-get update

  Or

  sudo apt-get upgrade to upgrade the software
- To install any software or package use

  sudo apt-get install X

  where X is the name of the software
- To remove any software or package use

  sudo apt-get remove X

  where X is the name of the software
- To fix the packages type this command

  apt-get -f install
- To fix the broken packages use this command

  dpkg –configure -a
- To get the version of Ubuntu operating system use this command

  lsb_release –a
- To get the version of kernel use this command

  uname -r
- To get all kernel information use this command

  uname -a
- To covert the command line interface to GUI edition we can use this command sudo apt-get install Ubuntu-desktop
- To view the network configuration type this command

  Ifconfig

- To display information from wireless type this command

  iwconfig

- To start the network interface up

  ifup

- To stop the network interface

  ifdown

- To scan the wireless networks use this command

  Sudo iwlist scan

- To manually configure the network use this command

  /etc/network/interfaces

- To restart the network use this command

  sudo /etc/init.d/networking restart

- To download files from internet use wget

  wget —url of the content—

- To shutdown the computer from terminal use

  shutdown –h

  where h is the time

- To make an iso file from a directory containing other files and sub-directories via the terminal then use

  mkisofs -o image.iso -R /path/to/folder/

- To check the architecture of CPU as 32 or 64 bit use

  arch

- To disable wifi or Bluetooth in Ubuntu we can use the rfkill command line tool

  rfkill block wlan

  rfkill block Bluetooth

  to unblock again use the keyword unblock instead of block

- IPTraf is a command line utility that allows to monitor network activities in real-time. Install it in Ubuntu with this command

  sudo apt-get install iptraf and use it as

  sudo iptraf

- To force close an unresponsive software, run xkill from the terminal then click the software window to close it.

  xkill

- To capture your screen and record it in a video, use ffmpeg

  sudo apt-get install ffmpeg

  ffmpeg -f x11grab -s wxga -r 25 -i :0.0 -sameqoutput.mpg

- The dtrx tool allows to extract most archive files without the hassle of memorizing the various extraction commands. To install it, run this command

  sudo apt-get install dtrx and use it as

  dtrx file.zip
- To check read/write speed of your hard drive on the terminal, use this command

  sudo hdparm -tT /dev/sda
- To get the maximum read speed of your optical drive with this command

  eject -X
- To increase/decrease read speed of a CD/DVD inserted into your optical drive, enter this command followed by the desired speed

  eject -x 4
- To check the speed of the RAM from terminal use

  sudo dmidecode -t 17 | awk -F":" '/Speed/ { print $2 }'
- To get the current temperature of your processor, use this command

  acpi –t
- To check CPU temp in real-time, run this command

  watch -n 1 acpi –t
- To check for how long your computer or laptop has been running since you powered it on, use this command

  Uptime

  Some of the other privileges commands in Ubuntu include
- **sudo su** - open a root shell
- **sudo su user** - open a shell as user
- **sudo -k -** forget sudo passwords
- **gksudo command** - visual sudo dialog (GNOME)
- **kdesudo command** - visual sudo dialog (KDE)
- **sudo visudo** - edit /etc/sudoers
- **gksudo nautilus** - root file manager (GNOME)
- **kdesudo konqueror** - root file manager (KDE)

Some of the application commands in Ubuntu include:

- **nautilus** – it is used to handle the File Manager operations (GNOME)
- **dolphin** – it also used to handle File Manager operations (KDE)
- **konqueror** – it opens the specified URL of the website (KDE)
- **kate** – it opens the text editor (KDE)
- **gedit** – it also opens the text editor (GNOME)

some malicious commands, do not use without knowing them exactly

This commands will erase your hard drive

sudo mkfs

sudo mkfs.ext3

sudo mkfs.bfs

sudo mkfs.cramfs

sudo mkfs.ext2

sudo mkfs.minix

sudo mkfs.msdos

sudo mkfs.reiserfs

sudo mkfs.vfat

This commands can damage your operating system.

sudo rm -rf / - This will delete all your files on your system

sudo rm -rf * - This will delete all the files in the current folder

rm -rf * or rm -rf *.* - This will delete all the files in the current folder

rm -rf ~/ & - This will destroy your home directory

Still many more commands are available but we have discussed only some of the important ones and those helpful in cloud installation. Working in a command prompt looks difficult first but later we will get used to it.

8.3 UBUNTU ENTERPRISE CLOUD

In the previous section, we saw in detail about the overall functioning of the Ubuntu operating system. We also saw the working of various commands and their usage in command line interface operating system. In this section, we see the integration of the cloud tool with the Ubuntu.

Quite before 2010 the Eucalyptus cloud was the most famous cloud tool. It was used by many researchers, educational institutions and other IT companies respectively. It was installed under the CentOS platform of Linux. It included several commands and took at least four hours to install the cloud controller. Then we again install the cloud node separately with several commands using all the required networking changes and the suitable hardware. It was very tedious, time consuming and required many networking settings. Thus this form of installation was not user friendly. It was very rigid and hardly only few people had known the secrets of cloud installation. It was always a mystery and was not easily shared to everyone or people never knew the actual and a standard steps to be fallowed in installing Eucalyptus cloud. To be more clear the Eucalyptus cloud installation in CentOS was very clumsy and a hard path to achieve success.

Thus to overcome the hard path in cloud installation and to solve the mystery in it Ubuntu combined with the Eucalyptus cloud company and designed an operating system called *Ubuntu Enterprise Cloud* popularly known as UEC. The UEC was a very user friendly and a simple way to configure the private cloud using the Eucalyptus tools. The Eucalyptus cloud tool was merged into the Ubuntu operating system to give UEC. Thus a whole new operating system was designed to install only cloud. One can easily configure the cloud controller and node using the UEC installation. The whole process was as simple as operating system installation. With the revolution of UEC the CentOS installation of cloud was avoided by all the users. Ubuntu was purely seen as the future of cloud from this stage. More and more cloud tools and solutions began to arrive in Ubuntu platform. Almost all the other Linux operating system lost their competition to Ubuntu in terms of its cloud computing technology revolution.

Figure 8.4 Ubuntu enterprise cloud.

Similar to Eucalyptus, UEC also had five components with various functions in cloud they include

Node Controller (NC)

A UEC node is a VT enabled server capable of running KVM as the hypervisor. UEC automatically installs KVM when the user chooses to install the UEC node. The VMs running on the hypervisor and controlled by UEC are called instances. Eucalyptus supports other hypervisors like Xen apart from KVM, but Canonical has chosen KVM as the preferred hypervisor for UEC.

Node Controller (NC) runs on each node and controls the life cycle of instances running on the node. The NC interacts with the OS and the hypervisor running on the node on one side and the Cluster Controller (CC) on the other side.

Its major function include:

- Collection of data related to the resource availability and utilization on the node and reporting the data to CC
- Instance life cycle management.

Cluster Controller (CC)

Cluster Controller (CC) manages one or more Node Controllers and deploys/manages instances on them. Cluster Controller also manages the networking for the instances running on the Nodes under certain types of networking modes of Eucalyptus. CC communicates with Cloud Controller (CLC) on one side and NCs on the other side.

Its Functions include:

- To receive requests from CLC to deploy instances
- To decide which NCs to use for deploying the instances on

- To control the virtual network available to the instances
- To collect information about the NCs registered with it and report it to the CLC

Walrus Storage Controller (WS3)

WS3 provides a persistent simple storage service using REST and SOAP APIs compatible with S3 APIs.

Its Functions include:

- Storing the machine images
- Storing snapshots
- Storing and serving _les using S3 API

WS3 should be considered as a simple storage system.

Storage Controller (SC)

SC provides persistent block storage for use by the instances. This is similar to the Elastic Block Storage (EBS) service from AWS.

Its Functions include:

- Creation of persistent EBS devices
- Providing the block storage over AoE or iSCSI protocol to the instances
- Allowing creation of snapshots of volumes

Cloud Controller (CLC)

The Cloud Controller (CLC) is the front end to the entire cloud infrastructure. CLC provides an EC2/S3 compliant web services interface to the client tools on one side and interacts with the rest of the components of the Eucalyptus infrastructure on the other side. CLC also provides a web interface to users for managing certain aspects of the UEC infrastructure.

Its Functions include:

- Monitor the availability of resources on various components of the cloud infrastructure, including hypervisor nodes that are used to actually provision the instances and the cluster controllers that manage the hypervisor nodes
- Resource arbitration – Deciding which clusters will be used for provisioning the instances
- Monitoring the running instances

In short, CLC has a comprehensive knowledge of the availability and usage of resources in the cloud and the state of the cloud.

The UEC involves generally two server machines to manage cloud and a single client machine. Generally we require some 2 to 4 GB of RAM to install UEC. The disk space of about 50 to 100 GB is also required. The high speed internet without any firewall is required as we enter a command in the terminal it downloads all the required packages and software from the repositories. Even if a single package is not downloaded properly the whole installation fails. We must enable the virtualization only then UEC installs else it will fail during installation itself. In order to install UEC we need to assign the required IP range and gateway respectively. We need to connect them using the LAN cable.

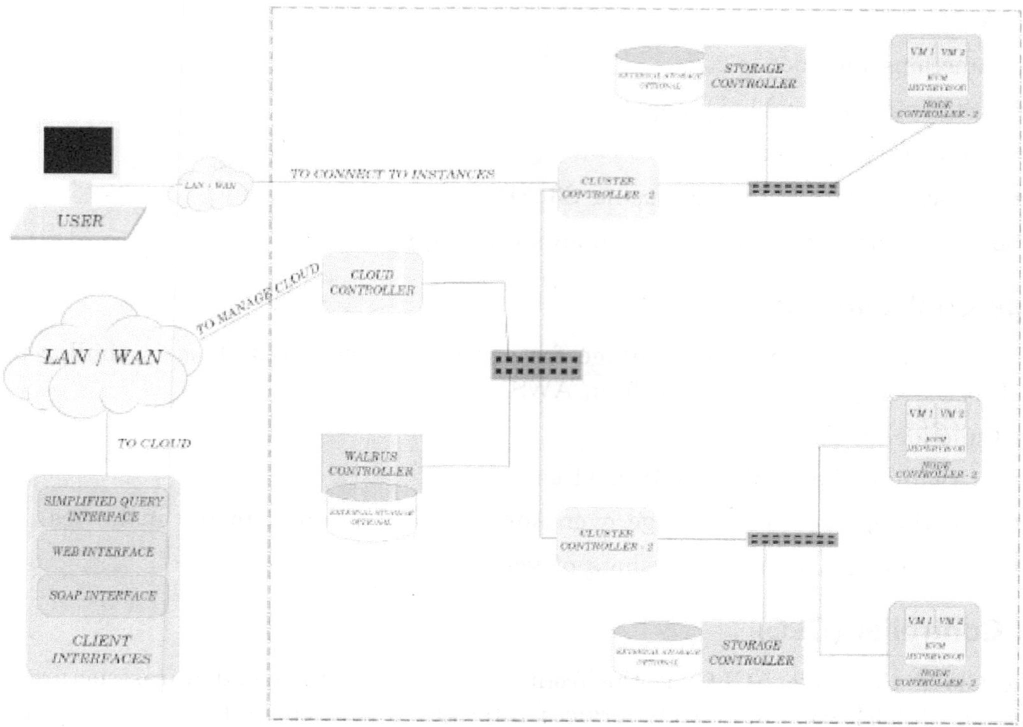

Figure 8.5 Ubuntu enterprise cloud.

With the cloud installation one can practically understand all the networking concepts and have hands on working experience. Without knowing any basic commands in Linux installing cloud is a fatal mistake on the user part. If the user is caught in some problem then it is very difficult to resolve them. Linux is quite a new and a vast world hence one must not underestimate it with just as a common operating system.

UEC can be installed in virtual OS software too instead of physical machines. Installing cloud in virtual OS can be a good start to learn the technology and understand all the basics. Virtual OS has same functionalities as the physical machine. But it is preferable to install in physical machine at later stages as virtual OS is just a virtual form of operating system inside the software. To some extent we can say virtual OS has some limitations compared to physical machines. While working with physical machines the user must have thorough knowledge to work with all networking components like LAN cable, switch, router and etc.

Finally the output is viewed in the web browser by entering the concerned IP address. Ultimately using all these cloud tools we run the virtual instance of a tiny operating system commonly known as image. Speaking technically the image actually migrates from the server machine to the client machine. In a real time we view the concept of virtualization and distributed by these cloud tools. It is a very good experience to work in real time and understand all the networking concepts. The output of UEC and OpenStack cloud almost resemble similar at some stages.

Some of the common errors in UEC installation include:

- Hardware virtualization error
- Failure in installation of anyone of the component
- Mistake in assigning the proper IP and gateway
- Authentication error at dashboard login
- Dashboard display error at the IP address
- All or few cloud services unavailable or failed
- Unable to create the users or project
- Image unavailable in cloud
- Image is inactive in state
- Lesser RAM in the physical machine to create instance
- Lesser disk space in physical machine to run UEC
- Failure in launching the instance of the image
- UEC software itself might have some problem leading to failure in installation

And so on are other errors too. The errors may be due to some underlying bugs or due to any other failure at the time of installation. The failure can be due to supported packages unavailable or have not been installed initially.

There are many interactive forums, discussion websites, tutorials, videos and other blogs available on cloud installation. In case of any error one can post their queries there and ask for solution from them. It may also be possible that many people already got same error before and the solution is made available. We can use such hints while we are caught in some issues.

8.4 UBUNTU AND OPENSTACK

In the previous section, we saw the Eucalyptus cloud with Ubuntu platform. We saw how Eucalyptus cloud shifted from CentOS platform to Ubuntu and made the revolution as UEC. Now in this section let us see the integration of Ubuntu with another cloud tool called OpenStack. This is the current trend as of 2013 in the cloud computing technology. Ubuntu and OpenStack have a bright future at least in the upcoming few years from now.

Eucalyptus cloud was doing its peak with the IT industry in 2010 but it lost its hold later. From late 2011 Eucalyptus began to decline due to various technical and other issues. By 2012 OpenStack cloud began to make its wide impact in IT industry. OpenStack was used by large sections of the people for cloud installation. OpenStack combined with Ubuntu to give many more cloud tools and solutions respectively.

HP, AT & T, Ericsson and Rackspace they all have build their clouds on Ubuntu plus OpenStack, the platform of choice for organizations deploying large scale cloud IAAS service model as of today. Today OpenStack is the buzzword in cloud technology. Almost all the IT companies and the business organizations are aligning with them to set up the cloud infrastructure. Ubuntu also has the depth and quality to stand up a large scale cloud infrastructure. Whether the user is focused on moving grid applications to a cloud, or integrating clouds or combining other advanced networking technologies together or finding efficiencies in central IT provisioning systems, Ubuntu has been used by companies to achieve their goals for private cloud. thus in the upcoming year we would see many more large companies too using the Ubuntu infrastructure to design, deploy, test and analyze a real time cloud.

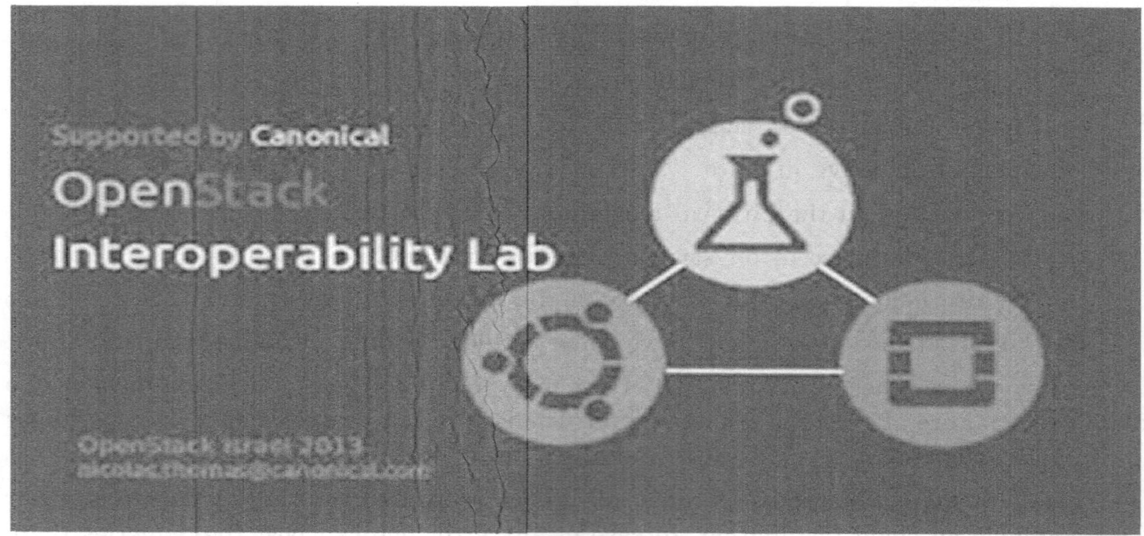

Figure 8.6 Ubuntu and OpenStack.

Ubuntu is the reference operating system for the OpenStack project, making it the easiest route to an OpenStack cloud, whether for private use or as a commercial public cloud offering. All OpenStack code is freely available under the Apache 2.0 license, so anyone can run it, build on it, or contribute to the project. This development model has fostered a vibrant community, with the largest ecosystem of tools, solutions and service providers. People get the latest updates and security fixes fast. OpenStack is tested every day on Ubuntu by the developers of OpenStack itself, making Ubuntu the platform with the widest testing of OpenStack's latest code. Thus Ubuntu is seen as the right platform to install the OpenStack cloud as of 2013 and UEC is outdated, no more seen as right choice for cloud.

The relationship between Ubuntu and OpenStack is so significant that both the brands are focused on high quality governance, platforms for mass computing, predictable schedules and robust releases. The release schedules of the two projects are synchronized, ensuring that OpenStack updates and releases are immediately available on widely deployed releases of Ubuntu. Thus both the Ubuntu and OpenStack are interlinked to each other in many ways.

Ubuntu has included IAAS service model of cloud since 2009. That's why more clouds are built on Ubuntu than any other platforms of Linux operating system. Though other operating systems are also working in cloud technology equally but Ubuntu has taken a way ahead of all of them. Since 2011 they have included the latest version of OpenStack in every Ubuntu release, as well as making it available for the most recent LTS. So once the user has deployed OpenStack on an LTS release of Ubuntu, the user can move to newer versions of OpenStack without changing the production OS. Thus the integration of OpenStack and Ubuntu is very user friendly atmosphere to all the users of cloud technology.

Ubuntu's OpenStack IAAS covers compute, storage and networking, just like Amazon's EC2 and S3. The Awsome component from Canonical provides APIs for OpenStack that are also implemented by Amazon's Web Services.

Ubuntu provides several advantages to the deployment of IAAS cloud by the end user or business organization. It is offered with two levels of support which include Standard and Advanced.

As we have already learnt the importance of standard in every technology. Standard cloud support is ideal for organizations considering cloud computing, along with those who have just begun deploying a private cloud for evaluation purposes. Standard cloud support provides business-hours support for a small base of machines. It offers support per physical machine and an unlimited number of additional Ubuntu machine images. Without standard the technology is never accepted by any organizations on a long run.

Advanced cloud support provides 24-hour support for production IT environments. It provides complete and comprehensive coverage of the Ubuntu Cloud Infrastructure platform including all physical machines and an unlimited number of additional Ubuntu machine instances. Customers get direct support from Ubuntu cloud experts ensuring critical applications and services are constantly available.

Some of the other advantages Ubuntu provides with the integration of cloud tools include:

- Legal assurance by Ubuntu
- New and advanced tools to manage cloud platforms
- Good knowledge base
- Better networking services
- Good server security
- Good package repository
- Clustering of technology
- High availability in spite of failure.

OpenStack has very active forum to discuss all the problems, issues, technical help, technology awareness, advancement and report all the bugs directly there. There are multiple technical people, researchers and other organizations working all over the world to expand and advance open source cloud technology of OpenStack. Every year from time to time OpenStack conferences are held where all the issues and problems of OpenStack are discussed.

All the suggestions are taken and the cloud tool is updated to give a new advanced one to all the users.

Today as of 2013 OpenStack cloud tool has tied with up Red hat Linux platform and also with Fedora Linux platform to develop the highly user friendly cloud installation process. Apart from Ubuntu slowly other Linux Platforms are also developing many more cloud solutions and tools. We can expect lot more new and advanced features from other Linux platforms too. We will see in last chapter on how to install and work with OpenStack cloud under the case study.

8.5 CLOUD TOOLS IN UBUNTU

In this section let us see some of the cloud tools developed by the Ubuntu. Ubuntu has made lot of efforts in revolutionizing cloud. It first tied up with Eucalyptus then with OpenStack. It has made lot of contribution to cloud technology by designing many cloud tools. Let us see the various tools features and its functionalities respectively.

Some of the cloud tools developed by Ubuntu include:

- Juju
- Metal as a service (MAAS)
- Landscape
- Jumpstart

And so on. Each tool has its own functionality and its feature.

JUJU

The speed with which capacity can be provisioned in the cloud shifts the bottleneck on efficiency from the provisioning stage to the deployment stage. For develops, the speed with which new iterations of business applications can be developed, tested and deployed is a critical measure of competence, competitiveness and effectiveness. In cloud technology deployment of apps also need to be paid more attention apart from designing and testing the application. Ubuntu further solved the deployment problem with a new orchestration tool called juju.

Juju is a quite unique tool designed by the Ubuntu platform. It is a single orchestration tool that works with private and public cloud deployments respectively. Juju packages the intelligence of installing, configuring, connecting and managing the services you are deploying. Juju is all about reuse and composition you can re-use other people's juju formulas with no modifications or changes, and you can couple multiple services together composing a bigger deployment that works as a single unit. Juju formulas can express deployment best-practices, and through sharing and collaboration, juju allows those best practices to spread through a community very efficiently. Thus using juju the deployment in cloud is becoming far easier and a dynamic one.

Core to the juju vision is a public repository of reusable juju formulas for popular application deployment scenarios. Those formulas are produced collaboratively, like a traditional Linux distribution, and follow the same pattern of governance as Ubuntu. Whatever you need to deploy, start by looking for a formula you can improve on, or start your own. With juju you can deploy services across multiple cloud or physical servers and manage those services via a handful of commands, built on the strong foundation of Ubuntu Server.

Juju is all about distilling infrastructure best practices into code, and sharing that code with peers. That allows for many benefits such as having a repeatable, reliable, auditable, and automated infrastructure-as-code procedures, as well as being able to stand on the shoulders of giants, reusing the work experience previously created.

Another attractive feature of juju is the use of charms. Charms give the real meaning to the usage of juju. Juju enables you to use Charms to deploy your developed application architectures to EC2, OpenStack, Azure, HP your data center and even your own Ubuntu based operating system. They encapsulate application configurations, define how services are deployed, how they connect to other services and are scaled. Charms are easily shared and there are several of them made available in Charm store.

Some of the commonly used charms include word press, Hadoop, Cassandra, ceph, mangoDB, mysql, mediawiki, rails and so on. One can easily work with juju start with deploying services and building relations immediately. Just find a charm and add it to your canvas to get your environment started. It is quite simple.

When you choose to build an infrastructure model as juju services, you are reusing the infrastructure experience of the Juju community. What is even more interesting perhaps is that juju does not force you to learn yet another domain specific language to model your infrastructure. Rather, juju provides you with command-line tools that are callable from any programming or scripting language. Very soon juju will also provide launchpad integration enabling the community to search for and leverage formulas written by other community members. One can think of it as PPAs for Infrastructure services.

One must install the juju first. It supports the Ubuntu platform, apple and windows operating system respectively. One can also work in demo version in the web browser itself. One can work with juju both in command prompt and also on GUI mode. Each component of your cloud deployment is deployed with a single command. Each component can be scaled up or down, with a single command. Each relationship between components is a single command. And all of those can be saved as a reusable stack. Thus it all works as simple as hitting a command in terminal.

Let us see the various steps for juju deployment:

- First choose the charm that you want from the charm store

  $charm search mysql

- Configure the selected charms by providing the number of instances, CPU power and the name

  $juju set mediawiki skin = monoblock name= 'cloudapp'

- Finally deploy the services

  $juju deploy mysql

- After several are running and active build relations among them. Each charm knows how to connect to each other

  $juju add-relation mysql wordpress

- Monitor the status of the deployed charm, in case of any failure the proper notification is issued

  $juju status

- Juju provides the details of all the activities going on with a well defined logs

  $juju debug-log

- With Juju you can simply scale applications by adding or removing service units knowing connections to other services are all taken care of automatically.

  $juju add-unit postgres -n 10

With juju you can easily save and export your environment to move it another cloud, move between dev, test and staging or share your set up with others in your organization. Juju makes your entire architecture completely portable.

Metal as a Service (MAAS)

In the chapter 6, we saw the various service models and its functionalities. Similarly Ubuntu has designed a service model which is MAAS. Metal as a Service (MAAS), a system that makes it quick and easy to set up the physical hardware on which to deploy complex scalable services, like Ubuntu's OpenStack cloud infrastructure. With MAAS, your new hardware can be part of your working infrastructure within minutes.

When a new node in cloud infrastructure boots up, MAAS steps in supplies all the information the node requires, reboots it and provides an Ubuntu image to install in it. In addition, MAAS can take care of hardware specific tasks such as burn-in tests, firmware and RAID upgrades and checking whether your hardware is Ubuntu certified. Thus it is much more automated and dynamic in managing the cloud node. MAAS provides enough abstraction to overcome hardware incompatibilities, saving you from costly upgrades and vendor lock-in. As we have already said before service models are cost effective and very user friendly one.

Metal as a Service (MAAS) provides a physical management layer that serves up machines on demand. Together which Juju, it enables you to deploy workloads onto physical metal that have all the same behaviors as workloads in the cloud, without the virtualization layer.

With Juju you can deploy, orchestrate and scale services in your MAAS cluster in seconds. We need not spend hours planning and implementing a service deployment. Just choose how many nodes your new service needs then apply a pre-written charm. When your needs change, you can monitor, scale and adjust deployment parameters in real time, and when you're finished with a service, Juju can remove it without a trace. We already saw the working of juju above in the same section.

Landscape

Landscape is an another unique tool from Ubuntu. It allows you to monitor your cloud environment, manage updates, and produce timely and accurate compliance reports. The rich, web-based GUI gives you an instant overview of everything going on in your cloud, from hardware to workloads. It is one of the best cloud management tools from Ubuntu.

Landscape is the systems management tool for Ubuntu, OpenStack included with Ubuntu. It allows you to manage, audit and report on your Ubuntu OpenStack cloud and services running within it easily as one, making your entire environment more cost-effective. There are numerous other OpenStack management tools are also available.

With the Landscape systems management tool, you can automate updates and manage physical, virtual and cloud-based systems from a single interface. It's easy to set up, easy to use and requires no special hardware. It features include:

- Management at scaling of cloud
- Deploy or rollback security updates into cloud
- Compliance reports
- Role based access
- Informative monitoring.

With Landscape you can manage your machines from anywhere and with a fully scriptable API, you can integrate it with your current Linux management tools, extending their capabilities and giving you the power to do more with fewer resources. Landscape is already used to manage hundreds of thousands of machines around the world, both physical and virtual, saving our customers money every day. Thus it a another well designed cloud management tool.

Jumpstart

Cloud Jumpstart is a fast, low-risk route to deploying private cloud infrastructure on your premises. Jumpstart builds your private cloud on your own hardware over the course of five days of on-site training, delivered by a Canonical services engineer. Jumpstart gives you a private cloud compatible with that architecture, on the hardware of your choice. The resulting cloud will be adapted to your preference for storage, network and compute and will remain compatible with our reference cloud for all workloads. Thus, it is a well designed cloud tool for private cloud. The engagement includes:

- A planning framework in which to make essential, core architecture decisions
- A seed Ubuntu OpenStack Cloud deployment, on up to 20 of your servers
- Training on tools and processes to support your cloud

Compatible with the Rackspace, HP and Amazon public clouds, Jumpstart starts from $9,000 and is guaranteed to take just five days, delivering a usable cloud that you can scale by adding additional nodes for compute and storage.

The scope of our standard Jumpstart engagement is limited to cloud deployment and training. Additional support, assurance, consulting, integration and professional services are available on a bespoke basis, both from Canonical and third-party providers.

8.6 LIVE CLOUD

In the last section of the chapter, let us see in detail about the configuration of *live clouds*. This is a quite different feature and a new way of setting a cloud. We will also see the demo of live cloud of OpenStack in Ubuntu.

The word *live* refers to the something that is currently available or exists and vanishes or goes offline later. Similarly to speak technically today many live solutions are available to learn or analyze some technology solutions.

For cloud computing installation instead of doing all the networking settings, fallowing all the steps, using all the commands and so on live cloud is far easier and readymade cloud. Live cloud is the easiest form to learn the cloud technology and it is too handy as it is a readymade. The live clouds are similar to the cloud installed in physical machines and virtual OS software but they disappear once we shut down the system. Live cloud is already pre built cloud tool in it. Which means the user need not fallow any installation step or do any networking settings. It is all already done and ready to use.

Now let us see the demo of OpenStack live cloud inside the VMware workstation software. VMware workstation is proprietary which means it is not free one has to pay money and use them. But there is a free trail of 30 days to use the software freely.

Figure 8.7 Ubuntu live cloud.

To start the live cd installation of OpenStack cloud in Ubuntu the user must download the operating system in the iso or other concerned format. We boot the downloaded operating system into the VMware workstation software and the installation starts from here.

The first screen looks like this like an Ubuntu desktop environment with a notepad file giving us the hints on the live cd.

In the terminal type the command to start configuring the OpenStack cloud components.

$ nova-setup.sh

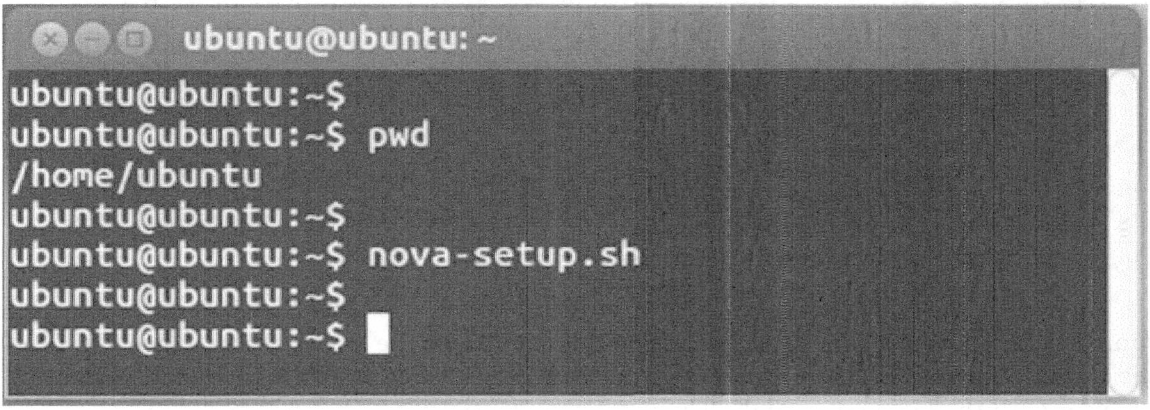

```
ubuntu@ubuntu: ~
ubuntu@ubuntu:~$
ubuntu@ubuntu:~$ pwd
/home/ubuntu
ubuntu@ubuntu:~$
ubuntu@ubuntu:~$ nova-setup.sh
ubuntu@ubuntu:~$
ubuntu@ubuntu:~$
```

Figure 8.8 Ubuntu command prompt with OpenStack command.

Then make some networking setting by using these commands.

By default this system uses standard network manager for network configuration. If you have DHCP server on your network, it will automatically set an IP and you can skip this step. In case you don't have DHCP server or you only have a WiFi connection, you need to set up the network manually. You can do that by using network manager or by using standard CLI tools:

$ sudo ifconfig eth0 192.168.99.100 up

In case you don't have any other connection on this machine add default route too

$ sudo route add default gw 192.168.99.1

Once network is set up, it's time to start nova and glance services.

$ start-OpenStack.sh

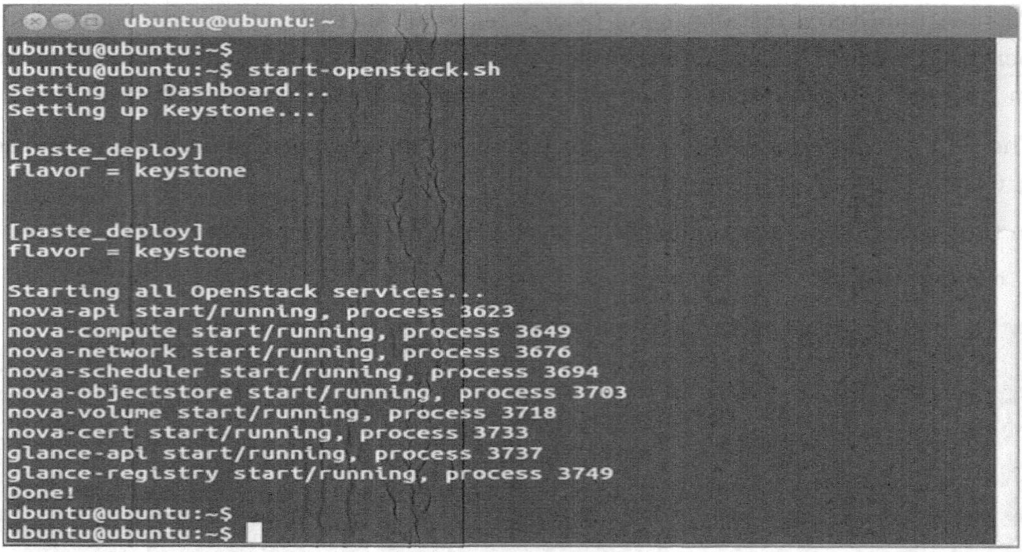
ubuntu@ubuntu: ~
ubuntu@ubuntu:~$
ubuntu@ubuntu:~$ start-openstack.sh
Setting up Dashboard...
Setting up Keystone...
[paste_deploy]
flavor = keystone
[paste_deploy]
flavor = keystone
Starting all OpenStack services...
nova-api start/running, process 3623
nova-compute start/running, process 3649
nova-network start/running, process 3676
nova-scheduler start/running, process 3694
nova-objectstore start/running, process 3703
nova-volume start/running, process 3718
nova-cert start/running, process 3733
glance-api start/running, process 3737
glance-registry start/running, process 3749
Done!
ubuntu@ubuntu:~$
ubuntu@ubuntu:~$

Figure 8.9 OpenStack installation completed.

Hence all the components of cloud are installed and the OpenStack cloud is ready to run. Now the output of the OpenStack cloud is viewed in the web browser. Type the IP of the virtual machine in the web browser, the OpenStack cloud is ready to launch prompting the user with the login credentials. The default credentials include username as Ubuntu and password as Ubuntu123.

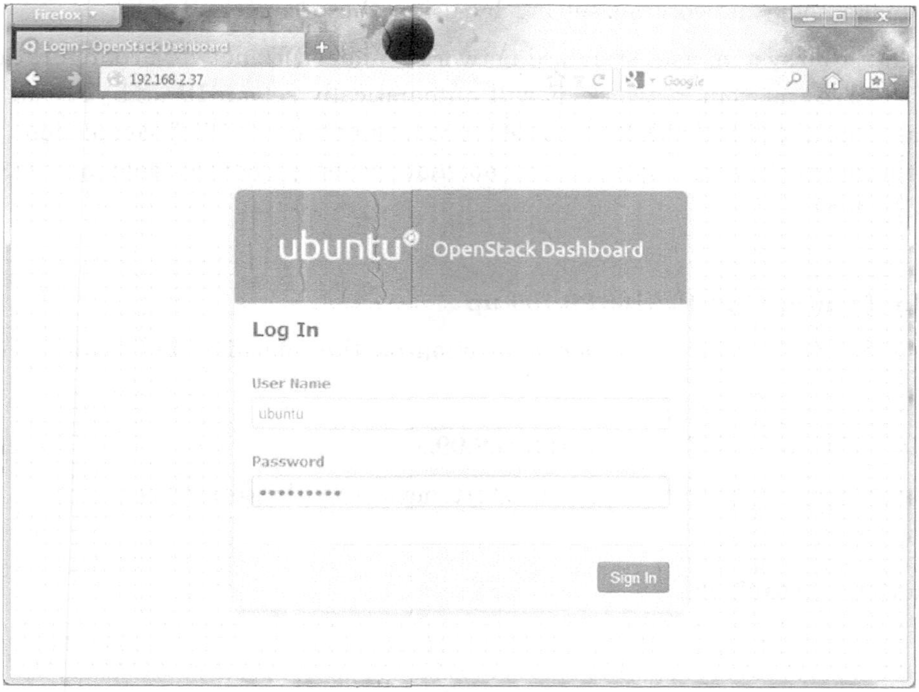
Firefox
Login - OpenStack Dashboard
192.168.2.37
ubuntu OpenStack Dashboard
Log In
User Name
ubuntu
Password
Sign In

Figure 8.10 OpenStack log in window.

Thus the cloud is configured. As of now we stop the discussion with the OpenStack installation. In the chapter 15, we will see in detail about how to work with OpenStack cloud.

SUMMARY

- *Ubuntu is an African word meaning humanity to others or I am what I am because of who we all are. The Ubuntu symbol in the official logo is called Circle of Friends, and represents freedom, collaboration, precision and reliability.*
- *Canonical Limited, the commercial company behind Ubuntu, is famously known as a virtual company with no national and geographic boundaries. According to its official source, Canonical has over 600 employees in nearly 200 cities across 30 countries, while the company has offices only at six locations.*
- *Ubuntu One, which is personal cloud storage integrated with Ubuntu, runs on Amazon S3. According to thecloudmarket.com, Ubuntu Linux is ranked first on Amazon EC2 in terms of the number of EC2 images created by users; 54% of created EC2 images are Ubuntu images.*
- *Terminal is a core part of Linux working environment. While in GUI mode of operating system everything is seen in the form of icons or visible one. But in Linux though most of them are in the form of icons too but working with commands in terminal is seen as the right way of handling several operations.*
- *Ubuntu combined with the Eucalyptus cloud company and designed an operating system called Ubuntu Enterprise Cloud popularly known as UEC. The UEC was a very user friendly and a simple way to configure the private cloud using the Eucalyptus tools. The Eucalyptus cloud tool was merged into the Ubuntu operating system to give UEC.*
- *A UEC node is a VT enabled server capable of running KVM as the hypervisor. UEC automatically installs KVM when the user chooses to install the UEC node. The VMs running on the hypervisor and controlled by UEC are called instances.*
- *By 2012 OpenStack cloud began to make its wide impact in IT industry. OpenStack was used by large sections of the people for cloud installation.*
- *HP, AT & T, Ericsson and Rackspace they all have build their clouds on Ubuntu plus OpenStack, the platform of choice for organizations deploying large scale cloud IAAS service model as of today.*
- *Ubuntu is the reference operating system for the OpenStack project, making it the easiest route to an OpenStack cloud, whether for private use or as a commercial public cloud offering. All OpenStack code is freely available under the Apache 2.0 license, so anyone can run it, build on it, or contribute to the project.*
- *The relationship between Ubuntu and OpenStack is so significant that both the brands are focused on high quality governance, platforms for mass computing, predictable schedules and robust releases.*

- *Today as of 2013 OpenStack cloud tool has tied with up Red hat Linux platform and also with Fedora Linux platform to develop the highly user friendly cloud installation process.*
- *Juju is a quite unique tool designed by the Ubuntu platform. It is a single orchestration tool that works with private and public cloud deployments respectively. Juju packages the intelligence of installing, configuring, connecting and managing the services you are deploying.*
- *Another attractive feature of juju is the use of charms. Charms give the real meaning to the usage of juju. Juju enables you to use Charms to deploy your developed application architectures to EC2, OpenStack, Azure, HP your data center and even your own Ubuntu based operating system.*
- *Metal as a Service (MAAS), a system that makes it quick and easy to set up the physical hardware on which to deploy complex scalable services, like Ubuntu's OpenStack cloud infrastructure. With MAAS, your new hardware can be part of your working infrastructure within minutes.*
- *Metal as a Service (MAAS) provides a physical management layer that serves up machines on demand. Together which Juju, it enables you to deploy workloads onto physical metal that have all the same behaviors as workloads in the cloud, without the virtualization layer.*
- *Landscape is the systems management tool for Ubuntu, OpenStack included with Ubuntu. It allows you to manage, audit and report on your Ubuntu OpenStack cloud and services running within it easily as one, making your entire environment more cost-effective.*
- *Cloud Jumpstart is a fast, low-risk route to deploying private cloud infrastructure on your premises. Jumpstart builds your private cloud on your own hardware over the course of five days of on-site training, delivered by a Canonical services engineer. Jumpstart gives you a private cloud compatible with that architecture, on the hardware of your choice.*
- *Live cloud is already pre built cloud tool in it. Which means the user need not fallow any installation step or do any networking settings. It is all already done and ready to use.*

Chapter 9

Mobile Cloud Computing

OBJECTIVE

- *To learn about the intersection of mobile and cloud technology*
- *To distinguish between mobile cloud and regular cloud*
- *To know architecture of Mobile Cloud Computing (MCC)*
- *To identify the pros and cons of MCC*
- *To resolve the issues in Mobile Cloud Adoption*

So far, we have seen about the various features, types, real time cloud, various open source of cloud computing. Let's look the cloud in different dimension. This arise a question in our mind "Why not merging the cloud concepts with mobile?" This understanding gives rise to new domain of computing **"Mobile Cloud Computing"**.

9.1 OVERVIEW OF MOBILE CLOUD COMPUTING

As we all have greater understanding of cloud, we will be able to figure **"What is Mobile Cloud Computing?"** Cloud is used in mobile apps for app development as well as hosting. The unique characteristics of mobile cloud apps makes the mobile cloud computing, a quite different domain from the regular cloud apps. Mobile Cloud is internet based data, applications and services accessed through laptop computers, tablets, smart phones and other portable devices. Mobile web has serious problems like limited memory and storage, small display screens, flaky browsers and flaky connections. Thus, Mobile apps rely on cloud mainly for computing, memory or storage, communication fault tolerance features. Mobile cloud computing is the combination of cloud computing and mobile networks in which the mobile applications are built, powered and hosted using cloud computing technology. Since Android is an open source which has greater advantage over other mobile operating systems, we will be seeing the merging of cloud with mobile especially Android in next chapter.

Figure 9.1 Mobile cloud computing.

Significance of Mobile Cloud Computing

Mobile cloud computing makes the app developers to build applications designed specifically for mobile phones. Mobile cloud apps which are available in the remote webserver are generally accessed through mobile browser. These types of apps does not need any installation of client application on the recipient phone. This type is also referred to as MoClo, which is derived from the word MObileCLOud.

Corporate Companies are moving to the mobile cloud by demand. Mobile users are demanding cloud applications for their smart phone and tablet applications so they can access companies' key applications. Employees of the IT companies are demanding access from their mobile devices. BlackBerry took an advantage on this need with its popular cloud-based mobile e-mail program. Because of this features of mobile cloud, work pattern are also changing in corporate sectors. Pew Internet Project surveyed many industrialists who think that by 2020, most people who use the Internet will work primarily through mobile applications on remote servers accessed through networked devices.

With changing patterns and work habits, the mobile ecosystem will consists of trillion cloud-ready devices. IBM predicts that by 2015, there will be 1 trillion cloud-ready devices. Mobile cloud computing can be thought as a mash up of mobile development and cloud computing. Cloud backed infrastructure provides the mobile user a rich featured application thorough internet. Intensive computing power and software platform support are crucial factors for most mobile applications. Storage and platform supports are must for these applications which is made available through cloud.

9.2 MOBILE CLOUD VS REGULAR CLOUD

Understanding the key differences between the mobile cloud and regular cloud helps in figuring out the new technology **"Mobile Cloud computing"**. Receiving cloud services on the go is termed as Mobile cloud. Apart from the basic differences between mobile cloud and regular cloud, there exist characteristic differences between the two which are listed below.

Differences	Mobile Cloud	Regular Cloud
Adjustments	Adjustments needed based on what the mobile device being used is.	No adjustments needed
Accessibility	Mobile devices go out of range at any time while the service is being delivered from the mobile cloud.	Stand-alone devices do not move out of range.
Fault Tolerant Communication	Extra precautions are taken to design mobile cloud, as there might be chance of frequent breaking communication.	Fault tolerance is not a concern in regular cloud.
Memory	Fixed memory in mobile devices	Memory expandable
Network latencies	Sensitive	Non-sensitive
Energy availability	Major concern	Not a crucial concern.
Testing	Addition testing is essential to test the synchronization of data on cloud and mobile device.	No addition testing required.

9.3 MOBILE CLOUD APPS VS NATIVE APPS

The key differences between native applications and mobile cloud applications are as follows.

Native Apps

A native app is one that is installed directly on a smart phone. In developer's perspective, it is an app that is stored on the mobile device or it is downloaded from an app store and installed on the mobile device. App developers create this native apps taking into the version of mobile device, PCs or tablets. This kind of App is developed for a particular device and its operating system. Data associated with this native app is also stored on the device. Latest technology available on mobile devices like GPS and camera can be used by native Apps.

Mobile Cloud Apps

Mobile cloud apps can be related to Web-based applications. Similarities among mobile cloud apps and web apps are that they both run on servers and require the use of a browser on the mobile device to display app User Interface. In addition, they both are targeted for multiple mobile devices unlike native apps which are targeted for single mobile device. Both Web apps and cloud apps go hand in hand. Cloud based apps is an application running in cloud which is providing requested services to the recipient mobile devices through web apps. Unlike mobile devices, Cloud ready devices run cloud-based Web apps rather than native apps.

Mobile Users subscribe to cloud services and access remotely stored applications and their associated data over the Internet. The current trend is increasingly toward the mobile cloud even though mobile devices run a mix of Web-based cloud apps and native apps. There is no need to download and install Mobile cloud apps on mobile devices. Mobile cloud app UI can be viewed by users in a browser window on the remote device. An Internet connection is needed to use mobile apps running on a cloud.

To transfer data between a mobile device and a mobile cloud app, JSON over HTTP is used. **JSON** stands for Java Script Object Notation is an ideal data-interchange language. It is language independent. Few organizations offer both a native and mobile cloud versions of their applications.

Differences	**Mobile cloud Apps**	**Native Apps**
Downloading App	Not needed	Needed
Accessibility	Access applications present remotely	Cannot access remote applications
Targeted Audiences	Multiple mobile devices	Single mobile devices
Mobile App	Running on Mobile cloud server	Running on Mobile Device
Notifications	Not Supported	Supported
Access to latest technologies	Indirect access through API	Direct Access to on-device features such as GPS, Sound, Camera
UI Speed	Comparatively Slower	Faster

9.4 MOBILE CLOUD COMPUTING (MCC) ARCHITECTURE

Data processing and storage services are provided to the mobile users by Mobile Cloud Computing. All complex computing modules can be processed in clouds. Thus the recipient do not need any powerful configurations. Mobile devices are connected to the mobile networks through different base stations like base transceiver station (BTS), access point, or satellite that establish and control the connections and functional interfaces between the networks and mobile devices. Mobile users' requests and information like ID and location are transmitted to the central processors that are connected to servers providing mobile network services. Mobile network operators can provide services to mobile users as AAA which accounts to Authentication, Authorization, and Accounting based on the Home Agent (HA) and subscribers' data stored in databases. With the help of Internet Service Providers, Mobile networks can get connected to cloud computing servers. After that, the subscribers' requests are delivered to a cloud through the Internet. In the cloud, cloud controllers process the requests to provide mobile users with the corresponding cloud responses or services.

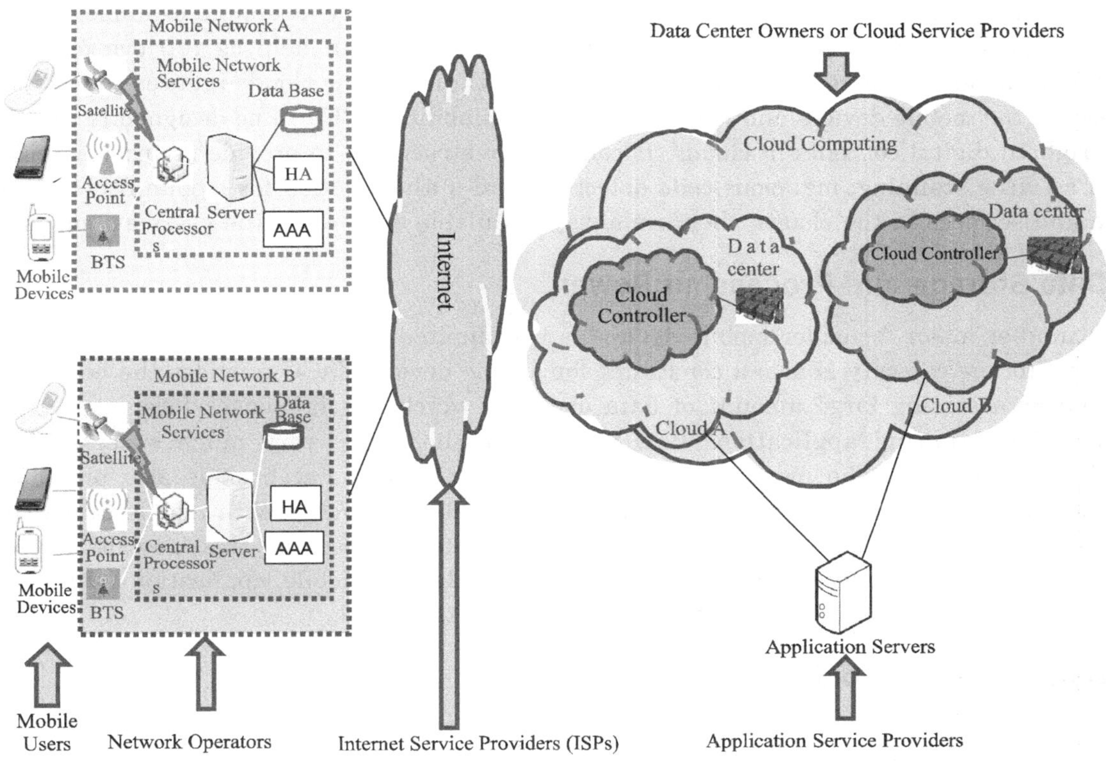

Figure 9.2 MCC Architecture.

9.5 ADVANTAGES OF MCC

There are certain advantages in making cloud to work in par with the mobile devices. Mobile computing itself has to diminish its own demerits like lower battery life, less storage capacity and comparatively worse processing power with the help of cloud computing. There exists a mutually beneficial relationship between mobile and cloud technology. Thus, it turns out to be the advantage of Mobile Cloud Computing. In the following, lets discuss how the cloud computing turns the mobile computing in to more advantageous.

1. Extending Battery Lifetime

Most essential factor for mobile devices is its battery life. To extend the battery life of mobile devices, lot of researches have been made. One profitable solution to this is offloading of computations and data. This type of offloading can be done by transferring the huge and complex calculations from recipient devices to the powerful servers on cloud. This idea helps to avoid complex calculations being done on mobile devices which lead to reduced time and power consumption.

2. Reliability and Availability

Since there are greater chances of losing data on mobile devices, cloud provides a solution for this problem too. All the data are stored and backed up in cloud, which minimizes the risk of losing data on mobile. Hence this improves reliability. A simple example is that backing up all contact details of a mobile device on cloud can help as retrieve our lost contacts whenever necessary. Keeping data and application in the clouds reduces the chance of lost on the mobile devices and hence improves availability.MCC can be designed to protect copyrighted digital contents in clouds. It can also be structured to provide security services such as virus scanning, malicious code detection, and authentication for mobile users. With data and services in the clouds, then are always available even when the users are moving.

3. Data Storage and Processing Power

Another major factor for mobile devices is very limited storage capacity and processing power. Storage capacity is also a constraint for mobile devices. MCC provides the benefit of storing or accessing large amount of data on cloud which has immense storage capacity. Many photo sharing applications like Flickr and ShoZu are very much successful in implementing MCC. The most popular social networking site Facebook is also providing cloud facility for its mobile users who share nearly 400 million/day. With mobile cloud, the users can save considerable amount of energy and storage space on their mobile devices since all images are shared and processed on the clouds. Mobile applications take the advantage of cloud since their data now is stored on the cloud.

4. Dynamic Provisioning

Mobile users have the provision of firing the service requests at anytime, anywhere. Advanced MCC reservation for invocation of services on cloud is not at needed with this on-demand accessibility. MCC is highly enough to support dynamic on-demand provisioning of resources on a fine-grained, self-service basis.

5. Scalability

With the scalability option on cloud, multiple users can subscribe to a service. Mobile applications can be performed and scaled to meet the unpredictable user demands. Service providers can easily add and expand a service. One of the key benefits of cloud computing is its scalability. Both up-scaling and down-scaling the services are possible as and when required. For example, most cloud service providers will allow increasing the existing resources to satisfy increased business needs or changes. Scaling the existing infrastructure is also on-demand which causes no expensive changes to your existing systems.

6. Flexibility

MCC allows IT employees to be more flexible — both in and out of the workplace. Employees can access files using mobile devices such as smart phones, laptops and notebooks. The ability to simultaneously share documents and other files over the Internet can also help support both internal and external collaboration. Many employers are now implementing "bring your own device (BYOD)" policies. A BYOD policy, or bring-your-own-device policy, is a set of rules governing a corporate IT department's level of support for employee-owned PCs, smart phones and tablets. In this way, mobile cloud computing provides high flexibility.

7. Multi-tenancy

Multi-tenancy is an architecture in which a single instance of a mobile application serves multiple customers. Each customer is called a tenant. Tenants may be given the ability to customize some parts of the application, such as colour of the user interface (UI) or business rules, but they cannot customize the application's code. Since application development and maintenance costs are shared, multi-tenant architecture is economical. It can be contrasted with single-tenancy which is an architecture in which each customer who has their own software instance and may be given access to code. With a multi-tenancy architecture, the provider only has to make updates once. Thus multi-tenancy supports synchronization. Service providers can share the resources and costs to support a variety of applications and large no. of users.

8. Ease of Integration

Multiple services from different providers can be integrated easily through the cloud and the Internet to meet the users' demands. In the cloud, software integration is usually something that occurs automatically. This means that you do not need to take additional efforts to customize and integrate your applications as per your preferences. This aspect usually takes care of itself. Not only that, cloud computing allows you to customize your options with great ease. Hence, you can handpick just those services and mobile applications that you think will best suit your mobile devices.

9.6 APPLICATIONS OF MCC

1. Mobile Commerce

Mobile Commerce simply called as M-commerce is the buying and selling of goods (commercial transactions) conducted electrically through mobile phone. It allows business models for commerce using mobile devices. Examples for such commercial transactions include Mobile financial, mobile advertising, mobile shopping. M-commerce applications face various challenges like low bandwidth, low processing speed. Integrated with cloud can help address these issues. Combining 3G and cloud yields a better result which increases data processing speed and security level.

Figure 9.3 Mobile Commerce.

2. Mobile Learning

M-learning provides the learning in one's own packet. This combines e-learning and mobility. Traditional m-learning has limitations on high cost of devices/network, low transmission rate, limited educational resources. Cloud-based m-learning can solve these limitations. It offers enhanced communication quality between students and teachers. This helps students learn distant study materials. M-learning set up a natural environment for collaborative learning. Several corporates are providing this king of training to their employees.

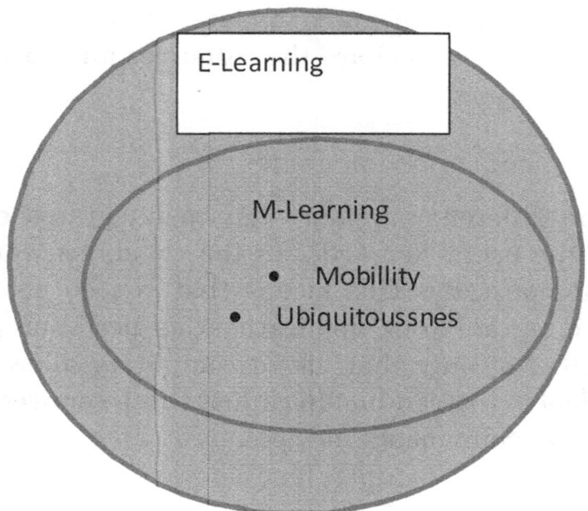

Figure 9.4 Mobile Learning.

3. Mobile Healthcare

Even though Mobile health care is at its infancy, many common tasks using M-healthcare are maintaining schedules, appointments and interacting with nurses, accessing patient records are done with the help of smart phones. The main benefits of using M-healthcare are to minimize the limitations of traditional medical treatment like limited storage, security/privacy, medical errors, and unreachable surgeons. M-healthcare provides mobile users with convenient access to resources like patient records.

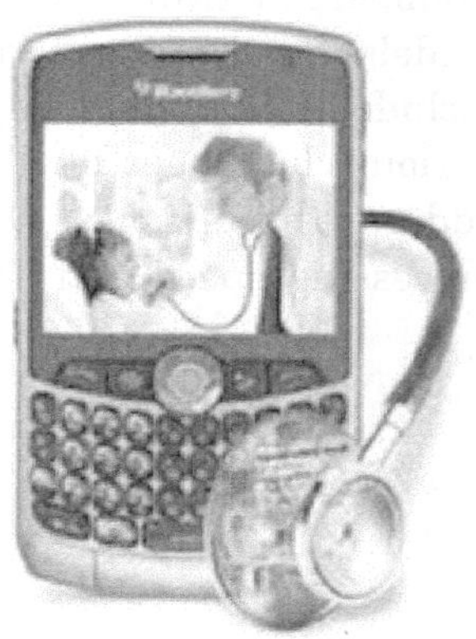

M-healthcare offers hospitals and healthcare organizations a variety of on-demand services on clouds. Examples: Comprehensive health monitoring services, intelligent emergency management system, Health-aware mobile devices that can able to detect pulse-rate, blood pressure, alcohol level and so on.

This type of health care is used to fill in the lack of hospital and medical care in rural or underdeveloped areas. IBM is joining hands with Boston's Children hospital for putting pediatrics in cloud. Cloud-based systems like OPEN Pediatrics help to access the knowledge which provides better care for patients all over the world. Prevention of new infections can be spread to facilitate general awareness to the people. Doctors are very much interested to adapt to this new technology since it can save lives irrespective of the distance.

4. Mobile Gaming

Mobile games vary from simple free games to paid games. M-game is a high potential market that can generate revenues for service providers. It's a kind of online gaming. The most interesting scenario is M-gaming provides multiplayer game environment, unique nick name selection and saving points and game levels in the game for continue playing. There are mainly two types of cloud gaming such as video streaming and file streaming.

In video streaming, the actual game is run on cloud server. Processing speed of this kind of games is extremely faster as every bit of processing is done on the cloud. File streaming is exact opposite where actual game is run on user's mobile device. In this small part of the game is initially downloaded to client machine for initial play. Users play, meanwhile the remaining part of the game will be downloaded.

5. M-Business

Since the burden of managing the hardware and software is not there with mobile cloud, all businesses are driven towards cloud. To business anywhere anytime, mobile cloud is inevitable. Scaling up and down the business is easy. Upgrades are automatic. Business magnets can save lots of money since they are going to pay what they need. Many different kinds of business apps like Customer Relationship Management (CRM), HR, accounting, purchasing, finance and much more are running in cloud. The latest innovations in cloud computing are making the business applications even more mobile and collaborative by popular social networking sites like Facebook and twitter. Marketers are now analysing the needs of the customers through social channels.

6. Other Applications

Mobile Cloud provides facilities like sharing photos/videos. Real time experience like travel, shopping and event management can be done with this mobile cloud. Other practical applications include different types of searching like Keyword-based searching, voice-based, tag-based searching. With mobile cloud, we can monitor different corners of a building, detecting traffic lights and currency reader for visually impaired. Cloud print android app help to print documents that stored on cloud. For storing and securing passwords, logins and other sensitive information, Safe Wallet password manager app is specially designed for smart devices. Automatic backing up contacts, pictures and videos and synching it to the cloud are also possible.

9.7 BRING YOUR OWN DEVICE (BYOD)

A BYOD policy, or bring-your-own-device policy, is policy in which corporate companies extend support for employee-owned PCs, smartphones and tablets. This helps in promoting "Work at Home". With this, employees can easily access the company's data stored in company's server from his/her own mobile device. A BYOD policy can take many different forms.Organizations can save money on corporate-issued PCs and laptops, instead giving employees a stipend to purchase and maintain technology equipment of their choosing. The access levels of crucial company's data often vary depending on a user's role in the organization.

B.Y.O.D.

(Bring Your Own Device)

Figure 9.6 BYOD.

9.8 ISSUES FOR MOBILE CLOUD ADOPTION

The way we perceive computing and mobility has changed a lot. Computing will provide the basic level of computing service that is considered essential to meet every day needs of the people. Cloud Computing is the latest paradigm proposed to deliver this vision. It has proved to be a promising solution for mobile computing for many reasons such as mobility, communication and portability. Due to the increased speed of the processors, larger screen size of mobile devices, battery consumption has also increased. Thus, battery life of mobile devices remains a key limiting factor in the design of mobile applications.

The two main contributors are limited battery capacity and an increasing demand from users for energy-hungry applications. User demand for battery usage is increasing by the day for resource intensive applications, like online video games, streaming video and sensors equipped on mobile devices that produce continuous streams of data about the user's environment.According to Microsoft's own telemetry data, almost 50% of a laptop's power goes to the LCD screen. Battery life is mainly drained by bigger and brighter panels. The rest of the energy output is almost equally divided by the CPU, hard disk, graphics card, network card, and chipset.

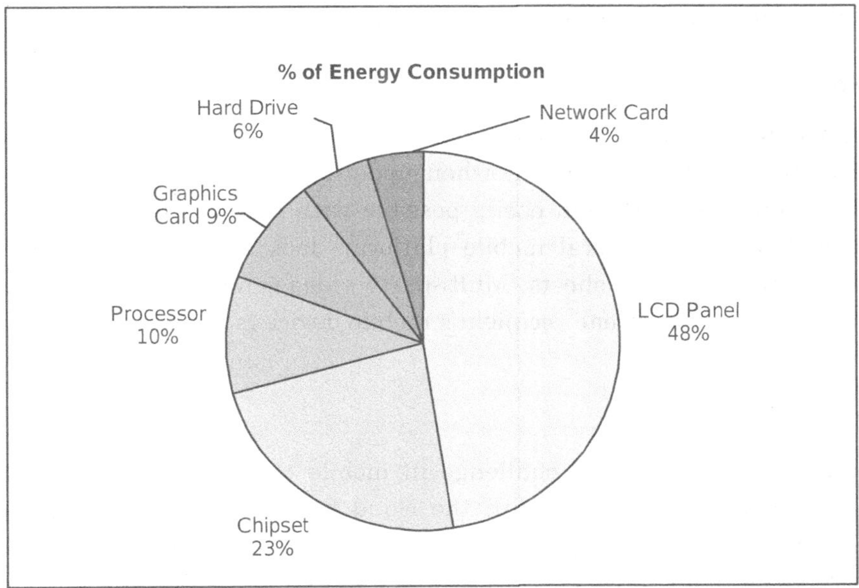

Storage is also another concern in mobile. Storage consumption depends up on the numbers of applications in mobile. Storage and energy consumption are the main concern when we talk about mobile computing alone.

Even though mobile cloud is rapidly growing with the increase in mobile users, there are certain challenges in adopting the mobile cloud. The following shows the limitations, both mobile and cloud are merged.

1. Security

Many mobile cloud applications are dealing with sensitive information. Securing this type of crucial information is extremely important. Data loss, data stealing by malwares, data leakage, unreliable Access Points (APs), unsecured market places are some of the security concerns. Secured Socket Layer (SSL) and digital certificates are some of the built-in security measures. MobileCloud offer the option to remotely wipe data in stolen mobile devices to avoid data misuse.

2. Interoperability

Mobile devices vary in its operating systems like Android, IOS, and Symbian etc. Each mobile OS has several versions. When cloud app is developed for mobile devices, developers should ensure that which type of mobile device that particular app is targeted. Moreover, Companies which allow the BYOD policy typically need to deal with interoperability challenges.

Since BYOD policy may involve different mix of mobile devices including iPhone, Android phones, BlackBerry and others as per employees' choice, interoperation between different kinds of mobiles with company's server should be considered.

3. Collaboration

Collaboration among different departments of IT like engineering, sales teams, developers and deployment team is very important when updating a related document in cloud. This type of collaboration is even though easily possible with regular cloud, its implementation is difficult in mobile cloud. Several mobile platforms lack sophisticated document editing tools like word, excel or spread sheets. Multi-party video conferencing among employees is a bit of tedious task when even one recipient's mobile device is of small screen size or having flaky connections.

4. Integrity

Maintaining integrity is main challenge in mobile cloud. Employees in BYOD policy typically need to sync their devices with the cloud to maintain data integrity. When an employee in an organization pulls a document for updating and fails to sync it back to cloud, it creates discrepancy. Thus other employees when accessing the document will get an older version instead of newer version. Enterprise as a whole will get affected by integrity issues.

5. Reliability

Not only is this, in the mobile phone's perspectives, many other challenges needed to be faced by the mobile cloud techies. When we access the cloud from mobile, there might be connection loss due coverage gaps. Unlike fixed network where a physical link supports consistent network bandwidth, wireless connectivity is characterized by variable data rates and intermittent connectivity due to gaps in coverage. The dynamic nature of mobile networks result in throughput demands, subscriber mobility and uncontrollable factors like weather can cause bandwidth capacity and coverage to vary. Moreover, mobile networks generally have longer network latency than fixed network.

6. Access

If a private cloud is in native mobile, it is challenging to provide access to multiple mobile devices since the private cloud is dependent on the local platform. While enterprises can add a security features to public and hybrid networks using firewalls and VPNs, providing access across private cloud can often be difficult task.

Despite of all the challenges in the mobile cloud technology, it is growing extremely faster with the growth of mobile phone market.Gartner predicts that mobile cloud computing will reach a market value of US$9.5 billion by 2014.

9.9 SOLUTIONS FOR MOBILE CLOUD ADOPTION

To reduce power consumption, several solutions have been implemented. These solutions, however, require changes in the structure of mobile devices or require new hardware.

Reducing Energy Consumption

To make energy aware applications, we need to figure out which type of applications that consume more energy.Video and game applications can consume 50 to 70 watts by themselves.Our games, cameras, maps and streaming videos are welcome and celebrated additions to our daily routines, but we need to sacrifice energy required by their bright animation.Use these applications for a few hours, and you will inevitably be in need of a charger.

Computation offloading is a technique to migrate the large computations and complex processing from resource limited devices to resourceful devices, thus avoiding mobile devices to consume more time and energy. Remote execution may be a solution for energy hungry applications which can be done by MAUI (Mobile Assistance Using Infrastructure).Remote execution of large tasks can reduce their power consumption by upto 50%. MAUI to migrate mobile components to servers in the cloud can save 27% of energy consumption for computer games and 45% for the chess game.

Enhancing Storage Capacity

Storage is also a major concern for mobile devices. Mobile Cloud Computing is developed to enablemobile users to store and access large amounts of data on the cloud. Amazon Simple Storage Service is one such example. It provides a simple web services interface that can be used to store and retrieve any amount of data, at anytime from any where on the web. Flickr and Facebook are applications based on MCC. It allows users to upload and share photos through mobile devices and web. MCC also helps reduce the running cost for compute-intensive applications. Cloud computing efficiently supports various tasks for data-ware housing, managing and synchronizing multiple documents online. Thus, mobile devices are no more constrained by storage capacity because their data is now stored on the cloud.

Division of Application Services

The mobile devices have inherently limited resources. Thus the applications have to be divided in order to achieve a particular performance target like low latency, minimization of data transfer, fast response time etc. Optimal partition of application services across cloud and mobile devices is one basic idea for large tasks. Adaptive monitoring of network conditions to optimize network and device costs should also be done to resolve the issues in mobile cloud adoption.

SUMMARY

- *The central idea of this chapter is about mobile cloud computing and its significance.*
- *Receiving cloud services on the go is called 'Mobile Cloud'.*
- *Mobile Cloud differs from regular cloud in adjustments, accessibility, fault tolerant communication, memory, network latencies, energy availability and testing methodologies.*
- *Mobile cloud apps differs from native apps in downloading features, accessibility, targeted audiences, Mobile apps, notifications, access to latest technologies and UI Speed.*
- *All complex computing are done at cloud servers, the process information are sent back to the mobile which is described in Mobile Cloud Computing architecture.*
- *Mobile Cloud Computing takes the advantages of both Mobile and Cloud technology.*
- *Advantages of MCC leads to development of applications in various fields like M-Commerce, M-Learning, M-Healthcare, M-Gaming, M-Business and other applications.*
- *Many companies are providing Bring Your Own Device (BYOD) feature for the betterment.*
- *Issues in MCC adoption like security, interoperability, collaboration, integrity, reliability and access are identified.*
- *For improving Mobile Cloud adoption, energy consumption by mobile can be reduced, storage capacity can be enhanced and optimal partition of application services among mobile and cloud devices can be enforced.*

10

ANDROID IN CLOUD

OBJECTIVE

- *To learn about impact of Android phones in market*
- *To identify the basic concepts of Android*
- *To merge cloud computing with android devices*
- *To see the existing Cloud based Android Apps in market*
- *To know about Mobile Back end starters*
- *To recognize the traditional Android Cloud technology called Cloud 2 Device Messaging (C2DM)*
- *To acquire knowledge on recent Android Cloud concept called Google Cloud Messaging (GCM)*
- *To migrate from C2DM to GCM*

10.1 SMART PHONES

Today, smart phones become a body part of younger generations. Android phones made such an impact in the hearts of world people. Such types of phones are used by all people without any age bar. Starting from sending / receiving e-mails, instant messaging, finding GPS location to variety of fun filled Apps like Angrybirds, WhatsApp, TalkingTom, etc, Smart phones can do anything. Most important thing is it is available at cheaper cost. Android rules the smart phone world and by estimates it will account for well over 50 percent of worldwide sales in the next 3 years. By 2015, 50% of the handsets sold worldwide will be powered by Android. For one who is new to the world smart phones it can be quite confusing at first. There is, however some basic features of smart phones which are common to pretty much all devices in this category of technology.

Figure 10.1 Smart phones.

One of the first basic features of a smart phone is that it has the ability to not only to receive phone calls, text messages, and voicemail, but that it also had the ability to access the Internet, play online games, access digital media. Most smart phones have a built-in browser, which is proprietary to the maker of the phone. However, recently major browsers have begun to develop versions of their software which will run on smart phone operating systems. This allows the user to choose what Internet browser they are most comfortable with. The smart phones can be able to run small computer programs called apps. These apps can perform wide variety of functions. Number of android apps in Google play store has crosses 1 million. These smart phones have the capability of installing and uninstalling the apps as and when required. There is, however dozens more features available to smart phones which vary from manufacturers to manufacture. These phones are capable of doing advanced computing which paves the way for Cloud computing to merge with. The most famous mobile operating systems in modern smart phones include Google's Android, Apple's iOS. Such operating systems can be installed on many different phone models, and typically each device can receive multiple OS software updates over its lifetime. Smart phones have become a core piece of technology in the modern world. In the forthcoming chapters we will be discussing about Android and its cloud facility.

10.2 WHY ANDROID TECHNOLOGY?

The two tech giants in the mobile world are Android and IOS. Hence, we are going to compare our most favorite Android with the immediate IOs. Android is a more open mobile operating system than most other operating systems. Because of its flexibility and diversity, it is easily handled. Apple's iPhone is not open source, in which its Operating System more commonly called as IOS can be put inside only its own phone called iPhone or iPad. Apple has to approve each and every app that is published for their system. The Android software is managed by Google, which then releases the open-source to device manufacturers like Samsung, HTC, Motorola, Sony, LG, Huawei, ZTE etc., who develop the phones and tablets and tailor the basic Android software from Google to their devices. That means there is much more device diversity. Android phones and tablets can be found with many different screen sizes, with or without keyboard, user-friendly and also of low cost. Moreover, most apps are available free of costs. Below comes the graph showing the number of low quality, regular apps and all apps as of 2014.

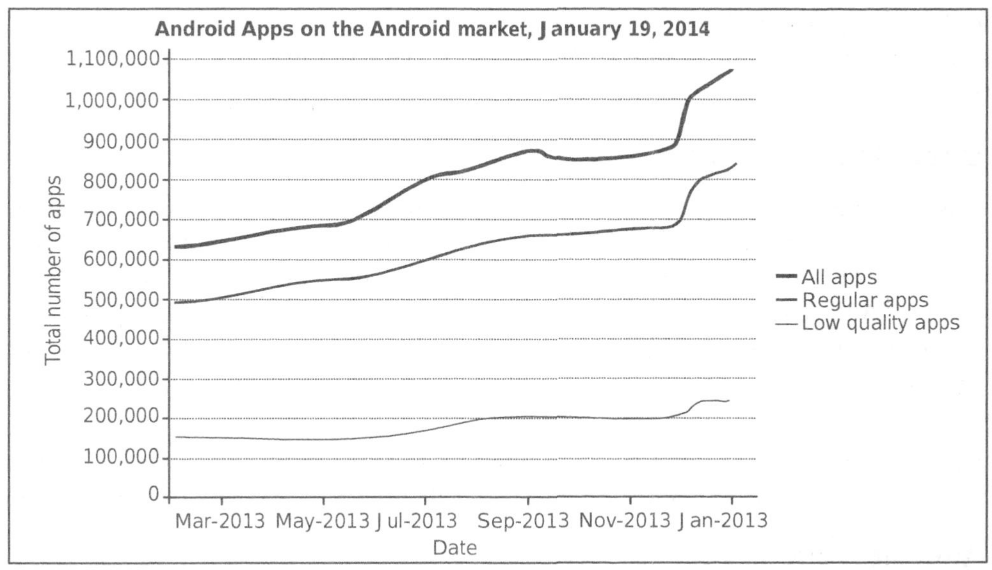

Figure 10.2 Android apps in market.

Number of free apps in the google market has crossed 850000 which are far greater than the number of free apps in iPhone. Thus free Android apps outnumber the free iPhone Apps. The ability to run million apps in android is just the same like iPhone but the choice of the phone depends upon the user. This facility drives us to take up Android as a platform to include cloud features.

10.3 OVERVIEW OF ANDROID OPERATING SYSTEM

History of android was quite interesting! You may wonder who actually founded android. Many of us think its Google's innovation. But Android Incorporation was originally founded by Andy Rubin in 2003. In 2005, Google took over Android Incorporation which had planned to penetrate into the mobile phone market with the weapon "Android". Interesting! Is not it?

On November 5, 2007, the Open Handset Alliance, a bunch of several companies which include Broadcom Corporation, Google, HTC, Intel, LG, Marvell Technology Group, Motorola, Nvidia, Qualcomm, Samsung Electronics, Sprint Nextel, T-Mobile and Texas Instruments expose themselves in front of media itself. The aim of the Open Handset Alliance is to develop open standards for mobile devices. On the same day, the Open Handset Alliance also unveiled their first product, Android, a mobile device platform which is built on the Linux kernel (version 2.6).On 9 December, 2008 14 new members accompany, including ARM Holdings, Asustek Computer Inc, Garmin Ltd, Huawei Technologies, PacketVideo, Atheros Communications, Vodafone, Sony Ericsson, Toshiba Corp.

Android, this word means a lot from non-techie to a techie guy. Today smart phones are known for its operating system "Android". Android created a reputed place in the mobile market in a very short span of time. Let's see more about techie dimension of android. What is Android actually? Android is a linux-based operating system. It is designed primarily for touch screen mobile devices such as smart phones and tablet computers. Android provides tools and API's required to begin developing applications on the Android platform. Many of us think what is SDK? Its Software Development Kit which gives us a platform to make new applications, games and other software.

10.3.1 Open Source Android

Another fascinating thing about Android is it is an Open Source! Android became an open source initiative that is led by Google under OpenHandset Alliance's umbrella with Apache License. This open source code and permissive licensing allows the software to be freely modified. Additionally, Android has a large community of developers writing code that extend the functionality of the operating system. Not only code for modifying operating system, but also free applications for android devices are developed by this community of developers.

The goal of the Android open source project is to provide an open platform to improve the mobile experience of users. Android is the first complete, open, and free mobile platform.

10.3.2 Android Versions

With open source availability of code, Android operating system versions are dynamically changing. Google is releasing the updated version of operating system then there. Android versions have been developed under a codename and released according to alphabetical order. Let's see the various versions, API Level and code name of android OS.

Release Date	Platform Version	API Level	Codename
November 5, 2007	Beta		
September 23, 2008	Android 1.0	1	
February 9, 2009	Android 1.1	2	
April 30, 2009	Android 1.5	3	Cupcake
September 15, 2009	Android 1.6	4	Donut
October 26, 2009	Android 2.0	5	Éclair
December 3, 2009	Android 2.0.1	6	Éclair
January 12, 2009	Android 2.1	7	Éclair
May 20, 2010	Android 2.2	8	Froyo
January 18, 2011	Android 2.2.1	8	Froyo
January 22, 2011	Android 2.2.2	8	Froyo
November 21, 2011	Android 2.2.3	8	Froyo

December 6, 2010	Android 2.3	9	Gingerbread
December, 2010	Android 2.3.1	9	Gingerbread
January, 2011	Android 2.3.2	9	Gingerbread
February 9, 2011	Android 2.3.3	10	Gingerbread
April 28, 2011	Android 2.3.4	10	Gingerbread
July 25, 2011	Android 2.3.5	10	Gingerbread
September 2, 2011	Android 2.3.6	10	Gingerbread
September 21, 2011	Android 2.3.7	10	Gingerbread
February 22, 2011	Android 3.0	11	Honeycomb
May 10, 2011	Android 3.1	12	Honeycomb
July 15, 2011	Android 3.2	13	Honeycomb
September 20, 2011	Android 3.2.1	13	Honeycomb
August 30, 2011	Android 3.2.2	13	Honeycomb
	Android 3.2.3	13	Honeycomb
December, 2011	Android 3.2.4	13	Honeycomb
January, 2012	Android 3.2.5	13	Honeycomb
February, 20121	Android 3.2.6	13	Honeycomb
October 19, 2011	Android 4.0	14	Ice Cream Sandwich
October 21, 2011	Android 4.0.1	14	Ice Cream Sandwich
November 28, 2011	Android 4.0.2	14	Ice Cream Sandwich
December 16, 2011	Android 4.0.3	15	Ice Cream Sandwich
March 29, 2012	Android 4.0.4	15	Ice Cream Sandwich
July 9, 2012	Android 4.1	16	Jelly Bean
July 23, 2012	Android 4.1.1	16	Jelly Bean
October 9, 2012	Android 4.1.2	16	Jelly Bean
November 13, 2012	Android 4.2	17	Jelly Bean
November 27, 2012	Android 4.2.1	17	Jelly Bean
February 11, 2013	Android 4.2.2	17	Jelly Bean
August 22, 2013	Android 4.3	18	Jelly Bean
October 3,2013	Android 4.3.1	18	Jelly Bean
October 31, 2013	Android 4.4	19	KitKat
December 5, 2013	Android 4.4.1	19	KitKat
December 9, 2013	Android 4.4.2	19	KitKat

Android versions are named after food items and also in alphabetical order. Google named it with desserts' names. Giving fancy and interesting names to different versions is a kind of marketing techniques.

10.4 ANDROID ARCHITECTURE

As an android user, one must know about the basic mobile functions like making a call, sending a text message, capturing image/video using camera options, changing the system settings, install or uninstall apps etc. All these details are made available to a normal user of android mobile by user maunal. But as a developer we need to know the nuts and bolts of android apart from the normal activites. The starting step of android are well explained in the below picture. Lets have a look at the architecture of android.

APPLICATIONS
Home
Contacts
Phone
Browser
...
APPLICATION FRAMEWORK
Activity Manager
Window Manager
Content Providers
View System
Package Manager
Telephony Manager
Resource Manager
Location Manager
Notification Manager
LIBRARIES
Surface Manager
Media Framework
SQLite
OpenGL | ES
FreeType
WebKit
SGL
SSL
libc
ANDROID RUNTIME
Core Libraries
Dalvik Virtual Machine
LINUX KERNEL
Display Driver
Camera Driver
Flash Memory Driver
Binder (IPC) Driver
Keypad Driver
WiFi Driver
Audio Drivers
Power Management

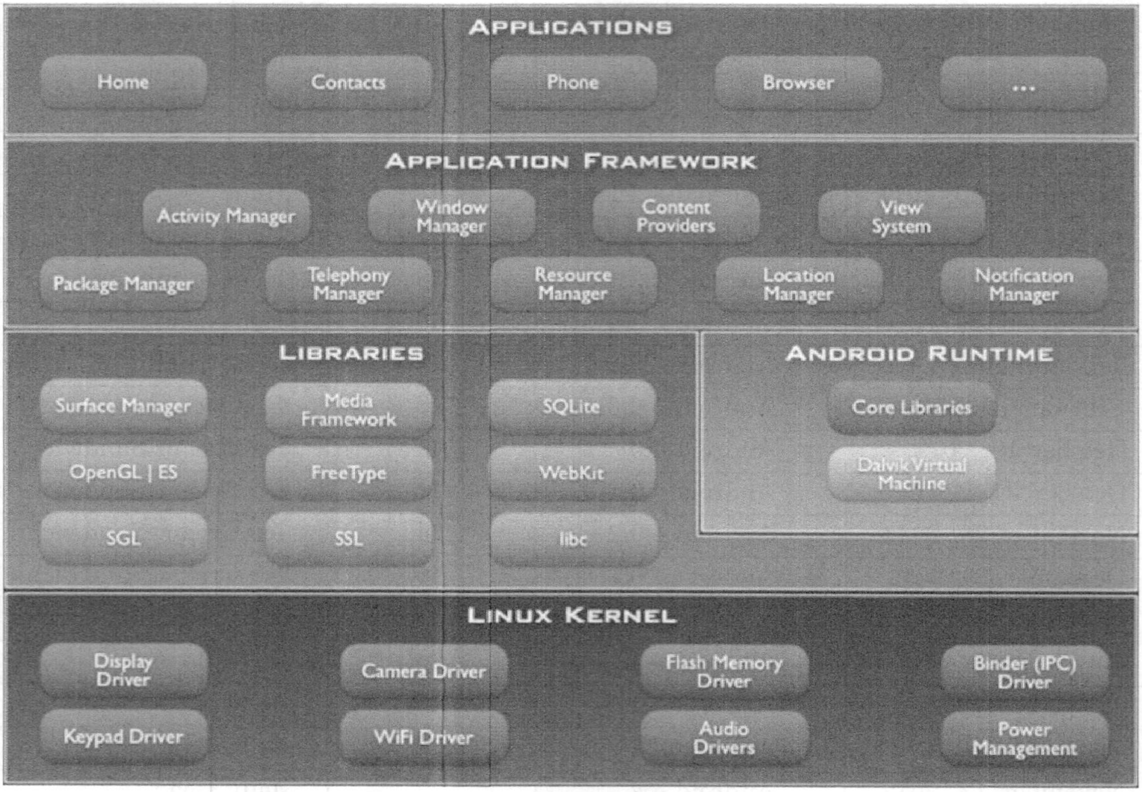

Figure 10.3 Architecture of Android.

Android OS is a software stack with multiple layers in it. Android OS is a software stack with multiple layers in it. We can see the individual layer deeply separated by borders and colours. Android architecture is sliced into layers for better understanding. In the following section, we will see the usage of individual layers.

10.4.1 Applications

APPLICATIONS
Home
Contacts
Phone
Browser
...

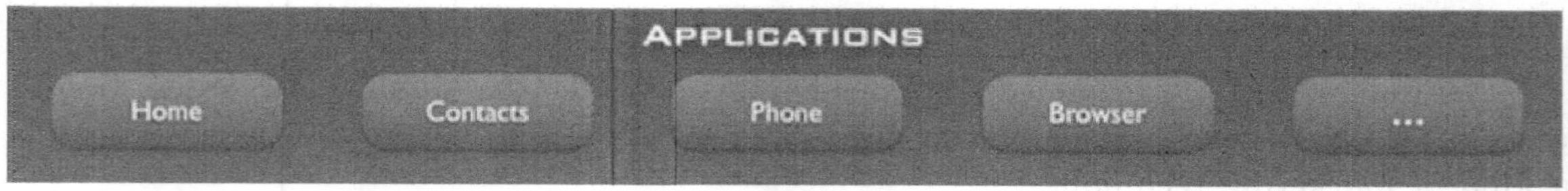

The top layer in android architecture is collection of applications. This layer is where our new application will fit into.

Core applications that are preinstalled in a new mobile are:

- Email Client
- SMS Program
- Dialer
- Calendar
- Maps
- Web Browser
- Contact Manager

It is possible for a developer to write his/her own app or he/she can modify the existing app. We are not limited to access any particular feature. We are free to modify the app the way we want it. Thus, android opens up a new dimension to existing apps.

10.4.2 Application Framework

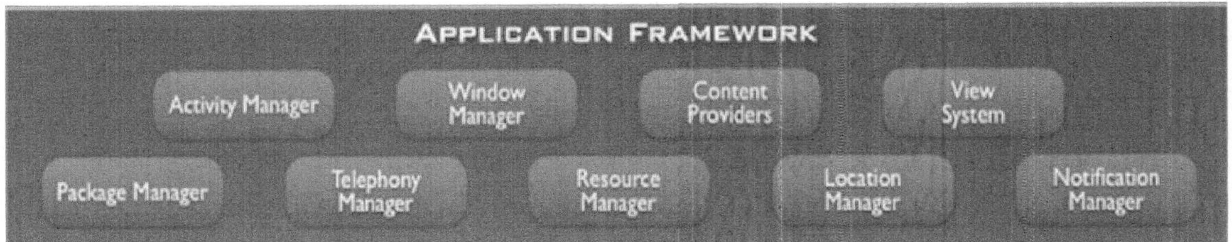

Application framework is the block that our applications directly interact with. It is designed to simplify the use of components. Any application can publish its capabilities and any other applications may then make use of those capabilities. This framework manages the basic functions of a mobile phone like resource management, voice call management etc.

- **Activity Manager** – manages states of different activities.
- **Window Manager** – responsible for organizing the screen.
- **Content Providers** – Enabling applications to access data from other applications or to share their own data.
- **View System** – manages UI elements
- **Package Manager** – manages application packages that are current installed on the device.
- **Telephony Manager** – handles making and receiving phone calls.
- **Resource Manager** – Providing access to non-code resources (localized strings, graphics, and layout files)
- **Location Manager** – obtains the device's position.
- **Notification Manager** – Enabling all applications to display customer alerts in the status bar.

10.4.3 Libraries

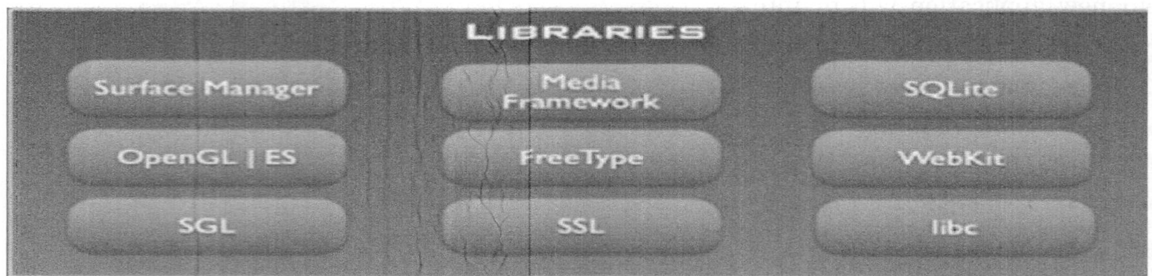

The next layer is the libraries. Android includes a set of C/C++ libraries used by various components of Android system.

- **Surface Manager** – manages access to the display subsystem.
- **Media framework** – allows the recording and playback of different media formats such as audio, video and static image files.
- **SQLite** – a powerful and lightweight relational database engine available to all applications.
- **OpenGL** – Used to render 2D or 3D graphics content to the screen.
- **FreeType** – bitmap and vector font rendering.
- **WebKit** – It is the browser engine used to display HTML content.
- **SGL** – stands for Scalable Graphics Library. It is graphics subsystem used by android. It is the low level graphics library implemented in native code that handles rendering.
- **SSL** – stands for Secure Socket Layer which provides security for communications over networks.
- **libc** – A standard C system library.

10.4.4 Android Runtime

10.4.4.1 Core Libraries

- The core libraries are written in Java Programming language.
- These are different from Java SE and Java ME libraries. However these libraries provide most of the functionalities defined in the Java SE libraries.

- The core libraries contain collection classes, utilities, IO.
- APIs inside core libraries include:
  - Data Structures
  - Utilities
  - File Access
  - Network Access
  - Graphics
  - Etc

10.4.4.2 Dalvik Virtual Machine

Dalvik Virtual Machine is a type of JVM used in android devices to run applications. It does not run .class files rather it run .dex files. Android applications are usually written in Java.

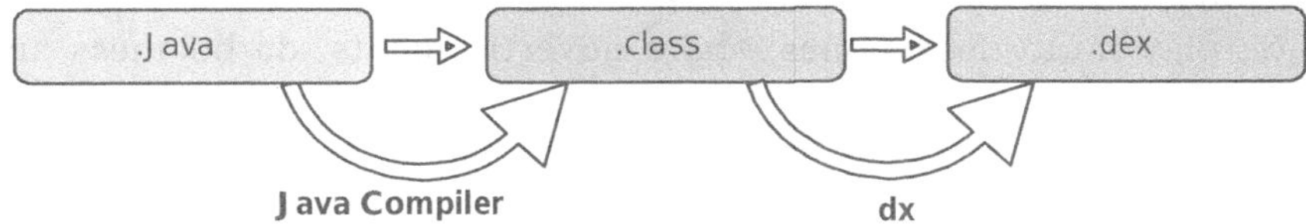

Written applications run on Dalvik, a custom virtual machine designed for embedded use which runs on top of a Linux kernel..java files are converted to.class files by Java Compiler.. class files are then converted to.dex (DalvikExecutables) by Dalvik virtual Machine (Dalvik Executer).

10.4.5 Linux Kernel

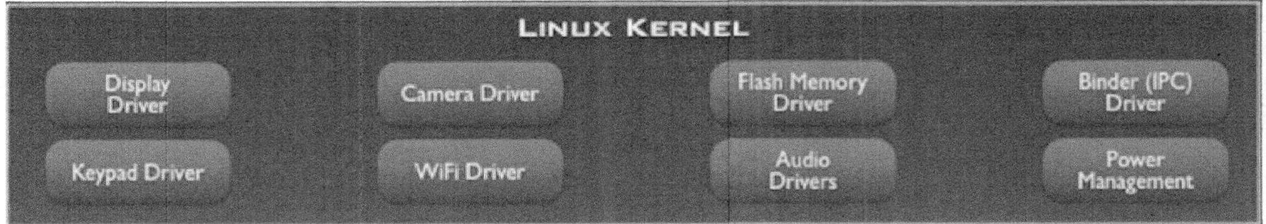

The bottom most layer is the Linux kernel which forms the strong basement for Android. Android OS as a whole is built on top of the Linux 2.6 Kernel with some changes made by Google. The Linux Kernel is responsible for functions like Power Management, Memory Management, Driver Model and Security. It provides an abstraction layer between the hardware and the rest of the software stack.

So far, we have discussed each component in software stack of Android architecture. In the next section, we are now going to see about the **CLOUD COMPUTING** with android devices.

10.5 CLOUD COMPUTING WITH ANDROID DEVICES

For Android users, Cloud plays an important role. Cloud change the way we think about smart phones and PCs. Cloud computing has successfully set up its realm in the arena of technology. Sharing information and data is no more a trouble even if you do not have a PC, a Smartphone is all you need and no matter wherever you are, you stay updated and connected with the real world. When cloud computing merged with mobile computing, Android phones received greater advantage. We use smart phones for sending and receiving emails, making phone calls probably with internet. Previously, for backing up contacts, frequently get updates, we need USB to connect your PC and mobile phone. In the era of cloud computing, mobile is much more than a phone. Most of the cloud computing features can be got when a smart phone is connected to the Internet using 3G or Long Term Evolution or 4G or by connecting via WiFi. Synching your contact details, calendar, tasks and emails with one's email account. With this feature, one can share status, images, and videos straight to social networking sites such as Google+, Facebook and Twitter. Cloud also provides the facility of searching databases, getting the local weather report, book tickets, make payments, play multi-user games, share advertisements, do business and so on.

Figure 10.4 Workings of Cloud with Android.

This type of smart phones can not only replace old PCs but also other electronic gadgets like Camera, MP3 players, GPS navigation system, pocket translator, handheld game device, etc. Android Cloud apps are both educational and recreational.

10.5.1 Backup API

Android cloud is highly useful in situations where the volume of data is less than a megabyte, like the user's preferences, notes, game high scores or other status, the Backup API provides a light weight solution. Backup API or cloud storage API is an application program interface that connects a native application to a cloud-based storage system, so that a user can send data to it and access and work with data stored in cloud. To the application, the cloud storage system is just another storage device. To put in another word, if a new user purchases a new mobile or resets his existing mobile, this backup API used to restore the user's previous apps back to the new mobile or reset one. During the initial setup, the previous data associated with the app restores as well. The lack of using cloud API can make it difficult to move data from cloud to target device.

10.6 CLOUD BASED ANDROID APPS – OVERVIEW

Cloud computing has been used to develop various mobile applications. Many product based companies are developing cloud based Android apps. Mobile application software's are application software's embedded on mobile phones. There are many cloud computing applications for android. Both as a developer as well as consumer of these mobile cloud apps, we should be aware of such apps.

Mobile cloud computing involves the introduction of cloud computing in a mobile phone environment. It provides a situation where data processing and storage happen outside a mobile device. Following are some apps of Cloud Computing for Android.

1. Google Drive

Google Docs is the part of Google Drive. This is a cloud computing application that enables a reader to read or write a document on line while collaborating with the other users live. Cloud computing enables the user to access the documents that is stored in the cloud and facilitate him/her reading it without having a copy on his mobile phone. By using this cloud computing app, you can upload files like photos, Images, Videos and share with others. This application is a freeware developed by Google supported by android operating system and is one of the best android cloud computing apps.

Figure 10.5 Google Drive.

2. Emails

It is similar to delivery of emails services on mobiles phones. Mobile phones email services enables the users to access their email inbox's, compose new emails and perform other email services. The awesome feature in it other the regular tasks is cloud provides storage for all email messages. This facility reduces the storage requirements on an android phone hence it becomes one of the most fascinating apps in Android.

Figure 10.6 Emails.

3. Google Cloud Print

Google Cloud Print Android App helps you to print and fax documents stored over cloud. You can easily print files and e-mails. There are various apps like Cloud printer, Easy print, Fiabee, Cloud Print beta available under Google Cloud print for your android devices.

Figure 10.7 Google Cloud Print.

4. Sugar Sync

Sugar Sync is a cloud service that enables active synchronization of files across computers and other devices for file backup, access, syncing, and sharing. This is an android application that enhances file sharing stored in a phone without using the internet. This is done through the use of wireless system. Cloud provides temporary storage of the information to be shared across the network. Sugar sync application is very popular with smart phone users.

5. Safe Wallet

Safe wallet is an android application that enables a user to securely store encrypted information like passwords or PIN numbers in the desktop. Through the cloud one is able to synchronize the document with his/her smart phone. It's also a popular android application. Safe Wallet is developed for android devices which keep your credentials safe and secure from identity theft and fraud. Safe Wallet password manager is the cloud computing app, you can use to store your passwords, logins and sensitive information. It helps in never forgetting your important passwords as well as in providing security.

Figure 10.8 Safe Wallet.

In addition, Evernote, Spring-pad, Dropbox, Icloud and mint are also best cloud computing applications for android mobiles. Adding to these common apps, many developers are developing still more fascinating apps for the Android mobile devices.

10.7 MOBILE BACKEND STARTERS

Smarter experiences in many of the mobile app are powered by services in the cloud. Android developers have taken the convenience and scalability of Google's cloud platform in their businesses. The tremendous growth and spread of mobile devices is leading to changes in the architecture of mobile applications. Mobile back end starter is an application that takes in benefits of both Backend as a Service (BaaS) and Platform as a Service (PaaS).

Backend as a Service (BaaS) is a type of cloud service that facilitates the integration between their mobile clients and their backend services. WithBaaS, it reduces the effort required for developing backend servers. Platform as a Service is also a type of cloud service which is used to rent hardware, operating systems, storage and network capacity over the internet.

The Mobile Backend Starter solution provides the benefits of BaaS as well as PaaS. It combines these benefits with the advantages of Platform as a Service (PaaS), such as high scalability, availability, and extensibility.

Mobile Backend Starter is an application you deploy and run on Google App Engine with a single click. App Engine is a complete development stack that uses familiar technologies to build and host applications on the same infrastructure used at Google. Mobile Backend Starter provides powerful backend features that are instantly available to your mobile application. There is no need of any server-side coding. Mobile Backend Starter is an application that runs on App Engine. Mobile Backend Starter comes with a number of functionalities. Using the client library, you can develop an Android app that integrates seamlessly and securely with the backend functionalities.

A mobile application built using the Mobile Backend Starter consists of the following components:

- A Mobile Backend server application deployed on Google App Engine
- Android client libraries and APIs for accessing the Mobile Backend
- Android client application developed using the Mobile Backend client library.

Definition of Mobile Backend Starter

Mobile Backend Starter is a one-click deployable, complete mobile backend that allows you to reap the benefits of a cloud backend. It provides a ready-to-deploy, general purpose cloud backend and a general purpose client-side framework for Android.

Without needing to write any backend code, you can able to set up a back end for your apps with the help of Mobile back end starter. It includes a server that stores your App data and a client library and sample app for Android that makes it easy to access that data. To keep user data secure, Mobile Backend Starter also includes built-in security support for Google Authentication.

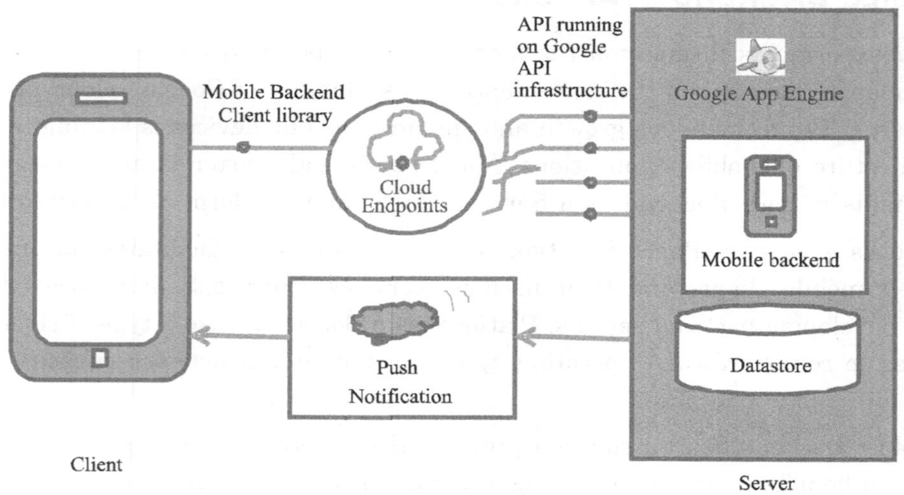

Figure 10.9 Mobile Backend Starter.

Features of Mobile Backend Starter

- **Cloud data storage:** Cloud offers large amount of storage space to its customers. It allows storing any amount of data per user in the cloud to be accessed from anywhere.
- **Pub/Sub messaging:** It is possible to send or receive data from one device to another, to any or to all other devices in the cloud. This feature is useful for various applications including social apps, forums, chat, gaming, and group collaborations.
- **Push notifications:** Data updated on one device is automatically pushed to all devices available in cloud with Google Cloud Messaging (GCM) for Android.
- **Continuous queries:** Automatic updates to the clients are done with the queries running continuously on server.
- **Google authentication and authorization:** Authentication and Authorization of cloud data promotes secured access to the data. It is possible to keep data isolated per user or shared among multiple users.
- **Free to get started, scales with your needs:** It is initially free to use for nearly hundreds of clients, and the services can be scaled to any number of customers.

10.8 CLOUD TO DEVICE MESSAGING (C2DM)

Cloud to Device Messaging (C2DM) is an Android service that helps sending data from servers to applications on Android devices. This is a simple, light weight mechanism which the applications can get updated data from server at any time anywhere.

Workings of C2DM

- Third-party application servers can send lightweight messages to target Android applications running on target device. The goal of this messaging service is only to send a notification to the target device about the updated data on server not to send huge user content.
- C2DM notifies about the data updated in the server. It does not bother about the delivery and order of messages.
- When the message arrives, C2DM wakes up the application via Intent broadcast. But the application will waked up only when the broadcast receiver and permissions are properly set. Thus an application on an Android device doesn't need to be running to receive messages.
- No built-in user interface or other handlings of message data are done with C2DM. C2DM simply passes raw message data received straight to the application. It is the task of the application to transform the raw data and to make it displayed with custom user interface.
- The target mobile devices should be running on Android 2.2 or higher version and should have Google account set up.

10.9 GOOGLE CLOUD MESSAGING FOR ANDROID

Google Cloud Messaging allows sending data from the server to target device and from device to server. Unlike C2DM, GCM allows large messages to be transferred between the server and the mobile device. GCM supports notification to the target mobile device when the information is updated on the server.

Features of GCM

- GCM helps in sending information from a 3rd party applications to the mobile app.
- GCM supports waking up an Android Application via Intent Broadcast and hence the application is not needed to run all the time.
- Similar to C2DM, it does not support built-in interface. So the task of displaying the raw data is left for the Android application.
- It needs Android 2.2 or higher version with Google Play store libraries installed.
- If the device is less or equal to 3.0 devices, it needs an existing Google account. Google account is not needed for android mobile with version higher or equal to 4.0.4.

10.10 DIFFERENCE BETWEEN C2DM AND GCM

Features	**C2DM**	GCM
API Key	Client Login Auth Token. But it is deprecated.	Simple API from Google API's console.
Sender ID	It is just an email address.	Project number obtained while creating the project in Google console.
JSON	Does not suppot JSON.	Supports JSON
Multicasting	Not supported	Supported
Multiple Senders	Not Supported	Multiple senders can send messages to the same app with one common registration ID
Time to Live	Not featured.	Ranges from 0 to 4 weeks. GCM will store the messages until they expire. A message with a time-to-live value of 0 will not be stored on the GCM server.
Messages with payload	It sends light weight messages probably to tell the application that a new data is available on the server.	Deliver messages up to 4Kb.
Canonical Registration ID	Not supported.	Supported.

10.11 MIGRATION FROM C2DM TO GCM

So far, we have seen the differences between C2DM and GCM. We migrate from C2DM to GCM mainly to use the cloud features with ease and to use battery efficiency. Rich set of new APIs are provided with GCM which paves way for moving from C2DM to GCM. Let us see the steps to migrate from C2DM to GCM.

Migration from C2DM to GCM is very easy two replacement process. One is to replace email account in C2DM with project number. And another is to replace ClientLoginAuth with the API key.

Since the sender ID in GCM is project number, the email account in C2DM is replaced by the project number that we get from the Google Console. Another major change is to change the deprecated ClientLoginAuth token with the API key that we obtained from the Google Console. Below are the snapshots that show how to get project number and API key for GCM.

Type the URL https://cloud.google.com/console/project in your browser. You need to enter the user credentials for your Google Account.

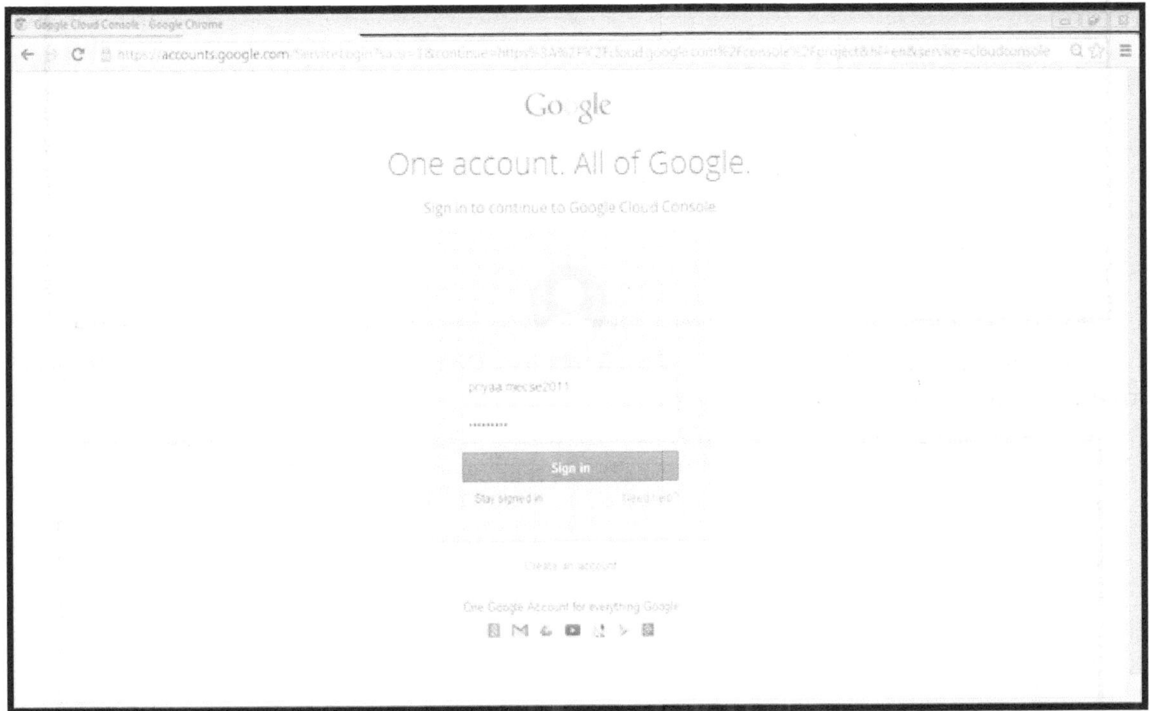

As of now, You don't have any projects as shown in the below snapshot. Click on the button "Create Project" to create a Project.

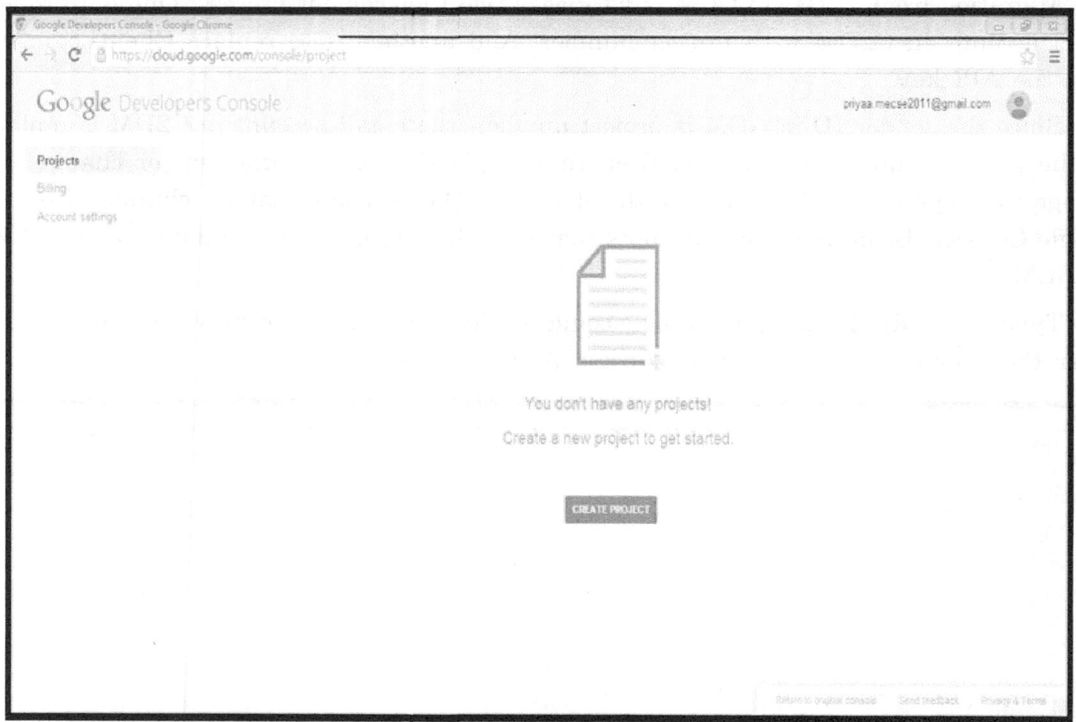

You can give any Project name of your choice. Default Project name is "My Project". Project ID can be reloaded if you wish.

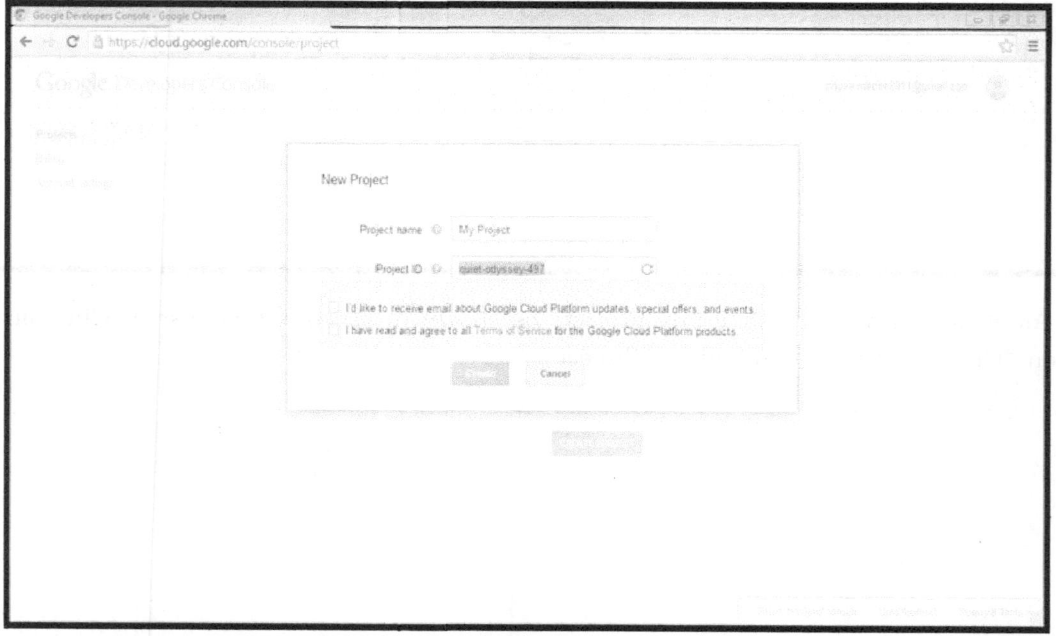

Check on the two checkboxes as shown below. Check box 1 is optional. Click on create.

Below you can see the Project ID and Project number which you need to note when creating your Android Cloud Applications.

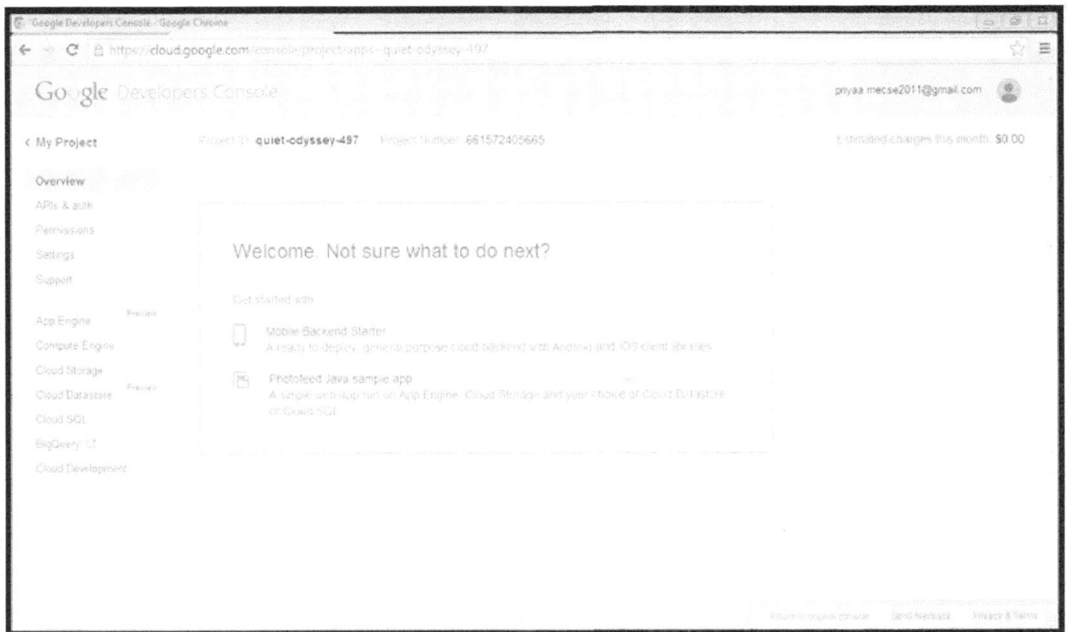

As of now We have got the project number. For getting the API key for GCM applications, Click on APIs and auth and then click on Credentials as in the below snapshot. Click on create new key.

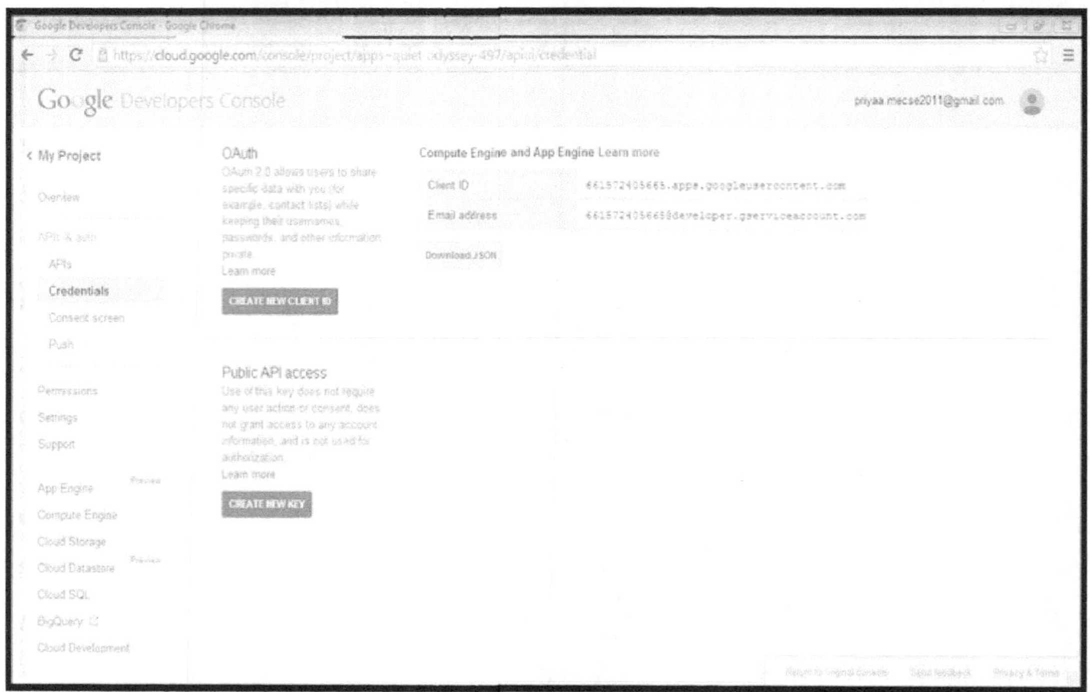

A dialog will appear as below. Based up on the type of Applications like Server, browser, Android or IOS, different API's can be generated.

Below snapshot is for creating a API key for server applications. When nothing is provided in the server IP Address box, the application will allow any IP address. Click on create.

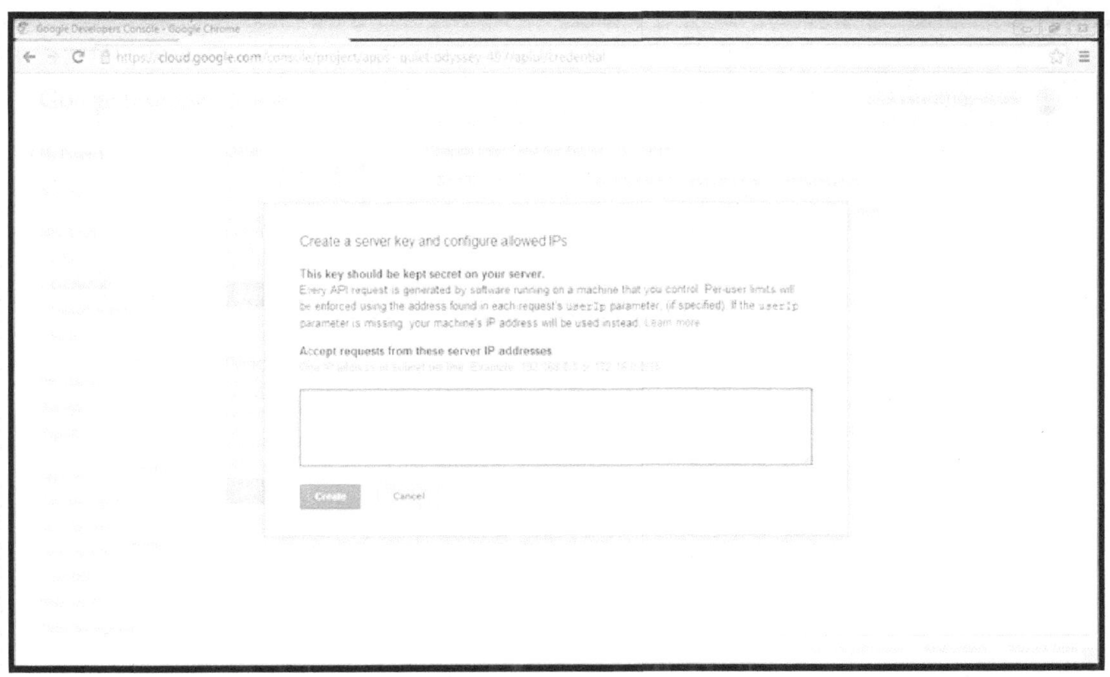

In the below snapshot you can note an automatically generated API for server applications. This is noted for developing the server application.

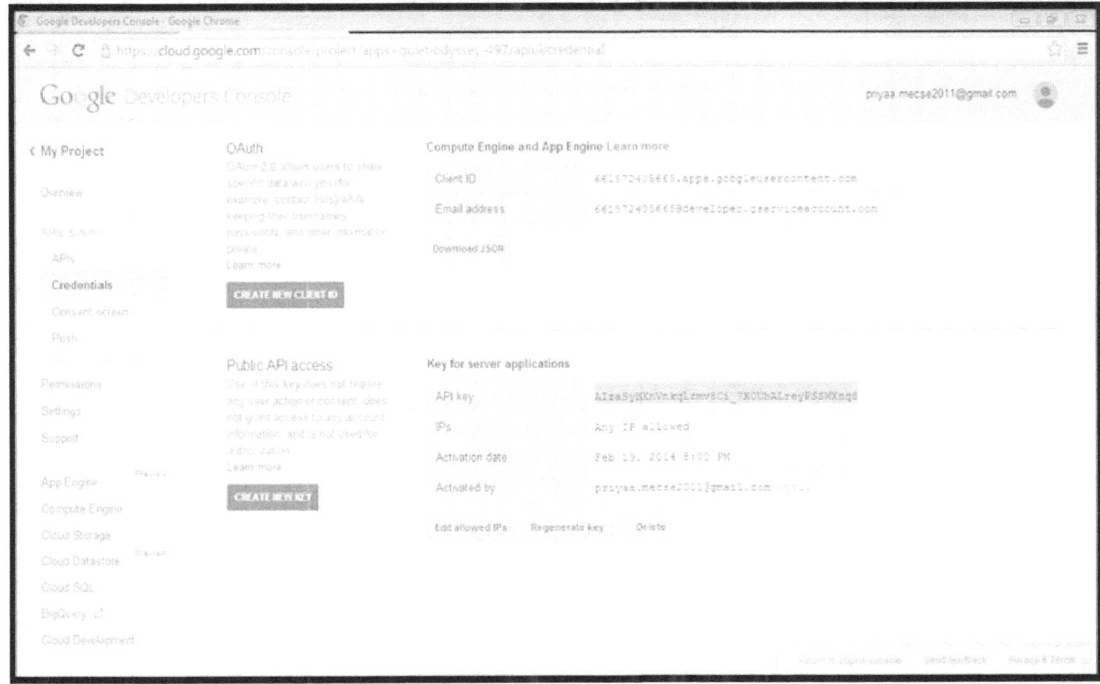

Following shows the Browser API key creation. You need to give a URL for sending requests. When nothing is given, it will accept requests from any URL.

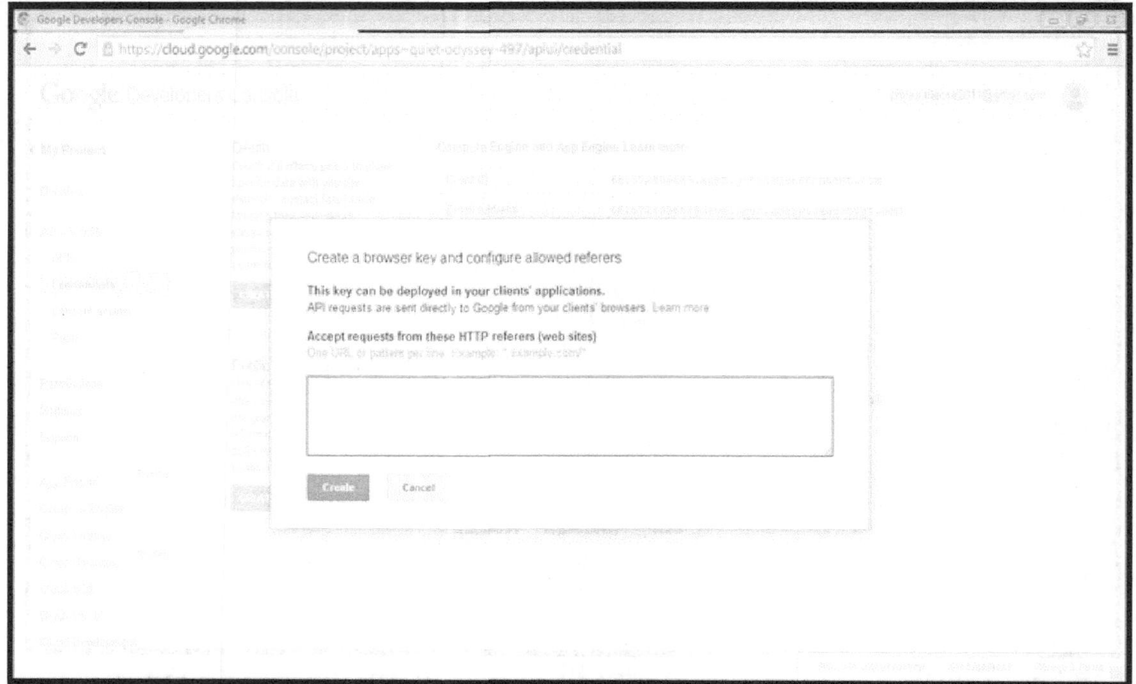

Below is the auto generated API key for browser applications.

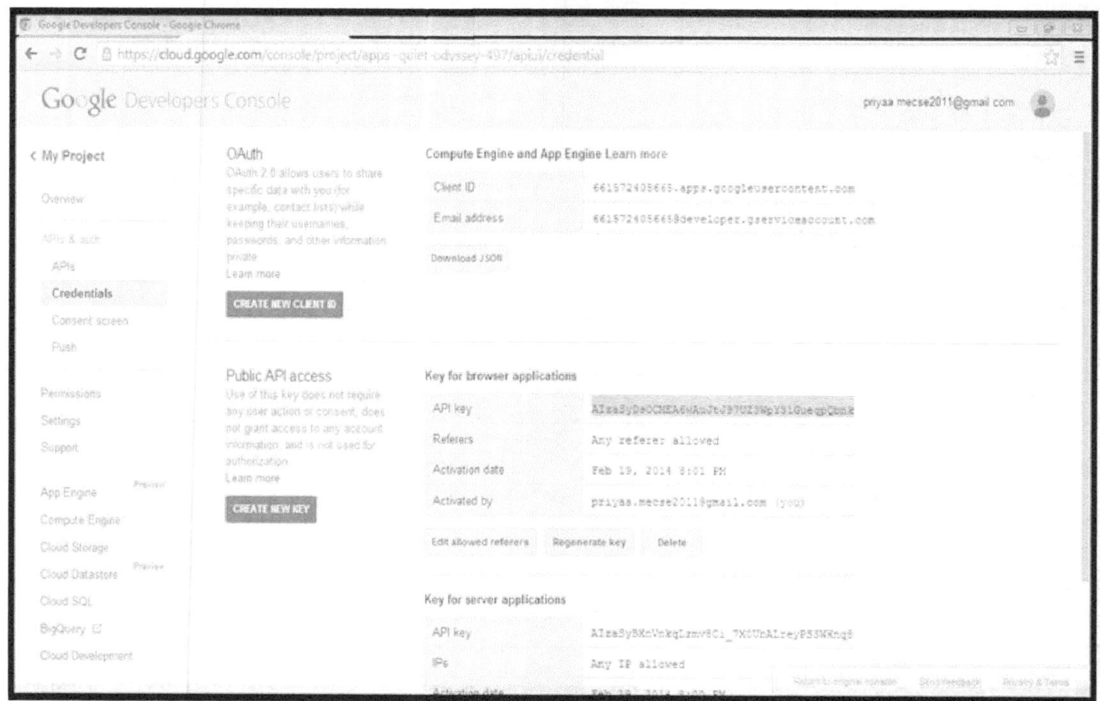

Similarly, Android and IOS keys are generated as below. For Android SHA1 certificate fingerprint is needed. Without this, it accepts requests from any Android applications.

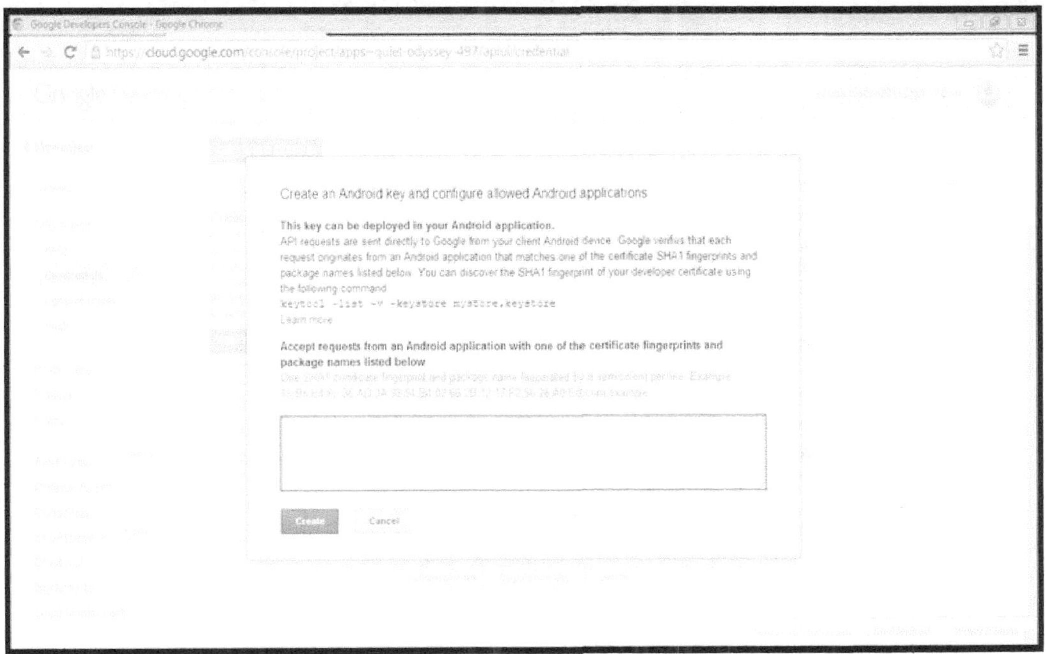

Thus API key for Android application is generated as shown below.

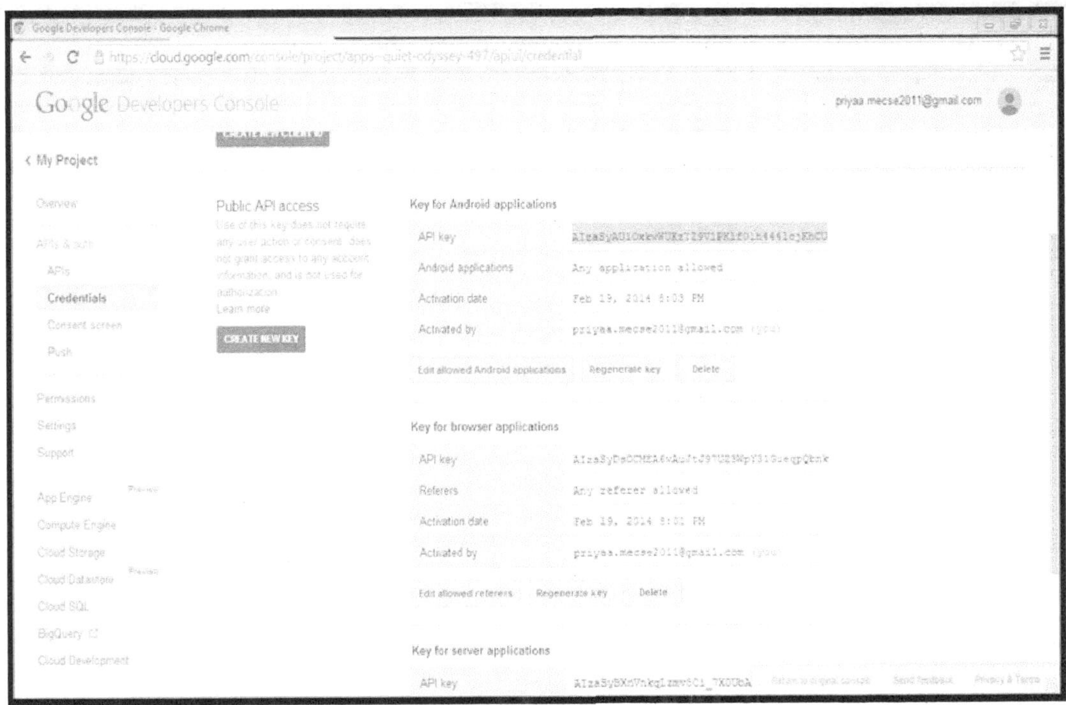

For IOS,bundle identifier is needed. Without this, it accepts requests from any IOS applications.

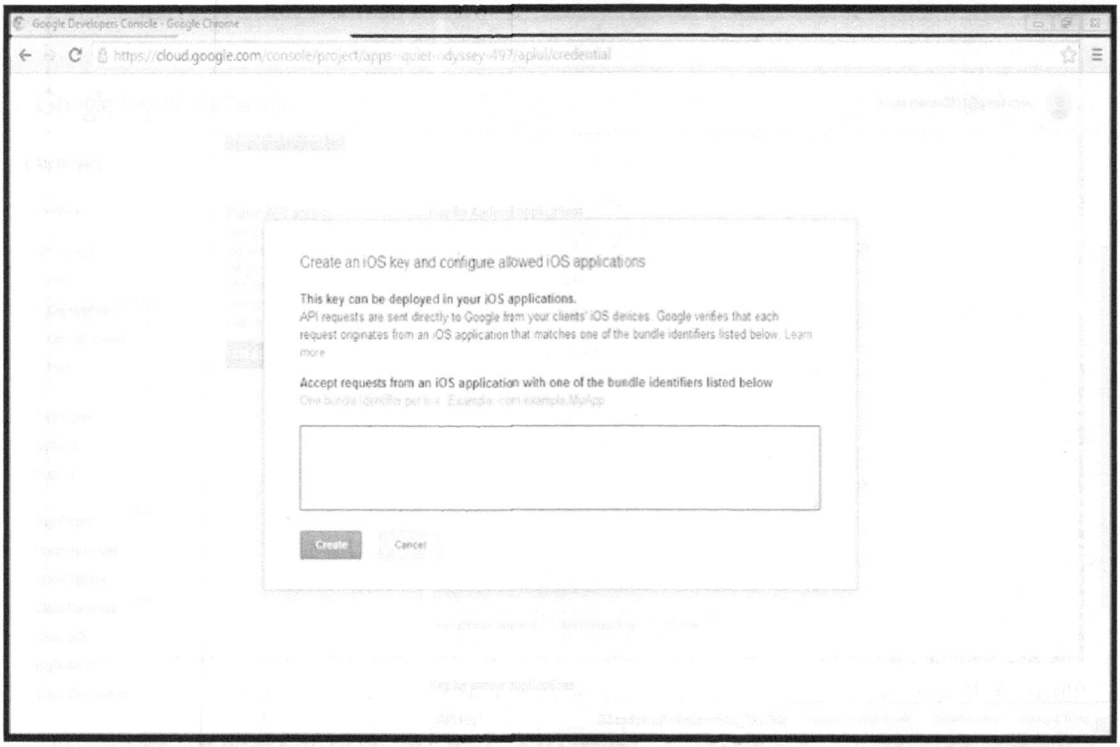

Thus API key for IOS application is generated as shown below.

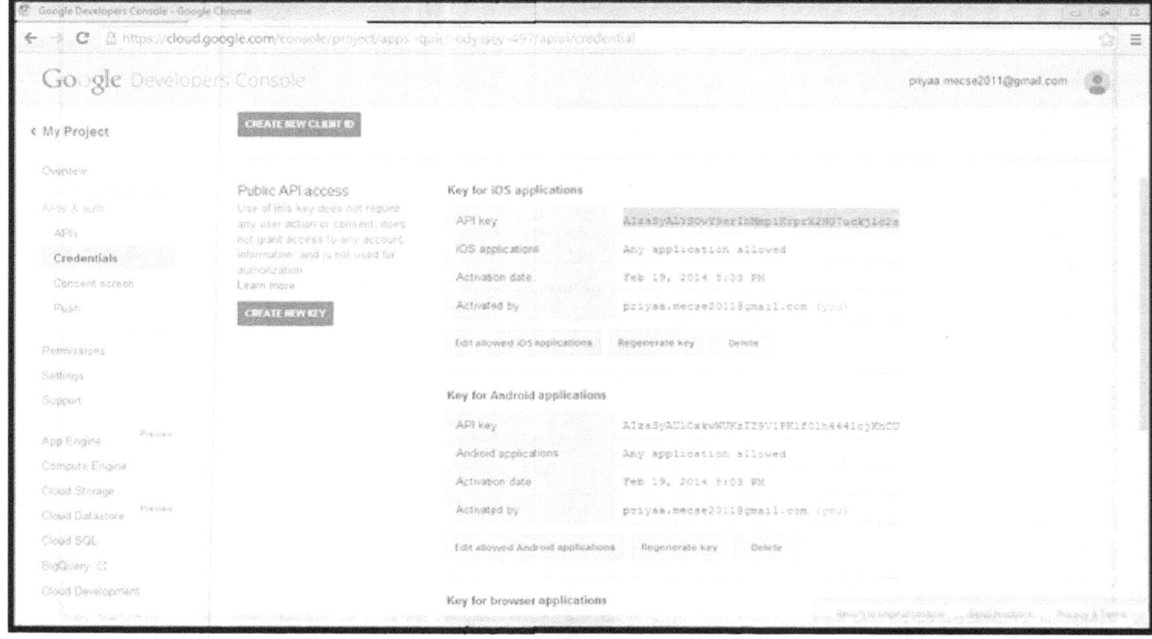

C2DM is replaced by GCM by Google. GCM has not only replaced C2DM, but also offers additional features as earlier said. We have seen about how to get a Project number and

API key that is necessary for building successful GCM applications. In the next chapter, more about GCM, its architecture and implementations are discussed.

SUMMARY

- *Android phones made greater impact in mobile phone market because of its cheaper cost.*
- *Android operating system is open source which paves way for developing different versions of OS.*
- *Google acquired Android in 2005, which was developed by Andy Rubin in 2003.*
- *Android versions are given dessert names in alphabetical order. As of now, it has reached 'K' which is referred as 'KitKat'.*
- *Android architecture includes some core parts like Application, Application framework, Libraries, Android Runtime and Linux kernel.*
- *More fascinating mobile cloud apps like Google Drive, Emails, Google Cloud Print, Sugar Sync and Safe Wallet are developed.*
- *Mobile Backend Starter is an application you deploy and run on Google App Engine with a single click.*
- *Cloud 2 Device Messaging (C2DM) is a deprecated Android service which helps in sending data from servers to application on Android devices.*
- *Google Cloud Messaging (GCM) is the current Android service which helps in sending data from server to device and from device to server.*
- *Migration from C2DM to GCM can be done effectively by simple two replacements.*

11

Google Cloud Messaging (GCM) For Android

OBJECTIVE

- *To learn about components and credentials of GCM*
- *To know the architecture of GCM*
- *To identify the life cycle of GCM*
- *To implement GCM*
- *To make a mobile device register with GCM*

11.1 CONCEPTS IN GCM

There are two major concepts.

1. Components which play a key role in GCM.
   (a) Client Application is the GCM-enabled Android Application that is running in target device or an emulator.
   (b) Third party Application Server – The application server which send information to the client app running on the target via GCM Connection server.
   (c) GCM Connection Servers – This is an intermediary between the client application and 3rd party application server. This is Google-provided servers which take the message from 3rd party application server to target device and vice versa.
2. Credentials which ensure that all parties are authenticated and authorized.
   (a) Sender ID – This is the project ID that we got from Google console. Refer to the snapshots for getting the project ID in Chapter 11.
   (b) Application ID – This is to uniquely identify an Android application.
   (c) Registration ID – This is the ID to identity the target device which receives the messages from the server. It is issued by the Google Server.
   (d) Google User Account – If the device is running a version lower than Android 4.0.4 at least one Google Account is needed for GCM to work.

(e) Sender Auth Token – This is API key. For getting API key refer to Chapter 11 snapshots. For Server authorized access to Google Services, API key is needed.

11.2 ARCHITECTURAL OVERVIEW

GCM implementation includes 3rd party app server, GCM Connection Servers and Android client app running on target device. GCM Connection Servers helps in sending messages from Client App to 3rd Party App Server and vice versa.

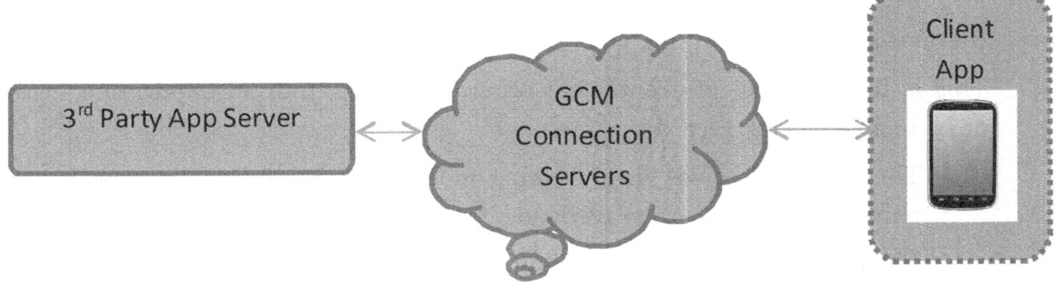

Figure 11.1 GCM Architecture Computing.

Component Interaction

- GCM Connection Servers send messages from 3rd party app server to client app that is GCM enabled. HTTP and XMPP are connection servers provided by Google.
- 3rd Party App Server sends messages to GCM connection server, which in turn en-queues and stores the message and sends to the target device when it comes online.
- To receive the stored GCM messages, client app must register with GCM and get a registration ID. If XMPP Connection server is used, client app can send message back to connection server which results in up-streaming.

11.3 LIFE CYCLE FLOW

- Enable GCM

  An Android application running on a mobile device has to register with GCM to receive messages.
- Send a message – Below are the sequence of events triggered while sending message.
  1. The 3rdapplication server sends a message to GCM servers.
  2. Google connection server en-queues and stores the message in case the device is offline.
  3. When the device is online, Google connection server sends the message to the device.

4. Up on receiving the message, the device broadcasts the message to the specified Android application via Intent broadcast with proper permissions, so that targeted Android application gets the message. The Android application does not need to be running beforehand to receive the message. Intent broadcast will wake up the exact application even though it not running.
5. The targeted application will then process the message.
6. A registered Android application can unregister GCM if it no longer wants to receive messages.

- Receive a message.

  This is the sequence of events that occurs when an Android application installed on a mobile device receives a message:

  1. The system receives the incoming message and extracts the raw key/value pairs from the message payload, if any.
  2. The system passes the key/value pairs to the targeted Android application in Intent as a set of extras.
  3. The Android application extracts the raw data from the Intent by key and processes the data.

11.4 GCM IMPLEMENTATION PROCEDURES

Let's see the requirements for GCM implementation

Creating a Google API Project

We have already seen in the previous chapter about how to create a Google API project. Steps for creating Google API are given below. For more information, refer to the snapshots of Chapter 11.

To create a Google API project:

1. Open the Google Developers Console.
2. Click Create Project.
3. Type your project name and click Create. Once the project has been created, a page appears that displays your project ID and project number.
4. Copy your project number for later use. Below is the screen shot to identify project number.

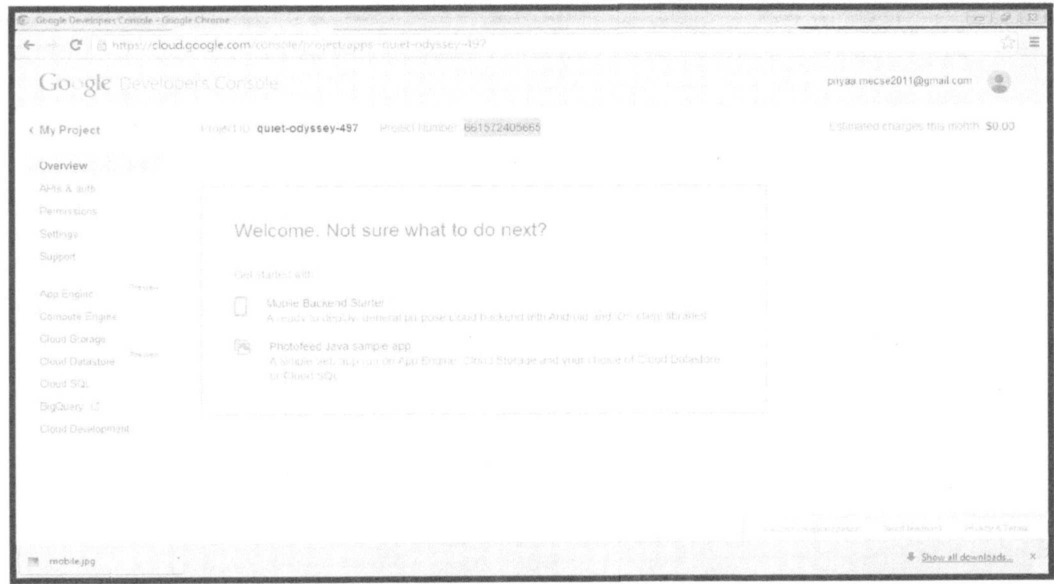

Enabling the GCM Service

Two steps to enable the GCM service:

1. In the sidebar on the left, select APIs and auth.
2. In APIs tab, turn the Google Cloud Messaging for Android toggle to ON.

The snapshots show how to enable Google Cloud Messaging for Android. For enabling it, agree the terms Google API and GCM for Android services as shown.

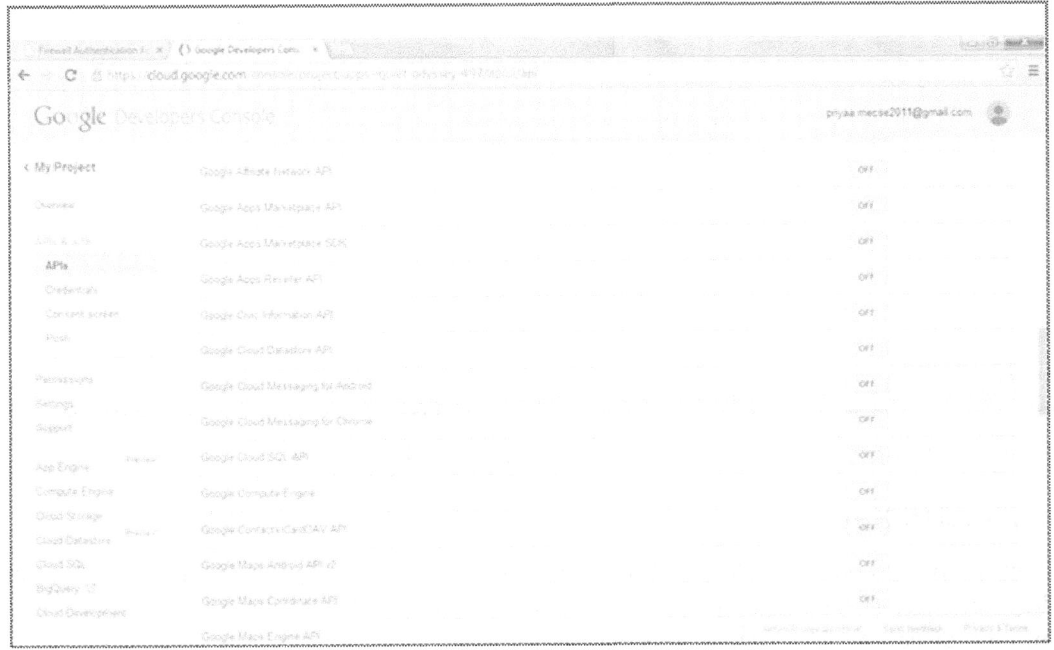

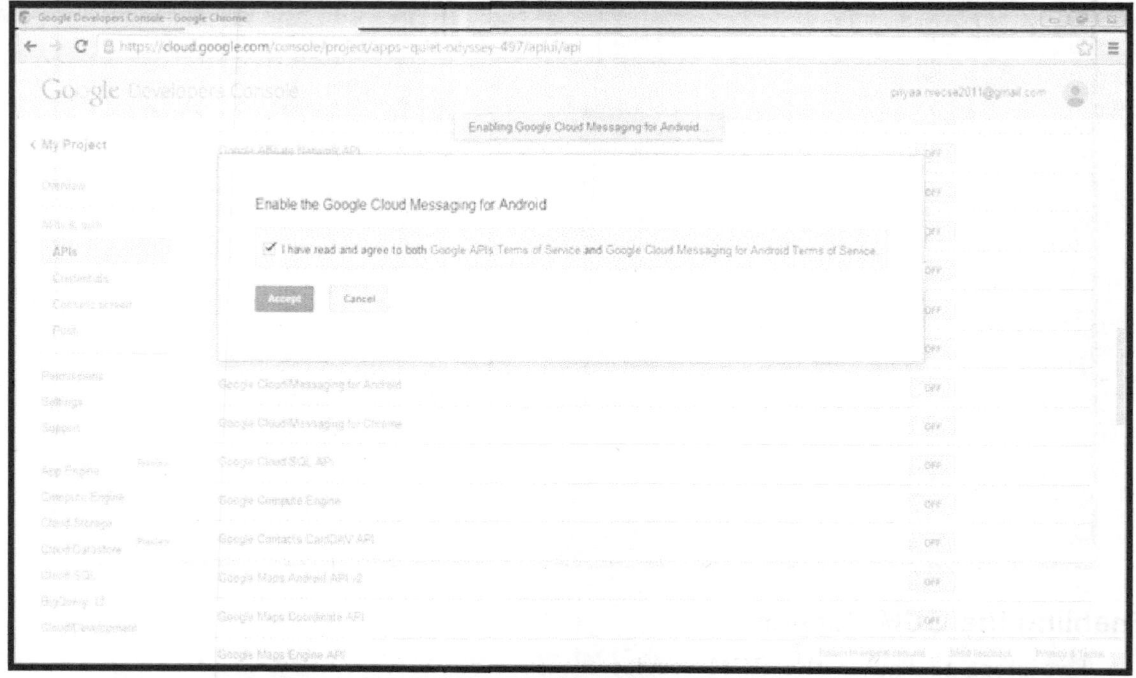

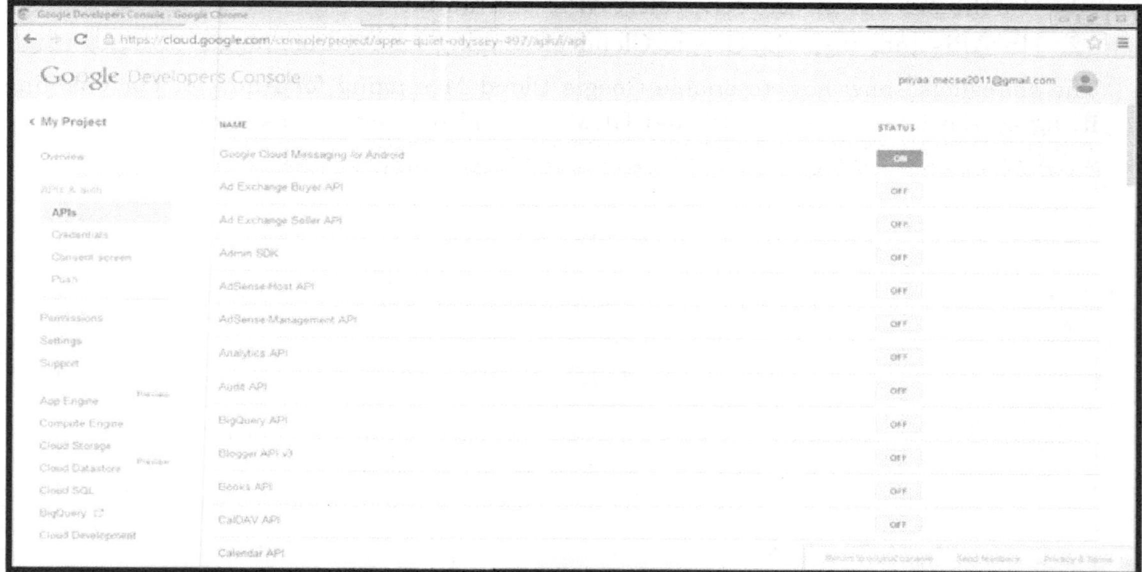

Thus enabling the GCM services on Google console is done.

Obtaining API Key

Next step is to obtain API key. We have already seen in chapter 11 about how to obtain API key for variety of Applications like server, browser, Android and IOS. Let's see the obtainment of server key API in steps.

1. In your project console, select **APIs & auth and then Credentials**.
2. Click **Create new key under public API access**.
3. In the **new key** dialog, click **Server key**.
4. In the resulting configuration dialog, supply your server's IP address. When not set, it will allow all IP addresses.
5. Click **Create**.
6. In the upcoming page, copy the API key. This API key is needed later on for performing authentication in your application server. If necessary new API key can be regenerated.

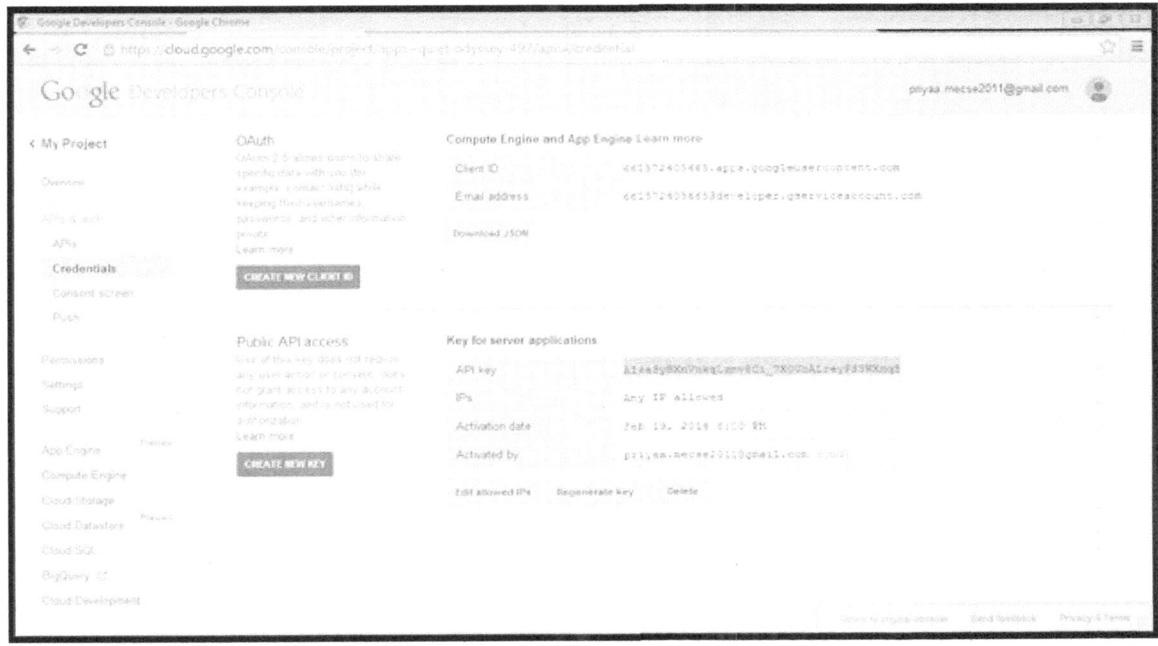

The API key above is generated for server applications. This key will allow all IP Addresses as you can see. Allowed IPs can also be edited.

With project number, GCM service enabled and API key generated, we can start implementing GCM. Here is an overview of the basic steps:

1. Choose a GCM connection server HTTP or XMPP (CCS).
2. Implement a 3rd-party application server to interact with your chosen GCM connection server.
3. Write your client app.

11.5 GCM REGISTRATION

So far, we have seen what the requirements for GCM implementation are. Let's see how to register a mobile device with GCM server.

It is assumed that you have already installed Eclipse for Android using ADT bundle. For implementing Client side code, Google Cloud Messaging API is needed for which Google Play Services should also be installed. To install Google Play services, double click on the Android SDK Manager 'SDK Manager.exe' file at the root of the Android SDK directory. Select Google Play Services in Android SDK Manager as below and click on install to install the package.

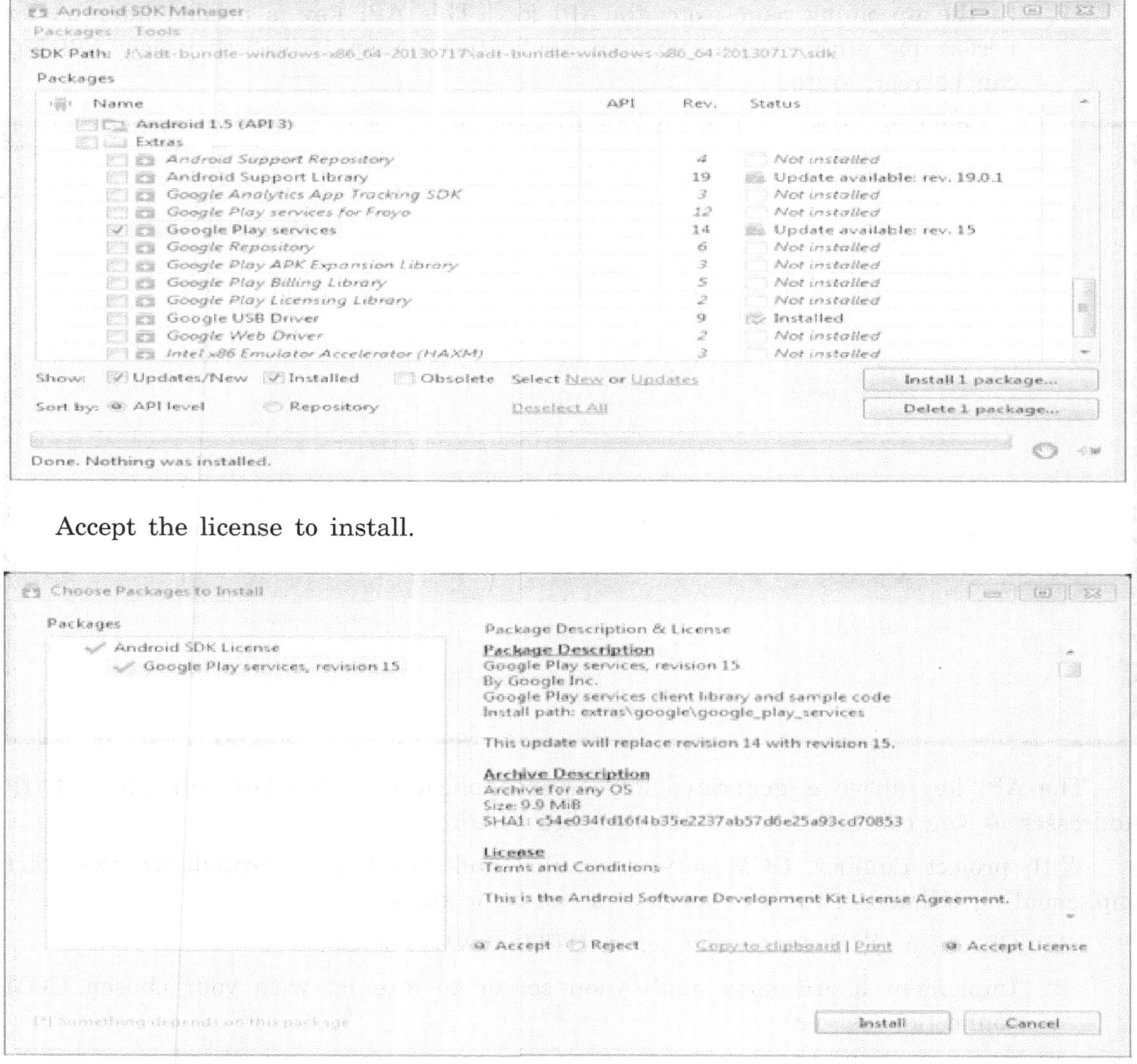

Accept the license to install.

It might take several minutes to install. Then install compatible version of Google API as shown below.

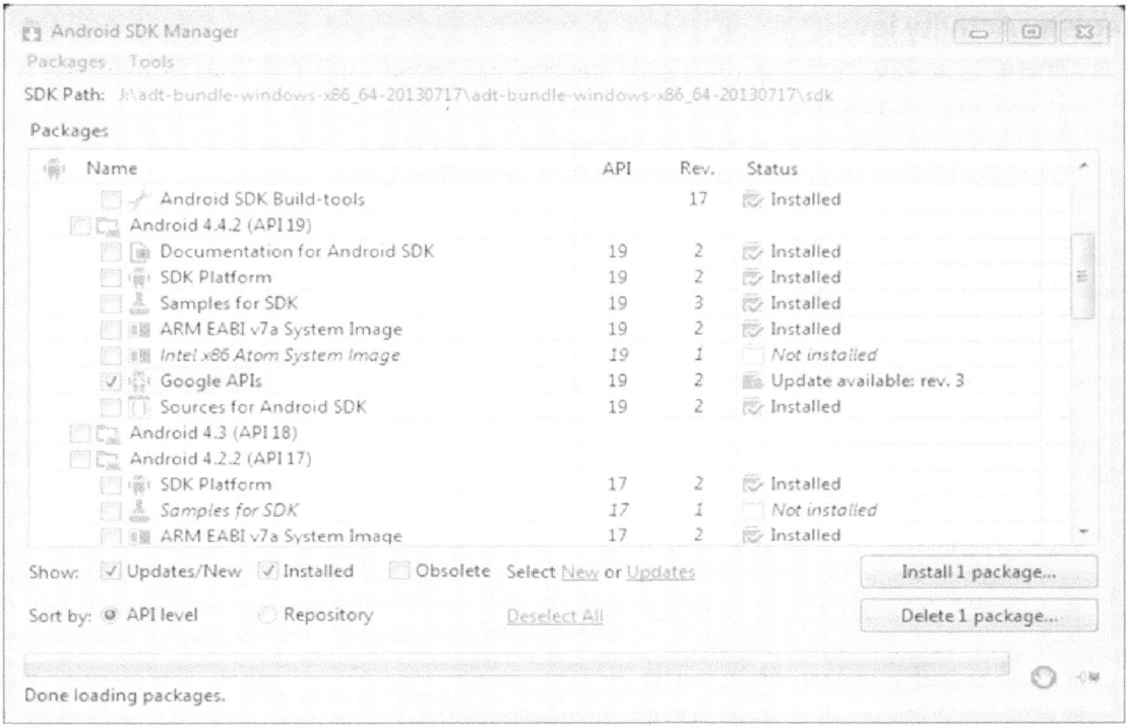

Click Install selected number of packages. Agree the terms to install the GoogleAPIs.

Let's see about how to register a mobile device with GCM. Create a simple Android Project. Make the project with the target Google APIs. To do so, right click on the project -> Build Path -> Configure Build Path -> Android. Then set the target to Google APIs. Below is the Project layout.

RegisterActivity.java

```
//This is a java file which helps in GCM registration of a mobile device.
packagecom.priyaa.gcm;

importstaticcom.priyaa.gcm.CommonUtilities.SENDER_ID;
importandroid.app.Activity;
importandroid.os.Bundle;
importandroid.util.Log;
importandroid.widget.TextView;
importcom.google.android.gcm.GCMRegistrar;
publicclassRegisterActivityextends Activity {
private String TAG = "Register Activity";
privateTextViewReg_ID;
  @Override
publicvoidonCreate(Bundle savedInstanceState) {
super.onCreate(savedInstanceState);
   //Call to checkNotNull method
checkNotNull(SENDER_ID, "SENDER_ID");
GCMRegistrar.checkDevice(this);
GCMRegistrar.checkManifest(this);
setContentView(R.layout.activity_push_android);
Reg_ID = (TextView) findViewById(R.id.textView1);
   //Checking Registration ID
final String regId = GCMRegistrar.getRegistrationId(this);
Log.i(TAG, "registration id ===== " + regId);
if (regId.equals("")) {
GCMRegistrar.register(this, SENDER_ID);
   } else {
Log.v(TAG, "Already registered");
   }
   //Setting the registration ID to TextView
Reg_ID.setText("Your Device Registration ID : "+regId);
  }
  //Checking Sender ID is not null
privatevoidcheckNotNull(Object reference, String name) {
if (reference == null) {
thrownewNullPointerException(getString(R.string.error_config,
name));
   }
  }
  @Override
protectedvoidonPause() {
super.onPause();
   //Unregistering with GCM
```

```
    GCMRegistrar.unregister(this);
      }
     }
```

GCMIntentService.java

```
    //This is a java file which act as Intent service. You can see the file being
added at //AndroidManifest.xml as a service.
    packagecom.priyaa.gcm;

    import static com.priyaa.gcm.CommonUtilities.SENDER_ID;
    importandroid.content.Context;
    importandroid.content.Intent;
    importandroid.util.Log;

    importcom.google.android.gcm.GCMBaseIntentService;

    public class GCMIntentService extends GCMBaseIntentService{

       publicGCMIntentService() {
                 super(SENDER_ID);
       }
    private static final String TAG = "GCMIntentService";
    @Override
    protected void onRegistered(Context arg0, String registrationId) {
                     Log.i(TAG, "Device registered: regId = " + registrationId);
       }
    @Override
    protected void onUnregistered(Context arg0, String arg1) {
               Log.i(TAG, "unregistered = "+arg1);
    }
    @Override
    protected void onMessage(Context arg0, Intent arg1) {
               Log.i(TAG, "new message= ");
    }
    @Override
    protected void onError(Context arg0, String errorId) {
               Log.i(TAG, "Received error: " + errorId);
    }
    @Override
       protectedbooleanonRecoverableError(Context context, String errorId) {
       returnsuper.onRecoverableError(context, errorId);
       }
    }
```

CommonUtilities.java

```
//This file is to set the project ID (got from Google Console) as SENDER_ID.

packagecom.priyaa.gcm;
publicclassCommonUtilities {
        //Intializing Project ID as Sender ID
        staticfinal String SENDER_ID = "661572405665";
}
```

AndroidManifest.xml

```
<?xml version="1.0" encoding="utf-8"?>
<manifest xmlns:android="http://schemas.android.com/apk/res/android"
package="com.priyaa.gcm"
android:versionCode="1"
android:versionName="1.0" >
<uses-sdk
android:minSdkVersion="8"
android:targetSdkVersion="19" />
   <permission
        android:name="com.priyaa.gcm.permission.C2D_MESSAGE"
        android:protectionLevel="signature" />
<uses-permission android:name="com.priyaa.gcm.permission.C2D_MESSAGE" />
<uses-permission android:name="android.permission.GET_ACCOUNTS" />
<uses-permission android:name="android.permission.WAKE_LOCK" />
<uses-permission android:name="android.permission.INTERNET" />
<uses-permission android:name="com.google.android.c2dm.permission.RECEIVE" />

<application
android:icon="@drawable/ic_launcher"
android:label="@string/app_name"
android:theme="@style/AppTheme" >
<activity
android:name="com.priyaa.gcm.RegisterActivity"
android:label="@string/app_name" >
<intent-filter>
<action android:name="android.intent.action.MAIN" />
<category android:name="android.intent.category.LAUNCHER" />
</intent-filter>
```

```
</activity>
<receiver android:name="com.google.android.gcm.GCMBroadcastReceiver"
         android:permission="com.google.android.c2dm.permission.SEND" >
<intent-filter>
<action android:name="com.google.android.c2dm.intent.RECEIVE" />
<action android:name="com.google.android.c2dm.intent.REGISTRATION" />
                <category android:name="com.priyaa.gcm" />
         </intent-filter>
         </receiver>
         <service android:name=".GCMIntentService" />
</application>
</manifest>
```

activity_push_android.xml:

```
<RelativeLayoutxmlns:android="http://schemas.android.com/apk/res/android"
android:layout_width="fill_parent"
android:layout_height="fill_parent" >


<TextView
android:id="@+id/textView1"
android:layout_width="wrap_content"
android:layout_height="wrap_content"
android:layout_alignParentLeft="true"
android:layout_alignParentTop="true"
android:layout_marginTop="88dp"/>

</RelativeLayout>
```

Strings.xml:

```
<?xml version="1.0" encoding="utf-8"?>
<resources>

<string name="app_name">GCM</string>
<string name="action_settings">Settings</string>
<string name="hello_world">Hello world!</string>
<string name="error_config">Error</string>
<string name="RegId">Your Device Registration ID</string>

</resources>
```

Creating new AVD (Android Virtual Device)

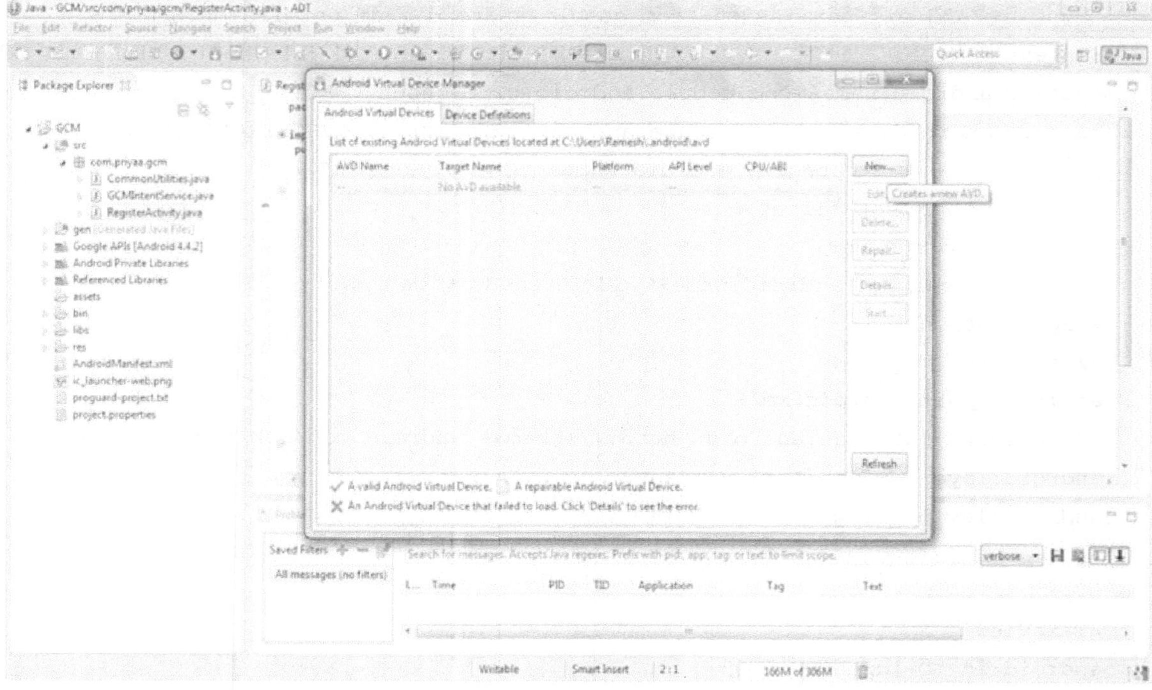

Give AVD name of your choice. Select the device type. Select Google API as Target. Remember GCM runs on Google API target alone.

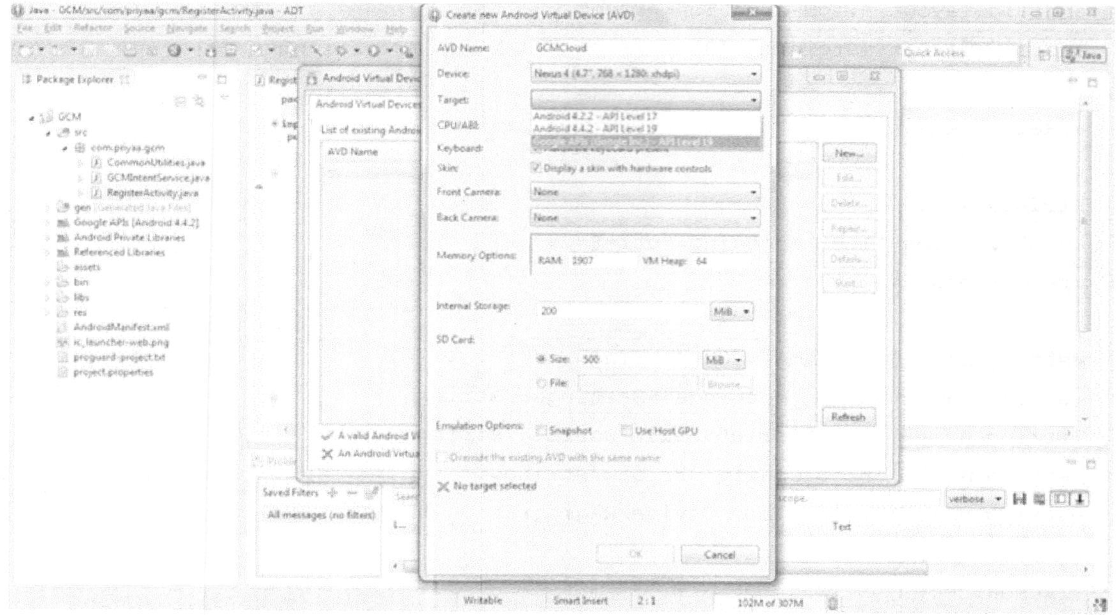

Set memory options, internal storage and SD card size of your choice.

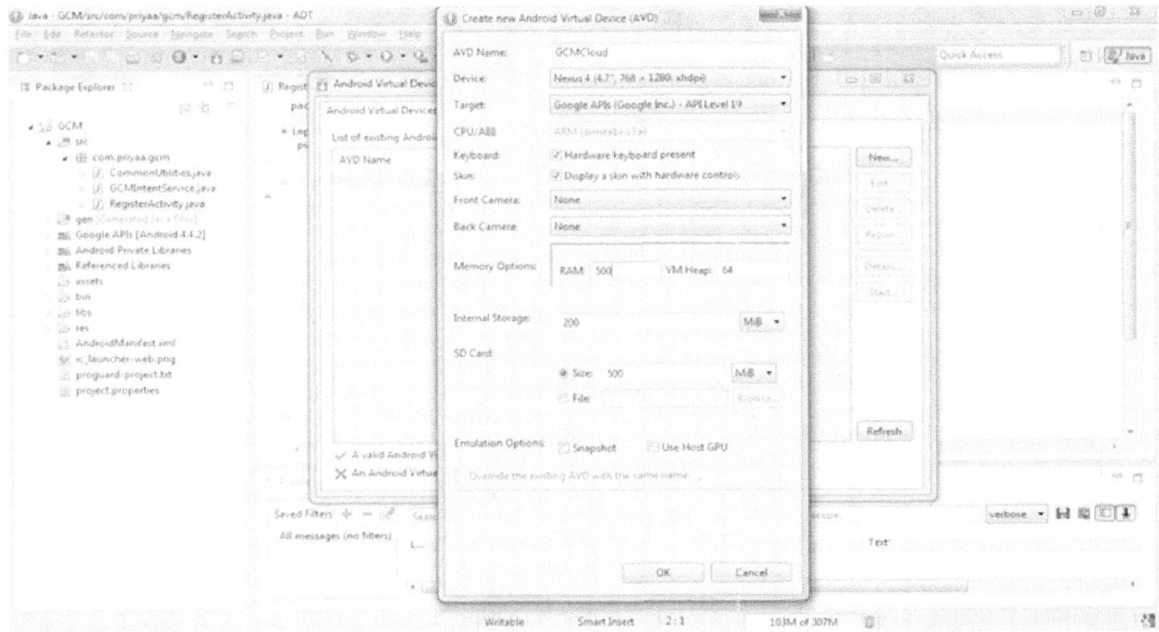

Thus a new AVD is created with Google API as tartet.

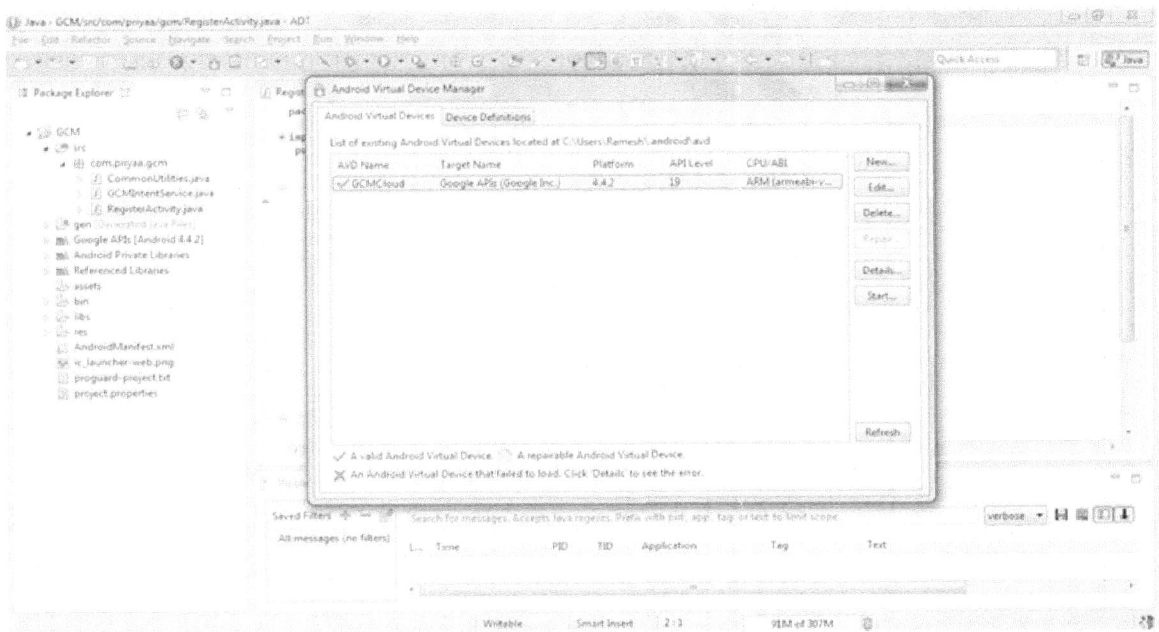

Launch the newly created AVD

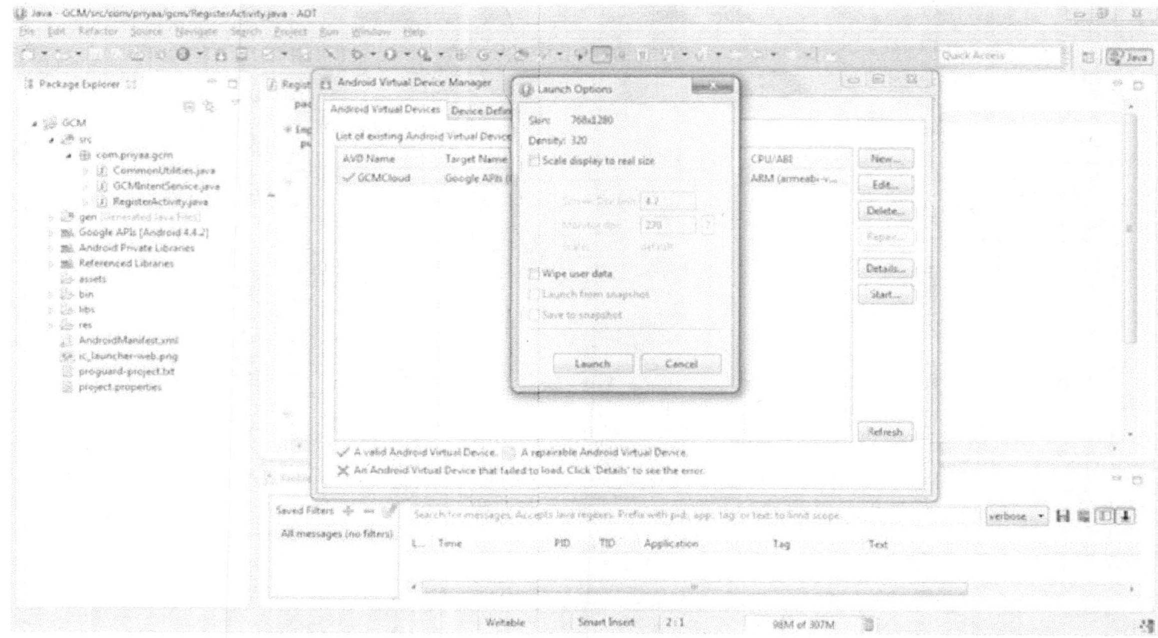

Starting the emulator.

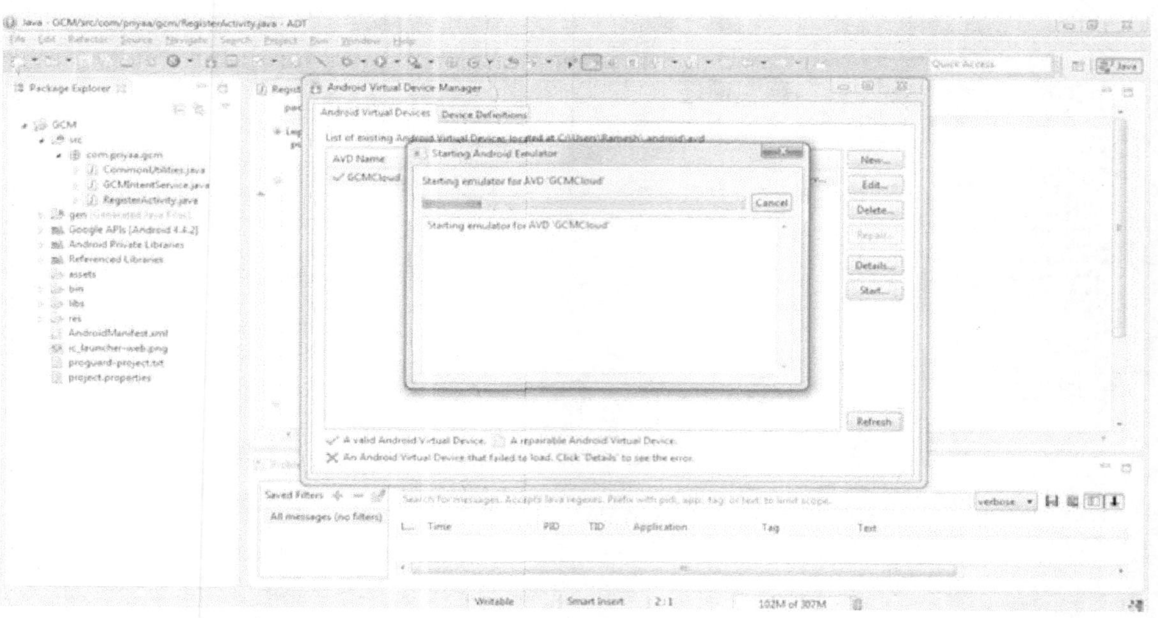

Output

Thus the device is registered with a registration id. Thus this device is ready to receive messages.

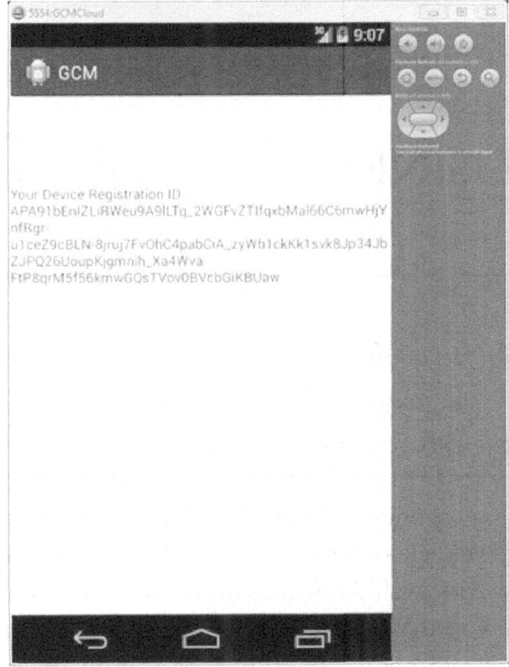

With the Device registration on, device can receive messages from GCM Connection Server.

SUMMARY

- *Components and credentials are the two major concepts of GCM.*
- *Client application, third party application servers and GCM connection servers form the components of GCM.*
- *Sender id, application id, registration id, Google User Account, Server Auth tokens are the credentials which helps in authentication and authorization.*
- *GCM connection server which acts as intermediary between client app and 3rd party app server.*
- *Enabling GCM, sending and receiving messages are the three key activities in GCM life cycle flow.*
- *Google Play Services are installed to benefit the feature of Google Cloud Messaging (GCM) API.*
- *Google API project is created in Google console which generated project id, which will be used to register a mobile device with GCM.*

12

Business Cloud Computing

OBJECTIVE

- *To learn and analyze about the term enterprise cloud computing*
- *To get exposed to the usage of cloud computing in the business domain*
- *To know about the future perspective of cloud computing.*

In the last chapters, we saw in detail about the cloud computing technology. We saw the various principles, applications, classification of clouds and various service models. We also saw how cloud computing works with Android and Linux platforms respectively. We saw the list of cloud tools to setup a real time cloud. Now in this chapter let us see in detail how the cloud technology is used and has made impact to the business world. We will deal with the business oriented and corporate meaning of cloud technology in this chapter. We also see in detail how a unique business oriented service model in cloud is used by the corporate IT companies.

12.1 ENTERPRISE CLOUD COMPUTING

In this section let us see in detail about the term enterprise cloud computing. We will see how cloud computing technology is of the business oriented and how it has changed the whole corporate IT sector.

Every technology has a value in it. Every technology value must be user friendly and business friendly in a very broader picture. To speak technically apart from theoretical and research every technology must be implemented in real time to the human kind and solve all their issues. When a technology is ultimately used by the people its full value is attained and there is real meaning behind the technology. For a technology to be fully operational by users it needs the full support from industry. Only industrial experts can ultimately help in the real time implementation of any technology. For every industry profit is the major goal or a part of the whole business strategy itself. Thus every technology must be industry oriented and supported rather than a research topic every time.

For industrial oriented term of cloud computing we say it as *enterprise cloud computing*. The word enterprise cloud computing refers to the business related operations and the usage of cloud computing technology for all their work. Cloud computing service models and its types are becoming the new way of working in a corporate IT sector. Every major corporate IT companies are moving towards this technology. The close alignment of business related corporate IT sector and cloud computing has given a new dimension to term enterprise cloud computing. Today cloud computing has changed the whole work culture in the corporate sector. Things have advanced very fast and have become more reliable. Gone are all the traditional and simple way in handling all problems and solution to them. Business related operations and solution are well handled and managed using the advanced remote cloud infrastructure and its unique capabilities.

The term enterprise cloud computing also refers to all the business related critical operations and functionalities. Enterprise computing encompasses all the various types of enterprise software, like company related business tools and solutions, database management, programming, testing, quality assurance, relationship management and so on. It also includes the companies hardware and the mass IT infrastructure to handle all the client projects and solutions to them. Enterprise computing is usually seen as a collection of big business software solutions to common problems such as resource management and streamlining processes. Every IT company must have vast amount of employees, infrastructure both physically and technically, technical experts, managing experts and distinguished leaders to run the mass organization, withstand any major problem. They also must have well defined business managers to manage the overall business operations in a well defined manner and negotiate all the business dealings in a win - win situation to both the company and client.

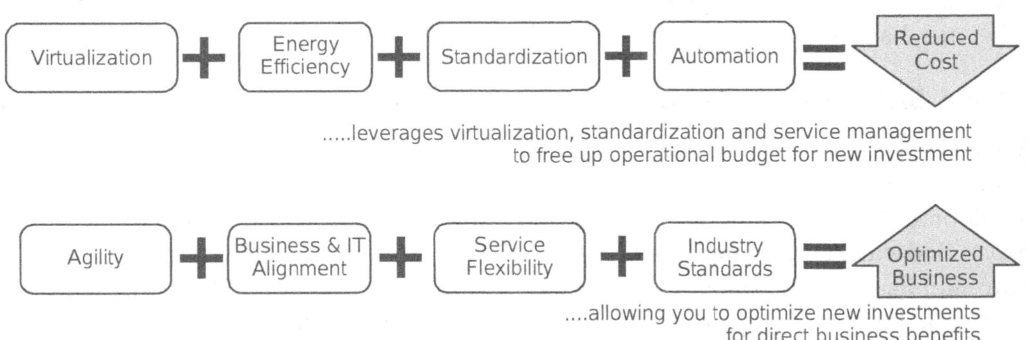

Figure 12.1 Economics of cloud computing.

Enterprise cloud computing is sometimes sold to business users as an entire platform that can be applied broadly across an organization and then further customized by users within each area, based on their specific need. As we already know cloud computing is a purely service oriented technology involving the migration of various resources and workspaces from the cloud vendor to the end user. This means the analytics, reporting, database management and other applications are standard across the system, while the application packages are used and the data being accessed in each area will be different. In this sense, enterprise cloud computing is a departure from finding single software solutions to specific business problems, such as inventory or accounting software. Instead enterprise cloud computing is intended to offer integrated solutions to these problems. Thus such form of integrated solution is the need of the hour in today competitive and dynamically changing business world.

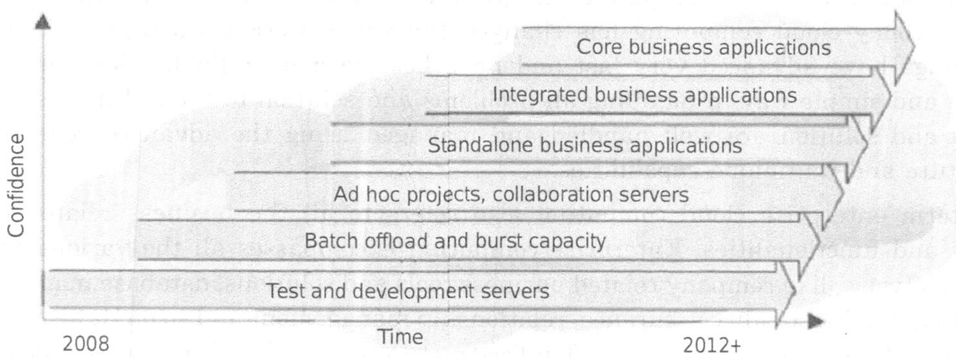

Figure 12.2 Enterprise cloud computing.

When we are talking about enterprise cloud computing there are four major terms that we need to need to understand. An enterprise cloud has changed the overall software development process from the traditional approach way. An enterprise cloud also provides the list of various cloud services for all business activities, solutions in real time to end user issues and client projects. The overall management of the cloud also needs to be handled by the company. Cloud management tools help in the overall performance and efficiency of cloud. Let us discuss each one of them in detail.

Enterprise Software Development

When we are talking about IT companies and all the business operations we must not forget the term *software development*. Today there are millions of IT companies working in the development, management, testing and supporting of various software. The term Enterprise Software Deployment refers to all of the activities that must take place to make a software application available to the end users. Enterprise Software Deployment technically begins after a software application has been written, tested, packaged and delivered to an enterprise. Enterprise Software Deployment is a recurring phase of the software development lifecycle since software is constantly being upgraded, to fix bugs or add new features. An iterative approach is the best way in the software development model. This fact makes Enterprise Software Deployment a core element in the administration of IT services within an enterprise.

The traditional method of software deployment places a heavy burden on enterprise IT resources, as they must devote a significant amount of time and attention to the installation and maintenance of all applications that exist within the enterprise computing environment. A far worse situation occurs when there is any problem in the underlying software. Conversely under a SaaS (Software as a Service) model of software delivery the cloud architecture provides a SaaS provider with a mechanism to easily deliver software over the Internet there by eliminating the need to deploy software to each application user as required under the traditional model of software delivery. The SaaS model of software delivery promises enormous savings opportunities for the enterprise in terms of labor utilization and operational expenses for software deployment and maintenance. Thus the cloud service model of designing and implementation of software is a very easy and simple task.

It is important to mention the relation between SaaS and SOA (Service Oriented Architecture) in an enterprise development. We already know that cloud computing is a perfect service oriented technology. SOA is a quite very unique feature of this computing technology. SaaS and SOA are the perfect pairing as SOA enabled SaaS providers have the capacity to serve thousands of clients from a single instance of an application that is pushed out to an enterprise cloud. This makes the delivery of software a seamless event due to the additional level of flexibility, scalability and version control that is available when SOA is coupled with SaaS. Thus the cloud delivery becomes a very easy task using SOA concepts.

SOA (Service Oriented Architecture) provides a framework where software components are delivered as services which significantly reduce the cost of software deployment and maintenance. SOA facilitates the integration of individual software components into an unlimited number of applications on demand. Each component is maintained by its owner. This provides organizations with the ability to virtually build entire applications without a need to ever worry about software updates or upgrades as this is handled by the web service providers. Organizations can use the various web services and APIs made available by various web service providers to build a variety of SaaS solutions to be delivered via the enterprise cloud. Thus one can simply say the SaaS service model of cloud has changed the overall software development process inside an IT company. It has made the things a far more simple and user friendly.

Apart from the SaaS (Software as a Service) model other service models in cloud like PaaS (Platform as a Service) or IaaS (Infrastructure as a Service) also help for the IT companies and their functions in all aspects. Well one can say with full confidence that cloud computing is certainly a full fledged business oriented technology. This has proved as a big tool in solving many problems and issues inside the corporate IT sector. In the past few years of its revolution alone things have been fast changing and are aligned to this cloud technology.

Enterprise Cloud Services

Enterprise Cloud Services refers to the extension of software, hardware, infrastructure and platforms as a service, within a private cloud computing environment. We already know cloud computing is a service oriented technology. Enterprise Cloud Services may be delivered internally using on-premise IT resources or may be delivered externally by a third party enterprise cloud services provider. Enterprise Cloud Services can provide a variety of benefits to an organization which contribute to its increasing use and popularity as an alternative to traditional methods of delivering IT services within an enterprise. We already saw in detail about private cloud and how they are useful inside an organization.

Organizations of all sizes can realize a significant cost savings for IT services, such as lowered IT operational costs and lowered capital expenses for IT assets, by deploying enterprise cloud services. Especially the small business unit ones are getting full advantage of this technology. Organizations who use enterprise cloud services no longer need to invest in server hardware network infrastructure or security tools. Instead these IT resources can be purchased on a subscription basis from a third party enterprise cloud services provider for a fraction of the cost thereby freeing up capital for other business uses. Thus the pay as you go model or renting of services in cloud has turned out to be a boon for all IT companies.

In addition many software applications will no longer need to be maintained or upgraded since software can also be purchased on a subscription basis. This provides a significant cost savings to any enterprise that has been previously saddled with the need to constantly upgrade or replace on-premise software applications, etc. New business start-ups and small businesses in particular have a great deal to gain from using enterprise cloud services since they typically have smaller budgets available for the procurement of IT resources. Thus one simply say, cloud computing is a very solution to IT company mainly due to huge cost savings.

A variety of operational benefits may be realized by organizations who deploy enterprise cloud services including a capacity to rapidly deliver new or enhanced software an ability to rapidly meet an increased demand on IT hardware resources during times of peak use and the ability to optimize the utilization of on-premise IT resources by introducing virtualization, automation and service management methods into the private cloud computing environment. The private cloud also has proved to be a right medium for communication and sharing of resources inside a company. In addition another benefit of enterprise cloud computing services when hosted on-premise is that many of the advantages of public cloud services can be gained without sacrificing security. This is because unlike public cloud services an on-premise private enterprise cloud can be firewalled to limit the threat of malicious attacks against organizational IT resources. Private clouds are far more secured inside the organization than a publically open public cloud. What's more externally hosted enterprise cloud services provide a higher level of fault tolerance and a capacity for disaster recovery that simply cannot be rivaled by most enterprise IT departments.

An Enterprise Cloud Solution is a term that may refer to a cloud service platform or it may refer to the various service models in cloud like SaaS (Software as a Service), PaaS (Platform as a Service) or IaaS (Infrastructure as a Service) offerings delivered via a cloud service platform. When an Enterprise Cloud Solution is not a cloud service platform, it typically follows the traditional model of IT service delivery like it is designed to handle a specific business operation such as accounting, document storage, electronic message delivery, software development, etc. there is a lot more difference between the cloud computing based highly advanced operation and the traditional model of IT work culture.

Enterprise Cloud Solutions that serve as cloud service platforms are distinguished from the SaaS, PaaS or IaaS offerings that they deliver, in the following way like they extend the actual cloud infrastructure services and cloud application services that are required to successfully deliver SaaS, PaaS or IaaS offerings to an enterprise. Regardless of the application an enterprise cloud solution must ultimately provide all of the resources needed to perform the required business functions in an integrated manner within the framework of the cloud architecture that delivers the solution. The cloud solution also must be highly robust and reliable as the entire business transaction is dependent on it. In any case the major goal of any enterprise cloud solution is to provide the necessary tools to manage or support a specific set of business functions systems or resources.

An Enterprise Cloud Solution can be implemented in a private cloud or in a public cloud. It has no major restriction on which cloud we must proceed. When a private cloud is used an organization takes full responsibility for the delivery of each cloud solution within its enterprise private cloud. As the private cloud is under the control of the organization it is their duty to provide all the cloud solutions in a more effective and user friendly manner. Private clouds are also a well secured environment for all business activities inside a company. Conversely when an organization uses a public enterprise cloud the external vendor has to extend the required cloud platform to the Internet to facilitate the delivery of its enterprise cloud solutions to each customer or organization. One must not forget the overall security issues involved in the publicly open public cloud platform. As the business data are very confidential one must be aware of all the security issues in handling them while processing in a public cloud. The external vendor can deliver any type of cloud solution to an enterprise including a private enterprise cloud within a public cloud that is only accessible by a single organization or entity.

Enterprise Cloud Management

Apart from enterprise cloud services and solutions, management of a cloud is also a quite big task in an enterprise. We have already mentioned cloud is a very vast technology with a huge set of pooled resources into it and is accessed by multiple users at a time. Enterprise Cloud Management refers to the execution of the requisite tasks associated with the establishment and delivery of enterprise cloud services to end user or client in a very easy and reliable manner. Whether an organization has a need to manage a private cloud or a hybrid cloud it will need to employ cloud management tools to facilitate the management of its enterprise cloud resources. Enterprise Cloud Management tools provide a platform and interface for centralized administrative control over enterprise cloud service delivery. An enterprise can effectively manage internal and external cloud resources including virtualized resources and business policies deployed to the enterprise cloud using enterprise cloud management tools. Above all the cloud management tools helps in the overall performance of the cloud in a very effective manner. Enterprise Cloud Management facilitates increased IT efficiency and cost savings for the enterprise in a variety of ways as follows:

- Cloud management tools allow the organizations to easily establish and change automation rules for their entire enterprise cloud resource pool and other usage policies from time to time resulting in a more efficient and cost effective utilization of IT resources.

- Cloud management tools may be used to deliver Infrastructure as a Service (IaaS) thereby enabling provisioning and configuration of IT resources on demand. Moving to a self-service or automated model of delivery for many IT services can eliminate a variety of time consuming and repetitive administrative IT tasks allowing IT personnel to focus their energy on higher level IT concerns. As we already know cloud computing involves the overall migration of the workspace or the technical infrastructure to accomplish the end user task. Enterprise cloud management tools can also be leveraged to deliver data security services on demand including password recovery assistance and so on.
- Enterprise Cloud Management tools can facilitate increased IT efficiency through the availability of web service management tools. Such tools provide an interface to a centralized repository of all available web services that exist in an enterprise cloud. IT administrators can easily track web service dependencies and web service versions to more efficiently handle configuration and change management tasks within the enterprise cloud computing environment.
- Enterprise Cloud Management tools also provide a capacity to automate IT auditing tasks that may be required for operational compliance with industry regulatory agencies. Organizations can use cloud management tools to automate IT audit processing based on various data access events, which reduces the need for manual IT monitoring of processes applications and data for audit purposes. The potential economic benefit to an enterprise can be huge, since compliance failures can lead the incursion of massive fines or legal expenses to defend an enterprise against lawsuits for data breeches, etc.

Today millions of cloud tools and solutions are available for the business operations inside the companies. Some are free of cost while some are proprietary and so on. As of 2013 some the commonly used cloud computing tools inside the business organization include:

- ***GitHub*** – It is a very powerful collaboration, review, and code management for open source and private development projects. GitHub is the best way for all coding aspects of the cloud technology. Most of the cloud tools codes are found in github platform only.
- ***Bitbucket*** – It store all of your Git and source code in one place. Includes issue tracking, wiki, pull requests, unlimited repositories and is free for the first 5 users.
- ***Vagrant*** – It is used to Create and configure lightweight, reproducible, and portable development environments. Run a single command vagrant up and then Vagrant puts together your complete development environment. Say goodbye to the workplace machine excuse as Vagrant creates identical development environments for everyone on your team.
- ***New Relic*** – New Relic is the all in one web application performance tool that lets you see performance from the end user experience through servers and down to the line of application code.

- ***Cloud 66*** – Cloud 66 is the easiest way to deploy, monitor and manage your Ruby on Rails applications on your servers or your cloud.
- ***Capistrano*** – Open source tool written in Ruby for running scripts on multiple servers its main use is deploying web applications. It automates the process of making a new version of an application available on one or more web servers, including supporting tasks such as changing databases.

12.2 CLOUD COMPUTING IN BUSINESS UNIT

In the last section, we saw in detail about the term enterprise cloud computing. We saw how the enterprises provide the various cloud services, solutions and the various management aspects that help in the business operations inside the companies. Now in this section let us see in detail how cloud computing is used inside a business unit of companies. We will also see how the cloud is very useful for small scale industries.

Cloud computing solutions can bring benefits to all industry sectors, and to both large and small companies. Switching information systems to the Cloud platform thus abolishing the need for extensive in company infrastructure, traditional approach and altering the way Business Intelligence is used to support decision making which will enable firms to speed up their product development processes and to achieve profitability much more rapidly. It can change the overall work culture and the functioning procedures inside the company. This is what many business leaders and analysts feel.

In today's growing computer age cloud computing is used by everyone from individuals to private and public organizations including educational systems and governments not just limited to major corporate IT sector or computer solutions limited. In business cloud systems are used by organizations of all shapes and sizes from small businesses to multinational corporations. This advance computing technology has made so much impact in the recent times to every sector. More and more people are getting exposed or accessed to this new advanced networking cloud technology day by day. With the exposure of cloud people are ready to shift or move towards this technology rather stick to the traditional and outdated approach.

Cloud computing has made a new revolution inside the business oriented IT companies. Its service models, cloud types and applications are well suited for the business purposes. This technology is closely aligned to needs and requirements of any major business solution company. The overall working process or the technology functioning is closely associated with the business operations and critical decisions. The critical approach or operations inside the business workspace are well suited to handle this advanced cloud approach. When we are talking about cloud computing one must not forget the previous or traditional approach that was used in the business approach earlier. A move to the cloud platform is inevitable now. Domestic infrastructure facilities served the organization for decades but it is not suitable for it now, when other business units expect services to be delivered quickly and without problems. With traditional infrastructure facilities can take months to get going. Meanwhile, the original business opportunity has come and gone with no effect. With the cloud opportunities can be exploited quickly. With growing demand and advancement the business units need to shift towards this technology.

Every new technology must be so user friendly and collaborative in nature such that it must support the transformation of all the previous work or technologies used earlier into the new platform. All the previous work must be supported into the new technology platform. Not that there is no relation or any forms of support by the new technology and the traditional method. In this aspect cloud is far collaborative and supportive. Cloud supports all previous techniques and helps in the easy synchronization of it. Cloud is also platform independent technology.

Businesses use cloud computing to access information anywhere using any compatible device. Unlike storing information on your computer or a server in your office, cloud computing stores data on the Internet in a remote virtual data. It works by making information available from a central Web-based hub that gives anyone access from any location with a high speed Internet connection with proper credentials. Cloud computing also synchronizes data for all devices connected to the cloud, keeping them updated with real-time information.

In the cloud environment, users can access all types of files, software, hardware and even workspaces. As we already know the various service models of the cloud help in the migration of all the resources even the currently working workspaces and the platform. A single project is divided into various modules and in each project multiple people are working into it which may be also from different locations. The higher officials and employee may also be from different locations. In such situations of remote working atmosphere cloud technology is a powerful tool in the business operation. The employees can use applications as though they were in the office and even collaborate remotely while working on the same project or presentation on their device as someone on the other side of the globe. Even if you're away from work or your office server is inaccessible data in the cloud is always up-to-date and always available wherever whenever. Thus cloud helps in the project work independent of the location. Cloud computing services can range from data storage to functional programs, including accounting, customer-service tools, remote desktop hosting and more.

According to a study an IT research firm that focuses on cloud technology, 54 per cent of organizations use cloud computing. Of these organizations, 74 per cent use some combination of different types of clouds, with 40–50 per cent of them using multiple services of the same type of cloud.

An another survey by the analyst firm Research found that 92 per cent of CIOs and IT professionals think the cloud is good for business. The same survey also found that only 31 per cent of companies that describe their infrastructure are mainly based on the cloud, indicating a rejection among most organizations to take positive steps towards cloud adoption.

Apart from all these discussion let us see how cloud computing is helping or is advantage inside the business unit of the organization in other ways too:

- ***Rented software and hardware*** – One the biggest advantage to the business world from cloud computing is the renting of resources in a very cheaper way.

It involves the pay as you go or metering model of paying. It is very cheap compared to the actual cost in purchasing dedicated resources.

- ***Better feature and more performance*** – Since cloud providers are providing services to many different companies they buy large high-performance systems that offer performance levels much higher than a small company can afford to run internally. They typically have the most capable versions of software and site licenses so they will also have access to features at much lower costs than one get from dedicated purchase of them. Their experienced administrators are more likely to know how to optimize performance than the users.
- ***Overall expenditure*** – By the cloud services and models the overall capital expenditure of the organization is reduced. Mainly due to the renting of resources. After all one must not forget profit and economy is the ultimate goal in any business.
- ***Business agility*** – The cloud services and the underlying technology helps the organizations by tuning themselves to the demands and needs of the growing dynamic market expectations.
- ***Automation*** – Instead of having to invest in IT support to keep your file storage system updated and maintained most applications that use the Cloud automatically update themselves.
- ***Ease of use*** – With the renting of software and hardware the biggest task of maintaining, updating or troubleshooting in case of any problem are no more required inside the business unit of the company. Thus the company can spent valuable energy towards the development purpose.
- ***Platform independence*** – Another advantage to all the business companies from cloud computing is that this technology is purely platform independent. It supports and gives full collaboration to all other platforms.
- ***Backup and file sharing*** – Cloud can be extensively used for the storage of all confidential data related to the critical business operating from any failures or disaster. Such data can also be easily shared to the concerned person or client in a very user friendly manner.
- ***Staffing efficiency*** – Cloud services helps in maintaining the right proportion of staffing by outsourcing the key technical specifications and rest being handled internally.
- ***Green dimension*** – There is also a green aspect in the cloud that can help companies achieve their business objectives in corporate social responsibility. This is because cloud providers can invest in data centers in a large scale. Which offer companies a green alternative to the conventional approach for IT. Furthermore by putting more cloud services material waste is reduced as less hardware is required. In addition fewer infrastructures on site means less equipment to manage or upgrade them.

- ***Business approach*** – The cloud technology allows companies to increase redundancy infrastructure in all parts of the business. Decentralization allows applications and data, and this increases business flexibility and streamlines disaster recovery and network. New approaches to scalable application computing to simplify your IT infrastructure by merging many essential elements including storage, load balancing, database and caching in equipment clearly managed or cloud instances.

  Business owners generally use three types of cloud services to store their data and provide them with services public, private and hybrid.
- ***Public cloud*** – A public cloud service is built on an external platform run by a cloud-service provider. With this off-site cloud service users get their own cloud within a shared infrastructure. The provider offers everything from system resources to the security and maintenance of your cloud system. Since it is managed by an outside company specializing in cloud services for a large range of customers a public cloud system is great for organizations that want more elasticity, cost-effectiveness and the latest technology.
- ***Private cloud*** – A private cloud service is a cloud platform built within your own walls on your own hardware and software. Since a private cloud is managed by your own internal IT team it is ideal for businesses that want exclusive access more flexibility and greater control over their cloud. To use a private cloud service however organizations build their own data centers making it a costlier cloud option.
- ***Hybrid cloud*** – A hybrid cloud service employs both private and public clouds. In a hybrid cloud system an organization's own IT team manages part of the cloud in-house and the rest off-site. For instance a hybrid cloud system is perfect for an organization that wants to manage business-related data such as customer files in-house but wants to store less-sensitive information with a third party. Hybrid cloud systems are used by all types of organizations but are 46 per cent more likely to be used by larger organizations with more than 1,000 employees according to the research.

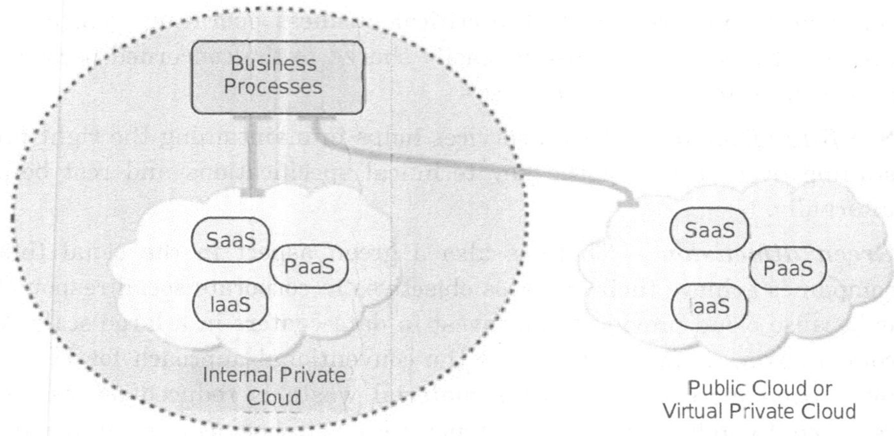

Figure 12.3 Cloud computing in a business unit.

Now to speak from the improvement aspect of cloud computing to the existing business structure, cloud offers far new features which can be used to improve the overall performance and productivity of a company. Some of them include:

- ***Data duplication*** – Unlike physical servers that can cost a lot to maintain let alone buying backups, cloud computing allows companies to have multiple copies of information on various virtual servers meaning work flow won't be affected by technical glitches.
- ***Access control*** – With the right amount of skill an intruder can access a physical server and damage or steal data. This kind of access is impossible under cloud as security is much tighter and is quite advanced compared to the traditional internet.
- ***Innovation*** – Businesses like banks and training institutions get a platform using which they can build new products and services that are easily accessible to the consumer.
- ***Outsourcing*** – Clouds make it easier for a business to outsource non core business activities like customer care to offsite and even overseas locations which is more cost effective. Thus they can concentrate on the major issues.
- ***Tele-working*** – It enables workers to carry out their jobs at convenient locations reducing fixed costs brought about by hiring premises and transport cost. Cloud computing is anytime, anywhere technology.
- ***Efficient data handling*** – Unlike in conventional situations where data access maybe slow or hampered by excessive traffic to one server, the cloud doesn't suffer from this. Cloud computing is based on virtualization and distributed principles.
- ***Increase technical capability*** – Cloud computing allows deployment of specialized software and tools that would have otherwise cost too much to use in the traditional setting.

Now to speak from a small business companies point of it cloud computing is a very big early source to the start up. For a small business organization cloud provides the right startup launch pad by all its business friendly advantages and service oriented concepts. Unlike all the traditional approach cloud platform is the right stage to kick start the business and then expand in all other directions. Using cloud technology small companies can grow in a big shape and dimension in just few years of its start. It can expect good profit and growth too from the beginning itself. Cloud computing saves the overall expenditure to start and run the small business. All the required tools for initial business can be easily rented using the cloud services. Cloud technology is far ease of use, scalable, flexible and agile to the growing needs and changing dynamics of the market for the small businesses.

The Cloud is scalable, so it allows small businesses to create a plan for growth that utilizes the benefits of the Cloud without a significant up-front investment. You can start small, and gradually increase your usage over time, while only paying incrementally for the services and access you need. The Cloud is also self-managed by the apps that provide the services, so you can eliminate or at least reduce the need for an in-house IT staff to manage your technology. Small business owners who want to reduce costs without sacrificing their ability to do business and compete with larger companies are using the Cloud. If you are ready to put the Cloud to work for your business, you can start small so you can see the benefits without making major changes to your operations. Over time, you will discover new ways to use and benefit from the Cloud.

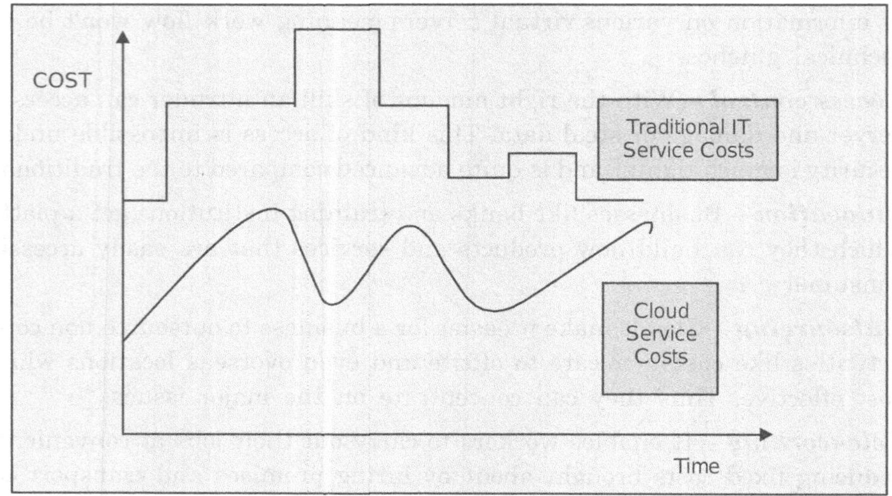

Cost Saving derived from:
- Efficiency of upscaling/downscaling as demand changes
- Reduced underutilization from sharing services

Figure 12.4 Cloud computing advantage to the business companies.

Large organizations are also adopting cloud technology for many of the same reasons as of the smaller organizations. The cloud can in many cases lower the cost of computing resources on the basis of price, but it also eliminates wasteful expenditures, because the company only pays for the computing resources it needs. They have been attracted to the idea of renting rather than owning computing resources greater flexibility and cost savings, resiliency in the event of natural disasters, and the ability to try new technologies without having to commit to them. And while they acknowledge concerns about cyber security, they believe they can safely pursue their cloud strategies while taking appropriate precautions.

Data gathered by IT companies from clients who make use of its Cloud Computing services and its approaches reveals that the primary use of Cloud Computing technology is currently helping to design mobile apps. Fully 80% of the firms analyzed use the Cloud for this purpose as it leads to cost reductions of up to 30% for app development. This approach can moreover make sense financially across a wide range of industries. Some 20% of the firms using Cloud solutions are today in the Retail sector, followed by 18% Media & Advertising firms, and 11% that are in Healthcare systems or Science-oriented fields. For major corporations the choice will be driven by their experience while for smaller firms switching to cloud computing will be less dependent on past experience or necessity and more a matter of choice, since Cloud Computing will prove to be extremely easy to adopt given their existing structures.

	Type of savings	Amount of savings
SaaS	• PaaS benefits + avoid software maintenance fees and costly upgrades	• 25-40% implementation costs savings • Operating costs savings • 50% + total cost savings
PaaS	• No need to run a datacenter • No need to maintain infrastructure software (database and applications)	• 30% savings on operating costs • 2-3x time-to-market improvement
IaaS	• Difference of efficiency between internal data data center vs. that of IaaS Provider	• Savings depend on use case and alternative costs • Savings might not be significant if an enterprise has a well-managed large data center

Figure 12.5 Cloud service models savings to companies.

12.3 BUSINESS PROCESSING AS A SERVICE

In the last section, we saw in detail how cloud computing is used inside the business unit and all its advantages them. To further understand how cloud computing is used inside the business organization there is a one more separate service model called *business processing as a service* (BPaaS). Let us discuss in detail how this service model helps for business organization.

While every one of us knows cloud computing is a service oriented technology. It has several service models whose ultimate goal is to provide service to the end user by the various underlying principles of cloud computing. We already discussed the list of various service models. We also saw the various advantages and the overall usage of these models in the accomplishing of end user task. There is one more service model exclusively meant from the business point of view whose goal is for all the critical business operations. One such business service models in cloud computing is *business processing as a service (BPaaS).*

Business processing as a service (BPaaS) refers to the various business services and processes being provided as a service in the cloud. It is one among the service models of the cloud. Its sole purpose is to provide the service to the end user. It is also based on the service oriented technology like other service models of cloud. It is used by all the users and the major IT companies. With the advent of cloud computing the overall approach in business world is starting to change. Increasingly companies are looking at a more service-oriented approach than to the traditional approach. Rather than assume you need a packaged application that includes business logic, data, and processes it is possible to select a process application that is not tied into a single application. BPaaS is a quite a big business tool for small companies at least in the initial stage of its start up. The term BPaaS is also closely associated with the term called *business process management* (BPM).

Business process management is an approach that aims to make a company's workflow more effective, efficient and adaptable to new developments. It deals with the overall agility of the business sector. This kind of workflow enables businesses to be more flexible and to decrease their spending. It also refers to the overall management of the business and its dynamic changes in the market flow from time to time.

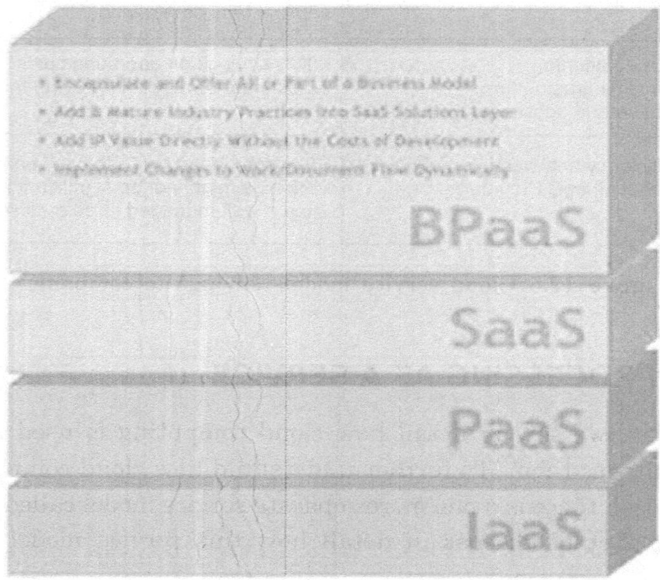

Figure 12.6 Business processing as a service (BPaaS).

Traditional Business Process Management Systems (BPMS) integrate business processes and keep track of running instances of these processes. A BPMS coordinates the execution of a business process step by step. Each process instance is monitored by the BPMS and provides users insights into each processes progress and show if they are completed successfully, or if they have crashed. In case of a crash the BPMS shows where the process had issues. By monitoring, evaluating and identifying where business processes fail companies have the opportunity to act proactively and optimize their processes. This will ultimately lead to lower costs and better customer satisfaction.

A Business Process as a Service (BPaaS) is any business process or service delivered as a service through cloud technology solutions and its service models. With BPaaS one or more business processes are uploaded to a cloud service that performs and monitors them. Like any other cloud environment, BPaaS gives companies the opportunity to use cloud software in a pay-per-use model, instead of having to invest in hardware and maintenance. It is just same as the other service models like SaaS, IaaS, PaaS and so on.

The difference between traditional packaged applications and BPaaS is that BPaaS is designed to be service-oriented one under the cloud technology. So BPaaS is likely to have well-defined interfaces. In addition, a BPaaS is a standardized service for use by many different organizations. Because these services are much more optimized to deliver a service consistently they can leverage automation, standardization, and repeatability in the way the services are used and delivered.

It is dependent on other services like Software as a Service (SaaS), Platform as a Service (PaaS), and Infrastructure as a Service (IaaS) and other services of the cloud computing too. Similar to other services in cloud BPaaS is also accessed using the internet in a client machine from the remote virtual cloud. It is viewed in the web browser. BPaaS also fallows all the principles and characteristics of cloud computing.

Business Process as a Service (BPaaS) and BPM solutions blend traditional business process outsourcing (BPO) solutions with cloud computing technology to deliver value added business outcomes with few IT resources and less IT infrastructure. These solutions help in managing the fragmented businesses of an enterprise across the regions from a central node while also ensuring flexibility in terms of accessibility, deployment and scalability of the solutions. BPaaS is the outcome of the evolution of cloud services thereby enabling the automation of business processes to assure the consistency of business outcomes. Although the benchmarking criterion of Business Process as a Service and BPM solutions remains an ambiguity amongst organizations due to privacy, security and compliance concerns, enterprises are slowly realizing the benefits of these solutions. Global adoption trends and pervasiveness across most verticals are clear indications of a positive growth, as early adopters are already edifying the various advantages of this cloud service.

The list of various services offered via the BPaaS model include:

- Customer management
- Finance and accounting
- Human resources
- Industry operations
- Supply management

It also includes the various other administration, advertising, marketing and industry related processes. The BPaaS service model is a standardized service for use by many different organizations. Because these services are much more optimized to deliver a service consistently they can leverage automation, standardization, and repeatability in the way the services are used and delivered.

When these services are delivered from the cloud it changes the overall economic dynamics. Particularly from the user perspective, one moves away capital expenditure (CAPEX) discussion to the operational expenditure (OPEX) discussion during business case calculations. This in the IT world is called as a paradigm shift, shift towards utility computing, where you pay as you go even within the walls of the enterprise and extended value chain. This shift is highly advantage to the business organization as it brings down the overall expenditure and even the required infrastructure to support them.

Some of the features of the BPaaS service model of cloud computing include:

- The BPaaS service model of cloud is on top of the other three foundational cloud services SaaS, PaaS, and IaaS. All the service models of cloud are integrated to each other and are very much useful in solving the end user task.

- A BPaaS service is configurable based on the process being designed and required by the end user or the business organization. The BPaaS model must be highly agile to the changing needs and demands of the market.
- A BPaaS service must have well-defined APIs so it can be easily connected to related services.
- A BPaaS must be able to support multiple languages and multiple deployment environments because a business cannot predict how a business process will be leveraged in the future. Business platform and underlying technology might change from time to time. The cloud service models must be supportive and collaborative to them.
- A BPaaS environment must be able to handle massive scaling. The service must be able to go from managing a few processes for a couple of customers to being able to support hundreds if not thousands of customers and processes. The service accomplishes that objective by optimizing the underlying cloud services to support this type of elasticity and scaling.
- The provision of enterprise (not consumer) business process offerings that encompass integrated optimization of process, technology, and people.
- Typical business processes include horizontal functions such as payroll, order-to-cash, procure-to-pay, hire-to-retire. Processes can also include industry specific vertical business process, such as healthcare claims processing, trade settlements, clinical data management, etc.
- These offerings of BPaaS are underpinned by complete applications that can be customized by clients and delivered over the Internet via either public or private cloud computing.
- The client does not manage the underlying software, platform, or infrastructure including networking, operating system, database management systems, storage, processing, storage, networking, security and so on. It is all provided as a service in cloud. After all cloud is a purely service oriented technology.
- The client only has one service provider touch point which caters to the entire business process delivery in a utility model. Thus the BPaaS service delivery model is very efficient and user friendly.
- The client typically will pay for the service via a subscription model that can be modified at any time based upon volume and usage requirements. This is one of the important characteristic of cloud computing known as pay as you go model.
- The BPaaS offering delivers measurable outcomes in terms of cost, compliance, risk and quality.

And still there are many more characteristics of the BPaaS model.

Now one has to imagine that there are millions of IT companies, with infinite number of employees working in several projects under various technologies. How does the BPaaS service provider exactly provide the specific required service to them?

In the first step, it requires service providers to develop more solution or consultative selling behaviors. Service providers will need to invest time to identify the few target markets where they intend to specialize and to develop a deep understanding of the business processes that are essential to these target markets. The service provider must make a deep study into all the technical and business requirements of all end users and corporate IT companies. The service provider must think of in both present and future technologies too. Business requirements and needs are highly agile in nature. Thus considering all the issues only the cloud vendor must think of the BPaaS model of delivery in cloud.

Once the critical business processes have been identified the service provider then needs to understand how these can be supported and can be provided as a service in cloud. Hopefully the cloud service model must have other additional client benefits and all other cloud services too. The services provided by the vendor must cover all the aspects of the client requirement. It is also must be of platform independent. It must support all the technologies and different project domains required by the industry. The BPaaS model solution must be a very high complete solution to the end user and all other stakeholders too. Here the service provider does not need to work alone but can also consider engaging an ecosystem of specialist vendors to develop a more complete solution. Thus the combination of vendors can further give more attractive feature and a very good solution.

There must also be a practical reason to select a business process service. First, an organization can select a process that matches their business policy and overall requirement. It can then be used in many different application environments and several other projects. This ensures that a well-defined and more importantly a consistent process exist across the organization. A trial period can also be given to the organization by the vendor initially to test all the features and their requirement. For example, a company may have a complex process for processing payroll or managing shipping. This service can be linked to other services in the cloud, such as SaaS, as well as to applications in the data center.

Like SaaS cloud services, business processes are beginning to be designed as a packaged offering that can be used in a hybrid manner. After all business processes are the steps you take or the activities you perform to facilitate the delivery of products or services to your customers or stakeholders. These business processes can really be any service that can be automated, including managing e-mail, shipping a package, or managing customer credit.

Business Process as a Service (BPaaS) and Business Process Management (BPM) solutions are fast gaining pace in the current business environment. It is predicts that BPaaS will grow from $84.1B in 2012 to $144.7B in 2016, generating a global compound annual growth rate of 15%.

These solutions bring in the economies of cloud computing technology and are positioned as flexible and scalable solutions which are focused on enhancing the value of business outcomes delivered by the efficient execution of business processes across all verticals and other regions. BPaaS and BPM solutions bring various other benefits beyond cost effectiveness and ease of access anywhere anytime.

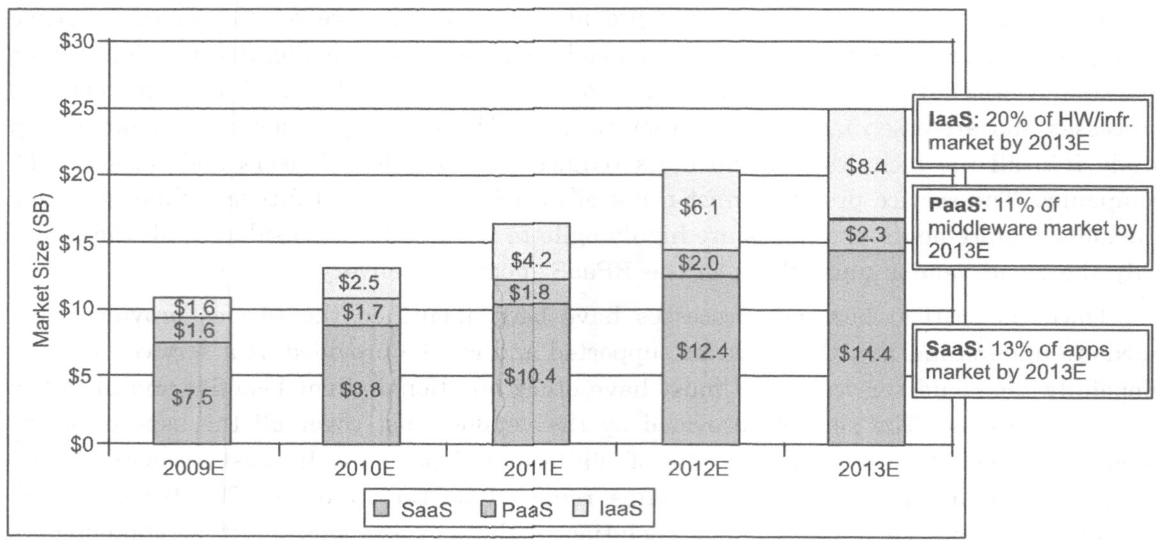

Cloud Layers	Market Size, $B (Gartner)				Investable spaces
	2009E	2013E	CAGR (2009E-2013E)	% of total market (2013E)	
SaaS	$7.5	$14.4	18%	13%	On-demand companies
PaaS	$1.6	$2.3	9%	11%	On-demand companies
IaaS	$1.6	$8.4	52%	2%	Networking and storage vendors Hosters, SI's, enablers

Source: LCM, Gartner

Figure 12.7 Market size of cloud service models.

12.4 CORPORATE COMPANIES CLOUD AND THEIR USAGE

Now in this section, we will see in detail how private cloud computing is used the corporate IT companies. What are their goals, services, strategy and all other internal information about their cloud. This will help us in better understanding how do companies have a real time projects in their workspace.

Today there are millions of IT companies using the cloud computing. Each one has developed their own tool, technology and other service models to satisfy their own company needs. In this section, we will see in detail about two major IT companies which are *Accenture* and *Cisco*.

Accenture Company

Accenture is a global management consulting technology services and outsourcing company, with approximately 281,000 people serving clients in more than 120 countries. Combining unparalleled experience, comprehensive capabilities across all industries and business functions, and extensive research on the world's most successful companies, Accenture collaborates with clients to help them become high-performance businesses and governments. The company generated net revenues of US$28.6 billion for the fiscal year ended Aug. 31, 2013.

Cloud Platform

Accenture helps mitigate the challenges associated with cloud integration, governance and service delivery by providing a platform that accelerates the successful adoption and integration of cloud services without compromising quality, standards or security. The Accenture Cloud Platform aggregates, integrates, automates and manages cloud services. It can be accessed in an on-demand fashion or as an asset for on-premise deployments.

Through a centralized storefront and service catalog, organizations can deploy and manage Accenture's growing suite of cloud computing services, and integrate them with services offered by other providers. The platform itself enables service automation and orchestration, consumption-based metering and billing, and centralized governance.

The Accenture Cloud Platform is founded on Accenture's leadership in the cloud space and its extensive experience in helping global clients sort through the complex cloud choices in the market. We sit within a strong cloud ecosystem, with knowledge of and access to a host of cloud providers.

As a result, our clients benefit from our unbiased knowledge and experience on all aspects of the cloud ecosystem, our unwavering focus on security, our deep skills at commercializing cloud opportunities and the insights we've gained by successfully deploying platform solutions for ourselves and clients around the world.

The solution delivers benefits in three main areas:

- Simplicity of oversight and stronger governance
- Increased business agility
- Reduced total cost of ownership.

Among the specific services offered on the Accenture Cloud Platform are:

- Big Data Analytics
- Data Decommissioning
- Infrastructure as a Service Provisioning and Management
- Testing-as-a-Service (TaaS).

Cloud Infrastructure

Accenture provides our cloud infrastructure clients with benefits such as:

- Technology independence
- A strong and varied partnership ecosystem
- A next generation data center roadmap and extensive implementation experience
- Our global delivery network

- Implementation through run experience
- Remote managed services strategy
- Accenture helps its clients deliver.

Private Cloud – Accenture helps clients gain agility and flexibility with an integrated private instance of a private cloud.

Cloud Infrastructure Services for Service Providers – Primarily for telecommunication companies, this solution allows our clients to lay down an external-style capability for their clients.

Cloud-Integrated Enterprise Services – Accenture helps clients seamlessly integrate cloud services (private /public) and legacy data center environments to create an integrated managed, end-to-end capability.

Accenture offers Data Center Services and Cloud Enterprise Services to help organizations transform their infrastructure to a virtualized, automated, service-based model. This model is the starting point for integrating cloud services. Depending on client need, Accenture can help build and enable private, public or hybrid clouds. We will help you determine which best fits your organization's needs, implement the right technologies and facilitate the running of your hybrid environment.

Cloud Applications and Platforms

Changing your applications, whether building new ones or rebuilding/replacing existing apps, can be expensive and time consuming. Designing, building, testing and deploying the technology platforms and architectures that will underlie the application requires a significant budget. As CIOs and their business clients grapple with issues of IT cost, legacy complexity, speed and agility, they are increasingly considering cloud application and platform technologies as a vehicle for change.

Accenture believes that cloud will become the primary platform and enabler for application development and management and replatforming within three to five years. The number of cloud platform choices both in the private and public spaces keeps growing as virtually all middleware vendors are moving to this space.

Our Agile Application and Platform Services solution focuses on the use of cloud of three ways first, Platform as a Service (PaaS), second, Application Modernization, and, third, Cloud-Enabled Systems Integration. In each case we are able to leverage assets, methods, delivery capabilities, and alliance relationships that in combination provide Accenture with a uniquely differentiated client value proposition.

Cloud Strategy

Accenture's Strategy Solution includes five key assets:

- ***Cloud Opportunity Assessment Tool*** – A toolset to support the assessment of your organization's applications and infrastructure to determine potential cloud opportunities, define a target application and infrastructure architecture, and develop road maps.

- ***Cloud Market Insight*** – Accenture continually monitors the global cloud marketplace to assess solutions for infrastructure, platform, software and business process as a service, as well as supporting tools and technologies. The team also maintains a knowledge repository that captures Accenture's collective cloud strategy expertise.
- ***Cloud Strategy Methodology*** – A proven methodology used to support the development of your cloud strategy, focusing on the alignment between business and IT, understanding the business and IT strategy and imperatives, the target cloud architecture, implementation road maps and business cases, and impacts to the IT operating model.
- ***Cloud Enterprise Architecture*** – A cross-industry cloud enterprise architecture representing what a future application and infrastructure architecture might look like. This enterprise architecture is maintained by a dedicated team as the cloud marketplace evolves.
- ***Cloud-Enabled IT Operating Model*** – A proven blueprint for how an IT organisation operates and how IT services are provided to the organization, including functions, processes, governance, roles and organisational models. This operating model is constantly refreshed.

Accenture SaaS Service Model

Accenture SaaS Business Solutions Suite

The Accenture SaaS Business Solutions Suite is used to help organizations address how SaaS can be used across strategy and planning, execution and operations. With SaaS, it is important to think about all three of these areas together versus sequentially. The Accenture SaaS Business Solution Suite can be applied to:

- Help organizations assess and plan their SaaS strategies, and integrate SaaS solutions with existing systems in complex, global environments.
- Many computing platforms, across all industries, by department or enterprise-wide.
- Address pressing business issues in human resources, customer service, indirect and direct sales and back-office functions.

In addition, Accenture has the methods and tools needed to help clients deliver third-party SaaS Solutions from strategy and planning to execution and ongoing operations.

Strategy and Planning

- ***Application Portfolio Assessment Toolkit*** – it helps analyze the technical, functional and financial information required to determine which applications are candidates for the cloud, including mapping to vendor solutions, and the different approaches your organization can use to retire, migrate, replatform and retain key applications. Used as key input for an overall application blueprint and roadmap for how to implement the changes.

Agile Execution

- ***SaaS Proof of Value Accelerator*** – It is a pilot approach your organization can use to validate specific metrics prior to scaling for a larger implementation helping you to deliver proven results faster.
- ***Accenture SaaS Delivery Toolkit*** – It assists in providing a disciplined approach to deliver SaaS solutions consistently, regardless of whether the work is performed on-shore or off-shore, including a method to estimate, scope, plan and deploy resources for initial and subsequent releases and enhancements. Use of the toolkit helps reduce risk and improve the quality of the solution.
- ***SaaS Global Deployment Accelerator*** – Helps provide your organization with an efficient and effective way to drive consistency in a global or enterprise deployment—for both the core solution and delivery, while accounting for regional variances in both, such as cultural approaches, regulatory issues and go-to-market channels.
- ***Accenture Partner Relationship Management Quick Start Tool*** – It helps enable your channel programs in as little as four weeks, using predefined leading-practice processes, business requirements, training, communication templates and job aides, and common business drivers and metrics.
- ***Accenture Cloud Application Factory*** – It is an industrialized delivery approach that makes it easier to migrate or build applications on a Cloud platform at lower cost using repeatable delivery processes, scalable delivery resources and proven delivery and development tools.

Ongoing Cloud Operations

- ***Cloud Application Maintenance*** – It helps your organization to get the most out of your SaaS solutions, including the structure to maximize the number of releases per year you can achieve, while minimizing costs and amplifying value.

Cloud Security

Our specific security services fall into four broad categories:

- ***Security strategy and risk services*** – We help clients assess their security and risk tolerance, determine the right level of security for their cloud ambitions, and design a comprehensive strategy and architecture that supports their business goals.
- ***Application and infrastructure security*** – Our infrastructure security solutions start by getting foundation security services right across the extended enterprise and cloud ecosystem. Our application security solutions help clients design, develop and deploy secure cloud-based applications.
- ***Identity and access management*** – We implement processes and tools that centralize and streamline access to cloud and enterprise services and applications.

- ***Data protection/active defense*** – Our data protection solutions determine the right data to migrate, providing balanced, protective measures required to enable business growth, in any cloud model, while keeping within established risk tolerances.

Cisco Systems

Cisco systems is an American multinational corporation headquartered in San Jose, California, that designs, manufactures, and sells networking equipment. It is the leader in networking area and is very popular. Let us discuss its private cloud features.

Cisco's Cloud Strategy

Cisco's cloud strategy is a set of capabilities that uniquely combines cloud business applications and services with Cisco Unified Data center and Cloud Intelligent Network. It brings together computing, networking, and storage resources within the data center and connects clouds between data centers to deliver a high-quality cloud experience to the end user.

The Cisco portfolio works with technologies from industry-leading ecosystem partners to offer integrated solutions and services including collaboration, security, IaaS, and video delivery that are pretested for private, public, and hybrid clouds.

Cisco cloud security helps customers reduce risk through the Cisco SecureX Architecture®, which delivers consistent security policies and enforcement, up-to-date threat intelligence, greater scalability, and improved performance. Cisco cloud security helps remove cloud barriers so that customers can achieve the economies of scale and efficiency of cloud computing.

The Cisco cloud portfolio is delivered to customers by Cisco partners: trusted experts who will listen to your challenges and design and implement a solution that will help your business thrive and adapt to change. Cisco's cloud strategy is supported by a portfolio of cloud enablement services (professional services) to help design, build, and manage cloud solutions and services offered by Cisco and our partners.

Cisco Unified Data Center

Cisco Unified Data Center unifies compute, networking, storage, and management into a common platform designed to automate deployment and management across physical and virtual resources for superior delivery of IT as a service. Cisco Unified Data Center architecture has three main components: Cisco Unified Fabric, Unified Computing, and Unified Management:

- ***Cisco Unified Fabric Solutions*** – Flexible and comprehensive data center network solutions for delivering network services to servers, storage, and applications, providing transparent convergence, scalability, and sophisticated intelligence.
- ***Cisco Unified Computing Solutions*** – A next-generation data center system that unites computing, network, storage access, and virtualization into a cohesive system designed to reduce total cost of ownership and increase business agility.

- ***Cisco Unified Management Solutions*** – Transparent management across physical and virtual resources to simplify and accelerate delivery of IT services within the data center or in a cloud environment. Cisco offers the industry's only self-service, open management platform for integrating all data center resources, including resources for computing, applications, network services, security, storage, and cloud computing.

Cloud Intelligent Network

The network is a critical component of your success, as it links clouds together and virtualizes connections within the cloud, between clouds, and beyond the cloud to the end customer. The Cisco Cloud Intelligent Network exposes the intelligence in the network to allow smarter decisions and service offerings and provide a consistent and secure user experience regardless of user location and the number of cloud platforms involved in the service delivery:

The Cisco Cloud Intelligent Network strategy encompasses three essential capabilities to support your cloud services:

- ***Cloud-to-Customer Connectivity*** – Facilitates the delivery of enterprise-class services from the service delivery source to the ultimate user, while securely promoting service quality with business-oriented policy controls and context-aware security capabilities.
- ***Cloud-to-Cloud Connectivity*** – Addresses the growing need to connect clouds and optimize the sourcing of data and content from the decentralized delivery centers within the cloud. This requires extending the data center fabric across data centers and clouds as well as implementing technologies that support the network's close integration with the cloud delivery.
- ***Network Management and Automation*** – Of critical importance for cloud services due to the ever-increasing requirements for agility resulting from the dynamic nature of the cloud.

Cloud Applications and Services

IT focus is shifting to service delivery as content and applications are increasingly being delivered on demand and to mobile users. The critical factors are making sure your service delivery works and making sure your teams can work. Cisco is focused on providing a compelling user experience with every service delivered from the cloud. These services can be provided anywhere, on any device, at any time with the security, performance, and reliability previously possible only with traditional on-premises deployments.

Cisco offers a portfolio of cloud-based business applications and services for enterprises to consume directly or as a service from a Cisco partner or service provider:

- ***Cisco's Collaboration Cloud Portfolio*** – An innovative set of applications and services that allow users to enjoy a rich, interactive, and compelling experience delivered by the industry-leading suite of Cisco Unified Communications, Cisco

TelePresence®, and other applications that provide services such as customer contact, meetings, and instant messaging.

- ***Cisco Videoscape*** – An innovative service-provider solution that reinvents the delivery of television experiences.
- ***Cisco Cloud Security*** – Solutions that provide effective, scalable, and always-updated web and email security. Cisco ScanSafe Cloud Web Security analyzes web requests for malicious, inappropriate, or acceptable content. Cisco IronPort Cloud Email Security helps protect organizations from spam, viruses, and blended threats.
- ***Extensive Portfolio of Third-Party Cloud Services and Applications*** – Pretested for Cisco's cloud portfolio.

Cisco Cloud Applications and Services help companies give users what they need to collaborate, when, where, and how they need it. With flexible deployment models based on cloud provisioning, Cisco solutions support the mobile, social, visual, and virtual aspects of effective collaborative environments.

Cloud Enablement Services

The Cloud Enablement Services portfolio supports the accelerated deployment of cloud solutions and applications, and includes professional and technical services to facilitate optimal operation of collaboration and video technologies in a cloud. Cisco and our partners offer deep expertise in cloud strategy, cloud planning and design, cloud implementation, and cloud optimization. Cisco and our partners have the services experience and expertise to help accelerate time to market, reduce costs, and quickly realize a return on cloud investment.

- Cloud Enablement Services for Building IaaS Clouds provides customized strategy, planning and design, implementation, and optimization. Drawing on extensive experience delivering secure end-to-end virtualized data centers, Cisco provides a comprehensive, architectural approach to IaaS that considers the people, processes, and technologies involved across network, compute, and storage resources. Services include Cloud Strategy Service, Cloud Planning and Design Service, Cloud Implementation Service, and Cloud Optimization Service, all with a focus on cloud security.
- Cloud Enablement Services for Adopting Clouds delivers the expert help you need to accelerate the adoption of a public cloud model based on your current environment and business goals. The service allows businesses to optimize existing infrastructure to realize the full benefits of a public cloud. To facilitate your decision making about a cloud migration, Cisco provides Cloud Adoption Strategy Services and Cloud Adoption Planning Services.

12.5 FUTURE OF CLOUD COMPUTING

At the last leg of our discussion is the future of cloud computing and how this technology will be in the upcoming years. Let us discuss the future aspects of cloud in detail in this section.

For every major decision or any major activity in life one has to think about the *long term strategy*. We must not restrict ourselves with the present time alone. We must have a very broad minded future scope and future planning well in advance. Things around us keep on changing and we must be prepared to all these changes. Certain future changes can be for good or may be bad. Some situations push it to the good corner while some to a very bad experience. Hence we must be prepared to face all this.

To speak from the technology and technical aspects technologies keep on updating from time to time. Today's new technology is tomorrows outdated one. Advancement and upgradation is all about technology. A brand new technique is ready to beat the older one it with advanced features or characters. Thus this iteration goes on. One must never overestimate or underestimate things. One must never restrict a technology. Allow it to grow, test it, view all features, identify the drawbacks and this cycle must goes on. By this time a brand new technology gets evolved in the market. Some technologies have a long scope and are unbeatable. While some of them loose their competition in the half way through the revolution of them. A good technology is a one that must keep on upgrading from time to time, support other technologies, must be collaborative and platform independent. The iterative model of technology improvement is the best one to survive the competition and in the future. Today's computer field is a very agile and dynamic market. It keeps on changing from time to time. The market needs and expectations keep on changing from time to time. Thus such rotation goes on.

Cloud computing an advanced networking technology which came into full use just less than a decade ago but today it has changed the life so much. There is a huge advancement in every sector that has applied cloud. Today the whole business IT sector is aligned to it. Apart from IT sector there are many more other sectors which are also moving towards this technology. A simple statement for future of cloud is:

"The biggest news for cloud computing is that it will not be news. It's the way we do computing today."

Let us see what the future holds for cloud computing. There are several future predictions for cloud which include:

- ***Personal cloud to replace personal PC*** – The research firm Gartner believes that the personal cloud will replace the PC as the center of our digital lives sooner than one might think by 2014 itself. Major trends in client computing have shifted the market away from a focus on personal computers to a broader device perspective that includes smart phones, tablets and other consumer devices. The days of depending on single machine are gone and the trend is moving towards a perfect dynamic personal cloud for everyone.
- ***Hybrid cloud revolution*** – Just as the transition to the private cloud was the last big Information Technology trend for the past few years. Many companies developed their own private cloud. But from now the future prediction will be hybrid cloud or the combination of both private and public cloud services. It is predicted that

half of the major organizations will deploy hybrid cloud solutions by 2017. It is recommended that companies begin adopting the hybrid cloud now and students should consider companies with the competitive advantage of hybrid cloud services when exploring internships and careers.

- ***Mobile apps and cloud*** – With the already revolution of Android based working environment. It is predicted that more and more cloud based apps which contains highly advanced features for all business oriented and practical approach is all set to enter the market in the upcoming years. And it is also predicted that mobile applications will perfectly tune into the growing needs and agility of the cloud platform.
- ***Shifting of power*** – With the rise in cloud adoption the role of Chief Information Officers (CIOs) and IT specialists will continue to change. IT experts will move away from developing new technologies, instead acting more like internal consultants that access and manage how technological services provide benefits to different industries. CIOs will focus less on the construction of new micro technologies and concentrate more time on the macro identification of technologies that provide the most strategic value to the enterprise.
- ***Business growth*** – It is predicted that small and medium sized businesses spending on cloud solutions are expected to grow by 20% in the next five years. These businesses cite the security benefits that cloud solutions have provided as well as the ability to fund new activities like better customer service because of the time and cost savings by using the cloud, according to a recent Microsoft study. Perhaps the reason that cloud adoption is ramping up in the small and medium sized market is due to the earlier adoption of the cloud by larger enterprises and therefore smaller businesses are fallowing their footsteps for success. Additionally, there is a tendency toward cutting-edge technology and forward thinking disruption when a company is still in its small, emerging start-up phase.
- ***App. developers role*** – For every technology to grow the application developers play a very crucial role. Without their development or advancement the technology will not revolutionize. Since the cloud makes applications more crucial to business and many other sectors, it is only logical that the role of app developers becomes equally vital for revenue growth. In the past companies were quick to rethink on the app development because of its high cost many organizations removed app development from their business and instead outsourced app services. However, the agility that cloud computing provides to data collection has begun to outweigh its cost and thus it is likely that more app developers will be hired at major companies or specialized agencies that subcontract cloud services will grow in 2014. Thus in the upcoming years we can see many more cloud related apps in the market which will be further used by all the IT companies.
- ***Cloud specialization*** – While Amazon Web Services (AWS) is seen as the clear leader in the cloud computing, tech professionals await the development of more

differentiated cloud solutions, such as services targeted specifically to healthcare, finance, government and many other sectors. Until recently most of the cloud technology developed there has been on the general purpose platforms and solutions only. The emergence of companies with community cloud solutions or services specialized for particular industries has been slow to mature but is expected to break ground and expand in 2014.

- ***Retail shopping in cloud*** – According to a study the retail cloud market is predicted to go more than triple from $4.2 billion in 2011 to $15.1 billion in 2015. With such growth, CIOs can enhance business capabilities for retail shoppers. Using the cloud, former data about customers that were placed in silos throughout the company will be consolidated for efficiency. Because the customer expects the company to know the shopper, the streamlining of customer data across all retail channels will enhance merchandising decisions, marketing tactics, and sales promotions. In India itself the trend of shopping has considerably changed with large retail outlets into the market in the last few years.
- ***Australia's cloud trend*** – Based on the recent Research, Australia comes in number two place as a leading country in public cloud solution fallowed by the United States. Although Europe alone as a whole outweighs Australia's IT growth, the country is quickly developing its public cloud market much in the same way its adoption of virtualization and smart phones followed by that of the US. The report also says China still lags behind Australia, remaining in the early stages of virtualization and consolidation.
- ***Cloud security*** – Well every one of us know that security is a big issue in cloud. With the recent discovery of the government's access to cloud provider networks, many companies will likely switch to automated security that allows management of their own encryption keys, versus lending that responsibility to cloud vendors. With the rise of hybrid cloud, companies will seek providers that guarantee to secure both private and public cloud services. By the end of 2014 it is expected that unencrypted data will virtually disappear.

12.6 PROJECTS AND RESEARCH IN CLOUD COMPUTING

In this section, we list some of the ongoing projects in cloud across the world. One can understand the importance and the ongoing research in the field of cloud computing by this list of projects.

- ***StratusLab Enhancing Grid Infrastructures with Virtualization and Cloud Technologies*** – StratusLab is focused on applying cloud technologies to grid infrastructures such as the European Grid Infrastructure (EGI) to enhance their use. The project is developing a complete, open-source cloud distribution that allows grid and non-grid resource centers to offer and to exploit an "Infrastructure as a Service" cloud.

- ***VENUS-C Virtual Multidisciplinary Environments Using Cloud Infrastructures*** – VENUSC aims to explore how cloud computing can be used in European scientific settings. It brings together industrial partners and scientific user communities to develop, test and deploy an industry-quality cloud computing service for Europe. The project currently supports research into bioinformatics, systems biology, drug discovery, civil engineering, civil protection and emergencies and data for science.
- ***RESERVOIR Resources and Services Virtualization without Barriers*** – The RESERVOIR project worked to enable massive scale deployment and management of complex IT services. The OpenNebula open source toolkit, a key outcome of this project, is now being used as an open reference stack for cloud computing by several new European projects including StratusLab, BonFIRE and 4Caast.
- ***BonFIRE Building service test beds for Future Internet Research and Experimentation*** – The BonFIRE Project will design, build and operate a multi-site cloud facility to support applications, services and systems research targeting the Internet of Services community within the Future Internet. The BonFIRE Project aims to give researchers access to an experimental facility which enables large scale experimentation of their systems and application.
- ***4CaaSt*** – The 4CaaSt project aims to create an advanced PaaS Cloud platform to support optimized and elastic hosting of Internet-scale multi-tier applications. 4CaaSt will enable applications from different providers to be tailored to different users, mashed up and traded together. It will provide an easy to use Infrastructure, greatly simplifying design and delivery of tailored services.
- ***Contrail*** – The Contrail project aims at removing some constraints that are currently present in cloud systems. It will federate clouds allowing companies and research organizations to easily switch between cloud providers. Contrail will develop a complete, secure cloud computing stack, including Platform-as-a-Service and Infrastructure-as-a-Service.
- ***mOSAIC Open-Source API and Platform for Multiple Clouds*** – The mOSAIC project aims to develop an open-source platform that enables applications to negotiate Cloud services as requested by their users. mOSAIC hopes to tackle the issue of provider lock-in by developing a platform to demonstrate how users can determine and access the cloud provider that offers the best services for them.
- ***QMUL Cloud Legal Project*** – The Cloud Legal Project at Queen Mary University in London is a three year project which aims to undertake academic research in relation to legal issues in cloud computing. The project will produce a series of papers to act as informative and practical guides to the legal issues that need to be addressed by customers, providers and regulators of cloud computing.

- ***VISION Cloud*** – VISION Cloud aims to build a scalable and flexible infrastructure for data-intensive storage services and enablers. This infrastructure will facilitate a new data model to raise the abstraction level of storage, data mobility, computational and content-centric access to storage as well as mechanisms for cost-efficiency with provisions for QoS and security guarantees
- ***TCLOUDS*** – TCLOUDS puts its focus on privacy protection in cross-border infrastructures and on ensuring resilience against failures and attacks. TCLOUDS aims to build prototype internet-scale ICT infrastructure which allows virtualized computing, network and storage resources over the Internet to provide scalability and cost-efficiency. In prototype development, it is a priority to address the challenges of cross-border privacy, end-user usability, and acceptance that are essential for widespread acceptance of such an infrastructure.
- ***S-CUBE*** – S-Cube the European Network of Excellence in **Software Services and Systems** will establish an integrated, multidisciplinary, vibrant research community. This will enable Europe to lead the software-services revolution, and help to shape the software-service based Internet.
- ***REMICS (Reuse and Migration of legacy applications to Interoperable Cloud Services)*** – The main objective of the REMICS project is to develop a tool- supported model-driven methodology for migrating applications to interoperable service cloud platforms. REMICS also aims to develop and extend several standards related to knowledge discovery, service interoperability, service modeling in the cloud, and testing and runtime management of services.
- ***gSLM*** – The gSLM project works on Service Level Management (SLM) and Service Delivery Management (SDM), seeking to bring experiences and approaches from commercial ITSM and provide ways to provide them in the grid and e- Infrastructure domain.
- ***Cloud4SOA*** – Cloud4SOA aims to face new challenges investigating new service engineering paradigms, methods and tools supporting the development of the Cloud Governance Application in PaaS context. This development includes the process of decision making, criteria and policies involved in the semantic setting-up, construction, negotiation, acquisition, development, deployment, operations, management of a cloud computing capability.
- ***OPTIMIS*** – OPTIMIS is aimed at enabling organizations to automatically externalize servicesand applications to trustworthy and auditable cloud providers in the hybrid model. Consequently, OPTIMIS believes its activities will support and facilitate an ecosystem of providers and consumers that will benefit from the optimal operation of services and infrastructures.

Some of the major universities and education centers across the world working in the field of virtualization and cloud computing area include:

Boston University

The Researchers at Boston University are exploring the merits of "Colocation Games" (CGs) as a novel, economically-sound framework upon which emerging cloud architectures could be implemented. This work is funded by a National Science Foundation (NSF) grant. It introduces Colocation Games as the basis of a general framework for modeling, analyzing, and facilitating the interactions between the various stakeholders in distributed/cloud computing environments, where resources are offered in an open marketplace to independent, rational parties interested in setting up their own applications.

Carnegie Mellon University

Carnegie Mellon University is actively involved in several cloud computing research programs and is one of the test sites for the Open Cirrus program. Their research includes studies on Multi-Tier Indexing for Web Search Engines, Integrated Cluster Computing Architecture, and others.

Duke University

The researchers at Duke University are conducting research funded by the National Science Foundation (NSF) in collaboration with NCSU, UNC Chapel Hill, and NCAT State University to explore and test Trustworthy Virtual Cloud Computing.

Florida International University

Florida International University (FIU) researchers are leveraging cloud computing, using a National Science Foundation (NSF) grant on the Google/IBM Cloud, to analyze aerial images and objects to help support disaster mitigation and environmental protection.

IBM/Google Academic Cloud Computing Initiative (ACCI)

The IBM/Google Academic Cloud Computing Initiative (ACCI) is a joint university initiative to help computer science students gain the skills they need to build cloud infrastructures and applications. The IBM/Google initiative aims to provide computer science students with a complete suite of open source based development tools so they can gain the advanced programming skills necessary to innovate and address the challenges of the Cloud Computing model—which uses many computers networked together through open standards—and thereby drive the Internet's next phase of growth.

Indiana University

The researchers at Indiana University are working on several cloud computing projects with grants from the National Science Foundation (NSF) and the National Institute of Health (NIH). Their research includes: Large-Scale Distributed Scientific Experiments on Shared Substrate; Exploring the use of cloud techniques to overcome current medical computing obstacles such as long computation time and large memory requirements; and The Future Grid project that will provide an experimental platform that accommodates batch, grid and cloud computing.

Massachusetts Institute of Technology (MIT)

The team at MIT is working in collaboration with Yale University and the University of Wisconsin at Madison on a comparative study, funded by a National Science Foundation (NSF) CLuE grant, of approaches to cluster-based, large-scale data analysis. In addition they are also independently studying Cloud Computing Infrastructure and Technology for Education.

NESSI

The Networked European Software and Services Initiative (NESSI) is the European Technology Platform dedicated to Software and Services. The overall ambition of NESSI is to deliver NEXOF, a coherent and consistent open service framework leveraging research in the area of service-based systems to consolidate and trigger innovation in service-oriented economies.

North Carolina Agricultural & Technical State University

The team at the North Carolina Agricultural & Technical State University is conducting research, funded by a National Science Foundation (NSF), in collaboration with NCSU, Duke University, and the University of NC at Chapel Hill to explore and test Trustworthy Virtual Cloud Computing.

North Carolina State University

The researchers at North Carolina State University are working on several cloud computing projects funded by the National Science Foundation (NSF). They include two collaborative studies on Trustworthy Virtual Cloud Computing and Hybrid Opportunistic Computing for Green Clouds. In addition, NetApp has contributed hardware, software and services to NCSU to expand their Virtual Computing Lab (VCL) and build the next generation of cloud computing environments.

Open Cirrus

Open Cirrus is an open cloud-computing research testbed designed to support research into design, provisioning, and management of services at a global, multi-datacenter scale. The open nature of the testbed is designed to encourage research into all aspects of service and datacenter management. In addition, they hope to foster a collaborative community around the testbed, providing ways to share tools, lessons and best practices, and ways to benchmark and compare alternative approaches to service management at datacenter scale.

Purdue University

The Purdue University team is investigating linguistic extensions to MapReduce abstractions for programming modern, large-scale systems, with special focus on applications that manipulate large, unstructured graphs. They also provide a cloud computing testbed called Wispy to TeraGrid users.

Tsinghua University

Tsinghua Cloud is an all-in-one Cloud Computing solution developed at the Grid Computing Division of Tsinghua University in China. The Cloud is composed of three components: Nova (virtual computation system: computing cloud), Carrier (distributed file system) and Corsair (distributed file manager based on Carrier: storage cloud), which can be utilized independently or in combination.

Umea University

The Umeå University research on flexible and scalable IT infrastructures covers a range of topics central to cloud computing. Research drivers are compute and data intensive applications requiring, e.g., elastic locality-aware infrastructures to meet the rapid capacity and locality variations of industrial services and large-scale distributed environments that enable coordinated use of federated resources for eScience. Research outcomes include autonomic infrastructure management systems and sophisticated tools for creating cloud-enabled applications.

University of California San Diego

The National Science Foundation has awarded a grant to researchers at SDSC to explore new ways to manage extremely large data sets hosted on massive clusters, which have become known as computing "clouds". This research will use the LiDAR topography data hosted by Open Topography as a test case and will focus on how cloud computing can aid the management and processing of massive spatial data sets.

University of California Santa Barbara

The University of Santa Barbara is actively pursuing several advancements in cloud computing. Their Massive Graphs in Clusters (MAGIC) project is focused on developing software infrastructure that can efficiently answer queries on extremely large graph datasets. They have also designed an open-source implementation of the Google AppEngine interface.

University of Maryland at Baltimore

The Institute for Genome Sciences at the University of Maryland's School of Medicine has developed a virtual appliance that integrates state-of-the-art genomic tools on Cloud Computing platforms in a robust, user friendly, and automated package called CloVR. By providing a set of push-button pipelines for applications in viral, prokaryotic, metagenomic and eukaryotic sequencing projects, CloVR will facilitate the further integration of genomics into environmental and biomedical research.

University of Maryland College Park

The research team at the University of Maryland's Cloud Computing Center at College Park is working on a range of projects funded by the National Science Foundation (NSF). They include: A Hadoop Toolkit for Distributed Text Retrieval; Data-Intensive Text Processing; Commodity Computing in Genomic Research; and a series of other independent studies.

University of Melbourne

The Cloud Computing and Distributed Systems (CLOUDS) Laboratory, formerly GRIDS Lab, is a software research and development group within the Department of Computer Science and Software Engineering at the University of Melbourne, Australia. The CLOUDS Lab is actively engaged in the design and development of next-generation computing systems and applications that aggregate or lease services of distributed resources depending on their availability, capability, performance, cost, and users' quality-of-science requirements. The lab is working towards realizing this vision through its two flagship projects: Gridbus and Cloudbus.

University of North Carolina at Chapel Hill

The researchers at the University of North Carolina at Chapel Hill are conducting research, funded by a National Science Foundation (NSF), in collaboration with NCSU, Duke University, and NCAT State University to explore and test Trustworthy Virtual Cloud Computing.

University of Virginia

The team at the University of Virginia is working on several cloud computing projects funded by the National Science Foundation (NSF). They include, Feedback-Controlled Management of Virtualized Resources for Predictable eScience and Image Super-Resolution Using Trillions of Examples.

University of Wisconsin, Madison

The team at the University of Wisconsin Madison have designed the Hierarchically-Redundant, Decoupled storage project (HaRD) to investigate the next generation of storage software for hybrid Flash/disk storage clusters. They are also working with MIT and Yale University on a comparative study, funded by a National Science Foundation (NSF) CLuE grant, of approaches to cluster-based, large-scale data analysis.

Virginia Polytechnic Institute and State University

The team at Virginia Tech is collaborating with NC State University on studying Hybrid Opportunistic Computing for Green Clouds. This project, funded by the National Science

Foundation (NSF), explores a new computing model of offering cloud services on active nodes that are serving on-demand utility computing users.

Wayne State University

At Wayne State University they are working on developing a unified learning approach, namely URL, to automate the configuration processes of virtualized machines and applications running on the virtual machines and adapt the systems configuration to the dynamics of cloud. This research is funded by a National Science Foundation (NSF) grant.

Yale University

The team at Yale University is working in collaboration with MIT and the University of Wisconsin at Madison on a comparative study, funded by a National Science Foundation (NSF) CLuE grant, of approaches to cluster-based, large-scale data analysis.

SUMMARY

- *For industrial oriented term of cloud computing we say it as enterprise cloud computing. The word enterprise cloud computing refers to the business related operations and the usage of cloud computing technology for all their work.*
- *Enterprise computing encompasses all the various types of enterprise software, like company related business tools and solutions, database management, programming, testing, quality assurance, relationship management and so on. It also includes the companies hardware and the mass IT infrastructure to handle all the client projects and solutions to them.*
- *The term Enterprise Software Deployment refers to all of the activities that must take place to make a software application available to the end users. Enterprise Software Deployment technically begins after a software application has been written, tested, packaged and delivered to an enterprise.*
- *Enterprise Cloud Services refers to the extension of software, hardware, infrastructure and platforms as a service, within a private cloud computing environment.*
- *Enterprise Cloud Services may be delivered internally using on-premise IT resources or may be delivered externally by a third party enterprise cloud services provider.*
- *An Enterprise Cloud Solution is a term that may refer to a cloud service platform or it may refer to the various service models in cloud like SaaS (Software as a Service), PaaS (Platform as a Service) or IaaS (Infrastructure as a Service) offerings delivered via a cloud service platform.*
- *Enterprise Cloud Management refers to the execution of the requisite tasks associated with the establishment and delivery of enterprise cloud services to end user or client in a very easy and reliable manner.*

- *Cloud Computing solutions can bring benefits to all industry sectors, and to both large and small companies. Switching information systems to the Cloud platform thus abolishing the need for extensive in company infrastructure, traditional approach and altering the way Business Intelligence is used to support decision making.*
- *Cloud computing has made a new revolution inside the business oriented IT companies. Its service models, cloud types and applications are well suited for the business purposes. This technology is closely aligned to needs and requirements of any major business solution company.*
- *Business processing as a service (BPaaS) refers to the various business services and processes being provided as a service in the cloud. It is one among the service models of the cloud. Its sole purpose is to provide the service to the end user. It is also based on the service oriented technology like other service models of cloud.*
- *Traditional Business Process Management Systems (BPMS) integrate business processes and keep track of running instances of these processes. A BPMS coordinates the execution of a business process step by step. Each process instance is monitored by the BPMS and provides users insights into each processes progress*
- *Cloud computing an advanced networking technology which came into full use just less than a decade ago but today it has changed the life so much. There is a huge advancement in every sector that has applied cloud. Today the whole business IT sector is aligned to it.*
- *The biggest news for cloud computing is that it will not be news. It's the way we do computing today.*

13

Issues and Risk in Cloud Computing

OBJECTIVE

- *To know about the various issues and risk in cloud computing*
- *To know about the effective security management techniques in cloud*
- *To know about the views of the cloud technology in survey*

Till now we saw all the positive features and advancement of cloud computing. We saw in detail about the cloud architecture, service models and its uses for business community. In this chapter let us see the other face of cloud computing, the issues involved in cloud computing. Every technology has some drawbacks, everything cannot be fully satisfied. Similarly cloud too has some major loopholes in the form of overall security. Today the biggest research in the field of cloud computing is the overall security to this new technology in all aspects. Various security features and advanced algorithms are being designed to satisfy the end user and the business community. Some of the questions we need to answer include:

- *Are clouds safer enough to guard all the user data and their personnel confidential contents?*
- *Are there no intruders or spies looking for confidential business data of corporate IT sector in the cloud?*
- *Are the service oriented technologies an tool for the next generation computers ignoring all the dedicated resources?*
- *Is it a wise choice in all aspects to shift to cloud technology?*
- *Is cloud technology trustworthy in moving all the previous technologies and concepts into the service model based cloud?*
- *Is the cloud technology of well defined standard, after all its recent trend technique only having been less than a decade in full action?*
- *From future perspective can we rely only on cloud technology, ignoring all previous networking technologies?*

Thus, these are the issues we need to consider for making the cloud technology safer and trustworthy one. We must never underestimate or overestimate a technology, as time changes there are advancement in everything. After all one must not forget that cloud computing itself is evolved from various other computing techniques of the past. Now let us discuss in detail all the security issues, risk along with how to tackle them.

13.1 ISSUES IN CLOUD COMPUTING

Today as of 2013 cloud computing has emerged as the recent trend in networking area. It is adopted by all the corporate IT companies. Its service oriented model with other technologies has made the end user task very easy and user friendly. But we have forgotten a major issue, how about the security and other privacy loop holes of the technology. IT companies deal with huge confidential business related data and many internal information, which cannot be disclosed to even another project employee of the same company. There is a separate security management team in every IT company whose only function is to guard the overall companies confidential and business data from a wrong person.

There are several layers of security check adopted in every IT company in a very well-defined standard format. If this much of security layers and standards are defined for an IT company, then there has to be similar ways to guarantee security in every technology and products the company uses. Companies also have to make wise choice in choosing the right technology and platform based on various business friendly parameters and even the user friendly one. In case the technology is full of issues then it is a total flop model and it is rejected by the corporate IT companies. They need to make a wise choice in choosing the underlying foundation technology, only upon which all the other major activities takes place inside the company. Hence let us see the overall issues concerning cloud platform first:

- ***Security*** – as we all know cloud computing is completely based on internet, which is vulnerable to all forms of security attacks and risks. But the cloud is much more dynamic and powerful than the static internet. It involves principles like virtualization and distributed, making it a perfect advanced networking model. Cloud being in remote location, handling millions of users and the tasks, pooled resources and storage of user data we need to ensure security in cloud. Even for mobile cloud computing we need to ensure the similar security problems. Today millions of security solutions and algorithms are available to provide the solution to security problem, but as the technology grows so as the negative technology to break them grows. More and more advanced and highly knowledge intruders and hackers are out to destroy the peace of the computer world daily.
- ***Compatibility issue*** – the other issue in cloud is the compatibility with the other technologies. It is universally acknowledged today that cloud computing works out to be the most cost efficient option for companies. However, the problem arises out of the fact that the company would have to replace much of its existing IT infrastructures in order to make the system compatible on the cloud. For these many years companies have been working with other technologies and platform,

but suddenly today they need to transform to cloud which is quite practically very difficult and to some extent very tedious. Thus, there is a need of a mass transformation in overall infrastructure in order to migrate into cloud, which is quite an issue in the initial stage for every company. Migration to a new technology also involves the training and providing all the skills to the employees about the new technology.

- ***Data loss*** – as we all know the entire operation in the cloud takes place in a remote virtual server, what happens if the main virtual remote server itself gets affected by some mischievous activity or some bad operation. The overall cloud is affected and the whole technology is under a big problem of a major flop. Much of a company's data, which is essentially stored on multiple servers in the cloud, sometimes spanning across several countries and continents is affected. Apart from company data all other individual user data is also affected. Thus all the data are in accessible till the server is fully functional again from the blockage. This means that if a certain center in cloud develops an issue and it cannot be accessed, it might pose a serious problem for the company involved. This problem would intensify if the data is stored in a server of a different country or the inter cloud technology is used. One can imagine the impact of such disaster if there are multiple clouds connected to each other to form the inter cloud concept. This being a potential issue, companies need to discuss it with their providers much in advance of beginning work on cloud computing. The company needs to clarify if the provider can totally guarantee service availability even during periods of any crash or bandwidth interruption and similar other issues. Data loss can be a very big issue for the company if it is not checked at a right time.
- ***Standardization*** – every technology must have a well-defined standard so that anyone can access the quality and overall picture of it. It can act as a parameter in judging the technology in overall aspect. A very real problem associated with cloud computing is the present lack of standardization in the system. Since no proper standards for cloud computing are set yet, it becomes almost impossible for a company to ascertain the quality of services they have been provided with. In order to avoid this potential trap, the company needs to find out if the provider uses standardized technology. In case the company is not satisfied with the quality of services rendered, it can change the provider without having to incur additional costs for the same. However, this point too has to be clarified by the company in its initial contract.
- ***Monitoring issue*** – the other issue with the cloud computing is the monitoring of the data in the cloud. In the cloud storage all the data are stored in the remote virtual cloud. Thus making it an issue of accessing, tampering or manipulation with the data. Once a company hands over cloud computing responsibility to a service provider, all the data would be handled by the latter. This could create a monitoring issue for the company, especially if the proper processes are not set in place. The business data are quite confidential. If revealed or manipulated can severely affect the company. Thus there needs to be a proper standard to handle

the issue of data monitoring in the cloud. Every year companies are spending millions of dollars by the security violations in the data security. Many business secrets are spied and reveled badly affecting the company. Corporate scams due to mass hackers and intruders are on the rise.

- ***Viruses*** – well we must never forget the fundamental threat in every networking technology, the virus attacks. The virus is a malicious software program whose ultimate objective is to cause the harm to all the computer resources and user work. The far more impact of virus is the fast spreading of it to other uninfected ones in a far replication process. In cloud computing if one file is infected by virus attack all other files stored in the remote virtual cloud is affected. It may pass on to other clouds in case of the inter cloud and cause a mass devastation to the computer field if this iteration goes on. Viruses are coded in so powerful way that they even change the overall functioning of a particular system itself. Viruses are causing enormous loss to the corporate IT sector every year and there is a huge data loss because of them. Some viruses are very powerful and fast in its actions that they are very difficult to manage them.

13.2 SECURITY ISSUES IN CLOUD

Now in this section let us see in detail about the various security threats and the risk associated with cloud. Some of them include:

- Data Integrity
- Data Theft
- Privacy issues
- Infected Application
- Data loss
- Data Location
- Security on Vendor level
- Security on user level
- Security on cloud infrastructure

Let us see each one of them in detail.

- ***Data integrity*** – as we all know the data is stored in cloud computing in the remote location. As multiple users are getting connected to it. Hence what happens if someone modifies or manipulates the data?. Hence there is an integrity constraint in such cases. As far as in cloud more than the data we even store and utilize many dynamic software and workspaces. If some overrides their functionality or misuses the work in the workspace environment, it can prove to be a disaster for a computer techie. From a corporate IT sector point of you integrity of any entity must be maintained, not that just leave it open for anyone. Many confidential business applications are designed using the cloud platform, if they are manipulated or tampered then it can prove to be a big disaster for the company.

- ***Data theft*** – today for every unique work done there are people to copy and reproduce the same, claiming to be their own work. As far as storing such confidential work in cloud is concerned we need to be careful. We must be aware that our data is not getting used or manipulated by any other intruder from our account. The internet is full of hackers and to other malicious attacks. In corporate IT sector many confidential data are spied and are stolen every year.
- ***Privacy issue*** – apart from data integrity and theft, we need to maintain the privacy of our own data in the cloud. The cloud Vendor must make sure that the Customer Personal information is well secured from other operators. As most of the servers are external, the vendor should make sure who is accessing the data and who is maintaining the server thus enabling the vendor to protect the customer's personal information. There must be a proper identity management of all the users in the cloud. Most of the business data are confidential which cannot be disclosed to others. Thus, we need to maintain the privacy of all the user data in cloud.
- ***Infected application*** – if the data or application or workspace is affected by any malicious attacks, if such data is stored or shared in cloud. It can prove to be a big problem for the cloud vendor and all other users. The high powerful viruses these days are so active that they affect all the other application easily. Their spreading is unlimited and cannot be contained so easily too. Thus cloud vendors must provide layers to check the data being uploaded or shared in cloud.
- ***Data loss*** – as we already discussed the loss of data in cloud. If suddenly a vendor shuts down the company or the server is down or the server is attacked, all the stored data is lost. It could prove to be a big problem for the cloud user. For a corporate IT company data loss can prove to be disaster as it can affect the entire project. It is highly impossible to build the whole project from the scratch after the data loss. The project specific data and related documents are very important for maintaining, testing and support to the existing project. Cloud must be robust enough to overcome such issues.
- ***Data location*** – When it comes to location of the data nothing is transparent, even the customer don't know where his own data's are located. The Vendor does not reveal where all the data's are stored. The Data's won't even be in the same country of the Customer, it might be located anywhere in the world. Cloud is a very vast network, the concept of migration is so broad that the data location is always a mystery in the cloud. The service providers have their data center situated at various places and such locations are very vast in structure.
- ***Security on vendor level*** – Vendor should make sure that the server is well secured from all the external threats it may come across. The vendor must provide all forms of check in at the security level. The vendor is responsible to maintain a strong and a robust cloud infrastructure which is well secured and satisfies all the requirements of the end user. After all cloud users are paying money for all this to the vendor. Vendor must manage all the cloud users, their

account, data, pooled resources and others from any malicious attacks or intruders. Vendor must detect any suspicious activity happening, if so the proper security alert and the mitigation system be designed to handle them. A Cloud is good only when there is a good security provided by the vendor to the customers.

- ***Security on user level*** – Even though the vendor has provided a good security layer for the customer, the customer should make sure that because of its own action, there shouldn't be any loss of data or tampering of data for other users who are using the same Cloud. The cloud user or customer must be matured enough that they must not involve in any suspicious work either knowingly or unknowingly that can lead to the vendor taking the action against the user. In case of such security alerts the vendor may suspend the user account, put on hold all the user activities in the cloud and must issue an security alert message to the user. This can be a big problem for the cloud user. The cloud user must not tamper with resources or any other activities which are against the governance of the cloud from the vendor perspective.
- ***Security on cloud infrastructure*** – as we all know cloud is accessed using internet. If the huge cable wires passing through the continents is affected or is down due to technical reasons, the entire cloud structure is a failure. As all the data, workspace, pooled resources and other contents in cloud cannot be accessed by the cloud user. The cloud vendor company must provide such a robust and a strong system to overcome any such failure. The servers in cloud must also be far secured from outside threats and other virus attacks on them. The pooled resources must not tamper with any outside materials, it must work in all atmospheres to satisfy the user requirement. Overall the cloud structure should overcome any failure or misinterpretation in a short span of time and must be manageable in any worst environment so that the end user does not get negative impression on cloud.

13.3 SECURITY MANAGEMENT IN CLOUD

In the previous sections, we saw the various issues and the risks associated with the cloud. We saw how sensitive the cloud is in various aspects. The security of cloud lies in user, vendor and other levels too. In this section let us see how to manage the security in cloud. The various techniques considered to maintain the security in cloud are discussed in detail in this section. While some of the steps that are required to be taken in order to maintain security in cloud includes:

- Ensure effective governance, risk and compliance in the overall process
- Audit operational and business processes in the cloud
- Manage people, roles and identities of the people involved in the cloud
- Ensure proper protection of data and information in the cloud
- Enforce privacy policies in order maintain the confidential contents

- Assess the security provisions for cloud applications
- Ensure cloud networks and connections are secure
- Evaluate security controls on physical infrastructure and facilities
- Manage security terms in the cloud service level agreement
- Understand the security requirements of the process.

In order to maintain the security in cloud we broadly classify them into two domains. This includes Governance domains:

- Governance and enterprise risk management
- Legal issues
- Compliance and audit
- Information lifecycle management
- Portability and interoperability.

Operational domains:

- Security and data recovery
- Data center operations
- Incident response, notification and remedy
- Application security
- Encryption and key management
- Identity and access management
- Virtualization.

Let us discuss each one of them in detail.

Governance and Enterprise Risk Management

Every organization be it a small or a giant corporate IT sector must have a well-defined governance and standards. Only then certain formalities and the proper functioning of the organization can be expected at all levels. Speaking from the cloud security issue each company must have their own well-defined governance policies to overcome any security violations. Well-developed information security governance processes should result in information security management programs that are scalable with the business, repeatable across the organization, measurable, sustainable, defensible, continually improving, and cost-effective on an ongoing basis.

The fundamental issues of governance and enterprise risk management in Cloud Computing concern the identification and implementation of the appropriate organizational structures, processes, and controls to maintain effective information security governance, risk management, and compliance. Organizations should also assure reasonable information security across the information supply chain, encompassing providers and customers of Cloud Computing services and their supporting third party vendors, in any cloud deployment model.

Today every giant corporate IT companies have a strong set of security team. Whose sole purpose is to monitor all the activities inside the company. Security team is well trained to check all the intrusion into the system. All the project workspaces and the client data are preserved at a well secured atmosphere. No one cannot manipulate or tamper with them under any circumstances. The employee official webmail cannot contain or transmit any unofficial materials so easily even inside or outside the company. Every member inside company needs security access to move from off shore development center (ODC) to another ODC which is the working environment of every project. Only the employees of that concerned project are given access in that ODC.

Information Risk Management is the act of aligning exposure to risk and capability of managing it with the risk tolerance of the data owner. In this manner, it is the primary means of decision support for information technology resources designed to protect the confidentiality, integrity, and availability of information assets.

Some of the issues need to be considered for security governance in cloud includes:

- A portion of the cost savings obtained by Cloud Computing services must be invested into increased scrutiny of the security capabilities of the provider, application of security controls, and ongoing detailed assessments and audits, to ensure requirements are continuously met.
- Both Cloud Computing service customers and providers should develop robust information security governance, regardless of the service or deployment model.
- User organizations should include review of specific information security governance structure and processes, as well as specific security controls, as part of their due diligence for prospective provider organizations. The provider's security governance processes and capabilities should be assessed for sufficiency, maturity, and consistency with the user's information security management processes. The provider's information security controls should be demonstrably risk-based and clearly support these management processes.
- Collaborative governance structures and processes between customers and providers should be identified as necessary, both as part of the design and development of service delivery, and as service risk assessment and risk management protocols, and then incorporated into service agreements.
- Security departments should be engaged during the establishment of Service Level Agreements and contractual obligations, to ensure that security requirements are contractually enforceable.
- Metrics and standards for measuring performance and effectiveness of information security management should be established prior to moving into the cloud. At minimum, organizations should understand and document their current metrics and how they will change when operations are moved into the cloud, where a provider may use different (potentially incompatible) metrics.
- Wherever possible, security metrics and standards (particularly those relating to legal and compliance requirements) should be included in any Service Level

Agreements and contracts. These standards and metrics should be documented and demonstrable (auditable).

Legal Issues

Cloud computing creates new dynamics in the relationship between an organization and its information, involving the presence of a third party the cloud provider. This creates new challenges in understanding how laws apply to a wide variety of information management scenarios.

A complete analysis of Cloud Computing-related legal issues requires consideration of functional, jurisdictional, and contractual dimensions.

- The functional dimension involves determining which functions and services in Cloud Computing have legal implications for participants and stakeholders.
- The jurisdictional dimension involves the way in which governments administer laws and regulations impacting Cloud Computing services, the stakeholders, and the data assets involved.
- The contractual dimension involves the contract structures, terms and conditions, and enforcement mechanisms through which stakeholders in Cloud Computing environments can address and manage the legal and security issues.

Cloud Computing in general can be distinguished from traditional outsourcing in three ways the time of service (on-demand and intermittent), the anonymity of identity of the service provider and anonymity of the location of the server involved. When considering IaaS and PaaS specifically, a great deal of orchestration, configuration, and software development is performed by the customer so much of the responsibility cannot be transferred to the cloud provider

Compliance with recent legislative and administrative requirements around the world forces stronger collaboration among lawyers and technology professionals. This is especially true in Cloud computing, due to the potential for new areas of legal risk created by the distributed nature of the cloud, compared to traditional internal or outsourced infrastructure. Numerous compliance laws and regulations in the United States and the European Union either impute liability to subcontractors or require business entities to impose liability upon them via contract.

Courts now are realizing that information security management services are critical to making decisions as to whether digital information may be accepted as evidence. While this is an issue for traditional IT infrastructure, it is especially concerning in Cloud Computing due to the lack of established legal history with the cloud.

Some of the issues we need to consider include:

- Customers and cloud providers must have a mutual understanding of each other's roles and responsibilities related to electronic discovery, including such activities as litigation hold, discovery searches, who provides expert testimony and so on.

- Cloud providers are advised to assure their information security systems are responsive to customer requirements to preserve data as authentic and reliable, including both primary and secondary information such as metadata and log files.
- Data in the custody of cloud service providers must receive equivalent guardianship as in the hands of their original owner or custodian.
- Plan for both expected and unexpected termination of the relationship in the contract negotiations, and for an orderly return or secure disposal of assets.
- Pre-contract due diligence, contract term negotiation, post-contract monitoring, and contract termination, and the transition of data custodianship are components of the duty of care required of a cloud services client.
- Knowing where the cloud service provider will host the data is a prerequisite to implementing the required measures to ensure compliance with local laws that restrict the cross-border flow of data.
- As the custodian of the personal data of its employees or clients, and of the company's other intellectual property assets, a company that uses Cloud Computing services should ensure that it retains ownership of its data in its original and authenticable format.
- Numerous security issues, such as suspected data breaches, must be addressed in specific provisions of the service agreement that clarify the respective commitments of the cloud service provider and the client.
- The cloud service provider and the client should have a unified process for responding to subpoenas, service of process, and other legal requests.
- The cloud services agreement must allow the cloud services client or designated third party to monitor the service provider's performance and test for vulnerabilities in the system.
- The parties to a cloud services agreement should ensure that the agreement anticipates problems relating to recovery of the client's data after their contractual relationship terminates.

Compliance and Audit

With Cloud Computing developing as a viable and cost effective means to out source entire systems or even entire business processes, maintaining compliance with your security policy and the various regulatory and legislative requirements to which your organization is subject can become more difficult to achieve and even harder to demonstrate to auditors and assessors. Of the many regulations touching upon information technology with which organizations must comply, few were written with Cloud Computing in mind.

Some of the recommendations include:

- Involve Legal and Contracts Teams. The cloud provider's standard terms of service may not address your compliance needs; therefore it is beneficial to have both legal and contracts personnel involved early to ensure that cloud services contract provisions are adequate for compliance and audit obligations.

- Right to Audit Clause. Customers will often need the ability to audit the cloud provider, given the dynamic natures of both the cloud and the regulatory environment. A right to audit contract clause should be obtained whenever possible, particularly when using the cloud provider for a service for which the customer has regulatory compliance responsibilities.
- Analyze Compliance Scope. Determining whether the compliance regulations which the organization is subject to will be impacted by the use of cloud services, for a given set of applications and data.
- Analyze Impact of Regulations on Data Security. Potential end users of Cloud Computing services should consider which applications and data they are considering moving to cloud services, and the extent to which they are subject to compliance regulations.
- Review Relevant Partners and Services Providers. This is general guidance for ensuring that service provider relationships do not negatively impact compliance. Assessing which service providers are processing data that is subject to compliance regulations, and then assessing the security controls provided by those service providers, is fundamental.
- Auditor Qualification and Selection. In many cases the organization has no say in selecting auditors or security assessors. If an organization does have selection input, it is highly advisable to pick a "cloud aware" auditor since many might not be familiar with cloud and virtualization challenges. Asking their familiarity with the IaaS, PaaS, and SaaS nomenclature is a good starting point.
- Cloud Provider's SAS 70 Type II. Providers should have this audit statement at a minimum, as it will provide a recognizable point of reference for auditors and assessors. Since a SAS 70 Type II audit only assures that controls are implemented as documented, it is equally important to understand the scope of the SAS 70 audit, and whether these controls meet your requirements.
- Cloud Provider's ISO/IEC 27001/27002 Roadmap. Cloud providers seeking to provide mission critical services should embrace the ISO/IEC 27001 standard for information security management systems. If the provider has not achieved ISO/IEC 27001 certification, they should demonstrate alignment with ISO 27002 practices.
- ISO/IEC 27001/27002 Scoping. The Cloud Security Alliance is issuing an industry call to action to align cloud providers behind the ISO/IEC 27001 certification, to assure that scoping does not omit critical certification criteria.

Information Lifecycle Management

One of the primary goals of information security is to protect the fundamental data that powers our systems and applications. As we transition to Cloud Computing, our traditional methods of securing data are challenged by cloud-based architectures. Elasticity, multi-tenancy, new physical and logical architectures, and abstracted controls require new data security strategies.

Some of the key recommendation includes:

- Understand how integrity is maintained and compromise of integrity is detected and reported to customers. The same recommendation applies to confidentiality when appropriate.
- The Cloud Computing provider must assure the data owner that they provide full disclosure regarding security practices and procedures as stated in their SLAs.
- Ensure specific identification of all controls used during the data lifecycle. Ensure there specifications of to which entity is responsible for each control between the data owner and cloud services provider.
- Maintain a fundamental philosophy of knowing where your data is. Ensure your ability to know the geographical location of storage. Stipulate this in your SLAs and contracts. Ensure that appropriate controls regarding country location restrictions are defined and enforced.
- A system of service penalties should be included in the contract between the data owner and the cloud service provider. Specifically, data that would be subject to state and international data breach laws should be protected by the cloud service provider.
- It is the data owner's responsibility to determine who should access the data, what their rights and privileges are, and under what conditions these access rights are provided. The data owner should maintain a "Default Deny All" policy for both data owner employees and the cloud service provider.
- Cloud services providers should offer contractual language that warrants the denial of access to data as a fundamental philosophy (*i.e.*, "Default Deny All"). This specifically applies to cloud services employees and their customers other than the data owner's employees and authorized personnel.
- The data owner's responsibility is to define and identify the data classification. It is the cloud service provider's responsibility to enforce the data owner's access requirements based on data classification. Such responsibilities should be in the contract and enforced and audited for compliance.
- Identify trust boundaries throughout the IT architecture and abstraction layers. Ensure subsystems only span trust boundaries as needed and with appropriate safeguards to prevent unauthorized disclosure, alteration, or destruction of data.
- Understand what compartmentalization techniques are employed by a provider to isolate its customers from one another. A provider may use a variety of methods depending upon the types and number of services offered.
- Understand the cloud provider's data search capabilities and limitations when attempting to view 'inside' the dataset for data discovery.
- Understand how encryption is managed on multi-tenant storage. Is there a single key for all data owners, one key per data owner, or multiple keys per data owner? Is there a system to prevent different data owners from having the same encryption keys?

- Data owners should require cloud service providers to ensure that their backed-up data is not commingled with other cloud service customer data.
- Understand cloud provider storage retirement processes. Data destruction is extremely difficult in a multi-tenant environment and the cloud provider should be using strong storage encryption that renders data unreadable when storage is recycled, disposed of, or accessed by any means outside of authorized applications, processes, and entities.
- Understand cloud provider policies and processes for data retention and destruction and how they compare with internal organizational policy. Be aware that data retention assurance may be easier for the cloud provider to demonstrate, while data destruction may be very difficult.
- Negotiate penalties payable by the cloud provider for data breaches to ensure this is taken seriously. If practical, customers should seek to recover all breach costs as part of their provider contract. If impractical, customers should explore other risk transference vehicles such as insurance to recover breach costs.
- Perform regular backup and recovery tests to assure that logical segregation and controls are effective.
- Ensure that cloud provider personnel controls are in place to provide a logical segregation of duties.
- Understand how encryption is managed on multi-tenant storage. Is there a single key for all customers, one key per customer, or multiple keys per customer?

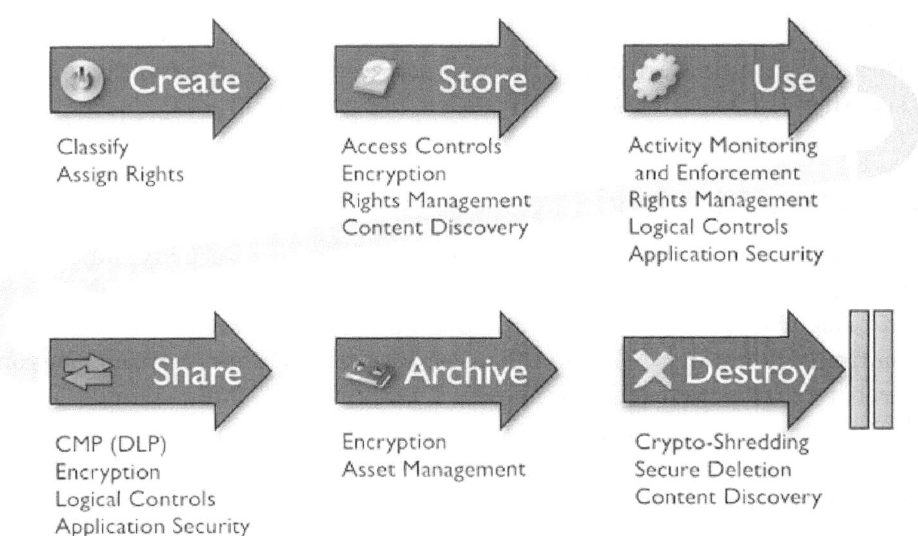

Figure 13.1 Data security life cycle.

Portability and Interoperability

Organizations must approach the cloud with the understanding that they may have to change providers in the future. Well one cannot stick to the same cloud provider if the user feels the service is quite not good. Portability and interoperability must be considered up front as part of the risk management and security assurance of any cloud program. Large cloud providers can offer geographic redundancy in the cloud, hopefully enabling high availability with a single provider. Nonetheless, it's advisable to do basic business continuity planning, to help minimize the impact of a worst-case scenario. Various companies will in the future suddenly find themselves with urgent needs to switch cloud providers for varying reasons, including:

- An unacceptable increase in cost at contract renewal time.
- A provider ceases business operations.
- A provider suddenly closes one or more services being used, without acceptable migration plans.
- Unacceptable decrease in service quality, such as a failure to meet key performance requirements or achieve Service Level Agreements (SLAs).
- A business dispute between cloud customer and provider.

Some of the key recommendations include:

- Substituting cloud providers is in virtually all cases a negative business transaction for at least one party, which can cause an unexpected negative reaction from the legacy cloud provider.
- Understand the size of data sets hosted at a cloud provider. The sheer size of data may cause an interruption of service during a transition, or a longer transition period than anticipated. Many customers have found that using a courier to ship hard drives is faster than electronic transmission for large data sets.
- Document the security architecture and configuration of individual component security controls so they can be used to support internal audits, as well as to facilitate migration to new providers.

Security and Data Recovery

The body of knowledge accrued within traditional physical security, business continuity planning and disaster recovery remains quite relevant to Cloud Computing. The rapid pace of change and lack of transparency within Cloud Computing requires that traditional security, Business Continuity Planning (BCP) and Disaster Recovery (DR) professionals be continuously engaged in vetting and monitoring your chosen cloud providers. Our challenge is to collaborate on risk identification, recognize interdependencies, integrate, and leverage resources in a dynamic and forceful way. Cloud Computing and its accompanying infrastructure assist to diminish certain security issues, but may increase others and can never eliminate the need for security. While major shifts in business and technology continue, traditional security principles remain.

Some of the key recommendations include:

- Cloud providers should consider adopting as a security baseline the most stringent requirements of any customer. To the extent these security practices do not negatively impact the customer experience, stringent security practices should prove to be cost effective in the long run by reducing risk as well as customer-driven scrutiny in several areas of concern.
- Providers should have robust compartmentalization of job duties, perform background checks, require/enforce non-disclosure agreements for employees, and limit employee knowledge of customers to that which is absolutely needed to perform job duties.
- Customers should perform onsite inspections of cloud provider facilities whenever possible.
- Customers should inspect cloud provider disaster recovery and business continuity plans.
- Customers should identify physical interdependencies in provider infrastructure.
- Ensure there is an authoritative taxonomy stated in contracts to clearly define contractual obligations related to security, recovery, and access to data.
- Customers should ask for documentation of the provider's internal and external security controls, and adherence to any industry standards.

Data Center Operations

The number of Cloud Computing providers continues to increase as business and consumer IT services move to the cloud. There has been similar growth in data centers to fuel Cloud Computing service offerings. Cloud providers of all types and sizes, including well known technology leaders and thousands of startups and emerging growth companies, are making major investments in this promising new approach to IT service delivery.

Sharing IT resources to create efficiencies and economies of scale is not a new concept. However the cloud business model works best if the traditionally enormous investments in data center operations are spread over a larger pool of consumers. Historically data center architectures have been deliberately oversized to exceed periodic peak loads, which means during normal or low demand periods, data center resources are often idle or underutilized for long stretches of time. Cloud service providers, on the other hand, seek to optimize resource usage, both human and technological, to gain competitive advantage and maximize operating profit margins.

The challenge for consumers of cloud services is how to best evaluate the provider's capabilities to deliver appropriate and cost-effective services, while at the same time protecting the customer's own data and interests. With the common carrier model of service delivery, which Cloud Computing is a form of, the service provider normally has little or no access to or control over the customers' data or systems beyond the contracted level of management. Certainly this is the correct approach to take, but some cloud architectures might take liberties with customers' data integrity and security that the customer would not be comfortable with if they became aware. The consumer must educate themselves about the services they are considering by asking appropriate questions and becoming familiar with the basic architectures and potential areas for security vulnerabilities.

Some of the key recommendations include:

- Regardless of which certifications cloud providers maintain, it is important to obtain a commitment or permission to conduct customer or external third-party audits.
- Cloud customers should understand how cloud providers implement Characteristics of Cloud Computing and how that technology architecture and infrastructure impact their ability to meet service level agreements.
- While the technology architectures of cloud providers differ, they must all be able to demonstrate comprehensive compartmentalization of systems, networks, management, provisioning, and personnel.
- Understand how resource democratization occurs within your cloud providers to best predict system availability and performance during your business fluctuations. If feasible, discover the cloud providers' other clients to assess the impact their business fluctuations may have on your customer experience with the cloud provider. However this is no substitute for ensuring the service level agreements are clearly defined, measurable, enforceable, and adequate for your requirements.
- Cloud customers should understand their cloud providers' patch management policies and procedures and how these may impact their environments. This understanding should be reflected in contract language.
- Continual improvement is particularly important in a cloud environment because any improvement in policies, processes, procedures, or tools for a single customer could result in service improvement for all customers. Look for cloud providers with standard continual improvement processes in place.
- Technical support or the service desk is often a customer's window into the provider's operations. To achieve a smooth and uniform customer support experience for your end users, it is essential to ensure that the provider's customer support processes, procedures, tools, and support hours are compatible with yours.

Incident Response, Notification and Remedy

The nature of Cloud Computing makes it more difficult to determine who to contact in case of a security incident, data breach, or other event that requires investigation and reaction. Standard security incident response mechanisms can be used with modifications to accommodate the changes required by shared reporting responsibilities. This domain provides guidance on how to handle these incidents.

The problem for the cloud customer is that applications deployed to cloud fabrics are not always designed with data integrity and security in mind. This may result in vulnerable applications being deployed into cloud environments, triggering security incidents. Additionally, flaws in infrastructure architecture, mistakes made during hardening procedures, and simple oversights present significant risks to cloud operations. Of course, similar vulnerabilities also endanger traditional data center operations.

Technical expertise is obviously required in incident handling, but privacy and legal experts have much to contribute to cloud security. They also play a role in incident response regarding notification, remediation, and possible subsequent legal action. An organization considering using cloud services needs to review what mechanisms have been implemented to address questions about employee data access that is not governed by user agreements and privacy policies. Application data not managed by a cloud provider's own applications, such as in IaaS and PaaS architectures, generally has different controls than data managed by a SaaS provider's application.

The complexities of large cloud providers delivering SaaS, PaaS, and IaaS capabilities create significant incident response issues that potential customers must assess for acceptable levels of service. When evaluating providers it is important to be aware that the provider may be hosting hundreds of thousands of application instances. From an incident monitoring perspective, any foreign applications widen the responsibility of the security operations center (SOC). Normally a SOC monitors alerts and other incident indicators, such as those produced by intrusion detection systems and firewalls, but the number of sources that must be monitored and the volume of notifications can increase exponentially in an open cloud environment, as the SOC may need to monitor activity between customers as well as external incidents.

An organization will need to understand the incident response strategy for their chosen cloud provider. This strategy must address identification and notification, as well as options for remediation of unauthorized access to application data. To make matters more complicated, application data management and access have different meanings and regulatory requirements depending on the data location. For example, an incident may occur involving data in Germany, whereas if the same data had been stored in the US it might not have been considered an issue. This complication makes incident identification particularly challenging.

Some of the key recommendations include:

- Cloud customers need to clearly define and communicate to cloud providers what they consider incidents (such as data breaches) versus mere events (such as suspicious intrusion detection alerts) before service deployment.
- Cloud customers may have very limited involvement with the providers' incident response activities. Therefore it is critical for customers to understand the prearranged communication paths to the provider's incident response team.
- Cloud customers should investigate what incident detection and analysis tools providers use to make sure they are compatible with their own systems. A provider's proprietary or unusual log formats could be major roadblocks in joint investigations, particularly those that involve legal discovery or government intervention.
- Poorly designed and protected applications and systems can easily overwhelm everyone's incident response capabilities. Conducting proper risk management on the systems and utilizing defense-in-depth practices are essential to reduce the chance of a security incident in the first place.

- Security Operation Centers (SOC) often assume a single governance model related to incident response, which is inappropriate for multi-tenant cloud providers. A robust and well maintained Security Information and Event Management (SIEM) process that identifies available data sources (application logs, firewall logs, IDS logs, etc) and merges these into a common analysis and alerting platform can assist the SOC in detecting incidents within the cloud computing platform.
- To greatly facilitate detailed offline analyses, look for cloud providers with the ability to deliver snapshots of the customer's entire virtual environment firewalls, network (switches), systems, applications, and data.
- Containment is a race between damage control and evidence gathering. Containment approaches that focus on the Confidentiality-Integrity-Availability (CIA) triad can be effective.
- Remediation highlights the importance of being able to restore systems to earlier states, and even a need to go back six to twelve months for a known-good configuration. Keeping legal options and requirements in mind, remediation may also need to support forensic recording of incident data.
- Any data classified as private for data breach regulations should always be encrypted to reduce the consequences of a breach incident. Customers should stipulate encryption requirements contractually.
- Some cloud providers may host a significant number of customers with unique applications. These cloud providers should consider application layer logging frameworks to provide granular narrowing of incidents to a specific customer. These cloud providers should also construct a registry of application owners by application interface (URL, SOA service, etc.)
- Application-level firewalls, proxies, and other application logging tools are key capabilities currently available to assist in responding to incidents in multi-tenant environments.

Application Security

Cloud environments by virtue of their flexibility, openness, and often public availability challenge many fundamental assumptions about application security. Some of these assumptions are well understood; however many are not. This section is intended to document how Cloud Computing influences security over the lifetime of an application from design to operations to ultimate decommissioning. This guidance is for all stakeholders including application designers, security professionals, operations personnel, and technical management on how to best mitigate risk and manage assurance within Cloud Computing applications. Cloud Computing is a particular challenge for applications across the layers of Software as a Service (SaaS), Platform as a Service (PaaS) and Infrastructure as a Service (IaaS). Cloud-based software applications require a design rigor similar to applications residing in a classic DMZ. This includes a deep up-front analysis covering all the traditional aspects of managing information confidentiality, integrity, and availability.

Some of the key recommendations include:

- IaaS, PaaS, and SaaS create different trust boundaries for the software development lifecycle; which must be accounted for during the development, testing, and production deployment of applications.
- For IaaS, a key success factor is the presence of trusted virtual machine images. The best alternative is the ability to provide your own virtual machine image conforming to internal policies.
- The best practices available to harden host systems within DMZs should be applied to virtual machines. Limiting services available to only those needed to support the application stack is appropriate.
- Securing inter-host communications must be the rule; there can be no assumption of a secure channel between hosts, whether in a common data center or even on the same hardware device.
- Managing and protecting application credentials and key material are critical.
- Extra care should be undertaken with the management of files used for application logging and debugging, as the locations of these files may be remote or unknown and the information could be sensitive.
- Account for external administration and multi-tenancy in the application's threat model.
- Applications sufficiently complex to leverage an Enterprise Service Bus (ESB) need to secure the ESB directly, leveraging a protocol such as WS-Security. The ability to segment ESBs is not available in PaaS environments.
- Metrics should be applied to assess effectiveness of application security programs. Among the direct application security-specific metrics available are vulnerability scores and patch coverage. These metrics can indicate the quality of application coding. Indirect data handling metrics, such as the percentage of data encrypted, can indicate that responsible decisions are being made from an application architecture perspective.
- Cloud providers must support dynamic analysis web application security tools against applications hosted in their environments.

Encryption and Key Management

Cloud customers and providers need to guard against data loss and theft. Today, encryption of Personal and enterprise data is strongly recommended, and in some cases mandated by laws and regulations around the world. Cloud customers want their providers to encrypt their data to ensure that it is protected no matter where the data is physically located. Likewise, the cloud provider needs to protect its customers' sensitive data.

Strong encryption with key management is one of the core mechanisms that Cloud Computing systems should use to protect data. While encryption itself doesn't necessarily prevent data loss, safe harbor provisions in laws and regulations treat lost encrypted data as not lost at all. The encryption provides resource protection while key management enables access to protected resources.

Encrypting data in transit over networks – There is the utmost need to encrypt multi-use credentials, such as credit card numbers, passwords, and private keys, in transit over the Internet. Although cloud provider networks may be more secure than the open Internet, they are by their very architecture made up of many disparate components, and disparate organizations share the cloud. Therefore, it is important to protect this sensitive and regulated information in transit even within the cloud provider's network. Typically this can be implemented with equal ease in SaaS, PaaS, and IaaS environments.

Encrypting data at rest – Encrypting data on disk or in a live production database has value, as it can protect against a malicious cloud service provider or a malicious co-tenant as well as against some types of application abuse. For long-term archival storage, some customers encrypt their own data and then send it as cipher text to a cloud data storage vendor. The customer then controls and holds the cryptographic keys and decrypts the data, if necessary, back on their own premises. Encrypting data at rest is common within IaaS environments, using a variety of provider and third party tools. Encrypting data at rest within PaaS environments is generally more complex, requiring instrumentation of provider offerings or special customization. Encrypting data at rest within SaaS environments is a feature cloud customers cannot implement directly, and need to request from their providers.

Encrypting data on backup media – This can protect against misuse of lost or stolen media.

Ideally, the cloud service provider implements it transparently. However, as a customer and provider of data, it is your responsibility to verify that such encryption takes place. One consideration for the encryption infrastructure is dealing with the longevity of the data. Beyond these common uses of encryption, the possibly of exotic attacks against cloud providers also warrants further exploration of means for encrypting dynamic data, including data residing in memory.

Existing cloud service providers may provide basic encryption key schemes to secure cloud based application development and services, or they may leave all such protective measures up to their customers. While cloud service providers are progressing towards supporting robust key management schemes, more work is needed to overcome barriers to adoption. Emerging standards should solve this problem in the near future, but work is still in progress. There are several key management issues and challenges within Cloud Computing

Secure key stores – Key stores must themselves be protected, just as any other sensitive data. They must be protected in storage, in transit, and in backup. Improper key storage could lead to the compromise of all encrypted data.

Access to key stores – Access to key stores must be limited to the entities that specifically need the individual keys. There should also be policies governing the key stores, which use separation of roles to help control access; an entity that uses a given key should not be the entity that stores that key.

Key backup and recoverability – Loss of keys inevitably means loss of the data that those keys protect. While this is an effective way to destroy data, accidental loss of keys protecting mission critical data would be devastating to a business, so secure backup and recovery solutions must be implemented.

There are a number of standards and guidelines applicable to key management in the cloud. The OASIS Key Management Interoperability Protocol (KMIP) is an emerging standard for interoperable key management in the cloud. The IEEE 1619.3 standards cover storage encryption and key management, especially as they pertain to storage IaaS.

Identity and Access Management

Managing identities and access control for enterprise applications remains one of the greatest challenges facing IT today. While an enterprise may be able to leverage several Cloud Computing services without a good identity and access management strategy, in the long run extending an organization's identity services into the cloud is a necessary precursor towards strategic use of on-demand computing services. Supporting today's aggressive adoption of an admittedly immature cloud ecosystem requires an honest assessment of an organization's readiness to conduct cloud-based Identity and Access Management (IAM), as well as understanding the capabilities of that organization's Cloud Computing providers.

Identity Provisioning – One of the major challenges for organizations adopting Cloud Computing services is the secure and timely management of on-boarding (provisioning) and off-boarding (deprovisioning) of users in the cloud. Furthermore, enterprises that have invested in user management processes within an enterprise will seek to extend those processes and practice to cloud services.

Authentication – When organizations start to utilize cloud services, authenticating users in a trustworthy and manageable manner is a vital requirement. Organizations must address authentication-related challenges such as credential management, strong authentication (typically defined as multi-factor authentication), delegated authentication, and managing trust across all types of cloud services.

Federation – In a Cloud Computing environment, Federated Identity Management plays a vital role in enabling organizations to authenticate their users of cloud services using the organization's chosen Identity provider (IdP). In that context, exchanging identity attributes between the Service Provider (SP) and the IdP in a secure way is also an important requirement. Organizations considering federated identity management in the cloud should understand the various challenges and possible solutions to address those challenges with respect to identity lifecycle management, available authentication methods to protect confidentiality, and integrity; while supporting non-repudiation.

Authorization & user profile management – The requirements for user profiles and access control policy vary depending on whether the user is acting on their own behalf (such as a consumer) or as a member of an organization (such as an employer, university, hospital, or other enterprise). The access control requirements in SPI environments include establishing trusted user profile and policy information, using it to control access within the cloud service, and doing this in an auditable way.

Virtualization

The ability to provide multi-tenant cloud services at the infrastructure, platform, or software level is often underpinned by the ability to provide some form of virtualization to create economic scale. However, use of these technologies brings additional security concerns. This domain looks at these security issues. While there are several forms of virtualization, by far the most common is the virtualized operating system, and this is the focus in this version of our guidance. If Virtual Machine (VM) technology is being used in the infrastructure of the cloud services, then we must be concerned about compartmentalization and hardening of those VM systems.

The reality of current practices related to management of virtual operating systems is that many of the processes that provide security-by-default are missing, and special attention must be paid to replacing them. The core virtualization technology itself introduces new attack surfaces in the hypervisor and other management components, but more important is the severe impact virtualization has on network security. Virtual machines now communicate over a hardware backplane, rather than a network. As a result, standard network security controls are blind to this traffic and cannot perform monitoring or in-line blocking. These controls need to take a new form to function in the virtual environment.

Commingling of data in centralized services and repositories is another concern. A centralized database as provided by a Cloud Computing service should in theory improve security over data distributed over a vast number and mixture of endpoints. However, this is also centralizing risk, increasing the consequences of a breach.

Another concern is the commingling of VMs of different sensitivities and security. In Cloud Computing environments, the lowest common denominator of security will be shared by all tenants in the multi-tenant virtual environment unless new security architecture can be achieved that does not "wire in" any network dependency for protection.

Some of the key recommendations include:

- Identify which types of virtualization your cloud provider uses, if any.
- Virtualized operating systems should be augmented by third party security technology to provide layered security controls and reduce dependency on the platform provider alone.
- Understand which security controls are in place internal to the VMs other than the built in hypervisor isolation — such as intrusion detection, anti-virus, vulnerability scanning, etc. Secure by default configuration must be assured by following or exceeding available industry baselines.
- Understand which security controls are in place external to the VMs to protect administrative interfaces (web-based, APIs, etc.) exposed to the customers.

- Validate the pedigree and integrity of any VM image or template originating from the cloud provider before using.
- Have a reporting mechanism in place that provides evidence of isolation and raises alerts if there is a breach of isolation.
- Be aware of multi-tenancy situations with your VMs where regulatory concerns may warrant segregation

13.4 SECURITY SURVEYS IN CLOUD COMPUTING

At the last section lets us see some of the interesting surveys in cloud computing. These survey results gives us some idea about how efficient is the cloud technology and how have the people responded to it. The survey was taken by CA Technologies and Ponemon Institute.

Following is a summary of the most salient findings from the study.

- The majority of cloud computing providers surveyed do not believe their organization views the security of their cloud services as a competitive advantage. Further, they do not consider cloud computing security as one of their most important responsibilities and do not believe their products or services substantially protect and secure the confidential or sensitive information of their customers.
- The majority of cloud providers believe it is their customer's responsibility to secure the cloud and not their responsibility. They also say their systems and applications are not always evaluated for security threats prior to deployment to customers.
- Buyer beware – on average providers of cloud computing technologies allocate10 percent or less of their operational resources to security and most do not have confidence that customers' security requirements are being met.
- Cloud providers in the survey say the primary reasons why customers purchase cloud resources are lower cost and faster deployment of applications. In contrast, improved security or compliance with regulations is viewed as an unlikely reason for choosing cloud services. The majority of cloud providers in our study admit they do not have dedicated security personnel to oversee the security of cloud applications, infrastructure or platforms.
- Providers of private cloud resources appear to attach more importance and have a higher level of confidence in their organization's ability to meet security objectives than providers of public and hybrid cloud solutions.
- While security as a "true" service from the cloud is rarely offered to customers today, about one-third of the cloud providers in our study are considering such solutions as a new source of revenue sometime in the next two years.

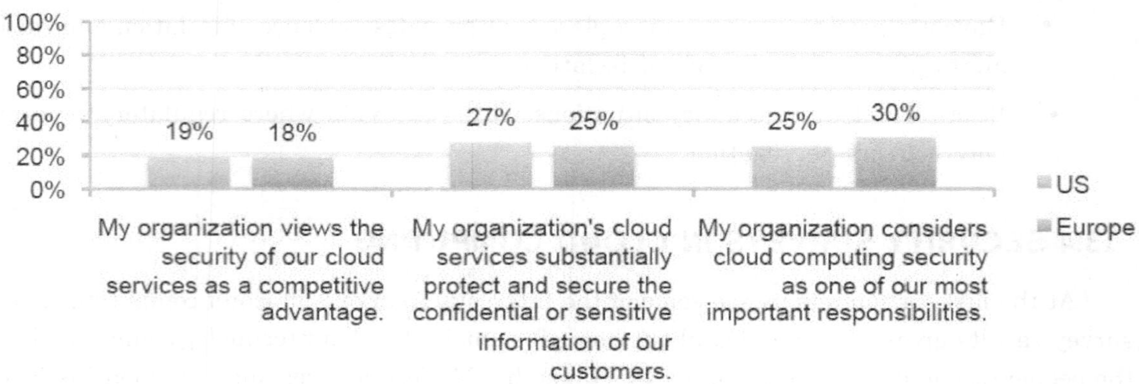

Figure 13.2 Bar chart 1.

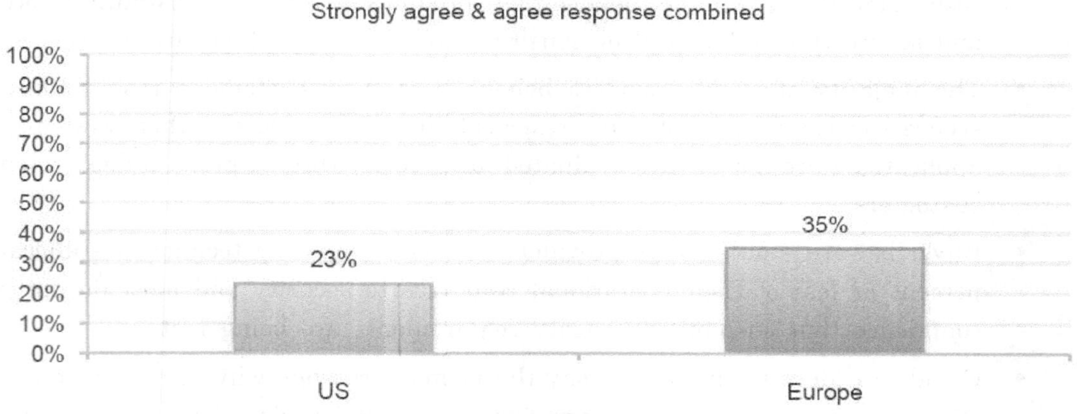

Figure 13.3 Bar chart 2.

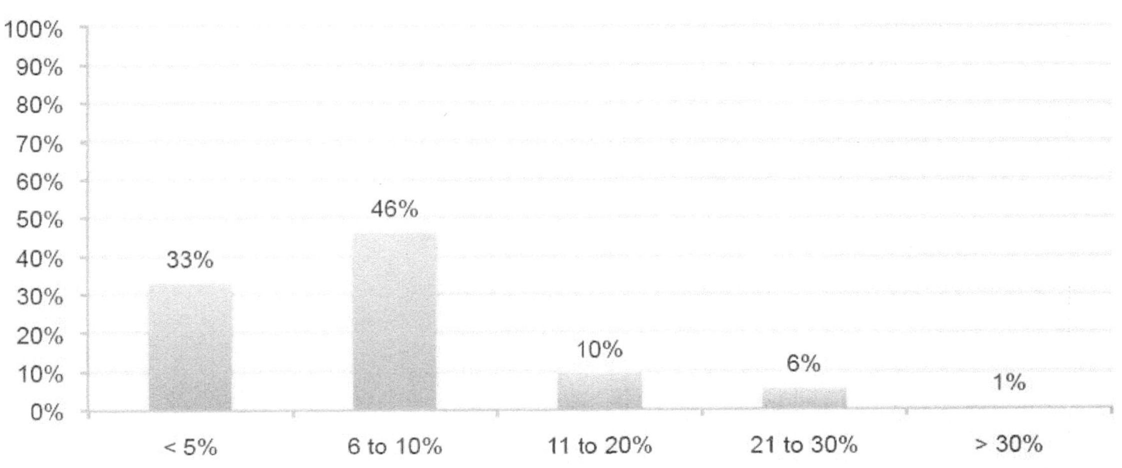

Figure 13.4 Bar chart 3.

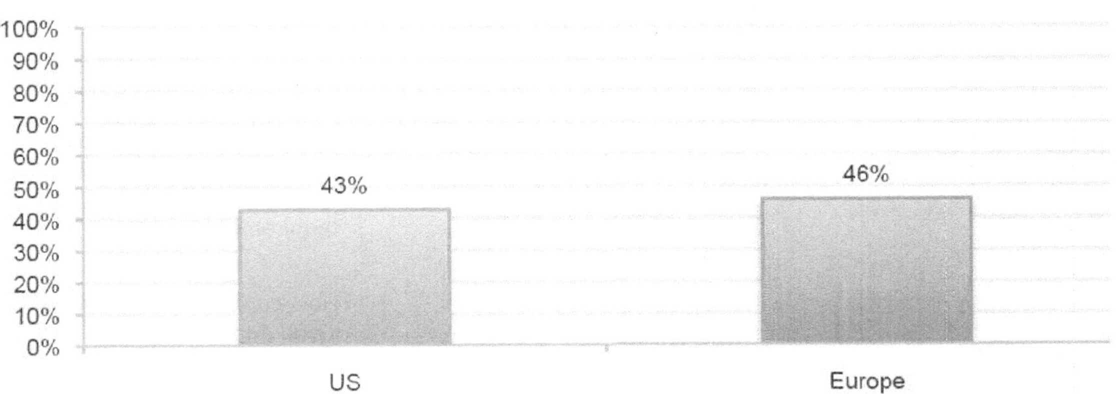

Figure 13.5 Bar chart 4.

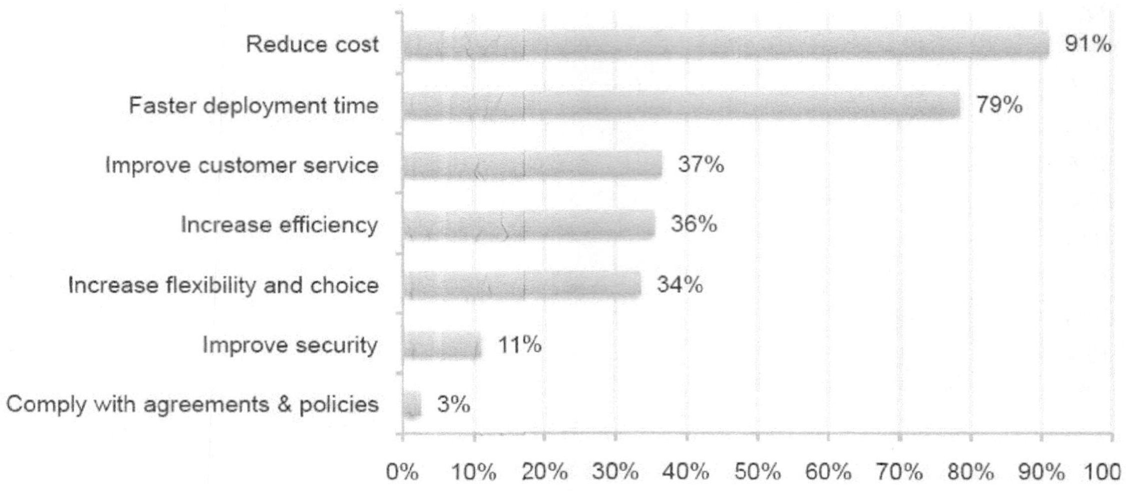

Figure 13.6 Bar chart 5.

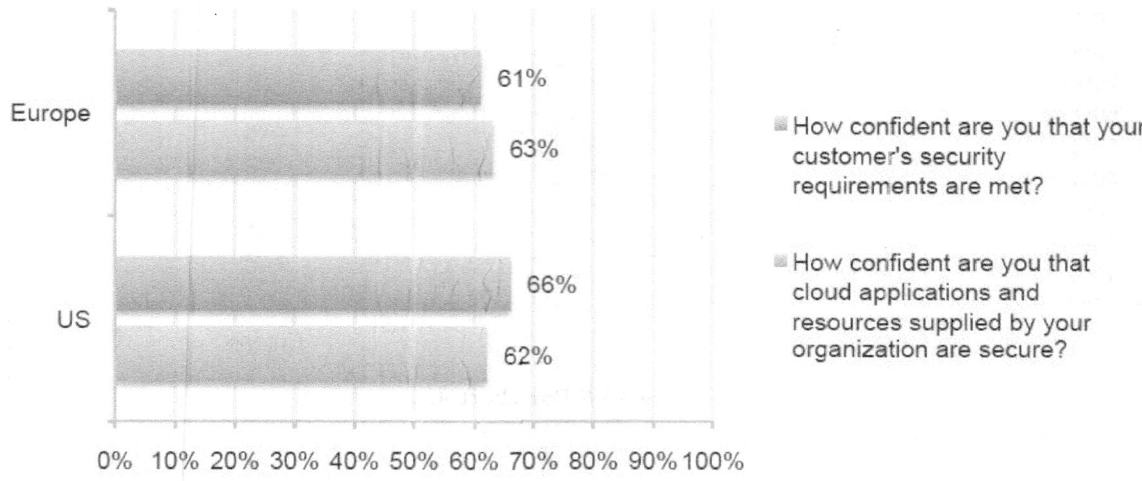

Figure 13.7 Bar chart 6.

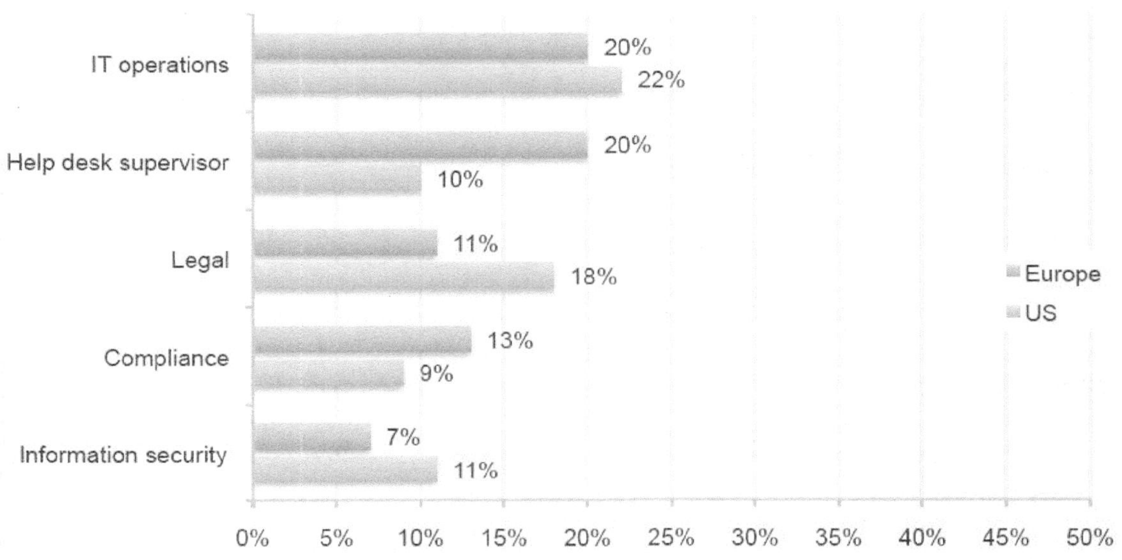

Figure 13.8 Bar chart 7.

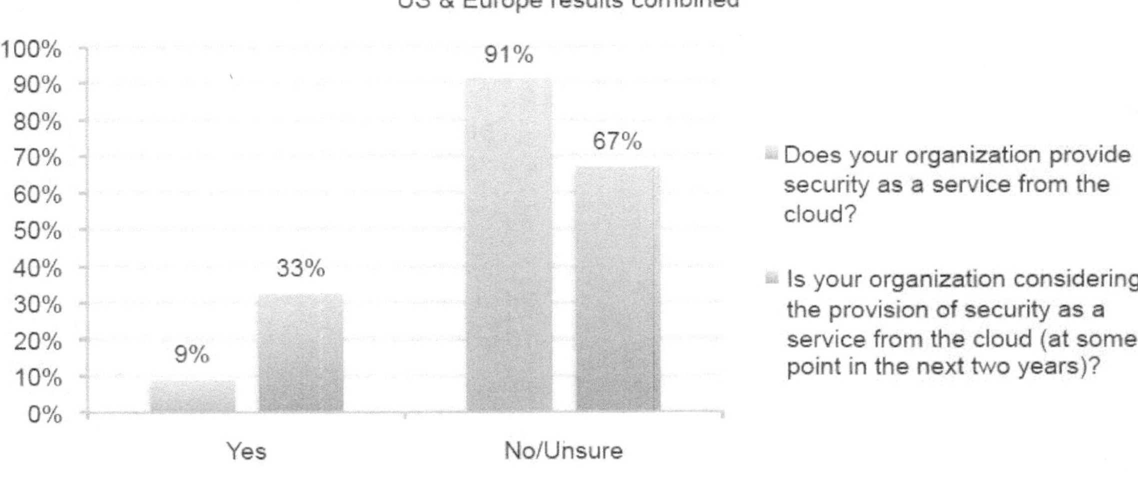

Figure 13.9 Bar chart 8.

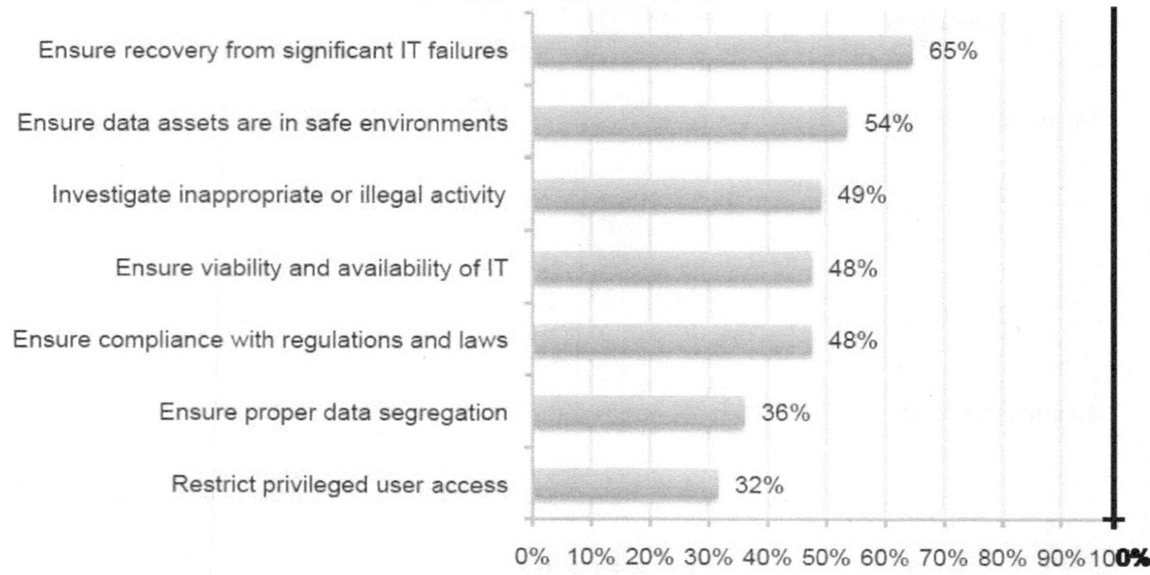

Figure 13.10 Bar chart 9.

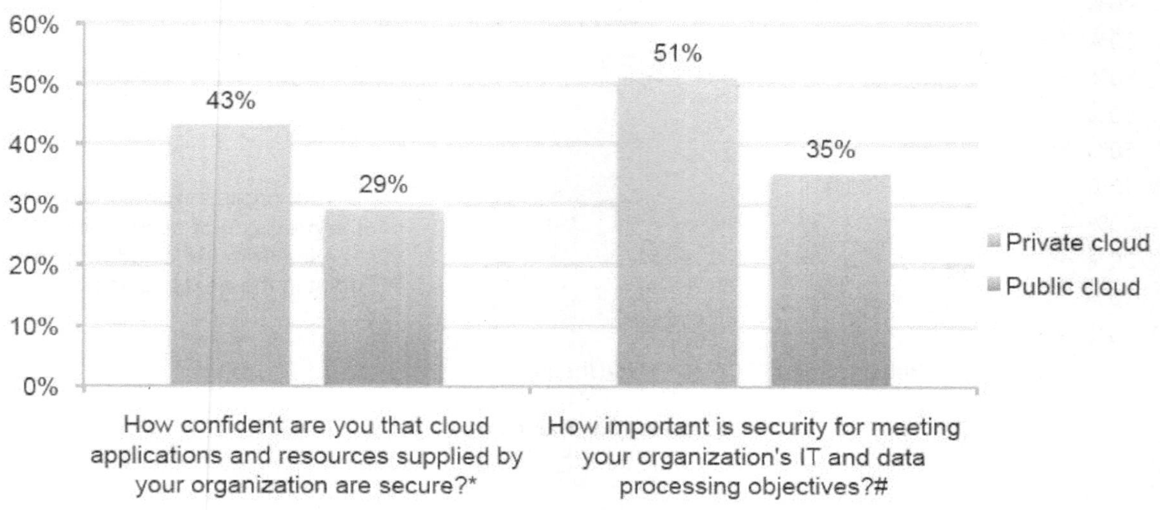

Figure 13.11 Bar chart 10.

SUMMARY

- *Companies have to make wise choice in choosing the right technology and platform based on various business friendly parameters and even the user friendly one. In case the technology is full of issues then it is a total flop model and it is rejected by the corporate IT companies.*
- *Cloud being in remote location, handling millions of users and the tasks, pooled resources and storage of user data we need to ensure security in cloud. Even for mobile cloud computing we need to ensure the similar security problems.*
- *Once a company hands over cloud computing responsibility to a service provider, all the data would be handled by the latter. This could create a monitoring issue for the company, especially if the proper processes are not set in place.*
- *The virus is a malicious software program whose ultimate objective is to cause the harm to all the computer resources and user work. The far more impact of virus is the fast spreading of it to other uninfected ones in a far replication process. In cloud computing if one file is infected by virus attack all other files stored in the remote virtual cloud is affected.*
- *As far as in cloud more than the data we even store and utilize many dynamic software and workspaces. If some overrides their functionality or misuses the work in the workspace environment, it can prove to be a disaster for a computer techie. From a corporate IT sector point of you integrity of any entity must be maintained.*
- *As far as storing confidential work in cloud is concerned we need to be careful. We must be aware that our data is not getting used or manipulated by any other intruder from our account.*
- *If suddenly a vendor shuts down the company or the server is down or the server is attacked, all the stored data is lost. It could prove to be a big problem for the cloud user. For a corporate IT company data loss can prove to be disaster as it can affect the entire project.*
- *The vendor must provide all forms of check in at the security level. The vendor is responsible to maintain a strong and a robust cloud infrastructure which is well secured and satisfies all the requirements of the end user.*
- *In order to maintain the security in cloud we broadly classify them into two domains which are the governance domain and operational domain.*
- *For the cloud security issue each company must have their own well defined governance policies to overcome any security violations. Well developed information security governance processes should result in information security management programs that are scalable with the business, repeatable across the organization, measurable, sustainable, defensible, continually improving, and cost-effective on an ongoing basis.*

- *Cloud computing creates new dynamies in the relationship between an organization and its information, involving the presence of a third party the cloud provider. This creates new challenges in understanding how laws apply to a wide variety of information management scenarios.*
- *Portability and interoperability must be considered up front as part of the risk management and security assurance of any cloud program. Large cloud providers can offer geographic redundancy in the cloud, hopefully enabling high availability with a single provider. Nonetheless, it's advisable to do basic business continuity planning, to help minimize the impact of a worst-case scenario.*
- *The challenge for consumers of cloud services is how to best evaluate the provider's capabilities to deliver appropriate and cost-effective services, while at the same time protecting the customer's own data and interests.*
- *Cloud environments by virtue of their flexibility, openness, and often public availability challenge many fundamental assumptions about application security.*
- *Cloud customers and providers need to guard against data loss and theft. Today, encryption of Personal and enterprise data is strongly recommended, and in some cases mandated by laws and regulations around the world. Cloud customers want their providers to encrypt their data to ensure that it is protected no matter where the data is physically located.*
- *Supporting today's aggressive adoption of an admittedly immature cloud ecosystem requires an honest assessment of an organization's readiness to conduct cloud-based Identity and Access Management (IAM), as well as understanding the capabilities of that organization's Cloud computing providers.*

14

CASE STUDIES

In the last chapter of the book, we present you some real time projects in the form of case studies. These case studies can help you better understand all the concepts of cloud computing. They can further help you in creating many more projects in cloud. The ultimate objective of these case studies is to motivate people to do real time projects in cloud computing.

14.1 CASE 1: WORKING WITH OPENSTACK CLOUD AND BOOTING A TINY GUEST OS

In chapter 7, we saw the detailed description of the cloud tool OpenStack and in chapter 8, we saw how Ubuntu platform supports OpenStack cloud and the live cloud installation of it. Now in this case study we explain you in detail about the configuration of OpenStack cloud and its function.

There are several ways to configure the OpenStack cloud. It is getting updated from time to time. There is a simple and easy way of cloud installation using the script files which we will use here to install cloud. Script file installation is an easy and a simple way of installing cloud. All the commands are put in a single file, running this file finishes the whole installation.

Devstack Method

The popularly used script method installation of cloud is Devstack method of OpenStack cloud. It installs the OpenStack Folsom version of cloud. Though other versions are also available but one must check it properly at the time of installation. One must not get confused with various versions of a cloud tool and the operating system versions too. They get updated from time to time. One must enable virtualization technology in the system before installing any cloud tool or it will fail in the installation step itself. One can install cloud in a physical machine or even in virtual operating system software. We can easily configure cloud in just few steps using the script file method. But this method is not recommended for any product development or for any other major research purpose. In such cases one needs to fallow the standard procedure in installing cloud from the respective company installation steps.

One of the major requirements of cloud installation is the high speed internet without any blockage of firewalls.

We start the cloud installation by the following steps:

- To install OpenStack cloud first select the Linux OS. Devstack method supports only Ubuntu 12.04 (Precise), Fedora 20 and CentOS/RHEL 6.5. OpenStack also runs and is packaged on other flavors of Linux such as OpenSUSE and Debian. Install the respective operating system. We use Ubuntu 12.04 in this case study.
- In the first step update the Ubuntu operating system by this command. It downloads all the required packages.

  apt-get update

- Install the git package as it is required for Devstack method.

  apt-get install -qqy git

- In the terminal of Ubuntu 12.04 download the script file of Devstack method by typing this command

  git clone https://github.com/OpenStack-dev/devstack.git

- It creates a new directory called Devstack. Move to that directory

  cd Devstack

- Now we are ready to start the script file installation of cloud by a single command

  ./stack.sh

This is a very big step as it involves all the steps in the OpenStack cloud installation. It involves downloading many packages and all the components required for the OpenStack cloud tool. This step requires a very high speed internet and may take about 2 hours to get completed. At the end OpenStack cloud is configured and it is ready to be used. The user can see a URL at the terminal paste this URL in the web browser you can see the ultimate cloud output in the web browser or use the default localhost 127.0.0.1 also to view the output.

Now we discuss the output of the OpenStack cloud using all the output images.

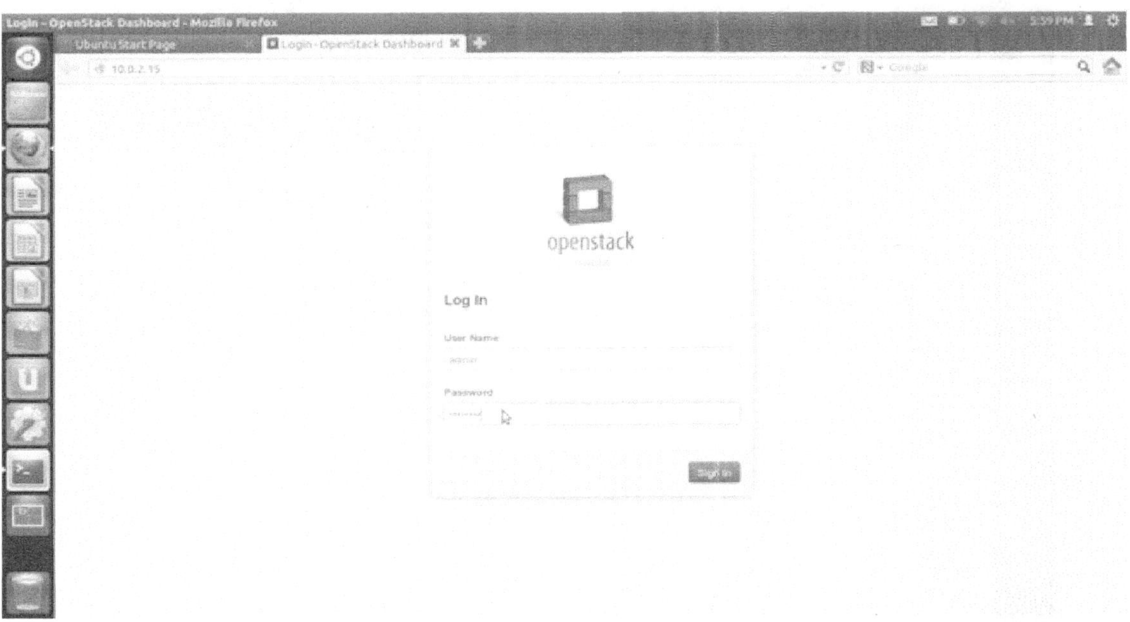

In the first step enter the OpenStack cloud with the admin credentials. It is displayed at the end of the installation in the terminal.

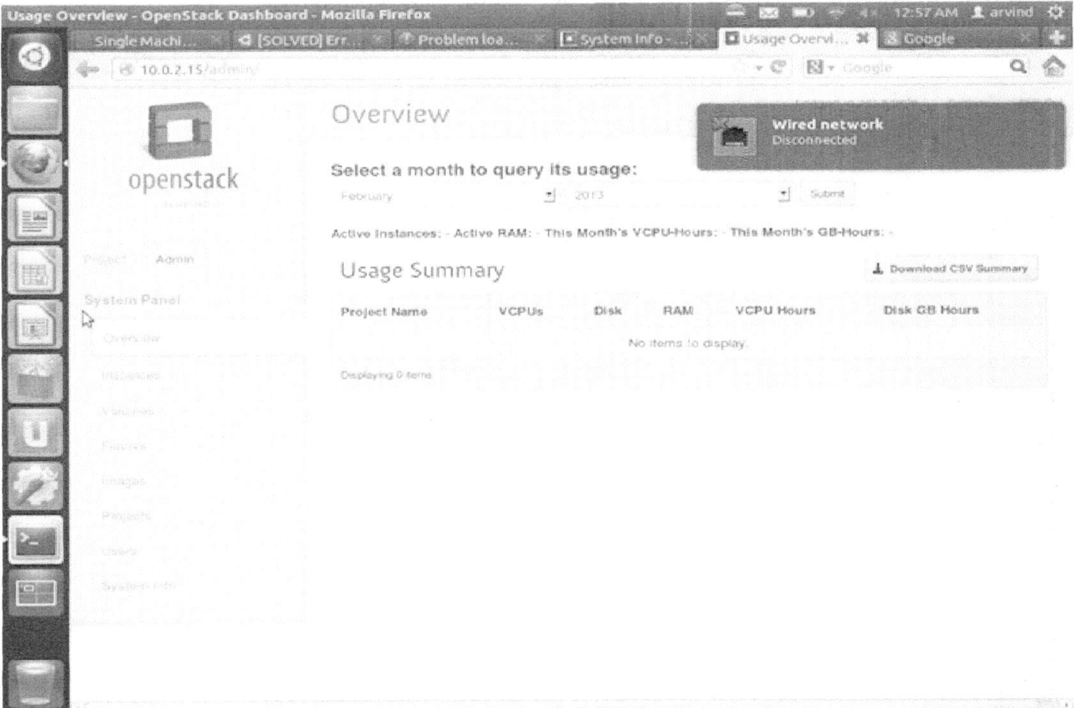

Initial overview of cloud without any users or instances created. It is any empty cloud at first

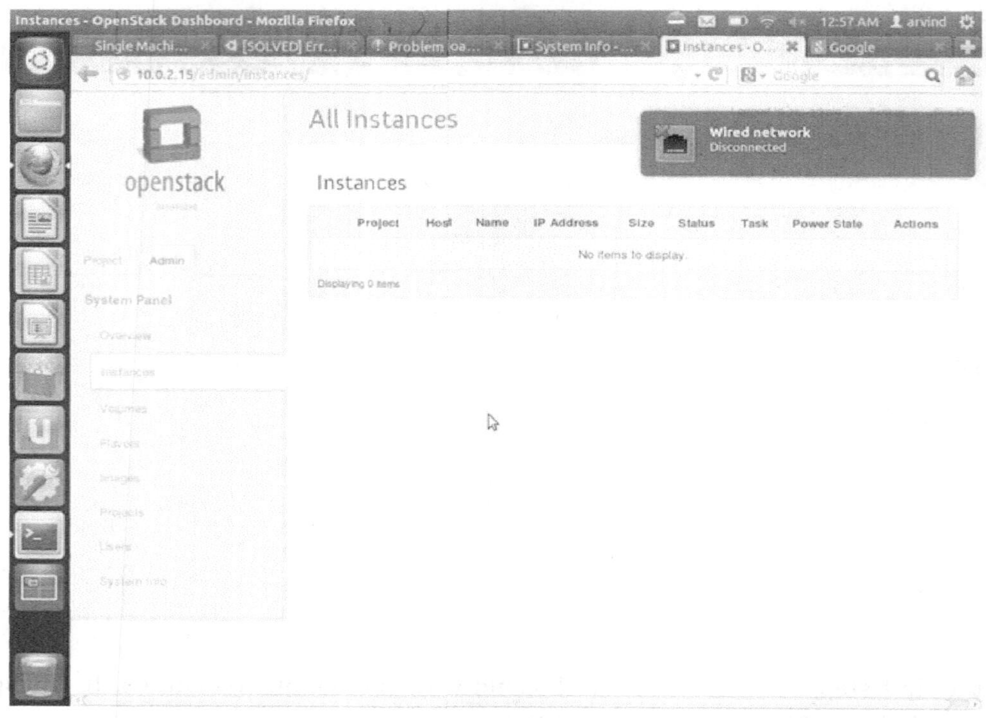

Initially no instances are created in the cloud. It is empty.

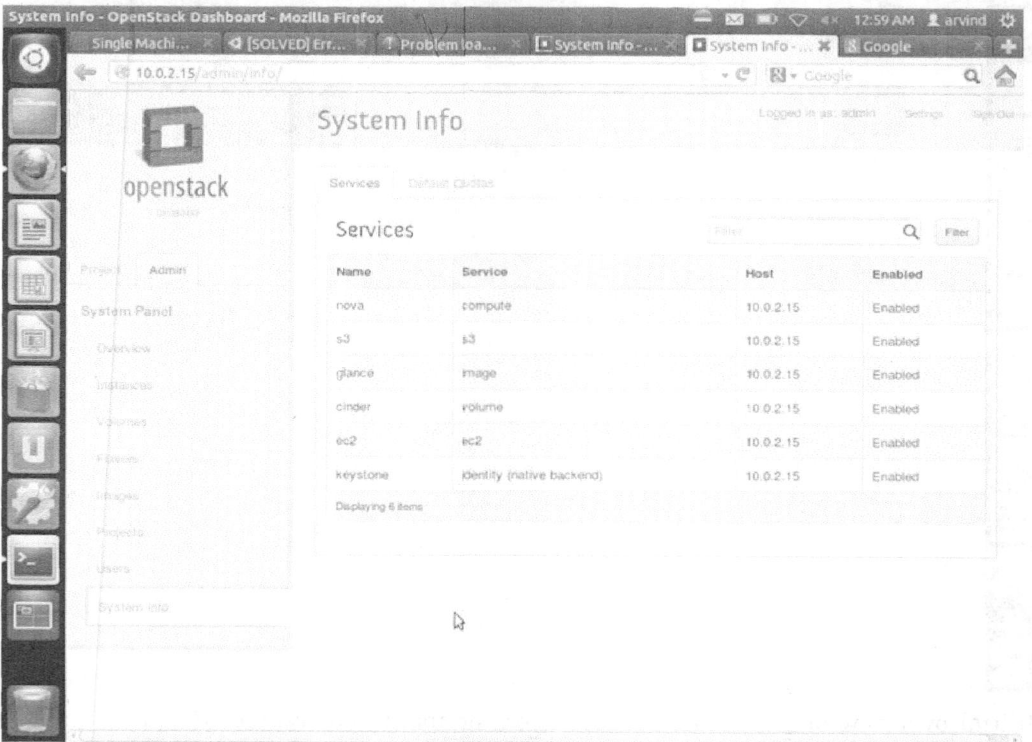

The various services provided by the cloud are displayed. One can see all the components of OpenStack cloud here.

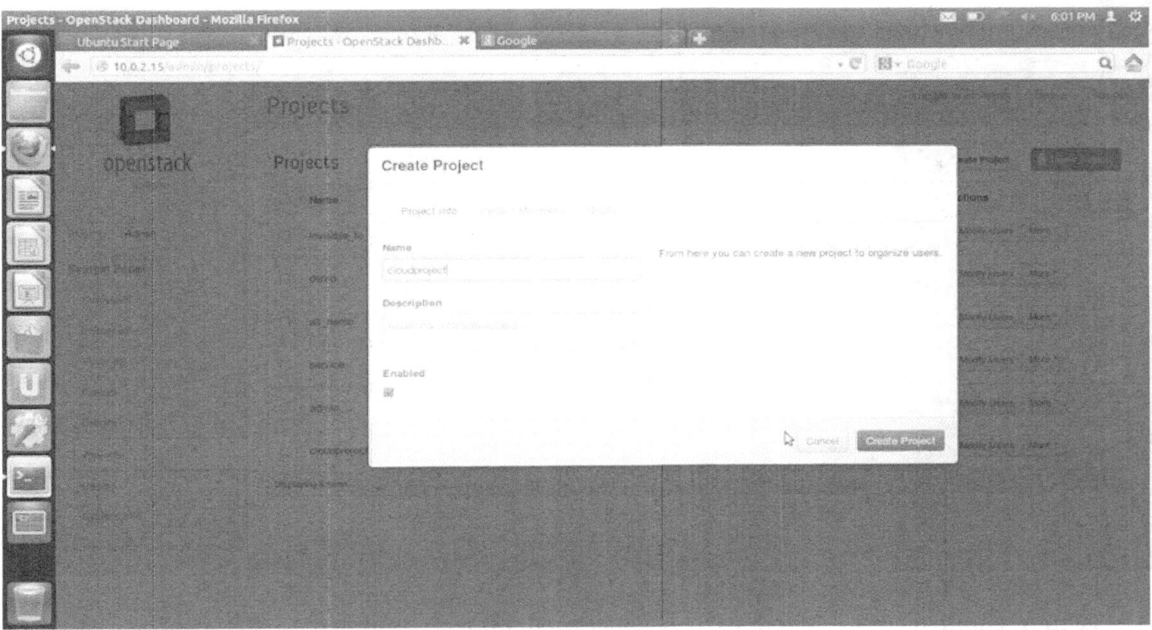

The admin creates a new workspace called project for the user. It is the first step in making cloud functional and providing service.

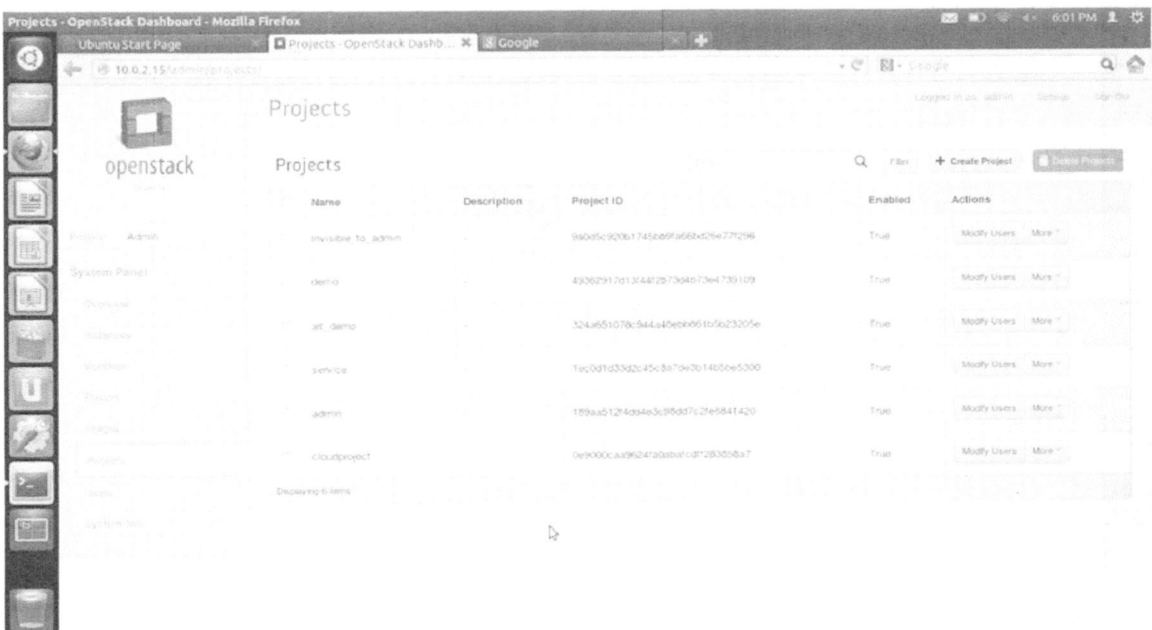

List of all projects along with the default one is displayed. Click create project to create a new project.

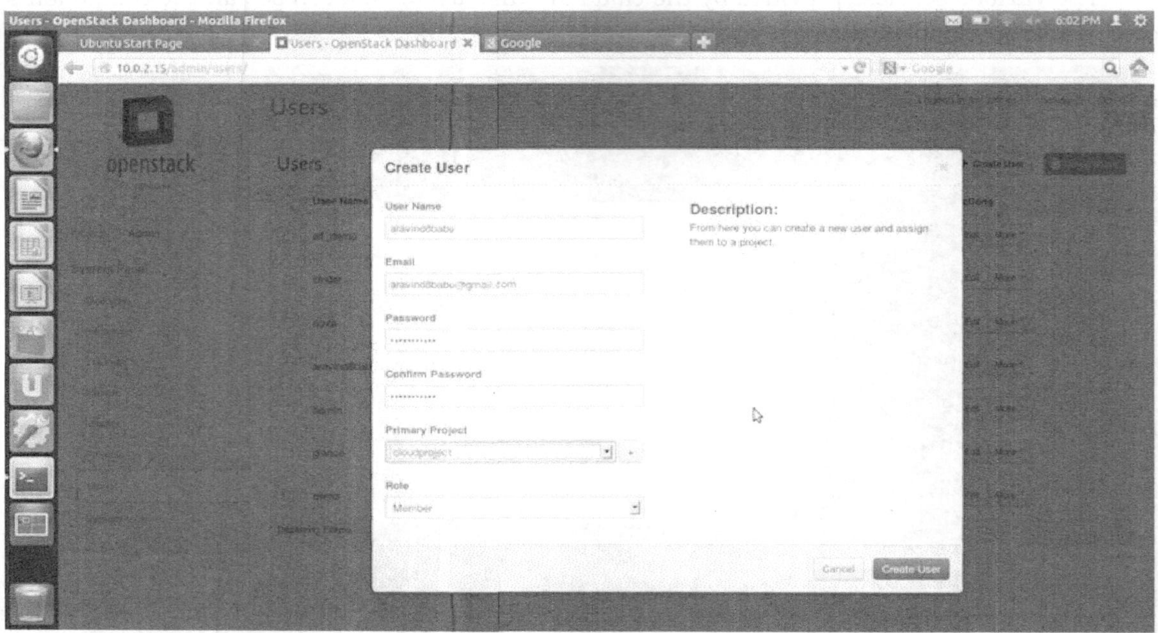

A new cloud user is added with a concerned project assigned to the user.

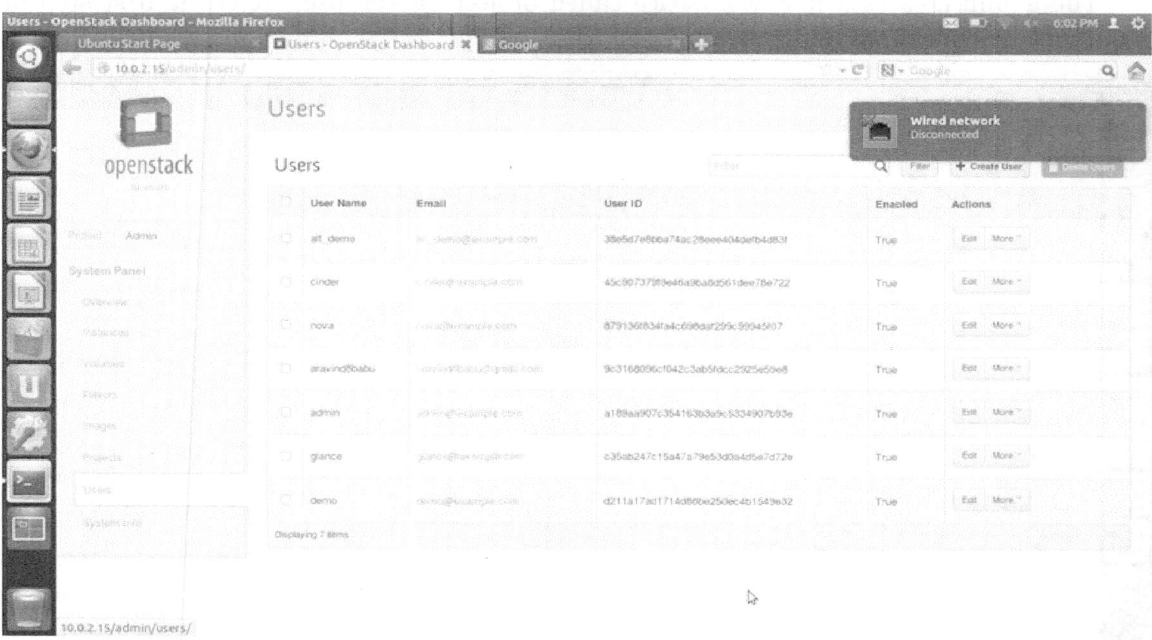

List of all cloud users along with default one are displayed along with the newly created one.

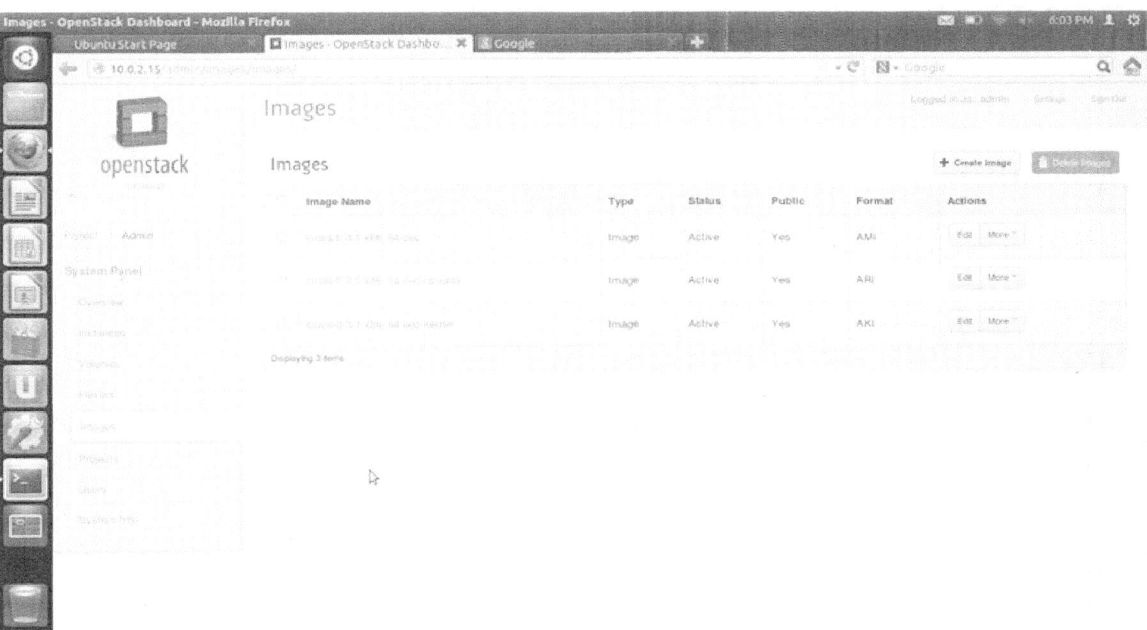

The available images or the cloud applications in the cloud are displayed. The default one is Cirros operating system. It gets uploaded at the time of installation itself.

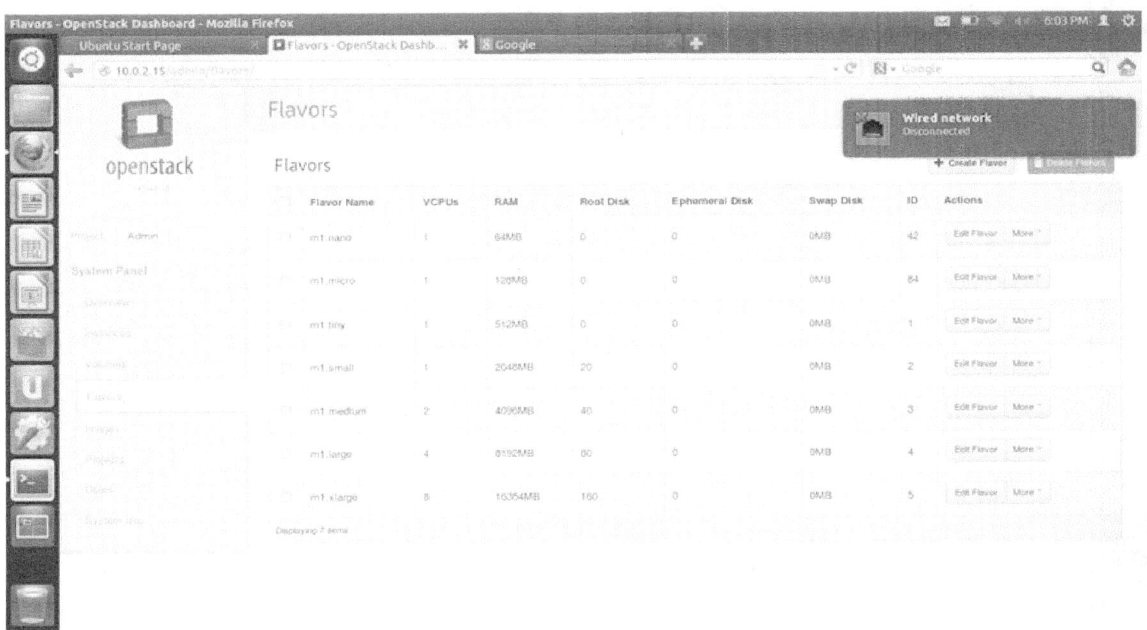

The various flavors available for running the virtual instance of the application are displayed. We can choose based on our requirement.

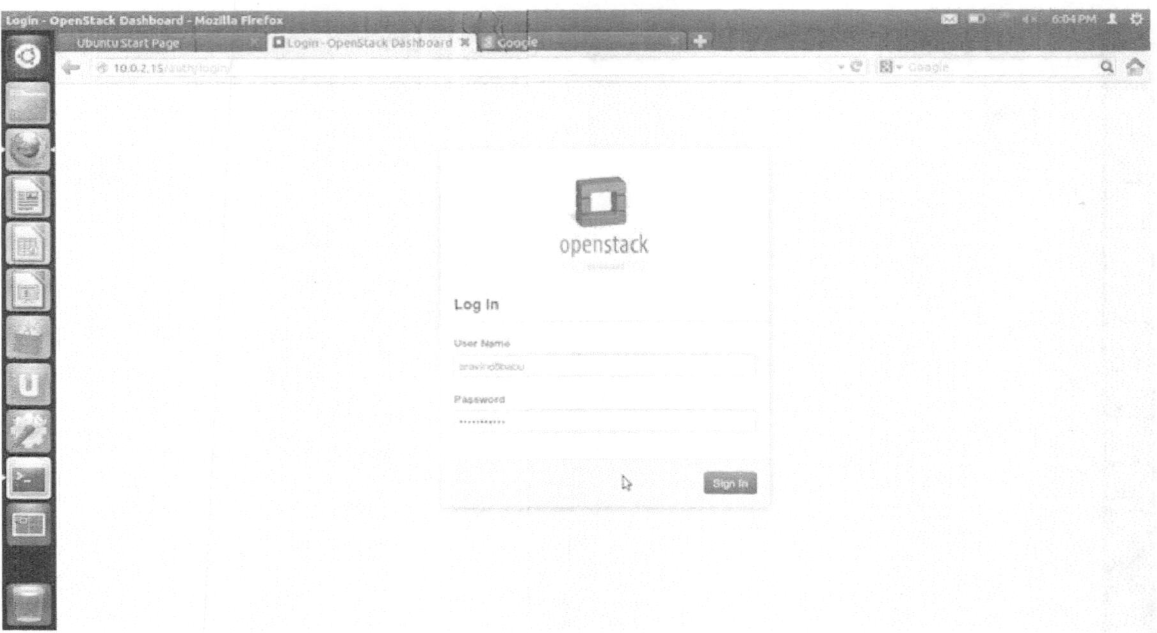

Finally the registered cloud user logs in with the respective credentials. This marks the full usage of cloud by registered user.

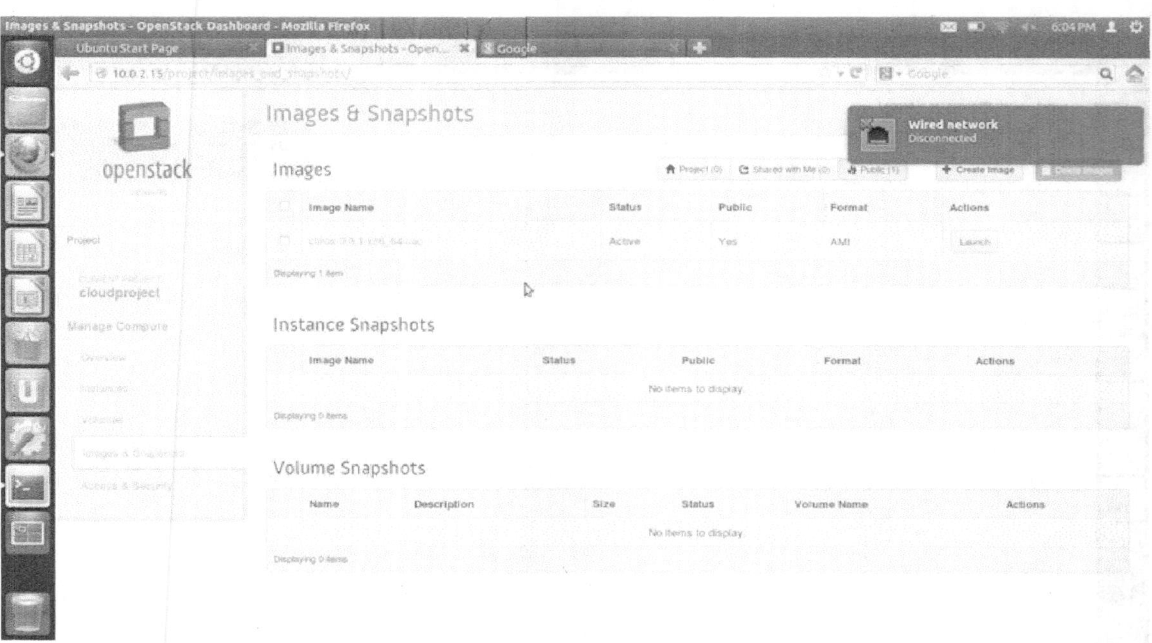

The user can see the available cloud application or image after the log in. We can also add other applications using the create image options provided they are based on the inbuilt accepted format of OpenStack cloud.

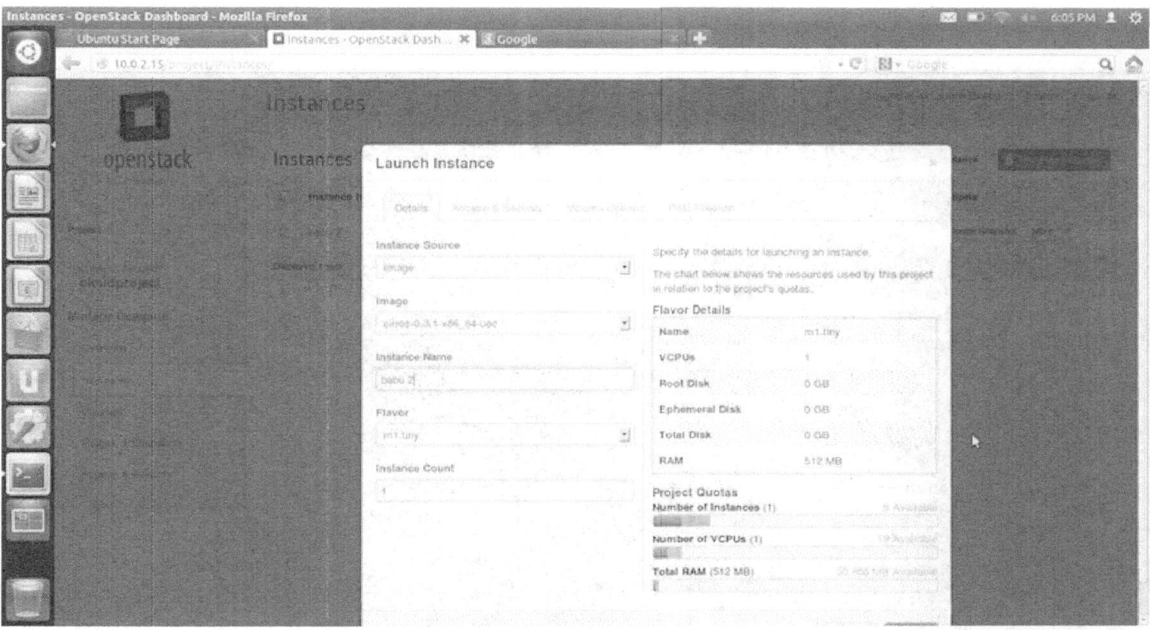

Finally the user launches the virtual instance of the cloud application by specifying the required flavor.

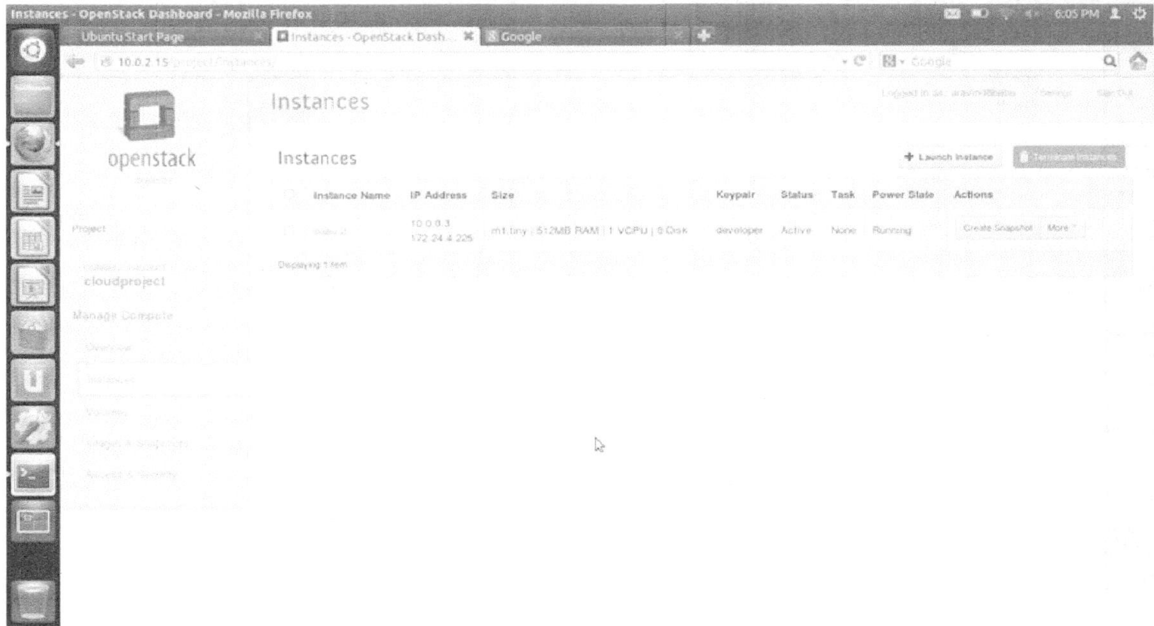

The instance is successfully created and it is active.

```
Booting from ROM...

login as 'cirros' user. default password: 'cubswin:)'. use 'sudo' for root.
cirros login: _
```

We can see the Cirros tiny guest OS in the console getting booted..

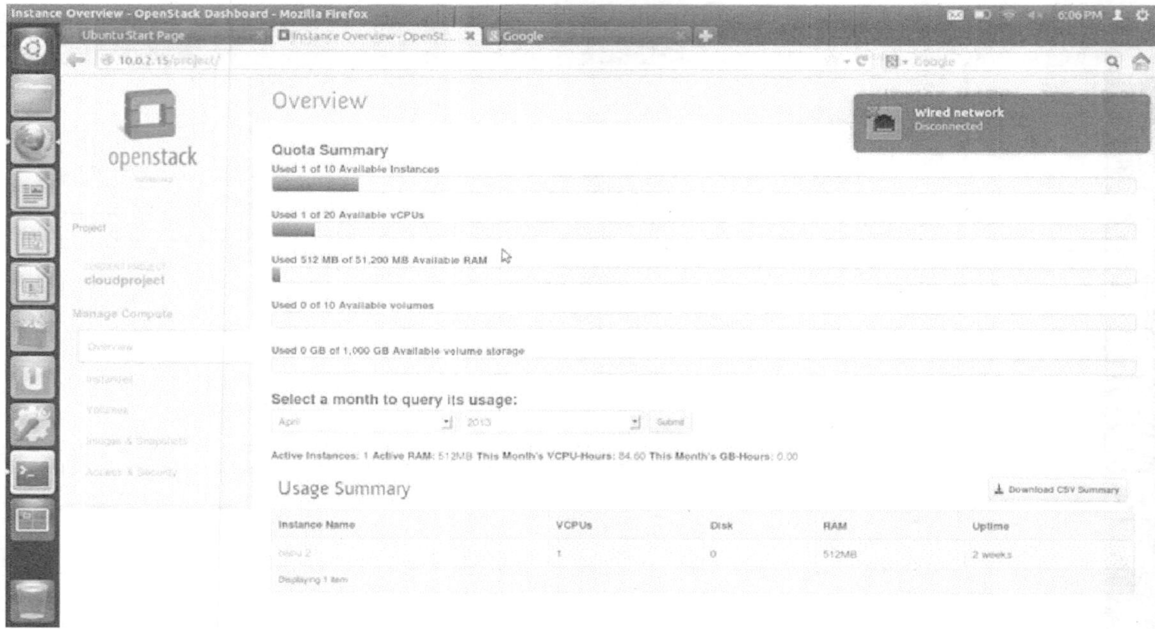

The user can view the overall summary of their account and the active instance.

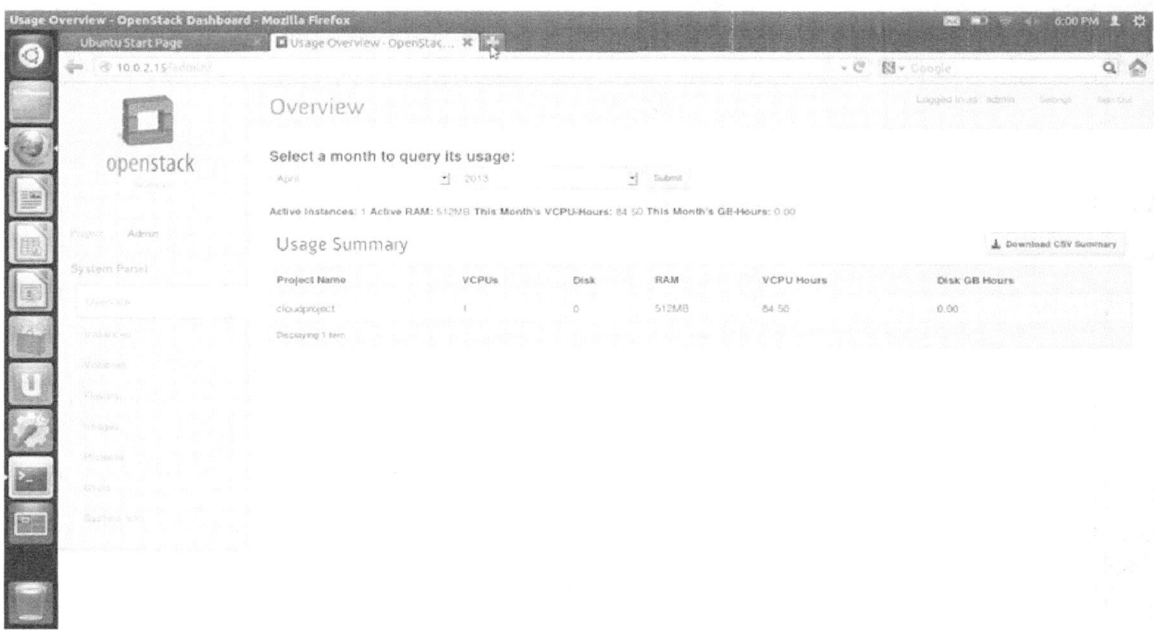

Under the admin tab the list of all active users, their instance details can be seen under the admin account.

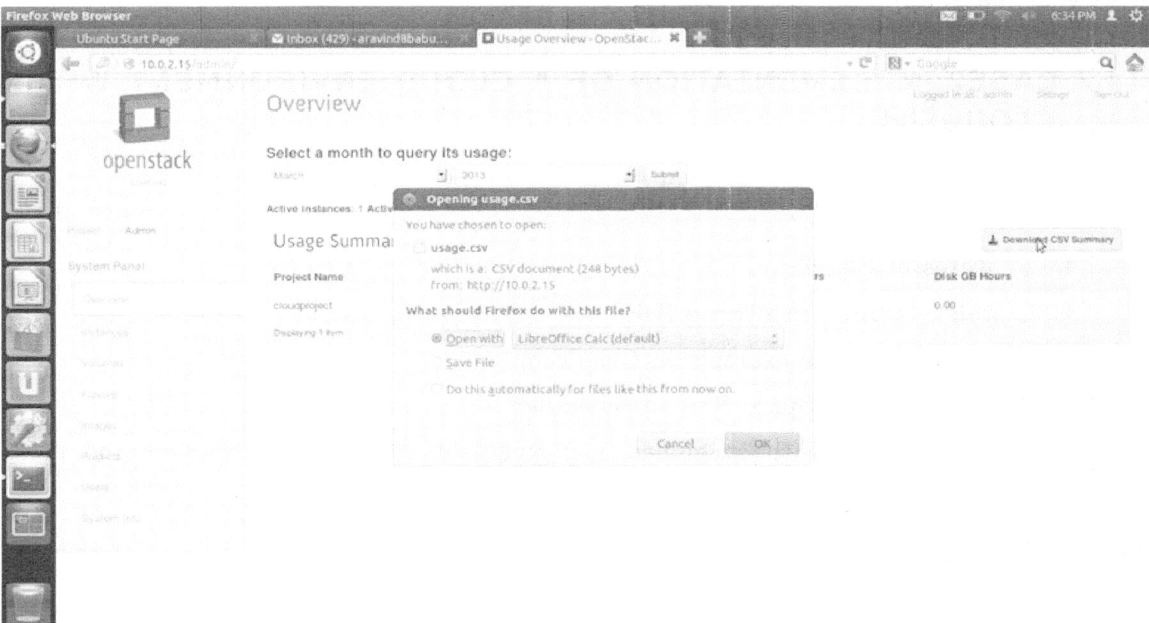

The admin can download and view the usage summary of all users in the cloud.

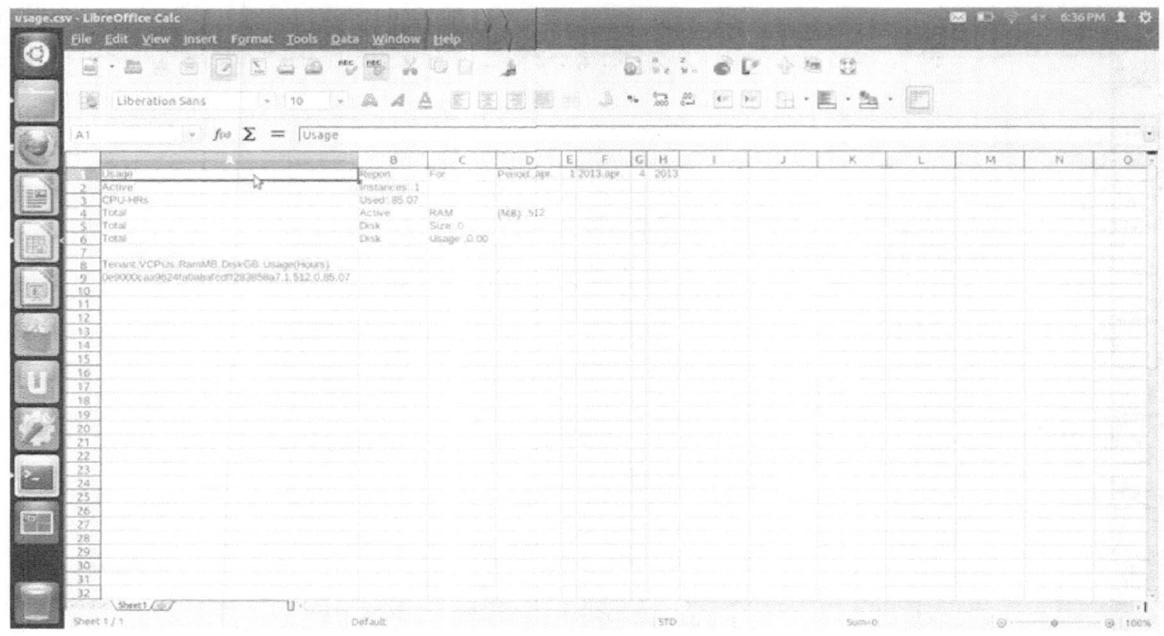

The usage summary is downloaded and seen as a spreadsheet.

We can also use SSH key and ping the virtual instances. Thus, this is how OpenStack cloud is configured and governed by an admin.

14.2 CASE2:IMPLEMENTATION OF A CLOUD ENVIRONMENT WITH CLOUDSIM

At the end of this case study, you can able to figure out:

- What is CloudSim?
- Features of CloudSim.
- Install CloudSim in Eclipse IDE
- Running a sample example in CloudSim.
- Time Shared Vs Space Shared scheduler.
- Simple example with 3 cloudlets usingspaceshared policy for cloudlets and VMs.

We will explain the whole process using the worked out snapshots.

What is CloudSim?

CloudSim is an open source simulation tool kit that helps in modeling and simulation of Cloud Computing scenarios. This tool kit was originally found by the GRIDS laboratory of University of Melbourne. For users, who are unaware of Simulation, Simulation is the process which provides the users with practical feedback when designing real world system.

In this case, the real world system is cloud system. Before the system is constructed, CloudSim allows the designer to determine the correctness and efficiency of a design. The overall cost in designing the real cloud computing system can be reduced to certain extent, since the problem with the design can be solved in the simulation phase itself. This rejects the need of developing a whole cloud environment for testing your algorithm in which the cloud setup is very costly and time consuming. The main goal of CloudSim is to provide a generalized and extensible simulation framework that enables modeling, simulation and experimentation of fore coming Cloud designs. CloudSim is flexible to its users, since it allows the users to focus on specific system design that they are researching, without knowing the low level details like Cloud infrastructure and services.

Benefits of CloudSim

There are many features that are provided by CloudSim.CloudSim being available at free of cost, can support the modeling and simulation of the following.

- CloudSim helps in simulating Data Centres hardware on a single computing node. A data centre is a centralized repository for storing, managing and dissemination of data and information pertaining to a particular business. This helps in simulating physical machines composed of processors, storage devices, memory and internal bandwidth.
- Creation, simulation and destruction of virtual machines can also be done. Virtual machine is software which does not physically exist but created to emulate the behaviour of a computer.
- Energy Aware computational resources can be built using CloudSim. Virtualization makes cloud run multiple Virtual Machines on single node, which leads to the design of energy aware computational resources. This brings enhanced modelling of power-aware and energy efficient Cloud computing.
- This supports modelling of internal data center topologies and message-passing applications.
- It helps in simulating federated clouds. Federated cloud is the deployment and management of multiple external and internal cloud computing services that perform a common action.
- Dynamic insertion of simulation elements can also be done with CloudSim. Simulation can be stopped and resumed.
- Allocation of hosts and hosts resources to VMs is also supported by CloudSim.

Install CloudSim in Eclipse IDE

Download Cloudsim from https://code.google.com. CloudSim-3.0.3.zip is the recent version. This version of CloudSim brings enhanced modelling of power-aware and energy efficient Cloudcomputing, and also a new package allowing modelling of internal data center topologies and message-passing applications.

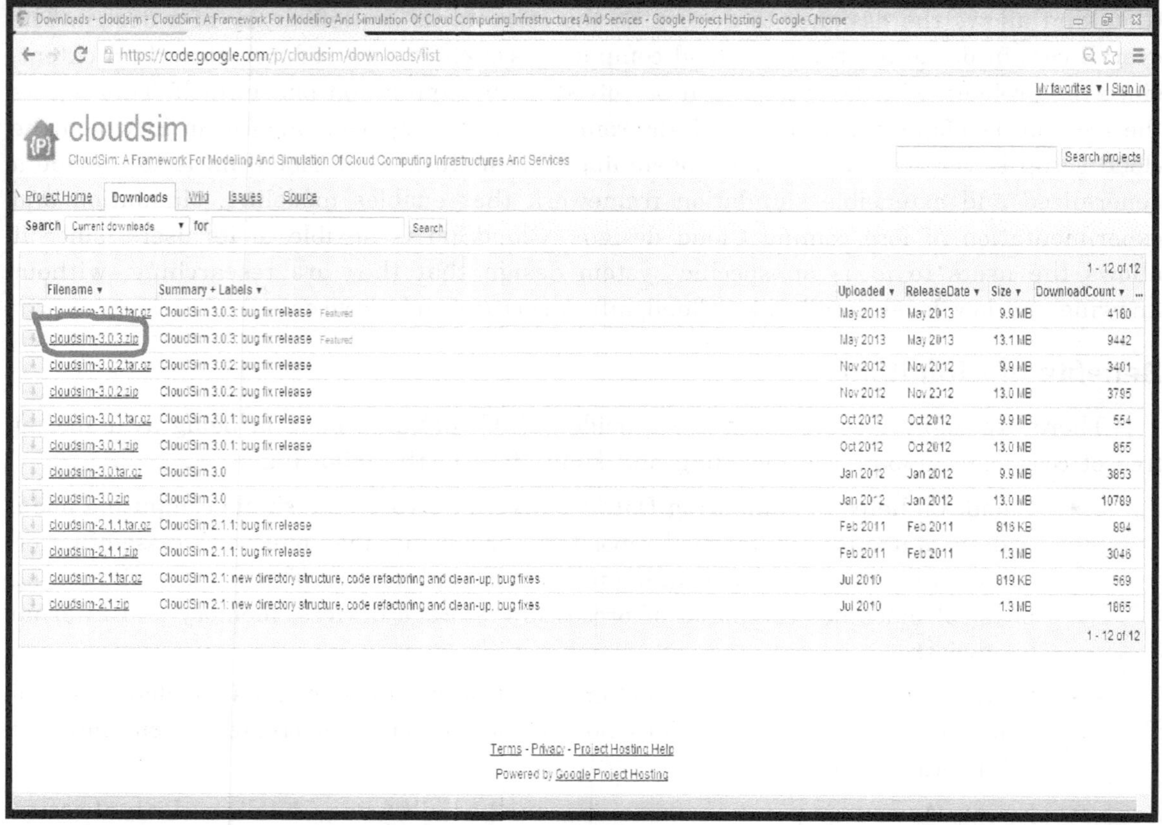

Directory structure of the CloudSim Toolkit

bin/	-- Precompiled class files
cloudsim/	-- top level CloudSim directory
docs/	-- CloudSim API Documentation
examples/	-- CloudSim examples
jars/	-- CloudSim jar archives
sources/	-- CloudSim source code

This CloudSim-3.0.3.zip will need commons-math3-3.2 for error free execution. Commons-math3-3.2 can be downloaded from commons.apache.org/proper/commons-math/download_math.cgi as shown below.Commons-math3-3.2 is used to do multiple convenient math functions like finding variance, median, and average and also for performing regression analysis which is the statistical process for estimating the relationships among variables.These mathematical evaluationsare used in forming cloudlets.

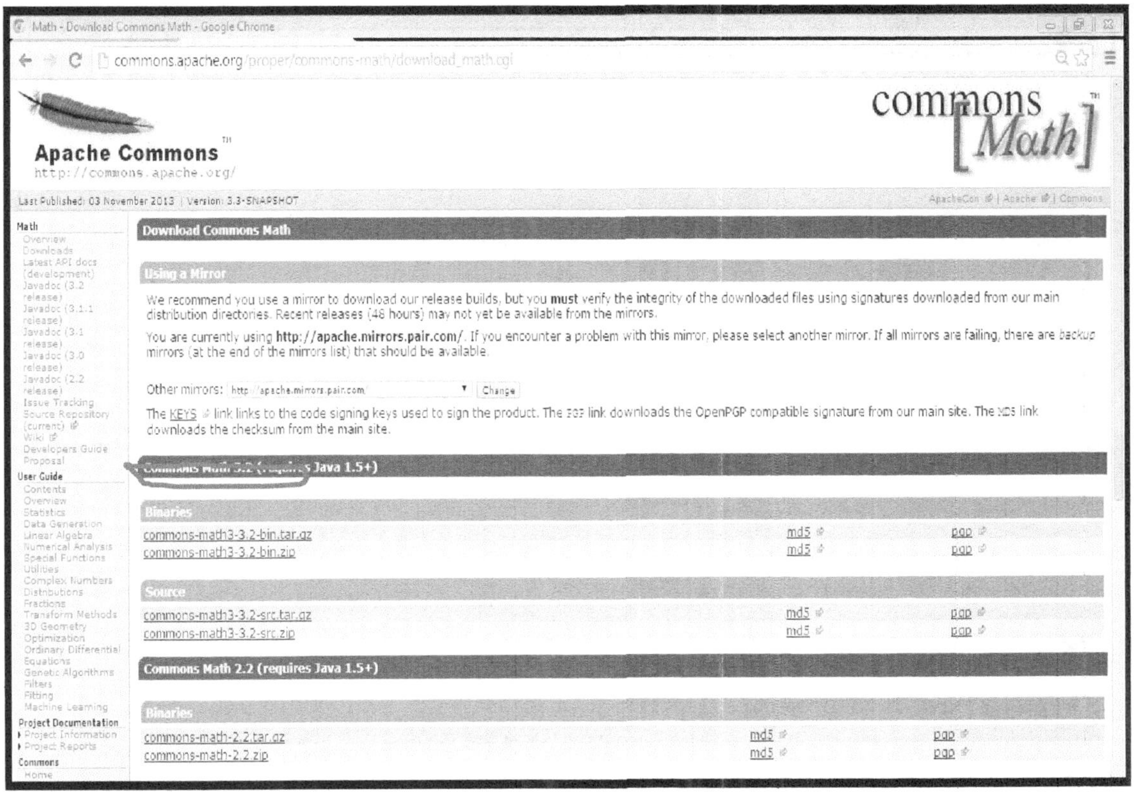

Math - Download Commons Math - Google Chrome

commons.apache.org/proper/commons-math/download_math.cgi

Apache Commons
http://commons.apache.org/

commons [Math]

Last Published: 03 November 2013 | Version: 3.3-SNAPSHOT

Math: Overview, Downloads, Latest API docs (development), Javadoc (3.2 release), Javadoc (3.1.1 release), Javadoc (3.1 release), Javadoc (3.0 release), Javadoc (2.2 release), Issue Tracking, Source Repository (current), Wiki, Developers Guide, Proposal

User Guide: Contents, Overview, Statistics, Data Generation, Linear Algebra, Numerical Analysis, Special Functions, Utilities, Complex Numbers, Distributions, Fractions, Transform Methods, 3D Geometry, Optimization, Ordinary Differential Equations, Genetic Algorithms, Filters, Fitting, Machine Learning

Project Documentation: Project Information, Project Reports

Commons: Home

Download Commons Math

Using a Mirror

We recommend you use a mirror to download our release builds, but you **must** verify the integrity of the downloaded files using signatures downloaded from our main distribution directories. Recent releases (48 hours) may not yet be available from the mirrors.

You are currently using **http://apache.mirrors.pair.com/**. If you encounter a problem with this mirror, please select another mirror. If all mirrors are failing, there are *backup* mirrors (at the end of the mirrors list) that should be available.

Other mirrors: http://apache.mirrors.pair.com [Change]

The KEYS link links to the code signing keys used to sign the product. The PGP link downloads the OpenPGP compatible signature from our main site. The MD5 link downloads the checksum from the main site.

Commons Math 3.2 (requires Java 1.5+)

Binaries

commons-math3-3.2-bin.tar.gz	md5	pgp
commons-math3-3.2-bin.zip	md5	pgp

Source

commons-math3-3.2-src.tar.gz	md5	pgp
commons-math3-3.2-src.zip	md5	pgp

Commons Math 2.2 (requires Java 1.5+)

Binaries

commons-math-2.2.tar.gz	md5	pgp
commons-math-2.2.zip	md5	pgp

Put the two zip folders just downloaded in a directory and extract it in the same directory. In our case, we have extracted it to D:\Cloud Setup.

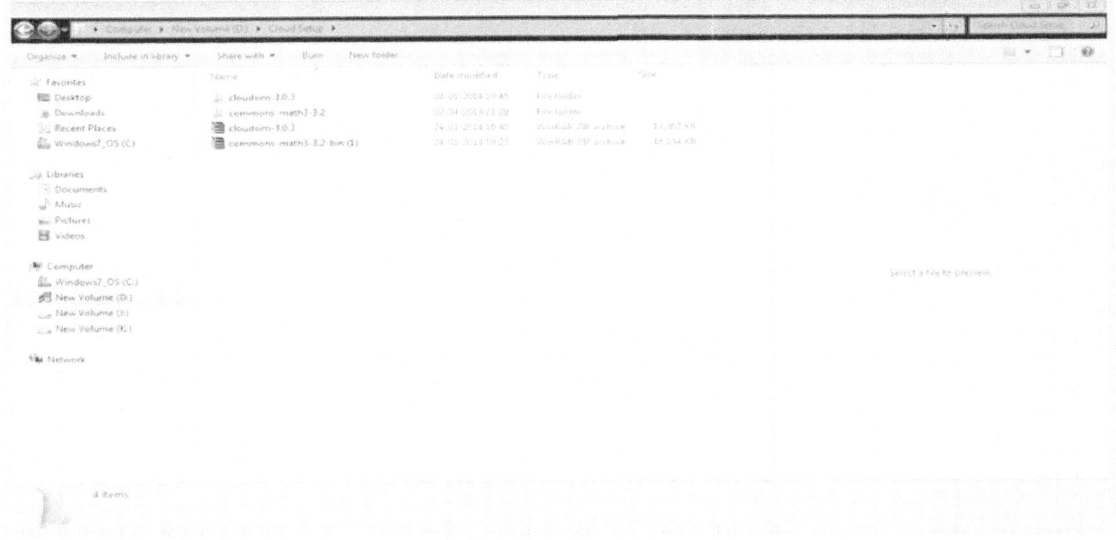

Open an Eclipse IDE. Make sure that the Java version is 1.6.0 or newer.

Create a new Java project.

Give a Project Name. In our case, it is 'Cloud'. Deselect the checkbook 'Use default location'. Click on Browse button to browse the downloaded and extracted cloudsim-3.0.3 folder. Click on 'Next'.

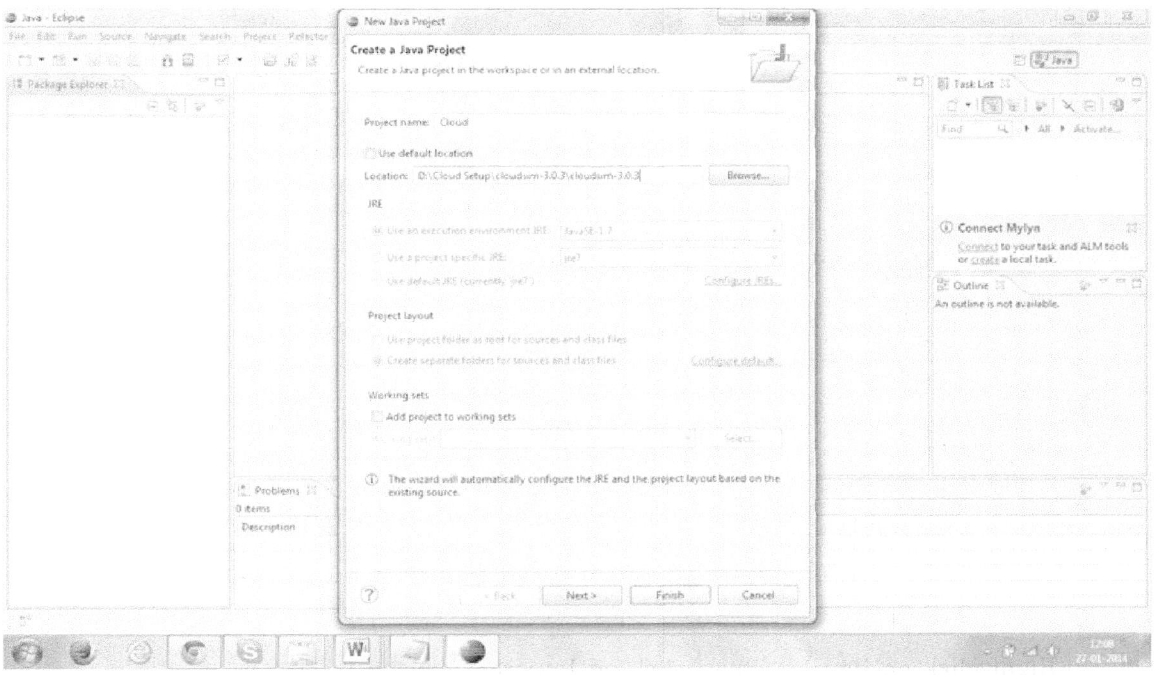

You can see the folder structure of the cloudsim-3.0.3 directory. Click on 'Finish' button.

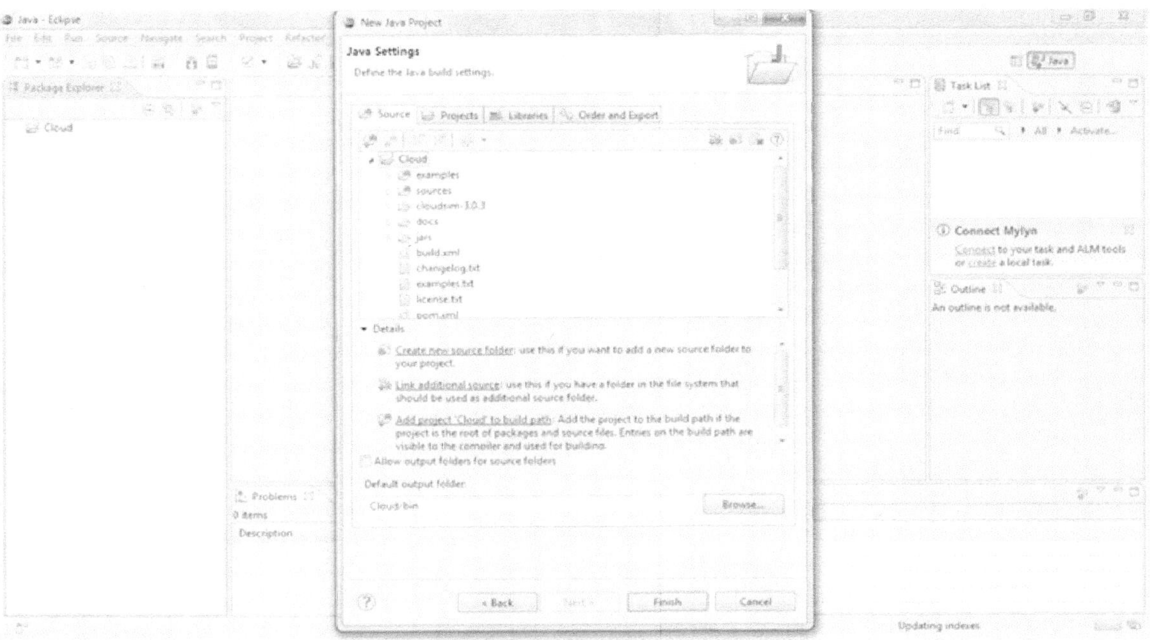

Thus, it has created a Java Project which the CloudSim Project. But still, this project requires the jar files mainly for mathematical calculations.

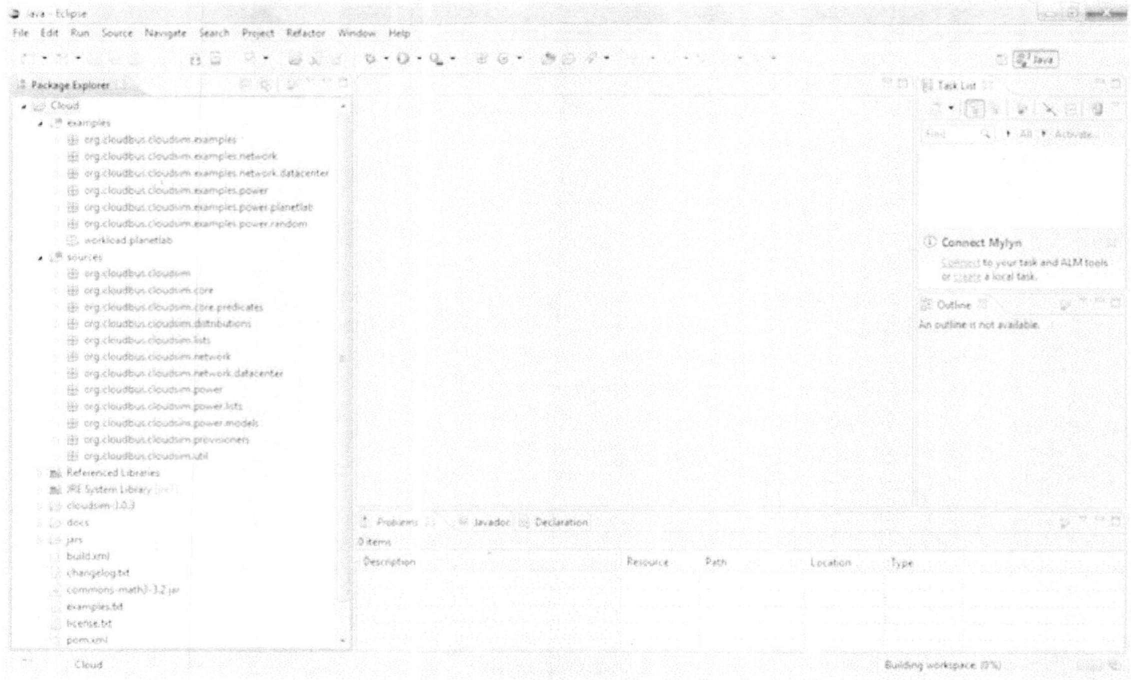

Right click on the jar folder, click on Import as shown below.

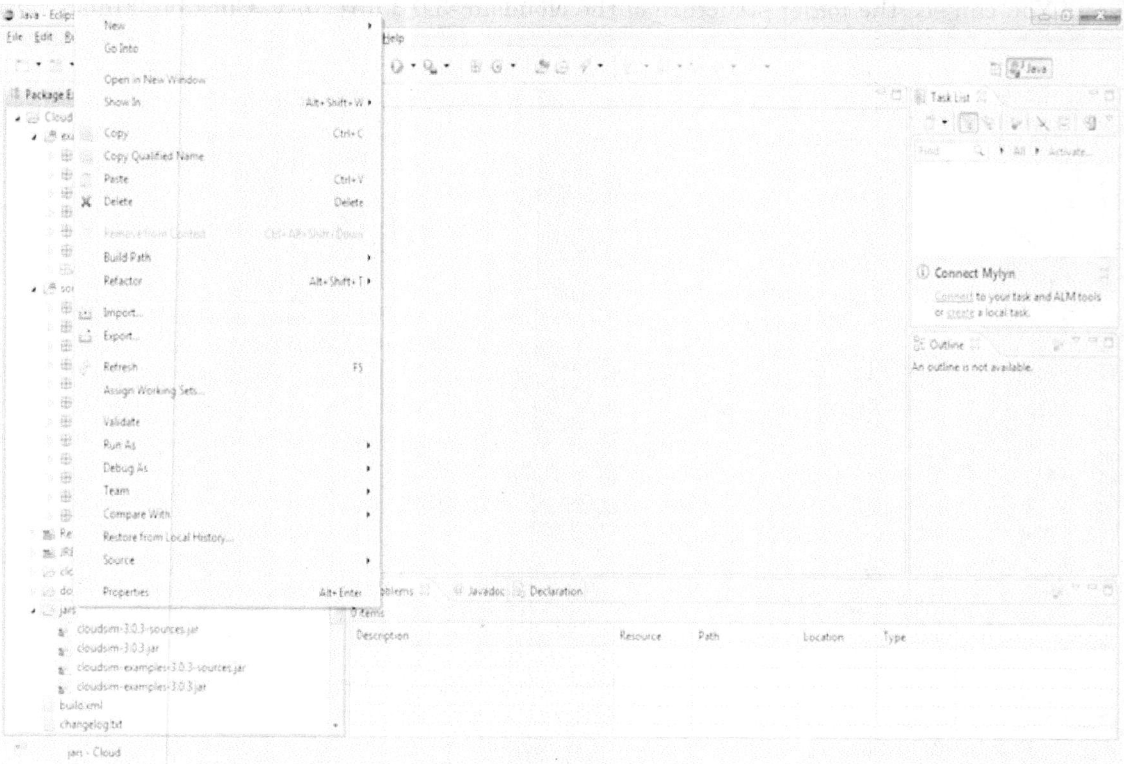

It opens up a panel for selecting import.Click General ->FileSystem.

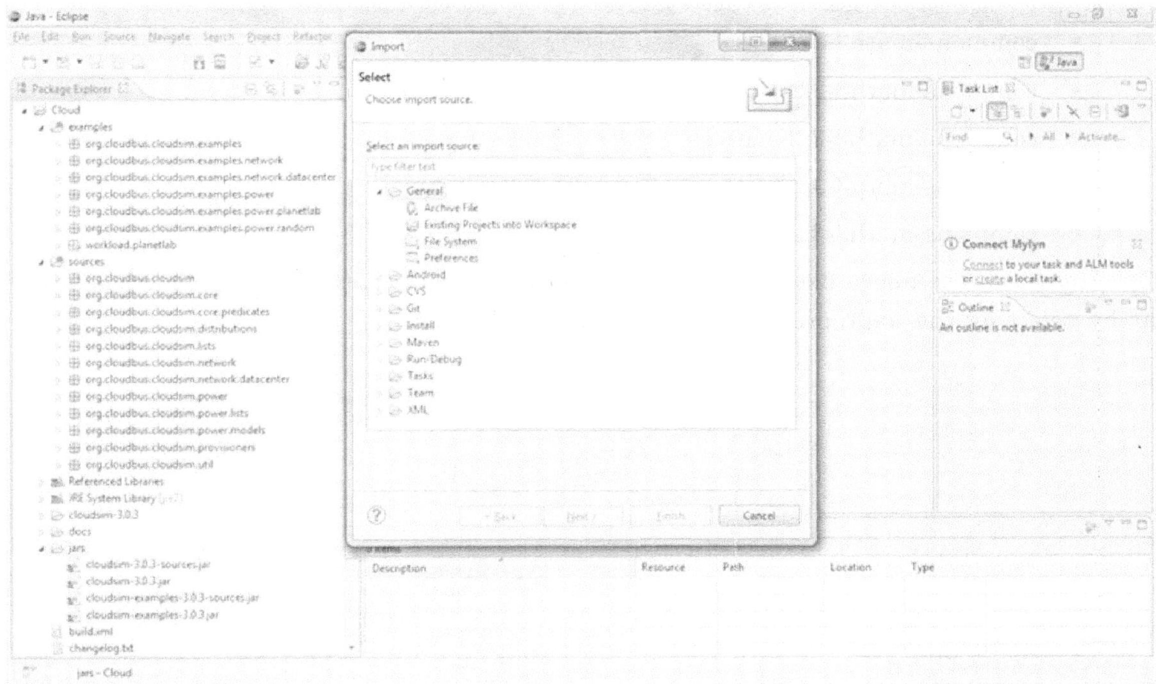

Select the commons-math3-3.2 folder that we have downloaded previously. Click on 'Ok'.

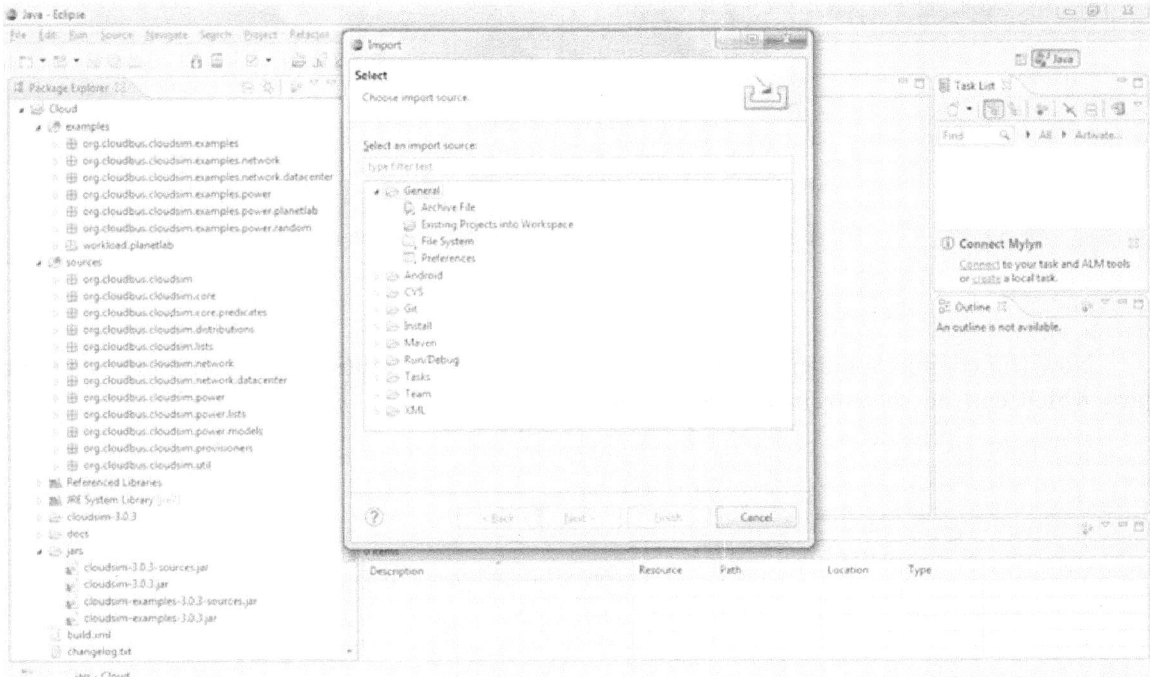

Below are the list of jars available in the common-math3-3.2.

- commons-math3-3.2
- commons-math3-3.2-javadoc
- commons-math3-3.2-sources
- commons-math3-3.2-tests
- commons-math3-3.2-test-sources

Among all the above list of jars, we need only commons-math3-3.2 jar file. Include the jar by selecting the appropriate checkbox. Click on 'Finish'.

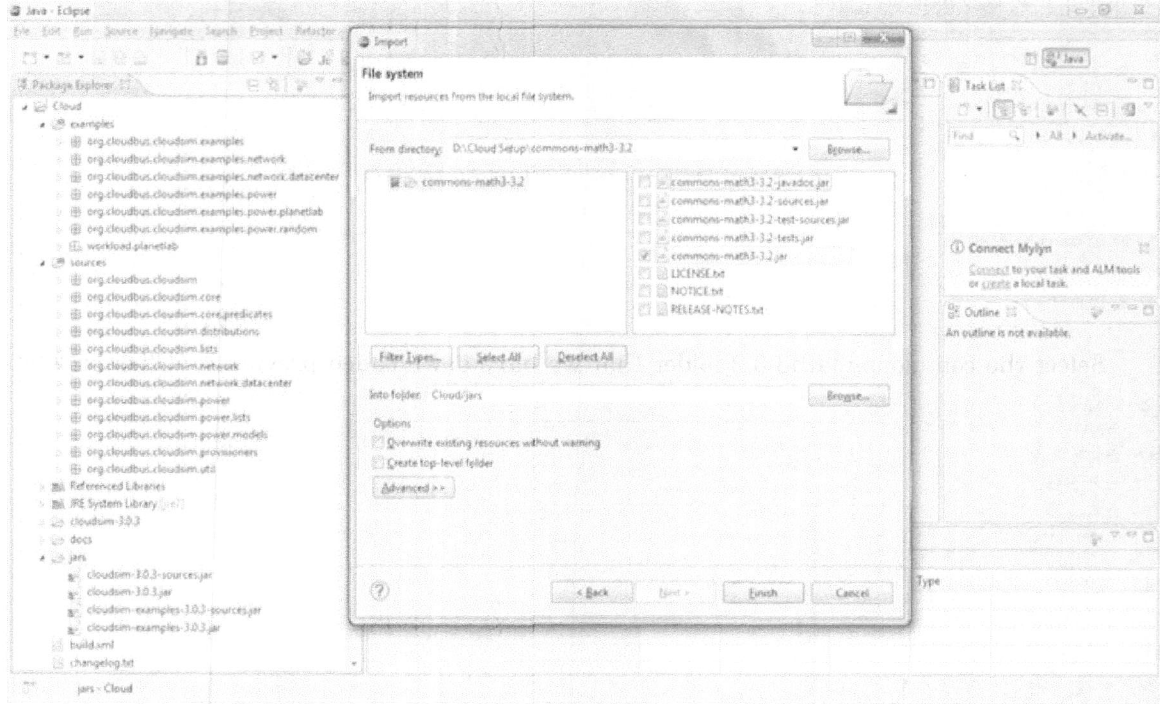

Now the commons-math3-3.2 jar has been included in addition to the already available jars which can be seen from the below snapshot.

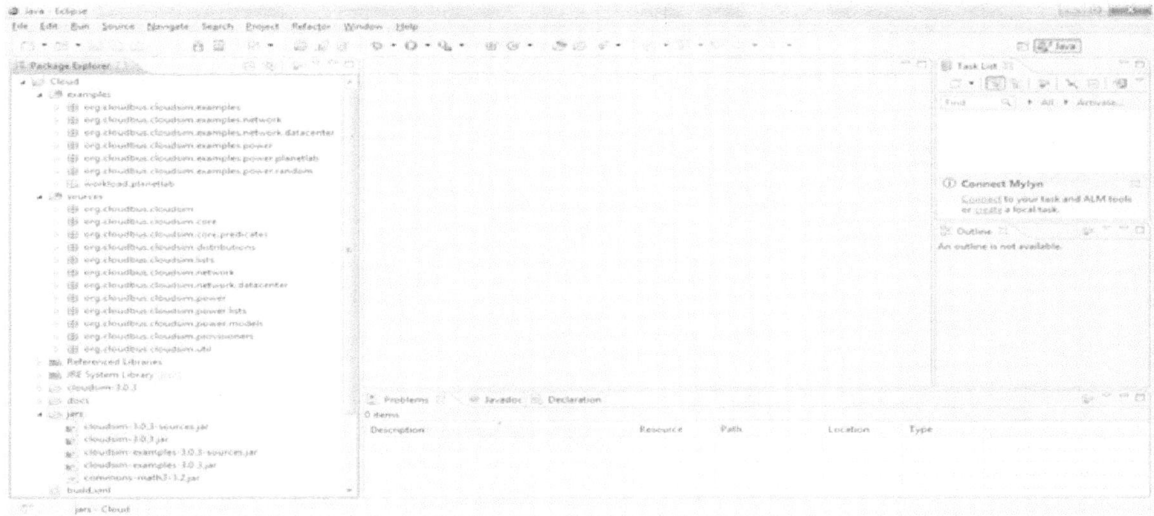

For building the java path, right click on the project click on properties which opens up a options to include the imported jar.

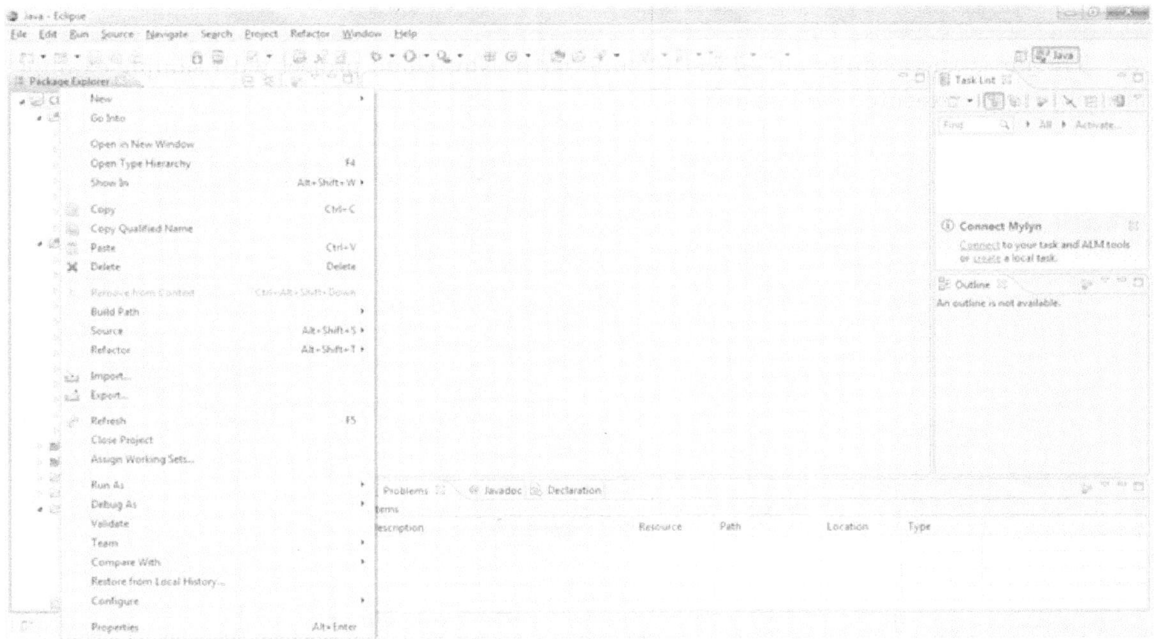

Include the imported jar by click Libraries tab and then 'Add JARs'. Select the commons-math3-3.2.jar we have just imported. Click on 'Ok'.

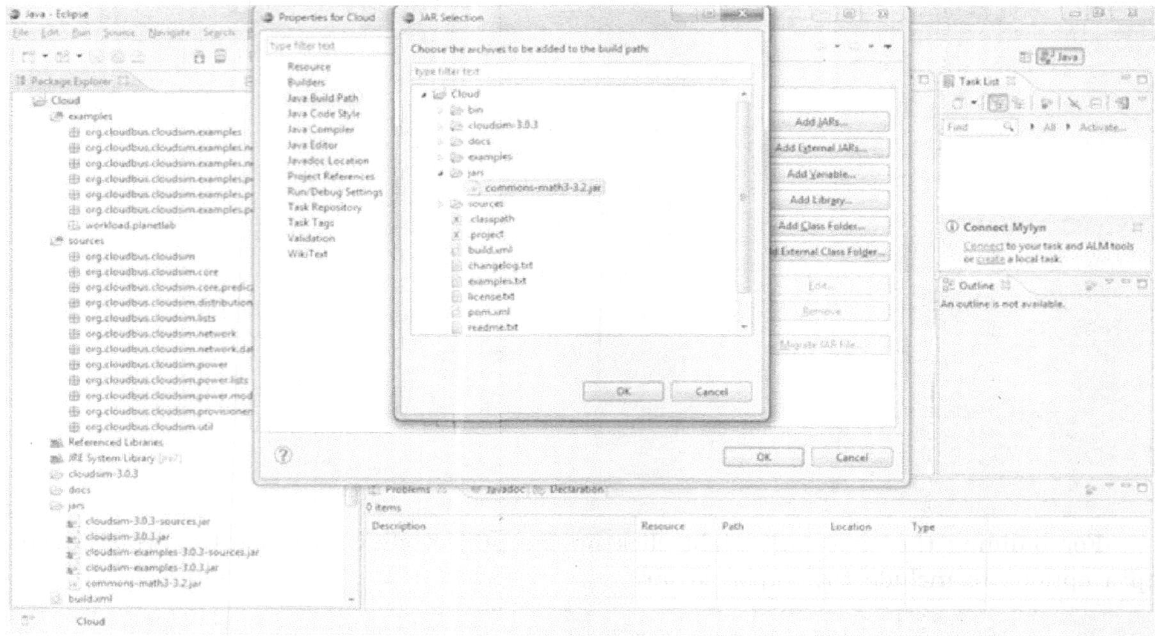

The jar is successfully added to the build path. Now cloud project with sample examples is ready to be executed and tested.

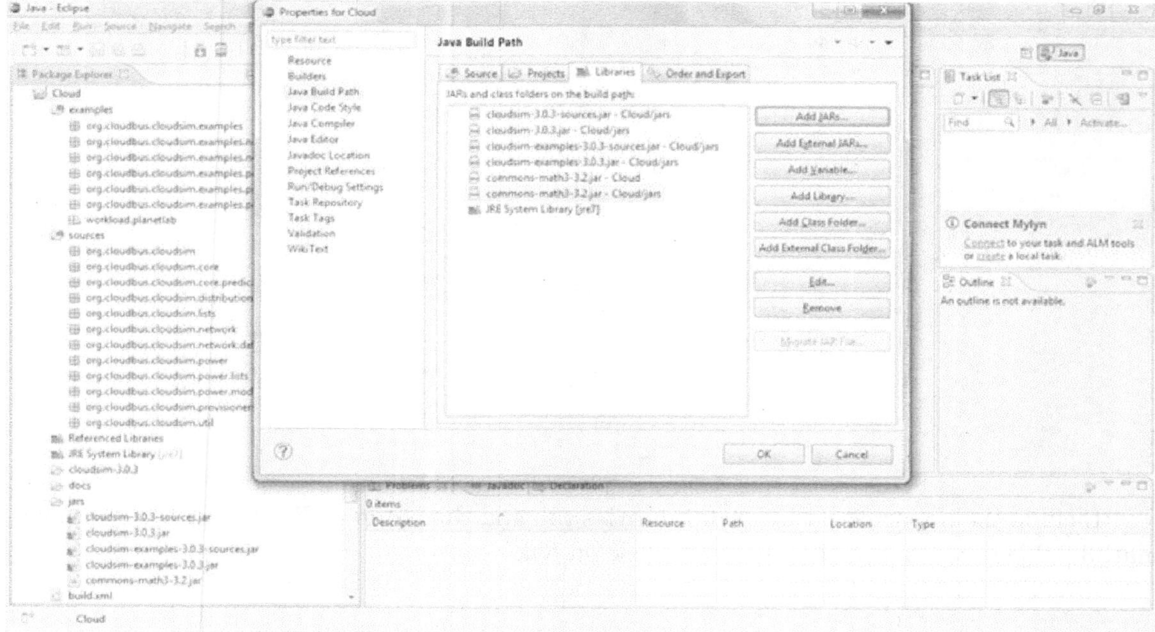

How CloudSim Works?

A Datacenter can consists of a set of hosts. Host can instantiate Virtual Machine (VM) scheduler. VM schedular allocates the processors to VMs. Cloudlets are tasks that will be executed in VMs. We can add as many cloudlets as we can in a VM.

Below are the step by step execution of simulating a cloud in CloudSim.

1. Initialize CloudSim Package by using init() method. The init() method is used to initialize the CloudSim library.
2. Create datacenter by createDatacenter() method. This is an essential step since any cloudlet to be executed; we need to create a datacenter.
3. Create Broker by createBroker() method. Broker is an interface between the consumer and provider.
4. Create virtual machines and add VMs to VM list. We can create as many virtual machines as we need.
5. Create cloudlets by setting properties like id, length, filesize. Add the created cloudlets to the cloudlets list.
6. Submit cloudlist to broker.
7. Start simulation
8. Stop simulation
9. Show Output

Running a sample example in CloudSim.

Lets see how to execute the CloudSimExample1 which is available in examples folder under the package 'org.cloudbus.cloudsim.examples'. CloudSimExample1.java is a simple example showing how to create a datacenter with one host and run cloudlet on it.

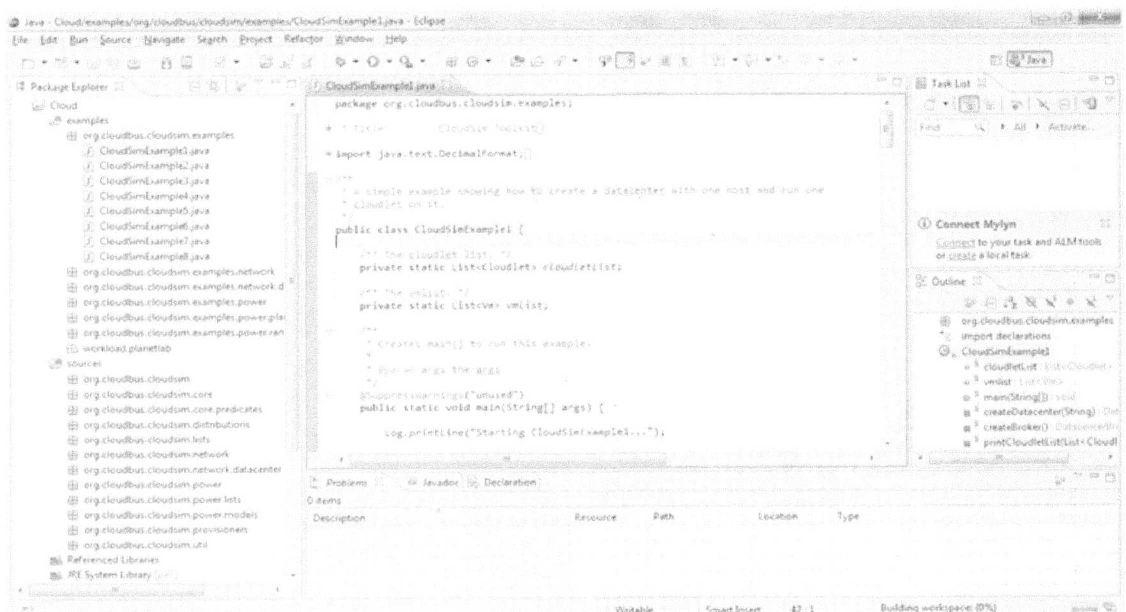

Run the CloudSimExample1.java by clicking on the java file->Run As->Java Application.

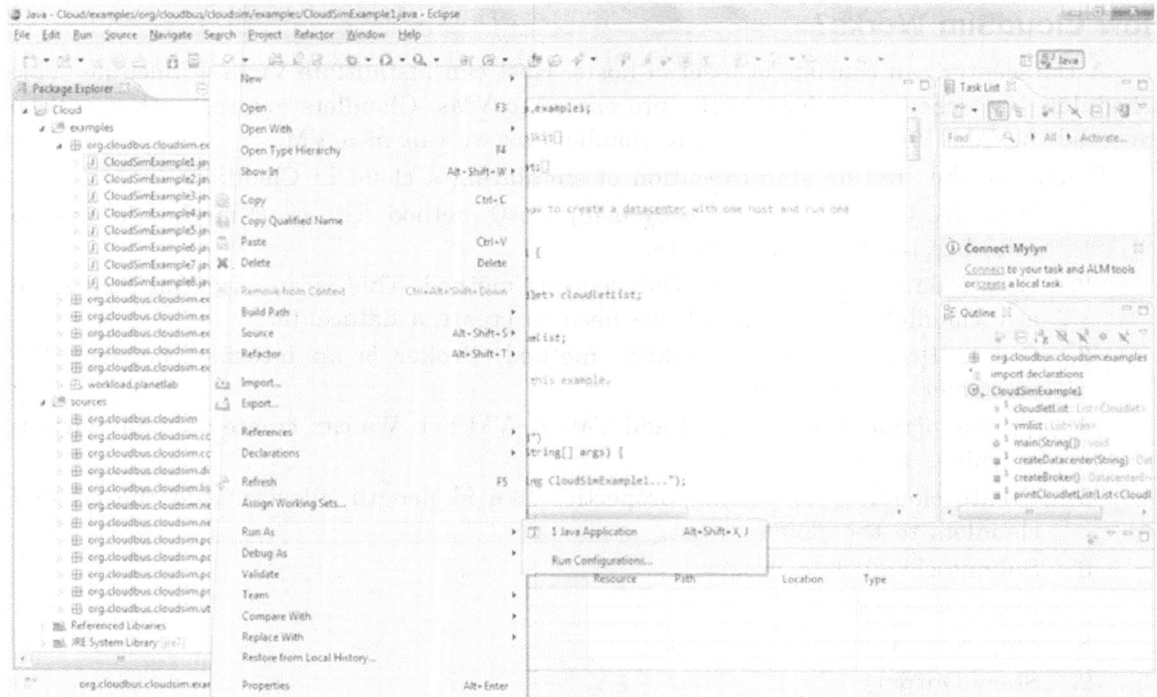

As you can see in the Console Window, it has started DataCenter. Broker is trying to create a Virtual Machine (VM). A Cloudlet is created and executed. Finally in the output, a CloudLet with ID '0' is created in VM with ID '0' which is running in DataCenter with ID '2'. CloudLet's execution status, its time to execute, start and finish time are also displayed.

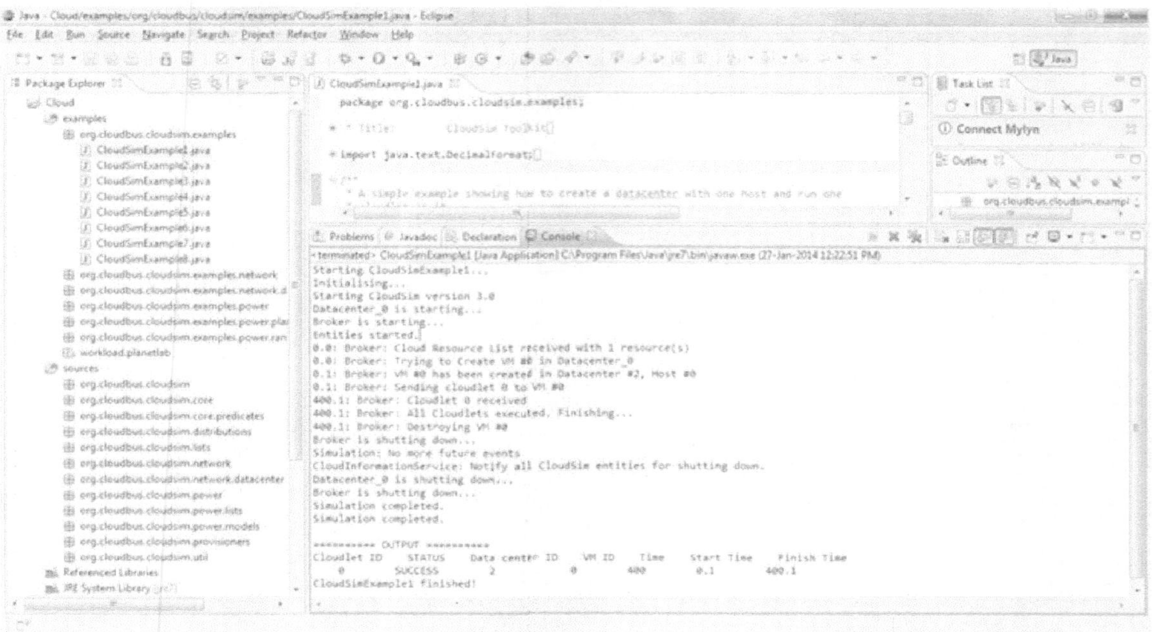

In the similar way, we can execute remaining 7 examples available in org.cloudbus.cloudsim.examples package. This package contains basic java classes included with fundamental cloud simulation functionalities.

In the second example in cloudsim example package, it helps to create a datacenter with one host. The host contains two VMs which execute two cloudlets one in each.

In the third scenario, one datacenter with two hosts is created. The 2 hosts contains 2 VMs one in each which in turn execute 2 cloudlets, one in each.

In forth example, it helps you in creating multiple data centres with one host, one VM and one cloudlet in each datacenter.

5th example is similar to 4th but the difference is to create two consumers who try to execute 2 cloudletsone in separate data center. Here each data center is having one host, one VM as in previous example.

6th example helps in creating list of virtual machines and running list of cloudlets.

In the 7th example, it shows how to pause and resume the simulation, and create simulation entities like Data center Broker dynamically.

8th example shows how to create simulation entityDatacenterBroker in run-time using a global manager entity (GlobalBroker).

Time Shared Vs Space Shared Scheduler

Time shared policy helps to Share the computing resource among many users. This helps in multiprogramming. Spaceshared policy divides the resources among many tasks so that no execution of task can affect other task execution. There are four scenarios possible with these scheduling policies.

1. Space shared for both Cloudlets and virtual machines.
2. Time shared for both Cloudlets and virtual machines.
3. Space shared for Cloudlets and Time shared for virtual machines.
4. Time shared for Cloudlets and Space shared for virtual machines.

Simple Example with 3 Cloudlets using Spaceshared Policy for Cloudlets and VMs

```
packageorg.cloudbus.cloudsim.examples;

importjava.text.DecimalFormat;
importjava.util.ArrayList;
importjava.util.Calendar;
importjava.util.LinkedList;
importjava.util.List;

importorg.cloudbus.cloudsim.Cloudlet;
importorg.cloudbus.cloudsim.CloudletSchedulerSpaceShared;
```

```
importorg.cloudbus.cloudsim.Datacenter;
importorg.cloudbus.cloudsim.DatacenterBroker;
importorg.cloudbus.cloudsim.DatacenterCharacteristics;
importorg.cloudbus.cloudsim.Host;
importorg.cloudbus.cloudsim.Log;
importorg.cloudbus.cloudsim.Pe;
importorg.cloudbus.cloudsim.Storage;
importorg.cloudbus.cloudsim.UtilizationModel;
importorg.cloudbus.cloudsim.UtilizationModelFull;
importorg.cloudbus.cloudsim.Vm;
importorg.cloudbus.cloudsim.VmAllocationPolicySimple;
importorg.cloudbus.cloudsim.VmSchedulerSpaceShared;
importorg.cloudbus.cloudsim.core.CloudSim;
importorg.cloudbus.cloudsim.provisioners.BwProvisionerSimple;
importorg.cloudbus.cloudsim.provisioners.PeProvisionerSimple;
importorg.cloudbus.cloudsim.provisioners.RamProvisionerSimple;

/**
 * A simple example showing how to create a datacenter with one host and run
   three
 * cloudlets on it.
 */
public class ThreeCloudletsinDC {

   /** The cloudlet list. */
   private static List<Cloudlet>cloudletList;

   /** Thevmlist. */
   private static List<Vm>vmlist;

   /**
    * Creates main() to run this example.
    *
    * @paramargs the args
    */
   @SuppressWarnings("unused")
   public static void main(String[] args) {

          Log.printLine("Starting ThreeCloudletsinDC...");

          try {
                 // First step: Initialize the CloudSim package. It should be
                    called
                 // before creating any entities.
                 intnum_user = 1; // number of cloud users
```

```
Calendar calendar = Calendar.getInstance();
booleantrace_flag = false; // mean trace events

// Initialize the CloudSim library
CloudSim.init(num_user, calendar, trace_flag);

// Second step: Create Datacenters
// Datacenters are the resource providers in CloudSim. We need
   at
// list one of them to run a CloudSim simulation
Datacenter datacenter0 = createDatacenter("Datacenter_0");

// Third step: Create Broker
DatacenterBroker broker = createBroker();
intbrokerId = broker.getId();

// Fourth step: Create one virtual machine
vmlist = new ArrayList<Vm>();

// VM description
intvmid = 0;
intmips = 1000;
long size = 10000; // image size (MB)
int ram = 512; // vm memory (MB)
longbw = 1000;
intpesNumber = 1; // number of cpus
String vmm = "Xen"; // VMM name

// create VM
Vmvm = new Vm(vmid, brokerId, mips, pesNumber, ram, bw, size,
vmm, new      CloudletSchedulerSpaceShared());

// add the VM to the vmList
vmlist.add(vm);

// submit vm list to the broker
broker.submitVmList(vmlist);

// Fifth step: Create one Cloudlet
cloudletList = new ArrayList<Cloudlet>();

// Cloudlet properties
int id = 0;
long length = 400000;
longfileSize = 300;
```

```
            longoutputSize = 300;
            UtilizationModelutilizationModel = new UtilizationModelFull();

            //Added 3 cloudlets to cloudletlist
            Cloudlet cloudlet1 = new Cloudlet(id, length, pesNumber, fileSize,
outputSize,        utilizationModel, utilizationModel, utilizationModel);
            cloudlet1.setUserId(brokerId);
            cloudlet1.setVmId(vmid);
            id++;

            Cloudlet cloudlet2 = new Cloudlet(id, length, pesNumber, fileSize,
outputSize,        utilizationModel, utilizationModel, utilizationModel);
            cloudlet2.setUserId(brokerId);
            cloudlet2.setVmId(vmid);
            id++;

            Cloudlet cloudlet3 = new Cloudlet(id, length, pesNumber, fileSize,
outputSize,        utilizationModel, utilizationModel, utilizationModel);
            cloudlet3.setUserId(brokerId);
            cloudlet3.setVmId(vmid);
            id++;

            // add the cloudlet to the list
            cloudletList.add(cloudlet1);
            cloudletList.add(cloudlet2);
            cloudletList.add(cloudlet3);

            // submit cloudlet list to the broker
            broker.submitCloudletList(cloudletList);

            // Sixth step: Starts the simulation
            CloudSim.startSimulation();

            CloudSim.stopSimulation();

            //Final step: Print results when simulation is over
            List<Cloudlet>newList = broker.getCloudletReceivedList();
            printCloudletList(newList);

            Log.printLine("ThreeCloudletsinDC finished!");
        }
        catch (Exception e) {
            e.printStackTrace();
            Log.printLine("Unwanted errors happen");
        }
```

```
    }

    /**
     * Creates the datacenter.
     *
     * @param name the name
     *
     * @return the datacenter
     */
    private static Datacenter createDatacenter(String name) {

            // Here are the steps needed to create a PowerDatacenter:
            // 1. We need to create a list to store
            // our machine
            List<Host>hostList = new ArrayList<Host>();

            // 2. A Machine contains one or more PEs or CPUs/Cores.
            // In this example, it will have only one core.
            List<Pe>peList = new ArrayList<Pe>();
            intmips = 1000;

            // 3. Create PEs and add these into a list.
            peList.add(new Pe(0, new PeProvisionerSimple(mips))); // need to store
Pe id and MIPSRating

            // 4. Create Host with its id and list of PEs and add them to the list
            // of machines
            inthostId = 0;
            int ram = 2048; // host memory (MB)
            long storage = 1000000; // host storage
            intbw = 10000;

            hostList.add(
                    new Host(
                            hostId,
                            newRamProvisionerSimple(ram),
                            newBwProvisionerSimple(bw),
                            storage,
                            peList,
                            newVmSchedulerSpaceShared(peList)
                    )
```

```
        ); // This is our machine

        // 5. Create a DatacenterCharacteristics object that stores the
        // properties of a data center: architecture, OS, list of
        // Machines, allocation policy: time- or space-shared, time zone
        // and its price (G$/Pe time unit).
        String arch = "x86"; // system architecture
        String os = "Linux"; // operating system
        String vmm = "Xen";
        doubletime_zone = 10.0; // time zone this resource located
        double cost = 3.0; // the cost of using processing in this resource
        doublecostPerMem = 0.05; // the cost of using memory in this resource
        doublecostPerStorage = 0.001; // the cost of using storage in this
        // resource
        doublecostPerBw = 0.0; // the cost of using bw in this resource
        LinkedList<Storage>storageList = new LinkedList<Storage>();

DatacenterCharacteristics characteristics = new DatacenterCharacteristics(
                    arch, os, vmm, hostList, time_zone, cost, costPerMem,
                    costPerStorage, costPerBw);

        // 6. Finally, we need to create a PowerDatacenter object.
        Datacenter datacenter = null;
        try {
                datacenter = new Datacenter(name, characteristics, new
        VmAllocationPolicySimple(hostList), storageList, 0);
        } catch (Exception e) {
                e.printStackTrace();
        }

        return datacenter;
}


/**
 * Creates the broker.
 *
 * @return the datacenter broker
 */
private static DatacenterBrokercreateBroker() {
        DatacenterBroker broker = null;
        try {
```

```
                broker = new DatacenterBroker("Broker");
        } catch (Exception e) {
                e.printStackTrace();
                return null;
        }
        return broker;
}

/**
 * Prints the Cloudlet objects.
 *
 * @param list list of Cloudlets
 */
private static void printCloudletList(List<Cloudlet> list) {
        int size = list.size();
        Cloudlet cloudlet;

        String indent = "  ";
        Log.printLine();
        Log.printLine("========== OUTPUT ==========");
        Log.printLine("Cloudlet ID" + indent + "STATUS" + indent
                        + "Data center ID" + indent + "VM ID" + indent + "Time" +
indent
                        + "Start Time" + indent + "Finish Time");

        DecimalFormatdft = new DecimalFormat("###.##");
        for (int i = 0; i < size; i++) {
                cloudlet = list.get(i);
                Log.print(indent + cloudlet.getCloudletId() + indent + indent);

                if (cloudlet.getCloudletStatus() == Cloudlet.SUCCESS) {
                        Log.print("SUCCESS");

                        Log.printLine(indent + indent + cloudlet.getResourceId()
                                        + indent + indent + indent +
                                                        cloudlet.getVmId()
                                        + indent + indent
                                        + dft.format(cloudlet.getActualCPUTime())
                                                                + indent
                                        + indent +
                                         dft.format(cloudlet.getExecStartTime())
                                        + indent + indent
```

```
                                + dft.format(cloudlet.getFinishTime()));
                        }
                }
        }
}
```

Screen Shot

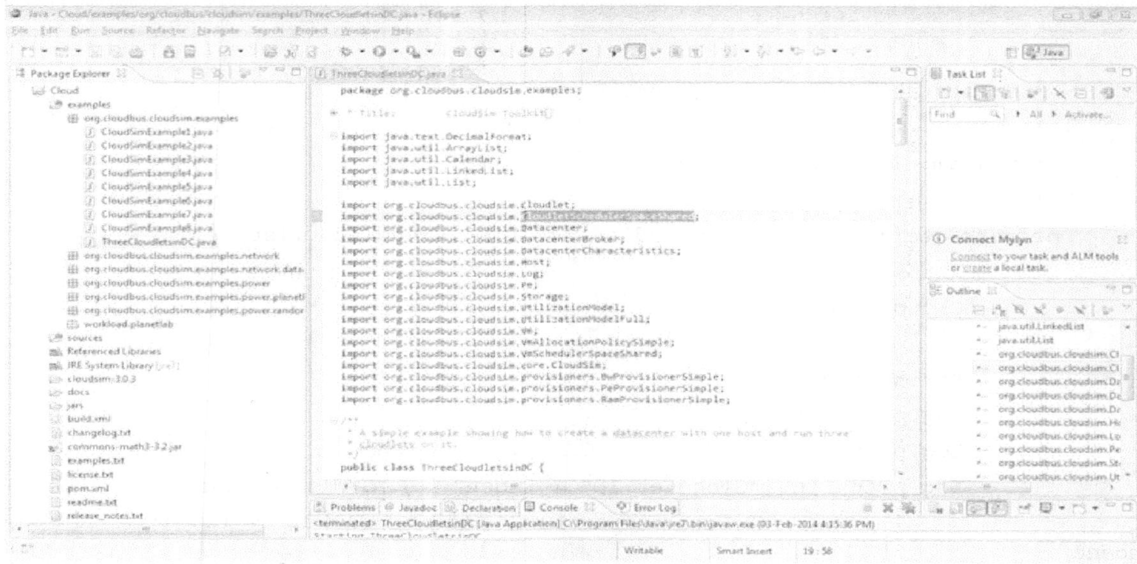

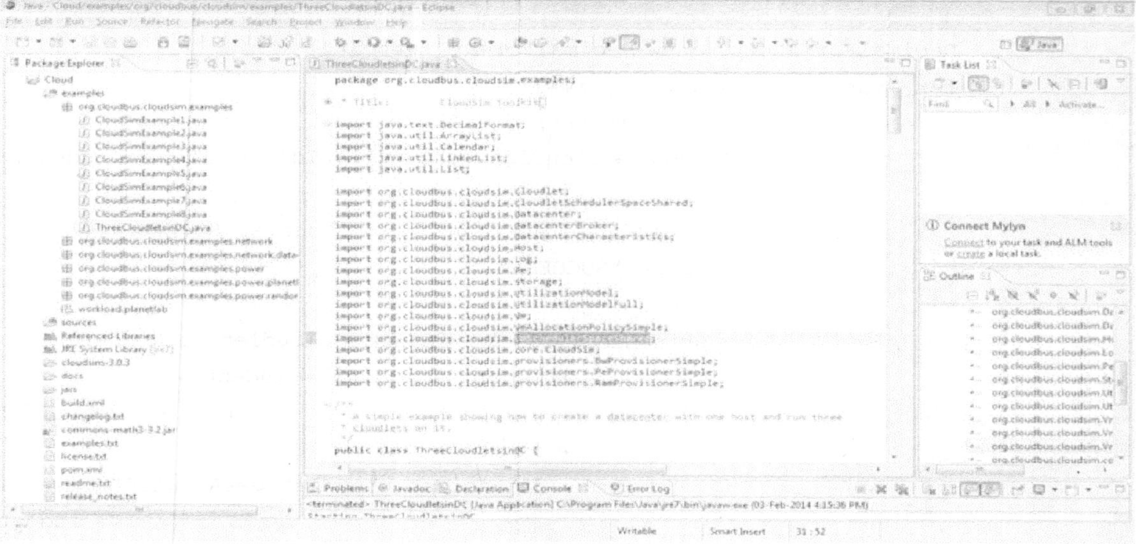

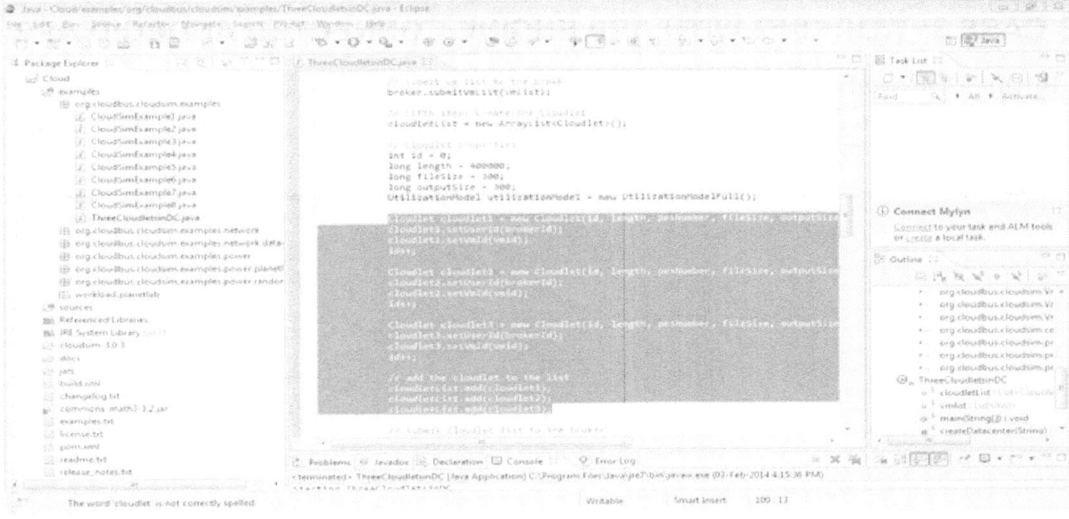

Output:

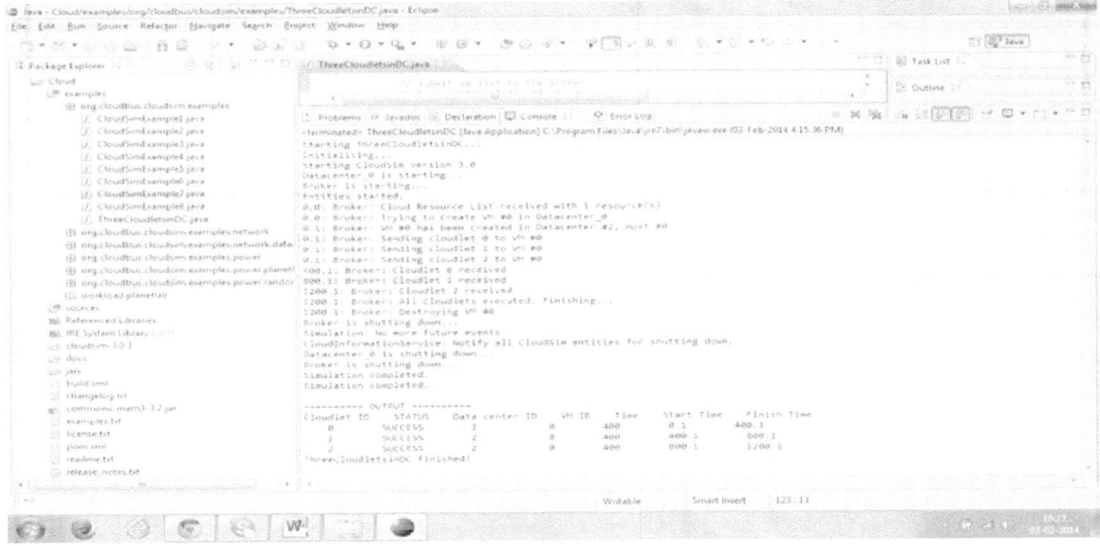

As you can see in the output, it has created 3 cloudlets with id 0,1,2 which are executed in VM with ID 0. All the 3 cloudlets take 400 as the execution time. Since this is space shared policy, the resources are allocated for each cloudlet execution. Once a cloudlet finished its execution, the resource is allocated to the next cloudlet and so on.

Many research ideas in cloudcomputing can be investigated by extending the cloudsim features. Task Scheduling, VM scheduling and load balancing algorithms can be simulated with cloudsim. Energy or power aware techniques can be implemented to simulate energy aware cloud computing systems. Different topology models can be designed to create virtualized, network-traffic free data centres. Cloudsim is a simulator which helps in simulating large scale cloud computing infrastructure free of cost. Moreover, cloudsim helps in fine tuning the performance issues before deploying on real clouds.

14.3 CASE 3: WORKING WITH APP ENGINE CONNECTED ANDROID APP

In this case study, we are going to see the steps in creating an App Engine Connected Android App. Create a Project in https://cloud.google.com/console. For more information on creating a console project refer to Chapter 11.

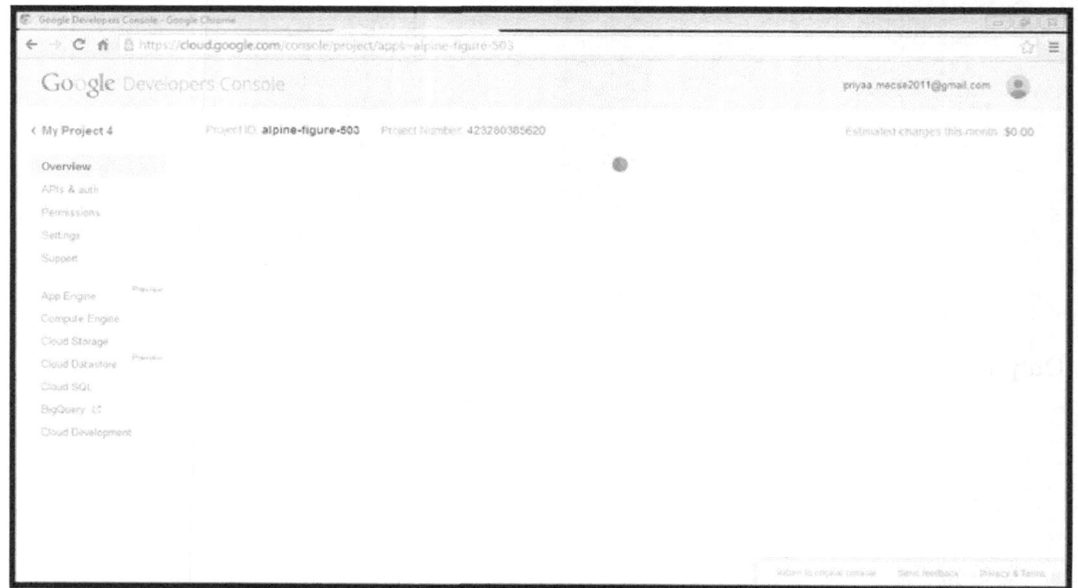

Go to APIs under APIs &auth, enable the Google Cloud Messaging for Android on.

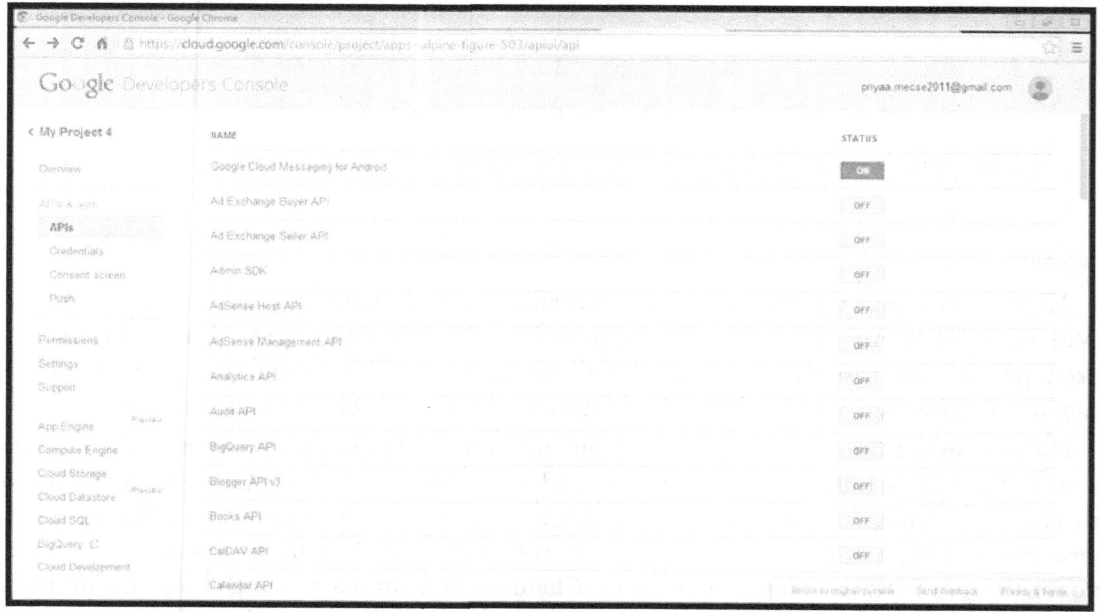

Create a server key API. For more details on creating server key, refer to chapter 12.

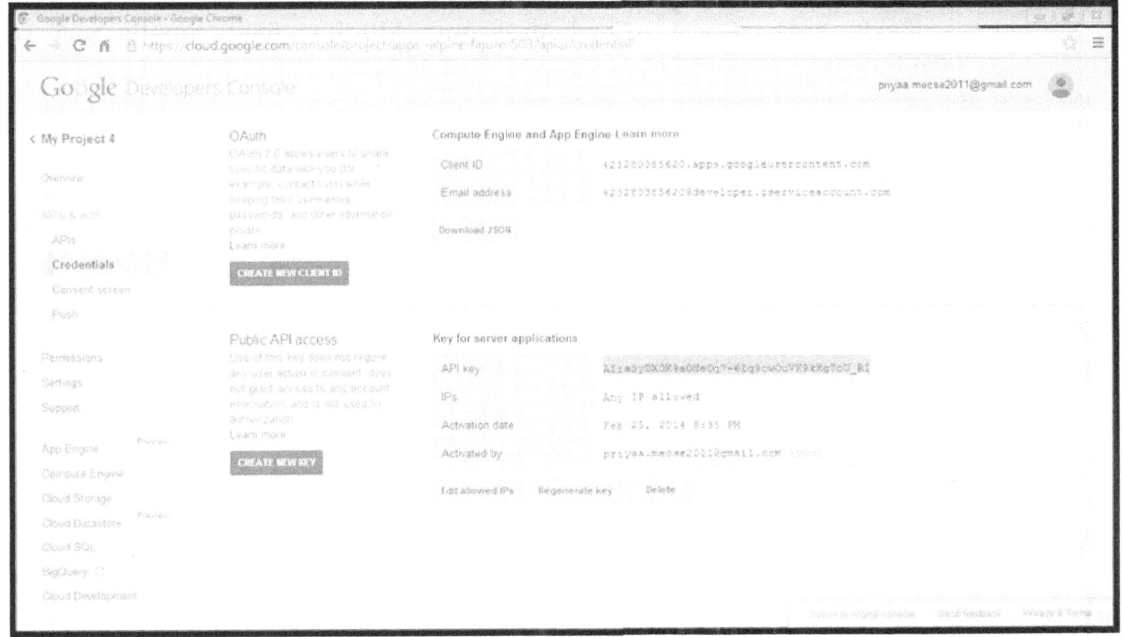

Deploy your backend. You can redeploy the backend as and when needed. Deployment will take some time. After successful deploy, you can see the snapshot as below. Next to accept incoming requests click on “Settings” link.

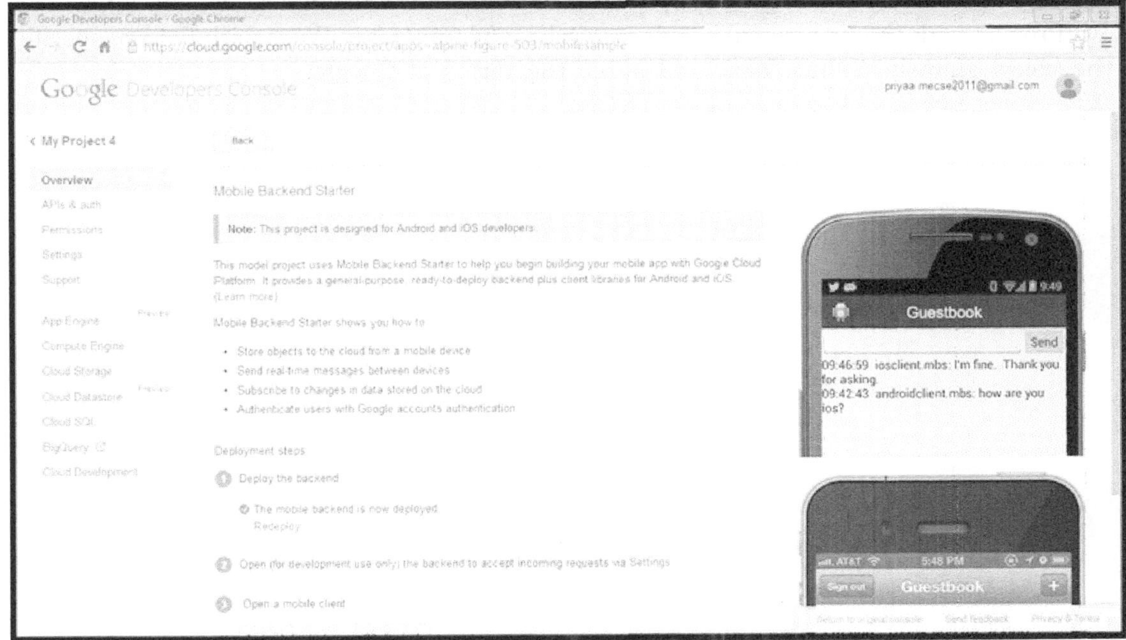

Under settings, click on the Open (development use only) radio button which is under Authentication / Authorization. Initially this will be set to Locked Down (Access disabled).

Then enable the Google Cloud Messaging as shown below. Provide with the Server API key that we got previously in the Google Cloud Messaging API Key field. Finally save the settings with save button.

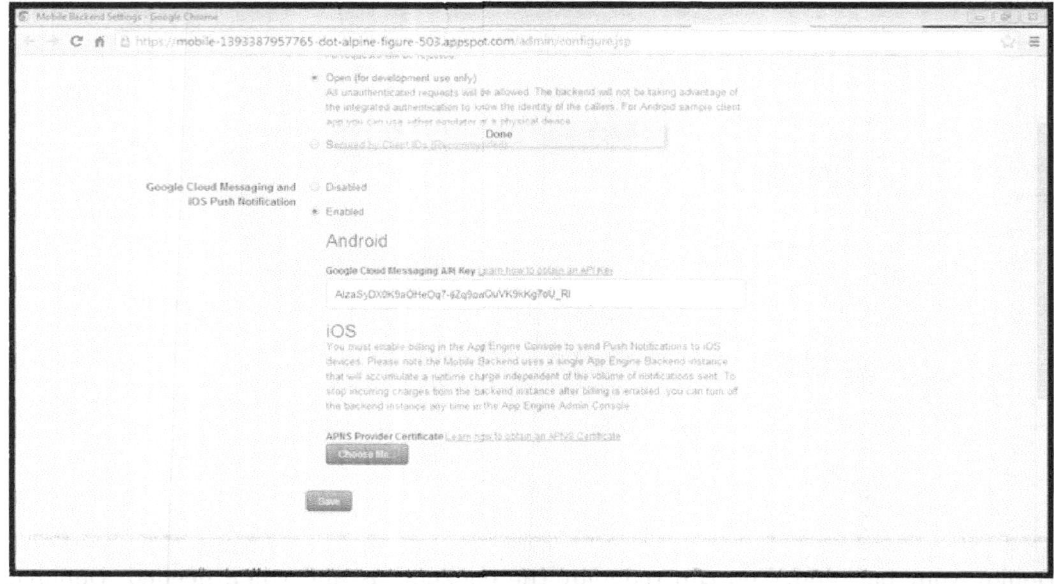

For creating AppEngineConneted Android project you need to install Google Play Services and Google API. Refer to Chapter 12 for installing these two. In addition you need to configure your SDK by clicking on Help -> Install New Software. Dialog box will appear like below. Provide with the urlhttp://dl.google.com/eclipse/plugin/4.2 in Work with field as specified in the below snapshot. Click next and agree the terms of Google.

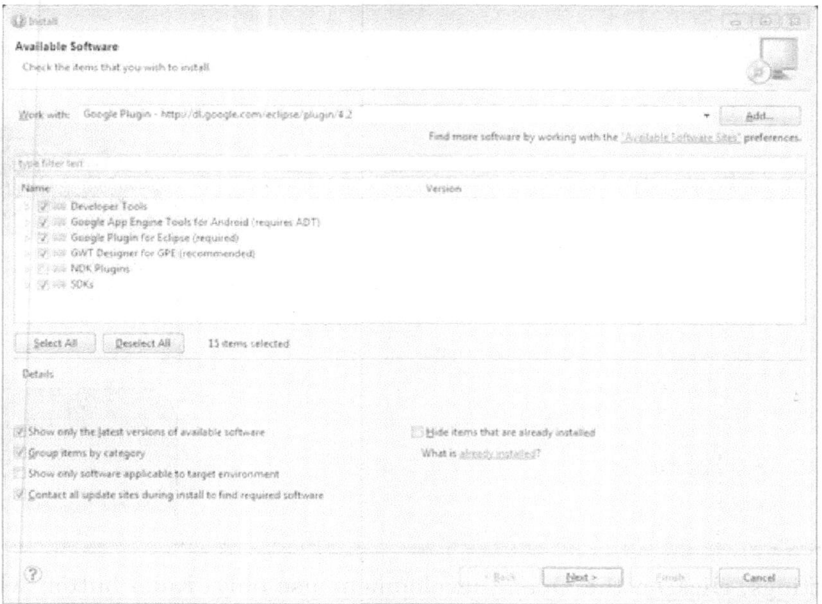

Now you are ready to create the AppEngine Connected Android Project. Create an AppEngine Connected Android Project by right clicking in your Eclipse package explorer-> New->Other.

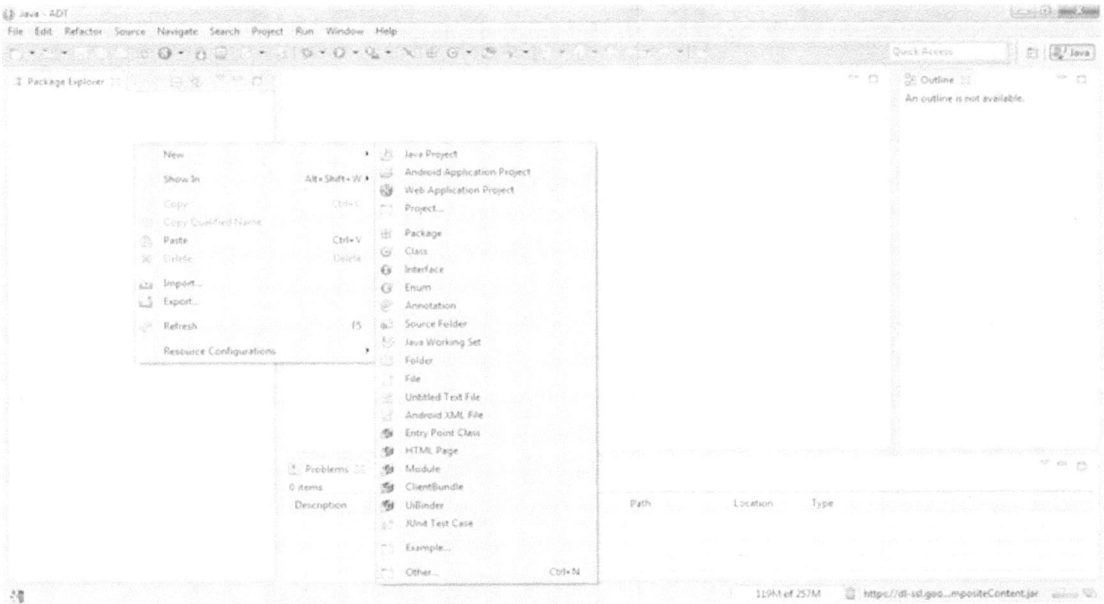

To create an App Engine Connected Android project, click on App Engine Connected Android Project available under Google. Click on next.

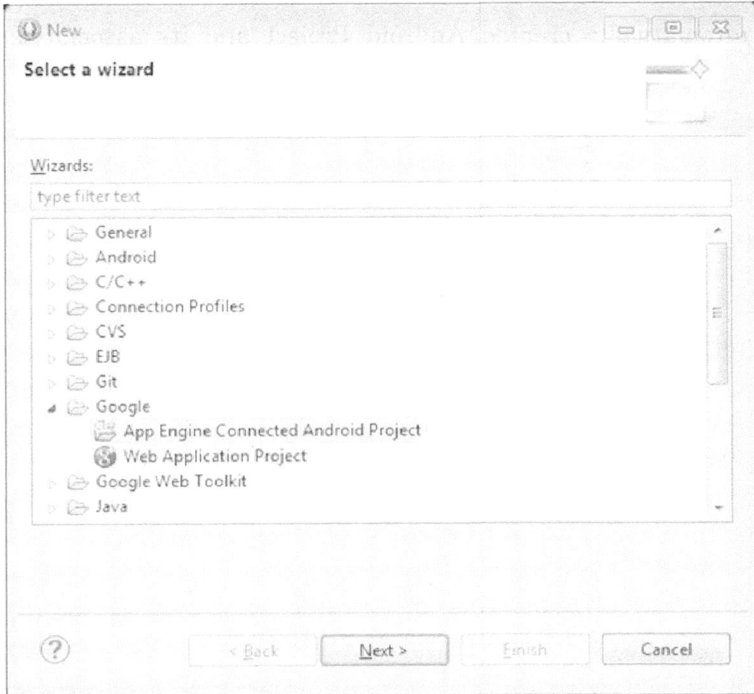

Give a project and a package name of your choice. It is time to use the API key and project number that we have created previously from Google Console.

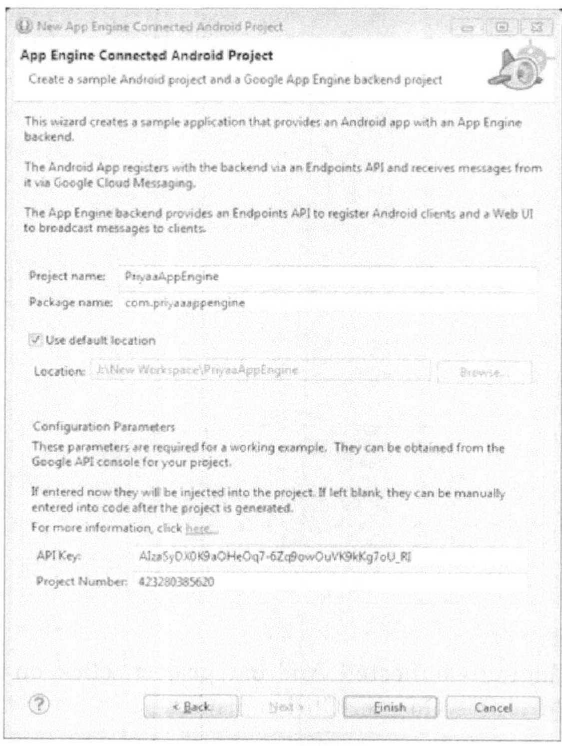

Now it has automatically created Android Project and its associated AppEngine as below.

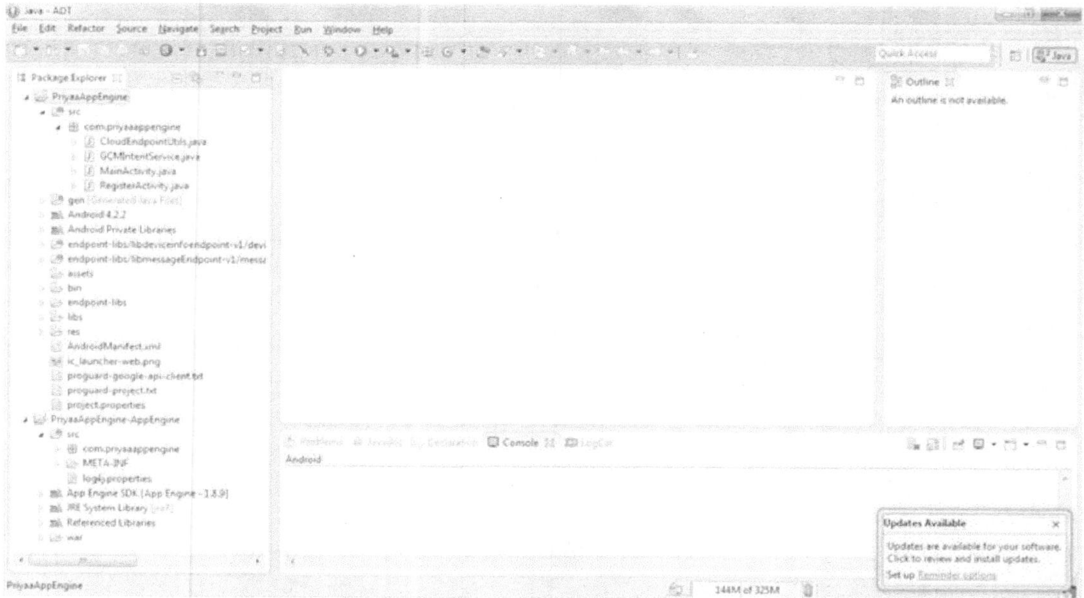

In the auto generated CloudEndpointUtils.java class available in the Android Project change the LOCAL_ANDROID_RUN as true.

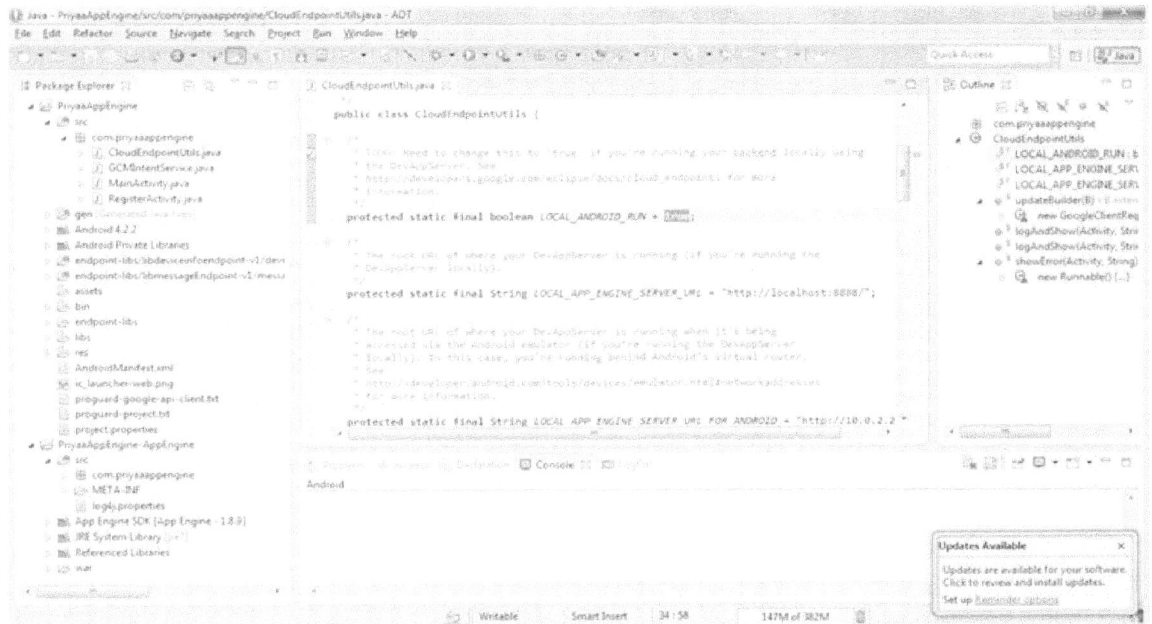

Right click on AppEngine Project->Google->Generate CloudEndpoint Client Library.

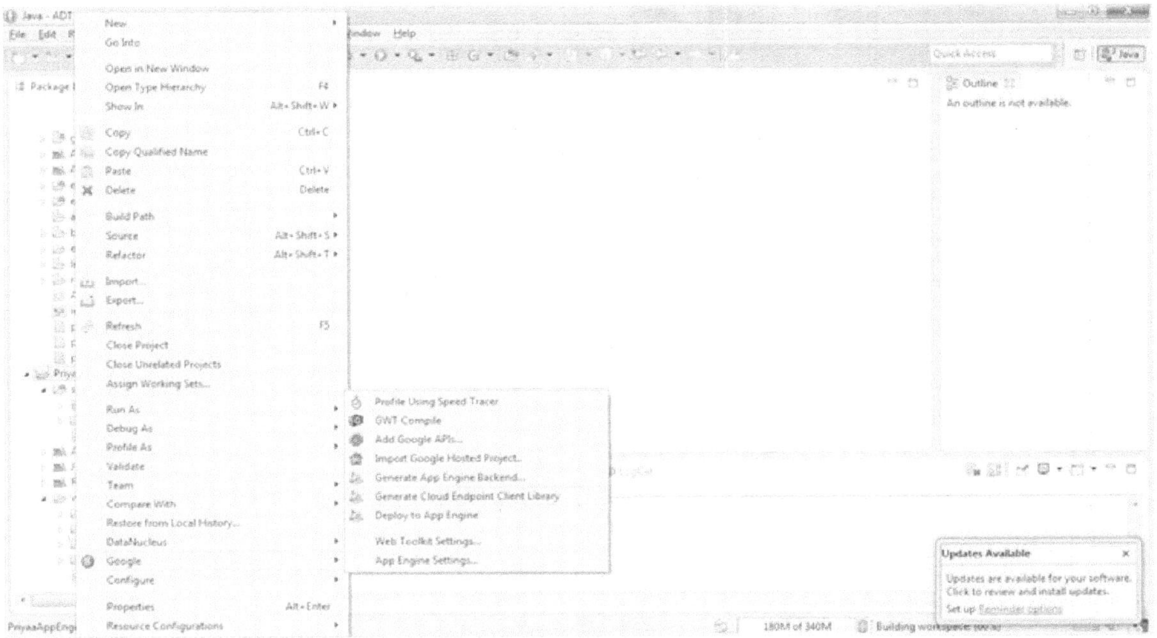

Generating Client Libraries.

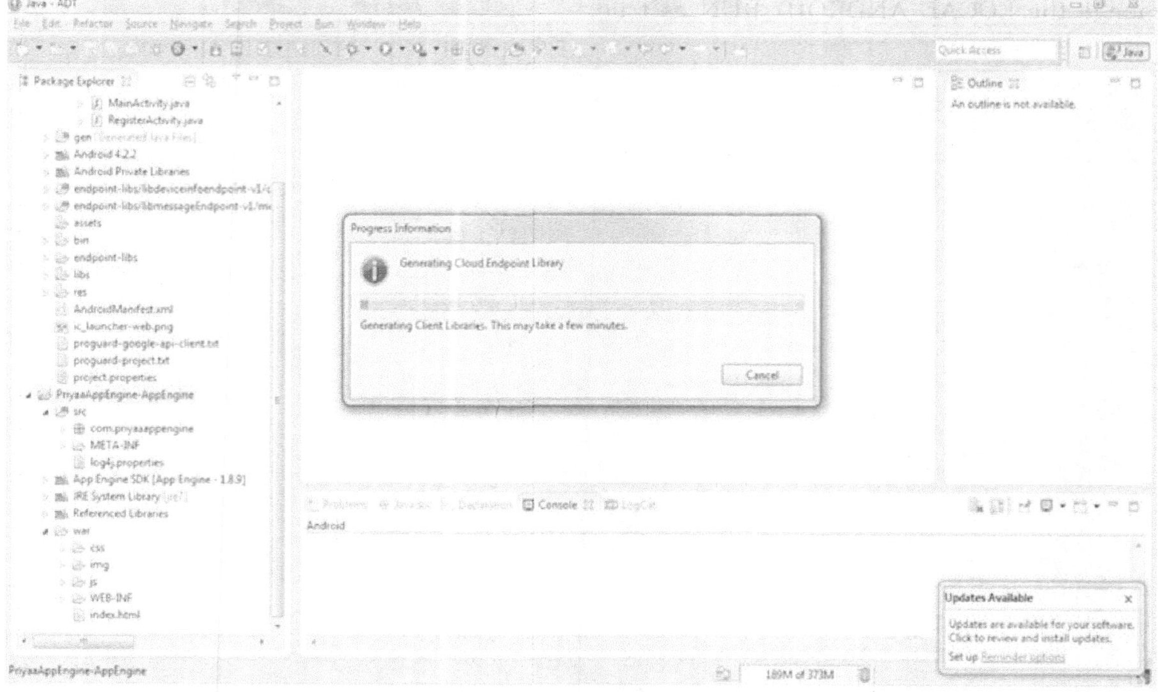

Deploy the AppEngine Project to App Engine by Google -> Deploy to App Engine.

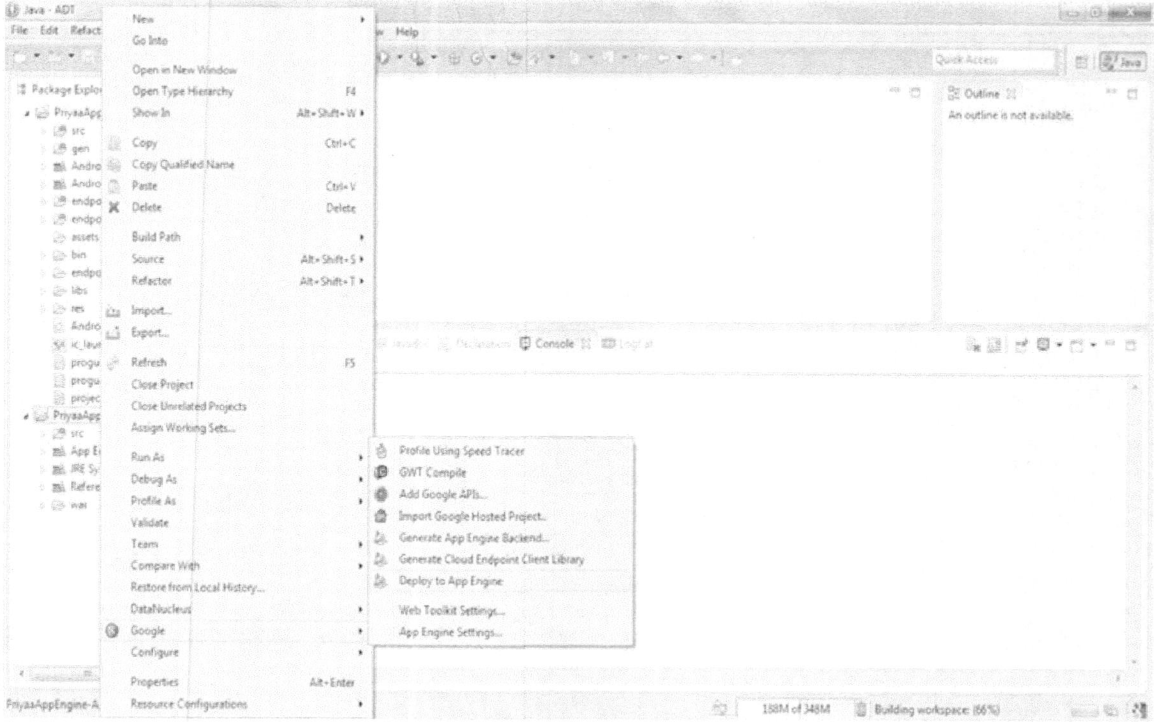

AppEngine Project is deployed successfully. Remember to sign in to the Google Account from the Eclipse.

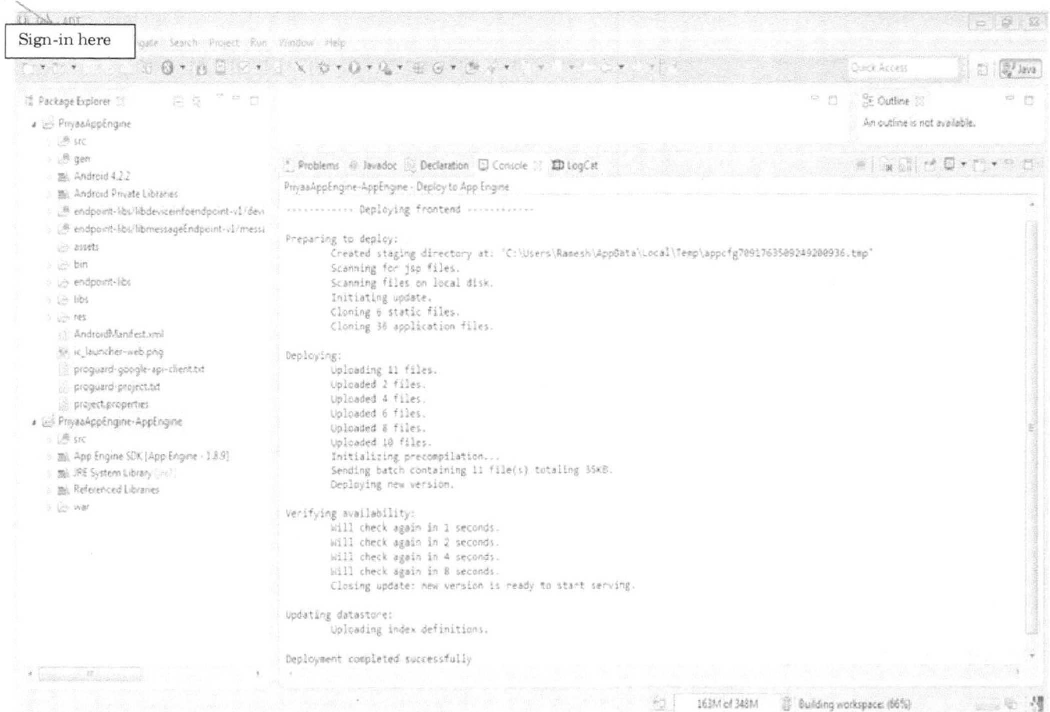

Right click on AppEngine Project->Run as->Web Application.

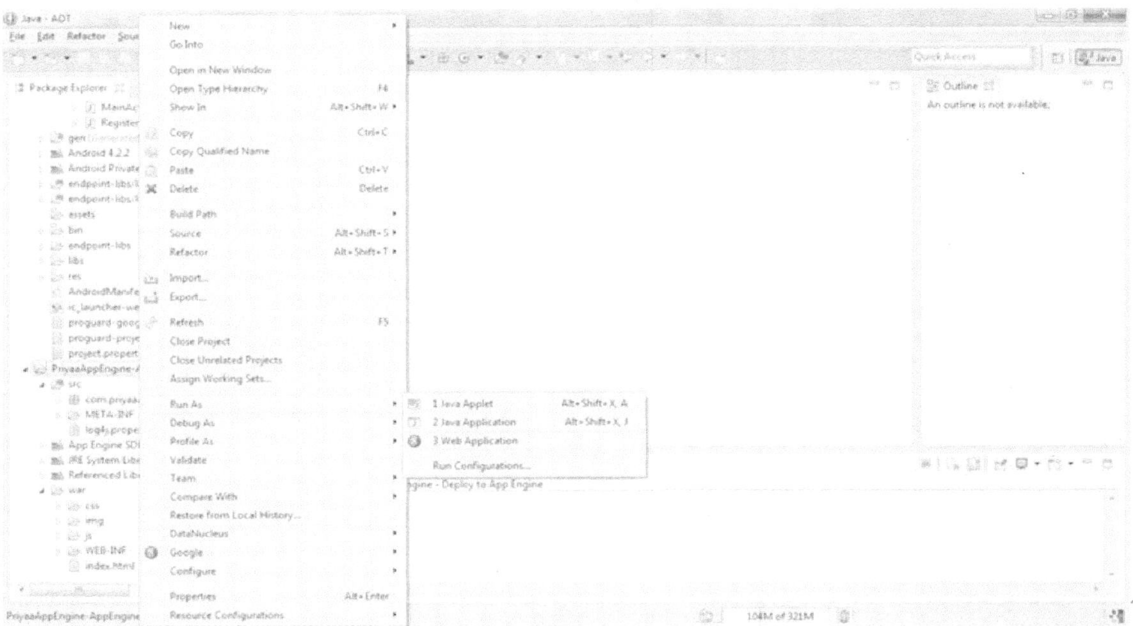

Now local AppServer is running.

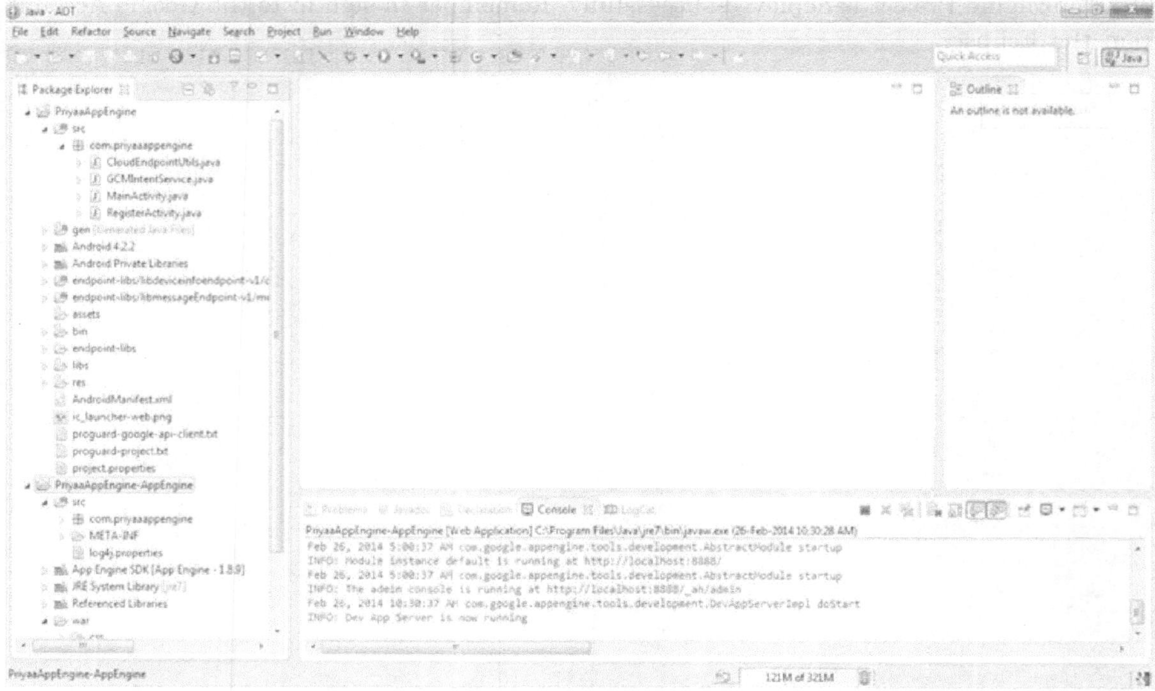

Run the Android Project : Run As -> Android Application.

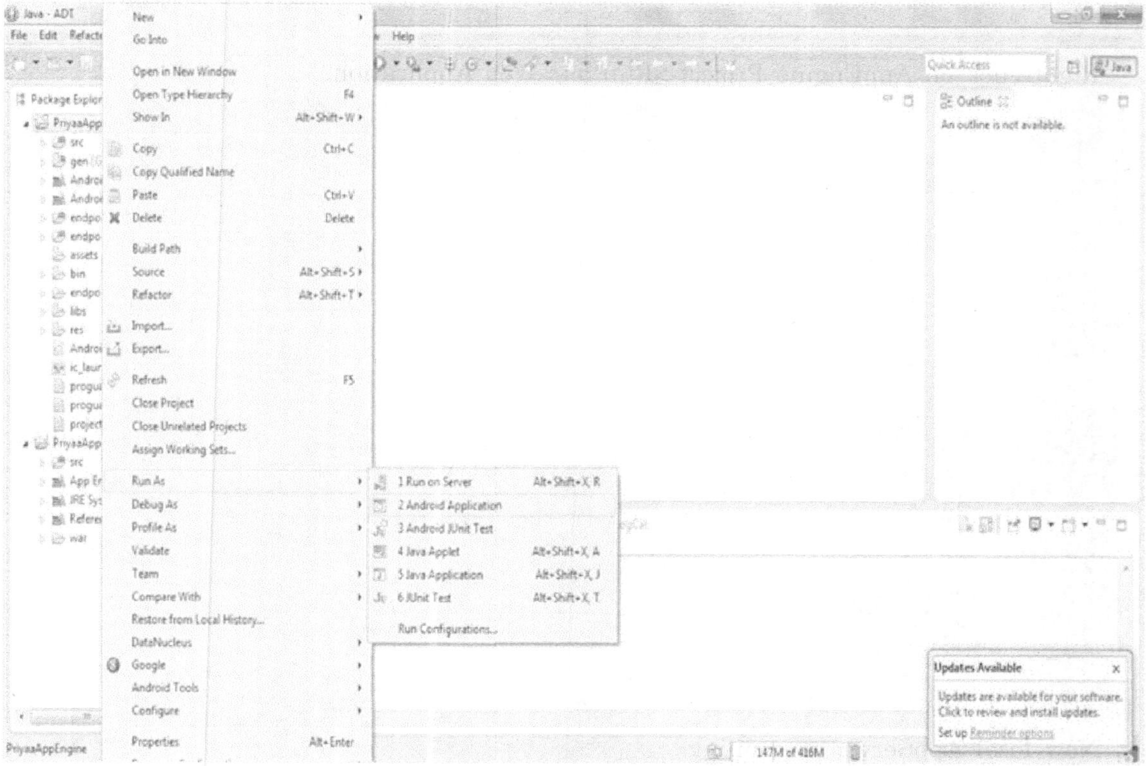

Create an Emulator with target as Google API. Run the Android Application on the emulator with target set to Google API.

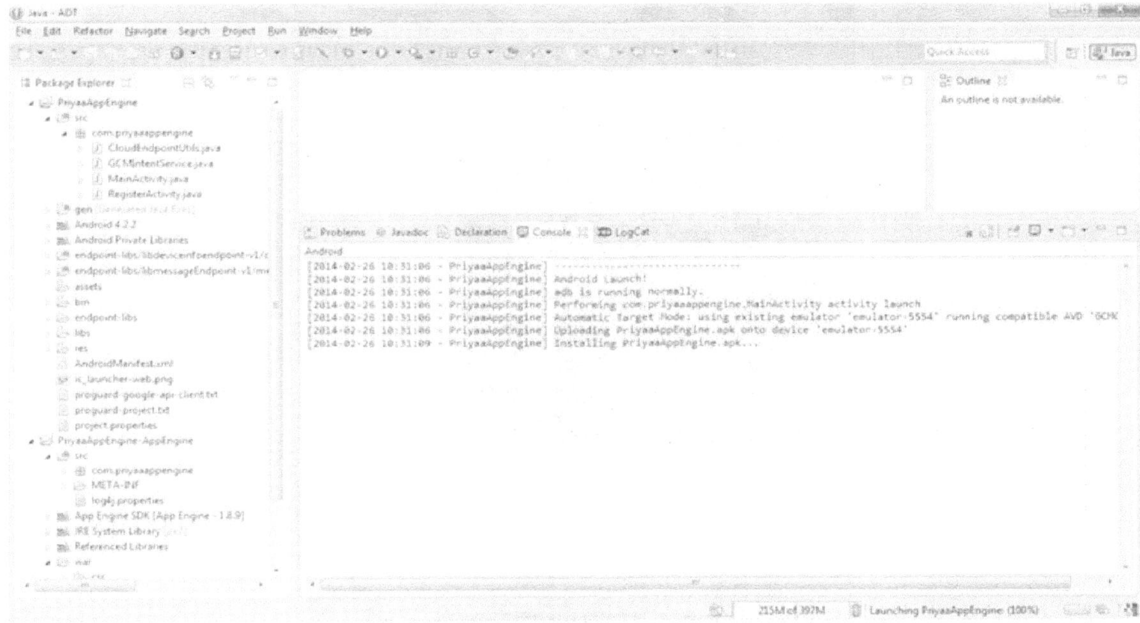

Output:

Click on Register to register the device to cloud.

Dialog box showing that the device is just registered with GCM.

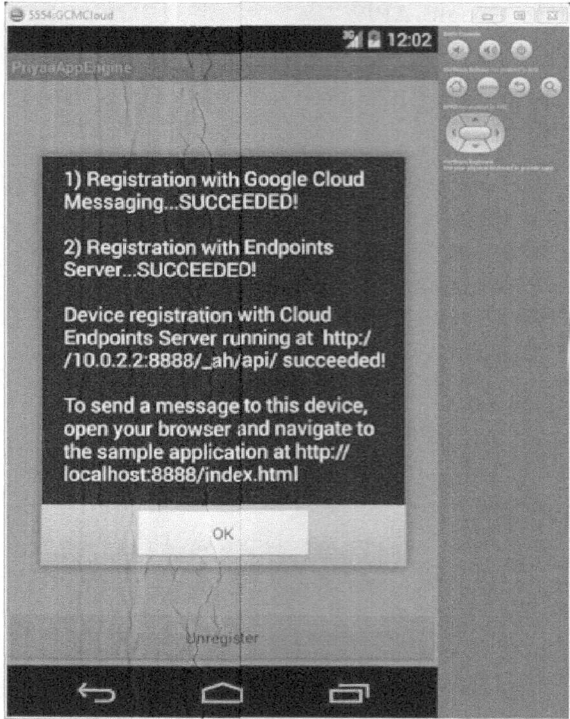

Go to localhost:8888/index.html to see the Registration Id of registered devices.You can send messages as well.

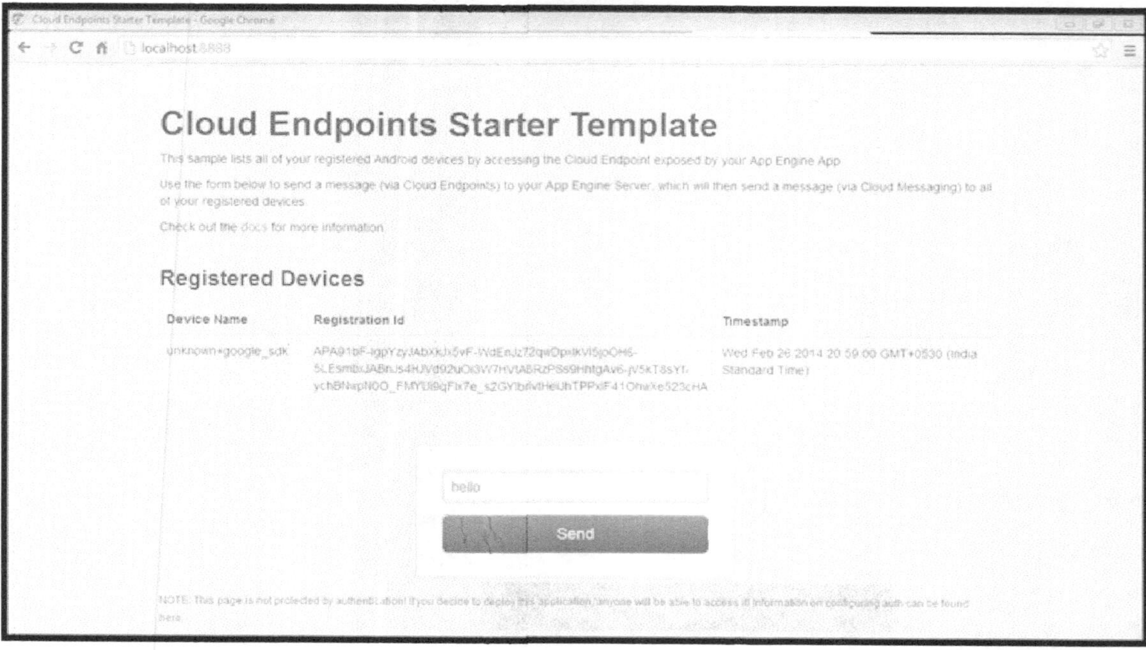

Note that an alert dialog appears to notify the registered device about the Google Cloud Messaging. Remember to sign in with your gmail account (project created account) to receive the GCM messages.

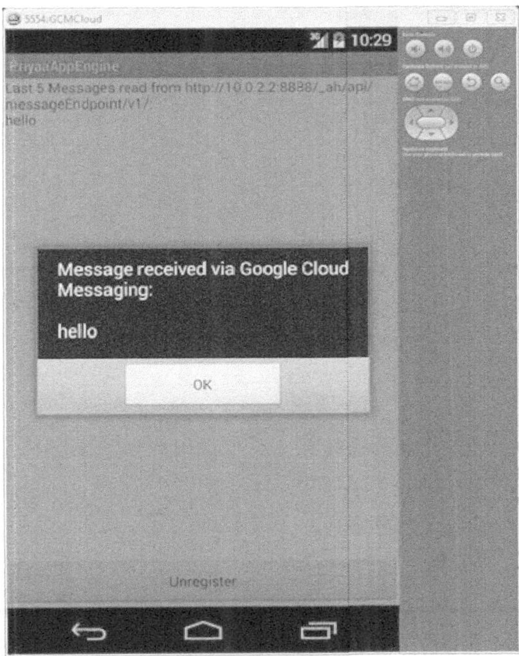

Messages are being displayed with the server endpointurl.

Go to local server url http://localhost:8888/_ah/admin/datastore?kind=MessageData to find the GCM messages that are sent to the registered devices.

Go to url http://localhost:8888/_ah/admin/datastore?kind=DeviceInfo to find the registered device information.

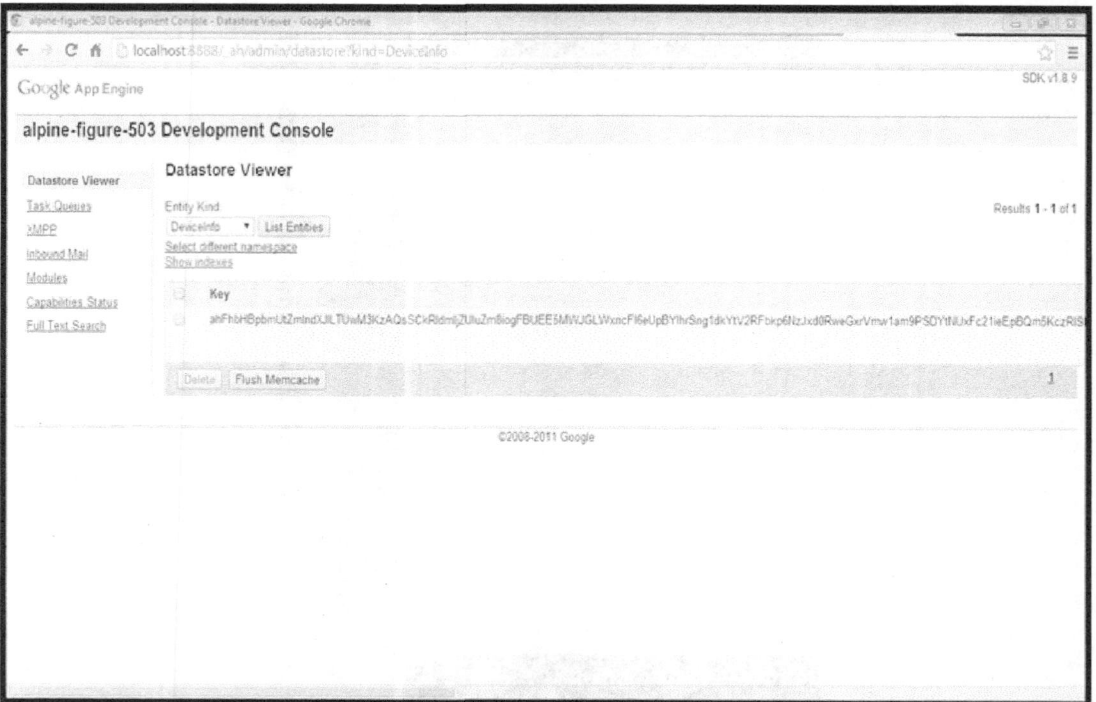

Click on Unregister for unregistering with GCM.

Below is the snapshot showing success dialog for unregistering with GCM.

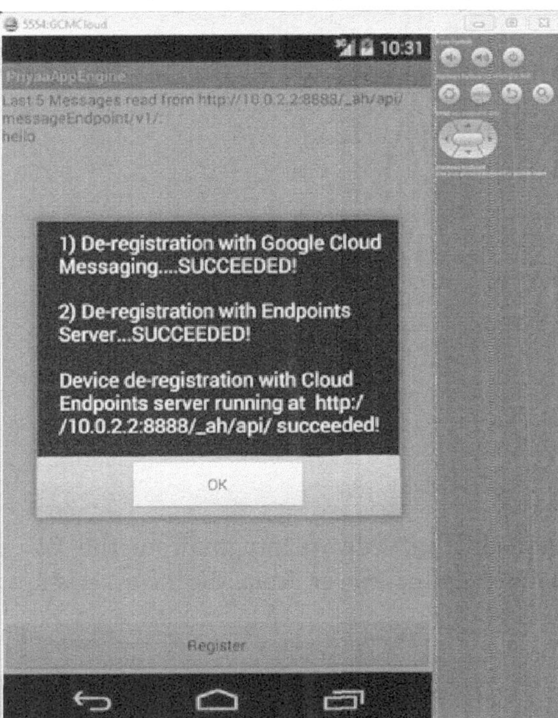

Depending on the need, the Android applications can be modified and redeployed the modified application in Google Console.

14.4 CASE 4: WORKING WITH VMWARE CLOUD FOUNDRY INTEGRATION WITH ECLIPSE

In this case study let us see in detail about the platform as a service (PaaS) concept by the VMware product cloud foundry integration.

VMware cloud foundry provides the platform for the user to design and host the application into the remote VMware cloud. The user must have a account to start up it is free unlike all other VMware products are charged. We can install this tool either in Eclipse or Spring tool suite. In this case study we use Eclipse.

The Cloud Foundry Eclipse Plugin is an extension that enables Cloud Foundry users to deploy and manage Java and Spring applications on a Cloud Foundry instance from Eclipse or Spring Tools Suite (STS). The plugin supports Eclipse v3.8 and v4.3 (a Java EE version is recommended), and STS 3.0.0 and later.

We will explain the PaaS concept of VMware cloud foundry using the various output images.

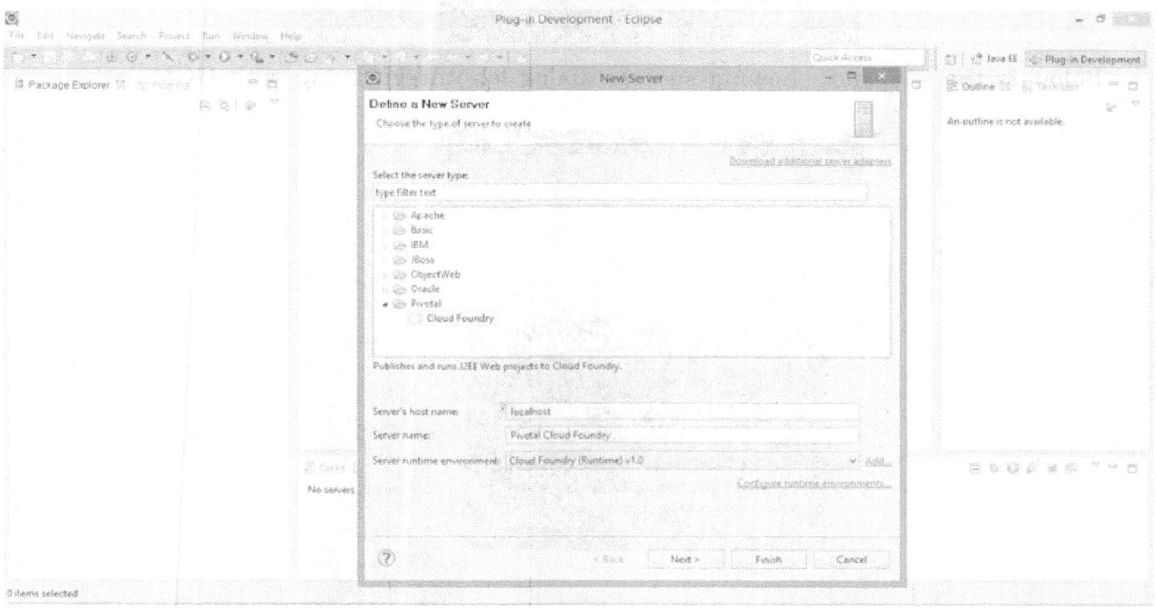

In the first step download the VMware plugin from the Eclipse market place. Then create a new VMware cloud foundry server from the new server wizard.

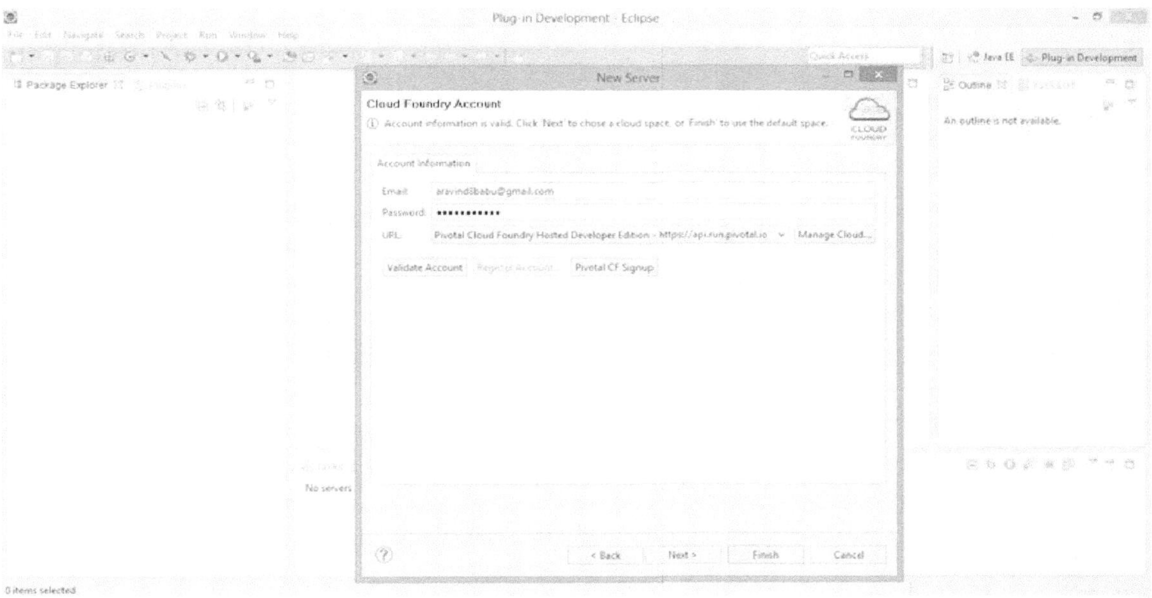

It prompts for the user account credentials, validate the account and finish the server configuration.

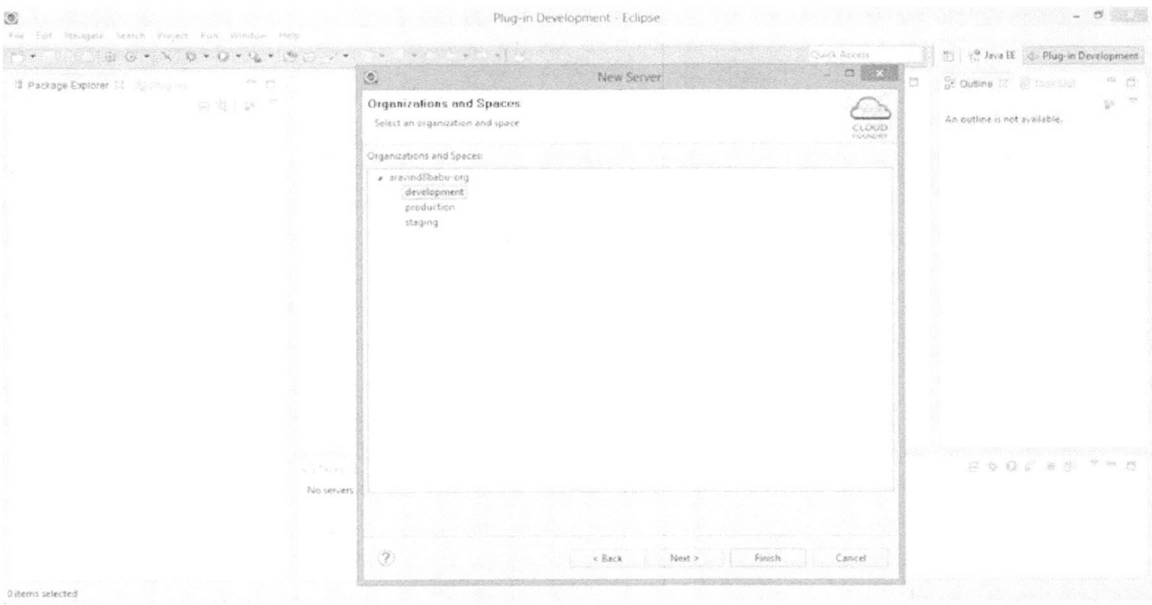

Select the development option under the organization and space step so as to design and host the app.

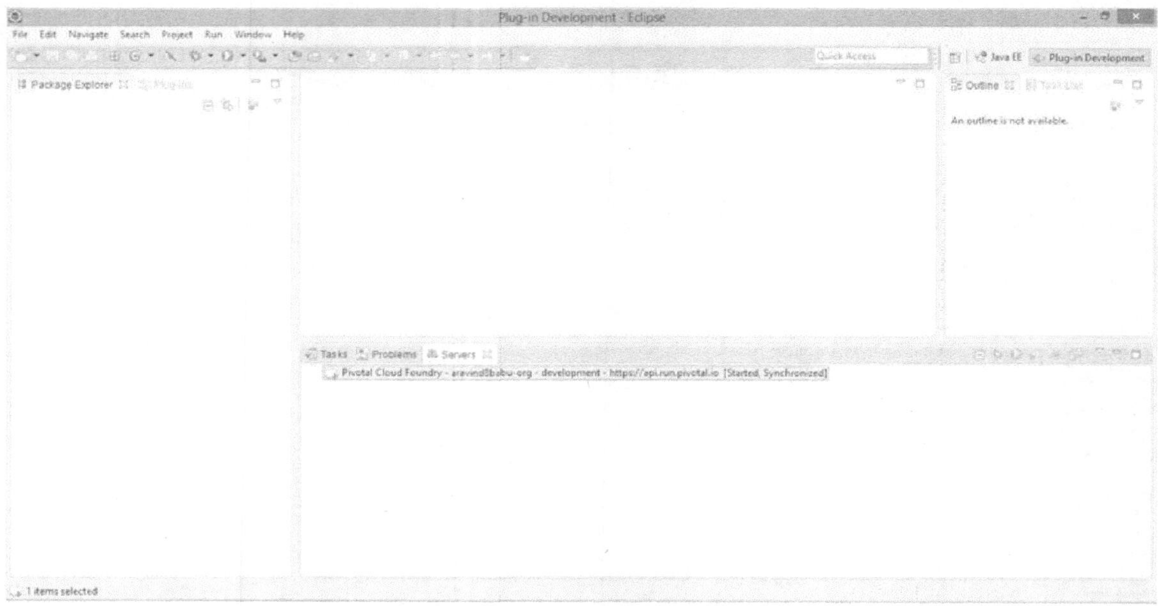

The new cloud foundry server is ready and it is started.

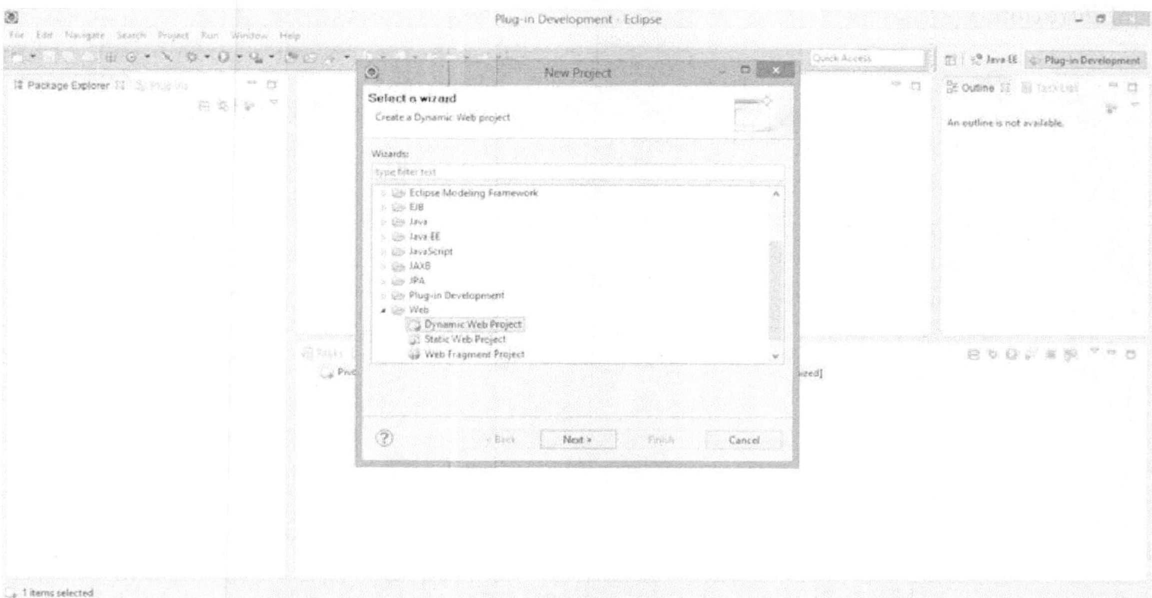

Create a new dynamic web project so that a suitable application is designed and hosted in the cloud.

The new project is created and is seen in the project explorer.

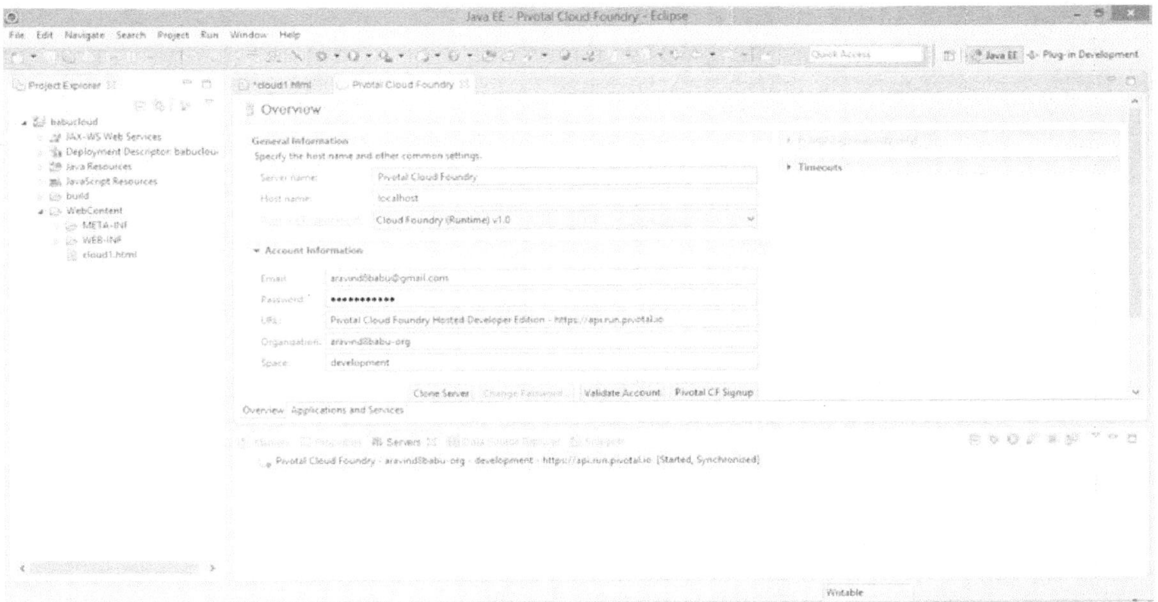

Create the required application under the project. Double click the VMware cloud foundry server and view all the details.

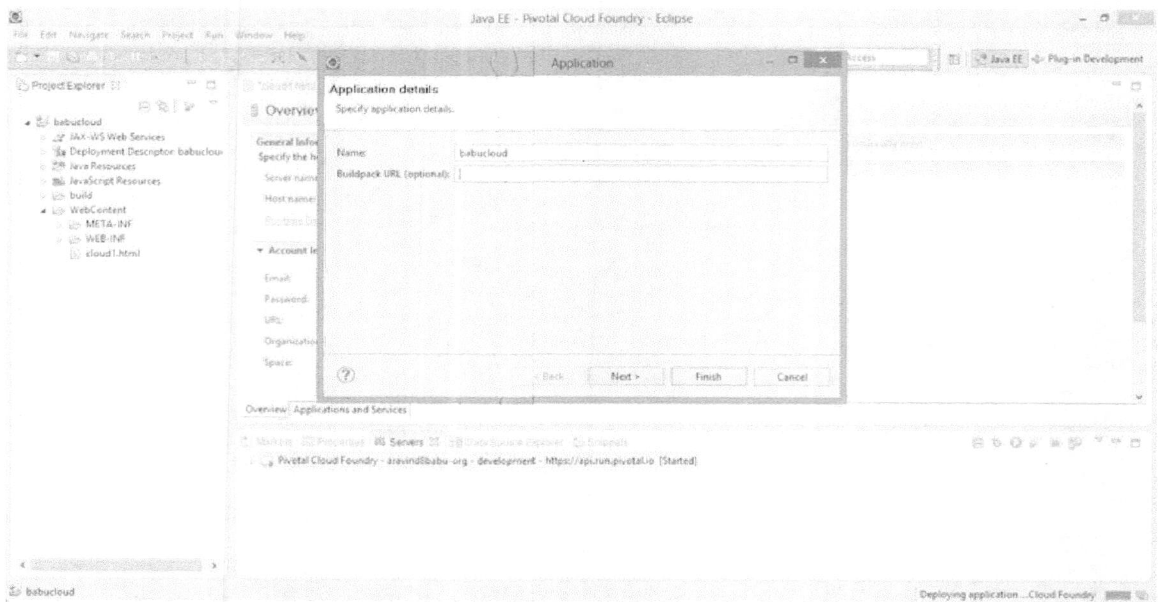

Now we can publish the application into the cloud. Just move the application into the cloud foundry server. It prompts the name.

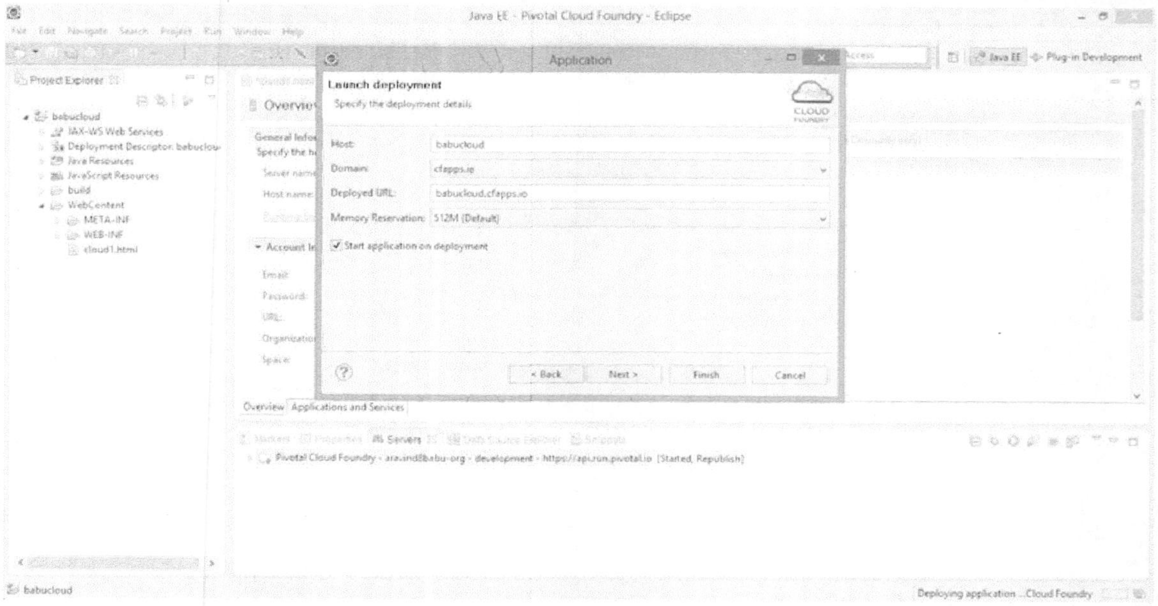

Specify the URL and memory required to host the application into the cloud.

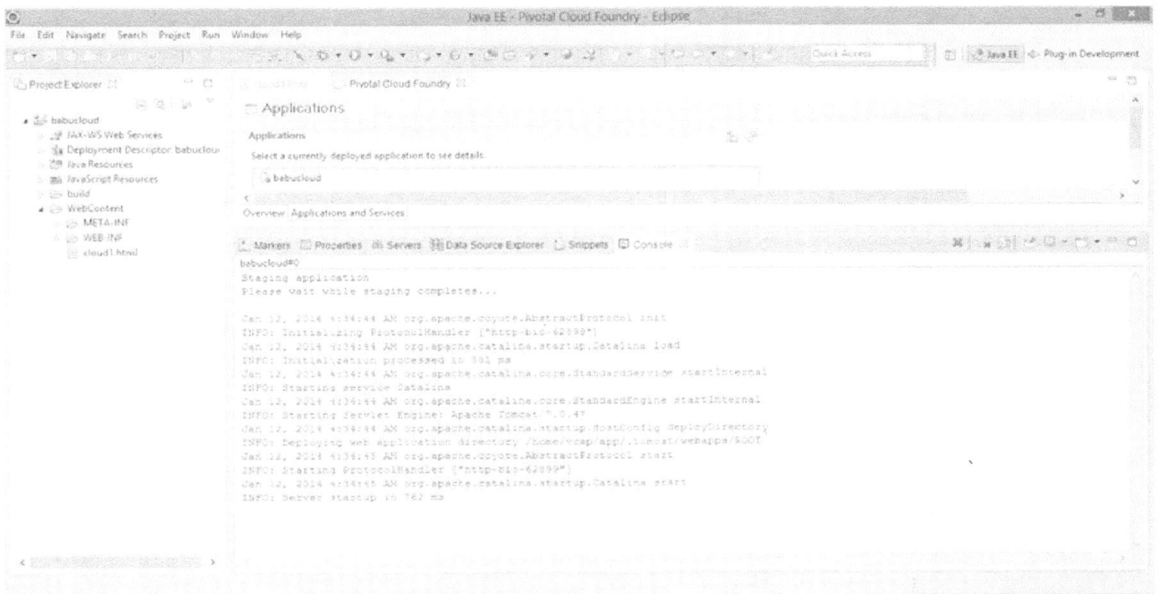

The application designed by the user is deployed into the cloud. We can see the console tab about all the activities.

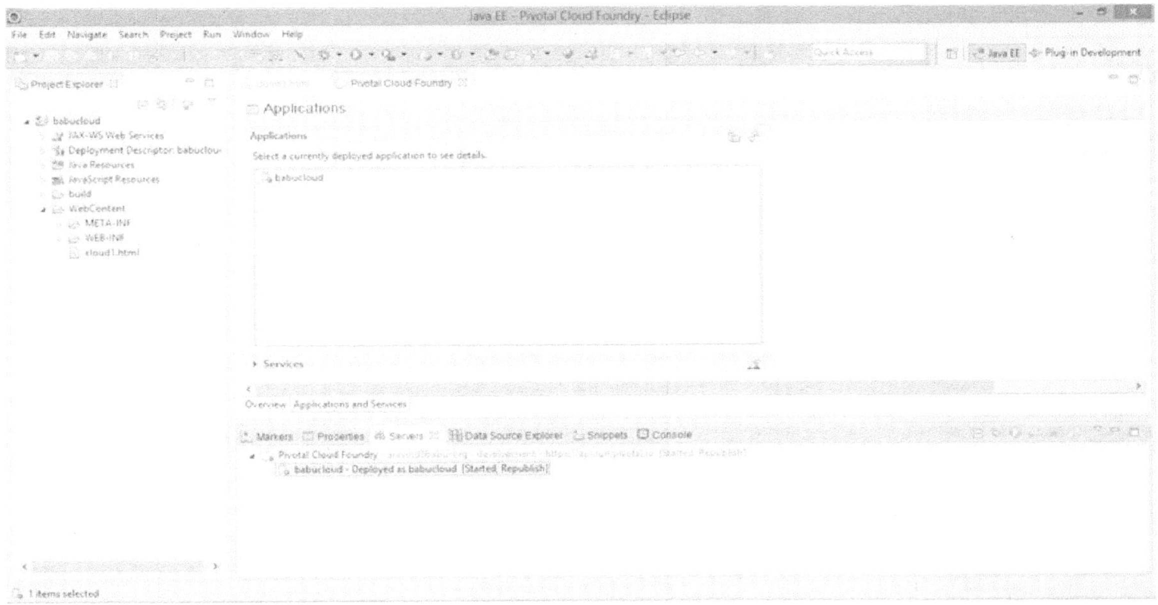

Finally the application is deployed into the cloud and it is started to run in the server.

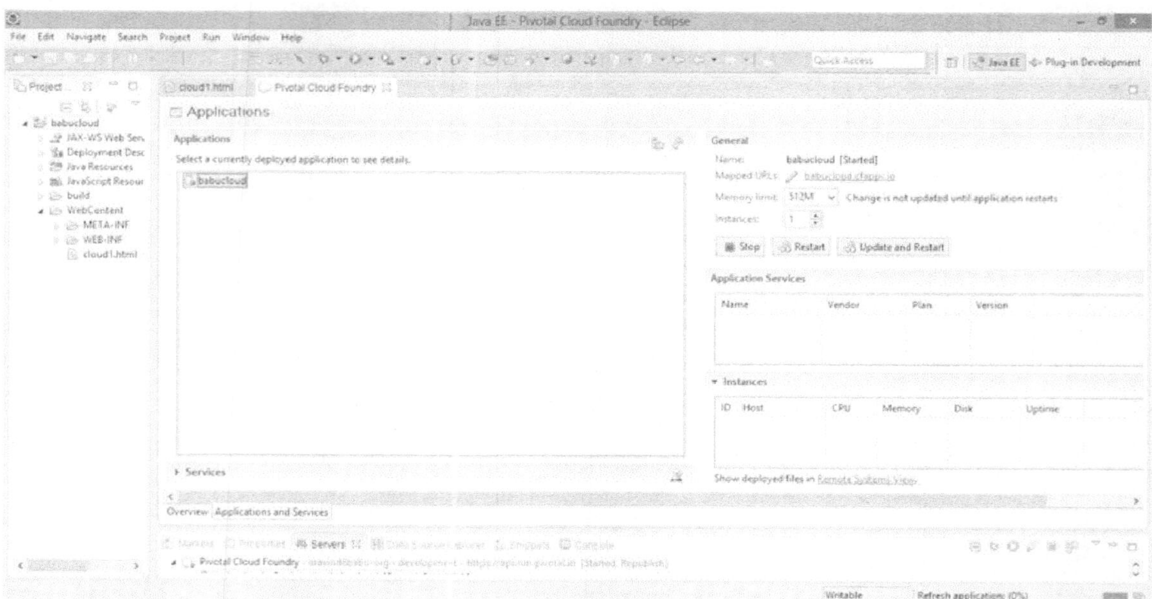

Click on the deployed application to see all the details like services, instance count, mapped URL and so on.

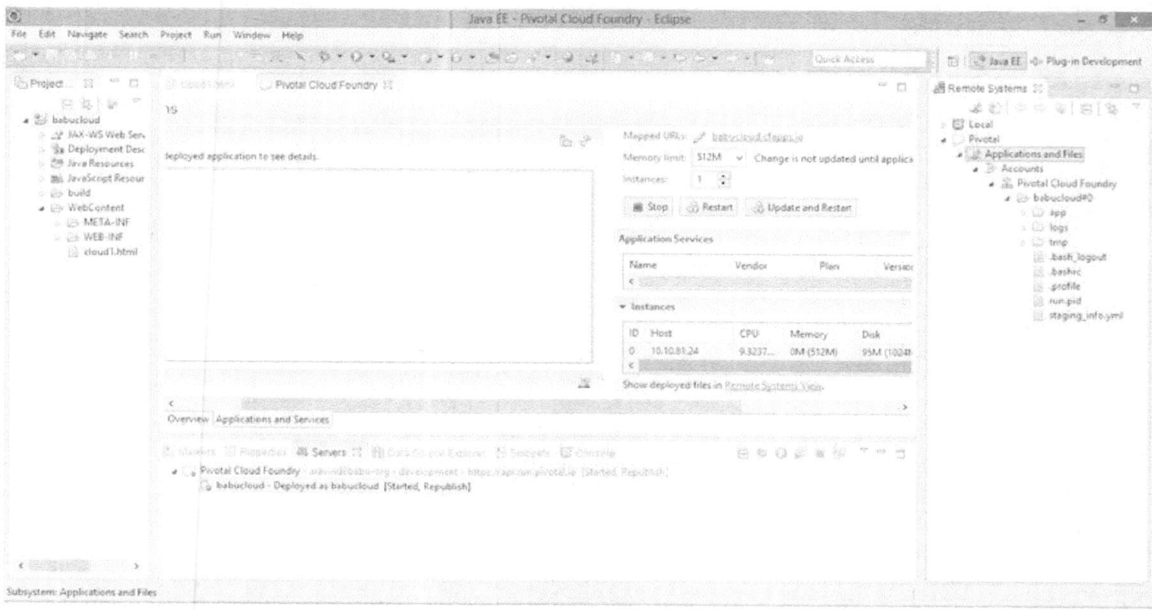

Once we choose the number of required instances we can start the application. We can also make some changes and then click update and restart option to restart the cloud foundry server again.

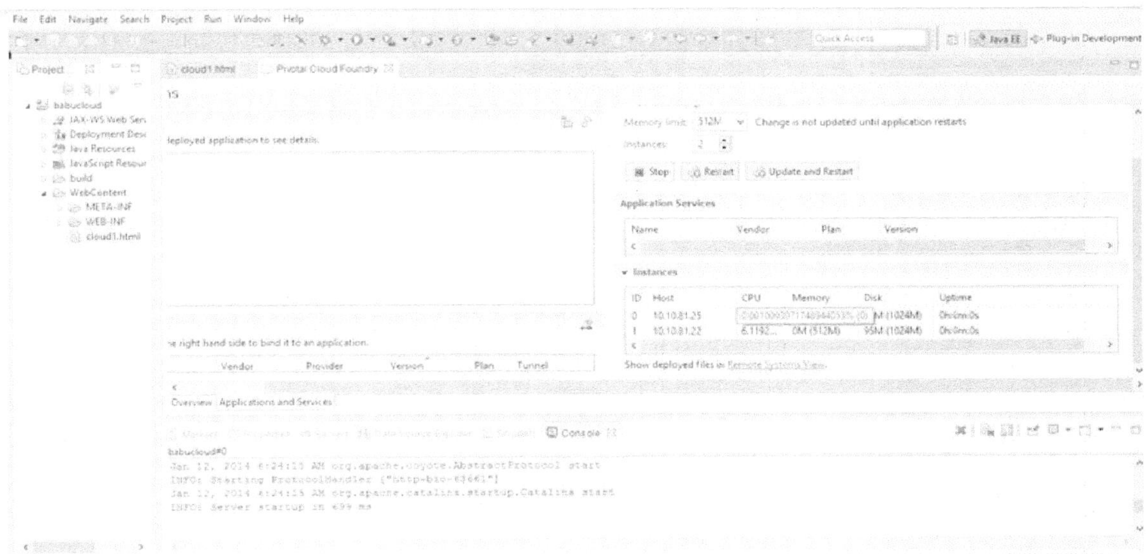

We can again see the console when we restart the server. We can also see the instances of the cloud running.

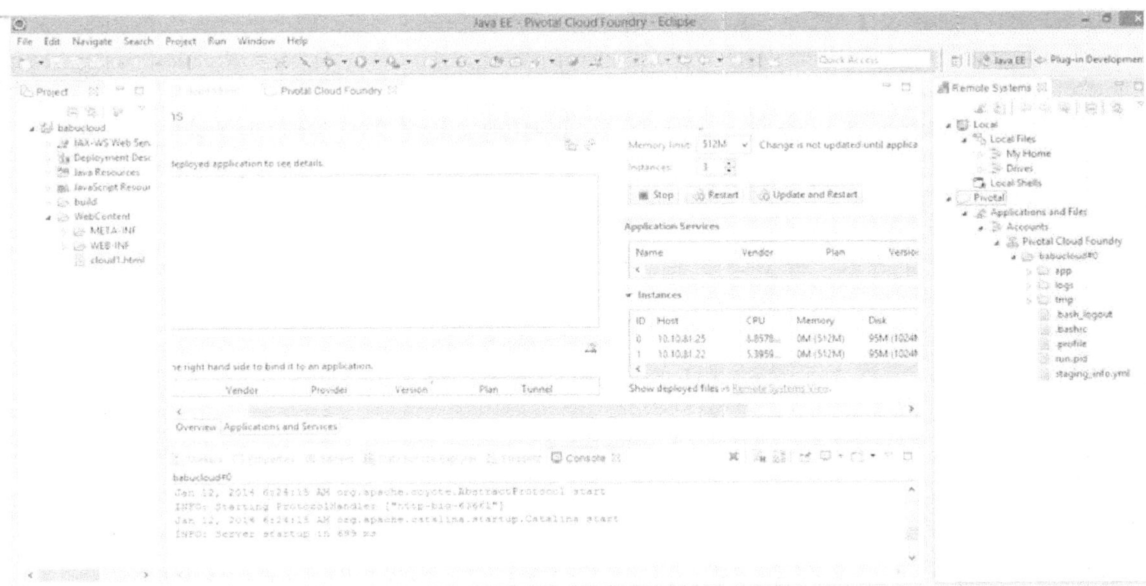

In the remote view we can see both the front end machine and the back end server with the instances of the application.

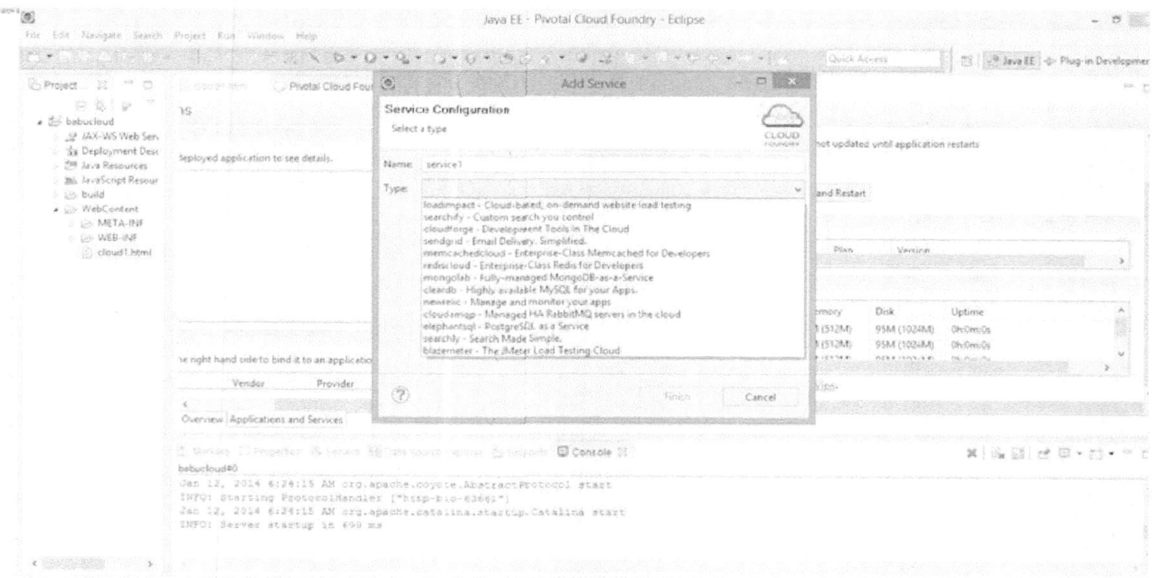

We can also add some services to our deployed application in the cloud.

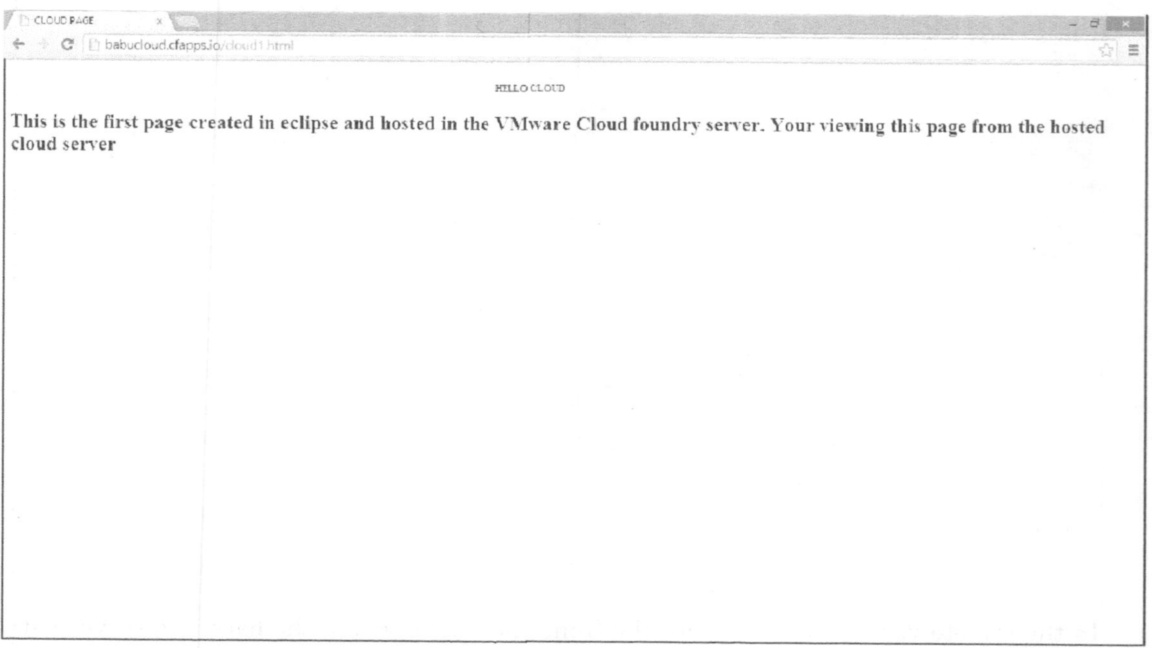

At last we can view the deployed application in the server using the mapped URL of the application.

Thus this how the PaaS concept works by setting up the development platform, design the app and finally host the app into the remote cloud server.

14.5 CASE 5: WORKING WITH GOOGLE APP ENGINE AND HOSTING THE APPLICATION

In this case study, we will see the another PaaS concept of cloud computing using the google product google app engine. We have already seen in the chapter 7 about all the google cloud products.

Google app engine comes under the platform as a service (PaaS) concept which provides the required platform to design the application, host the application into the google cloud. In this case study, we use the Eclipse software to work with the google app engine.

We will explain the whole process using the worked out images.

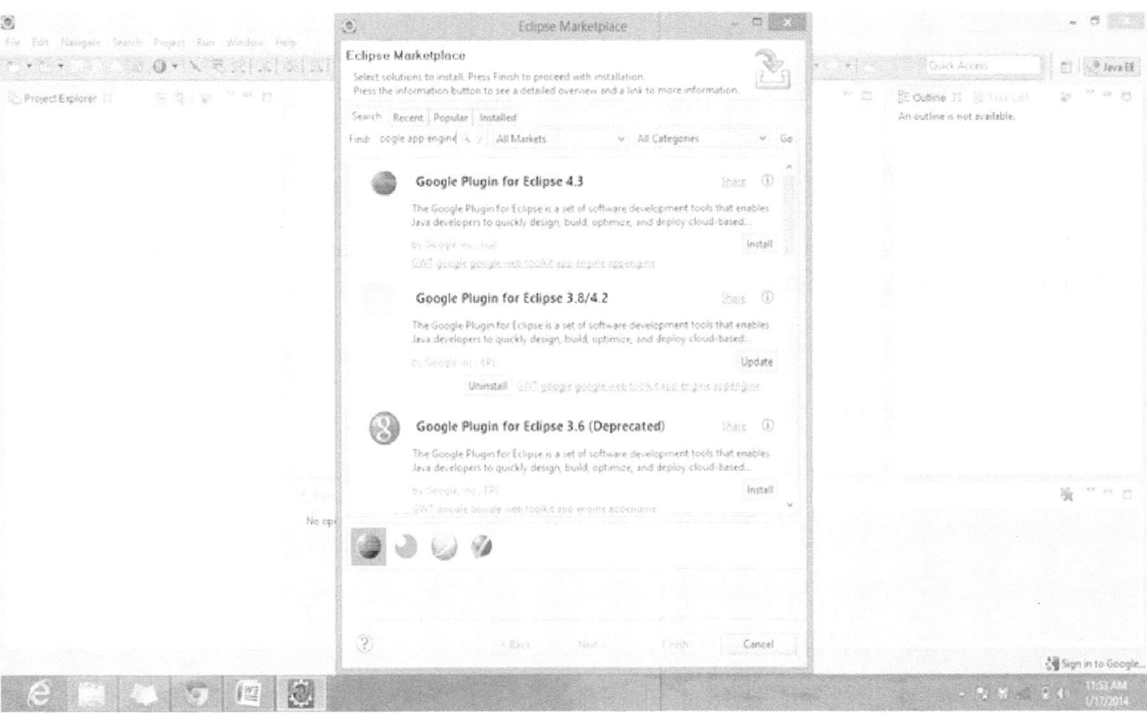

We work with Eclipse software, we download the Google plugin from the eclipse marketplace. It takes time to download and install the required packages into the Eclipse. It depends on the speed of the internet and there must be no firewall blockage.

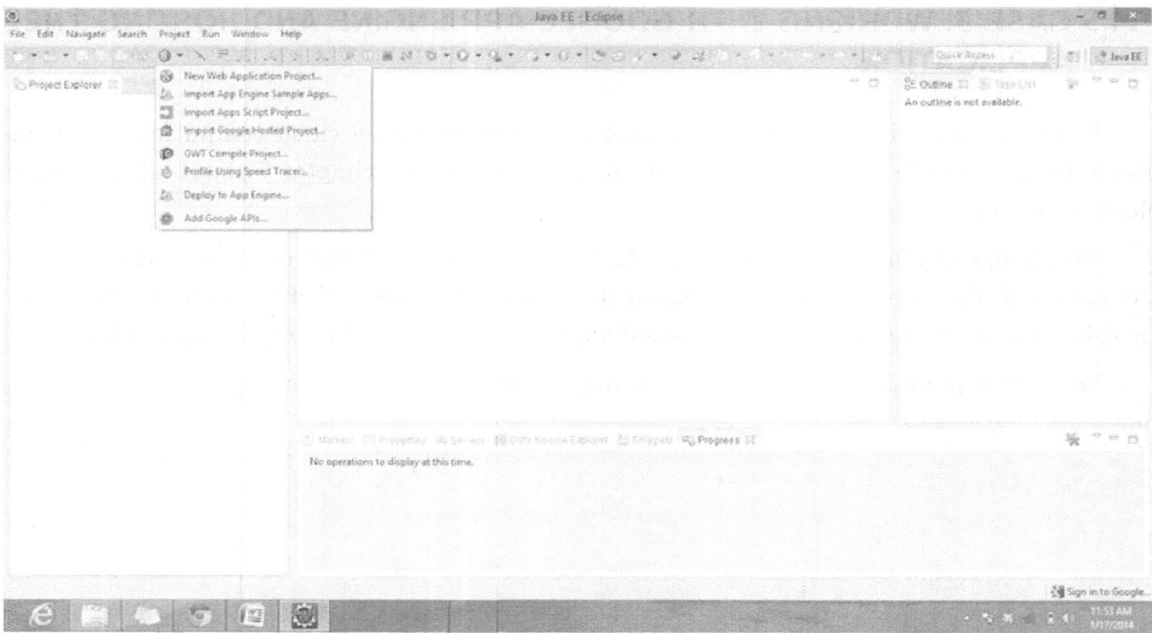

After the installation a new icon with the G symbol is created which contains all the functions for google app engine.

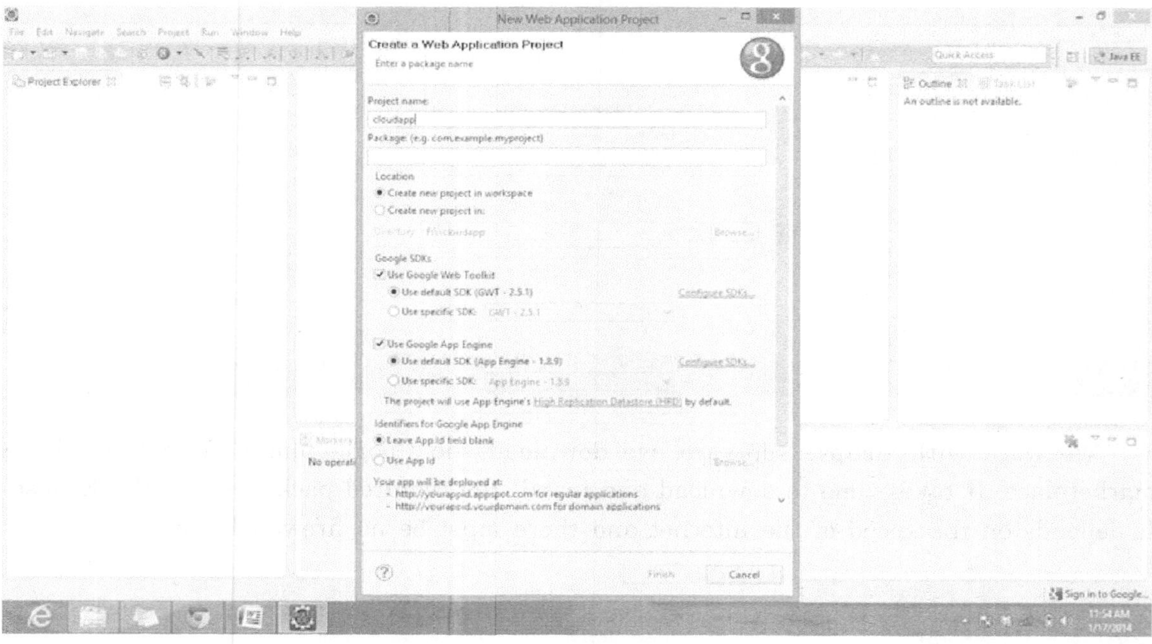

Select the create new web application project to create a new application to design and host in the google cloud. Select the project name and package, click finish to create the new web application project.

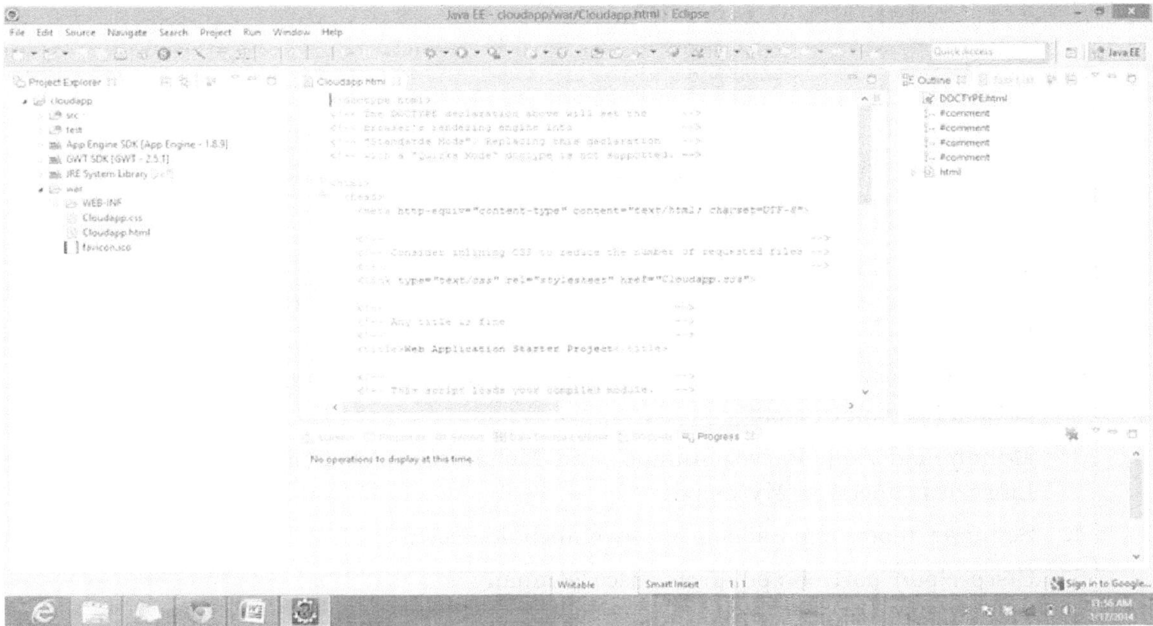

We can see the new project in the project explorer which is the workspace to design the application.

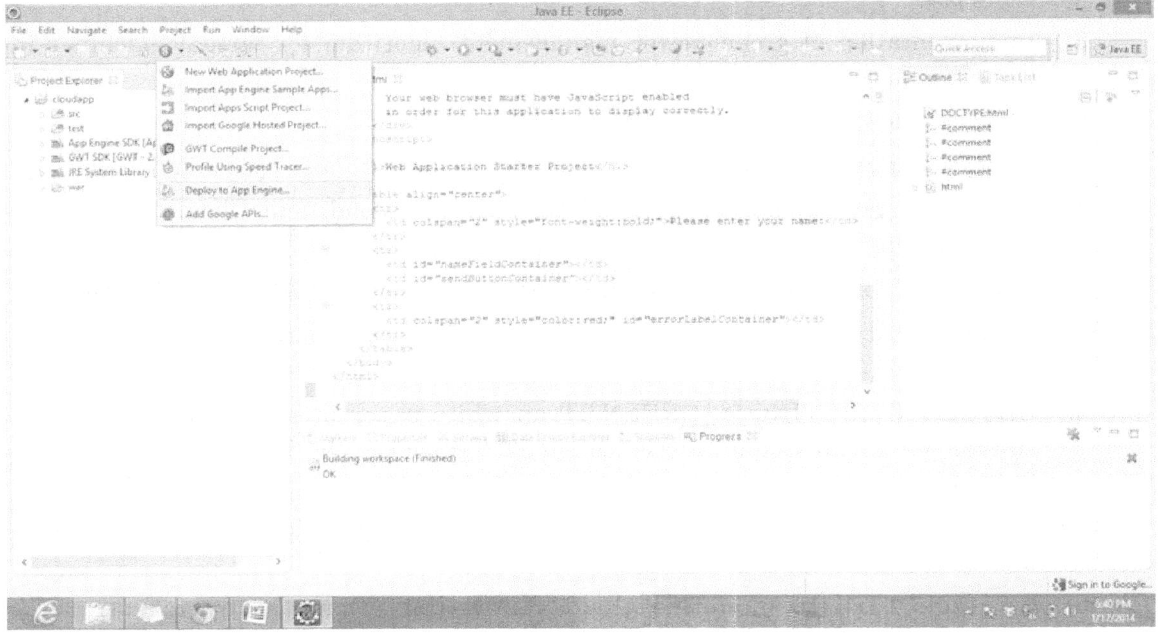

When the user has finished coding the required application, deploy it into the google cloud. To deploy the application click on the option deploy to app engine.

References

1. Introduction to cloud computing. Pdf by office of the privacy commissioner of Canada
2. 11v5-IT-Governance-and-the-Cloud-Principles-and-Practice-for-Governing-Adoption-of-Cloud-Computing.pdf
3. Mohammad Aqil, Parvez Ahmad, and Mohammad Asad Siddique - Web 2.0 and Libraries: Facts or Myths.pdf
4. Seminar report on hadoop by www.techalone.com
5. Cisco cloud portfolio.pdf from cisco company
6. The Cloud – The New Paradigm in Enterprise Computing.pdf by lizart company markets
7. A dynamic resource allocation model for virtual machine management for cloud.pdf
8. Implementation of green power management algorithm for virtual machines in cloud computing environment.pdf
9. Cloud framework from C-DAC
10. Cloud Computing: Concepts, Virtualization, IaaS and PaaS by sanjay chaudhary
11. Designing and Implementing Cloud Governance: Cloud, and Cloud Governance, are Emerging Capabilities by Eric Marks
12. Exploring Cloud Computing Services and Applications by Ahmed E. Youssef
13. Cloud security alliance – security guidance for critical areas of focus in cloud computing
14. CLOUD COMPUTING & GREEN IT an white paper presented in the national summit on Cloud Computing & Green IT Technology by Daman Dev Sood and Shiv Kumar
15. Cloud computing security for telecommunication applications by nokia Siemens network
16. Strategic turn to monetize cloud computing – case study for strategic management.pdf
17. Smart Metering the Clouds Singh, T.; Vara, P.K.; Enabling Technologies: Infrastructures for Collaborative Enterprises, 2009. WETICE '09. 18th IEEE International Workshops on June 29 2009-July 1 2009 Page(s):66 – 71

18. Cloud Computing: Does Nirvana Hide behind the Nebula? Erdogmus, Hakan; Software, IEEE Volume 26, Issue 2, March-April 2009 Page(s):4 – 6

19. Multi-tenant Cloud Computing: From Cruise Liners to Container Ships Kaliski, B.,Trusted Infrastructure Technologies Conference, 2008. APTC '08. Third Asia-Pacific 14-17 Oct. 2008 Page(s):4 – 4

20. Web Semantics in the Clouds, Mika, P.; Tummarello, G.; Intelligent Systems, IEEE Volume 23, Issue 5, Sept.-Oct. 2008 Page(s):82 – 87

21. The Case for Cloud Computing, Grossman, R.L.; IT Professional Volume 11, Issue 2, March-April 2009 Page(s):23 – 27

22. Cloud Computing and IT as a Service: Opportunities and Challenges Lin, G.; Dasmalchi, G.; Zhu, J.; Web Services, 2008. ICWS '08. IEEE International Conference on 23-26 Sept. 2008 Page(s):5 – 5

23. Cloud Computing: New Wine or Just a New Bottle?, Voas, Jeffrey; Zhang, Jia; IT Professional Volume 11, Issue 2, March-April 2009 Page(s):15 – 17

24. What Networking of Information Can Do for Cloud Computing, Ohlman, B.; Eriksson,A.; Rembarz, R.; Enabling Technologies: Infrastructures for Collaborative Enterprises, 2009. WETICE '09. 18th IEEE International Workshops on June 29 2009-July 1 2009 Page(s):78 – 83

25. CCOA: Cloud Computing Open Architecture, Zhang, Liang-Jie; Zhou, Qun; Web Services, 2009. ICWS 2009. IEEE International Conference on 6-10 July 2009 Page(s):607 – 616

26. Lasica, J.D.; Identity in the age of cloud computing; Pearson Publications.

27. www.sun.com/cloud

28. Cloud Computing Guiding Principles. pdf by business security alliance

29. The Future of Cloud Computing Opportunities for European Cloud Computing Beyond 2010 by Keith Jeffery and Neidecker Lutz

30. Cloud computing security by Ngongang Guy Mollet, Helsinki Metropolia University of Applied Sciences

31. Dynamic Resource Allocation using Virtual Machines for Cloud Computing by EnvironmentZhen Xiao, *Senior Member, IEEE,* Weijia Song, and Qi Chen

32. Priority Based Dynamic resource allocation in Cloud Computing by Chandrashekhar S. Pawar and Rajnikant B. Wagh

33. Economic Benefits of Cisco's Cloud Strategy by ACG research

34. A Comparison and Critique of Eucalyptus, OpenNebula and Nimbus by Peter Sempolinski and Douglas Thain, University of Notre Dame

35. Empirical Exploitation of Live Virtual Machine Migration by Jon Oberheide, Evan Cooke, Farnam Jahanian, University of Michigan

36. Thin clients.pdf from www.citrix.com

37. Enterprises show signs of adopting Business-Process-asa-Service (BPaaS) as modular components.pdf by equa terra

38. Global Open Versity Cloud Computing Hands-on Labs Training Manual - Step by step install guide eye OS cloud computing operating system by Kefa Rabah, Global Open Versity

39. Getting started.pdf from ubuntu live cloud

40. Guiding Principles on Cloud Computing in Law Enforcement by International Association of Chiefs of Police

41. How cloud computing works by Jonathan Strickland

42. Bogatin, Donna. "Google CEO's new paradigm: 'cloud computing and advertising go hand-in-hand.'" ZDNet. Aug. 23, 2006. Retrieved March 11, 2008. http://blogs.zdnet.com/micro-markets/?p=369

43. Brodkin, Jon. "IBM unveils 'cloud computing.'" Network World. Nov. 19, 2007. Vol. 24, Iss. 45. pg. 10.

44. Carr, Nicholas. "'World Wide Computer' is on horizon." USA Today. February 25, 2008.

45. Hickins, Michael. "Cloud Computing Gets Down to Earth." eWeek. January 21, 2008. pg. 14.

46. "IBM Introduces Ready-to-Use Cloud Computing." IBM. Nov. 15, 2007. http://www-03.ibm.com/press/us/en/pressrelease/22613.wss

47. Lohr, Steve. "Cloud Computing and EMC Deal." New York Times. Feb. 25, 2008. pg. C 6.

48. Lohr, Steve. "Google and I.B.M. Jon in 'Cloud Computing' Research." New York Times. Oct. 8, 2007. pg. C 8.

49. Lohr, Steve. "I.B.M. to Push 'Cloud Computing,' Using Data From Afar." New York Times. Nov. 15, 2007. pg. C 7.

50. McAllister, Neil. "Server virtualization." InfoWorld. Feb. 12, 2007. Retrieved March 12, 2008. http://www.infoworld.com/article/07/02/12/07FEvirtualserv_1.html

51. Markoff, John. "An Internet Critic Who Is Not Shy About Ruffling the Big Names in High Technology." New York Times. Apr. 9, 2001. pg. C 6.

52. Markoff, John. "Software via the Internet: Microsoft in 'Cloud' Computing." New York Times. Sep. 3, 2007. pg. C 1.

53. "Middleware." Carnegie Mellon Software Engineering Institute. Retrieved March 12, 2004. http://www.sei.cmu.edu/str/descriptions/middleware_body.html.

54. Naone, Erica. "Computer in the Cloud." Technology Review. Sept. 18, 2007. Retrieved March 12, 2008. http://www.technologyreview.com/Infotech/19397/?a=f

55. "Report sees big shift in IT delivery." IT Week. London. Nov. 5, 2007.

56. Swanson, Bret and Gilder, George. "Unleashing the 'Exaflood." Wall Street Journal. Feb. 22, 2008. pg. A 15.
57. How does cloud computing works? by Carl Mazzanti, CEO, eMazzanti Technologies
58. Hybrid Clouds: Comparing Cloud Toolkits Seminar Paper by Prof. Dr. Martin Schader, University of Mannheim
59. Cloud Computing: Infrastructure as a service by Md Yazid Mohd Saman and Jabatan Sains Komputer
60. Cloud Computing presented by IBM developer works Breaking through the hazeDan O'Riordan IDR La Gaude, France, IIC Architects
61. Getting cloud computing right the key to business success in a cloud adoption is a robust, proven architecture IBM Global Technology Services Thought Leadership White Paper
62. IBM Market Insights. Cloud Computing Research, July 2009
63. 2010 IBM Tech Trends Survey. October, 2010. www-03.ibm.com/press/us/en/pressrelease/32674.wss
64. The Open Group SOA Reference Architecture.http://www.opengroup.org/soa/drafts/refarch.htm#_SOA_Reference_Architecture4,5,6
65. Peter Mell and Tim Grance, The NIST Definition of Cloud Computing,Version 15, October 7, 2009. http://www.nist.gov/itl/cloud/upload/cloud-def-v15.pdf
66. Install CloudSim with eclipse In Windows Machine
67. Introduction to Cloud Computing and Virtualization By Mayank Mishra and Sujesha Sudevalayam, IIT Bombay
68. A Virtualization Architecture for In-depth Kernel Isolation by Jiang Wang, Sameer Niphadkar, Angelos Stavrou, and Anup K. Ghosh Center for Secure Information Systems, George Mason University Fairfax, VA 22030
69. Linux Kernel Architecture SMP issues, locking primitives by Harald Welte
70. Managing a Zoo: Tools for Managing and Monitoring Distributed Systems from Cloudera by Alex Kozlov, Cloudera Inc
71. Architecture of the Kernel-based Virtual Machine (KVM) By Jan Kiszka, Siemens AG, CT T DE IT 1 Corporate Competence Center Embedded Linux
72. Introduction to Cloud Computing by Majd F. Sakr
73. http://code.google.com/edu/parallel/dsd-tutorial.html
74. http://www.ida.liu.se/~TDDD25/lecture-notes/lect1.frm.pdf
75. http://www.cs.rutgers.edu/~pxk/rutgers/notes/content/01-intro.pdf
76. http://www.computing.dcu.ie/~kpodesta/distributed/
77. http://www2.cs.uregina.ca/~hamilton/courses/430/notes/notes1.htm
78. http://www.cs.vu.nl/~steen/courses/ds-slides/notes.01.pdf

79. http://en.wikipedia.org/wiki/Middleware#Types_of_middleware
80. Linux: The Operating System of the Cloud By Amanda McPherson
81. Exploiting Live Virtual Machine Migration by Jon Oberheide, University of Michigan
82. Migrating to the cloud options and opportunities understanding the software, platform and infrastructure as a service
83. The Open Cloud Manifesto A call to action for the worldwide cloud community from www.opencloudmanifesto.org.
84. OpenNebula Tutorial by Constantino Vázquez and BlancoBorja Sotomayor, DSA-Research.orgDistributed Systems Architecture Research GroupUniversidad Complutense de Madrid
85. B. Rochwerger, J. Caceres, R.S. Montero, D. Breitgand, E. Elmroth, A. Galis, E. Levy,I.M. Llorente, K. Nagin, Y. Wolfsthal, "The RESERVOIR Model and Architecture for Open Federated Cloud Computing", IBM Systems Journal, Vol. 53, No. 4. (2009)
86. B. Sotomayor, R. S. Montero, I. M. Llorente and I. Foster, "Virtual Infrastructure Management in Private and Hybrid Clouds", IEEE Internet Computing, September/ October 2009 (vol. 13 no. 5)
87. Openstack Installation Guide.pdf
88. http://www.subnet-calculator.com/subnet.php?net_class=C
89. http://uksysadmin.wordpress.com/2012/03/28/screencast-video-of-an-install-of-openstackessex-on-ubuntu-12-04-under-virtualbox/
90. http://www.tikalk.com/alm/blog/expreimenting-openstack-essex-ubuntu-1204-lts-undervirtualbox
91. http://damithakumarage.wordpress.com/2012/06/26/openstack-essex-cloud-setup/
92. Setting a private cloud in ubuntu.pdf
93. KVM – KERNEL BASED VIRTUAL MACHINE from www.redhat.com
94. Fundamentals of Grid Computing by Viktors Berstis
95. Security for Cloud Computing 10 Steps to Ensure Success.pdf by Cloud Standards Customer Council
96. Security of Cloud Computing Providers Study Sponsored by CA Technologies Independently conducted by Ponemon Institute
97. Community Clouds – supporting business ecosystems with cloud computing by Siemens IT Solutions and Services
98. Cisco Cloud Portfolio: Enabling the World of Many Clouds by cisco
99. Distributed Computing: Utilities, Grids & Clouds by ITU-T Technology Watch Report 9
100. http://www.itu.int/ITU-T/studygroups/com17/history.html
101. http://gevaperry.typepad.com/main/2007/04/tower_of_babel.html

102. Foster, I. and Kesselman, C. "The grid: blueprint for a new computing infrastructure," Morgan Kaufmann Publishers Inc., San Francisco, CA, 1998

103. http://www.globus.org/alliance/publications/papers/chapter2.pdf

104. Tanenbaum, A. S. and van Steen, M. "Distributed Systems: Principles and Paradigms"

105. Anderson, R. "Security Engineering: A Guide to Building Dependable Distributed Systems," chapter 6

106. Buyya et al. "Market-Oriented Cloud Computing: Vision, Hype, and Reality for Delivering IT Services as Computing Utilities,"

107. http://www.gridbus.org/papers/hpcc2008_keynote_cloudcomputing.pdf

108. http://samj.net/2008/09/taxonomy-6-layer-cloud-computing-stack.html

109. http://gridguy.net/?p=10

110. Tutschku, K. et al. "Trends in network and service operation for the emerging future Internet," Int J Electron Commun (AEU) (2007)

111. Delic, K. A. and Walker, M. A. "Emergence of the academic computing clouds," Ubiquity 9, 31 (Aug. 2008), 1-1.

110. http://www.eu-egee.org/

111. http://www.cern.ch/

112. http://www.opensciencegrid.org/

113. http://www.ndgf.org/

114. http://www.itu.int/ITU-R/conferences/rrc/rrc-06/

115. http://unosat.org/

116. ECW is an enhanced compressed wavelet file format designed for geospatial imagery.

117. http://www.itu.int/emergencytelecoms

118. http://setiathome.berkeley.edu/

119. http://folding.stanford.edu/

120. http://lhcathome.cern.ch/

121. http://boinc.berkeley.edu/

122. http://www.forbes.com/lists/2008/18/biz_2000global08_The-Global-2000_Rank.html

123. http://www.computerweekly.com/Articles/2006/09/26/218593/how-grid-power-pays-off for-hsbc.htm

124. http://www.fsg-ship.de/

125. http://www.gridipedia.eu/grid-computing-case-studies.html

126. http://gigaom.com/2008/02/28/how-cloud-utility-computing-are-different/

127. http://www.akamai.com/

128. http://www.limelightnetworks.com

129. Jaeger et al. "Cloud Computing and Information Policy: Computing in a Policy Cloud?"

130. infoDev Quick guide: Low-cost computing devices and initiatives for the developing world, http://infodev.org/en/Publication.107.html

131. See UNCTAD Information Economy Report 2007-2008, http://www.unctad.org/Templates/webflyer.asp?docid=9479&intItemID=1397&lang=1&mode=highlights, and ITU World Telecommunication/ICT Indicators Database 2008 (12th Edition), http://www.itu.int/ITU-D/ict/publications/world/world.html

132 http://www.eweek.com/c/a/Messaging-and-Collaboration/SAAS-Email-From-Google-Microsoft-Proves-Cost-Effective-For-Up-to-15K-Seats/1/

133. http://www.3tera.com/

134. http://flexiscale.com/

135. http://www.mor.ph/

136. http://www.rightscale.com/

137. http://blog.jamesurquhart.com/2008/11/quick-guide-to-big-four-cloud-offerings.html

138. http://aws.amazon.com/what-is-aws/

139. http://code.google.com/intl/en/appengine/docs/whatisgoogleappengine.html

140. http://www.salesforce.com/

141. http://www.microsoft.com/azure/

142. Delaney "Google plans services to store users' data," Wall Street Journal

143. http://www.infoworld.com/article/08/07/02
Gartner_Seven_cloudcomputing_security_risks_1.html

144. Greenberg (Forbes.com) "Bridging the clouds," http://www.forbes.com/technology/2008/06/29/cloud-computing-3tera-tech-cio cx_ag_0630tera.html

145. http://samj.net/2008/08/cloud-standards-not-so-fast.html

146. http://www.oiforum.com/public/liaisons.html Cloud Software Program by tivit

147. Understanding Thin-Client/Server Computing by Joel Kanter

148. Deploying Ubuntu Enterprise Cloud Training Course Overview from ubuntu

149. Ubuntu Server Guide from ubuntu

150. Ubuntu openstack deployment from ubuntu

151. Ubuntu 11.04 server guide from ubuntu

152. http://www.opendatacenteralliance.org/

153. http://www.capgemini.com/ctoblog/2011/01/the_new_data_centre_is_not_you/

154. http://www.capgemini.com/ctoblog/2011/02/generation-data-centre/

155. http://www.intel.com/itcenter/products/xeon/7500/index.htm
156. http://www.intel.com/itcenter/products/xeon/5600/index.htm
157. http://software.intel.com/sites/datacentermanager/faqs.php
158. http://sites.amd.com/us/business/promo/server/Pages/opteron-6000-series-new-models.aspx?lid=New_Models_of_AMD_Opteron&lpos=HP_bottom_bucket
159. http://www.cio.com/article/638577/Virtualization_Meets_Its_Organizational_Limit
160. http://wiki.xensource.com/xenwiki/HVM_Compatible_Processors <—list of VT-x AND-V cpu's
161. http://southbrain.com/south/virtualization/3-xen-hypervisor-based-virtual.html (opening slide) // hypervisor pictures
162. http://elite-itsolutions.co.uk/images/diag-hyperv-arch.png // Hyper-V picture
163. http://en.wikipedia.org/wiki/Iscsi
164. http://open.eucalyptus.com/wiki/EucalyptusAdvanced_v2.0
165. http://www.canonical.com/sites/default/files/active/Whitepaper-UbuntuEnterpriseCloudArchitecture-v1.pdf
166. https://help.ubuntu.com/community/UEC/PackageInstallSeparate
167. http://software.intel.com/file/31966
168. Virtualization and Cloud Computing: Optimized Power, Cooling, and Management Maximizes Benefits white paper by Suzanne Niles and Patrick Donovan
169. Application Architecture for Cloud Computing white paper from rpath
170. ZSL's Innovative Services & Solutions in Ubuntu Platforms
171. http://www.huffingtonpost.com/ben-uretsky/the-future-of-cloud-hosti_1_b_4632226.html
172. http://www.cloudreviews.com/
173. http://www.cloudreviews.com/cat/cloud-hosting-services.html
174. http://www.cloud-lounge.org/EN/how-do-clouds-work.html
175. http://www.cloudbook.net/directories/research-clouds/cloud-computing-research.php
176. http://cdac.in/
177. http://apprenda.com/
178. http://www.unitiv.com/it-solutions-blog/bid/39318/4-Basic-Principles-of-Cloud Computing
179. http://www.webopedia.com/
180. http://www.techopedia.com/2/29691/trends/cloud-computing/5-things-to-consider-when-choosing-a-cloud-drive
181. http://www.businessnewsdaily.com/4553-cloud-based-tools-small-business.html

182. http://www.networkworld.com/supp/2013/enterprise3/060313-ecs3-private-cloud-failures-269845.html
183. http://gigaom.com/2009/11/06/10-top-open-source-resources-for-cloud-computing/
184. http://www.businessnewsdaily.com/4864-cloud-computing-terms.html
185. http://ss64.com/bash/
186. http://mally.stanford.edu/~sr/computing/basic-unix.html
187. http://oceanofwebs.com/architecture-of-linux-operating-system/
188. http://www.cloudpro.co.uk/private-cloud/3359/arriva-opts-for-private-cloud-to-deal-with-increasing-demands-on-ticketing
189. https://www.gartner.com/doc/2598916/building-government-cloud-lessons-singapore
190. http://blog.softlayer.com/author/jklink/
191. http://www.techrepublic.com/blog/the-enterprise-cloud/cloud-app-vs-web-app-understanding-the-differences/
192. http://www.businessnewsdaily.com/4427-cloud-computing-small-business.html
193. http://en.wikipedia.org/wiki/Main_Page
194. http://www.theguardian.com/media-network/media-network-blog/2013/oct/29/cloud-computing-hype-business-benefits
195. http://www.techradar.com/news/internet/cloud-computing-explained-1105688
196. http://www.colt.net/uk/en/index.htm
197. http://cloudtimes.org/
198. http://gevaperry.typepad.com/main/2008/08/new-cloud-compu.html
199. http://www.cloudbook.net/directories/product-services/cloud-computing-directory
200. http://www.cloudproviderusa.com/
201. http://venturebeat.com/2013/11/28/evolution-of-the-modern-cloud-how-the-clouds-value-proposition-is-changing/
202. http://howtoubuntu.org/how-to-execute-a-run-or-bin-file-in-ubuntu#.UvRHuBCSxps
203. http://www.hongkiat.com/blog/cloud-hosting-how-does-it-work/
204. http://www.computerweekly.com/Cloud-storage-basics-The-facts-about-cloud-storage
205. http://www.itnewsafrica.com/2011/04/cloud-vs-hosted-services/
206. http://www.computerweekly.com/news/1510117/Community-cloud-computing-benefits-and-drawbacks
207. http://socializedsoftware.com/2010/01/20/eleven-open-source-cloud-computing-projects-to-watch/
208. http://www.linuxjournal.com/content/effects-cloud-computing-open-source-compliance
209. http://www.itdonut.co.uk/

210. http://www.serverwatch.com/tutorials/article.php/3858961/Grow-Your-Own-Cloud-Servers-With-Ubuntu.htm

211. http://xmodulo.com/2013/10/interesting-facts-ubuntu-linux.html

212. http://searchstorage.techtarget.com/NetAppSponsoredNews/Is-OpenStack-Grizzly-Ready-for-Deployment

213. http://www.linfo.org/kernel_mode.html

214. http://oss.org.cn/ossdocs/linux/kernel/a1/index.html

215. http://oceanofwebs.com/architecture-of-linux-operating-system

216. https://help.ubuntu.com/community/KVM/Installation

217. http://www.techotopia.com/index.php/Managing_Xen_using_the_xm_Command-line_Tool

218. http://www.cloudpro.co.uk/

219. http://www.techrepublic.com/blog/the-enterprise-cloud/mini-glossary-cloud-computing-terms-you-should-know/2308/

220. http://www.cliqr.com/

221. http://www.2x.com/whitepapers/private-cloud-computing/

222. www.thecloudtutorial.com

223. www.yoyoclouds.com

224. http://www.networkworld.com/supp/2013/enterprise3/060313-ecs3-open-stack-269899.html

225. http://www.clouds360.com/paas.php

226. http://howtoubuntu.org/things-to-do-after-installing-ubuntu-12-04-precise-pangolin

227. https://blogs.oracle.com/constantin/entry/blog_migration

228. http://smallbusinessblog.infostreet.com/2011/04/top-10-list-top-cloud-computing-benefits-for-your-small-business/

229. http://www.upubuntu.com/2012/12/20-useful-terminal-commands-and-tools.html

230. http://blog.sudobits.com/2012/07/20/top-17-terminal-commands-every-ubuntu-user-should-know-about/

231. http://www.cloudpro.co.uk/paas/cloud-deployment/3653/red-hat-launches-enterprise-linux-openstack-40-platform

232. http://www.businessnewsdaily.com/4863-what-is-paas.html

233. http://www.businessnewsdaily.com/4793-what-is-saas-software-as-a-service.html

234. http://www.businessnewsdaily.com/4862-what-is-iaas.html

235. http://erpcloudnews.com/2010/07/web-based-saas-and-cloud-erp-benefits/

236. e-learning using cloud computing.pdf by utpaljyotibora and majidul ahmed

237. Using cloud computing for e-learning systems by paul pocatilu, felician alecu, mariusvetrici, economic informatics department academy of economic studies 6 piata romana, secot 1, bucharest, Romania
238. future polling system using cloud computing in support with smart client technology by b.perumal, m.pallikonda and rajasekaran, j.vigneswar
239. cloud computing and SOA convergence in your enterprise by David S. Linthicum
240. privacy in cloud computing – ITU-T technology watch report
241. handbook of cloud computing by Borko Furht · Armando Escalante
242. hadoop in action by chuck lam
243. cloud computing strategies by Dimitris N. chroafas
244. The Cloud at Your Service by Jothy Rosenberg and Arthur Mateos
245. Cloud Computing A General State of the Union by David F. Soll, Vice President and Chief Technology Officer Omicron Consulting
246. Cloud computing and software services by Syed A. hason and Mohammad Ilyas
247. Cloud computing principles, systems and applications by Nick Antonopoulos and lee gillam
248. www. Google.com
249. www. Wikipedia.org
250. www. Amazon.com
251. www. Microsoft.com
252. www. Apple.com
253. www.vmware.com
254. www.dropbox.com
255. www.Rackspace.com
256. www.salesforce.com

INDEX

D

E

F

G

H

I